JOHN H. GOLDTHORPE

Consensus and Controversy

Consensus and Controversy

Principal Editor, Falmer Sociology Series: *Jon Clark*

1 Robert K. Merton
2 Anthony Giddens
3 John H. Goldthorpe

Editors, Falmer Psychology Series: *Sohan Modgil and Celia Modgil*

1 Lawrence Kohlberg
2 Hans Eysenck
3 Noam Chomsky
4 Arthur Jensen
5 B. F. Skinner

Falmer International Master-minds Challenged
Series Editors: Sohan Modgil and Celia Modgil

JOHN H. GOLDTHORPE

Consensus and Controversy

EDITED BY

Jon Clark, Dr Phil

Senior Lecturer
Department of Sociology and Social Policy
University of Southampton

Celia Modgil, PhD

Lecturer in Educational Psychology
University of London

Sohan Modgil, PhD

Reader in Educational Research and Development
Brighton Polytechnic

Routledge
Taylor & Francis Group

LONDON AND NEW YORK

First published 1990 by RoutledgeFalmer

2 Park Square, Milton Park, Abingdon, Oxon OX14 4RN
711 Third Avenue, New York, NY 10017, USA

Routledge is an imprint of the Taylor & Francis Group, an informa business

First issued in paperback 2016

British Library Cataloguing in Publication Data

John H. Goldthorpe : consensus and controversy – (Falmer
   international master-minds challenged).
   1. Sociology. Theories of Goldthorpe, John
   I. Clark, Jon *(1949–)*   II. Modgil, Celia   III. Modgil,
   Sohan
   301.092

Library of Congress Cataloging-in-Publication Data

John H. Goldthorpe : consensus and controversy/edited by Jon Clark,
   Celia Modgil, Sohan Modgil.
      —(Consensus and controversy. Falmer sociology
   series)
      Includes bibliographical references
      1. Goldthorpe, John H.   2. Social classes.   3. Social mobility.
   4. Political sociology.   I. Clark, Jon, Dr. Phil.   II. Modgil, Celia.
   III. Modgil, Sohan.   IV. Series.
   HM22.G8G655   1990
   305.5—dc20   90-2785
                                                                          CIP

ISBN 978-1-138-97386-2 (pbk)
ISBN 978-1-85000-549-0 (hbk)

Jacket design by Caroline Archer

Typeset in 10/12 Times
by Mathematical Composition Setters Ltd, Salisbury, Wilts.

Contributors

Dr Jon Clark
University of Southampton

Dr Duncan Gallie
Nuffield College

Dr Gordon Marshall
University of Essex

Professor Göran Ahrne
University of Stockholm

Professor Giorgio Gagliani
University of Calabria

Rosemary Crompton
University of Kent

Dr Susan McRae
Policy Studies Institute

Dr Shirley Dex
University of Keele

Dr Anthony Heath
Nuffield College

Professor Dennis Kavanagh
University of Nottingham

Dr William Roche
*University College
Dublin*

Professor William Brown
University of Cambridge

Dr Niamh Hardiman
*Somerville College
Oxford*

Professor Josef Esser
University of Frankfurt

Professor Raymond Plant
University of Southampton

Professor John Westergaard
University of Sheffield

Professor Geoff Payne
Polytechnic South West

Professor Walter Müller
University of Mannheim

Dr Jonathan Kelley
Australian National University

Professor Karl Ulrich Mayer
*Max-Planck-Institut
West Berlin*

Professor Terry Johnson
University of Leicester

John H. Goldthorpe
Nuffield College

Acknowledgments

First and foremost we would like to express our thanks to the subject of this volume, John Goldthorpe, without whose committed support this project would simply not have been possible. Thanks, too, to all the contributors who achieved our final deadline, mostly as a result of commendable self-discipline, though bolstered in some cases by mild editorial nudges and in a few by slightly less mild editorial arm-twisting. Thanks are due to Oxford University Press for permission to reproduce at various points excerpts and tables from the 1987 edition of John Goldthorpe's *Social Mobility and Class Structure in Modern Britain*.

We owe a particular debt to the academic and clerical staff of the Department of Sociology and Social Policy at the University of Southampton for their support and encouragement throughout the project. Finally, we would like to express our gratitude to Malcolm Clarkson, Managing Director, Falmer Press, for his unswerving confidence in the Sociology Series and his encouragement to give absolute priority to high standards of scholarship in the editing and production of the individual volumes.

Jon Clark, Celia Modgil, Sohan Modgil
Hoe Gate and Old Windsor
October 1989

Contents

Part One: Introduction

I. EDITORIAL INTRODUCTION

1. John H. Goldthorpe: Consensus and Controversy

JON CLARK, CELIA MODGIL AND SOHAN MODGIL

THE ORIGIN AND RATIONALE OF THE SERIES

The origins of this volume on the work of John H. Goldthorpe can be traced directly, if somewhat paradoxically, to the publication in 1986–87 of a series of books on the work of leading contemporary psychologists: Lawrence Kohlberg, Hans Eysenck, Noam Chomsky, Arthur Jensen and B. F. Skinner. The success of these five volumes, edited by Sohan and Celia Modgil, persuaded the publisher, Malcolm Clarkson of Falmer Press, to initiate a parallel series of books on leading contemporary sociologists. In the autumn of 1986 Jon Clark was appointed principal editor of the new series.

The first major task was to choose the international contemporary sociologists who would be the subject of the first five volumes in the series. The choice was guided by a number of criteria. First and foremost the editors shared a fundamental belief in the distinctive intellectual interest in concentrating on the work of individuals as opposed to subject areas (education, religion, domestic life, work, mobility, health), concepts (class, power, structure, agency, gender) or 'schools' and approaches ('neo-functionalism', 'rational choice', Marxism, hermeneutics, positivism). The reader will have to judge whether this belief was justified or not. It was also agreed by the editors that the work of each scholar chosen had to be internationally recognized in the discipline; still relevant to the core of the discipline in the 1990s; extensive in thematic coverage; and at one and the same time consensus-generating and controversial. Finally, the aim was to choose a group whose work covered a range of fields of sociological interest and countries of origin. The outcome was the choice of Robert K. Merton, Daniel Bell, Anthony Giddens, John H. Goldthorpe and Ralf Dahrendorf. For a variety of reasons the volumes on Daniel Bell and Ralf Dahrendorf did not materialize. Nevertheless, we believe that the three remaining volumes demonstrate the breadth, richness and creativity of the discipline of sociology in the post-war period.

THE FORMAT OF THE SERIES

The format of the Sociology Series is broadly similar to that of the Psychology Series. In each case the subject of the volume was invited to participate in its design so as to reflect the consensus and controversy which have surrounded their work. At the outset themes were chosen which covered the major areas of knowledge represented in their research and publications, and pairs of distinguished academics were then invited to write papers taking either a 'predominantly positive' or 'predominantly negative' view of each major area. The paired contributions were then exchanged through the editors to provide an opportunity for both parties to make a short comment on the heart of the opposing paper. When the manuscript was complete, it was sent to the subject of the volume for a concluding comment.

The aim of the debate format and the interchange of chapters is to highlight points of consensus and controversy. It should be emphasized, though, that the terms 'predominantly positive' and 'predominantly negative' imply no more than that the writer of the relevant contribution agrees or disagrees *in the main* with, say, Goldthorpe's approach to class analysis—it does not imply complete agreement or disagreement, and allows contributors some degree of latitude to provide their own often more rounded view of the subject. Also, although the generic topics to be debated were determined by the editors, the contributors were given the freedom to focus on those aspects of the theme which were closest to their own research interests.

THE CONTENTS OF THE BOOK

The book, like Gaul, is divided into three parts. Part I provides a general introduction to Goldthorpe's work. In Chapter 2 Jon Clark outlines the main stages in Goldthorpe's intellectual biography, situating his various research projects and publications in the context of British and international developments in the discipline of sociology. He also gives a personal view of Goldthorpe's distinctive 'style' of sociology. In Chapter 3 Duncan Gallie reviews Goldthorpe's critique of liberal theories of industrialism. He suggests that much of Goldthorpe's work can be seen as a prolonged debate both with the general 'historicist' arguments of liberal theories and with their more specific predictions about social structural change.

Part II contains nine sets of paired contributions and one 'free-standing' chapter covering the main themes of Goldthorpe's writings. Chapters 4 and 5 discuss Goldthorpe's own original version of class analysis. In Chapter 4 Gordon Marshall traces the evolution of Goldthorpe's research on class structure, outlining the main components of what has come to be known as the 'Goldthorpe class schema'. He argues that, while there are still some difficulties surrounding the operational procedures for generating classes from occupational data as well as with the status of women, Goldthorpe's scheme is more reliable, and makes better sense of the relevant data, than all other alternatives. In contrast Göran Ahrne suggests that Goldthorpe's class schema, which he describes as a 'well-made commonsensical classification of occupations', lacks the explanatory power of more sophisticated theories of the development of class societies. He illustrates his case with a critical discussion of the concepts of 'service class', 'intermediate class' and 'working class', and a short discourse on the development of the petty bourgeoisie and the state in Sweden.

The next section continues this debate, concentrating more specifically on Marxist theories of class and historical development. In Chapter 6 Giorgio Gagliani defends Goldthorpe's critique of recent Marxist theories, in particular of those which argue that there is a general trend in industrial societies towards 'proletarianization' and deskilling. He also provides an extended discussion of 'shift-share analysis', a technique used by Wright and Singelmann to analyze changes in the degree of proletarianization in the USA. In Chapter 7, however, Rosemary Crompton, while accepting certain criticisms of the 'proletarianization' thesis, uses recent case study evidence to cast 'micro-sociological' doubt on aspects of Goldthorpe's 'macro-sociological' class scheme. In particular, she suggests that random sample surveys of the population at large cannot provide conclusive evidence relating to organizational structures and processes, and that micro-level qualitative and macro-level quantitative research are not alternatives, as Goldthorpe appears to suggest, but complementary explanatory strategies.

The next three sections look in more detail at particular themes within class analysis. In Chapters 8 and 9 Susan McRae and Shirley Dex discuss Goldthorpe's writings on class and gender, work which has given rise to major controversies within the British sociological community (and beyond). McRae gives a detailed exposition of Goldthorpe's wide-ranging contributions to the sociological study of women. She also argues that the study of sexual and class inequalities should be kept separate, not only because it is unlikely that both can be explained by one all-encompassing theory, but also because such separation 'is the only avenue presently available' for understanding the changes in class *and* sexual stratification which are likely to occur over the next decade. Dex, in contrast, challenges the 'conventional' separation of gender and class as supported by Goldthorpe. She suggests that a focus on the individual rather than the family as the unit of class analysis, and a longitudinal rather than cross-sectional perspective, would be more appropriate to understanding class and life-cycle variations in women's social mobility.

In Chapters 10 and 11 Anthony Heath and Dennis Kavanagh examine Goldthorpe's work on the relationship between class and political partisanship, a topic which—like class and gender—has aroused sustained controversy, in this case particularly between political scientists and sociologists. Heath begins by summarizing some of the main conclusions of the *Affluent Worker* study which impinge on questions of political attitudes and behaviour in Britain. These include the need to distinguish between the 'solidaristic' collectivism of traditional workers and the 'instrumental' collectivism of affluent workers; that affluence on its own does not lead to middle-class identity; the strong association between workers' experience of work and their disposition to support a Labour Party espousing 'collectivist' policies; that actual support for Labour is contingent on a belief that it will 'deliver the goods' if elected. Heath then presents data on the relation between affluence, class identity and voting behaviour in the 1980s which suggest that the conclusions of the 1960s study go a long way to explaining working-class political behaviour today. In contrast, Kavanagh believes that there is conclusive evidence that social class has declined in importance as a shaper of electoral choice in Britain (the 'class de-alignment thesis'). He argues that the fact that Labour has remained a 'class party' pursuing an 'egalitarian' strategy, as recommended by Goldthorpe (and by Heath, Jowell and Curtice, 1985, whose work is seen by Kavanagh as continuing the Goldthorpian tradition), has been one of the main reasons why it has been doing so much worse than most other centre-left parties in Western Europe. According to Kavanagh, the question of Labour's relatively poor electoral performance in the 1980s should be a prime focus for contemporary political and sociological analysis.

Chapters 12 and 13 turn to the question of the relation between class and industrial relations. Bill Roche suggests that 'orthodox' approaches to industrial relations tend to neglect what he calls the 'pre-institutional' foundations of the employment relationship. He argues that Goldthorpe's writings, from the *Affluent Worker* study through to essays of the mid-1970s and 1980s, make a major contribution to our understanding of the influence of social class on worker attitudes and systems of control at work. In Chapter 13 William Brown provides what both Goldthorpe and Roche suggest has so far been conspicuous by its absence, a reply from within the 'liberal-pluralist' tradition to Goldthorpe's critique of 'institutional' approaches to industrial relations. In a sense, Brown turns Goldthorpe's argument on its head, defending the 'problem-oriented' approach of industrial relations orthodoxy as a strength rather than a weakness and arguing that Goldthorpe's 'class-oriented' approach is a case of 'sociological bricks without institutional straw'.

The next three chapters broaden the thematic focus by looking at questions of political economy and the state since 1945. In Chapter 14 Niamh Hardiman draws on examples from a number of Western European nations to demonstrate the explanatory power of Goldthorpe's analysis of the post-war 'Keynesian era', in particular his interpretation of the problem of inflation, which he sees as the 'monetary expression of distributional dissent'. She also uses the distinction between 'corporatist', 'neo-laissez-faire' and 'dualist' strategies to examine developments in different countries in the 'post-Keynesian' era. In Chapter 15 Josef Esser covers the same ground as Hardiman, but argues that Goldthorpe's concepts and analysis are ultimately lacking in explanatory power because they are not grounded in a historical theory of the development of capitalism as a world system. He suggests that the concepts of 'Fordism' and 'post-Fordism' provide a more appropriate conceptual framework, illustrating his argument by a comparison of recent developments in Britain and West Germany.

In Chapter 16 political philosopher Raymond Plant also discusses questions of corporatism and neo-liberalism in Goldthorpe's work, but his particular interest lies in how different political actors (parties, governments and citizens, but also academic social scientists) deal with the question of distributive justice in modern industrial societies. He concludes that questions of distributive justice represent a central dilemma of modern democracies, but argues that Goldthorpe's 'Popperian' refusal, *qua* sociologist, to take on such normative questions not only prevents him from pointing a way out of the dilemma, but actually goes some way to supporting a neo-liberal view of the economy and society.

Chapters 17 to 20 are concerned with the analysis of social mobility, the theme which has dominated Goldthorpe's research over the past twenty years. In Chapters 17 and 18 John Westergaard and Geoff Payne look at Goldthorpe's work on social mobility in Britain. Westergaard begins with the paradox that social mobility research is to a certain extent 'marginalized' from mainstream sociology in Britain, yet it is of central relevance for understanding its prime concerns, namely social structure, continuity and change. He argues that it is among Goldthorpe's signal achievements to have demonstrated and pressed home the central relevance of mapping social mobility for the discipline of sociology, and that his prime interest in the implications of changing mobility patterns for class formation and mobilization is fully justified. Payne, in contrast, believes that Goldthorpe's concentration on *class* mobility leads to major weaknesses in his approach because it fails to recognize that classes do not directly control or cause social mobility. For Payne, Goldthorpe's research also evinces a degree of blindness to questions of gender, unemployment and early career transitions, and makes no empirical links to education. All in all, Payne concludes that Goldthorpe's influence has been to narrow rather than expand contemporary ideas of mobility.

These and other issues are also discussed in the next section, which looks at the state of research into comparative social mobility. In Chapter 19 Walter Müller suggests that John Goldthorpe has played a pivotal role in bringing comparative social mobility research to its present state of maturity. He argues that this is for three main reasons: Goldthorpe has made the study of mobility into a central element of the class analysis of industrial societies; he has made a crucial contribution to the improvement of methodologies for comparative analysis; and he has provided firm substantive answers to long-running debates on the nature and impact of social mobility across industrial nations. In Chapter 20, however, Jonathan Kelley, while recognizing Goldthorpe's achievement in helping to stand-ardize mobility data across a number of countries, argues that Goldthorpe's chosen 'paradigm' of analysis, log-linear modelling, is fundamentally flawed, because it (1) has a limited power in dealing with questions of hierarchy; (2) is unable to use continuous measurement; and (3) presents difficulties in incorporating variables such as education and income into the model. In his conclusion Kelley outlines an alternative model of social mobility which suggests that 'inequality in the distribu-tion of human and material capital' is the key factor influencing social mobility.

In the last main section of Part II, Karl Ulrich Mayer and Terry Johnson look at the relation between theory and research in Goldthorpe's sociology. In Chapter 21 Mayer argues that Goldthorpe's contribution is one of the best current examples of how sociology should be conducted in order to be scientifically valid, intellectually convincing, academically successful and politically meaningful. In an extended metaphor Mayer also locates the key to Goldthorpe's sociology (and personality) in what he calls the latter's 'Tennis Player View of Sociology and Society'. In Chapter 22 Terry Johnson also identifies a continuity in Goldthorpe's sociology, suggesting that it is based on an ideological 'interest' in social openness and individual choice. However, Johnson examines a number of Goldthorpe's major writings and con-cludes that the link between this ideological interest and its scientific expression in a 'social action' approach is never adequately elaborated, whether in terms of theoretical principles, methodological implications or research procedures. Ulti-mately, then, for Johnson, Goldthorpe's 'call to action' remains rhetorical.

In Part III John Goldthorpe responds to his critics. Rather than treat each essay or exchange separately, he addresses seven issues which cut across a range of contributions. They are the relation between sociology and politics; the distinction between concepts and hypotheses; questions of data and analysis; sociological 'problems' and sociological theory; social mobility; class formation and class action; and the political economy of capitalist societies. He concludes with a Popperian commitment to the idea of 'Consensus and Controversy', which he sees as the two modes of communicative action which lie at the very heart of the scientific method.

The volume concludes with biographical details about the contributors; an outline intellectual biography of John Goldthorpe and a consolidated bibliography (both prepared by Jon Clark); and author and subject indexes prepared by Lyn Gorman.

II. GENERAL INTRODUCTIONS

2. John Goldthorpe as Sociologist

JON CLARK

INTRODUCTION

John H. Goldthorpe has a special place in the development and standing of the discipline of sociology, both in Britain and internationally. This is due in no small measure to the quality and thematic importance of the research and book publications with which he has been associated, beginning with the three volumes of the *Affluent Worker* study (1968/69), followed by the elaboration of an innovative approach to *The Social Grading of Occupations* (1974) and two highly acclaimed edited volumes of international papers, *The Political Economy of Inflation* (1978) and *Order and Conflict in Contemporary Capitalism* (1984).

However, it is research into social mobility for which he is now best known and to which he has devoted himself almost continuously with various collaborators since 1969. The theme of social mobility has been one of the most important areas of sociological investigation in the post-war period. Indeed, in terms of certain criteria—such as the scale of projects, extent of international collaboration and sophistication of research techniques—it could well claim, as Goldthorpe himself has suggested, 'a position of pre-eminence' (1987a: 1). Goldthorpe's own detailed research in this area began in 1972 with a large-scale survey of social mobility in England and Wales. This led in 1980 to the publication of the first edition of *Social Mobility and Class Structure in Modern Britain* (*SMCS*). The reviews of this volume in the London *Times*—'... the most exhaustive survey ever carried out into social mobility in Britain during the twentieth century'—and *British Book News*—'This is the most important book on the British social structure to appear for a quarter of a century'—give a clear indication of the strategic importance of the research. Since the mid-1970s, however, Goldthorpe has extended his research horizons, becoming involved with various international collaborators in large-scale research on social mobility across twelve industrial nations covering four continents. Numerous articles and papers arising from the project have already been published, and a major comparative volume is promised (see Goldthorpe's concluding chapter in this volume).

The initial aim of this chapter is to outline the main stages in Goldthorpe's intellectual biography, situating his various research projects and publications in the context of British and international developments in sociology. The second part of the chapter will be devoted to identifying the distinctive character of his contribution to sociology by elaborating on the various components of his particular 'style' of sociological analysis. A good flavour of this style is contained in his 'Preface' to the second edition of *SMCS*:

> The reception given to *Social Mobility and Class Structure in Modern Britain* when first published in 1980 was in various ways encouraging. The book attracted the attention of the press, television and radio to a degree that was quite unanticipated; its findings were widely discussed in the political weeklies; and when reviews later appeared in professional journals, they were, for the most part, generous. A number of critical issues were of course raised, and in some instances these led to debates which I, at least, found enjoyable. The only reactions of an entirely hostile character came in equal measure from the dogmatists of the Marxist Left and of the 'new' Conservative Right—which was exactly as it should have been, and especially gratifying. But most rewarding of all has been the longer-term response in the form of new research projects which are currently pursuing various lines of inquiry that were initiated in the book, or which are replicating in other national societies the investigations and analyses that it reported. (Goldthorpe, 1987a: vii)

In commenting on this passage, it is perhaps sufficient at this stage to say that Goldthorpe's style of sociological analysis involves a strong emphasis on the interplay between theory and systematic empirical research combined with a commitment to combative debate as *a* (perhaps *the*) principal means of advancing social scientific understanding.

INTELLECTUAL DEVELOPMENT

Like many British sociologists of his generation, John Goldthorpe came to sociology after completing an undergraduate degree in another discipline. In his case it was history, which he studied at University College London from 1953 to 1956. As we shall see below, some of the distinctive aspects of his approach to sociology must be seen against his particular conception of the relation between history and sociology, in particular his emphasis on their different materials, techniques and forms of explanation, and above all his rejection of 'historicist' approaches in the social sciences.[1]

It was in 1956 that Goldthorpe first came into serious contact with the discipline of sociology when he became a research student in the Department of Sociology at the London School of Economics, the undisputed centre of British sociology and social policy at the time. At the LSE he became acquainted at first hand with the work of T. H. Marshall, David Glass (whose pioneering 1949 investigation into social mobility in Britain was published in 1954) and Richard Titmuss, and he was soon engaged in his first 'empirical' research project, acting as research assistant to John H. Smith in connection with a study of personnel policies in nationalized industries. Then, after three years from 1957 to 1960 as Assistant Lecturer in the Department of Sociology at the University of Leicester (itself a major seedbed of post-war British sociology), Goldthorpe was appointed to a fellowship at King's College, Cambridge, where he remained for nine years. During this time, as research fellow at King's, and then as University Assistant Lecturer (from 1961) and Lecturer (from 1963), he established himself as one of the leading figures in British sociology.

As Heath and Edmondson have noted in their study of 'Oxbridge Sociology' (1980), the University of Cambridge had 'flirted' with sociology in the 1950s, mainly by inviting a series of visiting sociology professors from the United States, including Lloyd Warner, Edward Shils, George Homans and Talcott Parsons. Although Parsons's presence in Cambridge 'is reputed to have put acceptance of the subject back by a decade' (Heath and Edmonson, 1980: 40), three appointments were made in the early 1960s: W. G. Runciman at Trinity College, Goldthorpe at King's College, and David Lockwood to a University Lectureship and a Fellowship at St John's. With the appointment of Goldthorpe and Lockwood began, in the words of Heath and Edmondson, 'one of the best-known partnerships in British sociology' (*ibid.*).

In 1962, just one year after Lockwood's appointment, they initiated what came to be known as the *Affluent Worker* study. Many of the contributions in this volume discuss the findings of the project and its relation to Goldthorpe's subsequent research. In this chapter discussion will be confined to some details of the conduct of the project and some first indications of what it tells us about Goldthorpe's approach to sociology.

The project had one overriding aim: to examine the widely held view that the 'affluent' workers of post-war Britain were becoming increasingly 'middle-class' in their attitudes and lifestyles (the so-called *embourgeoisement* thesis). Over 200 interviews with skilled and semi-skilled manual workers in three companies in Luton were carried out between October 1962 and February 1964, with funding from the Department of Applied Economics at the University of Cambridge and subsequent support from the Human Sciences Committee of the Department of Scientific and Industrial Research (forerunner of the Science Research Council). Two full-time research officers, Frank Bechhofer and Jennifer Platt, were engaged to work on the project (Platt beginning and ending a year before Bechhofer), and a number of other research staff were also employed at various stages (including one contributor to this volume, Rosemary Crompton).

The output of the research was published, first in a series of major articles (Goldthorpe and Lockwood, 1963; Lockwood, 1966; Goldthorpe, 1966b; Goldthorpe, Lockwood, Bechhofer and Platt, 1967), then in three books. The first, *The Affluent Worker: Industrial Attitudes and Behaviour* (Goldthorpe *et al.*, 1968a), was almost a 'by-product' (*ibid.*: 1) of the main study and contrasted 'traditional' orientations to work with the more 'instrumental' orientation of the affluent workers. The second volume, *The Affluent Worker: Political Attitudes and Behaviour*, was devoted to one particular aspect of the larger study—the relation between affluence and voting behaviour and attitudes—and suggested that, while the affluent workers overwhelmingly retained their support for the Labour Party, this support tended to be of an 'instrumental' and, by implication, conditional kind. The third volume, *The Affluent Worker in the Class Structure*, presented the overall findings of the project on the sociology of the affluent worker and addressed a whole range of issues concerned with the class structure of Western industrial societies, including the decline of the traditional manual working class, changing attitudes to work arising from the introduction of new technologies, and the breakdown of traditional working-class communities. The three volumes have been widely cited as exemplifying the use of an 'action frame of reference' in empirical research, and have attracted widespread, if not always uncritical, interest among social scientists (for a discussion of the reception and influence of the *Affluent Worker* study, see Platt, 1984; also Heath and Edmondson, 1980: 44–50; Eldridge, 1980: 71–9).

In 1969, the year of the publication of the final *Affluent Worker* volume, a number of events took place in Goldthorpe's academic life which confirmed his high prestige within the sociological community and also indicated the direction of his future research activity. First, he was appointed as Official Fellow at Nuffield College, Oxford, where he has remained ever since. In the same year he was appointed editor of *Sociology*, newly established as the official journal of the British Sociological Association, and became President of the Sociology Section of the British Association for the Advancement of Science. On arrival at Nuffield, he joined the 'Social Mobility Group' at the College, and started a programme of research on social mobility which has occupied him ever since.

In 1972 the Nuffield Social Mobility Group undertook a major inquiry funded by the Social Science Research Council covering 10,000 men in England and Wales between the ages of 20 and 64. The 1972 survey, whose 'principal investigators' were A. H. Halsey, Jean Floud (who left soon after to become Principal of Newnham College, Cambridge) and Goldthorpe, provided the entire database for a study of family, class and education in Britain, which was subsequently written up as *Origins and Destinations* (Halsey, Heath and Ridge, 1980); it also provided the main basis for a second study under Goldthorpe's direction. In this second study Goldthorpe and his collaborators—Catriona Llewellyn and Clive Payne—also drew on a 1974 follow-up study of subsamples of 1972 respondents, in which more detailed data on work-histories and lifestyles were collected. These were used to examine in more detail issues such as work-life patterns and the links between mobility and kinship relations. The first papers reporting the findings of the second study were published in 1977 and 1978 (Goldthorpe and Llewellyn, 1977a, 1977b; Goldthorpe, Llewellyn and Payne, 1978), and the first edition of the book on the research, *Social Mobility and Class Structure in Modern Britain*, was published in 1980.

In his introduction to the 1980 volume Goldthorpe situated the study in the context of the two 'classic' post-war sociological studies of mobility, the British study by Glass *et al.* (published in 1954) and the American one by Blau and Duncan (published in 1967):

> ... our treatment of social mobility in modern Britain is ... carried out essentially in terms of mobility between classes, or, to be rather more precise, between class positions. We would accept, with the same glosses as those suggested by Parkin [*Class Inequality and Political Order*, 1971], Blau and Duncan's view that in the advanced societies of the West it is now the occupational order that forms 'the backbone of the class structure'. But, unlike Blau and Duncan, we seek to follow through the logic of this argument by using occupation (understood in a more qualified way than usual) as an indicator of class position rather than of prestige or of socio-economic status. In having a 'class' rather than a 'status' basis, our analyses do indeed depart from the usual practice of post-war mobility research, which, as we have noted, was influenced chiefly by Glass's study of 1949: we return rather, and appropriately enough, to the

earlier tradition of inquiry conducted within the context of 'the debate with Marx'. (1987a: 29)

The overall intention of *SMCS* was thus explicitly stated: to shift the emphasis of mobility research from a focus on a continuum of status positions which individuals can attain (the 'status attainment' approach) to a focus on patterned movements between class positions defined in terms of occupation and employment status (the 'class structure' approach).[2] In this respect, then, Goldthorpe's approach to the study of social mobility has a distinctly Marxian (or, in his own favoured phrase, *marxisant*) character (see *ibid.*: 28).

Questions of class structure had, of course, been central to the *Affluent Worker* study. However, the system of occupational classification used there—an eightfold classification ultimately collapsed into the three categories of 'white-collar', 'inter-mediate' and 'manual'—had been largely derivative of previous British studies (see Goldthorpe *et al.*, 1969: 196). In the early 1970s, however, under the stimulation of the Oxford Mobility project, Goldthorpe, in collaboration with Keith Hope, began a process of redefining the conceptual framework of occupational grading and prestige. The initial result was an article in 1972 (Goldthorpe and Hope, 1972) and a book in 1974 (Goldthorpe and Hope, 1974). However, the 'Hope-Goldthorpe scale' developed in these publications still saw mobility as occurring within a social continuum, whereas Goldthorpe himself was becoming increasingly convinced of the need to see mobility in a 'class structural' context. Together with Catriona Llewellyn he thus set about constructing a new class schema as the basic framework for interpreting the data from the 1972/1974 surveys, aggregating categories from the collapsed 'H-G scale' of 36 categories into a sevenfold 'schema of class positions' (Goldthorpe, 1980a: 40–3).

This is not the place to evaluate in detail what is now generally referred to as the 'Goldthorpe class schema' (see on this Chapters 4, 5 and 17–20 below).[3] What is important to note here is the 'style' of sociology indicated by the procedure adopted by Goldthorpe, in which theoretically informed empirical research led to a rethinking of conceptual tools and the elaboration of a new set of categories deemed more appropriate to the research task in hand. The same reasoning and procedure led to the adoption of the distinction between absolute and relative mobility rates as a conceptual cornerstone of the analysis of social mobility (see, for example, Goldthorpe, 1987a: 29–31, 305–16).

Already by the time of the publication of the first edition of *SMCS* in 1980, Goldthorpe had embarked on a new research project, which aimed to broaden and deepen the findings of the England and Wales study, testing them against compar-able studies in other countries. This required an enormous amount of work to standardize the data using a common frame of class positions. It began with a comparison between the data on England and Wales and those of two other countries, France and Sweden. This collaboration led to the publication of a series of articles in the late 1970s and early 1980s (Erikson, Goldthorpe and Portocarero, 1979, 1982, 1983; Goldthorpe and Portocarero, 1981). By 1982 this collaboration was formalized into a proposal to establish a larger project concerned with the Comparative Analysis of Social Mobility in Industrial Nations, the so-called CASMIN Project (see Goldthorpe and Müller, 1982). The aim of the project was to bring into comparable form data from mobility studies undertaken in nine European nations—England and Wales, France, Hungary, Northern Ireland,

Poland, the Republic of Ireland, Scotland, Sweden and West Germany—and three non-European ones—Australia, Japan and the USA.

The origins of CASMIN can be traced directly to the work of the Social Stratification and Mobility Research Committee of the International Sociological Association. Goldthorpe joined this group in 1971 when it was refounded after a period of inactivity, acting as its Vice-President from 1974 to 1982 and as President from 1982 to 1985. Many of the members of the Committee were acknowledged in the 'Preface' to the 1980 edition of *SMCS* (*ibid.*: vii-viii), including his collaborators in the three-nation research project, Robert Erikson and Lucienne Portocarero, as well as two contributors to this volume, Walter Müller (with whom he drafted the proposal to establish CASMIN in 1982) and Karl Ulrich Mayer, with whom in 1984 he founded a new journal for comparative sociological research, the *European Sociological Review*. By the end of 1989 CASMIN had already spawned around fifteen working papers and numerous published articles, including three by Erikson and Goldthorpe (1985, 1987a, 1987b). [4]

Before concluding this section on Goldthorpe's intellectual development, mention should be made of other areas of research and scholarship to which he has made significant contributions. First, he has published a series of articles which could be regarded as 'spin-offs' from the class schema and social mobility research. They include widely cited articles on the 'service class' (Goldthorpe, 1982) following on the work of Karl Renner and Ralf Dahrendorf, and contributions to two debates in the journal *Sociology*, one with Roger Penn on his class schema (Goldthorpe, 1981) and the other with various authors on women and class analysis (Goldthorpe, 1983a, 1984c; Goldthorpe and Payne, 1986b; Erikson and Goldthorpe, 1988c).

Second, he has published a number of articles in the broad field of sociological theory. Mention has already been made of his various writings on the relation between history and sociology (e.g. 1962a, 1962b; see also note 1 below), but he has also published articles on Pareto and Spencer (1968), social stratification theory (1964, 1972b; Goldthorpe and Bevan, 1977) and phenomenology and ethnomethodology (Goldthorpe, 1973a). He has made much cited contributions to industrial relations theory and policy (Goldthorpe, 1974a, 1974b) and to the development of social action approaches in industrial sociology research (Goldthorpe, 1970a, 1972b). His contribution to the 'political economy' of Western industrial nations (see Hirsch and Goldthorpe, 1978; Goldthorpe, 1984a, 1984b) will be discussed in more detail in the next section.

The most important theme, apart from social mobility, which runs like a thread through his work—from an article on 'Social Stratification in Industrial Society' (Goldthorpe, 1964; republished in 1966 as the concluding chapter to the second edition of Bendix and Lipset's classic American reader, *Class, Status and Power*) through to his contribution to Haferkamp and Smelser's edited volume, *Modernization and Social Change* (Goldthorpe, 1990)—is the critique of liberal theories of industrial and post-industrial society. Given the importance of this theme for Goldthorpe's work, it is discussed by Duncan Gallie in a separate introductory chapter to this volume.

In concluding this section, note should finally be taken of Goldthorpe's 'institutional' recognition, above all through his election in 1984 to become a Fellow of the British Academy, the highest academic honour in the humanities and social sciences in Britain. He thereby joined a small but distinguished group of sociologists to be so honoured, including Tom Burns, Ralf Dahrendorf, Ronald Dore, Ernest

Gellner, David Lockwood and W. G. Runciman. Goldthorpe was awarded the Helsinki University Medal in the same year.

JOHN GOLDTHORPE'S CONTRIBUTION TO SOCIOLOGY

In this second section the aim is to make a more general assessment of Goldthorpe's contribution to sociology. I will begin with a characterization of his approach to sociology as highlighted by the *Affluent Worker* study. This will be followed by an assessment of his place within British sociology as it developed in the 1970s and 1980s. Finally, additional elements will be adduced from his more recent national and international research on social mobility and the political economy of Western nations. This will lead to the final section, a summary presentation of his 'style of [sociological] inquiry' (Goldthorpe, 1987a: 1) in the form of a series of ideal-typical statements and propositions.

The Affluent Worker Study: A 'Critical Case' of Goldthorpe's Sociology

The primary objective of the study was outlined by Goldthorpe and his colleagues at the beginning of the first volume reporting on the research:

> to test empirically the widely accepted thesis of working-class *embourgeoisement*: the thesis that, as manual workers and their families achieve relatively high incomes and living standards, they assume a way of life which is more characteristically 'middle class' and become in fact progressively assimilated into middle-class society. (Goldthorpe *et al.*, 1968a: 1)

In this collective statement of the authors of the *Affluent Worker* study we can identify features which are typical of a more general approach to sociological investigation and analysis. First, there is the choice of a research topic of social and political 'relevance', in this case whether the 'affluent worker' of the post-war period was 'turning middle-class' in attitudes and behaviour. This was a highly charged topic with important implications for the conduct of industrial relations, political attitudes and behaviour, and the future of traditional working-class communities. Second, the topic chosen was one on which, at the time of the research in the 1960s, there were strongly held views among politicians and in the media and public opinion, and yet where detailed and systematic data were lacking. In other words, there was a good chance that sociological inquiry could make an important contribution to social and political debate.

Third, the main source of the sociological contribution was to come from engaging in empirical research, in which the evidence would be systematically examined and the findings presented in a way which would enable them to be subject to public scrutiny. Fourth, as well as being politically relevant, the research topic was of theoretical and conceptual importance for the discipline of sociology, touching on questions of social stratification, occupational class structure and the possibilities of collective action. Fifth and finally, the research strategy and techniques were chosen because of their appropriateness to the goals of the research (see Goldthorpe *et al.*, 1969: Ch. 2). In the event a 'critical case' approach was adopted, i.e. a site was selected which was likely to be as favourable as possible to the *embourgeoisement* thesis. The location was prosperous and expanding Luton, around 30 miles to the north of London, and around 330 male workers in three relatively high-wage 'progressive' companies—in the automobile, ball bearing and chemical industries —were selected for in-depth interview.[5]

Some of the general features of the *Affluent Worker* study can thus be summarized as follows:

> *research topic*: to be of socio-political and sociological relevance;
> *research aim*: to generate knowledge and understanding of the patterns underlying individual behaviours and attitudes, thereby to inform public and academic debate;
> *research strategy*: to carry out systematic, theoretically informed empirical research with appropriate research methods.

As we will see below, many of these features of the *Affluent Worker* study have been continued in Goldthorpe's research in the 1970s and 1980s, albeit with some important extensions and modifications. However, before looking at this, we will trace the development of Goldthorpe's position inside British sociology, as this will highlight some additional aspects of his approach to the discipline.

Goldthorpe and British Sociology in the 1970s and 1980s

By the early 1970s Goldthorpe had reached an eminent position inside the 'institutional' framework of British sociology, most obviously through his editor-ship of *Sociology*, the journal of the British Sociological Association (BSA), and his position as Official Fellow at Nuffield College, which was fast becoming one of the most important centres for social scientific research in Britain. By the mid- to late 1970s, however, his disaffection with British sociology was palpable. He had resigned from the BSA, no longer attended its annual conference, and clearly felt more at home among his colleagues in the Stratification and Mobility Research Committee of the International Sociological Association. By the early 1980s he had become something of a *bête noire* among certain groupings within the British sociological community.

We have already noted above his undisguised pleasure that the first edition of SMCS was attacked by what he called 'the dogmatists of the Marxist Left...' (1987a: 1), and there is no doubt he felt distinctly out of tune with certain trends within the resurgent Marxism and neo-Marxism of the 1970s and early 1980s. While he has always shown respect for 'more sophisticated' contemporary Marxist sociologists, and has readily acknowledged the influence of the Marxian tradition on his own research interests and thematic concerns (see, for example, Goldthorpe, 1987a: 24–31), he has consistently argued against those Marxists who suggest, implicitly or explicitly, that the task of sociology—and of the other social sciences—is to develop general theories of social change and to identify the structurally determined role of particular actors in bringing about such change. Indeed, he holds such theories to be just as mistaken as the 'liberal' theories of industrial society with their claim to have discovered a seemingly inescapable process of liberal-democratic 'convergence' in all 'industrial' and 'post-industrial' societies (see on this Chapter 3 by Duncan Gallie).

In this stance Goldthorpe has identified himself unreservedly with Karl Popper's critique of 'historicism'—that 'approach to the social sciences which assumes that historical prediction is their principal aim and which assumes that this aim is attainable by discovering the "rhythms" or the "patterns", the "laws" or the "trends" that underlie the evolution of history' (Popper, 1957: 3). For Goldthorpe, as for Popper and for Max Weber, there are no such underlying trends; indeed, the belief that there are is distinctly 'unsociological'. In addition, Goldthorpe, like Popper and Weber, rejects the view that sociologists, or any other social scientists for that matter, can provide technical answers to normative questions such as the problems of inflation and unemployment, let alone solutions as to how society should develop in the future. In a now famous debate in 1977 he said:

> ...ultimately the problem of inflation is a political problem: one's approach to it depends on what kind of society one wants to have. And in this respect, I have no more to say, as a sociologist, than the man who cleans my street. This is a matter, ultimately, for political action. As a sociologist, I will offer analyses. I might even say 'If you want to get from A to B, you might try doing it that way'—though I don't see this as being my major role. As a political actor I will make my own political decisions and use what trifling amount of political weight I've got to push in the direction that I want to go. What I object to is economists thinking that inflation is just a technical matter and that they, in the light of economic science, can tell us what we ought to do. (1978: 215)

There were other trends, too, apart from what he termed 'dogmatic' Marxism, which led Goldthorpe to a disaffection with many aspects of British sociology in the 1970s and 1980s. These included the attractions of phenomenology and ethnomethodology (see Goldthorpe, 1973a), and in particular the growth of an increasingly influential 'feminist sociology' which tended to reject him and his research as 'gender-blind' and 'sexist'. For example, writing in a BSA volume dedicated to reviewing British sociology from 1950 to 1980, Margaret Stacey made the following terse criticism of his work and that of his close colleagues:

> The Nuffield Mobility Survey of 1972 only sampled men. Wives were included in 1974. The only discussion of women in the book Hope edited is about the 'marriage market' (see Hope, 1972; Goldthorpe and Hope, 1974; Goldthorpe, 1980a). It is clear that Goldthorpe and Halsey still do not understand how their topic choices make women invisible to sociology.... . (Stacey, 1980: 178)

This is not the place to review the arguments on this matter (see the extended debate in Chapters 4 and 7–9 below). However, it is important to note that at the heart of Goldthorpe's general disaffection with British sociology was not an obsession with particular 'isms' or 'ologies', but a particular conception of the discipline of sociology and of social scientific research.

This came to the fore in a letter he wrote in July 1982 to *The Times Higher Education Supplement*. In the previous week eight social scientists (seven of whom were sociologists) had been asked to comment on the future priorities for social science research, particularly against the background of the Conservative Government's view that research should be made more 'relevant' to the needs of industry and the economy. Goldthorpe's reply captures much of the essence of his view of sociology. He began by supporting the unanimous view of the eight respondents that it would be wrong to undertake a fundamental reorientation of research priorities towards 'users' needs' and away from the central thematic and theoretical concerns of academic disciplines. However, he then went on to express his concern that, with one exception, so little awareness had been shown by the respondents of the 'unsatisfactory' nature of the existing relationship between *research* on the one hand and *the development of the discipline of sociology* in Britain on the other. He continued:

> One reason why the relationship is unsatisfactory is... the preoccupation of far too many sociologists with types of 'theory'—often no more than mere word-spinning—which neither derive from problems actually encountered in the conduct of empirical inquiry nor result in propositions of an empirically testable kind. A second, complementary reason... [is] the rather scandalous disregard shown in British sociology over the last 10 to 15 years for maintaining standards of research expertise, and especially in the area of data analysis.... . It has of course been the standard ploy to divert attention away from inadequacies in this respect by attacks on 'positivism', 'number-crunching', 'technique for its own sake', etc. But this will no longer do. The post-1968 rhetoric is wearing thin and, more importantly, it is being demonstrated in one substantive field of sociology after another that the use of formal models and quantitative methods has a major part to play in the proper integration of theory and research... .
>
> Two practical requirements follow. First, graduate work in British sociology departments should be reorganized so as to contain a far larger element of research training... . Secondly,...research funding agencies need to undertake far more painstaking and detailed assessments than they now do of the merits of research proposals from the standpoint of their likely contribution to disciplinary concerns: in particular, of just what are the theoretical issues to be addressed, of just what are the techniques of data collection and analysis to be applied, and above all of just how theory and research connect. The SSRC could learn much here from the evaluation procedures followed by bodies such as the American National Science Foundation or the Volkswagen Foundation, but of course in the last analysis it is the composition of its committees that will count. Hence the importance of maintaining—and, if need be, in opposition to Margaret Stacey's claim for the equitable (= equal?) representation of women as much as to specifically political appointments—that one criterion should precede all others: namely, recognised—or, it might be safer to say—internationally recognised—ability and achievement in research in the field in question. If this is deemed elitist or sexist, so be it. (*THES*, 23 July 1982)

This extended quotation summarizes many of the characteristic features of Goldthorpe's approach, in particular the reaffirmation of the (in his view indispensable) connection between the development of theory and the conduct of empirical research. However, there are some important additional aspects of his 'style' of sociology which have come increasingly to the fore in the research of the late 1970s and 1980s.

Data Analysis and Comparative Cross-Disciplinary Perspectives

First, it is important to highlight Goldthorpe's growing interest in data analysis and the use of formal models and quantitative methods in sociological research, in many ways against the grain of much sociological research in Britain since the 1960s (see Husbands, 1980). Indeed, the use of large data sets and log-linear modelling techniques in the social mobility research of the 1970s and 1980s marked a shift of emphasis away from the 'critical case' approach of the *Affluent Worker* study.[6] Second, there was a growing stress on the need for British sociology to be more aware of the international standing and recognition of its sociological research. In the 1982 letter to the *THES* Goldthorpe was particularly concerned with the need for British sociologists to keep more abreast of international developments, particularly within US-American sociology. But by this time, too, his own work had come to exemplify a number of other features of the 'international dimension'.

First, he was involved in organizing three international conferences—one in 1977 on inflation, and two in 1982 and 1983 on order and conflict in Western Europe—which aimed to stimulate cross-disciplinary international understanding between sociologists, economists and political scientists of major issues within advanced industrial societies. The resultant books (see Hirsch and Goldthorpe, 1978; Goldthorpe, 1984a) demonstrated his commitment to a new kind of multi-disciplinary comparative conceptual framework for social scientific analysis, which can be conveniently brought under the general rubric of a 'new political economy';

> under which may be examined, in freedom from orthodoxies of any kind, the effect on the performance of modern economies of the political systems with which they are enmeshed and, in turn, of the larger social structures and processes which comprehend economy and polity alike. (Goldthorpe, 1984a: 1)

Clearly Goldthorpe envisages the discipline of sociology, with its interest in 'larger social structures and processes', playing a major role in such an enterprise.

A second aspect of the 'international dimension' has involved the search for international models of social mobility based on data sets from an increasingly wide range of countries. Here it is interesting to note the particular procedure or process of comparative investigation he and his research colleagues have adopted, beginning with national research—in which models and techniques are developed and tested and findings presented—then moving to comparative work involving a small number of countries—in which national data collected according to different principles and with different techniques can be 'standardized'—and then moving to larger-scale comparative analysis which becomes more and more extensive in coverage and sophistication.

Of course, this should not be seen as a totally linear development. For example, the first international and comparative meetings on social mobility attended by Goldthorpe took place in the early 1970s, and clearly informed the way in which the findings from the 1972 and 1974 British studies were interpreted and presented, as he himself has recognized (1987a: vii–viii). Ideally, too, it would clearly be preferable for the national studies—which provide the databases for comparative research—to be conducted from the outset on the basis of common principles and common techniques, thus obviating the need for exceedingly laborious standardization procedures. Underlying the development of Goldthorpe's research into social mobility, however, is some image of a maturing discipline, maturity in the coverage of countries and issues, the techniques of data analysis, and the reliability and accuracy of the substantive findings.

Before bringing these various strands together, it is important finally to highlight some general features of Goldthorpe's research practice which may be said to constitute his 'style of inquiry'. First, all his major research has been conceived and executed as teamwork. Second, there has clearly been more than one highly creative 'partnership of equals' in his career. For example, the work of the 1960s undoubtedly owes much to the creative partnership with David Lockwood, whereas the international mobility research has seen a range of fruitful partnerships, perhaps above all with Robert Erikson. Third, the processes of research and publication in which he has been involved tend to follow the same procedure, with empirical research followed by initial publication of findings in extended articles in learned journals, eventually leading to the production of a book on the research after many years' gestation following the completion of fieldwork.

CONCLUSION: A SUMMARY OF GOLDTHORPE'S STYLE OF SOCIOLOGY

This concluding section will summarize the previous discussion of Goldthorpe's style of sociological inquiry in the form of a series of ideal-typical statements and propositions. In this way it is hoped to capture the essence of his approach to sociology and to social scientific investigation more generally.[7]

1   There are no underlying social scientific laws or trends from which predictions about the future of industrial society can be read off. The future is open, and there are real choices to be made.
2   Sociological investigation can help us, however, to identify certain patterned features of industrial societies, for example, as they relate to the occupational structure and social mobility within and between generations. These patterned features provide a persistent if continually changing framework of inequality between different social groups, structuring both individual life chances and the possibilities and limits of collective action.
3   The scope for individual and collective action in industrial societies will differ from nation to nation as a result of their different class structures, economic structures and political systems as historically formed. Social scientists need, therefore, to develop a comparative 'political economy' of industrial nations incorporating insights from the disciplines of, in particular, sociology, economics and politics.
4   Social scientific knowledge is advanced by formulating theoretically significant propositions that can be examined empirically through systematic research using the techniques of data analysis most appropriate to the problem in hand. Speculative theoretical debate without an empirical reference point ('data-free' analysis) often degenerates into mere word-spinning. The aim of social science research is to contribute to an understanding of relevant contemporary issues, providing academic—and social and political—controversy 'with more and better material on which to feed' (Goldthorpe, 1987a: 1).
5   Social scientists can identify the implications of class structure, economic structure and political systems for the distribution of power in society and the possibilities for individual and collective action arising from this. However, they cannot establish which forms of social action should be taken or adopted. This is a matter for individuals as citizens and as members of particular social groups to decide.

ACKNOWLEDGMENTS

I would like to thank Gordon Causer, John Goldthorpe and Jennifer Platt for comments on an earlier draft of this chapter.

NOTES

1 His first major presentation at an international sociological gathering—the Fifth World Congress of Sociology in Washington, DC in 1962—was subtitled 'a sociological approach to a problem in historical explanation' (Goldthorpe, 1962a), and in the same year he published an article entitled 'The Relevance of History to Sociology' (Goldthorpe, 1962b). Nearly twenty years later, the title he chose for the 1989 T. H. Marshall Memorial Lecture at the University of Southampton was 'The Uses of History in Sociology', which included an attack on recent attempts (from Barrington Moore to Theda Skocpol and Michael Mann) at grand historical theorizing, all of which, he argued, lacked the appropriate factual underpinnings and methodological rigour.

2 It is important to note, however, that the Goldthorpe class schema allows differentiation between and across occupational function. Here it is possible to detect the strong influence of David Lockwood, particularly the latter's celebrated distinction between the two major components of class position, 'work situation' (based on occupation) and 'market situation' (based on employment status) (Lockwood, 1958: 15–16). Lockwood's influence in this connection is specifically acknowledged by Goldthorpe (1987a: 40).

3 The combinations of occupational and employment status groupings in the later version of the 'Goldthorpe class schema' were taken directly from the improved 1980 occupation classification of the British Office of Population Censuses and Surveys (OPCS), thus severing all connections with the 'H-G scale' (see Goldthorpe, 1987a: 254ff.; also his 'Response' in this volume, especially note 13).

4 One of the spin-offs of the CASMIN Project can be found in the second edition of *Social Mobility and Class Structure*, in which Goldthorpe published a completely new chapter entitled 'Class Mobility in Britain in Comparative Perspective' (1987a: Ch. 11). This represents a preliminary attempt to assess the extent of cross-national variations and similarities in social mobility (on this see in particular Chapters 17–20 in this volume). As noted in the introduction to this chapter, a major volume bringing together comparative data from the CASMIN Project is in preparation.

5 In the end around 77 per cent of the chosen sample agreed to a first interview in the workplace, and around 70 per cent agreed to a second interview in their own homes together with their wives.

6 This shift in emphasis was, of course, due in large part to the different sociological problems being addressed in the two projects.

7 From these extremely concentrated concluding statements and propositions it is possible to infer the three main intellectual influences on Goldthorpe's sociology: Karl Marx, Max Weber and Karl Popper. To these could perhaps be added a fourth, the British 'political arithmetic' tradition. The influence of this tradition is discussed in detail by Halsey, Heath and Ridge (1980: Ch. 1).

3. John Goldthorpe's Critique of Liberal Theories of Industrialism

DUNCAN GALLIE

The theory of industrialism has a strong claim to being the most systematically formulated and influential theory of longer-term social structural change developed in the post-war era. Much of John Goldthorpe's work can be seen as a prolonged debate with the theory, and particularly with its claims that there has been a tendency over time for advanced industrial societies to converge in terms of the organization of work, patterns of social stratification, forms of social conflict and the nature of political institutions. In contrast Goldthorpe has repeatedly stressed the powerful self-maintaining properties of social structures and hence the persistence of major sources of differentiation between societies.

While the most influential general statement of the theory was in Clark Kerr et al.'s *Industrialism and Industrial Man* (1960, 1973), its general assumptions were reflected in a wide body of more specialized work. They underlay, for instance, Robert Blauner's (1964) vision of the effects of the evolution of technology on work experience, Ross and Hartman's (1960) analysis of patterns of industrial conflict, Lipset and Zetterberg's (1959) research on social mobility and Wilensky's (1975) analysis of the determinants of welfare state development. The importance of this perspective lay in its provision of an integrative framework that avoided both the formalism of Parsonian meta-theory and the vacuousness of pure empiricism. It offered a counter-interpretation of societal development to that of Marx which appeared far better equipped to illuminate the great post-war expansion. At the same time, like Marxism, it offered an optimistic vision of the future in which economic growth would continue and the major social conflicts in society would be resolved. This, however, was a future in which neo-liberal rather than socialist values would ultimately triumph, with evolutionary change generating the structural conditions for individualism, equality of opportunity and political pluralism.

Goldthorpe's critique of the theory has developed on two fronts: an attack on the argument as a new form of 'historicism'; and empirical criticism of the theory's

29

more specific predictions about social structural change. In the first place, heavily influenced by the work of Popper, Goldthorpe rejects the very possibility of a scientific theory of a unique and total process, arguing that scientific theory is necessarily concerned with recurrent relationships between particular aspects of phenomena that are analytically distinguishable (1971: 277). Equally fundamentally, he argues, the theory fails to specify the linkages between economic change and social action. It provides no explanation of why the social actors, through whose agency change occurs, *should* act in the particular ways that are deemed to be functional for an advanced society (*ibid.*). In contrast, he argues for the independent efficacy of social action, and for the influence on the development of society of 'purposive, organized interventions, guided by different models of what the future *could* be like' (*ibid.*: 286). This fundamentally undercuts the type of futurological ambition embodied in the theory. For if social action cannot be 'read off' from social structure and regarded as merely epiphenomenal, then any basis for clear-cut predictions about the future is undermined. Social forecasting must limit itself to indicating the range of possibilities and to considering the conditions and consequences of diverse types of potential development.

Despite the centrality of these issues for the original objectives of the theory of industrialism, it is not my intention to dwell on them here. For in his major later restatement of his views—*The Future of Industrial Societies* (1983)—Kerr has effectively conceded much of the argument. Given the centrality of knowledge to evolution, and the inherent unpredictability of the future of human knowledge, the future, he tells us, cannot be predicted (*ibid.*: 110). Further, Kerr now accepts that social values may develop in ways that cannot be predicted from the imperatives of industrialization and that these may impinge crucially on the nature of society: 'New mentalities can change society just as can new knowledge; they can propel society into new ways' (*ibid.*: 123). Finally, even in the sphere of economic development Kerr now anticipates quite diverse possible future scenarios, ranging from the continuation of high economic growth (which would favour the spread of market mechanisms) to the advent of economic decline (which would encourage heavily controlled economies and political systems). He now explicitly recognizes the possibility that future societies could have quite different experiences of economic change and that, in such circumstances, 'great divergence could then take place between these two sets of nations' (*ibid.*: 116).

This modification of the claims of the theory of industrialism greatly narrows the area of contention. What is now at stake are the empirical claims about whether or not there *has* been a tendency over time for the advanced industrial societies to converge in their major institutional structures. We can distinguish two major claims about convergence between advanced societies embodied in the theory of industrialism. The first is that Western capitalist societies are becoming increasingly similar, and the second is that there has been a broad convergence between capitalist and state socialist societies. A major problem in assessing the merits of the convergence thesis is the dearth of good comparative data over time. This difficulty is particularly acute with respect to the comparison between East and West. Our knowledge of the organization of work, industrial relations or income differentiation in the Soviet Union is simply insufficient to allow any rigorous comparison with Western societies. The greater part of this discussion, then, will focus on the issue of convergence between capitalist societies, although I shall conclude with some general comments on the 'inter-system' convergence hypothesis.

THE ORGANIZATION OF WORK AND INDUSTRIAL RELATIONS

The focal interest of the research programme that inspired *Industrialism and Industrial Man* was the changing nature of labour and management; this was also the area in which the imperatives of industrialization were thought to be most decisive. The two central developments that Kerr *et al.* saw as flowing from industrialization were the growing similarity in the structure of the workforce and the growth of large-scale bureaucratized organizations with rule structures regulated through a system of pluralistic industrial relations.

There can be little doubt that there have been important commonalities in the ways in which the labour forces in the advanced societies have developed. In each of these societies there has been a decline in the agricultural sector, a tendency to incorporate the bulk of the labour force into paid employment and more recently a major increase in female participation in employment. For Kerr, this is clear evidence of the overall tendency to convergence.

Two developments, however, might lead one to pause before assuming that the composition of the workforces of the advanced societies has become much more similar. First, one feature of the rapid expansion in the post-war period of the Western capitalist economies was the widespread resort to immigrant labour to meet labour shortages. The particular sources of immigrant labour varied substantially between societies, and perhaps more fundamentally there were considerable differences in the institutional regimes within which such labour was welcomed (Castles and Kosack, 1973; Freeman, 1979; Layton-Henry, 1984). These differences related to past historical conditions (which had created different patterns of relations between countries) and different definitions of citizenship. There was, then, a very sharp difference between the position of Asian immigrants who arrived in Britain as British citizens and the Algerians who came to work, often illegally, in French factories or the 'guest' workers in Germany. Whereas the first could legitimately struggle for equal rights within the labour market, the last two were usually excluded by law from such rights and subject to a level of labour market vulnerability that was qualitatively different from that of British immigrants.

The rise in female labour market participation may also have been an important source of increased divergence between capitalist workforces. In the first place the extent of participation varied very substantially between societies of broadly similar levels of economic development. For instance, in 1984 in the Netherlands and in Italy 41 per cent of women were in the labour force. In contrast, in Denmark and Sweden the figures rose to 74 and 77 per cent (OECD, 1986). Further, the manner of women's incorporation in the labour force differed between societies. In some societies a high proportion of women entered the workforce as part-time workers; in others this was relatively rare. For instance, in 1981, 46 per cent of women in employment in Sweden were part-time workers, 44 per cent of Danish women, 54 per cent of Norwegian women and 37 per cent of British women. In France and Belgium, on the other hand, the figure was no higher than 16 per cent and in Italy it fell to a mere 6 per cent (Beechey and Perkins, 1987: 43). Overall, then, the inclusion in the workforce of major new pools of labour—whether immigrants or women—occurred under very different conditions in different countries and it seems likely that this resulted in increased heterogeneity in the structure of employment.

A second major development identified by the theorists of industrialism was the growth in scale and bureaucratization of work organizations, the development of an increasingly complex web of rules, and the emergence of pluralistic systems of decision-making for determining such rules (Kerr, 1983: 54). Since it is now widely recognized that the tendency towards the increasing size of workplaces has been reversed in the 1980s (Millward and Stevens, 1986; Piore and Sabel, 1984), I shall focus here on the issue of convergence in work rules and industrial relations. Kerr *et al.* were fully aware that, in an earlier phase of industrialization, indeed even in industrial societies in the 1950s, there were significant variations in the rules governing the workplace. They argued that this resulted from the fact that they had evolved 'from different industrial relations systems created under different types of elite' (1973: 242). Thus, within capitalist societies, there were important distinctions between societies with 'middle-class' elites, where the unions had an active role in workplace regulation and where authority in rule-making was pluralistic, and societies with 'dynastic' elites where the unions had little role in the workplace and where the state and management dominated the rule-making process. The authors linked these basic differences in the structure of the decision-making process to differences in methods of payment, wage structures and disputes procedures (*ibid.*: 240–1, 251–5).

However, the essential claim of the theory of industrialism is that with economic development such differences should disappear. Given the view that the divergence between rules was related to differences in industrial relations systems, the argument for convergence is ultimately founded upon a belief in the growing similarity of national industrial relations systems. In particular, these are held to be moving in the direction of greater 'pluralism', conceived as tripartite decision-making by employers, labour organizations and the state.

Goldthorpe has challenged this view by arguing that, rather than convergence towards a pluralist system, there were signs of divergence in modes of institutional regulation in advanced Western societies (Goldthorpe, 1984a: 12–13; 1984b). The growth of pluralism in the expansionary decades of the 1950s and 1960s, he maintains, has led not to the greater functional integration of Western societies, but to severe problems of economic management. It is the responses to this dilemma that have led to divergent patterns between the capitalist societies. In some societies the power of the unions has been given higher-level recognition and the national leadership has been integrated into the policy-making process. In others there has been a move to weaken union strength by the creation of a flexible sector of the workforce more directly exposed to market forces. The emergence of such a sector is facilitated by the influx of migrant labour, the subcontracting of services to small firms, and the use of temporary labour.

Goldthorpe has perhaps overestimated the similarity in the growth of shopfloor power in different capitalist societies in the first three post-war decades, and it is clear that the major sources of differentiation in employer and state attitudes to the role of trade unions predate substantially the inflationary crisis of the 1970s. Nonetheless, the arguments that quite different institutional patterns may be equally viable, and that there is no evidence of convergence, are surely correct. A substantial literature has highlighted the very different levels of involvement of the unions at national level in countries such as Austria, Sweden and Norway, compared to their equivalents in France and Italy. Further, it is clear that there are very substantial differences between societies in the influence of unions over workplace rules.

Contrast, for instance, the procedures for decision-making, the rules governing work allocation and the modes of supervision in the car factories of Citroën in France described by Robert Linhart (1981) with those in comparable Ford factories in Britain described by Huw Beynon (1973). Or consider the equally strong contrast that emerges from Dore's (1973) analysis of social relations in Japanese and British engineering firms. It might be argued that, in terms of the theory of industrialism, such differences would be expected to evaporate only in the most technologically advanced sectors. However, there is little evidence that this is the case. For instance, a comparison of oil refineries in France and Britain (Gallie, 1978) revealed that, even in plants owned by the same multinational company and deploying very advanced forms of automation, there were quite different rules in the two countries governing job classification, payment, work allocation and discipline and very different procedures for making decisions about the organization of work. These were rooted in major differences in forms of management and in patterns of industrial relations that quite faithfully reflected the broader institutional patterns characteristic of the two societies.

It is clear, then, from detailed research into workplace social relations, that there has been a persisting variability in the nature of work organization and of work rules between capitalist countries. While there have been important internal developments, the essential differentiating characteristics of industrial relations systems as diverse as the British, the French, the Japanese and the Swedish have remained largely unaltered over the last three decades.

SOCIAL STRATIFICATION

One of the central pillars of the theory of industrialism was the view that economic development leads to a progressive reduction of social inequality. In the first place it is believed to lead to a reduction in wage and salary differentials, as a result of education increasing the supply of skilled persons and reducing the availability of labour for more 'disagreeable' occupations (Kerr *et al.*, 1973: 271). Second, it is held to generate higher levels of social mobility: 'Industrialisation tends to produce an open society, inconsistent with the assignment of managers or workers to occupations or to jobs by traditional caste, by racial groups, by sex or by family status' (*ibid.*: 45). Twenty years later Kerr's views on these issues had been modified only mildly. As industrialism proceeds, he argues, economic rewards come to be based more on merit and seniority, and the distribution of income after taxes becomes more equal within individual nations (1983: 57). While there are signs of growing scepticism about the emergence of a purely meritocratic society, there is still a firm belief in the declining influence of family background on life chances.

Trends in Income Inequality

The main thrust of Goldthorpe's critique with regard to income inequality has been directed at the theory's assumption that previous trends towards greater equality manifested 'the operation of some process inherent in industrialism—of some general economic law—which will necessarily persist in the future and ensure a continuing egalitarian trend' (Goldthorpe, 1966c: 652). Rather, he has suggested that the trend might be checked at a point at which considerable economic inequality remains. Giorgio Gagliani (1987: 319) has underlined the 'grossly inadequate supply of appropriate data', the lack of adequate time series and the formidable work on data standardization that would be needed before any rigorous test could be made of the relationship between economic development and income distribution on a cross-cultural basis. At best, such evidence as we have might point to the existence of an inverted U-shaped 'band' rather than of any linear trend to greater equality. Moreover, the width of this band implies that rather different patterns are possible.

If we look at the British data, there are grounds for considerable doubt about the existence of an inevitable trend towards greater economic equality. In the 1970s there was a significant narrowing in the overall earnings distribution, resulting in good part from a decline in real earnings in many higher-paid occupations. This was particularly notable in the period of the Labour Government's flat-rate incomes policies. In the 1980s, however, the trend altered dramatically. Far from growing equality, there was a marked tendency to heightened inequality, with the decile ratio for men rising from 2.38 in 1979 to 2.88 in 1986 and for women from 2.28 to 2.61 (Department of Employment, 1988: 75–82).

Moreover, it is notable that this widening of earnings inequalities in the 1980s was not offset by fiscal redistribution. There was a marked rise in the ratio of the highest to lowest decile after income tax, national insurance contributions and child benefit were taken into account for all of the major family types other than single women. In its analysis of disposable income, *Social Trends* notes:

> the increasing margin that has opened up between earners in the lowest and highest decile group. Between 1971 and 1986 a married couple with two children in the lowest 10 per cent of earners would on average have seen an increase of 18 per cent in their real disposable earnings. Meanwhile a similar family in the highest decile would have enjoyed an increase of 31% in the same period. (CSO, 1988: 90)

If we consider total household income, the same picture emerges of widening inequality in the 1980s. The top 10 per cent of tax units have increased their share of post-tax income from 23.4 per cent in 1978/79 to 26.5 per cent in 1984/85 (CSO, 1987: 94). In contrast, the post-tax share of the lowest decile declined from 2.9 to 2.7 per cent.

It is not only Britain that has lacked any clear long-term linear trend in the distribution of earnings. For instance, in France salary inequalities increased over the period 1950–1966. This was followed by a particularly sharp reduction in inequalities in 1968 due to the improvement in incomes at the bottom of the ladder, a slower narrowing of the distribution between 1969 and 1980 and finally a stabilization between 1980 and 1983 (Centre d'étude des revenus et des coûts, 1985: 77). In the longer-term perspective what is striking is not a tendency towards progressively greater equality, but the stability of pattern. As the major report on incomes in France puts it: 'The salary hierarchy at the beginning of the 1980s proves to be very close to that observed at the beginning of the 1950s: the progressive widening of differentials between 1950–1967 has been virtually compensated by the inverse movement of a narrowing of differentials between 1968 and recent years' (*ibid.*: 76). The report notes the possible significance of continuing political action in reducing salary differentials since 1968, particularly through raising lower salaries.

Social Mobility and Equality of Opportunity

It is, however, primarily the theses of the theory of industrialism with respect to social mobility which came to constitute the central focus of Goldthorpe's own research. In his original critique of the theory Goldthorpe emphasized two points. First, he suggested that an increased rate of intergenerational mobility was likely to be associated with some limitation of intragenerational or career mobility, thereby reducing the openness of society for a large proportion of the population. Second, drawing on the work of S. M. Miller (1960), he argued that the apparent similarity of mobility rates in the advanced industrial societies, revealed by studies such as that of Lipset and Zetterberg (1959), was an artefact resulting from their concentration on 'mass' mobility across the manual/non-manual line. Once the range of mobility, as distinct from its mere frequency, was taken into account, sizeable differences emerge in mobility patterns between industrial societies (Goldthorpe, 1966c: 655). In his later work he became increasingly concerned with a third tenet of the theory of industrialism, namely, the view that societies were becoming progressively more open over time in terms of intergenerational mobility.

His initial work focused on the evidence for change in patterns of social mobility in Britain (Goldthorpe, 1987a). In one respect this confirmed the view that economic development was associated with increased upward mobility. The major pattern of structural change involved the expansion of the service class of professionals, administrators and managers and the contraction of the manual working class. This increase in the opportunities for mobility meant that, across different birth cohorts, men of all class origins became progressively more likely to move into the service class. This trend appears to have continued across the period 1972–83, when economic conditions had become very much more difficult (*ibid.*: 262). Further, the analysis of the British pattern did not confirm Goldthorpe's argument that increased intergenerational mobility was likely to be associated with decreased career mobility for those who start in lowly positions (a version of the counter-balance thesis). Rather, an increase in direct entry to the higher levels of the class structure for manual workers had occurred without any accompanying erosion of their chances of upward mobility through later career advances (*ibid.*: 55–8).

However, Goldthorpe's findings conflicted heavily with the assumption of the theory of industrialism that such mobility led to a more open society. The key measure of 'openness', he argued, was that of the relative mobility chances of children from different classes of origin. In this respect there was no evidence at all of greater social fluidity. Rather, the increasing number of higher-level jobs provided by the service class had been shared out more or less pro-rata among men of different class origins, while the contraction of the manual working class had been accompanied by a decline in the relative chances of those of service class origins entering manual work. Overall, a constant social fluidity model fitted the data well (*ibid.*: 77, 82). This general pattern of fluidity remained unaltered by the economic crisis of the 1970s and early 1980s. There was some sign that inequalities in chances of entering the service class diminished, but this was offset by a widening of the inequality of chances of being located in the working class (*ibid.*: 258–62, 265).

In his more recent work Goldthorpe has turned to the issue of the degree of similarity in mobility profiles between the advanced societies. Kerr (1983: 53) refers to Lipset's research in defence of the view that mobility rates had converged across industrial societies. In their influential analysis of comparative mobility rates, Lipset and Zetterberg (1959: 13) had concluded that 'the overall pattern of social mobility appears to be much the same in the industrial societies of various Western countries'. However, a first point to emerge from more careful comparative work was that such societies in fact differ quite substantially in their absolute mobility rates, largely as a result of past patterns of economic and social structural development. This has affected the total amount of mobility, the implications of mobility for the formation of particular classes, and the chances of mobility between specific class origins and destination (Erikson, Goldthorpe and Portocarero, 1979). Thus in comparison to Britain and France, Sweden was distinctive both in having higher rates of total mobility and in its higher rates of long-range upward mobility on the part of sons of working-class fathers; Britain was distinctive for its very high level of self-recruitment into the working class—with almost three-quarters of its members being second-generation, compared with just over half in Sweden and under half in France (*ibid.*: 430); while France was characterized by the higher level of self-recruitment of the service class and petty bourgeoisie (*ibid.*: 430, 435, 438). Although there was evidence of similar long-term trends of occupational change, the fact that these occurred at different paces and rhythms between societies meant that there were no good reasons for anticipating a convergence in class structures over time (Goldthorpe, 1987a: 322).

However, if there were major differences in absolute rates, there was a much more impressive commonality between industrial societies in terms of their relative mobility rates. An elaborated form of the common fluidity model proposed by Featherman, Jones and Hauser (1975) provided a sufficiently good fit for the mobility data of countries such as the United Kingdom, France, the Federal Republic of Germany, the Republic of Ireland, Poland and Sweden to suggest that there was not a series of distinctive types of fluidity regime deriving from particular levels of economic development or types of political regime (Erikson and Goldthorpe, 1987a, 1987b). Yet even this finding does not accord well with the theory of industrialism. For Kerr *et al.* had argued that societies would become steadily more similar as they became economically more developed. The picture that has emerged from comparative research, however, suggests that societies became similar in their relative mobility rates at an early stage in the process of industrialization, but that there is little evidence of subsequent convergence. By the same token there is no support for the view that there has been a common evolutionary tendency for societies to become more open with higher levels of industrialization.

Overall, the evidence from two decades of research on social mobility has confirmed that there has indeed been a major increase in opportunities for upward mobility in Britain in the post-war period and it has failed to support the view that this has been 'counter-balanced' by declining opportunities for worklife mobility. However, this did not mean in any way that Britain was becoming a more equal or open society. Rather, the notable finding was that relative mobility rates had remained very stable for half a century. Nor was there any serious evidence of a convergence between societies in their absolute mobility rates. Absolute mobility rates showed substantial differences between societies at broadly similar levels of economic development and there are few grounds for thinking that they will get closer in the future. Where industrial societies were much more similar was in their relative mobility patterns, but in contrast to the assumptions of the theory of industrialism, there is no evidence that they have become more similar with higher levels of industrialization.

CLASS AND SOCIAL CONFLICT IN CAPITALIST SOCIETIES

A third major theme of the liberal theory of industrialism is that of the progressive attenuation of social conflict and the growth of social consensus with industrial development. Thus: 'Consensus develops wherever industrialisation is successful. The labour force becomes committed to and settled into industrial life. The sense of protest subsides' (Kerr *et al.*, 1973: 266). Four factors were seen as particularly important in accounting for this. First, the pattern of structural development was one that undercut the traditional bases of class organization. The master trend in the occupational structure was towards increased differentiation and increased diversity of skills. This would reduce people's sense of class identity and lead instead to the growth of 'professional-type interests' and to an occupationally-based identity (*ibid.*: 272). Class, quite simply, 'will lose its meaning' (*ibid.*: 275). Second, it was argued, there was a tendency towards the institutionalization of industrial conflict through the growth of procedures for joint regulation in industry. This would channel conflicts away from the political arena and enable them to be resolved piecemeal, thereby diminishing the intensity of social grievances (*ibid.*: 222). Third, the spread of education would diminish inequalities of income, increase the proportion of those with 'middle incomes' and thereby expand the middle class. As Kerr *et al.* put it: 'Education brings in its wake a new economic equality and a new community of political outlook. This, in turn, along with many other developments, helps bring consensus to society' (*ibid.*: 271). Finally, the upward trend in the skill structure implies an increased dependence on employees' skills and motivation. Autocratic modes of authority will no longer be effective and instead cooperation must be achieved by giving people responsibility and by developing social consensus (*ibid.*: 53, 270).

In contrast, a persistent current of Goldthorpe's work has underlined the durability of class-based conflict and the continuing sources of structural strain in capitalist societies. In the *Affluent Worker* study (Goldthorpe *et al.*, 1969) one of the central conclusions was that increased affluence did not lead manual workers to adopt distinctively middle-class lifestyles or social values. Rather, the future trend suggested by the attitudes and behaviour of the 'prototypical' workers of Luton was that of an increased emphasis on the purely instrumental aspects of work and the adoption of a more privatized lifestyle. One might question whether later research has supported the view that these workers were in any way prototypical rather than manifesting the more general characteristics of British working-class culture (Gallie, 1988b), but the account given as to why higher incomes should not directly translate into middle-class social values was a persuasive one.

In his essays in the 1970s Goldthorpe proceeded to draw out the ways in which the instrumental orientations of manual workers might lead to heightened social conflict rather than to progressive social harmony. His point of departure was the high degree of resistance of the structure of social inequality to change in an egalitarian direction. In Britian such inequality does not lead to a general contestation of the social order, in part because of the mutually reinforcing processes of restricted comparative reference groups and socialization into a political culture that emphasizes trust in the political elite (Goldthorpe, 1974a). But if class inequality does not produce radical political action, it nonetheless generates chronic disorder in the economic sphere. As Fox and Flanders (1969) argued, British industrial relations are in an anomic state, with a proliferation of unrelated or divergent normative systems that are a seedbed of tension over relativities between employees and employers and between different sets of employees. For Goldthorpe, however, this could not be remedied by a rationalization of the procedures of collective bargaining, since it was ultimately rooted in the lack of any clear normative basis to the *wider* structure of inequality (Goldthorpe, 1974b). Indeed, the attempt to introduce an overarching incomes policy, rather than creating greater consensus, might well lead to a broadening of comparative reference groups and thereby produce greater resentment over the existing structure of incomes.

Further, Goldthorpe suggested that there were broader changes occurring in the social structure of advanced Western societies that made it likely that employees would increasingly exploit their market position to the full through heightened militancy in collective bargaining (Goldthorpe, 1978: 196). In the first place structural change has been undermining the traditional status order that served to legitimate class inequalities. Such status orders, he argues, had never been intrinsic to capitalism, but were residues of pre-capitalist culture. Urbanization and increased geographical mobility undercut local status group structures; increased social differentiation and mobility led to greater status inconsistency; notions of 'generalized' social worth and responsibility tended to break down (*ibid.*: 199). Consequently, the working class was no longer constrained by a belief in its own necessary inferiority, or by a sense that income differentials reflected real differences in social worth. Second, the growth of 'citizenship' undermined the acceptance of class inequalities through its embodiment of the counter-principle of equality. Thus workers' expectations, for instance with regard to regular employment, are not merely higher, but they are reinforced by the fact that they are now regarded as a right (*ibid.*: 203). At the same time the extension of citizenship rights had increased the organizational resources of employees through the development of trade union organization and collective bargaining, thereby encouraging them to contest. Third, the very character of the working class was being changed by its growing homogeneity in terms of social background and experience. Increasingly self-recruiting and second-generation, its members were unaffected by early socialization in the local status structures of small communities. Instead they had been brought up in a culture where trade union action was the normal way of defending and improving employment conditions and living standards.

In sum, social structural change was leading to 'an increasingly delegitimated structure of class inequality' and it was possible to speak of a 'crisis of legitimacy' now existing in the sphere of distribution (*ibid.*: 208, 209). A more self-confident, better organized and more resentful working class was pursuing its interests more aggressively. At an immediate level this could be seen as the major factor behind the rise of inflation in the 1970s; in the longer term it meant that the working class had the potential for 'action of a more concerted type, both industrial and political' (*ibid.*: 208). Government economic policies designed to give greater weight to market forces might well lead to sharper social conflict, the structuring of conflict on broad class lines and confrontation between organized labour and the government (*ibid.*: 209).

From the vantage point of the 1980s it is clear that such a scenario of the declining legitimacy of class inequalities, increased worker militancy and the expanding power resources of working-class organization reflected at best the conditions of a very specific historical period. Indeed, such evidence as we have suggests that the attitudes of British manual workers to class inequalities remained unchanged over the 1970s (Gallie, 1983). Moreover the working class did not provide the militant response to higher unemployment and to government attempts to reduce its existing rights that Goldthorpe had anticipated. Rather, the 1980s were to witness a sharp decline in militancy and a severe weakening of trade union organization. Yet the critique of the assumption of an emerging consensus remains relevant. The theory of industrialism assumes that the capitalist market is not a major source of structural conflict. Yet both the rise of trade union militancy in the 1970s, and the efforts of the Conservative Government to repress it in the 1980s, were clearly manifestations of the conflictual nature of the relations generated by the market. What Goldthorpe underestimated in these essays of the 1970s was the extent to which political action could effectively structure the ways in which the tensions generated by the market are expressed. In the 1980s, however, he was to give increasing weight to the significance of political factors within capitalist societies for determining institutional structures and life chances.

POLITICAL AGENCY AND SOCIETAL DIFFERENTIATION

The central weakness of the liberal theory of industrialism is its failure to take account of the continuing importance of political factors in shaping social structure. While the nature of elites and their strategies had been attributed a major role in generating the institutional systems that were still prevailing in the early post-war era, the predictions of the theory demanded a sharp and progressive curtailment of such factors in the future. The theoretical explanation for this shift in the relative weight of economic and political influences was never coherently spelt out and, empirically, it would appear to be poorly substantiated. Political factors remain of major importance in differentiating institutional structures both within capitalist societies and between capitalist and state socialist societies.

The Influence of Politics in Capitalist Societies

In seeking to understand the rather substantial differences between societies in the 1950s, Kerr *et al.* (1973) emphasized the decisive role of the industrializing elites and of the ideologies they fashioned to secure their objectives and to justify their leadership. As far as the advanced capitalist societies were concerned, it was the middle class and the dynastic elites that were of key importance. Their distinctive orientations derived from their social origins. The middle-class elites were members of a new rising class drawn from commercial and artisan groups that had supplanted the old elites. This path to power had led to the adoption of a pragmatic, individualistic and politically egalitarian ideology that favoured institutional systems based on consent, decentralization and power sharing (*ibid.*: 62). The dynastic elite, in contrast, was drawn from the traditional aristocratic elite, which had conserved its power by taking the lead in the drive for industrialization. It sought to maintain a strongly paternalistic institutional system based on tradition and the use of power (*ibid.*: 66). These diverse strategies had a major influence on the nature of management, the character of labour organization, the structures of decision-making and forms of social protest. But, over the longer term, the influence of such differences in elite strategy would diminish and institutional structures would converge under the pressures of industrialism.

In practice, there have remained considerable differences in the way in which elites have sought to manage capitalist societies and these have been reflected in persisting differences in institutional structure. For instance, there are very marked (and possibly increasing) differences in the extent to which organized labour has been actively involved in central decision-making processes and, as Goldthorpe has argued (1984b), this has major implications for the more general character of industrial relations and labour organization in the society (see also Hibbs, 1978; Shorter and Tilly, 1974: Ch. 12). This predictive failure of the theory of industrialism reflects in part the rather unsatisfactory account provided of the sources of variation in elite policies. It is implausible that the relative emphasis on hierarchical control or union involvement in institutional structures can be accounted for by the social origins of the early industrializing elites. The industrializing elites of France, Britain and Sweden were all 'middle-class elites' in the terms of the theorists of industrialism, but the systems of industrial relations prevailing in these countries are fundamentally different in the degree of institutional involvement of the trade unions. The explanation for the different policies adopted by elites is to be found more convincingly in the way in which power resources have been historically mobilized. In particular, it relates to the success of left-wing parties in gaining stable access to governmental power and to the membership strength, unity and organizational scope of the trade union movement (Panitch, 1977/9; Lehmbruch, 1979; Batstone, 1988b). These factors in turn would appear to have been heavily conditioned by the way in which political elites intervened in major historical crises (Jackson and Sisson, 1976; Gallie, 1983). What is clear is that, once established, these patterns of relations are self-reinforcing and have considerable durability across time. In short, the differences in institutional arrangements between capitalist societies are underpinned not by the relatively weak factor of some distant cultural legacy, which might well decline in influence, but rather by very different structures of power that are actively maintained over time.

Apart from their evident importance for the structure of industrial relations, research has increasingly shown that such political factors have a major influence over the way in which economies are managed and over the quality of welfare provision. For instance, David Cameron (1984) has shown how the access to political power of leftist parties and the nature of trade union organization crucially affected the response of advanced capitalist societies to the economic crisis of the 1970s. Those societies that had had prolonged periods of left-wing control over the period 1965–82, and that had strong centrally organized trade unions, managed to ride the crisis years of the 1970s with much lower unemployment rates, lower strike levels and lower rates of inflation. Further, Stephens (1979: 98–108; see also Castles, 1978) found that, in the advanced industrial societies, the length of time in government of socialist parties and the strength of trade union organization were the major determinants of variations in the level of welfare spending, the degree of equality of income distribution (especially the post-tax distributions) and the progressiveness of welfare state financing. Moreover, Esping-Andersen and Korpi (1984) have argued convincingly that once one probes below superficial similarities in welfare systems, one finds major differences in the extent to which their procedures reflect equal citizenship rights, serve to reinforce status divisions between occupational groups, curb or reinforce the primacy of market principles and expand or restrict the boundaries of what is considered to be within the scope of welfare. More detailed historical analysis shows that such differences can only be accounted for in terms of the specific power contexts within which policies are formulated, contexts that are heavily influenced by the organizational unity of labour and its access to the centres of political decision-making.

There is, then, little evidence that political influences are diminishing as a source of differentiation in capitalist societies, nor is there much sign that the political structures in these societies are converging towards some broadly similar model. The 1980s have witnessed, if anything, the emergence of a more pronounced choice between models of political action.

Convergence between Capitalist and State Socialist Systems

Goldthorpe's original critique of the neglect of the political in the theory of industrialism centred on its treatment of state socialist societies. Whereas in the West market forces were the crucial stratifying agency in society, and the major source of social inequality, the system of stratification in Soviet society was politically regulated. To a far greater extent than in Western societies, the pattern of social inequality was moulded by purposive political action. As examples of this, he pointed to the sharp rise of economic inequality under Stalin and the subsequent shift to more egalitarian policies in the 1950s. Income inequalities, then, were the direct outcome of political decisions and such decisions were taken with political as well as economic objectives. Stalin's concern to expand income differentials was part of a wider strategy of increasing his personal control through creating a privileged elite dependent upon him. Thus the underlying assumption of the theory of industrialism—that the economic has primacy over all other aspects of the social structure—is incorrect. While some forms of social inequality are clearly much more prevalent than might be anticipated on the basis of official values (Lane, 1978; Millar, 1987), later evidence on the impact of Kruschev's reform of the wages structure from 1956 provides support for Goldthorpe's view that, in the Soviet Union, political action can and did have a marked effect on income inequalities. Through a substantial increase in minimum rates and a simplification of the wage tariff system, differentials were generally reduced and, indeed, between 1956 and 1965 the most extreme differentials were reduced from 1 : 4.1 to 1 : 2.6 (Matthews, 1972: 73ff; Yanowitch, 1977: 25). Certainly by the early 1970s, when they came to reassess the state of the debate, Kerr *et al.* largely conceded the point:

> In particular, we accept the view of Goldthorpe that political considerations will have more impact on the life chances of persons in a strongly statist pluralism and that the class situation of individuals and groups, understood in terms of their economic power and resources, will have more effect on the life chances of persons in more market-oriented pluralism. (1973: 298).

It is notable that, in his later work, Kerr became very much more tertative about the likelihood of very substantial or continuing convergence in political or economic structures. Indeed, he acknowledged that 'we should have clarified that we were not necessarily implying the parallel development of pluralistic political structures' (Kerr, 1983: 28). Instead he became more sympathetic to the bipolar solution proposed by Pryor (1973), according to which the two systems might prove equally viable and be able to provide relatively stable alternative forms of social structure. The existing evidence suggested that, 'while there are some increasing similarities, there is no convergence as yet between socialist and capitalist nations at the most essential point—the distribution of ultimate political power' (*ibid*.: 64). Similarly, there was as yet little or no convergence in the economic structure, with the two types of system remaining sharply differentiated in terms of the relative importance of planning as against the market, the level of centralization of decision-making and the relative independence of worker organizations (*ibid*.: 62). Confronted with this prospect, Kerr sought to salvage the theory of industrialism by strengthening his earlier argument that the imperatives of industrialization may have a greater impact on certain aspects of society than on others (*ibid*.: 72–5). He suggested that convergence affected primarily the development of knowledge, the mobilization of the resources of production, patterns of work and the distribution of economic rewards, but not necessarily the economic and political structures—a view that involved a return to the earlier implausible assumption that major differences in political structure would have negligible consequences for wider life chances.

From the vantage point of the late 1980s Kerr might be seen as having been particularly unfortunate in having made such a substantial concession to his critics only two years before Gorbachov's accession to the General Secretaryship of the Soviet Communist Party. With its twin themes of economic reform and political restructuring, the new reform programme certainly re-poses in a fundamental way the issue of the likely long-term convergence between systems. In the economic sphere the emphasis is on the reduction of the decision-making powers of the central ministries and the encouragement of forms of decentralized decision-making more responsive to the market. At the political level there is the promise of greater pluralism, contested elections and a greater accountability of the political leadership.

The shift from a command to a more decentralized economy is the area in which some measure of partial convergence with Western societies would seem most plausible. This has been a proclaimed objective of a number of state socialist regimes, and in the case of Hungary there is some evidence that it can be achieved. At the same time the history of the major earlier attempt to decentralize the Soviet economy underlines the very considerable structural constraints that the programme will have to encounter. The economic reforms of the late 1980s bear in many respects a marked affinity to the ill-fated 'Kosygin reforms' of the 1960s. These set out to reduce central economic control and to enhance the decision-making power of enterprise management. The vast array of central ministry 'indicators', which laid down for enterprises the details of their workforce, pay structures, purchasing policies and production objectives, were to be cut back and replaced with a limited number of more global indicators which would give management greater autonomy. A system of incentives was to be introduced to encourage firms to increase their level and efficiency of production, and the opportunity was to be provided to sell in the market part of what was produced.

As Levine (1974) has pointed out in her detailed analysis of the reform programme, the reforms were in part designed to use market mechanisms to increase the efficiency of central planning (see also Nove, 1977: Chs 3 and 4). Yet even this limited reform proved exceptionally difficult to implement and foundered completely at the close of the 1960s. In part this reflected the deeply entrenched bureaucratic interests of the central ministries, which in many cases simply ignored directives to reduce the level of intervention in enterprise decision-making. However, more fundamentally, it is likely to have reflected a concern about the implications of economic reform for social and political stability. If enterprise managers were to be given any substantial freedom to raise productivity as they saw fit, this might well lead to major workforce reductions and rising unemployment. In a political system that had for decades emphasized the right to work, the centrality of work to personal development and the superiority of the socialist system in providing full employment, a sharp rise in unemployment might well prove far more damaging to political stability than had been the case in Western societies. While in the Soviet Union in the 1960s the reform programme was curtailed before its implications for increased social instability could be assessed, it would seem that similar factors have played a significant part in bringing an abrupt halt to the ambitious economic reform programme in China.

The distinctive aspect of the 1980s reform programme in the USSR is not economic reform but the emphasis on the restructuring of political institutions. While there has been long-standing disagreement about the effective degree of concentration or diffusion of power in the Soviet Union (contrast, for instance, Brzezinski and Huntingdon, 1968; Djilas, 1957/66; Lane; 1976: Chs 7 and 8), it seems clear that the regime could not be considered pluralistic even in the rather wide sense of the term used by the theorists of industrialism. The constitutional reforms of 1988—introducing a full-time parliament, an elected executive presidency and contested elections—represent a far bolder approach to the reinvigoration of representative institutions than any measure that emerged in the reform movement of the 1960s. But the critical question as far as the convergence thesis is concerned must be whether such changes are likely to introduce effective political pluralism. The longer-term future is necessarily unknown, but in the shorter term it would appear that considerable care has been taken in drawing up the new Constitution to limit such a development.

More fundamentally, it is far from clear that the implementation of these changes will involve a weakening of the role of politics in Soviet society. Many of the early stages of the Gorbachov reform programme could be seen as an attempt to reassert active central political control over a party bureaucracy that had become increasingly feudalized. The corruption purges revealed that, in areas like Uzbekistan, the official party apparatus had lost any effective control over local economic and administrative affairs. The emphasis on local participation can be seen as, in part, a method for monitoring local officialdom and ensuring that initiatives from the centre are implemented. Similarly, the constitutional changes of 1988 are not envisaged as implying a sharp reduction of central power. In his commentaries on the reform Gorbachov has stressed that central power must be strong, but should not concern itself with secondary issues (*Le Monde*, 22 November 1988). Indeed, the major effect of the constitutional changes may well be, as Sakharov has argued, to enhance greatly the personal power of the Soviet leader. The manner and speed with which the constitutional changes were introduced demonstrate once more that Soviet institutions allow a level of personal power and a capacity for political action for which there is no parallel in Western liberal democracies. With the combination of heightened legitimacy and the sweeping powers of decree, both provided by the new Constitution, the personal power of the

Soviet leader would appear to have been given an even more secure institutional foundation. This could easily undercut the 'democratic' objectives of introducing greater institutional constraints on party decision-making. Far from leading to a weaker state, political restructuring may provide the potential for a greater concentration of political power and for its more effective implementation.

The major progress towards political pluralism has been in the 'satellite' states of Eastern Europe rather than in the Soviet Union itself. This however, has little to do with the factors that lie at the heart of the theory of industrialism. There is little or no positive relationship between the level of economic development in these societies and the strength of pressures for political pluralism. Such pressures emerged far earlier, for instance, in Poland than in the economically more advanced East Germany. Any adequate explanation would need to turn to the crucial role of cultural and political factors. The essential point about the East European societies that have seen the earliest and strongest movements for pluralism—Poland, Hungary and Czechoslovakia—is that they had developed, through centuries of conflict, deeply embedded national traditions, rooted in distinctive cultures and in the experience of national sovereignty. Given the circumstances in which state socialist institutions were established in these societies in the aftermath of the Second World War, they were likely to be seen as imposed by an external, imperialist and even deeply hostile power. Their legitimacy, then, has been necessarily problematic throughout the post-war period. While the pressure for political pluralism must be understood primarily as the product of the conflict between past national traditions and an externally imposed institutional system, it was facilitated in part by economic difficulties, but much more fundamentally by the decision of the Soviet leadership to move away from military solutions to inter-state problems. In short, the move to pluralism in East European societies is the result not of the imperatives of industrialism, but of changes in the framework of international relations and of the persisting strength of the type of historic national tradition that the theorists of industrialism assumed would disappear.

CONCLUSION

The range of questions raised by the theory of industrialism lies at the core of much of Goldthorpe's contribution to sociology. It was in developing his critique of the theory that he formulated most clearly his views about the nature of social theory, the determinants of patterns of social stratification and social mobility, the significance of class in structuring social divisions and social conflict, and the importance of political factors in determining social structure. Rejecting the theory's deterministic scenario of the *necessary* convergence of the social structures of advanced industrial societies, Goldthorpe has emphasized the history-laden character of social institutions, the importance of patterns of social conflict and the capacity of social actors to influence the direction of change in their societies.

The debate over the neo-liberal theory of industrialism will no doubt be one of the more permanent features of the sociological landscape. The theory provides a powerful vision of the development of societies which, given the fluidity oı its time horizons, can never be definitively proved or disproved. Yet the evidence of the first three decades of the theory's history has tended to confirm many of Goldthorpe's early doubts about the core assumptions of the argument. In capitalist societies there is little sign of a convergence in industrial relations systems, there is little evidence of an inherent tendency to greater equality or greater openness, and class remains a major factor structuring life chances and social conflict. While it seems possible that there may be a move towards greater decentralization of the state socialist economies, the progress to date has been, in general, unimpressive. There is still little sign of the imminent disappearance of the strong state in the Soviet Union and the pressures for pluralism in East European societies derive from essentially political and cultural factors rather than from the imperatives of industrialism. In general, one of the major sources of the theory's shortcomings is its neglect of social values and political structure. Differences in power structures have led to very different patterns of social differentiation and social conflict between capitalist and state socialist societies, and research has increasingly suggested that they account for important variations in patterns of industrial relations and forms of social stratification *within* both types of society. Given the lack of any coherent argument as to why the significance of politics will decline, the deterministic scenario of the theorists of industrialism must be regarded as implausible. There may, in the future, be convergence between specific societies, just as there may be divergence. But in either case the critical factors will not be the imperatives of industrialism, but changes in the political values and strategies of the dominant groups, changes in the organization of power resources within societies and changes in the framework of international relations.

Part Two: Consensus and Controversy

III. CLASS ANALYSIS

4. John Goldthorpe and Class Analysis

GORDON MARSHALL

CLASS ANALYSIS AND MACRO-THEORIES OF SOCIETY

John Goldthorpe has been developing his own, highly original, version of class analysis since the early 1970s. Its origins are twofold: first, in his critique of liberal theories of industrial society; and, second, the subsequent extension of these criticisms to include neo-Marxist accounts of late capitalism.

The former perspective was popular among American sociologists during the 1950s and 1960s. Clark Kerr and other advocates of what is now known as the 'logic of industrialism' thesis argued that certain underlying processes of convergence in industrialized nations would, among other things, transform the class structures of Western democracies. The exigencies of modern technology would tend to generate uniformity in hitherto distinctively class (democratic capitalist) and mass (state socialist) societies, by increasing the number of occupational roles that required specialized training and skills, and decreasing those involving only routine tasks and minimal qualifications. This 'upgrading' of the occupational structure would expand the middle class—those commanding high economic rewards and prestige in their employment—and, in conjunction with progressive taxation and improved social welfare, lead to a general *embourgeoisement* of these societies. Relative homogeneity of living standards would, in turn, generate cultural homogeneity around middle-class values, norms and lifestyles. This new 'post-industrial' social order would be more meritocratic and therefore more consensual than early industrial societies. Moreover, it was to be achieved by evolutionary rather than revolutionary means. An expanded state would regulate competition and industrial conflict in the general interest; class stratification would give way to a fluid occupational structure based on expanding educational opportunities; and ideological battles succumb to a new conservatism that would be compatible with the new egalitarianism. In short, as Kerr and his colleagues put it, 'consensus develops'; class competition vanishes and is replaced by 'the bureaucratic contest of interest group against interest group' (1960: 282–96). [1]

Goldthorpe has never been convinced by this argument. One of his earliest published articles (Goldthorpe, 1964) challenged its central tenets by drawing on available studies of social inequality in the West to show that there was no significant general trend towards income equality; that classes having quite distinct class advantages, lifestyles, patterns of association and ideologies still persisted; and that the mobility profiles of industrial societies suggested they were no more open and meritocratic now than in the past. The classic *Affluent Worker* studies of the 1960s reinforced these criticisms with original research designed specifically to test the thesis of working-class *embourgeoisement*, a proposition which Goldthorpe and his colleagues rejected, since the critical test-case 'affluent' workers in Luton remained distinctively working-class in normative, associational and lifestyle terms.

However, Goldthorpe's opposition to the various theories of industrial society was principled as well as empirical. In particular he objected to the deterministic ethnocentrism of this approach. It started from an absolutely general theory of society, rooted in the theorist's own socio-political preferences, rather than in fact; purported to grasp an underlying or immanent logic to industrial developments; and in this way substituted ideological arguments for serious empirical inquiry. 'Facts' were introduced only insofar as they illustrated the propositions and categories of the entirely a priori analysis. In no sense was the theory *tested*, since data which did not fit were simply disregarded. Those displayed had been selected specifically because they could be interpreted as evidence of a secular trend towards some ultimate goal of history. Clearly, therefore, theorists of industrial society were guilty of, to use Goldthorpe's terms, 'wishful rather than critical thinking' (see Goldthorpe, 1962b).

It is this opposition to what he has called 'half-hearted and covert historicism' that justifies Goldthorpe's description of himself as a 'good Popperian'. He is fundamentally opposed to the practice of presenting ideological arguments in sociological disguise. Not surprisingly, therefore, he soon extended his critique to include the various neo-Marxist accounts which, in the 1960s, offered the principal alternative to liberal perspectives on social stratification in modern societies. Since these were overtly historicist and value-laden, they were, if anything, yet more cavalier in their treatment of empirical materials.

In the case of Marxism, of course, the Western working classes were the essential agency for achieving socialist (rather than liberal) socio-political objectives. In order to protect this particular assumption, theorists on the Left were predisposed to see changes in the labour process as evidence of a long-term trend towards proletarianization rather than *embourgeoisement* of the class structure. In their view work was progressively routinized and deskilling prevalent, with the result that alienation became intensified; the expansion of middle-class positions was more apparent than real, since the low level of expertise required for the new jobs rendered them indistinguishable from those performed by unskilled manual workers; so that putative rates of upward mobility from manual to non-manual employment served only to obscure the continuing class struggle between capital and labour. In due course, Marxists argued, the historical tendency of workers towards workplace and communal solidarism would overcome the mystification induced by the ideological and political apparatus of bourgeois hegemony, and class action by established and newly proletarianized workers alike would overthrow the structures of property and power which underpinned late capitalism.[2]

Goldthorpe was no more convinced by these arguments than by those of the liberals. Both perspectives sought to interpret the present characteristics of the occupational or class structure in the context of some developmental logic of industrial societies, rather than attempting serious empirical investigation of these structures, and both projected the particular socio-political goals of the theorist onto his or her working-class subjects. From the publication of the *Affluent Worker* studies onwards, therefore, he has treated both perspectives together as offering substantively opposed, though logically identical, but in any case equally implausible interpretations of the processes of social stratification and social integration in advanced societies (see, for example, Goldthorpe, 1971, 1979, 1990).

By the end of the 1960s, therefore, Goldthorpe was able to conclude that class inequalities persisted in advanced capitalist countries, despite the liberal-democratic project of making these societies more open through economic expansion, educational reform and redistributive welfare measures. 'In sum', as he put it, 'one may say that social inequality, as observed in present-day Britain, takes the general form of a substantially self-maintaining structure of social groupings differentiated multifariously and often extremely in terms of the power and advantage that their members enjoy'. However, he also insisted that the implications of such a structure for the patterning of social relationships and social integration must be a matter for empirical investigation, rather than *a priori* assumption. 'What, then', he asks, 'are the consequences of this inequality for the integration of British society; that is to say, for the extent to which the actions of individuals and groups tend regularly to comply with recognised norms, and to be thus consistent with, rather than in conflict with or unrelated to, the expectations and actions of other individuals and groups?' (1974a: 219). Extant studies seemed, to him at least, to provide only a partial and ambiguous answer to this question; they did not constitute a *systematic* test of the central propositions about class processes (or their demise) advanced by the liberal and Marxist theories of social change. Through his involvement with the Oxford and International Mobility Projects, from 1969 to the present day, John Goldthorpe has sought to provide precisely such a test.

THE GOLDTHORPE CLASS CATEGORIES

The Oxford Mobility Project of the 1970s was a collective enterprise and therefore pursued several disparate objectives in accordance with the different interests of those involved. However, its twin primary aims reflect perfectly Goldthorpe's longstanding concern with the relative merits of the liberal and Marxist perspectives, since these aims were to examine trends in intergenerational mobility in England and Wales, and then to compare the processes of occupational achievement uncovered in these countries with those already reported for the United States. In essence, this meant repeating the classic study by David Glass and his colleagues of *Social Mobility in Britain* (conducted in the late 1940s), and replicating in this country the inquiry by Peter Blau and Dudley Duncan into *The American Occupational Structure* (dating from the mid-1960s). Rather conveniently, from Goldthorpe's point of view, the latter study embodied all the major assumptions of liberal theory;

while the former, though scarcely Marxist in orientation, could nevertheless be interpreted in such a way as to provide ammunition for those on the political Left.

Blau and Duncan explored 'status attainment', that is, the extent to which the present occupational status of individuals was influenced by their family of origin or own earlier statuses, as against their other attributes such as education or qualifications. The results of their study purportedly show that structural shifts in the American economy—the expansion of professional, managerial and administrative occupations—created 'more room at the top' and so extended the opportunities for upward social mobility of individuals from working-class origins. Moreover, this was reinforced by a progressive shift from ascriptive to achievement criteria as the dominant factors determining status attainment, a movement towards meritocratic selection that, together with the prevailing high rates of mobility, undermined the potential for class formation and class conflict in the United States. Openness and equality of opportunity promoted social stability (see Blau and Duncan, 1967).

Glass and his colleagues, in contrast, started from the assumption that individuals were born into distinct 'social classes', membership of which tended to be life-long and to have clear consequences for life chances, values, norms, lifestyles and patterns of association. The overall impression produced by their study is one of a stable social structure showing a high degree of association between the status of fathers and sons. Although considerable mobility was found at intermediate levels, this tended to be short-range movement of a rather transitory kind. Moreover, birth-cohort analysis suggested that patterns of mobility (or perhaps rather immobility) had not significantly changed since the end of the nineteenth century, though education had become more important as a determinant of destinations. This seemed to suggest that the post-war expansion of educational opportunities might bring about greater openness in British society, though Glass and his team also noted that schooling and credentials were increasingly important in maintaining the privileged position of sons of high status fathers (see Glass, 1954).

So how 'open' (or 'closed') was the social structure of Britain by the 1970s? Had the Beveridge reforms of the 1940s and the Robbins expansion of higher education in the 1960s made Britain more like America? In addressing this question Goldthorpe and the other members of the Oxford team began by emulating the procedures of their predecessors. Both the Glass and the Blau and Duncan studies viewed mobility (be there lesser or greater amounts of it) in terms of individuals moving up or down a hierarchy of occupations reflecting differences in the 'prestige' or 'social standing' of the jobs involved. Since the (Hall-Jones) scale used in the earlier British study rested on assumptions about the public ordering of occupational prestige which had never been validated, and the American scale contained culturally specific evaluations, the obvious first step was to construct a new classification reporting a valid and reliable social grading of occupations for England and Wales. This was duly done and the resulting 'Hope-Goldthorpe' (or 'H-G') scale was unveiled in 1974.

The complex procedures by which this scheme was constructed need not be reported here. These involved a series of grading exercises, subject to numerous checks, in which members of the general public and professional experts alike were asked to rank occupational titles in an order corresponding to their 'social standing'. These evaluations were scaled and a composite value produced for each job. The crucial point to note is that the resulting classification purports to measure 'the "general desirability" of occupations, understood as a synthetic, emergent judgement from a specific population' (Goldthorpe and Hope, 1974: 132). A good deal of time and effort was expended on constructing this device. Not surprisingly, therefore, many people were (and continue to be) confused by the fact that, when the results of the Oxford mobility inquiry began to appear in print in the late 1970s, the H-G scale was not the instrument used for reporting and analyzing the data. Instead, mobility was understood to be between 'Goldthorpe classes', categories which had no relationship whatsoever to those of the earlier scale.

The new class scheme attempted, instead, to aggregate occupational groupings whose members shared similar 'market situations' and 'work situations'. Following the conception of class advanced by David Lockwood in *The Blackcoated Worker* (1958: 15–16), Goldthorpe now took these to be the two defining characteristics of class position. The Goldthorpe class categories therefore attempted

> to combine occupational categories whose members would appear...to be typically comparable, on the one hand, in terms of their sources and levels of income, their degree of economic security and chances of advancement [market situation]; and, on the other, in their location within systems of authority and control governing the process of production in which they are engaged, and hence their degree of autonomy in performing their work-tasks and roles [work situation]. (Goldthorpe, 1980a: 39)

Operationalizing this framework for class analysis therefore led in a direction quite different from that followed in the construction of the earlier H-G scale. The Goldthorpe class standing of any individual is determined by a simple threefold procedure. First, respondents are placed in occupational groups according to the content of their jobs; second, they are given an employment status that reflects their social relationships at work (self-employed without employees, manager in large establishment and so forth). In both cases the categories and definitions used are those adopted in Britain by the Registrar-General for the analysis of official statistics. (The British Office of Population Censuses and Surveys' *Classification of Occupations 1980* lists 549 occupational groups and nine employment statuses.) Goldthorpe thus takes occupational title as an indicator of market situation and equates employment status with work situation. Finally, a social class position is obtained for each individual by cross-classifying the relevant occupational title and employment status, each possible legitimate combination having previously been allocated a place within one of the seven Goldthorpe social class categories listed in Table 4.1.[3]

Why did Goldthorpe abandon the H-G scale in favour of this new classification? He has subsequently maintained that two factors explain the change of direction. The first is that the Oxford data themselves militated against viewing mobility as occurring within a *social continuum*, and suggested instead a context of *class structure*, since there seemed to be a systematic patterning of intergenerational and career trajectories which challenged the assumption that individuals were free to move up and down an ordered hierarchy according to their labour market capacities. Second, the international community of mobility researchers (with whom Goldthorpe has always been greatly involved) itself resurrected class structure as the conceptual context of mobility research during the 1970s, in response to a number of perceived theoretical, substantive and methodological weaknesses in the hitherto dominant status attainment paradigm represented by the work of Duncan and his associates. It was now seen that this rested on certain undemonstrated assumptions about the social relationships of deference, acceptance or derogation implied in socio-economic status scales; ignored the methodological difficulties caused by the

Table 4.1   *The Goldthorpe Class Schema*

SERVICE	I	Higher-grade professionals, administrators and officials; managers in large industrial establishments; large proprietors
	II	Lower-grade professionals, administrators and officials; higher-grade technicians; managers in small business and industrial establishments; supervisors of non-manual employees
INTERMEDIATE	IIIa	Routine non-manual employees in administration and commerce
	IIIb	Personal service workers
	IVa	Small proprietors, artisans, etc., with employees
	IVb	Small proprietors, artisans, etc., without employees
	IVc	Farmers and smallholders; self-employed fishermen
	V	Lower-grade technicians, supervisors of manual workers
WORKING	VI	Skilled manual workers
	VIIa	Semi-skilled and unskilled manual workers (not in agriculture)
	VIIb	Agricultural workers

Source: Adapted from Goldthorpe (1987a), p. 305, Table 11.1.

composite or synthetic nature of the scales themselves; and was incapable of distinguishing adequately the various structural influences on mobility from those which originated in personal attributes. Coincidentally, the emergence of the mathematical techniques of log-linear modelling offered critical mobility researchers, for the first time, a method for analyzing contingency tables which was as powerful as the path-analytic technique available to the status attainment orthodoxy, yet did not require ordinal data (and therefore prior assumptions) about a 'social hierarchy' (see Goldthorpe and Bevan, 1977: 299–302; also Goldthorpe, 1984d).

One suspects, however, that one other factor was crucial to Goldthorpe's change of perspective. Status attainment research was heavily influenced by liberal theories of industrialism. It envisaged a long-term decrease in social inequalities of opportunity and condition, the emergence of a structureless and fluid stratification hierarchy, and the consequent decomposition of classes as identifiable socio-cultural entities and collective actors. We have already noted that Goldthorpe had a longstanding objection to this interpretation of developments in the social structures of Western societies. Events in Britain during the early and mid-1970s would surely have reinforced his scepticism: significant strikes by miners and other organized groups of workers suggested that collective action by unionized employees showed no signs of withering away, while the renewed economic recession first highlighted, then exacerbated, the social inequalities masked by the ideology of post-war affluence. The language of this renewed conflict, if not explicitly that of class, was often close to it. Social class had patently not been abolished. Yet the underlying assumption of the status attainment perspective, and the various socio-economic scales of occupational prestige with which this operated, was that liberal theories of industrial society were essentially sound. Against this background it would indeed have been surprising had Goldthorpe *not* abandoned the concern with determinants of social standing, and framed mobility issues instead in terms of the processes of class formation.

CLASS STRUCTURE IN COMPARATIVE PERSPECTIVE

Throughout the 1980s Goldthorpe has applied his new class schema to the analysis of mobility data from various large-scale data sets. The principal findings of the Oxford study of mobility in England and Wales were collated and published as *Social Mobility and Class Structure in Modern Britain* in 1980. More recently, and sometimes in collaboration with others, he has developed the comparative aspects of his arguments: first, by looking at changes to mobility patterns in Britain occasioned by the recession of the 1970s, using data from the British General Election Surveys; and, second, by comparing the mobility profiles of various West European societies under the auspices of the CASMIN (Comparative Analysis of Social Mobility in Industrial Nations) Project of which he is co-director.

The substantive findings of his research are too numerous to mention in a short overview such as this. In any case most of the principal themes are discussed in subsequent chapters of this book, which look in considerable detail at Goldthorpe's specific conclusions about class formation and class action in Britain and Europe. We should perhaps confine ourselves here to the more general observation that, considered as a whole, these findings cast serious doubts on both liberal and Marxist theories of social change alike.

For example, Goldthorpe finds that there has been in most Western societies a significant growth in the so-called 'service class' (employees having high, secure and incremental incomes, and who exercise discretion or authority at work), from some 5–10 per cent of the economically active population during the early twentieth century to some 20–25 per cent today. The expansion of government, social welfare, management and the like, especially after 1945, created a demand for personnel which could be met only by a steady recruitment from other classes. The composition of the present-day service class is therefore remarkably heterogeneous. Only one-quarter to one-third of those currently in service-class positions come from service-class backgrounds: the majority have been upwardly mobile from intermediate and working-class origins. On the face of it, therefore, this particular finding lends credibility to liberal predictions of a more open society. However, the methodological innovation of log-linear modelling allows Goldthorpe to distinguish *absolute* from *relative* mobility; or, in other words, changes in mobility occasioned by shifts in the occupational structure from changes in social fluidity or openness as such. He finds that, in Britain for example, absolute levels of mobility have indeed changed significantly over the past half-century in accordance with the growth in service-class positions, but relative mobility chances have remained largely unaltered throughout this period. More room at the top has not ensured greater equality of opportunity to get there, since proportionately more of the new middle-class jobs have been captured by the children of those already in privileged class locations. As a result, the association between an individual's class of origin and eventual destination has remained remarkably stable across successive birth-cohorts, despite economic expansion, educational reform and redistributive social policies. There is, in fact, no obvious long-term 'loosening' of the class structure. This finding seriously damages, in Goldthorpe's eyes at least, the liberal claim that industrialization progressively entails egalitarianism.

On the other hand, the mobility profiles of all West European societies examined thus far also render untenable the Marxist argument that, except perhaps in the special case of the collective proletarianization of some hitherto middle-class groupings, social mobility occurs to only a negligible degree. The data from Britain again provide a good illustration. These show that the working class of manual employees has shrunk by anything between one-quarter and one-third over the course of this century. Moreover, the most obvious candidates for occupational deskilling (routine clerical and administrative workers) constitute a highly differentiated workforce, rather than a cohesive 'mass'. Some (mainly older unqualified men) enter routine non-manual employment from manual jobs late in life and stay there; others (notably young women with few qualifications) alternate spells of clerical work with periods of childcaring; while considerable numbers of credentialled men and women alike spend only a limited period in clerical jobs early in careers which take them into senior managerial and administrative (service-class) positions. Finally, the relative mobility chances of men and women can be shown to be very similar, as can those of younger and older groups of workers in a birth-cohort analysis. Against this background, therefore, it is difficult to see which groups within the class structure are being proletarianized.

These and other data relating to the mobility profiles of Western societies suggest to Goldthorpe that changes in the class structure are considerably more complex than is allowed within either liberal or Marxist accounts. Thus, for example, he has argued that comparative studies undermine the liberal contention that overall patterns of social mobility are much the same (indeed tend to converge) in Western industrial societies. On the other hand, while the growing 'demographic maturity' (self-recruitment) of British workers has encouraged working-class 'pushfulness' (for example, in making claims for higher wages), there is nothing to suggest that these demands go beyond mere militancy—far less that they do so in the direction of some historically appointed affinity with socialism.

Although limitations on space preclude detailed consideration of Goldthorpe's arguments, two summary observations can be made. The first is that his overall research programme constitutes an impressive, and probably unique, attempt to subject to systematic empirical inquiry the various liberal and Marxist claims about class processes in the West. Second, considered as a whole, Goldthorpe's empirical studies show that there is no immanent logic in either the technological development or the class structures of advanced societies; and that class processes are contingent upon historical particularities which, in any given society, might include purposive political interventions in (for example) the educational system, system of industrial relations, or legal framework of company law. The tendency to construct general theories of long-term social change upon the supposed functional exigencies of technology or the class struggle therefore betrays a persisting historicism which is invariably disappointed when matched against the historical record.[4]

TWO PROBLEMS: OPERATIONALIZING CLASSES AND THE UNIT OF ANALYSIS

From an initial position of neutrality, I have therefore gradually become convinced of the merits of John Goldthorpe's perspective and the robustness of his principal conclusions, a conviction enhanced by making systematic comparisons with other conceptions of social class—not only at the level of theory but also as part of a large programme of empirical research into class processes in contemporary Britain in which I have been involved. This revealed that Goldthorpe's scheme was more reliable, and that his approach 'made better sense' of data pertaining to socio-political preferences and collective action generally, than either Marxist or official (Registrar-General's) alternatives (see Marshall, Newby *et al.*, 1988, for details).

Of course, his approach to class analysis is not without its difficulties. Although I have (both here and elsewhere) defended Goldthorpe's general position, I would be the first to concede that many of his ideas are controversial, and certain of his detailed conclusions highly contentious. The most important questions, for me at least, surround the operational procedures for generating classes from occupational data, and his views on the status of women in class analysis. These two issues are closely related.

Goldthorpe's conception of class is rooted in the neo-Weberian notions of market situation and work situation. He claims to have assigned an appropriate class standing to each combination of occupational title and employment status 'in the light of the available information from official statistics, monographic sources etc., regarding the typical market and work situations of the individuals comprised: e.g. on levels and sources of income, other monetary and non-monetary benefits, degree of economic security, chances of economic advancement, and location in systems of authority and control' (Goldthorpe and Payne, 1986a: 21). In fact we are never shown the 'available evidence' in question. This omission becomes crucial when it is remembered that the class categories arrived at were designed explicitly for a study of social mobility among men only: it is male pay and conditions (market and work situations) which Goldthorpe has in mind when constructing his schema (see Goldthorpe, 1980a: 287–8).

Critics have observed that this operational logic makes the resulting class analysis (and the class categories themselves) sex-specific. They point to the generally accepted wisdom that the occupational division of labour is sex-segregated: women are concentrated in some occupations rather than others, and, within specific occupational categories, they tend to have inferior conditions of pay and service to corresponding males. Goldthorpe has always acknowledged this fact. But in defending himself from the so-called 'feminist critique' he does tend to alter the terms of the debate in a way that may have confused rather than clarified the issues involved.

His response rests on the distinction between 'the procedures which one carries out in attempts to produce a valid and reliable research instrument, and the evidence one is able to bring forward for the degree of validity and reliability that the instrument actually possesses'. According to Goldthorpe, 'constructional procedures have the sort of bearing on the success of a scale that scaffolding has on a building: the scaffolding may contribute to the erection of a sound and imposing structure, but the final judgement of the critical onlooker will be passed on the building when the scaffolding is no longer in view' (Goldthorpe and Hope, 1974: 1). In other words, if one can be permitted to switch metaphors, the proof of the pudding is in the eating. Starting from this premise, Goldthorpe then reminds his critics of the objectives of any class analysis; namely, to link the structure of class positions in societies to an understanding of observable patterns of collective action. This link is forged by the crucial intervening variable of class formation. The relevant processes here are of two kinds:

> First, those associated with the extent to which classes acquire a demographic identity—that is, become identifiable as collectivities through the continuity with which individuals and families retain their class positions over time; and, second, those associated with the extent to which classes acquire a socio-cultural identity—that is, become identifiable through the shared and distinctive life-styles of their members and their patterns of preferred association. (Goldthorpe, 1982: 171–2)

But, as he points out, all the available evidence suggests that families rather than individuals are the units both of demographic class formation (for example, the duration and timing of a wife's employment is typically conditioned by the class position and mobility experience of her husband), and also of socio-political class formation (thus the voting intentions and class identities of married women are generally a function of their husbands' jobs rather than their own occupational experiences). These and similar data confirm that the conjugal family remains the unit of class fate, class formation and class action. Goldthorpe concludes, therefore, that one can legitimately ignore women in a *class analysis* of social stratification because their experiences are irrelevant to the processes of class formation. The sex-specific nature of his class categories is, in his eyes, not an issue (see Goldthorpe, 1983a).

My own view of this matter is that the parties to the debate are in large measure talking past each other. Goldthorpe contends that the position of the family as a whole within the class system derives from the 'family head', or member having the greatest commitment to, and continuity in, the labour market; and that, empirically, it is usually husbands who are in this position. A good deal of supporting evidence has been generated by feminists themselves showing that women are (still) constrained to take primary responsibility for childrearing and household tasks; are invariably discriminated against in the labour market; and so placed in subordinate and disadvantaged positions relative to men. In challenging Goldthorpe on this point, his critics are caught in the dilemma of seeming to argue both that the family and labour market oppress women, yet their oppression is insufficient to support the logic of conventional class analysis.

On the other hand, Goldthorpe's insistence on the family as the *unit* of class analysis restricts unnecessarily the *scope* of class analysis, and in a manner not entirely consistent with his overall conception of that enterprise itself. His own interest is in the relationship between demographic and socio-political class formation. He concludes that, since women's class identities and votes (class socio-political traits) are largely a function of the occupational standing of the men to whom they are attached (class demographic characteristics), this then justifies an exclusive concern with the mobility experiences of the latter in any class analysis.

I do not agree. I would endorse Goldthorpe's approach in general, and especially his view that class structures are not static positions, but rather career-like trajectories through positions. However, a mass of data accumulated over the past decade or so confirms that the ways in which people are allocated to places in the structure over time—the very processes of demographic class formation themselves—are heavily influenced by gender, so that the career trajectories of men, and their associated life chances, cannot be explained without reference to the very particular ways in which women participate in paid employment. Men have higher absolute rates of mobility than women, receive higher rewards and get better returns to their credentials. Goldthorpe does not deny that this is the case: but he will not accept that this is part of the legitimate concerns of class analysis. For him, demographic class formation is interesting only to the extent that it sheds light on socio-political class formation; and, as the data show, certain (rather restricted) socio-political characteristics among women are conditioned primarily by the class standing of their husbands. In contrast, I would argue that the study of class formation needs to include any important mechanisms, including those of sexual inequality, which help to generate classes as persistent demographic collectivities. In other words, class structures are 'gendered', since the effect of women's employment is to privilege men. This means, of course, that an approach which takes the individual as the unit of class analysis is no less legitimate than one which takes families as the basic unit. Clearly, both are important (though perhaps for different purposes), since social classes are made up neither of individuals nor of families but of individuals in families.

The consequences of pursuing only Goldthorpe's 'conventional' strategy of allocating class positions to male heads of households are evident in Table 4.2. This shows the Goldthorpe class distribution of the Essex national sample as a whole; of males only within the sample; the percentages realized if all female respondents in the study are reclassified to the class position of their male cohabitees; and, finally, the results reported by Goldthorpe and his colleagues in their study of social mobility in England and Wales. It will be seen that the Essex 'male only' figures, derived by following Goldthorpe's strategy of sampling male heads of household, are similar to both the Oxford results and the figures for males within the Essex sample. But these are quite dissimilar to the Essex totals for men and women together, since a study of males only tends to inflate the proportions within classes I, IV, V and VI (where men predominate), while decreasing the relative importance of class III (of which women form the great majority). Arguably, therefore, the 'individualistic' strategy of sampling both men and women yields a more accurate—and complete—class map of modern Britain as the basis for any subsequent analysis of demographic class formation.

Most recently Goldthorpe has attempted to defend his position by switching attention from the pattern of absolute mobility rates to the matter of social fluidity. He has demonstrated, rather convincingly, that there is no difference between the mobility chances of women in competition with other women when compared with

Table 4.2 *'Goldthorpe' Class Maps of Britain, Excluding and Including Women*

		Men and women	Essex data Men	'Males only'	Oxford data (males only)
	I	9.4	13.1	13.8	13.6
	II	17.9	17.1	16.6	11.5
	III	19.5	6.0	5.7	9.2
SOCIAL	IV	8.7	11.4	12.0	9.4
CLASS	V	8.1	11.4	12.1	11.6
	VI	12.5	17.4	17.5	21.2
	VII	23.9	23.6	22.4	23.5
	Total	100.0	100.0	100.0	100.0

Source: Marshall, Newby *et al.* (1988), p. 86, Table 4.12.

men in competition with other men; and concluded that, since relative rates for the sexes are the same, one can on these grounds alone ignore women's occupational experiences in any class analysis (Goldthorpe, 1987a: 277–301). But the problem with this argument is that the competition for class places is not sex segregated. Women have to compete with men and in this competition their chances are not equal. It is rather as if one were to look separately at the chances of black and white people in South Africa achieving service-class positions from working-class origins, discover that these were broadly similar, and then conclude that blacks could be excluded from a class analysis of that country since looking at whites alone would not lead to any false conclusions. I do not think class analysis should be as limited as this. In the real world class and gender (and race) intersect and must be examined at these intersections.

Indeed, I confess to being somewhat puzzled by Goldthorpe's resolute defence of an exclusively conventional approach to class analysis, since he readily admits that 'the long-term change in the occupational distribution of males, and especially the growing proportion found in professional, administrative, and managerial positions, which emerges as the key dynamic element in mobility over the period we have studied, cannot be understood other than in relation to the trend and character of female employment' (1980a: 295). His only possible objection to an individualist strategy can be that it introduces a number of unresolved problems in classifying households where a husband and wife are both in paid employment. This is true, but seems to be simply one more instance of sociological theory lagging behind the reality it addresses. To embrace women's experiences within a class analysis is to retain useful information that is unnecessarily excluded if one pursues Goldthorpe's purely conventional alternative. The next task for class researchers must surely be to resolve the theoretical and methodological issues raised by the gender issue. I remain convinced that this will most readily be done by building on the impressive foundations laid by the Goldthorpe scheme in order to extend its capacity for distinguishing the market and work situations of men and women.

NOTES

1   See also Kerr (1983), Inkeles (1960), Moore (1963) and the variation on this general theme found in the 'post-industrial society' thesis advanced by Bell (1973) and others.

2   Controversy about the work of Braverman (1974) has made this general thesis rather fashionable of late, with debate focusing on the nature of the capitalist 'labour process'. In the 1960s, however, Goldthorpe's immediate targets were an older generation of somewhat disparate Marxists including Perry Anderson, André Gorz, Serge Mallet and John Westergaard.

3   The original sevenfold scheme has been modified over the years to meet specific research objectives. Agricultural workers were distinguished from others to facilitate comparative studies of social mobility involving countries having sizeable workforces on the land. The *petite bourgeoisie* was subdivided for the same reason (see Erikson *et al.*, 1979, 1982). To make the scheme more suited to the class allocation of women, Class III was divided into two, and since 1986 those in Class IIIb positions have been combined with Class VII on the grounds that their employment relations and conditions are more like those of semi-skilled and unskilled manual workers than routine clerical employees (see Goldthorpe and Payne, 1986a).

4   The most accessible recent summary of Goldthorpe's general conclusions is to be found in Part 2 of the second edition of *Social Mobility and Class Structure in Modern Britain* (Goldthorpe, 1987a: 251–355).

5. Class and Society: A Critique of John Goldthorpe's Model of Social Classes

GÖRAN AHRNE

WHY CLASS ANALYSIS?

Class is a contested concept, in the social sciences as well as in everyday life. It has political connotations which make its use in a scientific context a delicate task. It has been declared obsolete many times over by scholars of modern and post-modern society, particularly those studying Western welfare-capitalist nations. For example, in the late 1950s Ralf Dahrendorf wrote that the occupational role of the industrial worker had lost 'its comprehensive moulding force for his personality' (1959: 272); and in 1982 André Gorz bade farewell to the working class. However, these declarations were somewhat premature. Even though class cannot explain all aspects of human behaviour, it has been shown time and again to explain a significant amount of the variations in human actions and attitudes.

The main merit of class analysis is its ambition to connect scientifically the economic and social macro-structure with the everyday realities of human life. A class position must therefore be defined according to the conditions that determine both the development of production relations and the living conditions of ordinary people. Most of these positions are found in the sphere of work—for example, the ownership of the means of production, source of income, control over the labour process—which continues to be of utmost importance. Work affects where people live and their life at home. Conditions at work affect their health, their knowledge about the world and their attitudes towards other people. The size of their income from work determines their housing conditions and leisure activities. Being without work leads to financial difficulties and is a negative experience in terms of social identity. In short, I find it very hard to argue that work has lost its prime importance for determining the living conditions of ordinary people.

I have stressed the theoretical importance of the concept of class. The aim of class analysis can never be to find the maximum amount of variation in a set of variables. The ambition is rather to combine an interesting theoretical explanation with a reasonable variation in observed activities. The main *raison d'être* of class analysis is to give theoretical substance to long-term social changes. Class is therefore a natural component of historical sociology. One of the most outstanding examples of its uses in historical sociology is the book *Social Origins of Dictatorship and Democracy* (1966), in which Barrington Moore describes different roads to modernity in terms of class division and class alliances. Of particular importance here are the relationships between the landed upper classes and the rising bourgeoisie, whether they are antagonistic, as in France, or form a coherent political coalition, as in Germany. Moore's analysis demonstrates the intelligibility of a historical class analysis that combines a straightforward description of relations to the means of production with national and conjunctural conditions in political struggles over long periods.

The feasibility of the theoretical elaboration of class categories, such as they relate to the control of labour and the means of production spanning a long period, is demonstrated in Erik Olin Wright's book *Classes* (Wright, 1985). Wright has shown how different class categories may have varied functions and be of more or less importance in a 'trajectory of social formations' from feudalism and capitalism to statism, socialism and communism. While there are numerous problems in Wright's theoretical construction, it still provides a fruitful perspective on the historical meaning of class.

One of the main differences between a Marxist and a Weberian approach to class analysis is their historical scope. For Weber, class was a phenomenon to be found only in capitalist societies, whereas a Marxist analysis stresses its more or less universal nature. For Weber, different societies are characterized by different kinds of social relations. He claimed, for instance, that the main means of social stratification in feudal societies were status orders. This implies that, even though there may be similarities in the formal criteria for classes in capitalist societies in both Weberian and Marxist analysis, the logic for the use of those criteria is quite distinct (on this, see Wright, 1985: 108).

But a class analysis may also guide very specific and detailed analyses of lifestyles and tastes, as in the research of Pierre Bourdieu, presented in the book *Distinction: A Social Critique of the Judgement of Taste*. Bourdieu distinguishes between economic and cultural capital in his construction of a three-dimensional social space, 'defined by volume of capital, composition of capital, and change in these two properties over time' (Bourdieu, 1984: 114). Within this social space of class relations he traces indicators of various lifestyles—in a highly illuminating way—in terms of culture, ideology and leisure habits. The idea behind Bourdieu's project is to find connections between macro-social power resources and the most minute details of everyday life. There are some conceptual problems in his analysis, but they are not so great as to prevent his results from being highly significant.

THE OVERALL CHARACTER AND AIM OF GOLDTHORPE'S CLASS MODEL

The main sources for my discussion of Goldthorpe's class model are twofold: Chapters 1 and 2 of the book *Social Mobility and Class Structure in Modern Britain*, published in a revised version in 1987 (Goldthorpe, 1987a), and an article from 1982, 'On the Service Class, Its Formation and Future' (Goldthorpe, 1982). There is an important point in my identifying these sources, because what Goldthorpe has written on class theory and class analysis *per se* is in fact not much at all. In the book on social mobility and class structure, hardly more than ten pages are devoted to a discussion of class theory in general and only four pages are used to present his own class model.

The first chapters of the book of 1987 deal with social mobility and social interests. Here Goldthorpe discusses various motive forces behind mobility research. He argues convincingly that mobility research is not necessarily ideologically biased. He states that his own interest in mobility research originates in its implications for class formation and class action (1987a: 28). He goes on to say that this analysis may not be Marxist, but is at least of a '*marxisant* character'. Another reason for his interest in mobility studies is the desirability of greater openness in society. He also states, in contrast to much other mobility research, that mobility is something that occurs between classes or class positions. This is the reason for the class model.

In the article on the service class Goldthorpe's aim is to shed some theoretical light on the expansion of higher-grade white-collar employment, the class of professional, administrative and managerial employees. The concept of the service class is generated in an effort to come to grips with a problem that has been an important issue in the discussion of class theories over the last thirty years. But I would like to question whether the increase in higher-grade white-collar employment is still the most important question in class analysis today, as Goldthorpe seems to suggest.

On the whole class analysis in itself is dealt with very briefly in Goldthorpe's work. It is evident that his interest in class analysis does not stem from an ambition to examine the macro-social distribution of power and its implications for conditions of life in different classes or the nature of class conflicts. I find the form in which Goldthorpe presents his class model quite problematic. It gives the impression that the model itself is of minor importance to him. It takes up comparatively little space in the book and in Chapter 2 it is presented under the headline 'Data and the Class Schema'. The class model is presented as a sevenfold scale numbered from Class I to Class VII. Classes I and II are labelled the service class; Classes III–V are regarded as being 'an intermediate class—that is, as being structurally located between the service class and the working class' (1987a: 42). Classes VI and VII make up the working class.

The form of the model is ambiguous. The manner of categorization is certainly not one-dimensional, but it is presented as such. There is no logical multi-dimensionality in the model. There is nothing to explain why, for instance, the petty bourgeoisie is number IV and routine non-manual employees are number III. Is there a particular idea behind this or is it just a matter of chance? This question of numbers may seem trivial, but it is important for understanding how Goldthorpe thinks about the intermediate class. At the end of the section on data and the class schema, Goldthorpe mentions that the model should not be regarded as having a consistently hierarchical form. This is the message conveyed, however, especially when presented in the tables with only the numbers I–VII. In the text, too, classes are mostly named after their numbers. Even if this is not the intention, the class model lends itself very easily to an interpretation of the class structure as hierarchical and one-dimensional.

MARKET, WORK, OCCUPATION AND CLASS

The theoretical basis of the class model is not clearly elaborated and, moreover, it is neither very logical nor theoretically consistent. At best it may be regarded as a well-made commonsensical classification of occupations. Goldthorpe describes the overall guiding principle for his class model as the bringing together of 'occupations whose incumbents will typically share in broadly similar market and work situations' (*ibid.*: 40). Market and work situations are declared as the 'two major components of class position'. Market situation is described in terms of conditions of employment, such as sources and levels of income. Work situation has to do with authority and control in the production process. Even though this may seem quite sensible, the lack of any clarification of how to specify market or work situations is quite problematic. This is most apparent in the case of market situations. The mention of market and work situations is of course a way of alluding to a Weberian class theory instead of a Marxist one; but I am not going to criticize John Goldthorpe for this choice. What I will question is his way of not adequately elaborating a Weberian approach to class analysis; instead he uses it merely as a label.

For instance, what constitutes a market situation? In the class model under discussion it is employment status (whether one is self-employed or an employee) and income level that are supposed to characterize the market situation of a class position. Clearly though, Weber must have meant much more when he wrote that a class situation is a market situation. 'But always this is the generic connotation of the concept of class: that the kind of chance in the *market* is the decisive moment which presents a common condition for the individual's fate' (Weber, 1978: 928). It seems to me that the idea of market situation should include at least some connection to the supply and demand for labour power, which is of utmost importance in determining the life chances of people in different occupations. In this way class positions would change with economic recessions and booms. This is just one example of the fact that few, if any, of those claiming to apply a Weberian class theory have really succeeded.

Moreover, the operationalization of Goldthorpe's concept of market situation is not carried through in a coherent way. Despite its claims, the model does not bring together class positions with similar market situations. In the case of people with self-employment they may end up either in Class I in the service class or in Class IV in the intermediate class. There is little in the theoretical model to explain a classification of, for instance, a self-employed engineer into the service class and a self-employed electrician into the intermediate class. Work situation is dealt with in quite a conventional way, distinguishing between foremen and supervisors on one hand and rank-and-file employees on the other. Theoretically this is quite unproblematic, even though it may cause practical difficulties in the actual classification of occupations.

The vagueness of the underlying theoretical assumptions of the class model is further revealed when one reads the descriptions of the classification of the seven classes. Here two additional grounds for classification are introduced which are neither explained nor discussed. These are the distinctions between higher-grade and lower-grade and between manual and non-manual work. Within the service class a distinction is made between higher-grade and lower-grade professionals; higher-grade professionals are in Class I, while lower-grade professionals are in Class II. The terms 'higher-grade' and 'lower-grade' presumably have something to do with educational qualifications, but the concept of education is never mentioned in the text. The idea of manual versus non-manual is in fact quite problematic. It is introduced to distinguish between occupations in Class III and Classes V–VII. I will discuss this distinction below.

To summarize the argument so far, the class model as a whole does not contain any rigorous theoretical logic. It seems to be a mixture of practical and common-sensical considerations that may work for certain mobility studies, but whose application gives very little theoretical insight into the relationship between structurally derived power relations and everyday class realities.

THE SERVICE CLASS

In an interesting article of 1982 Goldthorpe has developed his argument concerning the service class. Having criticized some Marxist and non-Marxist attempts to overcome the prevalent theoretical obscurity regarding higher-level white-collar employment, he develops his own theoretical considerations linked to a discussion of Karl Renner's idea of a service class. The argument concerns the need for *trust* in the employment relationship between employers and their professional, administrative and managerial employees. The need for trust stems from the need to delegate authority and the need for specialist knowledge and expertise in order to exercise it (Goldthorpe, 1982: 168). To reinforce the service relationship, the employer needs to provide special rewards. These are of an 'essentially prospective kind: that is, as embodied in understandings on salary increments, on security both in employment and after retirement, and, above all, on career opportunities' (*ibid.*: 169). The notion of the service class is quite informative, and is similar to Wright's arguments on organizational and skill assets among higher managers and professionals.

In his article Goldthorpe also touches on the question of the boundary between the service class and 'those who, so to speak, stand over them' (*ibid.*: 170). In this connection it is stated that the ruling class, if this term be allowed, owe their positions to their own power, which may be economic, political or military. This is a fundamental insight which is lost, however, in the class model itself. Here Goldthorpe mixes those who have a power position of their own with that of their employees, thus omitting one of the most fundamental variables in class analysis.

Somehow Goldthorpe seems to be aware that there is a problem here, but in the description of Class I he says: 'However, the shortcoming is more apparent than real' (1987a: 41). This may be the case for mobility studies, but for a theoretically grounded class model such a statement is fatal. Moreover, Goldthorpe adds a further argument in defence of his mixing the service class with those who are being served, namely, that the latter category is of such a small number. Historically there is no doubt that ownership of the means of production, whether it is land or capital, has been of the greatest importance as a power resource. Through ownership of strategic economic resources, a small number of people have been able to wield very much power. When Goldthorpe leaves this distinction out of his class model, he also loses one of the most salient explanatory factors in class analysis.

THE INTERMEDIATE CLASS

One of the positive contributions in Goldthorpe's class model is that he does not treat white-collar employees as a unitary group. The distinction that he makes between the employed service class and routine white-collar employees is important. In this respect the distinction between the service class and an intermediate class seems to be a good suggestion. However, there is one serious problem in the conceptualization of the intermediate class. It is similar to the problem found in the Marxist model of Nicos Poulantzas, when the latter speaks about the old and the new petty bourgeoisie (Poulantzas, 1975); the only thing connecting the traditional and the new petty bourgeoisie is that they are both outside the main contradiction between labour and capital. In Goldthorpe's class model the only common denominator among Class groups III–V in the intermediate class seems to be their residual character.

In the intermediate class we find routine non-manual employees in administration and commerce (Class III) and technicians whose work is of a manual character (Class V). For Class III it seems that non-manual work is what distinguishes it from the working class. In the case of Class V, though, doing manual work is something that gives it an intermediate status in comparison to the service class. Below I will argue that the manual versus non-manual distinction is a very tricky one to make. My point here is simply to make clear the ambiguity in the theoretical explanation of the intermediate class. Classes III and V are admittedly both employees. However, Class IV in the intermediate class is composed of small employers, self-employed artisans and other own-account workers (Goldthorpe, 1987a: 42). In my view, then, Class IV adds to the confusion as regards the theoretical content of the intermediate class.

THE WORKING CLASS

According to the arguments offered, the chief characteristic of the working class is its market situation, first the sale of 'their labour power in more or less discrete amounts', and second their subordination in the work situation (*ibid.*: 42–3). These characteristics of the market situation are supposed to be quite different from the market situations of intermediate class positions, of which it is said that a majority provide high security of employment (*ibid.*: 41). This distinction between the intermediate class and the working class is highly questionable. Shop assistants, waiters and bar staff are considered to belong to Class III in the intermediate class, whereas postal workers and ambulance men, to mention just a few occupations, are part of the working class (see Goldthorpe and Hope, 1974: 140–1). This certainly does not hold for Sweden, where postal workers and other public employees in the working class have a more secure employment status than shop assistants and waiters. Moreover, workers in public employment sell their labour power 'in more or less discrete amounts' to a much lesser extent. They have monthly salaries, while shop assistants work largely on an hourly basis. In Sweden around 40 per cent of the working class (depending on how one defines this class) are publicly employed. Their market situation is without doubt better than that of a privately employed shop assistant, or a rank-and-file clerical employee for that matter. The effort to define the working class from their market situation does not work.

Empirical results from Britain seem to indicate that the work situation sales and service workers, in particular those in Class III, are very similar to those of the working class (see Marshall, Newby *et al.*, 1988: 121). This problem is so obvious that Goldthorpe, in a later chapter on the class mobility of women, has split Class III into two 'sub-classes', Class IIIa and IIIb (Goldthorpe, 1987: 280). One of the major occupations in Class IIIb is shop assistants. The explanation provided by Goldthorpe is that these occupations 'entail straightforward wage labour rather than displaying any of the quasi-bureaucratic features associated with other positions covered by Class III'. I find this a step in the right direction, but it does not solve the anomaly of the 'quasi-bureaucratic features' of the widespread public employment among the working class.

Another argument advanced in support of the distinction between the inter-mediate class and the working class, especially in the case of Class III, is the idea of manual versus non-manual work. (This is another argument that Goldthorpe has in common with Nicos Poulantzas.) My suspicion is that this distinction is used arbitrarily. In extreme cases, for example, in order to differentiate between the work of a psychologist and a carpenter, the concepts manual and non-manual may make sense. But how can one say that the work of a routine clerical employee is non-manual whereas the work of a postal worker is manual? And is not the work of a shop assistant today, putting up goods on shelves and marking prices, as much manual as the work of a storekeeper? But clerical employees and shop assistants are placed in the intermediate class, and postal workers and storekeepers in the working class.

It is very hard to find any criteria in Goldthorpe's model which categorize the working class coherently in comparison with the intermediate class. From the remarks above it follows that it cannot be market situation, it cannot be the distinction between manual and non-manual work, it is not skill, and it cannot be subordination, since Class III employees are also categorized as rank-and-file employees. If there is a motive for making a clear distinction between the working class and the intermediate class, it is not mentioned in the text.

THE PETTY BOURGEOISIE AND THE STATE IN SWEDEN

To substantiate my critical discussion of Goldthorpe's class model, I will mention two important features of the development of the class structure in Sweden, both of which have to do with the changing power structures in society which affect people's everyday life as well as the process of class formation, neither of which is dealt with adequately in his model. These significant trends within the Swedish class structure are the development of the petty bourgeoisie and the growth of public employment in the central and the local state (counties and municipalities).

In 1930 the petty bourgeoisie comprised around one-third of the labour force in Sweden (see Ahrne *et al.*, 1988: 16). A rough estimation of the share of the intermediate class (in Goldthorpe's terminology) in Sweden in 1930 would make it 40–45 per cent of the labour force. In 1968 the share of the intermediate class was 37 per cent and in 1981 it was 31 per cent (see Erikson and Widerberg, 1988). During these fifty years the intermediate class decreased its share of the labour force by about 15 per cent, from nearly half of the labour force to around one-third. This is a considerable change within the class structure. But to assert that there has been a decrease in the intermediate class in Sweden over the last fifty years is to conceal more fundamental changes. Theoretically, it would be more fruitful to regard these changes as different class processes taking place in different classes as expressions of dramatically changing power relations. Since 1930 the Swedish petty bourgeoisie has been reduced from around one-third to around one-tenth of the labour force. At the same time Classes III and V have increased their shares from less than one-tenth to one-fifth of the labour force. Thus behind the decrease of the intermediate class there are two more far-reaching class processes. The existence of a large petty bourgeoisie in Sweden until the 1930s and 1940s had a decisive influence on class formation in Swedish political life. Farmers' organizations and parties, in particular, have been of great importance in forming the historical compromise in Sweden, as well as in the other Scandinavian countries (cf. Ahrne *et al.*, 1988). The importance of the petty bourgeoisie is made theoretically more intelligible if we treat it as a separate social class with distinct power resources, interests and methods of mobilization.

Goldthorpe's article on the service class starts from the assumption that the rise of a class of professional, administrative and managerial employees is a general problem for class analysis today. In some ways this is true—it is a problem—but it is not an issue in its own right. It is connected with a more fundamental change in the power structure of modern nations, namely, the growth of state and public employment. I would argue that, when examining the problem of the class positions of higher white-collar employees, it is crucial also to consider the question of the state sector and the class structure. In Sweden, at least half of the employees in the service class are in public employment. It has also been shown that public employment is of particular importance for explaining interest formation and political attitudes among the service class. In the working class the difference between public and private employment is not as pronounced (see Ahrne and Leiulfsrud, 1984: 11–12). The implications of the service relationship are quite different in the private sector compared with the state sector. I should emphasize that the question of the state sector has not been treated successfully in any class odel; but my assumption is that this is a more fundamental challenge than the problem of the rise of white-collar employment *per se*.

CONCLUDING REMARKS

I find John Goldthorpe's easily applied commonsensical class model of little general interest. It has been too much adjusted to his very special research interest, namely social mobility. The idea behind the concept of the service class is valuable, but it should be developed further, particularly in relation to the different functions and roles of the service class in the capitalist versus the state sector. But the overall impression of the class model is that its categories are defined according to very different criteria, and thus the systematic theoretical logic of the model is lost. The service class is mixed up with those whom they serve. The petty bourgeoisie is put together with Classes III and V—which are themselves distinguished by their performing non-manual and manual work—into an intermediate class. The reference to the market situation of the class position is not adequately or consistently elaborated.

All theoretically grounded empirical class analysis has its difficulties. Finding concepts and measures that contain information on the macro-social distribution of power, as well as relevant facts about the work situation, and at the same time covering the whole of the labour market, is a formidable task. It is not to be expected that social scientists will ever be able to fulfil such ambitions. Nevertheless, empirical problems must not make the researcher give up all theoretical endeavours. A theoretically sophisticated model that explains some variation in strategic variables will still be of greater value to future research than a simpler, more commonsensical model that explains more of actual variation. Even if the simpler model 'explains' more variations at an empirical level, it is difficult to know what this explanation actually says about the nature of social reality.

Interchange

MARSHALL REPLIES TO AHRNE

I read Göran Ahrne's paper with great interest and am delighted to learn that we at least agree about something. Despite the fact that the concept of social class has been declared obsolete many times, it has indeed, as he puts it, 'been shown time and again to explain a significant amount of the variations in human actions and attitudes'. Unfortunately, where class is concerned, we seem to disagree about almost everything else.

I am, for example, frankly bemused by his claim that 'what Goldthorpe has written on class theory and class analysis *per se* is in fact not much at all'. If the Oxford Mobility Study and CASMIN Project are not part of class analysis, then I don't know what is. The underlying unity of John Goldthorpe's sociology is provided by his systematic testing of liberal and Marxist theories of long-term changes in the class structure. Consequently, therefore, almost everything he has written forms part of class analysis.

It also seems to me that Ahrne has misunderstood what one might call the 'practical application' of the Goldthorpe class scheme. The fact that the classes are numbered I to VII is unimaginative but unimportant. Anthony Heath has elsewhere labelled and collapsed them rather differently to yield the 'Salariat' (I and II), 'Routine non-manual' (IIIa), 'Petty bourgeoisie' (IV), 'Foremen and technicians' (V), and 'Working class' (IIIb, VI, VII) categories (Heath, Jowell and Curtice, 1985). In looking at aggregate mobility trends, Goldthorpe often (for technical reasons concerning statistical reliability) merges his Classes III, IV and V into an 'intermediate grouping'—but the schema does not have to be used in this way. There is, therefore, no reason in principle why a Goldthorpe-type analysis would fail to pick up the changing proportions of Classes III, IV and V in Sweden during the past fifty years. Indeed, since Goldthorpe's first step in an empirical class analysis is invariably to construct a 7 by 7 class-mobility matrix, it is certain that such changes would be identified in the marginal distributions of the basic inflow/outflow tables. The significance or otherwise of sectoral (public versus private) cleavages is an empirical issue that can be dealt with similarly.

The claim that Goldthorpe's concept of the service class is fatally flawed because it embraces both top employees and their employers is, of course, an old one. Roger Penn (1981) offered the same objection when the schema first appeared. On that occasion John Goldthorpe defended himself—rightly it seems to me—on pragmatic grounds. A national random sample is not an appropriate device for investigating 'the bourgeoisie', since very few capitalists will be selected for study.

Moreover, the distinction between employee, self-employed and employer is at this level rather ambiguous, as in the case of managers holding sizeable ownership assets. In Britain, at least, the distinction is often artificially introduced simply for income tax or national insurance purposes. Of course, Goldthorpe would be a fool were he to believe (as he clearly does not) that the Duke of Westminster and Gordon Marshall, both of whom would be placed in his service class, have identical 'market situations'. But, for the practical purposes of determining what large-scale changes (if any) have taken place in class mobility chances over the past fifty years, this is, unfortunately, the best one can do. What alternative research strategy for studying aggregate mobility does Göran Ahrne have in mind? In any case why would he *want* to investigate class formation among top people, since we already know a good deal about the elites in question: they are relatively closed; pass on their considerable wealth in the form of land and capital assets; wield power out of all proportion to their numbers; and are remarkably conservative in their political beliefs and outlook on life generally. What we did not know much about, at least until the results of the Oxford Mobility Project were published, were the relative mobility chances of the other 95 per cent of the population.

Enough. It would be tedious to take up every point of disagreement between Ahrne and myself. Behind all our differences, and behind his chapter itself, is the weighty theoretical presence of his mentor on the Swedish Class Project—Erik Olin Wright. Ahrne's basic objection to Goldthorpe's class analysis is that *Social Mobility and Class Structure in Modern Britain* is not prefaced by a huge 'theorization' of all hitherto existing class societies. Erik Wright, of course, has provided precisely such a theory (two, if you accept his auto-critique). Ahrne acknowledges in passing that 'there are numerous problems in Wright's theoretical construction', but insists that 'it still provides a fruitful perspective on the historical meaning of class'. Well, it depends what one means by 'fruitful'. The evidence from the British class project in which I have been involved shows clearly that, however impressive Wright's complex theorization of modes of production, his resulting class categories are so heterogeneous that they make little sense of almost any class-related phenomena in which one might possibly be interested (see on this Marshall, 1988a). The superiority of the Goldthorpe class categories, in this respect, cannot be dismissed merely by asserting that 'the aim of class analysis can never be to find the maximum amount of variation in ... observed activities'. Goldthorpe's concern for the *empirical* does not make him *empiricist*. His class analysis is grounded in a Weberian theory about the importance of the market for life chances. It is not, as Ahrne would have it, merely 'commonsensical'. I accept that Goldthorpe's approach has its own problems, indeed I ventured to suggest at least a couple of controversial elements in my chapter. But I would also like to know precisely what it is that makes Erik Wright's class analysis 'more fruitful' and 'of more value to future research' than that of John Goldthorpe.

AHRNE REPLIES TO MARSHALL

Gordon Marshall has stressed the fact that John Goldthorpe has been developing his approach to class analysis since the early 1970s. In my contribution, on the other hand, I pointed out that Goldthorpe has actually written very little on his own specific class model, hardly more than ten pages. This seems paradoxical; however, both observations may in fact be valid.

I believe the description presented in Marshall's article underlines my argument concerning the limited value of Goldthorpe's class model because of its adjustment to the agenda of mobility research. According to Marshall, Goldthorpe's aim has been to make systematic tests of some central propositions about class processes in order to falsify both liberal and orthodox Marxist assumptions about these processes. But in so doing it seems that he has relied too much on the power of the British data at the cost of elaborating and explaining his own class model. Even if he may have been right in his critique of some simplified statements from liberal and Marxist theoreticians, it is not evident that collecting data alone will tell you the essentials about class processes. It is also necessary to have a relevant theory. In this connection I find Marshall's discussion of why Goldthorpe abandoned the 'Hope-Goldthorpe' scale illuminating. It seems as if the shift to a class model was astonishing and sudden. It was an adjustment to the data as well as to the international community of mobility researchers. Moreover, another push-effect was the emergence of the log-linear modelling technique. Altogether this underlines the *ad hoc* character of Goldthorpe's class model.

Marshall does not go into the details of the model, and nothing that he writes contradicts my critique of the lack of consistency concerning the theoretical arguments in the model. However, he states as one of the merits of Goldthorpe's empirical work that it has been able to illuminate the complexities of changes in the class structure. He exemplifies this by mentioning the growth of the service-class and a proportionally decreasing working-class. I would say that the case of the growing service-class is largely indisputable, although this is hardly thanks to Goldthorpe's class concepts. On the other hand, the conclusions concerning the working class are highly uncertain and to a large extent dependent on the theoretical arguments in the model. Since I cannot find in Goldthorpe's discussion any conclusive justification for his distinction between the working class and two of the divergent parts of the intermediate class, I do not find his empirical results at all convincing in this respect. Moreover, in my initial contribution I described some severe limitations concerning the ability of the class model to elucidate long-term changes in the class structure. Placing the self-employed in the intermediate class between routine non-manual employees and technicians does not help to clarify the complexities of changing class structures. Nor is the model suitable for describing the effects on class structure of a decreasing petty bourgeoisie.

IV. CRITIQUE OF MARXIST THEORIES OF CLASS AND HISTORICAL DEVELOPMENT

6. Class and Economic Development: A Critique of Marxist Theories

GIORGIO GAGLIANI

My purpose in this chapter will be to support and, where possible, add fuel to John Goldthorpe's critique of the Marxist and post-Marxist account of some significant class-related changes associated with economic development.

Marxist thought is very diversified, to the point that it has become unclear how much *marxiser* is needed to retain membership rights.[1] The 'account' I shall deal with is thus a stylized one or, rather, a *leitmotif*. Most Marxists and their sympathizers would agree on capitalist development being characterized by a basic trend towards proletarianization, in at least one of the possible meanings of the term. Some point more particularly to a progressive deterioration in the class-relevant characteristics of certain non-proletarian occupational labels, to such an extent that their reclassification is called for. Others point to a progressive increase in the fraction of workers once-and-for-all classified as proletarian. The first section of this chapter is devoted to the former meaning, the second to the latter.[2] Goldthorpe's resolute criticism of both positions can be found in a variety of publications (e.g. Goldthorpe *et al.*, 1969: 24; Goldthorpe, 1972b: 354–5; 1985b, esp. 180–9; 1987a, 24–5, 258–9, 270–3; and 1990).

PROLETARIANIZATION VIA RECLASSIFICATION?

People, Positions and the Development Process

Is it appropriate to use the term 'proletarianization' when dealing with positions in the class structure? The answer appears to be no. It is better to talk of the downgrading of positions as distinct from the proletarianization of people, for the good reason that much of the former could take place without any of the latter. If the position *B* you occupy is downgraded to proletarian conditions, you are negatively affected. But if, as *B* is downgraded, you are able to move to position *A*, of a higher grade than *B*, why should you be concerned? For altruism, perhaps, as *I* will have to take *B*. But say that my previous engagement was in *C*, of still lower grade than *B* now is. In this case one position may have been 'proletarianized', but neither you nor I have been. In fact, we are both likely to feel better off, and thus temporarily prone to 'consensus', at least for as long as I do not perceive, or choose to neglect, the relative mobility issue (why are *you* in *A* instead of *me*?), or the inequality issue (is the difference in 'grade' between *A* and *B fair*?).[3]

It is the presence of absolute mobility which makes proletarianization and downgrading two not necessarily concurrent events. This holds both within and across generations. As an instance of the effect of ignoring mobility, consider the following passage:

> From about 1870 the growth of the service economy had increased the demand for clerks but the increase in supply more than matched this. Several factors need to be considered. First, the *type* of clerical work that this expansion generates required lower levels of skill in terms of numeracy and literacy than had previously been expected. Second, changes in the education system had improved general levels of numeracy and literacy. Third, it seems clear that the sons of skilled manual workers *were* attracted into clerical work and had the educational standards required. Finally, women and foreign male clerks entered the labour force. All of these factors, to varying degrees and at different periods, weakened the market position of the clerk. (Crompton and Jones, 1984: 21; original emphasis)

This typical account (a similar one may be found in Carchedi, 1977: 188–93; its most celebrated forebear is Braverman) aims to prove that workers belonging to an occupational label rightly considered as mainly non-proletarian in the nineteenth century should be reclassified as mainly proletarian now. Since the number of clerks has long been on the increase everywhere, and since no instances are normally given of counter-tendencies in other occupational groups, the implied resulting process is one of net intergenerational proletarianization of the labour force. But is it really? A look at some mechanisms characteristic of economic development, with their implications in terms of long-term mobility, suggests a different interpretation.

Economic development is made easier, not to say possible, when more than one group of actors derives a net advantage from it, relative to the *status quo*. The type of growth our ancestors saw in the nineteenth century owed much to the fact that, facing a group of capitalist entrepreneurs eager for profit, there were people who both considered working for a factory wage as a solution preferable to the available, often gloomy alternatives, *and* who could take up the new jobs being offered.[4] These jobs had to be designed to suit the characteristics of the existing supply, made up of mostly unskilled cheap labour. A virtuous circle could thus be set in motion, a simplified account of which may be the following. Workers newly employed in the factories could now start purchasing those products entrepreneurs could sell cheaply, while still making profits, thanks to high labour productivity, which more than compensated for high wages. High profits and high demand in turn would stimulate more investment and employment as well as keep raising real wages.

But were wages in the new factory jobs high or low? The answer is both, and neither. They were high compared to what workers could get elsewhere, and very high indeed if account is taken of existing or emerging unemployment or under-employment in the contracting sectors. They were low compared to (1) average productivity in the factories and (2) average incomes of the cream of self-employed craft workers engaged in *similar* production in the near past. But they were neither high nor low relative to existing *identical* occupations, as there were no such occupations with which they could be compared.

As to skills, it would be hard to compare their level in rural and factory tasks. Yet this is what would need to be done to be able to say anything about changes affecting *people*, since most factory workers came from the countryside. An unknown fraction of factory workers may have been less skilled than the craftsmen supplying the competing products which were displaced. A number of the latter, as well as many self-employed farmers and unpaid family workers, did become proletarians in the original connotation of the term.[5] But, in the absence of factories, most of the rural workers, by far the majority of the working population, would have had no chance to enter a craft. Rather than the degrading of *occupations* which did not exist, it is the intergenerational upgrading of labour force *entrants*, and the personal advancement of migrants, which were relevant to the long-run dynamics of class.

The great expansion in lower-level office jobs followed a similar pattern since, in the private sector, it had the same rationale. It was made possible by a similar virtuous combination of skill content, productivity, profits and pay, and by the fact that manual workers' children were (and still are) sufficiently 'attracted' by clerical work to be willing to invest in, and able to attain, those moderate amounts of 'numeracy and literacy' required for access. Thus persons destined to be farm or factory workers became, instead, non-manuals, whose pay and conditions were, again, good or bad, depending on the terms of comparison. The contention that skill requirements were expected to resemble those of 'the nineteenth century clerk' is unrealistic. First, the twentieth century equivalent of that clerk belonged to a much more sizeable and skilled 'service class', whose expansion was also fostered by economic growth. Second, the level of numeracy and literacy required of new entrants definitely surpassed that of their parents, whose pay, working conditions and prospects for advancement were also inferior. This was the veritable test for the direction of change. Whatever people expected before entering the office, their disappointment would scarcely be such as to make them wish 'to go back'. Running the risk of being proletarianized was likely to be more desirable than the certainty of remaining a proletarian.

Crompton and Jones's interpretive fallacy, shared by many others, is the result of the seemingly sound argument that when average conditions in an occupational category worsen to proletarian levels, this entails proletarianization of persons classified in that category. It is a common feature of economic development that, if an *average* worsening occurs at all (which is far from certain), it is due to an identifiable group of new lower grade occupations invading the particular category. However, since the options previously available to the workers involved were, normally, inferior, the use of a term implying that anyone in the category is now worse off makes no sense. Reclassification of the old category is thus misleading: an additional one is needed, together with an assessment of its class location.

The relationship between gender and class is analyzed elsewhere in this volume. Here we may note that, just as the expansion of factories had found its typical source of 'cheap' labour in families of the rural domestic and foreign peripheries, the growth of the office found its source of cheap labour in the large number of women first entering the labour force. The reasons why the female participation rate had been low were many. Prominent among them were the lack of viable alternatives and, in some countries, the influence of custom. Office growth provided an ample source of new jobs for women endowed with some degree of 'numeracy and literacy', more docile than males, willing to accept lower pay, and often forced by an unequal division of labour within the family to regard job security as a luxury reserved to men. Here, again, the necessary consequence was a drop in the average non-manual/manual pay ratio for females, especially in clerical jobs. But the appropriate class location of the new entrants is certainly less influenced by this drop than by the rise in their incomes above those characterizing the informal domestic labour from which they had emerged.[6] And unless domestic skills, with all that they imply, are valued 'more' than the numeracy and literacy required of newcomers, it is hard to see how female *work* may have been deskilled.

The argument, until now, was that upward mobility, whether intra- or intergenerational, would thwart the proletarianization of persons who enter the allegedly deskilled jobs (or, *a fortiori*, move away from them: see, on work-life changes, Stewart *et al.*, 1980, esp. 93, 112, 192; also Lee, 1981). As Goldthorpe observes, however, for the destinies of people and places to diverge, mobility does not have to be upward. To return to the initial example, suppose that, as your position *B* is downgraded, you descend to *C*, while I ascend from *C* to *B*. Suppose, also, that I will soon either go back to *C* or ascend further to *A*. Neither of us will be likely to react to these events as affecting 'members' of *B*. In fact, *B* has no permanent membership: it is, as it were, 'in constant flux'. Now, remarks Goldthorpe (1987a: 258), for any class-relevant process to occur within a given group, its members must possess some 'continuity of association ... with a given set of class locations', a continuity which, for his 'intermediate Class III', is largely missing. Whatever happens to Class III places (which, at any rate, needs to be demonstrated empirically), the allocation of people to them proves too transient to allow loyalties to form and alliances to cement.

Deskilling

All attempts to test the deskilling of the occupational structure have collided with massive obstacles. First, what needs to be found, via an analysis of all occupational categories, is *net* deskilling (Goldthorpe, 1987a: 275–6n22; 1990: 13–14). Second, the same problem is encountered within each category: detailed analysis of only some of the jobs in the category will not suffice, since the others may have been upskilled. As to net deskilling in single occupational categories (such as 'clerks'), note also that, questions of mobility aside, to equate deskilling with proletarianization requires proof that the registered subtraction of skill is sizeable enough for proletarian levels to have actually been reached. Some authors seem prone to an excessive underrating of numeracy and literacy. Observe, finally, that net deskilling of the occupational structure does not necessarily entail its net downgrading, since the loss suffered in terms of skill could be offset by favourable changes in working conditions and pay (for instance, by a reduction in weekly hours and unchanged weekly wage).[7]

A recent comprehensive survey of the literature on deskilling reaches very sceptical conclusions (Form, 1987; see also Attewell, 1987; Diprete, 1988). As to clerks, Crompton and Jones's claim (1984: 5, 210) to have found in their study of 'three large white-collar bureaucracies', 'that the work content of the majority of jobs was routine and "deskilled"', appears to be based on a too restrictive and static definition of deskilling as 'lacking control' (*ibid*.: 58–62) and, at least in its second part, simply cannot be accepted.

PROLETARIANIZATION WITHOUT RECLASSIFICATION?

Some Comparative Evidence

High levels of economic development in mixed-economy countries tend to be associated with a high proportion of non-manuals in the working population (Gagliani, 1985). As non-manuals increase their share, it is their top rather than bottom layers that are increasingly represented among them.

Table 6.1 derives from a statistical estimate based on 127 observations relating to 58 countries at various levels of development. The estimate postulates the existence of a time-series cum cross-sectional association between the ratio of professional and technical workers (PROF) and total non-manuals (NMT) to total employment. Together with (i) professional and technical workers, 'non-manuals' include (ii) administrative and managerial, (iii) clerical and (iv) sales workers. Group (i) has been taken as the top layer of non-manual occupations. Some of the occupations classified in the group—mostly in the health sector—would not qualify for membership of the 'service class', while those of group (ii) would. However, while subtraction of the former would have been impossible, inclusion of the latter would have implied a drastic reduction in sample size, due to the high cross-country variation in the statistical treatment of the administrative and managerial group (normally the smallest of the four). International comparisons do require concessions of some sort (scathing words on some of these 'sorts' may be found, alas, in Goldthorpe, 1985a: 554–5).

Table 6.1 *Percentage of Professional and Technical Workers among Non-Manuals (PTNM)*[a]

Non-manual (NMT) percentage	Total	Males	Females
20	22.0	22.5	31.7
30	24.9	26.8	30.9
40	29.4	32.5	30.4
50	34.5	38.7	30.2
53.06[b]		40.7	
54.4[b]	36.9		
70.39[b]			29.9

Notes:

[a] = fitted ratios (PTNM = PROF/NMT) from a statistical relationship between PROF (professional, technical and related workers/total workers) and NMT (all non-manual workers/total workers), estimated for 58 countries in various years (*n* = 127), in total and by sex. For further details, see note 8.

[b] = highest value of percentage of non-manuals among 127 observations.

Source: *ILO Statistical Yearbook*, various issues, Table 2B.

Table 6.1 presents the proportion of professional and technical workers in total non-manual employment (PTNM = PROF/NMT) at selected levels of NMT, estimated from the fitted equations, in total and by sex.[8] The ratio increases considerably with NMT when both sexes are considered. In particular, when non-manuals represent 20 per cent of the labour force, professional and technical workers account, on average, for 22 per cent of non-manuals, but when half the labour force is non-manual, more than one-third of that half is technical and professional. This is exclusively due to males, as the representation of professional and technical workers among non-manual females tends, instead, to decrease. This decrease is, however, remarkably slight (from 31.7 to 29.9 per cent of non-manual females as these rise from 20 to 70 per cent of the female labour force), and it would be even lower if only female professional and technical *employees* were considered (not shown). It is, moreover, strongly influenced by the cross-sectional element in the estimate, as it does not show up in most of the time series.

Columns 1 to 3 of Table 6.2 show average annual compound rates of change in the ratio of professional and technical workers to the non-manual labour force, in total and by sex. The rates, computed from the values in the initial and final years, refer to the 22 countries for which the ILO data used in the above cross-sectional estimate are available for an interval of at least 18 years (with the exception of Haiti). As can always be expected when even low levels of occupational disaggrega-

Table 6.2 *Average Annual Percentage Rates of Change in* (1) *Professional and Technical Share of Non-Manual Employment*; (2) *Same for Males*; (3) *Same for Females*; (4) *Real Gross National Product per Head*; (5) *Non-Manual Share of Total Employment*; (6) *Female Share of Total Employment* (*countries ranked by ascending value of column 1*)

Country	Period	(1)	(2)	(3)	(4)	(5)	(6)
El Salvador	1950–80	− 0.28	0.77	− 1.29	1.29	3.41	2.52
Korea	1955–80	− 0.14	− 0.09	0.35	4.96	4.27	− 0.35
Sri Lanka	1963–81	− 0.09	− 0.35	− 1.68	− 0.05	1.41	0.36
Japan	1950–80	− 0.02	− 0.13	0.11	6.90	2.13	− 0.07
Philippines	1960–81	0.47	0.71	0.04	2.22	3.27	1.77
Venezuela	1950–81	0.58	0.82	− 0.89	1.44	2.46	1.36
Thailand	1960–80	0.61	0.06	1.65	4.54	2.78	− 0.14
Ireland	1961–79	0.74	1.47	− 0.02	3.28	2.17	0.35
Germany FR*	1961–82	0.97	0.89	1.36	2.87	1.99	0.23
USA*	1950–82	1.05	1.78	− 0.70	1.81	0.99	1.39
New Zealand*	1961–81	1.08	1.81	0.21	1.44	1.02	1.49
Portugal	1960–81	1.21	2.45	− 2.00	4.88	2.69	4.00
Canada*	1951–83	1.21	2.06	0.22	2.24	3.04	2.00
Chile	1952–70	1.31	0.93	1.48	1.86	1.53	− 0.48
Peru	1961–81	1.46	2.52	− 0.19	1.60	3.14	0.22
Norway	1960–82	1.47	1.36	1.80	3.56	2.64	2.78
Guatemala*	1950–81	1.50	1.89	0.84	1.70	2.11	0.24
Netherlands	1961–81	1.61	2.28	0.47	3.06	1.84	1.23
Ecuador	1950–74	1.69	1.69	1.65	2.86	2.48	− 2.10
Singapore	1957–82	1.77	3.31	− 2.61	n.a.	1.02	6.50
Sweden	1950–82	2.35	2.13	2.92	2.56	1.91	1.74
Iran	1956–76	4.14	3.75	1.04	6.66	2.93	3.77

Note: an asterisk denotes final year for Y = 1980 instead of date shown.
Source: ILO, *Yearbook of Labour Statistics*, various issues, Table 2B; GNP per head: Summers and Heston (1984).

tion are attempted, differences in individual countries' experience (and classificatory practices) are very wide. However, the ratio for females *increases* in almost two-thirds of the cases (as against more than 80 per cent for males).[9]

Table 6.2 also presents average annual rates of change in per capita income in the non-manual share of the labour force and in the proportion of the labour force accounted for by women. It is of special interest to observe that, while no accurate statistical generalization can be inferred from the data, some kind of regularity exists concerning the alleged proletarianization of women and the feminization of the labour force. Specifically, and with the exceptions of Sweden and Norway, there is a tendency for the change in the professional and technical fraction of *non-manual* females to be inversely associated with the relative absorption of women. In fact, if the two mentioned countries were excluded, the negative coefficient between the two rates of change appearing in columns 3 and 6 would be highly significant. This tends to confirm that it is not the proletarianization of women, but a different process, that is at work as a concomitant of economic development (as analyzed in the first section of this chapter).

On the Fruitlessness of Shift-share Analysis

The analysis of changes in the degree of proletarianization is carried out by some authors by making use of an accounting technique known as 'shift-share analysis' (SSA). By applying the technique to changes in US employment, Wright and Singelmann (1982) claimed that in the 1960s employers acted so as to foster proletarianization (without reclassification).[10] Aggregate statistics would fail to show this, due to composition effects SSA was presumed to disentangle. Singelmann and Tienda (1985) and Wright and Martin (1987), in turn, using the same technique, found no evidence of employer-induced proletarianization in the second half of the 1970s (on these studies see Goldthorpe, 1987a: 271–2). Apart from the inconclusive results of SSA, however, it is the use one can make of it that is open to question.

The alleged rationale behind SSA is that an increase in the share of occupation x in total employment may be due to two logically separable sets of 'causes', one relating to the occupational, the other to the industrial structure of the economy. In the first case employers in some or all industries may choose to raise the proportion of workers engaged in x, thus increasing that proportion in the aggregate. In the second employment may increase more rapidly (or decrease more slowly) in industries using x intensively. SSA offers an arithmetical way of separating the former ('intraindustry', or 'intrasectoral') from the latter ('interindustry' or 'intersectoral') type of change. If asked why it should be useful to do so, shift-sharers would answer that intersectoral change, which has been very important in the past, is approaching an end. Such change consisted mostly of transfers of employment, at first away from agriculture and, later, away from manufacturing. Once the former sector is depleted and the manufacturing share stabilized, we shall 'have seen the better part of the sectoral transformation' (Singelmann and Browning, 1980: 259). Singelmann and Tienda (1985: 64) repeatedly refer to the 'completion' of such transformation into the 'service economy'. At that point events *within* each sector will be dominant in shaping the future. By extracting their past influence on proletarianization, SSA is thus expected to throw light on events to come. This claim is, however, unwarranted for two basic reasons associated with (1) the dependence of interpretation on the level of aggregation, and (2) the impossibility of isolating the role of any given group of agents from that of all other contributors to the aggregate outcome.

To look at (1) first, suppose intersectoral change effects in period t were computed for each of m groups of occupations (or classes), allocated across n sectors. If we now wanted to increase n via further disaggregation, and compute the intersectoral effects again, their magnitudes for each m would be unchanged only if, in t, absolute employment in each of the new subsectors changed at the same rate as in the larger sector to which it belongs. Apart from this quite exceptional case, the size of the intersectoral effects will depend on n, i.e. on the chosen level of disaggregation. Users of SSA should thus base their choice on some sort of theoretical analysis, lest their conclusions should be exposed to destruction by mere reclassification.[11]

The SSA authors consistently neglect this problem. In fact, most of them keep applying uncritically a 37-sector classification originally elaborated for a different purpose, admittedly underrating the transformative sector (Singelmann, 1978: 29ff.). Of course, in the real world the industrial transformation is never completed. Even the legendary 'service economy' would continue to register the customary incessant flux from one type of service to another. Continuous structural change is bound to have occurred also *within* each of the mere six manufacturing sectors (as against 20 in services) appearing in the classification. How much, for instance, of the measured degree of proletarianization in 'machinery' was 'due' to employment shifts between the many and sizeable machinery subsectors, thus having nothing to do with decisions taken at the level of production or organizational unit?[12] The shift-sharists end up counting as intrasectoral many changes other scholars could swear are intersectoral (and *vice versa*).[13] If the SSA kit is to be kept in the toolbox, a large warning label on the influence of classification should be made compulsory. A closer look at point (2) above, however, makes one wonder if it is not advisable to dispose of the kit altogether.

SSA can be used, with care, to describe the past. To interpret that past, let alone predict the future, some theory will be necessary. More specifically, SSA users must be confident that two distinct sets of determining forces exist and can be singled out, one for each type of change. For if facts X and Y are both found due to an undifferentiated *explanans* Z, their separate quantification would, by itself, explain little and predict nothing, as we would never be able to say—when Z occurs—whether X or Y, or which combination of them, should be expected to follow.

The 'ideal' case for SSA is thus one in which intersectoral shifts are solely due to the rising share of state employment, and intrasectoral ones to the capitalist entrepreneur's strategy of multiplying 'agents of social control within production' and of enlarging 'administrative apparatuses' in line with the 'increasing concentration and centralization of capital' (Wright and Singelmann, 1982: 188, 200). More or less implicitly, SSA authors tend to assume this to be the 'normal' case as well. Since, however, intersectoral change in mixed economies is, to say the least, strongly influenced by private operators, as is intrasectoral change by technical and cost considerations, the assumption is unrealistic.

An attempt at refinement by SSA advocates might consist in attributing intersectoral shifts to changes in *consumer* demand, and intrasectoral ones to the economic (as well as 'strategic') behaviour of *producers*, thus placing the distinction along the demand/supply divide.[14] Consumers would then be assumed to affect the industrial employment mix in response to changes in their incomes and tastes and relative product prices, while remaining indifferent or, at any rate, ineffectual as to *how* the objects of their desires are produced in each industry. Producers, on their part, would affect intrasectoral change on the basis not only of *divide et impera* strategies but also of the available technological blueprints, relative factor prices and price elasticities of factor substitution.

On closer scrutiny, however, separation along these lines also proves unfeasible. First, demand-based variables can produce intrasectoral effects: a change in tastes in favour of product *p*, for instance, will tend to raise the relative price of factors (hence types of labour) used intensively in *p* and, consequently, influence the occupational mix. Second, supply-based variables can have intersectoral implications: technical change, by raising product per head, determines whether employment will rise or not, in response to a higher demand for the products of that industry;[15] Schumpeterian entrepreneurs, by 'creating' not just new products but also their consumers, will operate directly on the industrial mix.[16] Third, the same event, whether on the demand or the supply side, can produce both kinds of effect at the same time. Technical change normally affects the industry's occupational mix as well.[17] Changes in relative pay will influence the occupational structure, but also the distribution of income and, through that, the pattern of consumption.

Fourth, and most fundamentally, the idea that components of individual behaviour can be extracted for separate analytical treatment belongs to social science fiction. In real life, around half the population belongs to the labour force: within this half, consumers and workers coincide. Neo-classical *homo oeconomicus*, or any normal individual at that, might well be indifferent as to how goods are produced by others, but will surely be concerned when it is he/she who is involved. What matters here is that his/her preferences will *not* be ineffectual. A rising number of applicants to attractive jobs previously protected by barriers to entry will drive down relative advantages enjoyed in those occupations. The adjustment often concerns pay. A drop in relative pay may stimulate employers not only to hire more of that kind of labour today (as hinted above), but also to reward technical progress conducive to a more intensive use of it tomorrow (Binswanger and Ruttan, 1978; for competing views see Elster, 1983a: 101–5). Two cogent illustrations of this are: (1) the disappearance of many products and of the associated occupations when, due to improved opportunities elsewhere, the remaining workers ask, as producers, prices most people are reluctant to pay as consumers; and conversely (2) the proliferation of new products and jobs where better working conditions counter-balance low pay.

To sum up, unless one is prepared to take a strictly non-market view of the workings and the development of an economy, consumers and workers must be seen as interacting with employers in the determination of *both* the industrial *and* the occupational structure. An intrasectoral shift may have the same determinants as an intersectoral change. An industry's occupational mix may change as a consequence of shifts in the demand for the product, just as sectors may grow *because* certain occupations are highly represented in them.[18] Until more solid theoretical support is provided, SSA will remain no more than an exercise in tabulation.

CONCLUSION

Many writers in the Marxist tradition more or less openly claim monopolistic rights to a scientific concern for the exploited, treating other views as unconcerned and/or incorrect. A non-secondary by-product of Goldthorpe's impressive work on mobility is its reassurance to students that they can feel concerned without being Marxist, and that they can be Marxist (or post-Marxist) without being correct. While Marx could have turned a blind eye to social mobility, but did not (Goldthorpe, 1987a: 4–7), most Marxists should not, and do (Goldthorpe, 1990). As soon as any sort of class boundary is drawn between groups of workers who own no property—an innovation many of our Marxist authors had, sometimes reluctantly, to accept—one only needs the assumption of equal abilities and tastes to understand the subversive role an increase in mobility can play. Yet the negative influence of mobility on class sedimentation, with its both favourable and unfavourable consequences for a society's 'degree of openness' (Goldthorpe, 1987a: Ch. 9), is systematically ignored or belittled (Goldthorpe, 1985b: 180–1) by the very authors who profess to be second to nobody when subversion is at stake.

At the root of this attitude seems to be the idea that a sound analysis of class positions can and should be kept distinct from the personal trajectories of those who occupy them (Poulantzas, 1974: 32–3; Carchedi, 1977; Wright, 1985: 17n4), an idea of tempting 'objectivity' which may even be practicable, but only in a timeless analytical world. For in a dynamic context the reproduction of positions and of agents are not independent of each other. This is so from two basic perspectives, which could be termed, for brevity, 'sociological' and 'economic'. First, for 'classes' to mean anything in terms of collective action (which is why we study them), one of their characteristics must be some degree of diachronic self-reproduction, some kind of Goldthorpian 'demographic identity', which can never be detected if persons, and their movements, do not matter. The well-known contention of Poulantzas (1974: 37) that if suddenly, tomorrow or in the next generation, the bourgeois swapped places with the proletarians, *rien d'essentiel ne serait changé au capitalisme*, would lose all meaning if a re-run of the swapping were staged the day after tomorrow (or in the following generation) and so on. In this case the only people left to identify class positions would be disoriented sociologists, unable to find the slightest trace of correspondence between fictional categories and real people.

Second, and from the 'economic' viewpoint, an increase in (relative) mobility entails an enhancement of the ability to compete of those for whom the dice were unfavourably loaded. Competition directed towards 'better' positions will have an effect, as it had in the past, both on their relative desirability, and on their relative availability. Positions determine the objective location/situation of agents, but agents do act on the structure of positions.

Typical of most Marxists, and consistent with the analytical framework of their more orthodox representatives, has also been the tendency to bank on the historical inevitability of an alliance between lower non-manual and manual workers, prompted by the proletarianization of the former. Fortunately, such a stand seems more and more to be a thing of the past.[19] While few post-Marxists would do away with the notion that proletarianization of lower non-manuals occurs on a significant scale, most now reckon that so many other ambiguous and/or contradictory events happen to a number of them that, on the whole, one cannot say *a priori* which way they, as a group, will go. Thus, albeit from a different route, some Marxists have taken a position which is not too dissimilar from that of Goldthorpe. All regard this alliance as crucial to the attainment of their basic goal which, for Goldthorpe (1987a: 327), is 'a genuinely open society' and, for the Marxists, is 'doing away with the rule of capital altogether' (Oppenheimer, 1985: 201). But all consider it as one which, in order to come about, will need all the political skills accumulated by working-class parties and organizations (Goldthorpe, 1987a: 350). [20]

The future may see more of these points of contact between post-Marxists and Goldthorpe. A basic difference will, however, persist. Much of the Marxist literature still resounds with dire predictions based on immanent laws of one sort or another. Thus a drop in the labour share is quickly taken as proof of the exploitative bias of capitalism; a rise, of its incumbent collapse. Goldthorpe's long-standing Popperian position is also non-Panglossian. There is no train of history. If one there is, it is of our own make. As such, of all the possible trains, it is certainly neither the best nor the worst.

ACKNOWLEDGMENT

I would like to thank Maurizio Franzini and Francesca Sanna-Randaccio for their comments on an earlier draft of this chapter, and CNR for financial assistance.

NOTES

1 If in doubt about oneself, knowing another Marxist may prove useful. Wright, for instance, was reassured that a recently confessed dislike of cognitive processes common to Marxism and theology—and an implicit pledge to abandon the former if a different theory provided better explanations, however disturbing and naive—are not enough. In fact, he 'will always be a Marxist' (Burawoy, 1987: 53, 70–1). The reason for this prediction is that 'Marxists who abandon Marxism because it is false are rationalizing a rejection based on other, usually political or moral grounds', and Wright must be known as incapable of reaching such political or moral troughs. On differences among Marxists see Wright (1980b), Abercrombie and Urry (1983: Chs 4 and 5).

2 A third, and most truly Marxian meaning concerned with the transformation from self- to paid employment has tended to step off the analytical stage. This is probably due to the observation that the drop in the number of the self-employed to an all-time trough did not coincide with an all-time peak of what could reasonably be defined as the proletariat.

3 If position *C* still exists, and is taken by a 'full citizen' (not, say, an illegal immigrant or a *saisonnier*), but with few prospects for mobility, both issues may be raised *vis-à-vis* the two of us as soon as the 'tunnel effect' is over (see Hirschman, 1973, for the inequality issue; on relative mobility see, of course, Goldthorpe, 1987a: esp. Ch. 3).

4 In the twentieth century a very similar type of development has taken place in some countries of Southern Europe and Asia. In fact, I would venture to say that development, or growth, is always based on a mechanism of this kind. What changes is the technology in use, the type of new jobs being created, the source of 'cheap' labour being tapped, the groups which are advantaged, and those which are disadvantaged.

5 See note 2 above.

6 Incomes, working conditions and, most certainly, skills were also higher when compared to the average female farm and factory job, as well as to that *formal* domestic work which in some countries and years accounted for more than a quarter of the entire female labour force.

7 One has to take a really hard structuralist line to explain why, if a job's skill content could drop by a sufficient percentage to plunge its holder into the proletariat, a simultaneous rise in its hourly wage by, say, twice or three times that percentage might not avert the danger.

8 I selected the functional shape of the association between PROF and NMT by increasing the degree of a polinomy in NMT until the gain from doing so became negligible, and by then proceeding backwards to eliminate superfluous terms. In fact, the best correlation was found with NMT for females and with squared NMT for males and the total. All coefficients of the independent variable are significant at the 1 per cent confidence level. The coefficient of determination ranges from 0.67 (males) to 0.82 (both sexes).

9   The increase registered for Sweden is so large as to generate doubts as to data comparability between 1950 and 1982 for that country.

10 In all co-authored articles Wright has applied his own definition of classes by which, for instance, more than half of clerical workers are counted as proletarians (Wright, 1980a: 207).

11 Suppose a new technology, which affects the occupational mix, is adopted by an entrepreneur to produce a new commodity. The ensuing occupational change will be registered as an intra- or intersectoral effect depending on whether the new commodity 'belongs' to the entrepreneur's sector or not. But since this 'belonging' depends on the classification being used, the most refined 'sector' being, in fact, a product, fiddling with digits would generate contradictory results.

12 Machinery and laundry receive identical treatment in Singelmann's classification, although in 1980 the former employed in the USA 19 times as many workers as the latter.

13 An interesting example of the possible confusions may be found in Singelmann and Tienda (1979: 761), who explain the decline in the female employment share in the personal service sector (given the classification, an intrasector effect) with the declining role of domestic service 'which almost exclusively employs women' (an intersectoral interpretation).

14 It must be stressed that no attempt along these lines is ever made by the shift-sharers, whose theoretical premises always remain unclear.

15 On this ever-present issue in economic analysis see Baumol, 1967; Pasinetti, 1981.

16 I owe this point to Francesca Sanna-Randaccio.

17 That is, technical progress is seldom 'neutral', in short, saving all types of labour in the same proportion.

18 This holds even more for public sector employment, whose expansion may be due to worker pressure to obtain certain kinds of public jobs no less than to consumer demand for certain kinds of public services.

19 It is to be remembered, however, that only ten years ago Poulantzas was impelled to insist, without much success, on the dangers implicit in the proletarianization thesis, not only for France (see Ross, 1978: 175), but also for Chile (Hunt, 1977: 116).

20 My own point of view is that such an alliance, even if stipulated, would stand very few chances of resisting conflicts centred on the division of labour (Gagliani, 1981: 279). A sceptical view of alliances *with the service class* is found in Goldthorpe (1982: 184).

7. Goldthorpe and Marxist Theories of Historical Development

ROSEMARY CROMPTON

The desire to understand both how modern societies arrived at their present condition and the likely direction of their future development is probably universal. One answer to this question was given in the nineteenth century in Marx's analysis (summarized in the *Communist Manifesto*) of the growth of the capitalist mode of production and his predictions for the future. He identified 'classes' as major forces in historical development, arguing that the bourgeoisie had assumed a 'revolutionary' role in the transition from feudalism to capitalism and that the proletariat was the emerging revolutionary class of capitalist society (Marx and Engels, 1962).

As is widely known, Marx did not provide a comprehensive definition of the concept of 'class'; the manuscript of *Capital* broke off at a point just where one was apparently forthcoming. However, there is no general shortage of definitions of 'class'; class schemes have been devised and used by government departments, psephologists, market researchers and advertizing agencies, as well as neo-Marxist and neo-Weberian sociologists. Such schemes vary in the extent to which they use production relations, consumption patterns, social standing and so on as elements in the classification process, but all, without exception, relate directly or indirectly to the occupational structure.

It is my contention that, although occupational class schemes are essential to the social science enterprise as a whole, they are rather inadequate as accurate longitudinal measures of long-term historical change.[1] This criticism would apply equally to neo-Marxist as well as to neo-Weberian class schemes. Both the occupational structure and the people located within it are in a state of constant flux as a consequence of technological change and economic booms and slumps, as well as factors such as changing rates of female employment and national and international migratory movements. Thus classifications deriving from this structure have to be continuously revised and updated, and longitudinal comparisons are made rather problematic (Crompton, 1980).

However, Goldthorpe would seem not to accept fully the requirement that occupational class schemes should be modified in the light of changing circumstances. This point may be illustrated with reference to his position on the issue of women and class analysis. (As this topic is the particular focus of the next chapters in this volume, I will not dwell on it here.) Goldthorpe (1983a) has argued that the proper unit of class analysis is the household, and where that household contains a 'male breadwinner', the class position of household members should be derived from this, whether or not women in the household are in employment. This is because the life chances of women in conjugal households are 'overdetermined' by the male head. The exclusion of women from consideration in class analysis is also required in order to preserve the location of Goldthorpe's Class III—routine non-manual workers—relative to the other classes in his scheme. Empirically, women are concentrated in Class III occupations, and have tended not to be mobile out of them. However, as men in such occupations have high rates of (upward) mobility, and women are not significant for class analysis, then Class III may still be safely described as 'being structurally located between the service class and the working class' (1987a: 42).

Recent trends in the distribution and extent of women's employment suggest that, contrary to Goldthorpe's arguments, women's own qualifications and skills are better indicators of their employment standing than the occupation of their conjugal partner (Britten and Heath, 1983; Marshall, Newby *et al.*, 1988). More fundamentally, it is recognized increasingly that the structure of *men's* employment is affected by the structure of *women's*, and that changes in women's participation in the labour force have affected the structure of 'class positions' (i.e. the occupational structure). As authors broadly sympathetic to Goldthorpe have recently argued: 'People are distributed to places through time according to processes that are powerfully shaped by gender. The structuring of opportunities itself is therefore a legitimate part of the subject matter for a class analysis concerned with demographic as well as socio-political class formation' (Marshall, Newby *et al.*, 1988: 84).

However, Goldthorpe shows no signs of accepting this argument, perhaps because, as suggested above, to take it on board would threaten the integrity of the sevenfold class scheme. Rather more is at stake, however, than the defence of a particular research instrument, for Goldthorpe uses evidence derived from occupational class data both to refute Marxist theories of long-term historical development and to question the validity of Marxist analysis as a whole. I would not wish to defend Marxist theories of long-term historical development on the evidence of occupational class data—and, as we shall see, the major 'Marxist' who has argued this position has recently abandoned it.[2] I would wish, however, to defend Marx's conceptual framework—including elements of his theory of history—from summary rejection. I would also wish to retrieve aspects of empirical research and evidence—often, though not invariably, of an interpretive non-quantitative kind —from the sociological wilderness to which Goldthorpe's arguments would consign them. First, however, his account of Marxist (and liberal) theories will be examined.

GOLDTHORPE AND THEORIES OF SOCIAL CHANGE

A parallel critique of 'liberal' and 'neo-Marxist' theories of the development of industrial societies has been a recurring feature of Goldthorpe's work. The strategy of the argument has remained the same over two decades: (1) presentation of liberal view; (2) presentation of Marxist view; (3) critique of liberalism; (4) critique of Marxism; (5) fault(s) common to both; and (6) Goldthorpe's alternative interpretation. However, the tactics have varied in response to intellectual developments in liberal, and more particularly Marxist, thinking, as well as in Goldthorpe's own work. This may be seen by comparing one of the earliest manifestations of the original argument—the concluding chapter of *The Affluent Worker in the Class Structure* (Goldthorpe *et al.*, 1969)—with the latest—'Employment, Class and Mobility: A Critique of Liberal and Marxist Theories of Long-Term Change' (Goldthorpe, 1990).

In 1969 the major focus was on the political behaviour of the *working* class in Britain. The 'liberal' perspective, according to Goldthorpe, argued that as the 'new worker' had been 'able to gain a good deal for himself within the existing system, [he would] move towards a conservative and individualistic, rather than a radical and collectivist, outlook on economic political issues', and a decline in support for the Labour Party was predicted. In contrast, Marxist commentators argued that profound alienation in work and growing commodity consciousness in the world outside denied the true needs of man in the midst of affluence, providing at least the conditions for protest and rebellion (Goldthorpe *et al.*, 1969: 165). This version of Marx, therefore, was the Marx of the *Economic and Philosophical Manuscripts* rather than the Marx of *Capital*. The *Affluent Worker* research provided empirical refutations of both arguments. The continuing adherence of the affluent worker to collectivism contradicted the liberal view on the one hand, whilst a lack of overt perception or expression of 'alienation' undermined the Marxist view on the other. *Both* theories were criticized as deriving from 'some kind of evolutionist position'. The chapter ended with a few pages of advice to the then Labour leadership.

In the most recent paper (1990), the focus is on the class structure as a whole rather than on the political future of the working class in particular. Three trends of change in the class structure are identified: (1) in the structure of employment; (2) in the class structure: and (3) in rates and patterns of social mobility within the class structure. In respect of these factors, the 'liberal view' (according to Goldthorpe) would emphasize the diffusion of skills and knowledge in the population and thus the growth of the middle classes, which is accompanied by an increasing 'openness' of society, expressed in high rates of social mobility. This characterization of the 'liberal view' is similar to that of 1969. In the case of the 'marxist view', however, the Marx of the *Economic and Philosophical Manuscripts* has given way to the Marx of *Capital*—or rather, Braverman's *Labor and Monopoly Capital* (1974).

Marxist theorists, Goldthorpe asserts, have argued (*contra* liberal theorists) that 'the long-term trends of change in western societies is for employment to be systematically degraded'. Following from this, the class structure is 'proletarianized' as the burgeoning middle layers of employment are progressively 'deskilled'. Finally, Marxist theorists regard social mobility as relatively unimportant (given that the 'structure' is not thereby transformed), except in respect of the 'proletarianization' of the 'new middle class'.

Liberals and Marxists are duly rejected by Goldthorpe; liberals because their model cannot accommodate rising levels of 'non-standard' and un-employment as well as the persistence of relative disadvantage in respect of class mobility. Marxists have been forced onto the defensive because ' ...the official employment statistics of the more advanced industrial nations...show...that the greatest increases in non-manual employment over recent decades have occurred not in relatively low level clerical, sales and personal service grades but rather in professional, administrative, and managerial occupations' (1990: 11). 'Degrading', even if it had occurred, would in any case be irrelevant as it is *women* who have been recruited to such jobs. As we have seen, the appropriate unit of class analysis is the household, and women's class is dependent on their 'household situation' rather than their 'work situation'. Thus women's employment may safely be omitted from considerations of the 'class structure'.

Liberals and Marxists are rebuked for their 'historicism'; that is, they are both 'theories which stem from an ultimate ambition of achieving some cognitive grasp on the course of historical development' (*ibid.*: 31). This shift in terminology, from 'evolutionism' to 'historicism', reflects a growing tendency for Goldthorpe to acknowledge explicitly the influence of Popper on his own work. Presumably because he wishes to practise what he preaches, Goldthorpe offers no political advice in this latest contribution to the liberalism/Marxism debate.

The contemporary authors who represent the 'Marxist view' are Braverman (1974), Carchedi (1977), Wright (1978, 1985) and Wright and Singelmann (1982). Erik Olin Wright, in particular, may be identified as having devised and implemented an empirical test of Marxist theories of long-term historical change. Indeed, Wright and Singelmann's discussion of changes in the American class structure between 1960 and 1970 includes a systematic contrast between 'Marxist' and 'liberal' theories of the development of the class structure which closely parallels that of Goldthorpe. Braverman's account of the degradation of the labour process in capitalist societies is a key reference through which they articulate their thesis concerning the 'proletarianization' of the American class structure.

Wright's discussion of the American class structure has been recently updated, using 1960, 1970 and 1980 census data from which Marxist class categories were estimated using 'good cross-sectional data on class structure gathered in mid-1980' (Wright and Martin, 1987: 8). Contrary to the predictions of the earlier paper, Wright concludes: 'In terms of the working class, ... the 1970s were a period of relative *de*-proletarianization... . In no case is there any evidence that the prolonged stagnation of the 1970s generated a tendency for the proportion of managers, supervisors and experts within sectors to decline...these results [run] consistently counter to our theoretical predictions...' (*ibid.*: 16). Indeed, all of the evidence points in the *opposite* direction: 'The implication of these analyses, then, is unmistakable: the results are more consistent with what we construe to be the post-industrial society thesis than the traditional Marxist proletarianization thesis' (*ibid.*: 18).

A major Marxist protagonist identified by Goldthorpe, therefore, would appear to have withdrawn from the fray. Wright has measured the American class structure using Marxist-derived class concepts, has discovered not degradation but *de*-proletarianization, and apparently conceded the superior predictive capacity of 'post-industrial' theories. It might seem reasonable to suggest, therefore, that there is little point in continuing with the argument.

Inasmuch as the argument relates to 'class structures' as described by trends in the employment/occupation structure, then this would be a reasonable conclusion. 'De-industrialization', or the 'post-fabricative economy' (M. Rose, 1985), has resulted in an increase in white-collar, non-manual employment, much of which is labelled manager, expert, supervisor, professional, etc. As far as the argument was ever about occupational trends as measured at the 'macro' (i.e. national) level, then the Marxist case has been lost.

If Goldthorpe's (or rather, Popper's) logic were to be strictly followed, then Marxists should, at this point, beat a more general retreat.[3] Their theory has generated a testable hypothesis which, upon testing, has been falsified. The falsification of the hypothesis justifies the rejection of the theory. However, although falsificationism does offer a set of practical guidelines for the conduct of empirical research in the social sciences, its limitations, deriving from the theory-dependence of observation, mean that it does not always provide a secure base from which to reject theories. Occupational class categories, in particular, do not exist independently of sociological theories of them.[4] This theory-dependence of observation also means that legitimate disputes may persist over the interpretation and/or significance of empirical results which are not themselves the object of contention. Wright, for example, does not appear to have rejected Marxist theory *in toto*, despite the failure of his original predictions, suggesting that the 'globalization of capitalist class relations and... the effects of post-industrial developments in the advanced capitalist world' (Wright and Martin, 1987: 25) explain the expansion of 'managerial and expert' class locations. In short, '...a theory can always be protected from falsification by deflecting the falsification to some other part of a complex web of assumptions' (Chalmers, 1982: 66). These arguments suggest that we should examine in more detail the nature of the evidence upon which these larger arguments rest, and this will be our next task.

OPERATIONALIZING SOCIAL CLASS

The most usual strategy through which 'class' is operationalized in British sociology is via the occupational structure. For example, Duke and Edgell (1987) have calculated that in recent years 90 per cent of articles in the main British journals containing empirical data with class as a variable used 'some form of the conventional conceptual scheme based on occupational class categories'.

Although there may be considerable disagreement as far as the theorizing of 'class' is concerned, a common thread in all accounts is that 'class' relates to production and/or market activities, and thus the division of labour and employment relations. It is hardly surprising, therefore, that occupational statistics should have been used to generate class categories. However, the very gathering of such statistics is theory-dependent, that is, the way in which even apparently straightforward data gathering takes place will tend to reflect the assumptions of the data gatherers about the nature of the society in which they are carrying out their task.[5] Wright (1980a) has criticized the use of occupational categories in respect of 'class', making a sharp distinction between 'class' and 'occupation'. 'Occupations are understood as positions defined within the *technical* relations of production; classes, on the other hand, are defined by the *social* relations of production'.[6]

An obvious response to the perceived inadequacies of official data sets, therefore, is for the sociologist to generate his or her own. As one of the strongest critics of the use of occupations as class categories, this is indeed what Wright has done, although, apparently, the operationalization of Wright's scheme also requires the use of an aggregated occupational variable (D. Rose and Marshall, 1986). Sociological surveys enable the investigator to inquire into, for example, authority relationships at work and the precise nature of the respondent's work task, information which enables the researcher to locate with confidence individuals in their 'correct' class categories.

Empirical discussions of 'social class', therefore, usually refer to a combination of 'purpose-gathered' material and official statistics. Occupational class schemes represent attempts to group together units which share certain important characteristics, on the assumption that these shared characteristics may be used to explain features of, or phenomena within, the society in question. The particular scheme employed will reflect the theoretical assumptions of those who devised it. Different theories and systems of allocation to occupational classes, therefore, can produce quite different descriptive accounts of the 'class structure' (Marshall, Newby *et al.*, 1988; Wright, 1985).

The basic move in the construction of an occupational class scheme is from the individual to the class, as in Figure 7.1. This move from the micro to the macro level corresponds to a transition between the first two 'trends of change' identified by Goldthorpe in his discussion of liberal and Marxist theories, from (1) the division of labour or structure of employment to (2) the class structure. As we have seen, there is some controversy concerning the appropriate unit of class analysis—should it be the respondent/individual or the household/family?—as well as the degree of coverage of the population—should the economically inactive be included or not? (see Duke and Edgell, 1987). These controversies, however, are independent of the exercise described in Figure 7.1, which has to be carried out in any case.

Goldthorpe's original sevenfold class scheme was formed by aggregating categories from the collapsed (36-category) version of the Hope-Goldthorpe occupational scale (see Goldthorpe and Llewellyn, 1977a: 259). A new version of the class scheme has been subsequently developed, but 'the objective of this new version was exactly the same as that of the old...: to bring together, within the classes distinguished, combinations of occupations and employment statuses whose incumbents would typically share in broadly similar market and work situations' (1987a: 255). The definition of class situation in terms of 'market' and 'work' situation is taken by Goldthorpe from the work of Lockwood:

> 'market situation', that is to say the economic position narrowly conceived, consisting of source and size of income, degree of job-security, and opportunity for upward occupational mobility... 'work situation', the set of social relationships in which the individual is involved *at work* by nature of his position in the division of labour. (1958: 15; emphasis supplied)

Employment status complements 'market' and 'work' situation in defining class allocation.

Individuals are allocated to classes within Goldthorpe's sevenfold class scheme, therefore, via a combination of occupation and employment status. Occupations are located within the scheme on the basis of evidence relating to the characteristic

Figure 7.1   The Construction of an Occupational Class

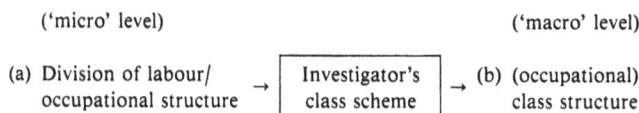

('micro' level)		('macro' level)
(a) Division of labour/ occupational structure	→ Investigator's class scheme →	(b) (occupational) class structure

'market' and 'work' situations associated with particular occupations. The kind of evidence taken into account includes: 'occupationally linked data on earnings, hours, fringe benefits, job stability, etc., as provided by such official sources as ... the *New Earnings Survey*...and also on the relevant monographic literature of industrial sociology and the sociology of occupations' (Goldthorpe and Llewellyn, 1977a: 283). Similarly, the revised scheme is described as being constructed

> in the light of the available information from official statistics, monographic sources etc. regarding the typical market and work situations of the individuals comprised: for example, on levels and sources of income, other monetary and non-monetary benefits, degree of economic security, chances of economic advancement, and location in systems of authority and control. (Goldthorpe and Payne, 1986a: 21)

This use of individual sociological judgment, informed by the available empirical evidence, to allocate occupations to class categories is a perfectly straightforward process. The aim in describing it has been to throw into relief the kinds of evidence used by the sociologist in making these judgments. Goldthorpe used a combination of official statistics and monographic evidence, as would others. Statistical sources such as the New Earnings Survey will certainly provide reasonably accurate information concerning official earnings levels, overtime working, occupational pension schemes, and so on, that is, information on aspects of the 'market situation' of particular occupations. However, one important element—opportunity for upward occupational mobility—will not be discernible from such statistics. Similarly, information relating to other non-monetary benefits such as physical working conditions, and the 'social relationships in which the individual is involved at work by virtue of his position in the division of labour' (Lockwood, 1958: 15), may only be established through the empirically grounded study of work organizations. In short, case studies of particular jobs and occupations were, and are, essential elements in the construction of Goldthorpe's—or indeed, any other— occupational class scheme.

Let us consider, therefore, the implications of the existence of case study material which apparently throws doubt upon the existing location of a particular occupation within an occupational class scheme. One obvious response is to reject the findings of such studies as unrepresentative of the occupation in question—as Goldthorpe has done.[7] Case study evidence may be judged as acceptable or not in the light of other empirical evidence, on the basis of common-sense notions of representativeness (e.g. should policy decisions relating to fishing in Cornwall be made on the basis of a study of fishing in Hull?), or even on personal knowledge of the skills and veracity of the case study investigator. Some kind of judgment, however, has to be exercised, there is no mechanical formula available. However, Goldthorpe does not rest his argument concerning the rejection of 'unrepresentative' case study evidence on his evaluation of 'representative' case study findings. Rather, he argues that:

> ...even quite indisputable evidence of degrading *derived from particular case-studies* can be of little value in defending the degrading thesis against the upgrading thesis *in so far as the argument is about class structures*...macro-sociological arguments can only be adequately discussed on the basis of macro-sociological data. (Goldthorpe and Payne, 1986a: 23; original emphasis)

However, as we have seen, these macro-sociological occupational class schemes are in part constructed on micro-sociological foundations. Once constructed, the basis from which they originated does not disappear.

This point may be illustrated by briefly considering the debate surrounding the work content of many of the occupations which Goldthorpe places in the 'subaltern positions of the service class'. Research in the sociology of work and organizations (some, but not all, stimulated by Braverman's analysis) has suggested that the impact of technological and organizational restructuring on these occupations has been both to centralize control within organizations and to remove discretionary content from many lower-level 'managerial' and supervisory tasks (for example, Child and Partridge, 1982; Crompton and Jones, 1984). The location of such occupations in proximate 'service-class' locations has therefore been questioned. However, Goldthorpe argues that if such occupations had been 'degraded', then one consequence should be a decline in the opportunities for mobility out of them (i.e. in their associated 'life chances'). However, this has not occurred. Thus micro-sociological evidence of apparent 'deskilling' is rejected using macro-sociological evidence of *mobility*. However, as has been argued elsewhere:

> ...the 'service class' content of an increasing proportion of managerial *jobs* is more apparent than real. This argument can only be explored empirically by examining the *jobs*, rather than the movement of people in and out of them. It is the *nature* of the hierarchy that we dispute, rather than the relative mobility chances of men located on its continuum. (Crompton and Jones, 1988: 81)

It could be suggested, as Goldthorpe has done, that if the 'degrading' thesis relates only to skill and job content, and not to employment relations, then this should be made clear (Goldthorpe and Payne, 1986a: 23n15). This is a fair point, but it could equally be argued that if Goldthorpe wishes to disregard empirical evidence of skill dilution and the concentration of control within organizations, then this should also be made clear. In brief, all occupational class schemes are sociological artefacts which reflect the theoretical orientations of their creators. If 'work situation' has been identified as a key factor in the construction of the original scheme, then evidence—including case study evidence—relating to 'work situation' which suggests that the scheme requires modification should not be summarily rejected.[8]

Goldthorpe has argued that 'macro-level concepts' (i.e. occupational classes) require testing with 'macro-level data'; it has been argued that these macro-level concepts in fact rest upon micro-level evidence in their initial construction. It is apparent that Goldthorpe would prefer not to have to deal with 'micro' case study evidence at all.[9] For example, work by Åberg in relation to deskilling is cited with approval as 'of importance in breaking with the case study approach which has so far been almost exclusively followed in research in this area' (1987a: 275n22).

The interesting possibility arises, therefore, of an occupational class scheme informed only by information gathered from individuals in the course of large-scale sample surveys. That is, data relating to the 'work situation' would reflect the replies of individuals to suitable questions. Sociologically, this must be regarded as an unsound procedure. Random sample surveys of the population at large cannot provide conclusive evidence relating to organizational structures and processes. In contrast to macro-level occupational class structures, labour processes *have* substantive realities which cannot be described in their entirety via questions directed at decontextualized individuals. In any case the survey investigator can only ask relevant questions given *some* prior knowledge of actual organizations and work situations. The impermeable barrier which Goldthorpe attempts to construct between 'micro' and 'macro' levels, between case study and survey analysis, simply cannot be maintained.

SOME QUESTIONS OF METHOD

The question arises as to *why* Goldthorpe should wish to deny the relevance of case study data to the macro-level empirical analysis of 'social class'. I would suggest that this position derives, at least in part, from his commitment to Popper's philosophy of social science and its associated methodology, that is, a modified form of positivism in which the world (for research purposes at any rate) must be seen to contain 'what might be called falsifiers, reasonably hard, self-sustaining facts' (Gellner, 1985: 32). In an illuminating metaphor Gellner has observed that such a world resembles '...a desert consisting of hard, discrete, isolable pebbles, each one of which can easily be separated from the others' (*ibid.*: 33).

Goldthorpe's setting out of Marxist theories of historical development, as we have seen in the second section above, corresponds to the application of *modus tollens*:[10] Marxist theory of historical development implies the degradation or 'proletarianization' of the class structure; empirical investigation of the occupational class structure demonstrates that this has not occurred; therefore Marxist theory is false. Testing this hypothesis requires falsifiers, which in this case are produced by an agreed-upon class schema which can unambiguously measure both the nature of the class structure and the fates of the individuals within it. Thus the question of social class is addressed in relative isolation from other factors.[11] One may have some sympathy with Gellner's arguments to the effect that the 'granular metaphysic' (that is, a world of hard, pebble-like 'falsifiers') and what it entails is a strategic assumption which facilitates empirical explorations in the social sciences. In my opinion, however, it would be a serious mistake to move from this convenient methodological strategy towards the assumption that the world is actually *like* that. Societies, as Mann has recently reminded us, 'are much *messier* than our theories of them' (Mann, 1986a: 4).

The methodology of the case study cuts directly across the granular metaphysic. Case studies have been described as 'a way of organising social data so as to preserve the unitary character of the social object being studied' (Goode and Hatt, cited in Mitchell, 1983: 191). Thus a commitment to methodological holism is implied in this strategy for empirical research which is apparently at variance with a (Popperian) positivist approach.[12] Some sociologists—and perhaps Goldthorpe is one of them —would regard case studies as suitable only for the role of suggesting hypotheses or interpretations for future quantitative investigation by 'survey methods'. (This point parallels the quantitative/qualitative distinction in sociology, but this avenue is not being pursued here; case studies can be, and often are, 'quantitative'.) However, because case studies *are* holistic, it may be suggested that they are the *most* suitable strategy for theoretical analytical research (see Mitchell, 1983).

In developing this argument, it is important that it is recognized that the idea of a 'case study' should not be restricted to small-scale ethnographic work. A 'case' can range from an individual through to a nation-state, or even the partitioning of the world ('north' versus 'south', 'east' versus 'west', etc.). It is not being argued that large-scale, methodologically individualistic and necessarily quantitative survey research is unimportant. However, it is the case that some crucial sociological concepts—for example, 'community' or 'organization'—can *only* be investigated using holistic case study methods. For example, it has been argued in the previous section that information relating to the characteristic 'work situations' associated with particular occupations can only be gathered *in situ*.

Case studies make a vital contribution not only to the construction of occupational class categories, but also to the interpretation of the data so gathered. Holistic case study evidence provides the context within which 'macro-level' class data are evaluated, and may be used to suggest explanations of particular macro-level outcomes. For example, Lockwood (1981), in his critique of Braverman, uses the evidence of Kornblum's (1974) case study of steel workers in Chicago to point out that both community relationships outside the workplace and status differentials within it worked against any homogenization of the 'working class' which might have been apparent at the 'macro' level.

This short excursion into questions of method has been in order to make the point that it is misleading to couch the argument, as Goldthorpe and others have done, in terms of micro-level, qualitative case studies *versus* macro-level, quantitative survey research.[13] Rather, the argument relates to different explanatory strategies, and the ultimate necessity for holistic explanations, in contrast to the granular metaphysic. The move from 'micro' to 'macro' levels characteristic of occupational class schemes presumes such a metaphysic—it actively *creates* the pebbles in question (or boulders perhaps?). I do not wish to reject the theoretical value of large-scale, quantitative, occupational class research. However, research on occupational class can only be enhanced if it is constantly open to modification in the light of analytic, holistic, empirical material.

THEORIES OF HISTORICAL DEVELOPMENT

So far in this chapter the emphasis has been upon the procedures through which Goldthorpe has set about the evaluation of theories of historical development rather than an exploration of these theories as such. I have tried to suggest that the logic of social investigation which Goldthorpe employs, while it has many strengths (a commitment to empirical investigation, the requirement that objectives should be clearly stated and so on), has also led to rigidities in the conceptualization and analysis of research data; a tendency to treat as unassailable 'facts' what are the constructs of the investigator; and the risk of the premature closing-off of potentially fruitful avenues of social investigation. These arguments may be relevant to sociology, but they have taken us some way from theories of social change.

Goldthorpe argues that both liberal and Marxist theories appear as so 'inadequate as a basis for understanding long-term trends of change in ...class stratification' because in both there is

> ...a persisting *historicist* strain. They are theories which stem from an ultimate ambition of achieving some cognitive grasp on the course of historical development which can then be used for normative and political purposes: that is to say, to show that certain political beliefs, values and commitments have an 'objective' superiority in being those that the movement of history favours, while others can be 'correctly' dismissed as historically outmoded. (1990: 31–2)

These are large questions to raise in the closing paragraphs of a short paper. However, when stated with such passion ('historicist endeavours' are further described as logically and morally defective), they cannot be simply passed over.[14] In brief, it may be suggested that if 'historicism' describes invariant, Stalinist, iron laws of history which determine political strategy and action both in the present and the future, then there are certainly 'Marxists' who are not 'historicists'. A current debate (Geras, 1987; Mouzelis, 1988) illustrates this point: 'One can...whole-heartedly agree...that there are no iron laws of history, no historical necessity for a proletarian revolution, no "special mission" for the working classes, and so forth. But this does not mean that everything goes, that all social movements are on a par...' (Mouzelis, 1988: 115). Mouzelis suggests, for example, that the working-class movement has a better chance of playing a transformative role than, say, the sexual liberation movement on account of its more central structural position in capitalist society. This position is, in practice, not too far from Goldthorpe's own.

It is possible, therefore, that there is room for genuine disagreements with Goldthorpe's analysis, and his suggestions as to current trends in the occupational class structure, which do not necessarily commit their perpetrators to a belief in iron laws of history. We have already seen above that to the extent that the debate relates to occupational structures as measured at the macro (i.e. national) level, then the empirical outcome would seem to point firmly in the direction suggested by 'liberal theorists'. It has also been suggested that, useful though macro-level occupational class classifications may be for making broad generalizations, the sociologist should be alert to the possibility that such measures may mask processes at variance with those indicated by macro-level data. A debate of some interest and one where, in my opinion, case study and other empirical material throws considerable doubt on Goldthorpe's conclusions, relates to the 'service class' and its 'cadet' or 'subaltern' ranks—Classes I and II in Goldthorpe's sevenfold class scheme.

As described above, it has been suggested that this expansion of the service class may be more apparent than real, as the content of many service-class jobs has been subject to increasing routinization and control. New technology has played an important role in these developments, in facilitating 'controlled decentralization'. These trends have been particularly marked in the area of financial services (one of the fastest growing areas of employment in Britain), where recent legislation (the *Financial Services Act* 1986) has increased competition between banks, insurance companies, building societies, broking agencies, etc. One manifestation of this competition has been the rising number of outlets marketing these services to the general public—building society branches, financial advice centres and so on. These developments have been made possible, in large part, through rapid developments in the computer field, notably the increasing capacity of micros (which operate as large and easily accessible stores of information) as well as interactive terminals linked to mainframes, which both facilitate and monitor flows of exchange. Thus the decentralization of financial marketing has been achieved without any loss of, or decline in, centralized control in respect of policy-making, power over resources and so on in the financial sector (see Gill, 1986; Rajan, 1987).

Although these satellite outlets cannot, in many cases, be described as the real *loci* of power and decision-making, they nevertheless have to be 'managed'; someone has to unlock the door in the morning, make sure that the counter is covered during the lunch period and so on. These managerial jobs involve responsibility and authority, but is it realistic to describe them as 'service-class' positions? To put the argument another way: when the nature of this managerial authority is examined *in its context* (note that such managers *do* have responsibility for the work of others, for property, etc.), it can be seen to be very different from that of, say, an old-style bank manager who held personal responsibility for customers, staff, lending and money.[15] At the very least one would have to conclude that this kind of evidence suggests considerable heterogeneity within the 'service class'.

This kind of case study evidence has been cited by Goldthorpe as a 'last ditch' attempt to 'save' Marxist theories of historical development by implying the 'proletarianization' of the 'service class'.[16] An alternative explanation might be that the exploration, at the organizational level, of the actual 'work situations' of supposedly 'service-class' positions reveals not only more attenuated levels of authority and control than might be immediately apparent, but also the potential for fragmentation and conflict within this grouping. This conclusion would also be supported by the recent evidence of a national sample survey (Marshall, 1988b). Fragmentation and conflict—including conflict along the gender dimension—have been predicted in our recent work (Crompton and Jones, 1984; Crompton, 1986). In contrast, Goldthorpe has argued that the service class, '…far from being threatened with any kind of decomposition, is rather at one and the same time expanding *and* consolidating' (1982: 178). Indeed, he predicts that the 'service class' 'will seek to use the superior resources that they possess in order to *preserve* their positions of relative power and advantage' (*ibid*.: 180). (Note that both protagonists in this argument are engaged in predictions relating to the future development of the occupational class structure.)

In summary, it would be pointless to attempt to defend in their entirety the predictions relating to the occupational structure made in the 1970s by Wright and Braverman. However, I would argue that it is important to defend (or rather, not reject) Marxism as a conceptual framework. A central argument within this framework is that capital, in order to create and realize surplus value, must secure control over the labour it employs. Braverman emphasized above all the significance of 'deskilling' and routinization; however, as many commentaries broadly sympathetic to Braverman have argued, 'deskilling' is only one strategy through which control over labour may be achieved (see, e.g., Thompson, 1983). Developments in respect of the organization of the labour process will in any case not have a direct and unmediated impact on the occupational structure; factors such as occupational and internal labour markets, gender segregation in employment, trade union and political strategies have all had a major impact on occupational roles. Thus the measurement of 'class' using occupational aggregations is fraught with practical, as well as theoretical difficulties, and macro-level class schemes are liable to be rather imperfect measures, requiring constant modification and updating in response to the kinds of factors summarized above. These are practical problems for the sociologist, rather than particular concerns of Marxist theory.

As a conceptual framework, Marxism has proved remarkably fruitful, and encompasses both those who would adhere to notions of 'iron laws' of history as well as many who would reject this position. I cannot deal with the major issues raised by the topic of 'historicism', but the final word I leave to E. H. Carr, who wrote over twenty-five years ago that:

> Progress in human affairs, whether in science or in history or in society, has come mainly through the bold readiness of human beings not to confine themselves to seeking

piecemeal improvements in the way things are done, but to present fundamental challenges in the name of reason to the current way of doing things and to the avowed or hidden assumptions on which it rests. I look forward to a time when the historians and sociologists and political thinkers of the English-speaking world will regain their courage for that task. (Carr, 1964: 155)

ACKNOWLEDGMENT

I would like to thank Gareth Jones, Martin Hollis, Stephen Edgell and Vic Duke for their comments on an earlier draft of this chapter.

NOTES

1 On the reasonable assumption that the longer the time period the more likely there are to have been significant changes in the occupational structure, short-term comparisons (e.g. from year to year) will probably be fairly accurate.

2 An explanation is perhaps in order. In past publications I have argued that (1) the 'class structure' (understood broadly as employment relationships) is largely 'determinate' of other social differentiations (Crompton and Gubbay, 1977: 97–8); and (2) that changes in the labour process (in this case with regard to the 'proletarianization' of non-manual work) are transposed into occupational class categories (Crompton, 1979). (However, I have *never* suggested that the move from changes in the labour process to occupational class categories has been direct and unmediated.) My own position on both of these topics has been modified, largely as a consequence of my attempts to understand the position of women within the occupational structure, and the interrelationship of theories of gender and class. In respect of (1), I would now recognize that employment relationships are shaped by the independent struggles of occupational groups (for example, professions, trade unions) as well as the demands of employers or 'capital', and that the forms these struggles take are shaped by a cultural context (which incorporates gender) which is not simply a 'reflection' of the economic base—in short these are not just 'secondary structural factors'. In respect of (2), although changes in the labour process clearly *do* have an impact upon both individual occupations and the occupational structure, their mediation through the cultural context might in some cases be equally important (Lockwood, 1981).

However, a growing sensitivity to this multi-factor structuring of occupations has also led to increasing difficulties with occupational class schemes: if occupational outcomes are multiply determined, then how can there be complete confidence in what is being measured at the 'macro level'? I would not seek to reject occupational class analysis on these grounds, but would be more cautious as to the claims I might make on the basis of such evidence. In particular, I would hold separate the discussion of empirically derived occupational class schemes on the one hand, and 'classes' as social forces—for instance, in history—on the other (Hindess, 1987).

3 'If theories are to have any informational and hence explanatory value, they must be open, either directly or through propositions derivable from them, to criticism and possible refutation in the light of empirical enquiry' (Goldthorpe, 1990: 40).

4 Chalmers (1982, Ch. 8). Goldthorpe anticipates this criticism, and argues as follows:

> ...empirical results which apparently disconfirm a proposition may themselves be called into question via the concepts and theories that guided and conditioned their production. However...such difficulties can be largely circumvented...by the proponents of a theory *being themselves prepared to state what empirical results produced in what way would lead them to regard their theory as no longer valid*. (1990: 40; original emphasis)

However, falsificationism is not thereby protected, as the theoretical proponents are at liberty to change their definitions. For example, the 'proletariat' could be defined as 'all employees'.

5   This argument is well illustrated in Hindess's discussion of Indian Census Statistics (1973: 29ff.).

6   In practice this distinction cannot be maintained. Occupational listings incorporate *both* 'social' *and* 'technical' elements. For example, in the Registrar-General's classification of occupations, 'manager' is an element in *occupational* categorization.

7   'Even if one accepts that...the studies...*do* indicate significant adverse changes in the class situation of professional, administrative and managerial employees— which I would think very arguable—the crucial question still remains of how far these studies can be taken as representative ones (why were the particular occupational groupings to which they relate selected for study in the first place?) and as a basis for generalization' (Goldthorpe, 1980a: 122).

8   Others seem to have accepted that the re-location of occupations within an occupational class hierarchy *is* appropriate. For example, a number of occupations have been re-classified in official statistics over the years, presumably in response to such considerations (see Hakim, 1980).

9   For example, acknowledgment of the use of monographic evidence in constructing the class schema is omitted from the republished versions of the original articles. Compare, for example, Goldthorpe and Llewellyn, 1977a: 283n8, with Goldthorpe, 1980a: 63n3; and Goldthorpe and Payne, 1986a: 21n2, with Goldthorpe, 1987a: 273n3.

10 As described by Gellner: 'suppose p; if p *entails* q, and if q is false, then p is false. In this schema, p is a theory, p *implies* q conveys the relationship of the theory to any one of its consequences, and q is the consequence which, through its experimental falsification, brings down the entire theory' (1985: 32).

11 In fact, Goldthorpe's approach does not follow this methodology strictly. For example, as we have seen in the case of women, 'major sexual inequalities, especially in regard to opportunities for labour market participation' (1983a: 469–70), are treated as intervening variables which, in combination with women's position in the household, mask the relationship of their market and work situations to the 'class structure'.

12 Methodological holism has frequently been associated with idealism. I do not wish to enter this argument except to state that I would not wish to be associated with this position. Popper has argued that he is not a 'positivist', but I am persuaded by Gellner's (1985) arguments to the effect that falsificationism entails important elements of a 'positivist' metaphysic. In any case 'positivism' in sociology has a variety of meanings (Halfpenny, 1982), which restricts its use as a *precise* descriptive term.

13 For example, D. Rose *et al.* have argued that 'arguments about the characteristic modes of social control under various so-called phases of industrial-capitalist society must necessarily be conducted in quantitative terms. Isolated ethnographies, though having complementary strengths elsewhere, are here illustrative rather than conclusive in tenor' (1987: 20).

14 In *The Poverty of Historicism* (1957) Popper's net is cast widely. Someone not entirely at one with Popper's approach to the philosophy of science, therefore, might find themselves sympathetic to some elements in his critique (e.g. of the tendencies leading towards national socialism and Stalinism), but not in complete agreement with, for example, his rejection of holism.

15 The confusion over 'management' is further demonstrated by the variations in job titles characteristic of these situations. For example, during research in the building society industry we found that the same functional role in different societies was carried out by a 'chief clerk', 'branch manager', 'assistant branch manager' and 'office manager'. See also Ashburner (1987: 135) for a discussion of the problem.

16 The term 'proletarianization' has certainly been used (Crompton and Jones, 1984) and is not being withdrawn. The non-manual labour process has, in many instances, been both routinized and fragmented into a series of minor operations (and occupations); that this has occurred is not without sociological significance.

Interchange

GAGLIANI REPLIES TO CROMPTON

First, no one would deny the need for periodic revision of the class location of occupations: time-proof social classifications have not yet been invented.[1] However, some care is needed in singling out the occupations to be relocated. Let us take an example in which criterion Z assigns occupations L1 and L2 to a given class under the common label L. If conditions in L2, but not in L1, then worsen in time, a straightforward aggregation problem arises.[2]

Goldthorpe's observation on 'macro-sociological arguments' (discussed in Crompton's paper) simply means that any statement concerning change in *aggregate* variables should be based on some sensible and reproducible procedure for aggregating changes in micro units to obtain *net* macro results. This is something wholly different from the construction of 'an impermeable barrier' between micro and macro levels: indeed, it is the opposite. The point made by Goldthorpe is that, at some moment in time the analysis of society as a whole *must* step from micro to macro variables, and that not all ways of doing so are equally acceptable.

His argument applies to *all* aggregate variables, i.e. not only to the class structure as a whole, but also to composite occupational subgroups such as 'clerks'. In our example, let L represent clerical jobs. A banal but correct reclassification procedure may be the following:

A   use criterion Z to reclassify L2, if necessary; as classes must be fewer than occupations, downgrading the latter does not automatically entail transgressing class borders;[3]

B   as L1 may have been upgraded, apply Z to it as well;

C   evaluate how representative L1 and L2 are of aggregate category L by means of some measure of 'representativeness' R;

D   combine Z and R to decide on L's *déclassement*.

Crompton and Jones's (1984) 'holistic case study analysis' amounts to a restricted application of their own inadequate Z to the L2 micro units they decided to pick (see below). Of steps A through to D above, only A is taken care of, and then only partially. Any conclusion derived from *this* procedure cannot be generalized.

Second, as acknowledged by Crompton, 'proletarianization' and 'deskilling' imply a change over time (Crompton and Jones, 1984: 17; see also their telling 'slightly different' restatement on page 210). Diachronic analysis, however, is hindered by the fact that most clerical positions are *new* positions. Thus a 'deskilled' job is taken to be one which 'lacks control' (*ibid.*: 61), so that intertemporal comparisons are defined away. As a surrogate, various characters are then enrolled to serve as fictional terms of reference. Present in all the Bravermanite literature, these *Charaktermasken* range from the 'independent farmer' and the 'self-employed craftsman' to the 'nineteenth century clerk'. Towards the end of Crompton's chapter they have been promoted to the 'old-style bank manager'. All of them, emerging from a sort of occupational Spoon River, are there to remind the oblivious sociologist of the good old times. Suppose, for a brief moment, that Crompton or other authors had managed to demonstrate the (net) intertemporal downgrading of clerical (or service class) positions. But the *déclassement* of a category does not entail the *déclassement* of people entering it (Goldthorpe, 1985b: 189). And since it is people, rather than positions, who vote, demonstrate, strike, create barriers to entry, demolish them and so on, for the student of long-run class change the issue is not of mere secondary importance. The questions such a student would still want to ask are: what (absolute) chance had a farm or factory worker's child of becoming a nineteenth century clerk or an old-time bank manager? And what chance does (s)he now have of becoming a (downgraded) twentieth century one? The old jobs were suppressed and replaced by others, some more complex and skilled, some less so. It is (hopefully) the analyst's task to quantify. But even if the less complex and skilled prevailed (as we are assuming now), a correct evaluation of the class location of those *people* cannot neglect where they came from. Failure to do so will make some aspects of their behaviour wholly unintelligible.[4]

Third, Goldthorpe does not reject 'the Marxist theory of development' *en bloc*, as Crompton suggests, on account of its unsuccessful prediction of proletarianization (see, for instance, Goldthorpe, 1987a: 28). What Goldthorpe rejects are theories resulting in 'iron' developmental laws of any kind. If net proletarianization occurred, it would be caused by a number of factors, some of which are modifiable by human intervention producing a different outcome.

Crompton protests that there are Marxists who are not historicists. This is easily agreed upon: there are Marxists of all possible kinds. Goldthorpe's critique is obviously directed against those whose teleological view of history mirrors that of (most of) Marx himself.

Fourth, Crompton agrees with Mann that societies are much messier than our theories. Goldthorpe would certainly assent, but I suspect he would add that some of our theories are messier than others. In the page quoted by Crompton, where Gellner (1985: 32) likens the empiricists' world to one made of 'hard, discrete, isolable pebbles', he goes on to say that holistic idealists, for their part, 'can only aspire to All or Nothing, or, in some characteristic Hegelian ecstasy, to both at once. But not to sober cognitive progress'. When Crompton tells us that 'this expansion of the service class *may* be more apparent than real, as the content of *many* service class jobs has been subject to increasing routinization and control' (emphasis supplied), we are left questioning whether the expansion is in fact more apparent than real or *vice versa*, and how many the 'many' routinized jobs are. Our hopes for an answer must still rest on isolable, perhaps, but hopefully also hard and sober, pebbles. The alternative, for now, is stepping on quicksand.

NOTES

1 Less convincing is Crompton's point that classifications should also be revised to account for booms and slumps. Categories used in studies of long-run change should be made as insensitive as possible to cyclical fluctuations.
2 Even if conditions in *both* L1 and L2 had worsened, we would still have an aggregation problem if the worsening in, say, L2 justified a *déclassement*, but that in L1 did not.
3 Crompton's observation that there is 'considerable heterogeneity within the "service class"' applies necessarily to all other classes as well.
4 Incidentally, one would not expect such neglect from authors supporting a 'holistic' approach.

CROMPTON REPLIES TO GAGLIANI

There is much in Professor Gagliani's paper with which I find myself in agreement. However, there are also important points where my arguments would be at total variance with those he advances.

Gagliani's discussion treats the 'Marxist' account of 'proletarianization' as falling into two categories: 'Proletarianization via Reclassification' and 'Proletarianization without Reclassification'. The former describes the 'progressive deterioration in class-relevant characteristics of non-proletarian occupational categories', which thus require reclassification; the latter refers to 'a progressive increase in the fraction of workers once and for all classified as proletarian'. However, one of the major arguments of my chapter is that this distinction cannot be maintained. The size of the fractions which are measured will depend on the nature of the classification. I can illustrate my point with an example drawn from Gagliani's own discussion. The work of Erik Olin Wright is taken to represent 'Proletarianization without Reclassification'. However, Wright's empirical work, as Gagliani recognizes, uses an especially devised class scheme in which more than half the clerical workers are counted as proletarians. As I and others have argued, empirical representations of the 'class structure' via the application of a class scheme to a national population are no more and no less than a reflection of the particular class scheme which has been employed; Wright's class scheme, for example, will generate more 'proletarians' than Goldthorpe's when applied to the same raw data (see Marshall, Newby *et al.*, 1988). Thus, it may be suggested, Wright has already engaged in 'Proletarianization by Reclassification' in advance, and there are not, as Gagliani suggests, two separate approaches to 'proletarianization', but two elements within a single approach.

Gagliani is correct to argue, in his discussion of 'Proletarianization via Reclassification', that an empirical description of this process of 'proletarianization' will be problematic, given that technological and other developments constantly produce 'new' occupations not strictly comparable with the 'old', whether these were proletarian or non-proletarian. As he observes in the second part of his chapter, '...in the real world the industrial transformation is never completed'. However, this difficulty is not peculiar to systems of classification informed by Marxist theoretical concepts. For example, Gagliani demonstrates that, on the basis of an international comparison using ILO data, the proportion of 'professional and technical' workers within the total non-manual employment category increases depending on the overall proportion of non-manual employment within the country in question. When non-manuals are 20 per cent of the total labour force, professional and technical workers account for under a quarter of the total, but for a third when the proportion of professional and technical workers rises to half. However, if this kind of evidence is to be used in support of Gagliani's more general arguments, then we have to assume that the work content, status, and material returns of 'professional and technical' occupations are similar at different levels of material development and between different countries; and indeed, that 'industrial societies' are all developing in much the same direction. I am rather sceptical of a table which treats the USA, El Salvador, Iran and Sweden as equivalents, but, in any case, is not this kind of argumentation (perish the thought) 'historicist'?

There are other points on which I would, if space permitted, take issue with Gagliani: I do not think that the expansion of lower-level office jobs within an industrial capitalist society may be legitimately compared with the transition from agricultural work (of all kinds) to industrial capitalist employment, and his discussion of 'skills' completely misses the point that technical skills are relative to their context. The fascination of the Robinson Crusoe myth, for example, lies in the awareness that, notwithstanding the sophistication of modern technology, we have lost the 'skills' to live without it. Nevertheless, his broader argument that 'consumers and workers must be seen as interacting with employers in the determination of *both* the industrial *and* the occupational structure' (original emphasis) is similar to that which I have argued at length elsewhere (Crompton, 1988) and not too dissimilar from conclusions reached on the basis of previous empirical work (Crompton and Jones, 1984: 210).

This stance, however, presents quite serious problems for Goldthorpe's approach to class analysis which Gagliani does not appear to recognize. Yes, the fluidity (or mobility) of persons should be taken into account, but so should the fluidity of positions. The techniques of social mobility research can take into account variations in the size of the aggregates of positions in question, but they assume that the ranking or structural location of the positions remains constant over time, as when, for example, the same coding frame is used to allocate the social class of a respondent's father—when the respondent was aged 14—and of a respondent—when the respondent may be aged up to 64 (see Goldthorpe, 1987a: 44ff.). The treatment of the occupational mosaic as relatively rigid is a weakness inherent in longitudinal research on social mobility, and thus of Goldthorpe's more general conclusions relating to the long-term development of industrial societies. This weakness does not necessarily invalidate the findings of social mobility research, or Goldthorpe's position as a whole, but it should be acknowledged.

In conclusion, has Goldthorpe's critique of Marxist theories of industrial societies been enhanced by Gagliani's arguments? Gagliani focuses on the critics, rather than on Goldthorpe's work. His discussion does reveal important problems, both of a technical nature, and of the difficulty of bringing analytical order to the historical flux which is the occupational structure.[1] However, Gagliani offers no solution to this latter problem, and appears to be unaware of the difficulties that it presents for Goldthorpe's own work. The comparative international evidence (presented in Tables 6.1 and 6.2) relating to the proportion of professional and technical workers among non-manual employees could be used to support what Goldthorpe has identified as 'liberal' theories of the development of industrial societies, but he is as critical of such theories as he is of the 'Marxists'. Gagliani's rationale for his own support for Goldthorpe's critique is, frankly, a weak one; that is, that it reassures students that 'they can feel concerned without being Marxist'. 'Concern' is not, and never has been, a prerogative of Marxists, and a generalized attack on 'most Marxists' for 'claiming monopolistic rights to a scientific concern for the exploited' makes little in the way of political or sociological sense.

NOTES

1 I find myself rather perplexed by Professor Gagliani's arguments on this point. He states that the worsening of average conditions in an occupation is usually due to an identifiable group of new lower-grade occupations invading the category. (This is indeed one of the processes which may occur, a useful example might be the short-lived occupation of key-punching, which was classified as 'clerical'.) Therefore, 'Reclassification of the old category is misleading: an additional one is needed, together with an assessment of its class location'. If this is not 'reclassification', what is?

V. CLASS AND GENDER

8. Women and Class Analysis

SUSAN McRAE

In their recent book, *Social Class in Modern Britain*, Marshall, Newby *et al.* specify gender as the most controversial issue confronting present-day class analysts (1988: 98).[1] Accepting this as true, and being a feminist committed to research on women's labour force participation *and* a feminist asked to present the supposed anti-feminist side of the controversy, I am sorely tempted to invoke W. C. Fields's 'All things considered, I'd rather be in Philadelphia', pack my bags and head for the nearest airport. Alas, as so often happens—both professionally and personally—second thoughts are allowed to prevail over initial impulses, and the proffered task is taken up. In this particular instance, however, hesitation soon turned into gentle irony as, in preparing to write a defence of Goldthorpe's views on women and class analysis, I realized afresh the variety and quality of the contributions he has made, however reluctantly, to our understanding of the position of women in society. For example:

1   Goldthorpe (1983a, 1987a; Erikson and Goldthorpe, 1988b) has provided further documentation, in Britain and across five other industrial nations, of the continued existence of sex segregation in the labour market, to the marked disadvantage of women. In comparison with men, women of all class origins are significantly more likely to experience absolute downward occupational mobility, with, moreover, nearly half of all women (and men) required to change places in the present occupational structure in order for equality in occupational attainment between men and women to exist.

2   Goldthorpe (1987a; and Erikson and Goldthorpe, 1988b) demonstrates that in contrast to much popular—and some sociological[2]—thinking, marriage in Britain and across five other nations does not provide women with an easier route to the higher social classes than is available to men through employment. On the contrary and with only minor variations, the pattern of

women's 'attainments' through marriage mirrors the pattern of men's attainments in the labour market, with women from service-class origins—in comparison to women from working-class origins—three times more likely to marry into the service class than into the working class. The class inequalities which separate men in the labour market, in other words, also separate women in the marriage 'market'.

3 Goldthorpe (1987a; and Erikson and Goldthorpe, 1988b) illustrates the effects of class inequalities, in Britain and across five other industrial nations, on women's employment chances in relation to other women in the labour market, demonstrating that like men, women from service-class families do significantly better in the labour market than women from working-class families. Far from 'sisterhood' cutting across class inequalities, women are instead divided from other women occupationally in much the same way and to much the same extent that men are divided from other men. Class inequalities, in other words, act in ways which are gender-blind.

4 Goldthorpe (1987a), through an analysis which allows for the dominance of wives' occupational participation over husbands' in appropriate cases, provides systematic evidence on the class mobility experiences of unmarried women, and of families in which wives exceed their husbands' occupational attainments, together with evidence about the class mobility experiences of families linked to the class structure via the husband's occupation. These data provide a valuable base line against which the implications of future changes in women's labour force participation for class analysis may be measured.

In addition, research undertaken by Goldthorpe and his colleagues shows that:

5 within families with intergenerationally stable husbands, wives of working-class men withdraw from paid employment after marriage more quickly than other wives; wives of intermediate class men are the slowest returners to paid work after childbirth; and wives of service-class men take the shortest period away from work for childbirth (Goldthorpe, 1983a).

6 women are more likely than men to be upwardly mobile into Class I from Class VI or petty bourgeois origins; and more likely than men to be upwardly mobile into Class II (teachers, nurses, etc.) from Classes V, VI, VII or blue-collar origins (Goldthorpe, 1987a).

7 class homogamy remains strong, with a significant association existing between the employment of husbands and wives when each are assigned to class positions on the basis of their own occupations (Erikson and Goldthorpe, 1988b).

I could go on, but I think the point has been made. It cannot help but add a dash of irony to my task of defending John Goldthorpe—the so-called 'sexist sociologist' and bane of so many feminists—to be able to present such an enviable list of contributions to the sociological study of women. Irony aside, however, it remains the case that Goldthorpe is one of the main protagonists in a debate about how women, and in particular married women, should be treated within class analysis. Explaining why this is so remains the task in hand.

In commenting upon the issue of women and class stratification, Bechhofer was careful to stress the following: 'The state of the art in studies of gender and stratification is somewhat confused and does not lend itself to a small number of sharply focused and neatly argued conclusions' (1986: 224). In consideration of this, and of the countless words already written on the subject, it seems a wise course to set out in advance my intentions for the remainder of this essay. I will not, with one exception, reproduce here the empirical data upon which the findings detailed above are based. These data are available to interested readers in the relevant publications. In any event, few sociologists question Goldthorpe's competence in carrying out quantitative research or in constructing and analyzing mobility tables, although some do disagree with his interpretations. Moreover, it is my belief that this debate is unlikely to be resolved—if it *is* to be resolved—on the basis of empirical evidence, however unfortunate or unsociological that may be. On the contrary, rather than evidence being the adjudicator of the issues, it appears that wishes, hopes or political beliefs about women's experiences in the family and in the workplace have come to dominate, with the unpalatable result that participants at best talk past each other, and at worst simply fail to listen.

Thus my primary aim here will be to present Goldthorpe's arguments regarding women and class analysis as simply and clearly as possible. One of Goldthorpe's criticisms of his critics is that they often fail to engage with the essentials of his arguments (1984c: 491); therefore, making his arguments clear is important. In addition, I will refer to some of the many critics of Goldthorpe's views, and in doing so, present my own arguments for the continuing validity of his approach to class analysis.

THE DEBATE

Stated simply, the debate about women and class rests upon the exclusion of women as actors in their own right from the analysis of class, whether it be called class inequality, class stratification, class structure or class mobility. This exclusion is neither fortuitous nor inadvertent. Instead, it is based upon the theoretical choice of the family as the basic unit of the class structure, on the grounds that the family is the primary means whereby advantage and reward are transmitted from one generation to the next, with the major class divisions in society running *between* but not *through* families. Further, the family is seen to be linked to the class structure via the occupational position of that family member who has the most enduring or continuous participation in the labour market (cf. Parkin, 1971: 15; Giddens, 1973: 288; Westergaard and Resler, 1975: 291). Empirically, this theoretical stance has meant that where women live in families, their class position is deemed to depend upon (derive from) the occupational position of the male head of household (husband or father); and that where women live alone they are generally omitted from consideration.

This approach to class analysis is usually labelled the 'conventional' view, and John Goldthorpe has been, and remains, one of its strongest advocates. Behind the challenge to this approach, and hence at the heart of the debate in question, is the increased labour force participation of women and especially married women. If, it is argued, married women participate in the labour market in their own right, should they not be regarded in class terms as more than passive recipients of their husbands' occupational attainments? Should they not, at the very least, be seen as co-determiners of their class fates? As such, should they not occupy places of their own in the analysis of class stratification? The debate arises because, changes in the labour force participation of women notwithstanding, adherents of the conventional approach to class analysis, Goldthorpe included, would answer negatively to each of these questions, at least with respect to the majority of married women. Moreover, they would do so wholly in respect of, first, their understanding of what is entailed by *class* analysis and, second, their recognition of sexual inequalities in both family life and the labour market. To show why this is the case, I turn first to a necessarily brief and schematic exposition of Goldthorpe's views on class analysis, followed by an equally brief and schematic examination of women's labour force participation.

GOLDTHORPE ON CLASS ANALYSIS

Although criticisms of the conventional approach to class analysis have been made on both sides of the Atlantic, Goldthorpe has laid great stress on the differences between American studies of stratification and his approach to the study of class which falls within the European tradition (see esp. 1983a). Unlike the American tradition with its emphasis upon multi-dimensional analyses of individual attributes or socio-economic status, the European tradition, with its roots in both Marx and Weber, seeks to understand social change in terms of the relations between labour and capital, in terms of power and the marketplace. Analysis thus focuses upon the formation or decomposition of social relationships or collectivities with which individuals or families are associated over time by virtue of their location in the social division of labour. In the European tradition the primary concern of class analysis, to use Goldthorpe's words, is with:

> ... certain social relationships in which individuals and groups are daily involved and which are believed to exert a pervasive influence on their lives. More specifically, one could say that class analysis begins with a structure of positions, associated with a specific historical form of the social division of labour, which is usually seen as being constituted in two main ways:
> (i) by basic employment relationships which differentiate employers, self-employed workers and employees; and
> (ii) by varying employment functions and conditions of employment which differentiate categories of employees—most importantly (a) those in subordinate positions who, via a labour contract, exchange more or less discrete amounts of labour for wages on a short-term basis and (b) those in positions involving some exercise of authority or expertise, whose conditions of employment imply the exchange of 'service' for 'compensation' in a more diffuse and long-term fashion. (1983a: 467)

Moreover, on the understanding that the analysis of *structure* is insufficient for examining *processes* of social change, this approach to class analysis manifests itself in Goldthorpe's work primarily through the study of class mobility, on the grounds that mobility plays a crucial role in the dynamics of class relations.

> For any such structure of positions, the empirical question can then be raised of how far classes have in fact formed within it, in the sense of specific social collectivities; that is, collectivities that are identifiable through the degree of continuity with which, in consequence of patterns of class mobility and immobility, their members have been associated with particular sets of positions over time; and, in turn, the further issue may

be pursued of the degree of distinctiveness of members of identifiable classes in terms of their life-chances, their life-styles and patterns of association, and their socio-political orientations and modes of action. (*ibid.*)

On Goldthorpe's view then, class analysis is concerned with both demographic class formation, or the extent to which stable collectivities have or have not developed, and socio-political class formation, or the extent to which these collectivities provide bases for social solidarity and conflict or for the development of collective class identities. Further, on Goldthorpe's view, class analysis is not concerned with the study of occupational mobility *per se*, but rather with processes of occupational *qua* class mobility and in particular its effect on class formation (1980a, 1987a); nor is it concerned to document the full range of socio-cultural variation that may exist within social classes (1983a, 1984c); nor yet again with accounting for the specific structure of occupations existing at any given period (1983a). Class analysis is, however, concerned with the existence of sexual inequalities in society and, in conjunction with many feminists, Goldthorpe sees the relations between husbands and wives within the family as the primary source of these inequalities (1980a, 1983a, 1987a; and Erikson and Goldthorpe, 1988b). It is in recognition of the pervasiveness and persistence of sexual inequality that married women, in the conventional approach to class analysis, are seen to be linked to the class structure, not through their own participation in the labour market, but through their position within the family via the occupation of their husbands. As Goldthorpe writes:

... married women are required by conventional norms to take major responsibility for the performance of the work that is involved in maintaining a household and rearing children. This requirement then in various ways restricts their opportunities and prospects in regard to paid employment and, more, forces them to a greater or lesser extent into a situation of economic dependence on their husbands. ... [Thus, the conventional approach] *stems from* a clear recognition of major sexual inequalities, especially in regard to opportunities for labour market participation, and of the consequent relationship of dependence that generally prevails between married women and their husbands. (1983a: 468, 469–70)[3]

And further:

... a valid understanding of the class position of women must start from a recognition of the fact that in industrial societies, at least up to the present stage of their development, it is the family, rather than the individual, that is the appropriate unit of class analysis. Although inequalities in resources and consumption standards may exist *within* families—whether between men and women or, for that matter, between members of different age-groups—we would argue that, conceptually, these inequalities are not usefully seen as being ones of class and that, empirically, they are in fact less extreme than the true inequalities of class that run *between* families.
   Members of the same family, at least to the extent that they live together in the same household, typically share in a broadly similar life-style—even if with gender- or age-related variations; and, moreover, they typically engage in joint or inter-dependent economic decision-making—even if with differing degrees of power and influence—as regards both their immediate and their longer-term futures. (Erikson and Goldthorpe, 1988b: 4)

However, despite the recognition of the major commitment made by the majority of women to their roles within family life, and of the inequalities which flow in consequence, this approach to class analysis is criticized as being 'andro-centric' or 'sexist' (Acker, 1973; Delphy, 1981; Roberts and Woodward, 1981).

Thus, it is argued that the conventional approach to class analysis misrepresents reality by disregarding the extent to which women themselves participate in the labour force and by ignoring those women who do not live in 'families', that is, who are themselves 'heads' of households without adult male members. Further, it is argued that the conventional approach eliminates from the legitimate concerns of class analysis the study of sexual inequalities which exist both within families and within labour markets. These criticisms of the conventional, and hence Goldthorpe's, approach to class analysis stem from a common complaint—the exclusion of women—but are nonetheless quite distinct. The former accepts the general aims of class analysis as interpreted by Goldthorpe (and others), but argues for the inclusion of women; while the latter seeks to overturn conventional class analysis itself. Given this distinctiveness, each will be considered separately, beginning first with an overview of women's labour force participation.[4]

WOMEN'S LABOUR FORCE PARTICIPATION

In Britain (as elsewhere) the initial impetus for the challenge to the conventional approach to class analysis arose as a result of the marked increase in the labour force participation of women, and especially married women, over the decades since 1950. From 1881 until 1951 the labour force participation rate of women in Britain remained constant at about 35 per cent. By 1987, however, some 50 per cent of women were in paid employment. For married women, the change has been rather more marked. Starting in 1911 with an activity rate of less than 10 per cent, married women increased their participation in the labour force between 1951 and 1979 to reach just over 50 per cent, a level at which it has since stabilized. Restricting the analysis to only those married women of working age (16–59), however, indicates that in 1985, the latest figures available, some 62 per cent of wives were economically active. During these years, then, the involvement of wives in paid employment changed from only one in ten working outside the home to well over one in two. Moreover, as these figures refer to the proportion of women/wives in the labour force in any given year, it is important to point out that virtually all married women will spend some part of their married lives in the labour force.[5]

As is well known, however, few women will, over the course of their married lives, mimic their husbands' 40 or more years of relatively continuous adherence to waged-work. Within marriage, women remain almost completely responsible for both childcare and housework, and this responsibility is reflected in their patterns of employment. For example, if observed at a selection of points in time over her lifetime, an individual woman could be a child-free partner in a dual-earner family, a non-working wife with dependent children, a part-time worker with dependent children, a full-time worker with grown children, or out of the labour force caring for an elderly parent (cf. Dex, 1984). In other words, *movement* through the life-cycle, and hence *change* in both family and employment circumstances, is the essence of the majority of women's lives. While one might like to argue that there are certain advantages to lives marked by change and movement (not all 40-year, full-time working lives are worth having), in the case of women's involvement in the labour force, specific disadvantages accrue.

It is now clear that the most important changes in women's working lives are consequent upon bearing children (Martin and Roberts, 1984; Dex, 1984, 1987; Joshi and Newell, 1987). Joshi and Newell (*ibid*.: 8–13), for example, calculate that childless women earn about 30 per cent more in lifetime earnings than mothers as a result of reduced employment experience, downward occupational mobility when returning to work after childrearing, and lower wage rates paid for part-time work. There is an overwhelming tendency for mothers' employment to be on a part-time basis, as Dex notes in her study of women's occupational mobility:

> Women's priorities ... appear to vary over their life-cycle. In their early years of working occupational preferences have priority, whereas during the family formation period women often trade-off their preferred occupation in order to obtain a job with fewer hours. Much downward occupational mobility resulted from women taking part-time jobs after childbirth. The hours of work thus become the main priority over family formation, superseding occupational preferences, although the latter can come to dominate again in later life. (1987: 122)

Moreover, the growth of part-time employment accounts for virtually all the increase in women's labour force participation since the 1950s, with the proportion of women in *full-time* employment remaining relatively stable at about 30 per cent, while the proportion of women in *part-time* employment rose from 5 per cent of all women in the labour force in 1951 to 27 per cent in 1981 (Joshi *et al.*, 1983). In 1987 over 4 million women were in part-time employment, representing 44 per cent of all employed women (*Employment Gazette*, July 1988). Married women, moreover, account for between 80 and 90 per cent of these part-time workers. *General Household Survey* (*GHS*) data for 1985 show 30 per cent of mothers with pre-school age children in employment: 22 per cent on a part-time basis; while among women whose youngest child had reached age 10, 60 per cent of mothers in employment continued to work on a part-time basis (*GHS*, 1985: 70, Table 6.13).

The *Women and Employment Survey* (*WES*), carried out in 1980, provides further detail about the working patterns of women with children. Until women have children, there is little to distinguish between the participation rates of married and unmarried women. Once becoming mothers, however, less than half of women's time on average is spent in paid employment, with only about one-quarter of this time spent in full-time work (Martin and Roberts, 1984: 123–32). Furthermore, multiple breaks from employment over the family formation phase and after childrearing is completed remain the norm for the majority of women with children, as Dex shows in her re-analysis of the *WES* data. Over 60 per cent of mothers surveyed aged 30–49 years had two or more periods of not working during the course of their working lives, rising to 74 per cent of mothers aged 50+ years. These figures contrast sharply with those for women without children; only about one-quarter of women aged 30–49 had taken more than one break from paid employment, rising to 38 per cent of women 50 years and older (Dex, 1984: 114). Thus, although there is some evidence that younger women are returning to paid work more often between births and more quickly after completing their families (J. Martin, 1986), it remains the case that the majority of women follow discontinuous or interrupted work patterns in order to accommodate paid employment with family life. It also remains the case that, as a result of breaks in employment, adverse consequences for future employment opportunities, including promotion chances, ensue for the majority of women.[6]

If the well documented segregation of women into low-level, often poorly paid occupations is considered alongside women's discontinuous work histories,[7] then the reasoning behind the choice of the husband's occupation as the best indicator of the family's class position by class analysts such as Goldthorpe becomes clear:

> While the proportion of married women who have at some time or another been engaged in paid employment has substantially increased, the adoption of a work-life perspective fully reveals the intermittent and limited nature of this employment—even discounting the considerable extent to which it is undertaken on less than a full-time basis. There can be little doubt that within the conjugal family it is still overwhelmingly the husband who has the major commitment to labour market participation. (Goldthorpe, 1983a: 481)

And further:

> In the context of class analysis, it is then the location of the family member who has the fullest commitment to participation in the labour market that is seen as the most reliable indicator of the location of the family as a whole.... . For despite the general tendency in modern societies for the participation of married women in the labour market to increase, their employment still tends to be more intermittent than that of men, is less often full-time, and is only rarely such as to place them in what could be regarded as dominant class positions relative to those held by their husbands. (1987a: 281)

In summation, then, the reasoning behind Goldthorpe's approach is the following: accepting the family as the basic unit of the class structure; and given the fundamental aim of class analysis—to determine how far classes have in fact formed as relatively stable collectivities with which individuals and families are associated over time; and given the widespread discontinuity of wives' occupational participation; then, *at least at the present time*, the use of husband's occupation as a proxy for the family's class position is warranted. Concomitantly, the study of men's mobility patterns is unlikely to be misleading from a macro-perspective insofar as the study of *class* mobility, and hence class formation, is concerned.

GOLDTHORPE AND HIS CRITICS

The empirical evidence brought forward by Goldthorpe to support this line of reasoning is considerable. Thus, he is able to refute the arguments of critics who suggest that a method of *joint classification*, with husbands' and wives' occupations considered together in the designation of family class position, should be used in place of husbands' occupations alone,[8] by demonstrating that spuriously high rates of mobility between various class positions are generated in this way because of the pattern of wives' labour force participation (1983a, 1984c), thus defeating the primary aim of class analysis. Further, two of the most used indicators of class formation—political partisanship and class identification—are more strongly associated, for women, with their husbands' class position (as measured by his occupation) than with women's own occupational-cum-class position (Erikson and Goldthorpe, 1988b).[9]

On the evidence he presents, Goldthorpe is also able to refute the arguments of those who advocate an *individual* approach to social class classification, wherein women and men are assigned unique places in the class structure on the basis of their own occupations, whatever their marital status. The individual approach is advocated on a multiplicity of grounds: sometimes because women—as a result of discrimination in the labour market—are said to be united in diversity, with the class experience of married women being, more often than not, proletarian (Stanworth, 1984); or because women's experiences in the labour market are said to be less closely tied to their social origins than men's (Heath, 1981); or because men-only studies of class mobility are said to distort reality grossly (Roberts and Woodward, 1981; Walby, 1986). In response to these arguments, however, Goldthorpe has demonstrated that, in Britain and across five other industrial nations, the *relative* intergenerational mobility chances of women parallel almost exactly the relative chances of men (1987a; and Erikson and Goldthorpe, 1988b). That is, despite the (well known) fact that women experience much greater *absolute* downward mobility than men in comparison with their fathers, i.e. occupational sex segregation is widespread and persistent, the relative class inequalities that exist between men in the occupational structure are shown by Goldthorpe to exist between women as well:[10]

> Although women overall confront at any one time a less favourable set of employment opportunities than do men, the forces making for class inequalities are not annulled among women. On the contrary, they appear to operate in a way that is quite blind to gender; and hence, women are divided by these inequalities to much the same degree and on much the same pattern as are men. (1987a: 288)

This is a finding that should be taken on board by any feminist interested in women's participation in the labour market: a point which will be discussed below.

In responding to critics' arguments, however, Goldthorpe has recently acknowledged two limitations of the conventional approach to class analysis. First, and by the very logic of the conventional approach, a full account of class mobility should include the study of women's marital mobility. In other words, if it is the case that women derive their class positions from their husbands, then investigation of the class mobility that results from women marrying should form part of any class mobility research. Therefore, women's marital mobility, which was not considered in the initial publication arising from the 1972 Nuffield mobility study (1980a), has been included in the second edition (1987a).

Second, the conventional approach is acknowledged as limited insofar as it neglects the study of women who live alone or are themselves 'heads' of households. Thus Goldthorpe has accepted a modification to the conventional approach first suggested by his colleague, Robert Erikson (1984). Within the 'dominance' approach to class analysis the unitary nature of the family within the class structure is retained and family class position is determined by the occupational position of that family member—male or female—whose labour market participation can be regarded as dominant in terms of work time and work position.[11] This modification not only overcomes the limitation noted above, its use in research also provides benchmark information against which future changes may be measured in the extent to which wives occupy positions as family 'heads' consequent upon changes in their labour force participation. Goldthorpe provides analyses of class mobility based on the dominance approach in his later work (1987a; Erikson and Goldthorpe, 1988b).

It is important to stress that, with regard to women's labour force participation *up to and including the present time*, Goldthorpe's approach to class analysis provides an accurate and hence adequate representation of the reality of the overwhelming majority of women's lives. Moreover, Goldthorpe has taken great care to point out that his position *vis-à-vis* women and class analysis is conditioned by the present patterns of women's labour force participation, or, in the case of the omission of women from the original Nuffield mobility study, by the pattern of women's labour force participation over the period to which the Nuffield data related, that is, up to 1972. Much of the debate—at least insofar as it has taken place within the confines of more or less orthodox class theory—has glossed over this important qualification to the conventional approach, perhaps in anticipation of future changes in women's labour force participation, or perhaps in reaction to the designation of men's labour force participation as somehow carrying a greater commitment to paid work then women's labour force participation (Goldthorpe, 1983a: 470; 1987a: 281). It is very clear that women, like men, are committed to paid work; many women, indeed, have no choice other than to be so committed: two facts of modern society Goldthorpe would be unlikely to deny.[12] However, women also (unlike most men) are committed to assuming responsibility for the myriad tasks attendant upon family life, including acting as carers and facilitators for children, husbands and sometimes elderly parents. Women strive to balance these two commitments; and up to the present day at least for most women the balance tips in favour of the family, to the disadvantage of their employment opportunities. Hence the current appropriateness of the so-called conventional approach to class analysis. However, should the balance tip the other way— as it easily might—then many more women than today will doubtlessly achieve occupational positions equal or dominant to their husbands' positions. If this happens—or perhaps one should say, when this happens—the dominance approach stands ready, largely because of the debate in question, to allow class analysts like Goldthorpe to measure what will be a major social change.

CLASS ANALYSIS CHALLENGED

Goldthorpe's movement to the conventional/dominance approach to class analysis seems likely to satisfy critics who work within the confines of orthodox *marxisant* or (neo-) Weberian class analysis, but who argue for the inclusion of women. It seems unlikely, however, that this movement will satisfy those critics who challenge the basic premises of class analysis. It was noted above that the conventional approach is attacked because it eliminates the study of sexual inequalities from the legitimate concerns of class analysis. Here critics argue, against Goldthorpe, that accounting for the specific structure of occupations at any given period is a legitimate aim of class analysis. Class theory should, but does not, account for the determinants and shape of the (given) class structure, especially in consideration of the fact that men's class chances are significantly conditioned by the nature of women's labour force participation (e.g. Mann, 1986b; Abbott and Sapsford, 1987; Marshall, Newby *et al.*,1988). Further, sexual inequalities, far from being ones not usefully thought of as class inequalities, must be understood and explained within a single theory encompassing both class and sex. Moreover, such a theory must address the sexual inequalities that exist within the family as well as those found in the labour market (e.g. Dex, 1987; Walby, 1984, 1986).

The challenge that class theory should explain the form and evolution of the class (occupational) structure appears to have arisen, at least in part, in response to the distinction made by theorists such as Goldthorpe between the patterns of women's *absolute* and *relative* mobility chances (see esp. Marshall, Newby *et al.*,

1988). Studies of absolute mobility demonstrate the distribution of persons to places in the occupational structure, and in the case of women clearly show their disadvantaged position *vis-à-vis* men. Investigations of women's relative mobility patterns, in contrast, reveal the labour market chances women have in comparison with other women, and, as has been mentioned, demonstrate the way in which class inequalities tend to divide women in much the same way as they divide men. Critics of Goldthorpe argue that this distinction makes a nonsense of class analysis, insofar as it ignores the impact that women's labour force participation has on men's class chances, and hence that the so-called 'gendered' structure of the labour market within which men and women compete must also be explained.

Goldthorpe acknowledges that the way in which women are distributed throughout the labour force has considerable importance for men's chances in the class structure and, indeed, suggests that he was among the first to do so (1980a: 58–9). In other words, he agrees that sex stratification in the labour market (or sexually differentiated rates of absolute mobility) operates to the advantage of men. However, he also argues that it is misleading to suggest that women's employment is the only, or even the most important, such class/structural influence on men's chances, and shows that across all classes of origin men's occupational destinations would change by only about 17 per cent should men and women compete equally (1987a: 299n23). Table 8.1 reproduces in full the previously unpublished data upon which Goldthorpe bases this conclusion.[13] As may be seen, under *present conditions*, that is, given present rates of men's and women's economic activity and present patterns of class inequalities within the current occupational structure, if sex segregation did not exist, fewer men would achieve higher non-manual occupations,

Table 8.1   *Sex Segregation and Men's Occupational Destinations*

Father's class		\multicolumn{8}{c}{Respondent's class}							
		I	II	IIIa	IV	V	VI	VII + IIIb	
I	M	33.7	30.6	8.8	8.5	3.8	8.8	5.8	15.9
	WM	23.2	31.5	23.4	6.2	3.5	6.0	6.1	
II	M	30.2	30.9	10.4	6.9	5.9	7.8	7.9	14.9
	WM	20.6	30.6	17.9	8.1	3.4	5.3	14.1	
IIIa	M	17.5	23.1	21.0	8.2	7.9	9.3	13.0	22.6
	WM	10.8	17.8	35.6	5.5	4.3	5.0	20.9	
IV	M	11.1	18.8	4.1	32.0	6.8	13.7	13.3	19.3
	WM	7.7	19.7	14.2	21.5	4.8	10.5	21.7	
V	M	21.5	10.5	3.5	12.7	6.1	23.6	22.1	18.6
	WM	14.3	13.3	14.1	10.1	3.9	17.0	27.5	
VI	M	11.9	14.1	6.1	7.4	8.3	28.7	23.4	16.8
	WM	8.0	13.5	15.8	4.9	6.7	20.6	30.4	
VII + IIIb	M	10.1	13.9	3.9	9.5	10.3	22.5	29.8	18.3
	WM	5.9	12.1	14.0	7.1	7.5	15.4	38.0	
	M	16.2	17.8	6.3	12.1	7.8	19.7	20.2	16.8
	WM	10.9	17.6	16.9	8.8	5.6	13.8	26.5	

Source: British General Election Survey, 1983 (see endnote 13).

as women took their places; and fewer women would be confined to clerical and junior non-manual jobs. In other words, an end to sex segregation tomorrow would have a markedly beneficial impact on women's employment opportunities. However, the differences made to men's chances, as noted by Goldthorpe, would not be overwhelming, in part because of the unequal labour force participation rates of men and women, but in part also because other structural factors influence the occupational distribution of men (and women). Moreover, as Goldthorpe argues further, such influences—the rate of expansion of higher occupations, trends in self-employment, the movement from an agricultural- to an industrial-based economy and so on—can have an impact on men's chances of at least a comparable magnitude to the pattern of women's labour force participation.

However, acknowledging the existence, and importance, of sex segregation in the labour market is not equivalent to assuming that it is the task of class analysis to account for its rise and persistence. Rather, and on the basis of evidence (Goldthorpe, 1988b) which suggests that, in Britain as in other industrial nations, processes of *relative* class stratification cut across sexual stratification (or, for that matter, stratification by religion, ethnicity and region), Goldthorpe argues that the task of explaining the existence of sex segregation in occupations, and hence the evolution of the class structure, lies outside the realm of class analysis:

> The forces that make for inequalities in relative mobility chances ... would appear to operate in a way that is for the most part blind to gender—suggesting, in turn, then, that if an adequate account is to be provided of the social processes that generate sex segregation in employment and thus restrict women's opportunities, it will be one that is developed largely outside the scope of class analysis. (Erikson and Goldthorpe, 1988b: 28)
>
> If, therefore, we wish to explain differences in absolute rates, we must be ready to explain differences in the form and evolution of class structures. And the question then arises is whether this is a task that macro-sociology has the theoretical resources to attempt—or whether it is one that should be left rather to the historians, to deal with on a more descriptive basis. For my own part, I would, for the time being at least, opt for this latter alternative. And to those who disagree, and would wish to be more ambitious, I can only say *Hic Rhodus, hic salta.* Let those who believe that general theories of class structural change can be developed set to work to produce them. (Goldthorpe, 1988b: 26)

In terms of the present debate, of course, asking for class analysis to provide explanations of the evolution of the class structure is tantamount to asking for class and sexual inequalities to be explained within one all-encompassing theory. Although I concur in general with Goldthorpe's dictum—if someone wants to, let them get on with it—in this particular case there appear to be valid reasons for keeping the study of sexual inequalities and class inequalities separate. Goldthorpe argues that the 'blindness' of class to gender is one such reason; in addition, I would argue that separation is the only avenue presently available for understanding the changes in both class and sexual stratification that are likely to occur over the next decade (cf. Cockburn, 1986; Stacey, 1986).

The challenge that class and sexual inequalities should be encompassed and explained within a single theory of stratification is not new. For the past twenty years feminists have attempted to create a unified theory of class and sexual oppression, largely without success.[14] In fact, it is difficult to envisage just what success in this endeavour would look like, at least in terms of conducting empirical research. Almost certainly, there would be serious methodological difficulties inherent in operationalizing any single grand theory of sexual and class inequality. Two recent attempts to provide such a theory by authors with similar approaches serve to exemplify my suspicion that unification remains a very distant goal indeed. Walby (1984, 1986) and Dex (1987) both argue that the relations between husbands and wives need to be seen in class terms, and hence should be incorporated into class analysis. While one is sympathetic to (and in general agreement with) the view that wives exchange unpaid labour and services (including sexual) within the home for goods, housing and income provided by husbands, it is more difficult to have sympathy for an approach to analysis that seems almost incapable of empirical investigation. For example, in elaborating her contribution to the issue, Walby argues:

> that housewives (both full-time and part-time) are a class exploited by their husbands who also constitute a class. This is not, however, a sufficient characterization of the class position of women. I do not believe it is appropriate to designate all women as a class. Not all women are housewives, and thus not all women have a class position in the patriarchal mode of production... many women also have a class position deriving from their participation in waged labour. Thus many women have a dual class position. Many women are engaged in distinct sets of relations of production. ... Sometimes this dual class location will be contradictory, sometimes in harmony: there are no *a priori* conclusions to be drawn here. (1986: 35–6)

Setting aside any worry about *a priori* conclusions, one wonders what *a posteriori* conclusions would follow from research designed to test this theory. If we assume, for example, that harmonious dual class relations entail exploitation at work and at home—given that, on Walby's reckoning, the housewife-husband relationship is by definition one of exploitation— then contemplating the amount of class mobility generated by the changes experienced by an average wife in her contradictory (and harmonious?) class locations as she moved through the various life-cycle stages (and changes in employment status) associated with marriage and children is rather staggering

However, it is obviously misguided to argue that a new theoretical perspective should not be developed simply because the task is too difficult or its implications presently untestable. Talented sociological thinkers are always on the horizon, ready to tackle old problems. More fundamental to an argument against the unification of sociological theories of sexual inequality and class inequality is the continuing need to explore the substantive differences in the processes which underlie these two aspects of social inequality. Moreover, I would argue that changes in the labour market over the course of the next decade or so—likely to change the processes of sexual inequality while reinforcing class inequalities—will only be properly researched and understood by retaining separate modes of analysis.

We are, in Britain at the end of the 1980s, on the edge of a potentially momentous social change. It is often the case that major change in society occurs only in response to crisis (Lipman-Blumen, 1973). Crises upset traditional ways of doing and thinking, and may thus challenge or overthrow established avenues to occupational success. Just such a crisis situation confronts Britain in the 1990s. Following a massive surplus of 18–24-year-olds during the mid-1980s, resulting in unprecedented levels of youth unemployment, the number of young people available to employers over the first five years of the 1990s is expected to drop by at least one million, or about 30 per cent (National Economic Development Office, 1988). In contrast, the number of women entering the labour market during this same period is expected to increase, with women likely to account for some 0.8 million of an anticipated 1.1 million extra workers. Women aged 25–44 years, returning to work following breaks for childcare, are projected to make up the largest single pool of new workers (Incomes Data Services, 1988: 29–31). In anticipation of these demographic changes many employers are increasing their provision of support services for women with families. Career breaks, retainer schemes, job-sharing, workplace creches—all relatively rare at present—may thus be expected to proliferate before the end of the century.

Furthermore, there is likely to be more room for women at the top of the occupational hierarchy. Most observers believe that the marked post-war increase in higher-level and professional occupations will continue well into the next decade and beyond. Of the 1.7 million new jobs anticipated by 1995, some one million will be in professional and related occupations, bringing the proportion of the labour force employed in these occupations to just under one-quarter by 1995 (Rajan and Pearson, 1986; Institute for Employment Research (IER), 1988). The likelihood of women taking up a major share of these new jobs at the top of the occupational structure is increased by the continuing trend among women to gain professional and higher-level qualifications (Crompton, 1986), and by past trends which suggest that the growth rate in representation of women at this occupational level has doubled that of men (IER, 1988). If it is true, in other words, that the labour market of the 1990s will be a seller's market, then women perhaps stand ready to bargain for greater equality. Thus women in the 1990s might make significant progress towards ending sexual stratification in some occupations. The social processes at work in those occupations and industrial sectors where they succeed in doing so—and, perhaps more importantly, where they fail—will need to be studied and explained by sociologists.

Furthermore, sociologists will also need to explain which women succeed and which women fail. As discussed above, Goldthorpe (1987a; Erikson and Goldthorpe, 1988b) has demonstrated, in his analysis of women's relative mobility chances, that the class inequalities that divide men can be shown to divide women as well. This is a crucial finding for feminists concerned to create a more equal, more open society. For, on this evidence, it seems certain that not all women will achieve occupational success—just as not all men do; rather, women from advantaged backgrounds will do much better than women from working-class homes: class will tell, in other words. These *class* differences between women will be as important an area of sociological investigation over the next decade as will be analyzing the ending (hopefully) of marked sexual segregation in the labour market. Moreover, this differential success among women from different class backgrounds in achieving professional and higher-level jobs will undoubtedly exacerbate existing class inequalities between families (cf. Westergaard and Resler, 1975) as, given the persistence of marked class homogamy, a rise in the number of dual-career families is witnessed. This too will be an area of investigation of some considerable importance for sociologists.

It is perhaps wholly understandable that, in attempting to bring women's experiences to the forefront of sociological analysis, researchers have emphasized the differences between women and men. This focus has led to the neglect of studies that investigate both the differences that exist between women and women, and the similarities that exist between some women and some men. Siltanen (1986) has made a start towards remedying these lacunae; and although she starts by arguing for a unified theory of stratification that encompasses sexual and class inequalities, her own work points to the value of keeping these two systems of discrimination apart:[15]

> While we need a theory of the distribution of people to jobs which can explain sexual divisions where they occur, this must be a theory which can account for those aspects of social processes which yield similar outcomes for women and men. Taking 'gender' or 'sexual divisions' as a general statement of social experience and the object of explanation, has had two deleterious consequences: the importance of similarity in women's and men's experiences has been neglected and social processes giving rise to sexual divisions have not been understood adequately. (1986: 102)

One might add that the study of class has become rather confused. However, to follow the lead provided by Siltanen, I would argue that we need rather more than an adequate theory of sexual stratification; we also need an adequate theory of class stratification. Perhaps the one interpreted and practised by John Goldthorpe might do.

ACKNOWLEDGMENT

I would like to thank Robert Erikson and Giorgio Gagliani for commenting on an earlier draft of this paper.

NOTES

1 The word 'gender' was originally introduced into the discourse on differences between women and men to complement the word 'sex', in the hope of escaping problems arising from the confusion of biological with social attributes: gender was to refer to culturally determined or learned aspects of a role; sex to biologically determined aspects. As Eichler notes (1980: 12), however, this distinction did not succeed, and many authors use these two words interchangeably. Eichler goes on to suggest that the difficulty in making this distinction lies, not in the inadequacy of the two terms, but in the nature of the link between the social and the biological itself. I would argue that few authors today think about this distinction between social and biological; and that more than 'gender' coming simply to replace 'sex' (which it largely has), it is now often treated as a theoretical category. As such, it can hinder rather than help empirical research. I concur with Siltanen, who argues (1986: 118) that gender and sexual divisions are issues to be addressed, not assumed. For these reasons, the present paper does not use the term.

2 See, for example, Glenn, Ross and Tully (1974); Chase (1975); also Heath (1981: 114), who argue that women are more mobile through marriage than are men through employment and work careers.

3 Within this debate discussion of the economic dependence of wives on husbands has taken two forms: first, it is argued that because of their participation in paid labour, wives should no longer be seen as financially dependent upon their husbands; and second, it is argued that despite their labour force participation, wives and husbands divide family resources unequally, with wives faring less well. In regard to the first of these somewhat contradictory claims, it may be noted that although in many families wives' incomes are important for keeping their families out of poverty (Layard *et al.*, 1978), the 1980 *Women and Employment Survey* (*WES*) shows that on average working wives earn only about half of what their husbands earn, with only 7 per cent earning the same or more (see Martin and Roberts, 1984: 99). Rainwater (1984), in examining national data for Britain for the years 1968–73, found that wives' contributions to family income across all levels of husbands' income stood at about 20 per cent of total family income; by 1988, wives' average contribution had risen to 27 per cent (*Family Expenditure Survey*, 1988). This difference in earnings between husbands

and wives arises in part from the shorter hours worked by wives and in part from women's generally lower hourly earnings relative to men (Martin and Roberts, 1984: 99). With respect to the second of these claims, very few supportive data exist. Given the duration of this debate, it is surprising that no one has yet attempted to provide nationally representative data following the leads suggested by J. Pahl (1980), Land (1983) and Wilson (1987). Certainly, claims such as the following by Delphy and Leonard (1986: 65) are wholly inadequate as a basis for social scientific research:

> Because the family has been taken to be 'the major unit of reward and class fate' by sociologists and 'of consumption' by economists, very few people have bothered to look at distribution *within* it. They have assumed, *against all the evidence of their own lives*, that there is a simple per capita division of money, goods and services ... However, existing evidence suggests that there is a marked hierarchy of consumption within families. (emphasis supplied)

One's own personal life and experiences often provide good starting points for research, however, they should not be allowed to act as substitutes for empirical data. Unfortunately, Delphy and Leonard provide no references for existing evidence they cite.

4   For reasons of space, the following discussion on women's labour force participation does not include lone mothers. There are approximately 900,000 women with children living in households without male partners, of whom 39 per cent were in paid work in 1983–88 (17 per cent part-time) (*General Household Survey*, 1985: 64, Table 6.6). On these figures Goldthorpe's suggestion that families comprising lone women with children, although increasing in number, remain statistically insignificant in comparison with other women in families, seems valid.

5   Sources for these figures include: Joseph, 1983; *OPCS Labour Force Survey 1981* (Office of Population Censuses and Surveys, 1982); *General Household Survey*, 1985. It may also be noted that in 1985, 89 per cent of men of working age (16–64) were in employment (*GHS*, 1985: 59, Table 6.1).

6   Domestic responsibilities continue to be the primary reason behind women's breaks from employment, especially having and rearing children (see Martin and Roberts, 1984: Chs 9, 10). However, as Dex shows in her re-analysis of the *WES* data, across all women's occupational groupings except semi- and unskilled, a significant association exists between changes in the location of husbands' jobs and wives giving up paid employment (1987: 68–80).

7   In 1971, 70 per cent of women were concentrated in service and clerical work, with 40 per cent of all women in occupations comprising 75 per cent or more women workers (Joseph, 1983), a situation which had changed little in 1985 (Equal Opportunities Commission, 1986). For a review of occupational segregation in Britain and comparisons with the situation in the USA, see Dex (1985).

8   Nicky Britten and Anthony Heath were among the first to present an alternative way of conceptualizing the class position of families while remaining within the tradition of orthodox class analysis. On the grounds that the existence of a new stratum within the class structure—comprising a significant number of *cross-class* families—is obscured by the conventional approach, Britten and Heath (1983; Heath and Britten, 1984) constructed a method of joint classification. Goldthorpe (1984c) argues that, in doing so, Britten and Heath revealed more detail about socio-cultural differences between families within the present class structure, the existence of which he never sought to deny. For a further critique of Britten and Heath, see McRae (1986).

9   Goldthorpe (Erikson and Goldthorpe, 1988b) re-analyzes data from Germany, Hungary, Sweden, Norway, the USA and Britain. For Britain, these data sets include Heath *et al.* (1985); Abbott and Sapsford (1986); and Marshall, Newby *et al.* (1988). A significant association is found between a wife's class position (as measured by her own occupation) and either class identification or party identification. Controlling for this, and for class homogamy, however, reveals in all cases but one (Germany) a stronger association for women between these two and husband's class position.

10   Although a significant fit is found in the model comparing men to women in part-time employment, the model fits much better for women in full-time employment (see Goldthorpe, 1987a: 298n21). Countries in which similar findings have been found include the USA, Finland, Sweden, Norway and France (see *ibid*.: 298–9n22).

11   Within this approach dominance is established first on the basis of work time, with full-time employment taking precedence over part-time, and part-time over no employment. On the second criterion, work position, higher qualified positions dominate lower qualified; non-manual dominate manual; and self-employed dominate employee. For a full discussion, see either Erikson (1984: 503–13) or Goldthorpe (1987a: 291–4).

12   For a review of studies investigating women's commitment to paid work, see Dex (1985: Ch. 2).

13 I would like to thank Anthony Heath for making available the data in Table 8.1 which are drawn from the 1983 British General Election Survey. The class categories used in the table are based upon Goldthorpe's seven-class schema (1980a; also reproduced in Chapter 4 above, eds), with Class IIIB—shop assistants, machine operators, etc.—collapsed into Class VII—non-skilled manual—on the grounds that little in the work or market situations of employees in Class IIIb jobs distinguishes their position from straightforward waged labour. The table has been created through a technique known as Mostellerisation (Mosteller and Tukey, 1977): the odds ratios are kept constant and the margins varied (in this case by the addition of women) in order to present a counter-factual representation of the distribution of men and women under conditions of equality.

14 For some early contributions to this attempt, see Kuhn and Wolpe (1978); Hamilton (1978); Eisenstein (1979); Hartmann (1979).

15 Siltanen provides an excellent account of the similarities and differences between men and women employed in the post office. All of respondents were in low-paid, low-autonomy jobs with no career prospects; yet within these obviously working-class jobs workers were stratified according to domestic responsibility, age and ethnicity, with some women having better jobs than other women and some men and *vice versa*. It is clear from her work that neither gender alone nor class alone can account for the differing recruitment outcomes. Also see Bechhofer's comments on Siltanen's work (1986: 227).

9. Goldthorpe on Class and Gender: The Case Against

SHIRLEY DEX

Goldthorpe set out his defence of the 'conventional view' of class analysis in 1983 in response to claims that this view represents a position of intellectual sexism. He has since elaborated his position, with some changes over time, in reply to the many critics who responded to his defence paper. He thinks that his critics are wrong on a number of counts: in their attack on the conventional view; in their view that their alternatives are better and constitute a case for abandoning the conventional view; and in that they fail to engage with the central thrust of the conventional view and his defence of it, sometimes by citing irrelevant empirical work.

This chapter sets out to construct a case against Goldthorpe's arguments by addressing a number of questions:

1   Is he correct about the conventional view? That is, if we take his view of what class analysis is about, should we then accept his position on gender and class?
2   Is he correct about his critics and is the conventional view better than the alternatives?
3   Are there other viable sorts of class analysis which could adopt a different view from that of Goldthorpe on gender and class?

The chapter argues that a case against Goldthorpe can be made in answer to all of these questions, although this is far from wanting to argue that his work is without value. The chapter starts by giving an overview of the debate which Goldthorpe's 1983 paper initiated. It then goes on to address the three questions in the order in which they are listed.

THE DEBATE SO FAR

Goldthorpe's defence of the conventional view of class analysis (Goldthorpe, 1983a) came in response to a number of attacks by United States and European sociologists, many of them feminists. Watson and Barth (1964) provided probably the first critical voice; others followed, up to and including Garnsey (1978), Delphy (1981) and Allen (1982).[1] The critics accused the traditional or conventional view of intellectual sexism because it had neglected women, rested on sexist assumptions in so doing, was out-of-touch with the changes in women's marital and employment statuses, had used male heads of households to represent the family's status and ignored sexual inequalities within the marriage. In addition, Britten and Heath (1983) had published a paper which provided an alternative set of class categories using both husbands' and wives' statuses.

Having formerly justified the exclusion of women on grounds of resource constraints (Goldthorpe, 1980a: Appendix), Goldthorpe's 1983 defence made a much stronger case for the conventional view.[2] He argued that there are both theoretical and empirical grounds for adopting the conventional view, which in his view ruled out the charge that sexism underpinned the analysis. He provided empirical evidence to support his case and argued that Britten and Heath's joint classification gave a misleading picture of Britain's class structure. Goldthorpe also threw out a challenge to the critics, that they should provide a case of the 'actual sociological inadequacy' (1983a: 470) of the conventional view rather than pursue ideological claims of sexism.

Since then many critics have responded and a debate has taken place, largely in the journal *Sociology*. Goldthorpe has replied on each occasion arguing a reasoned and empirically based opposition to the critical points made. Heath and Britten's (1984) and Stanworth's (1984) criticisms are replied to in Goldthorpe (1984c). Goldthorpe and Payne (1986b) provide further empirical support for Goldthorpe's original defence and his reply to critics. The reprinted version of Goldthorpe and Payne (1986b) in Goldthorpe (1987a: Ch. 10) offers some comments on Walby (1986) and Delphy and Leonard's (1986) criticisms. Leiulfsrud and Woodward's (1987) criticisms are replied to in Erikson and Goldthorpe (1988c). Erikson and Goldthorpe (1988b) provide empirical work from Goldthorpe's European social mobility study CASMIN, plus reworking of other researchers' results which counter some implied criticisms of Goldthorpe's position in Abbott and Sapsford (1987) and in the empirical work of Marshall, Newby *et al.* (1988) on women in Britain's class structure.

As far as the theoretical areas of debate are concerned, Goldthorpe's original defence was at pains to dissociate his position from that of the conventional American stratification or functionalist theories. Goldthorpe was not seeking to defend functionalist theories against the claims of his critics, but was locating himself within the European non-functionalist tradition of class analysis.[3] The subsequent debates and replies have accepted this narrowing and clarification of the debate and seem to have agreed with Goldthorpe that some confusion was injected early on through a failure to clarify which type of theory was being addressed.[4] In addition, Goldthorpe dissociates himself from a solely Marxist view of class analysis (1983a: note 5). He has also expressed a preference for the debate, as it has proceeded, to be conducted along lines which can be empirically tested.[5] To a large extent the critics who have persisted in arguing with Goldthorpe have done so on the basis of empirical work, although he has always been quick to respond, either questioning whether the empirical work cited is relevant to the debate or by producing more empirical work supporting his own position.

This is an overview of the debate up to July 1988, and it is not necessarily the end of the story, even excluding effects which the contributions in this volume may produce. Over the course of the debate several changes have occurred which are worth noting at the outset of this review. One is that Goldthorpe has clearly adapted, and in some respects changed, his position. Coinciding with his first paper defending the conventional view (1983a), a paper was published by Erikson (1984) arguing for the 'dominance approach' to the classification of family units for purposes of class analysis. Goldthorpe (1984c) gave some qualified support to this modification to traditional class analysis. However, in a later paper (Erikson and Goldthorpe, 1988b) he clearly accepts, seemingly without qualifications, the 'dominance approach'. Also by 1988 he seemed more established and strengthened in his position than he was in his first defence paper in 1983. His initial defence of the conventional view was to some degree an argument that since women were dependent upon men within marriages, and that women's occupational position did not appear to influence that of husbands to any great degree, classifying family units by the (usually) male head of household was an appropriate procedure for class analysis. Also it was one which would not lead to a misleading picture of Britain's class structure. He thought, too, that at that time the substantive issues had not been adequately treated from an empirical (or theoretical) standpoint (1983a: 465). Goldthorpe has since produced empirical work on women's class mobility which he claims shows that the neglect of women has not limited or distorted our understanding of class mobility, since, when they are included or examined, it either makes no difference or they give a misleading picture.

By 1988 the charge of intellectual sexism has dropped out of the debate. One might interpret this to mean that critics no longer think this an appropriate judgment for Goldthorpe's position as it has been elaborated. It is difficult to be sure about this assessment, since those who have persisted in criticizing Goldthorpe have been those who think that it can be done on empirical grounds. Those who made what they claimed were more theoretical criticisms have by and large left the arena. This is to be expected, although this does not imply that they were incorrect as suggested by Goldthorpe's contention that they offered merely vague and tendentious claims referred to as 'theory' (1987a: 297). Disagreements about theoretical approaches are not easy to resolve, and constant restatement does not usually help persuade one's opponent, nor is it likely to be accepted by academic editors.

This lengthy introduction has been necessary to set the context for this chapter, which aims to make a case against the Goldthorpe view of gender and class. What this review of the debate shows is that this paper follows a lengthy debate in which Goldthorpe's patient replies and painstaking empirical work have strengthened his position. In the process many debating points have been made by both sides. It is not the intention here to describe every point made or the reply, but rather to construct a case against Goldthorpe's conventional view in the light of the debate so far. Some of the points have been made before, some have not. As far as possible I have tried to acknowledge points made by earlier contributors to the debate. An examination and documentation of Goldthorpe's aims for, and definition of, class analysis will be an important first step in presenting the case.

GOLDTHORPE'S CLASS ANALYSIS

It is important to recognize that Goldthorpe's views on gender and class are located within his view of what class analysis is all about and why it is of interest. In this section, therefore, Goldthorpe's view of class analysis and its foundations is documented, using in the main his statements of his position in Chapter 1 of the second edition of the social mobility book (1987a) and his first defence of the conventional view (1983a).

Aims

The foundation for Goldthorpe's interest in class analysis also defines what class analysis is:

> We regard a particular pattern of mobility as defining a goal to which we have a value-commitment; namely, that of a genuinely open society. But at the same time, we believe that the likelihood of this goal being achieved, or more closely approximated, will importantly depend on the pattern of mobility that actually prevails: specifically, on how far this pattern, in deviating from openness, is conducive to class formation and action, and in turn to forms of class conflict, through which the class-linked inequalities of life-chances that are the denial of openness may be reduced. (1987a: 327)

The stages of class analysis then follow:

1 There is a given structure of positions called 'class positions' (*ibid*.: 29).
2 The occupational order forms 'the backbone of the class structure' (*ibid*.). I understand this to mean that it is occupational categories which determine the set of class positions and these are what are referred to as the class structure.
3 One cannot assume that classes have formed in any society. It is an empirical question, in fact the first empirical question which researchers interested in class analysis must address (1983a: 467; also 1984c: 491).
4 Classes have formed if a specific social collectivity is identifiable, that is, if the members of a class are associated with particular sets of positions over time (1983a: 467). Mobility is inversely related to class formation (1987a: 330).
5 If identifiable classes have formed, one can then investigate (it is assumed empirically), as a second step, the extent to which members of the class have the same life chances, lifestyles, patterns of association (with each other), political orientations or modes of action.

Goldthorpe thus appears to suggest that there is a sequence of causal relationships, such as that shown in Figure 9.1.

Thus Goldthorpe set out his empirical agenda: first, to see if classes have formed; and second, to see if members of the classes have the same life chances, lifestyles, political orientations and modes of action, etc. He suggests that the second empirical task is his ultimate interest (1987a: 335). One could add a necessary precondition, which often goes unmentioned in Goldthorpe's later works on class analysis: the need to construct a prior set or structure of class positions. Of course, Goldthorpe and his collaborators did just that in their earlier work. These three

Figure 9.1   The Relationship between Social Mobility and Class Formation

			Implication
High amounts of social mobility	→ low levels of class formation	→ low levels of class action or conflict	→ less chance of achieving openness, but already close
		and	
Low amounts of social mobility	→ high levels of class formation	→ high levels of class action or conflict	→ more chance of achieving openness, but far off

components constitute an empirical agenda which has occupied Goldthorpe over almost two decades. This is a tremendous coherent achievement, aided by a variety of colleagues along the way. No one could fail to be impressed with Goldthorpe for seeing it through. The criticisms levelled here should not be thought in any way to detract from these achievements.

It is to the operational details of this agenda that we now turn, since it is through these details that the issues about gender have come into class analysis. It will be argued that those issues are also rooted in Goldthorpe's rationale for doing class analysis as outlined above.

Operationalizing Class Analysis

The requirements for carrying out Goldthorpe's empirical agenda are as follows:

1. a set of class positions through which mobility between them can be empirically documented;
2. a sample chosen appropriate to the task in hand;
3. a mobility criterion or set of criteria for determining whether class formation has occurred;
4. if classes are identifiable in step 3, then criteria are required to identify what constitutes similarity in the characteristics of the members of these groups, especially in their attitudes to socio-political action.

Much of the debate about Goldthorpe's view of gender and class has revolved around point 2 above; this includes a decision about what is the appropriate unit of analysis through which to conduct this examination. Goldthorpe sees the debate in the following terms: 'The issue...is one of research practice: how should sociologists engaged in class analysis treat the conjugal family?' (Erikson and Goldthorpe, 1988c: 545). However, issues of debate have also concerned points 3 and 4. Since it is possible to make some points about gender with respect to all of these points, comments will be made in the order they are listed, but concentrating only on the first three.

Choice of Class Positions

Goldthorpe's set of class positions was derived from much painstaking work in the early 1970s, the details of which cannot be entered into here. The seven collapsed class categories which are most frequently used by Goldthorpe in subsequent empirical work are based on a combination of occupational categories (the backbone of the class structure) and elements of employment status (self-employed or employee, etc.). It is arguable that men's occupations alone formed the basis of the empirical work to devise the Goldthorpe class positions. It is a well known fact that women's occupations differ considerably from those of men. One might expect, therefore, that a set of composite aggregations of occupations (and statuses) based on women's occupations might look quite different from the set of class positions Goldthorpe and his colleagues derived.[6]

The procedure adopted by Goldthorpe *et al.* in constructing these class categories was entirely understandable and reasonable, since they were to go on to examine men's occupational or class mobility. That Goldthorpe believes that, in general, the choice of an appropriate classification is a necessary prior step, can be deduced from his reaction to Britten and Heath's use of the OPCS social class schema. He writes:

> ... the OPCS social classes are quite unsuitable for the purposes of class analysis—most obviously in that they fail to distinguish systematically either between employers, self-employed and employees or between supervisory grades and rank-and-file workers. Thus, for example, Britten and Heath's results will be biased in favour of their own arguments... . (1983a: 488)

This raises an important question. Is it permissible or justifiable to apply these (men's) class positions or categories to a set of women's occupations *and* draw conclusions about women's class formation or lack of it on this basis? This would seem to be at least a debatable procedure, for which good arguments in favour would need to be produced. Goldthorpe has engaged in this exercise as the gender and class debate has proceeded (e.g. Goldthorpe and Payne, 1986b; Erikson and Goldthorpe, 1988b, 1988c), but no justifying arguments have been provided. The conclusions reached were that there is no need to examine women's class mobility if there is a shortage of resources, since a focus on men is sufficient or at least not distorting of the class structure of modern Britain.

The problem which arises from wanting to recognize the differences between men's and women's occupations in constructing a set of class positions is that serious conceptual difficulties will need to be resolved. However, this should not be a reason to abandon the attempt. It may be a reason to accept an easier but recognizably imperfect (even conventional) alternative, so long as it is seen as such and is not heralded as a pinnacle of sociological achievement.

There are other implications of the set of class positions adopted for the amount of mobility discovered. The way in which occupations are aggregated, and their number, will influence the amount of mobility visible between the categories. One would usually expect that the finer the classification, the greater the amount of mobility and *vice versa*. Goldthorpe is aware of this problem, since he recognizes that the mobility he documented for men may be 'simply artefactual' (1987a: 212). His response to this problem is to suggest the use of two principles in deciding to adopt a particular scheme:

1 Judge the choice of scheme by its heuristic and analytical value for the interests being pursued (*ibid.*: 143).
2 Do further empirical work to see if
    a the classes discovered are meaningful groupings in the sense that

systematic differences in social relationships overlap and correlate with the 'class' membership.

b see if individuals' own perceptions of their class identification and/or mobility coincide with the way they have been classified (*ibid.*: Ch. 8).

At first sight these are reasonable procedures to adopt in difficult circumstances, but one must surely be careful to interpret one's conclusions in the light of them, especially since there is an inbuilt problem of circularity in the first step. It is presumably for heuristic and analytical value that Goldthorpe's empirical work collapses the class categories from the original thirty-six to the seven and ultimately to the three main positions for analysis of mobility, and not because the use of more categories led to the conclusion that there was no class formation because there was too much mobility. A decision to reduce the number of cells in a mobility table is often made on the basis of insufficient sample sizes to sustain the finer level of analysis. In this particular case, however, decisions of this kind carry other implications which can affect the results and conclusions in a serious way. One might expect both an analysis of the implications of making a decision to reduce the number of class positions examined, and a sensitivity analysis, to show the implications of changing the group membership of occupations at the margin, but neither is offered. This is all the more important since other class schemes which combine occupations in different ways produce different results (e.g. Marshall, Newby *et al.*, 1988).

The implications of all this for the debate on gender and class are as follows: Goldthorpe's conclusions about men's mobility and men's class formation, contingent upon that mobility, could be influenced to some extent by his choices of groupings and numbers of class categories. Conclusions drawn from comparisons between men's and women's class mobility, or between the various approaches compared in Goldthorpe and Payne (1986b), may also be contingent on the choices of initial class positions, especially if women's amount of mobility is affected differently from men's as a result of the choices made. This is not an unreasonable expectation in view of the segregation between men's and women's occupations.

There are also problems attached to conducting further empirical work to see if meaningful groups have been identified. Goldthorpe seems to be using his empirical work for two quite separate purposes. On the one hand, it is offered as support for the choice of class scheme adopted in the first place. On the other hand, it is the empirical examination he advocates as a second step of class analysis: 'And in turn, the issue may be pursued of the further degree of distinctiveness of identifiable classes in terms of their members' life-chances, their life styles and patterns of association, and their socio-political orientations and modes of action' (1983a: 467).

Admittedly Goldthorpe presents only a limited selection of correlations to act in this dual role, those which would be described as lifestyle or patterns of association. We might speculate that since he believes it is really the investigation of class action which is the important second stage of class analysis, he does not recognize the dual weight he is placing on these correlations about lifestyle. However, that is not the emphasis he actually gives to the various degrees of distinctiveness within class groups open for investigation. The dual purpose is important, because it has been a significant part of the debate over his view of gender and class (to be described below). That Goldthorpe sees the correlating of measures of socio-cultural variations with class-formed groups as a secondary task is repeated later in the first defence paper (1983a: 467). He criticizes Britten and Heath for thinking that their better correlations can in some way displace the conventional account of class formation.[7]

This raises a problem for Goldthorpe. If he wants his conventional analysis of class formation based on social mobility matrices to be taken seriously and thought to be more than artefactual, then he needs to incorporate the socio-cultural variation work, in which case Britten and Heath's better correlations should be taken seriously. If he wants to dismiss the view that evidence on class formation can be gained through examining socio-cultural variation, then he must leave open the possibility that his so-called class formation is artefactual. Some confusion is injected into Goldthorpe's position in a later reply paper, when he seems to place priority on explaining class effects rather than seeing them as a distinctly secondary issue. 'From this standpoint, then, the key questions that arise are essentially empirical ones concerning which approach can ... most fully reveal class effects while ... not generating spurious or artefactual effects—e.g. regarding class mobility' (Erikson and Goldthorpe, 1988c: 545).

When we examine the results of this further empirical work, two sets of results emerge. Goldthorpe finds 'fairly systematic differences' (1987a: 212) in social relationships between the class groups he identifies in the mobility analysis. On the question of whether individuals experience subjectively the mobility he identifies, there is *some* confirming evidence from 'those men who returned life-history notes' (*ibid.*: 247), who were a subsample of the whole sample and whose representative nature is not discussed. But Goldthorpe also adds, 'we must acknowledge that there are other types of subjectively significant mobility than that on which we have chosen to focus our attention' (*ibid.*). This evidence might reasonably be described as providing weak support of his claim to have identified meaningful class-formed groups. Goldthorpe himself suggests that his conclusions on the experience of social mobility are more 'tentative' and 'debatable' than most of his other results (*ibid.*: 246, 212). It might well be at the best end of the spectrum of what social scientists can expect.[8]

However, it seems reasonable to ask a number of questions: Is this categorization of Britain's class structure the best that can be achieved? Goldthorpe thinks it is better than the alternatives offered by his critics, and it is clear that this is an important issue. However, might it not be possible that other starting positions will produce more meaningful divisions between people by the criteria of empirical correlations? It is arguable that Britten and Heath's joint classification provides one such example of a set of categories which provides better correlations with aspects of socio-political or class behaviour than does Goldthorpe's, although the classification used clearly suffers from other problems.[9] One may then be in the position of having to choose between, on the one hand, a set of categories producing classes which does not confuse different types of mobility, but represents other socio-economic differences only weakly, and on the other, a set which confuses different types of mobility, but represents socio-political differences quite well. It would seem to be worth at least some debate as to whether the weaknesses of the conventional view might not constitute grounds for abandoning it, even apart from the gender issue. The currently available alternatives also have strengths as well as weaknesses. Goldthorpe's presentation of the issues sometimes give the impression that the conventional view does not itself have weaknesses. Once these weaknesses are remembered, the decision between alternatives is not so weighted in favour of the current view as Goldthorpe suggests.

Choice of Sample and Unit of Analysis

The need to choose an appropriate sample for a research project is an accepted principle for operationalizing any research endeavour. In the debate over the place of gender in class analysis, much time has been spent discussing which is the most appropriate unit of analysis: family units, individuals or some other. One might expect that the decision about the unit would inform the choice of what is the appropriate sample, that is, either a sample of families (or households) or a sample of individuals. However, for one reason or another, many of the data used in the debates over gender and class do not comply with these expectations.

Goldthorpe argues that the family is the appropriate unit of class analysis, and that married women's class position is dependent, for the most part, on their husbands. We presume that he would argue, on this basis, that although the appropriate sample would be one of households, a sample of men could be argued to represent the family units. A sample of individual men did constitute the data of the Oxford Social Mobility Study in the early 1970s, which forms the basis for Goldthorpe's (and others') subsequent class analysis of modern Britain. However, while a justification for using such a sample could be provided, none was forthcoming at the time. In fact, the exclusion of women from the sample was justified on resource grounds. We are left with the impression that both individual women as well as individual men would have been sampled had resources permitted. Thus either Goldthorpe would have gone against his own view at that point, or this issue had not been thought through sufficiently, and/or Goldthorpe came to his commitment to the family as the unit of analysis some time later. In the latest paper with Erikson (1988b: 50) he advocates the collection of men's and women's data. It is implied, but not made explicit, that this is individual-based and not household-based data. In fact, a sample of men's individual data forms the basis of all Goldthorpe's work on Britain's class structure. This is ideal for examining *men's* position in Britain's class structure, their class formation and class action, etc. It is less than ideal if the objective is to document the class position of families or households; for that task, a sample of households would seem to be the appropriate sampling unit. Certainly, if one were adopting 'the dominance approach' to class analysis, as Goldthorpe does in his more recent papers, a household sample would seem to be mandatory, although it is a men's sample which is in fact used. It is also less than ideal to use the wives of a men's sample to analyze women's class mobility, which Goldthorpe does on a number of occasions in this debate, although he does recognize these data deficiencies (1983a: 472).

We turn now to a focus on the unitary view of a family's class position. It takes a bit of unravelling to sort out what Goldthorpe intends by using this concept. He means that when families are the focus of analysis, they should be given one (and not a joint) class position. But this does not seem to preclude an analysis of individual women's class mobility (Goldthorpe and Payne, 1986b: 550). The women examined are a mixture of married and single women, so that he is not saying that only unmarried women's class mobility can be analyzed. Does he think, therefore, that one can examine families and individuals in the class structure? But why compare the results from the conventional and individual approaches as if they are alternatives (*ibid.*)? Also Goldthorpe recognizes that the approaches do give different results on occasions. The conclusion that must be drawn from collecting these points together is that what Goldthorpe is claiming for the unitary view is uncertain.

In the light of this uncertainty it is worth making some comments on how the unitary view is justified and what it implies. One of the main planks on which the unitary view of the family's class position is based is that class division and potential conflict run between and not through families (1983a: 469). In fact, it is debatable whether class conflict runs between but not through families, since it is individuals who engage in class conflict. The social mobility analyses based on men's data often refer to men and not family units.[10] To have maintained that the analyses are about *men's* social mobility would, in this author's view, be entirely coherent and acceptable and, moreover, consistent with the database collected and analyzed and even with its aims. (That such analyses would be limited to men and therefore incomplete would then be uncontroversial,[11] but this *could* be justified on the grounds that all research is inherently limited.) This position would have the virtue that it was what it claimed. Such a position would also be consistent with the aims Goldthorpe set out in starting to analyze social mobility. After all it is only individuals who can experience occupational mobility of either inter or intra varieties. In most cases, family businesses excepted, spouses are contractually employed (or not, as the case may be) as individuals. Also, in most cases, they engage in class action or conflict as individuals, most often through employment-based organization. As Goldthorpe rightly points out, 'In democratic societies, such conflict has in fact been typically initiated via labour movement...' (1987a: 329).

What is needed is a clearer framework of which unit of analysis is appropriate for what ends. In this respect I can do no better than quote from an article by Garnsey which preceded this debate with Goldthorpe by some years:

> In my view the attempt to identify a unique and exclusive base of analysis is misplaced. If the complexities of the stratification system are to be explored it is necessary to work with different bases for different purposes of enquiry. The salience of the family in the class system is not in question. Its importance in the transmission of social advantage to the next generation through the inheritance of property and preparation for occupational position is indisputable. It does not follow, however, that the family must be taken as the exclusive unit of analysis. In a system of individual wage labour, families are not engaged as units in the occupational division of labour. The family is in some respects a unit of consumption; its members may own property in common; but it is as individuals that its members are engaged in roles in the system of economic production ....Market and work situation deriving from occupation are essentially individual attributes. (Garnsey, 1978: 226)

In that Goldthorpe is concerned with the market and work situations in his class analysis and with class formation and class action, I offer this justification that he should appropriately be concerned with a class classification which takes the individual as its unit of analysis.

What is the implication of the above for analyses of individual women's social mobility? There are no reasons, in principle, why one should not address a similar set of questions to women as have been addressed to men.[12] One could do a similar set of analyses, addressing the same questions to a sample of individual women, about the extent to which classes have formed, and how far action or conflict results. Goldthorpe argues that this was not done prior to 1986, despite the availability of some data sources, because there had been uncertainty about what were the central issues to be addressed and what would be the appropriate conceptual approaches and analytical procedures to pursue (Goldthorpe and Payne, 1986a: 548). This is speculation. A variety of equally speculative plausible alternative explanations could be offered.[13]

An analysis of women's social mobility needs a longitudinal, as opposed to merely cross-sectional, perspective which can recognize life-cycle variations. The foundation for analysis of women's social mobility which can recognize class and life-cycle variation has now been laid (see Dex, 1985). No one to date, Goldthorpe included, has undertaken a study of women's social or class mobility which distinguishes or recognizes women's life-cycle occupational mobility, but this is not to say that it is impossible. Unfortunately, there is no time here to attempt such a development in detail. It is interesting to note, however, that Goldthorpe has used (married) women's life-cycle employment and occupational mobility as arguments against including them in class analyses or in constructing joint class-based positions. At the same time he seemingly happily paid no attention to such variations in his own analysis of women's class mobility (Goldthorpe and Payne, 1986b). That he thinks a longitudinal perspective important can be found in the first defence paper, where he criticizes others' research data: '...the data in question have at least two major shortcomings: first, they are of a cross-sectional nature and thus tell one little about the actual histories of employment or non-employment of particular women' (1983a: 472).

An analysis of women's social and class mobility may well require the development of new conceptual approaches and criteria, for example, of mobility and of class schema. There is no difficulty in posing questions about women's class action or conflict, or of the lack of it, through the traditional channels of the labour movement, and in this respect women, like men, participate as individuals. It is not the case, as Goldthorpe suggests (1983a: 469), that women lack the capacity to cause serious disruption of the production process. It would be relatively easy to cite cases of industrial disputes where women have done just that. That women do not use this capacity as much as men may well be the case. The extent to which women do use their potential power and what determines when and how they use it are empirical questions. Adopting the unitary view of the family would not encourage such issues to be examined, and would seem to encourage the gross overgeneralizations about women of the sort Goldthorpe cites (e.g. from Parkin, 1971) as part of his justification for his position.[14]

Women can undoubtedly also experience marital mobility (something which is receiving attention in this debate), but then surely so can men. Men's marital mobility has not received any attention. In this respect there is an asymmetry (some might call it sexist) in the conventional view as it has developed to incorporate marital mobility. The conventional view also includes the asymmetrical conclusion that women move *up* the class scale by marrying above them, but that men do not move down by so doing; nor do men move up, in the original conventional (non-dominance) approach, by marrying above them.

Lastly in this section, we will examine the implications of the practice which Goldthorpe has adopted in his work. What are the implications of taking a sample of individual men for an analysis which is intended to represent the class structure of modern Britain? Critics have claimed, of course, that this is a distorted and limited view of the class structure by virtue of the fact that it omits women. Goldthorpe's subsequent empirical work on married women suggests it does not distort their position to any great extent. We will return to this point of debate below. What does seem to be less contentious is that the use of a sample of men for analysis does limit the view of the class structure in excluding from the distribution households where a women is the single parent and/or unmarried. Also the distribution will include, but will not give any recognition to, married households where the wife's occupation is genuinely of a higher class than her husband's, that is, cross-class families. The size of the cross-class family group is subject to debate, a debate which is impeded by the lack of an appropriate set of class groupings for women's occupations.

Let us assume, as Goldthorpe argues, that genuine cross-class families are a small proportion of all households. It is still the case that they would be omitted by focusing on a sample of individual men's class positions alone. In his latest paper addressed to the debate (Erikson and Goldthorpe, 1988b) these limitations are recognized and some empirical work is offered which examines the implications. Erikson and Goldthorpe attempt to provide 'complete mobility tables' (*ibid.*: 44), that is, 'ones which display the mobility experience of national samples that are representative of the male and female adult populations together' (*ibid.*). Unfortunately, data of the kind required are unavailable for Britain (and for many other countries, Sweden being the only case where they are available). The conclusion drawn from these admittedly unsatisfactory databases is as follows: '...their comparison with "men only" tables serves in fact more to confirm than to undermine the general validity of the latter so far as the industrial societies of the mid-twentieth century are concerned' (*ibid.*: 50–1).

In view of the data shortages, we cannot place any confidence in these conclusions. What is interesting is that Goldthorpe, as part of this conclusion, advocates the future collection of data using (individual?) men's and women's data, a suggestion described as 'an innovation': 'Complete tables of the kind we have suggested represent an innovation which, we hope, will be increasingly used in future mobility studies' (*ibid.*: 50). It does not seem to strike these authors that the conventional view's traditional focus on men's social mobility, and the claim that a class analysis of married men encompasses their wives, may in the past have hindered data collection of the type which they now advocate and of the type which is actually necessary to advance some aspects of the debate in which they are involved. This author, and many of Goldthorpe's other critics, would, I am sure, agree wholeheartedly with the position on data collection he advocates in this paper with Erikson. The case offered against Goldthorpe in this contribution thus recognizes this new departure in his position, and one with which it is in agreement. However, the recognition of the need for new forms of data collection by Goldthorpe is viewed here as one of the successes of the critics in this debate.

As things stand, the adoption of the unitary view is not likely to give any better or worse or different picture of men's social mobility, class formation or class action. (A unitary view based on sample households might conceivably provide some differences in men's mobility.) The unitary view would fail to examine the effects on class action of cross-class families, however small in size these are. It might also tend to ignore altogether the effects of wives on husbands' class action. Although Goldthorpe might argue that this is not inherent to the approach, it could be argued to be a danger of treating the family as a unit. In an examination of industrial action, wives' employment and/or class may well play important roles in influencing men's *behaviour*. This sort of relationship has not been the subject of examination in this debate, since large-scale data on the topic are not available. Empirical work has been conducted on subjective class perceptions and it has tended to support Goldthorpe's argument that the husband's class influences wives more than vice versa, although there is a need for other approaches to confirm these findings.[15]

Goldthorpe's analysis of the marital mobility of individual women concluded that it did not lead to a view that society was more (or less) open than that obtained from the conventional unitary view. Presumably it could have, and adoption of the unitary view as a sole basis for class analysis would certainly preclude uncovering such potential differences. On the further point that inequalities are greater between rather than within families, one suspects tautology in Goldthorpe's use of this justification for the unitary view.[16] It is possible to argue that differences in individuals' jobs underlie family inequalities and are thus more fundamental. Also Stanworth (1984) has made the point that the conventional unitary view has the implication that, in the current days of high divorce rates, the class structure is changing considerably as women move in and out of marriage (what Goldthorpe would presumably call 'spurious' effects on the class structure and class formation). To repeat, the fact that all approaches have their problems has perhaps not been stressed sufficiently.

Mobility and Time in Class Analysis

As noted earlier, Goldthorpe's analysis of class formation rests on the amount of mobility individuals experience and is based on a certain period of time over which class members have to be immobile. Goldthorpe does not spell out criteria for the threshold amounts of immobility or for the necessary time period over which immobility should be visible, but clearly he does have criteria. Significant measures of association in absolute and relative mobilities, and low exit rates for a set of individuals' intergenerational plus intragenerational mobility, are used to conclude that two broad classes of men, the service class and the working class, have experienced class formation. Goldthorpe obviously thinks that intraoccupational mobility is important to examine.[17] Unfortunately, he is short of data in this respect. For men, he has their father's job, their first job, their first interview job, if employed in 1972, and for a smaller subsample, their follow-up interview job. For women, he only has one job from the election survey data, their current or last job, as well as their father's occupation. Even if the conceptual problems had been resolved, it would be difficult to conduct an adequate class mobility analysis of women with the available data. These are the unfortunate but common constraints of research.

There are ways in which these issues about the mobility criteria for class formation have a bearing on the gender and class debates. First, there is a question as to whether it is absolute or relative mobility which determines class formation; second, Goldthorpe draws on other studies of women's lifetime employment to argue that its intermittency poses severe problems for the alternative class schemas, suggested by his critics, especially Britten and Heath's joint classification system (see Goldthorpe, 1983a). We will consider these two problems in turn.

There appears to be a difference in the criteria Goldthorpe applies to men's and women's social mobility. In his study of men he makes use of both absolute and relative mobility rates to construct an argument about men's class formation. However, he seems to say that most weight is placed on the absolute rates (1987a: 29). When women are examined (Goldthorpe and Payne, 1986b), most emphasis is placed on relative rates. The conclusion that the analysis of women's class mobility does not lead to any difference in conclusions from the men's study rests on this

interpretation, since women's absolute rates of mobility lead to a different conclusion. Thus the use of different criteria appears to give results which favour
Goldthorpe's arguments.

On the issue of intermittency in women's employment histories, Goldthorpe
argues that, if one allows women to change their class position by virtue of a change
in employment status (in or out of employment), a lot of spurious class mobility will
result. There is a problem here whose implications reach beyond the issue of the
joint classification system. It applies equally to men who move in and out of
employment and especially to those who are recurrently unemployed. There has
been no suggestion that recurrently unemployed men should be either omitted from
class analysis or thought to have a derived class status from their wife's employment.
It is possible that Goldthorpe did not have to face these issues in his men's social
mobility study, partly because, at the cross-sections he examined, probably only
small proportions of men were unemployed (and they could probably be ignored)[18]
and he was still using cross-sectional data. Goldthorpe now thinks that unemployed
men can be allocated to a class position on the basis of their previous occupation.[19]

This still leaves a problem of the long-term unemployed and the young
long-term or even short-term unemployed who have never had a job. (In the early
1980s the proportions of 16-year-old school leavers who had never had a job were as
high as 20–25 per cent of the age group, the vast majority persisting in this state for
some time.) There are ways in which these groups can be given a class position,
possibly their father's position in the case of young men living at home. However,
it may also be necessary to recognize a long-term unemployed or 'underclass' or
'state-dependent' category for long-term unemployed men who are not dependent
on their spouse's employment, especially if they are a sizeable group, as is now the
case, and whether or not one takes the conventional view. It is also a feature of the
dominance approach to classifying families, now adopted by Goldthorpe, that a
man's change of employment status from full-time to part-time, while the wife
remained in full-time work at a lower class level, would involve a change of class.
One might conclude from this that problems of spurious class mobility are endemic
to all approaches to class analysis and yet these are the very fabric of individuals'
real work histories.

The problems of women's employment mobility could be resolved in similar
ways. In the case of short periods out of the labour market women could be given a
class position on the basis of their previous (possibly best) employment. Young
women living in the parental home who have never worked could be allocated their
father's social class, and married women who have given up ever working again
could be given either their husband's class if he is working or be allocated to the
'state-dependent' class if they rely long-term on state benefits. One has, of course, to
have criteria of short- and long-term periods out of employment, but this is a
situation common to men and women and can be resolved, if to some extent
arbitrarily, possibly by using existing empirical work to look for bimodalities in the
distribution. Also, the amount of information required to classify individual men
and women in these positions would be much increased.

The procedures which can be adopted to resolve issues of this kind in both
men's and women's class analysis will depend on the size of the problem and the
specific objectives of the analysis. In periods when the 'state-dependent' group has
been growing, it seems necessary for class analysis to recognize this fact. There
might now be intergenerational transfers of state-dependent 'class' positions. This

sort of immobility might be argued to constitute class formation, but the potential for class action and conflict is certainly different from that conventionally assumed. That this would describe real inequalities, however, cannot be doubted.

There is one further data problem worth highlighting concerning Goldthorpe's investigation of women's marriage mobility. The absence of information about women's and men's own class (occupation) at the point of getting married, and the use instead of her/his current or last job, mean that conclusions about women's marriage mobility need to be regarded as at best indicative and at worst possibly misleading.

Goldthorpe's Class Analysis: Conclusions

So far we have examined Goldthorpe's own view of class analysis and whether, given that view, he is correct in arguing that it is not important to incorporate gender division within it. In the examination of the necessary operational steps involved in pursuing Goldthorpe's own stated aims, some inconsistencies have been found both in his approach and in his arguments in support of neglecting married women's own class position. I would interpret this to mean that his case is far from proven. There are equally good reasons for adopting an individual approach to his sort of class analysis, and his practice, if not his statements, has done just that. Whether one would treat individual men's samples and individual women's samples separately or together for purposes of analysis will depend on the objectives of the investigation. Also, some of the grounds on which his case against alternative approaches rests apply equally to the conventional and dominance approaches to classifying individuals or families. It is undoubtedly true that there are conceptual problems to be resolved if the analysis of women's class mobility according to Goldthorpe's approach is to be undertaken; these encompass drawing up appropriate class positions for women's occupations, distinguishing class and life-cycle mobility and, of course, collecting better data. However, it is not only the alternatives to the conventional view which have their problems of analysis, but also the conventional view itself. We turn now, more briefly, to the remaining questions, notably, whether Goldthorpe is correct about his critics, and whether different definitions of class analysis are possible and underlie these debates.

GOLDTHORPE ON HIS CRITICS

Goldthorpe's first defence and subsequent reply to his critics has made two main points: first, that the critics failed to engage with the central thrust of his original argument; and second, that the alternatives they offer to replace the conventional view have so many problems of their own that they fail to constitute a basis for abandoning the conventional view. It is impossible here to go into all of the points made, but some summary points are worth noting. My assessment of the debate is that Goldthorpe has made a lot of valid points. However, the earlier sections of this chapter show that his own approach is not without problems. He also has superiority over many of his critics in quantitative statistical analysis. Before Goldthorpe gets more pleasure from his critics disagreeing with each other (1984c:

491), I would add that the critics have served a very useful purpose which even Goldthorpe may appreciate in retrospect. The critics have stimulated him into analyzing women's class mobility, and the debates have served to clarify the conceptual issues that still need to be resolved if women's social mobility is to be analyzed within his framework. One can hardly blame the critics for having only poor instruments when there has not been the same tradition of interest in women's employment as in men's. However, the claims of 'intellectual sexism' may well have been sounded too rapidly.

If one accepts Goldthorpe's view of what class analysis is about, and that the family is the appropriate unit of analysis, then there is a logic to his argument. In his view a consideration of women's lifetime social and employment status mobility, as part of assessing whether class formation of families is occurring, produces results which are difficult to interpret. The results suggest that families are forever changing their class status and that no class formation is occurring. Goldthorpe thinks this conclusion is erroneous, although on what grounds is not made clear. (If one dropped the necessity to deal with families, one would be free to interpret women's social mobility as indicating a low level of class formation among women, which might not be so obviously erroneous. However, more work on the conceptual issues and on a set of appropriate class positions is required before any firm conclusions can be drawn.) It is, therefore, largely Goldthorpe's definition of, and approach to, class analysis which are at the root of the differences. Other commentators have reached the same conclusions, for example, Marshall, Newby *et al.* (1988). Thus, while Goldthorpe has argued for the debate to take place on empirical (or research) grounds, the main issues which separate Goldthorpe and his critics are conceptual.[20] In which case we need to ask whether there are approaches to class analysis which both differ from Goldthorpe's and have a validity of their own.

OTHER CLASS ANALYSES

There are other types of class analyses than the one adopted by Goldthorpe. Marshall, Newby *et al.* (1988) provide one contemporary example, but there are many others. At this level of macro-sociological approaches I would expect that Goldthorpe would not want to argue to the contrary. However, critics have often implied, although not stated outright, that there is scope within a Goldthorpe-like, Weberian, structuralist framework for other approaches to class analysis, and ones which take a different view of the role of gender from Goldthorpe. It may be that some of the critics are arguing from within a different macro-sociological framework than Goldthorpe, but that has not been stated explicitly. If so, Goldthorpe might have accepted their position and agreed to differ. I am assuming here that the discussion is about, broadly speaking, a Weberian-structuralist's approach to class.

Three main questions have arisen over the approach to class analysis: first, whether class analysis can encompass an analysis of the sexual division of labour as a result of which women and men come to occupy different initial positions; second, whether class analysis can encompass analyses of relationships and inequalities within families and within marriage; third, whether class analysis should be wider than Goldthorpe suggests, for example, by addressing the questions of how far increased home ownership has relied upon women's earnings; how far savings and provision for old age or children's education are dependent upon women's earnings; to what extent the potential for class action is influenced by women's as well as men's employment histories or how women's own class position influences children's socialization and occupation? Stanworth (1984) has argued that many of these questions are important for class analysis to address.

On the first point about the sexual division of labour, Goldthorpe would argue that while this is of major sociological interest, it is not part of class analysis, although perhaps we should say it is not part of his definition of class analysis. Garnsey (1978) and Marshall, Newby *et al.* (1988) argue that there are good reasons why it should be. Clearly, to analyze the sexual division of labour is different from conducting Goldthorpe's class analyses as presently defined. However, it is a boundary problem as to whether the sexual division of labour lies inside or outside the scope of class analysis. Goldthorpe believes that whether or not the sexual division of labour lies beneath the set of class positions which is the starting point for his analysis is an empirical issue and open to question.[21] In this respect the argument is probably of little consequence and almost semantic.

Similar points to those made above about the sexual division of labour can be made about the issue of whether within-family inequalities should be part of the research foci of class analysis. On this point Goldthorpe argues more clearly against incorporating such analysis into class analysis because between-family inequalities are much greater than within-family inequalities (Erikson and Goldthorpe, 1988b: 4). If we are to evaluate whether Goldthorpe is correct on this point, we would need a clear statement of which are the important inequalities under consideration. As already indicated, Goldthorpe makes a confused statement on this point. He says in the text that it is 'resources and consumption standards' that he is considering, but then in a footnote (1988b: note 9) he says that it is class which determines living standards (which I take to include resources and consumption standards) and not *vice versa*. Thus we cannot assess, except in a tautological sense, whether inequalities between families are greater than those within families, and therefore deserve the label class, which must be denied within-family differences.

On the final point of whether other questions should be part of class analysis, Goldthorpe has no objections. However, he appears to want to argue that the label 'class analysis' be reserved for his approach. On this issue my assessment is that Goldthorpe is being unduly narrow. The sorts of questions raised by Stanworth (1984), for example, are concerned with the processes and mechanisms underlying intergenerational class transmission. Thus they underpin exactly what Goldthorpe is examining in his class analysis. While Goldthorpe does examine the class positions people occupy over time, he does not examine the routes via which they travel between the positions. These are two aspects of the same problem, and thus the case for calling the investigation of the *processes* 'class analysis', even according to Goldthorpe's definition, is a strong one.

NOTES

1 For a more complete list of critics, see Goldthorpe's (1983a) paper and a review in Dex (1985).
2 Goldthorpe restated the resources constraint as a justification for examining only men in Goldthorpe and Payne (1986b: 550).

3   'It is, moreover, in no way the aim of class analysis to account either for a structure of class positions or for the degree of class formation that exists within it in functional terms' (Goldthorpe, 1983a: 467).

4   For example, Stanworth: 'Two parts of Goldthorpe's argument serve particularly well to clarify the issues at stake in this debate. First by elaborating the positions of class analysis and of structural-functionalism...' (1984: 159).

5   In the second edition of *Social Mobility and Class Structure in Modern Britain* (1987a) Goldthorpe lists some initial contributions to the debate and comments: 'Issues arising from the debate are also taken up by several contributors [to Crompton and Mann, 1986] ..., but in a way which seems regressive: that is, by returning to large, vague, and tendentious claims (often referred to as "theory") rather than attempting to resolve issues by putting them in a form in which research findings might be brought to bear upon them' (1987a: 297n6). See also Erikson and Goldthorpe (1988c: 2).

6   See, for example, Dex (1987) for a grouping of occupational categories which is more appropriate for women, although it does not consider self-employment.

7   On this see Goldthorpe: '... it must be observed that to account as fully as possible for the range of socio-cultural variation existing in the population at large is *not* in fact the objective of class analysis as this would be understood by writers such as those earlier referred to in this paper' (1983a: 483).

8   There is no intention here of casting doubt on Goldthorpe's integrity, not least because all of these findings are openly reported.

9   The problems are noted in Goldthorpe (1983a, 1984c). Also, Goldthorpe notes that Britten and Heath's joint classification confuses class and life-cycle mobility.

10 For example, Erikson and Goldthorpe: '... in our previous analyses of the class mobility of men...' (1988b: 3); see also Goldthorpe: '... our investigations focussed on the class mobility of men...' (1987a: 329).

11 Goldthorpe makes this point himself in Goldthorpe and Payne (1986b: 550).

12 Abbott and Sapsford (1987) have done this, as, it could be argued, have Goldthorpe and Payne (1986b).

13 For example, secondary analysis of large-scale computerized data sets is not something with which many British sociologists are familiar, although skills in this field are increasing.

14 There are some very interesting questions which could be examined about the recent growth of white-collar militancy involving many women.

15 For example, the fact that Goldthorpe finds the husband's class position a better predictor of the wife's class identity than her own needs further analysis using alternative measures of wife's own class, e.g. her best occupation, or last occupation before childbirth, if Goldthorpe is not to attribute to class something which is in fact a life-cycle effect.

16 Goldthorpe makes the point about inequalities running mainly between families in a recent paper (Erikson and Goldthorpe, 1988b). An element of tautology can be identified when he says that 'Class inequalities are the true inequalities' between families. If one then asks, what are class inequalities, the reply is that they are *not* inequalities in living standards, since living standards are determined by class (*ibid.*: 58 n9). The answer implied, therefore, is that class inequalities are between-family inequalities, presumably by definition.

17 His criticisms of the use of cross-sectional data only (Goldthorpe, 1983a) have been mentioned already.

18 It is not clear what did happen to them in the study.

19 I cannot find this in Goldthorpe's writings, but I have heard him say this.

20 In the case of Stanworth, Goldthorpe makes this point himself: 'In other words, we are back to the conceptual divergence from which we began...' (1984c: 493).

21 Goldthorpe says, '... such questions are entirely left open—including that of what connections exist between the prevailing form of sexual inequalities and class relations...' (1984c: 498).

Interchange

McRAE REPLIES TO DEX

Although I can no doubt be fairly accused of having already made an overlong contribution to a debate that has itself gone on far too long, I trust that in the interests of clarification just a few more words will be forgiven. Dex acknowledges that one of Goldthorpe's criticisms of his critics is that they often fail to engage with the central thrust of his arguments (Goldthorpe, 1984c: 491). Despite this, Dex also fails to engage with what Goldthorpe actually argues, at least in some important respects. It should be said, however, that Dex's failure to do so appears to be based upon her misreading some of his arguments, rather than upon missing their importance. Given that one of my aims has been to make Goldthorpe's position within this debate as clear as possible, I have taken up my 'right of reply' in the hope of setting straight what I see as Dex's most important misunderstandings.

Throughout her chapter Dex acknowledges, and indeed emphasizes, the value of Goldthorpe's empirical contributions to this debate. Moreover, she points out that, in recent years at least, the debate has been conducted largely on the basis of empirical research, and that Goldthorpe's 'patient replies and painstaking empirical research have strengthened his position'. Yet in discussing the selection of a sample for the 1972 mobility studies—an issue of no small importance in any empirical work—Dex presents a misleading picture of the reasoning behind Goldthorpe's choice of a sample of men. On two occasions Dex notes that the exclusion of women was justified on resource grounds and suggests that Goldthorpe gives the impression that 'both individual women as well as individual men would have been sampled had resources permitted'. Resource considerations were undoubtedly as important in 1972 as they would be today, but nowhere does Dex mention what was in fact the primary theoretical reason behind the exclusion of women, although this was discussed by Goldthorpe in some detail:

> The second consideration, of chief significance from our own point of view, was of a more substantive kind. It concerned the degree of relevance that information on the occupational mobility of women would have for our interests, which ... were not in processes of occupational attainment as such but rather in occupational *qua* class mobility and, primarily, in its implications for class formation. In this respect, the conclusion we reached was ... that to concentrate attention on the experience of males is unlikely to bring one to very misleading conclusions, at all events so far as the historical period covered by our inquiry. ... The general grounds for this conclusion can best be stated in negative terms: it is difficult to envisage any factors which, over the period in question, would be likely to result in any *sizeable* number of women occupying *markedly* different class positions from those of the male 'heads' of their families, or

153

possessing attributes or engaging in activities which would in themselves materially influence the class position of the family unit. (1980a: 287–8)

Given the importance of the family as the relevant unit of analysis within the conventional approach to class analysis, to categorize Goldthorpe's sample choice of male family 'heads' as an after-the-fact-of-research justification, as Dex does in her contribution, is to mislead.

However, as Dex observes, the most profound differences between Goldthorpe and his critics rest not upon the facts of empirical research, but upon conceptual differences over where the boundary of class analysis is to be drawn—an observation with which I fully agree. In my own contribution I have argued that the investigation—both theoretical and empirical—of sexual inequalities and class inequalities should be kept separate, and I will not repeat those arguments here. Rather, I will suggest that Dex's arguments for altering the boundaries of class analysis are based upon two quite serious misreadings of Goldthorpe's position, and as such lend support to those, like myself, who prefer a more cautious, less ambitious approach to the study of sexual and class inequalities.

First, in asking whether class analysis should encompass study of the sexual division of labour which gives rise to sex segregation in the labour market, Dex writes that 'Goldthorpe believes that whether or not the sexual division of labour lies beneath the set of class positions, which is the starting point for his analysis, is an empirical issue and open to question', and offers, in a footnote, a partial quote from Goldthorpe as evidence of his position. She then categorizes his view as 'probably of little consequence and almost semantic'. In fact, Goldthorpe's position from the very beginning has been to recognize the relationship between occupational inequalities flowing from the sexual division of labour—sex segregation in the labour market—and men's class chances (1980a: 58–9; 1983a: 468). Far from considering it an open question *whether or not* the sexual division of labour underpins the class structure, Goldthorpe argues that it is the very existence of sexual inequalities within marriage—operating to the disadvantage of women in the labour market—which provides the fundamental justification for taking the family as the appropriate unit of class analysis and for taking the husband's occupation as an adequate proxy for the family class position. What *are* open questions are those directed at investigating the specific links between sexual inequalities and the class structure in any given society in any given period (which I take to be the meaning intended in the full version of the quote by Goldthorpe referred to by Dex). The 'list' of research topics provided by Dex—said to be 'closed off' by the conventional approach—seems to be exactly the kinds of questions that should, and could, be investigated by sociologists interested in the relationship between women's employment and social class analysis. To what extent has home ownership increased as a result of women's earnings, and with what effects? To what extent are family economic well-being or children's life chances dependent upon women's labour force participation? How is the potential for class action influenced by women's as well as men's employment? As Dex notes, these are some of the processes underlying intergenerational class transmission, and as such are waiting to be fully researched. Nothing in Goldthorpe's approach to class analysis prevents such an undertaking.

Second, in asking whether class analysis should encompass investigations of inequalities within families, Dex argues that Goldthorpe's position is both confused and tautological. Goldthorpe suggests (Erikson and Goldthorpe, 1988b: 4) that inequalities in resources and consumption standards which exist between husband and wife are (1) not usefully thought of as *class* inequalities, and (2) in any event less extreme than those found between families. Goldthorpe reserves the latter inequalities in living standards—those between families—as the true inequalities of class. Dex appears to believe that the difference in meaning intended by Goldthorpe is one of magnitude: if the resource and consumption inequalities within families were large enough, then they would become true class inequalities, but because they are less extreme than those found between families, they do not qualify. In fact, Goldthorpe is simply arguing that we have no reason to believe that inequalities within families are related to individual family members' relationships to the division of labour or means of production: a necessary precondition for *class* inequalities. Unequal divisions undoubtedly take place between family members. But why these should necessarily be based upon family members' economic roles outside the family is unclear: ethnicity, age, custom or religion might as easily provide sources of explanation. Inequalities in living standards between families, on the other hand, arise in capitalist society at least largely through that family's place in the hierarchical social division of labour.

The debate over women and class analysis has gone on for a very long time, too long in my estimation. It has been an important and extremely productive debate, both in its impact on the thinking of protagonists and antagonists alike and in its setting of new research agendas. Now, however, the time has come to end the debating and get on with some research.

DEX REPLIES TO McRAE

Susan McRae's contribution to this debate is mainly to reiterate Goldthorpe's position using a wider range of material. In this she draws attention to some of Goldthorpe's published opinions, most notably that his critics have failed to engage with his essential arguments. This I accept contains an element of truth. That there might have been a misunderstanding in the early rounds of this debate is also accepted; for example, that Goldthorpe's position was thought originally to be denying that women are exploited and dependent within marriage, which clearly he is not. However, as I tried to point out in my chapter, a closer inspection of Goldthorpe's justification of his whole approach and his definition of *class* inequality, which McRae repeats, reveals elements of circularity rather than coherence. McRae adds some new points in her contribution, partly through being able to cite Goldthorpe's most recent and unpublished work, to which I also had access. She also includes a more extended discussion than has previously been seen of the debate over whether the sexual division of labour falls inside or outside the boundary of class analysis. I am not offering any new arguments in this comment, either in criticism of Goldthorpe or in defence of my own position, partly because McRae has not offered any that Goldthorpe had not already stated. I merely reiterate a number of points which pertain to points McRae raises about Goldthorpe's position.

I agree with Susan McRae that Goldthorpe's contribution to the study of social mobility and class analysis is not to be minimized, and that more recently he has done much to contribute to analyses of women's social mobility. However, to put things in context, from the point of view of the critics of the conventional view, when the initial claims of sexism in class analysis were being made in the 1960s and

1970s, few, if any, studies of women had been conducted. Goldthorpe is to be commended for responding to the lack of analyses of women, and for providing some of the studies which now exist in this field. Most of the contributions for which McRae commends Goldthorpe are from his very recent, and as yet largely unpublished, material. One can hardly blame the critics for not fully appreciating the extent of these contributions. Critics might also reasonably argue that, but for their opening shots fired at the traditional view, we would not now be in the position of having Goldthorpe's contributions on women, although that is not to say that others would not have responded. However, there is the remaining difficulty about some of his conclusions from this work; in his analyses of women he has not attempted to separate class mobility from life-cycle mobility, a criticism Goldthorpe made of his critics. That this is a difficult task all parties would probably agree. But the idea that the work of Goldthorpe's critics suffers from this conflation, but that his work does not, is mistaken.

McRae also accepts that the family is the unit of class analysis on the grounds that inequalities are greater between families than they are within them. I argued that, taking the full range of Goldthorpe's objectives, which are to examine the extent of class formation and the contingent potential for class action, the individual is a more appropriate unit, at least for most of Goldthorpe's measures of class action, which are workplace-based actions. The empirical finding that class inequalities (measured by relative rates of mobility) are as great between women as they are between men is presented as an argument for not using the individual as a unit of class analysis by McRae in her contribution. (I understand this point to mean that because of the similarity between men and women, a picture of the class structure based on men only will not be distorting, as some critics had argued.) However, such a picture will tell us little about the potential for class action among almost the only growth sector of employment in Britain in the 1980s, women's employment. Furthermore, Goldthorpe has not aligned himself with the school which seeks to provide static pictures of the class structure of modern Britain (or anywhere else). In addition, there appears to have been an overly literal reading in McRae's chapter of critics' arguments on the homogeneity of women's experiences. If intergender group differences are great, it is not unreasonable to comment on the similarities, by contrast, of within-group experiences. This need not be taken as a failure to recognize intragender group differences, as McRae seems to suggest.

Finally, as to whether the sexual division of labour should be recognized as a subject of study under the heading of class analysis, McRae argues a stronger case than has previously been made for considering these two topics as separate and almost unlinked. I would argue that there is a clear link between these subject areas. For one thing, class mobility as measured by occupational mobility is dependent upon the range of possible moves. These moves are restricted for each gender because of the sexual division of labour. It is possible that alterations in the possible movements for each gender, whether equalizing or otherwise, would produce differing amounts of class mobility, either absolute or relative. I would argue that this is a fairly strong link between the two topics. However, I also accept that different sorts of questions can be addressed under each heading, as they are presently conceived. Thus I reiterate my earlier point, that this is primarily a boundary or definitional dispute, although to deny the links between the two areas is a mistake.

VI. CLASS AND POLITICAL PARTISANSHIP

10. Class and Political Partisanship

ANTHONY HEATH

This chapter concentrates on John Goldthorpe's work on the *Affluent Worker* study, in particular on the volume *The Affluent Worker: Political Attitudes and Behaviour* (Goldthorpe *et al.*, 1968b). While Goldthorpe's more recent work on class also makes important contributions to political sociology, the *Affluent Worker* study remains of considerable interest and deserves a fresh look. It was very influential at the time it was published (see the commentaries by Banks, 1969; Westergaard, 1970; Mackenzie, 1974), particularly in developing a sociological as opposed to a narrowly psephological approach to the study of political partisanship. It contains the seeds of much of Goldthorpe's later work on class and mobility; and the themes it dealt with have once again become highly relevant to our understanding of political change in Britain.

The *Affluent Worker* study was the product of a research team, not of a single individual. Teamwork is almost essential for the conduct of major empirical investigations in sociology, and it is important to acknowledge at the outset the contributions of Frank Bechhofer, David Lockwood and Jennifer Platt to the study.

THE AFFLUENT WORKER STUDY

The central concern of the *Affluent Worker* study was to test empirically the thesis of working-class *embourgeoisement*. This thesis 'in most versions embodied the claim that affluence brings about a change in the political orientations and party loyalties of the more prosperous sections of the working class' (*ibid.*: 1–2). The thesis was particularly popular at the end of the 1950s, when it appeared to offer a plausible account of the Conservatives' electoral successes and the decline of the Labour vote. For example, Abrams, Rose and Hinden in their famous booklet *Must*

Labour Lose? saw economic prosperity as a major source of change in working-class values: 'The old working-class ethos is being eroded by prosperity and the increasing fluidity of our society. People now know that they can improve their lot by their own efforts. And as they succeed, they change their values and cease to identify themselves with the class from which they sprang' (Abrams, Rose and Hinden, 1960: 106). These changes in working-class values, Abrams and his colleagues believed, meant that Labour's class appeal had become outmoded and that Labour had to change if it were to survive electorally. Arguments like those of Abrams and his colleagues postulate a process of *embourgeoisement*; that is, prosperity is held to detach workers from working-class identification and move them not only towards middle-class standards of living but also towards middle-class values and identities. It is this argument about the social and political consequences of affluence that became the main target for the Cambridge team.

As is well known, to test this thesis the Cambridge team followed the bold strategy of selecting a 'critical case' rather than selecting a representative sample of the national adult population. 'In planning the field investigations which formed the major part of the research, our first concern was to find a *locale* for these which would be as *favourable as possible* for the validation of the *embourgeoisement* thesis' (Goldthorpe *et al.*, 1968b: 2). The team believed that, if the affluent workers in the critical case did not display *embourgeoisement*, it was highly unlikely that such a process was occurring on any significant scale in Britain. The locale finally chosen was Luton. This was at the time a prosperous and expanding town, with a relatively large proportion of private housing and containing a high proportion of geographically mobile workers. It was not dominated by the more militant traditions of industrial relations of some older industrial areas, and its firms were noted for their high wages. The sample consisted of 229 male manual workers, aged between 21 and 46, married and living with their wives, and regularly earning at least £17 per week gross (data from October 1962). They were employed by Vauxhall (where assemblers were selected for interview), Skefko (machine operators, setters and craftsmen) and Laporte (process workers and craftsmen engaged in process maintenance). There was also a sample of 54 white-collar workers drawn from Skefko and Laporte. The interviews were conducted in 1963–64.

The Cambridge team found that, in the case of the workers they studied, there was indeed, as predicted by the *embourgeoisement* thesis, a modest relationship between particularly high earnings and the likelihood of not voting Labour (*ibid.*: 40). This relationship, however, largely disappeared when the extensiveness of a worker's white-collar affiliations was introduced into the analysis (*ibid.*: 41). The main finding of the study proved to be that 'our sample as a whole, while clearly affluent by comparison with lower white-collar and other manual workers, is strong and stable in its allegiance to Labour, as indicated both by voting history and by voting intention at the time of our interviews' (*ibid.*: 46). Thus 79 per cent of the manual sample intended to vote Labour at the next general election. This compared with the figure of 67 per cent (of men aged 21 to 45 and employed in well-paid manual work) found by National Opinion Polls Ltd in national surveys in 1963 (*ibid.*: 15) and 70 per cent of the working class as a whole who actually voted Labour in 1964 (Heath, Jowell and Curtice, 1985). (All these figures exclude non-voters.) Thus affluence did not on its own necessarily lead to an erosion of the Labour vote and appeared to be quite compatible with high levels of support for the Labour Party.

The central flaw in the *embourgeoisement* thesis, the Cambridge team went on to explain, 'lies in the assumption that a certain level of income and possessions (itself never very clearly specified) leads to a feeling of social marginality among manual workers' (*op. cit.*: 47). Individuals surely do not identify with abstract statistical collectivities such as 'the middle income bracket'. Being affluent does not mean that the worker becomes a member of middle-class society or even aspires to such membership. In explaining the failure of the *embourgeoisement* thesis the Cambridge team thus focused on workers' social relationships and on their experiences in the workplace. 'A worker's prosperity, or lack of it, is only one element entering into the formation of his class and political awareness ... the weakness of the affluence thesis is that it fails to take account of the workers' social relationships'. They went on to show that social relationships, and in particular the respondents' social origins and job histories, were important in understanding working-class conservativism. White-collar affiliations mattered more than white-collar levels of affluence. (The emphasis on mobility is taken up in Goldthorpe's later work.) The team concluded: 'The understanding of contemporary working-class politics is to be found, first and foremost, in the structure of the worker's group attachments and not, as many have suggested, in the extent of his income and possessions' (*ibid.*: 82).

In looking at group attachments, however, the team suggested that their sample exhibited rather different patterns from those of traditional workers. The Luton workers were more privatized in their social existence and showed little evidence of 'communal sociability'. Following on from this, the Luton workers did not exhibit 'solidaristic collectivism', an orientation in which voting Labour is merely one expression of community solidarity (*ibid.*: 74–5). Instead, they displayed 'instrumental collectivism'. Solidaristic collectivism, the team argued, is associated with communities based around the mining, docking, fishing and shipbuilding industries. The decline of these industries and their associated communities goes with a shift from communal sociability towards a more privatized form of social existence and a parallel shift towards more instrumental orientations: the economic advancement of the individual and his family become more important than membership in a closely knit local community (*ibid.*: 76). However, collective action may still be the chief means by which the worker can maintain and improve his economic position:

> For, despite his affluence, the worker's experience of the social divisions of the work place, of the power and remoteness of management, and of his own inconsiderable chances of ever being anything but a manual wage-earner, all generally dispose him to think of himself as a member of the class of 'ordinary workers', and to seek collective rather than individualistic solutions to his problems. (*ibid.*: 78)

The crucial point is that the *nature* of the affluent worker's attachment to the Labour Party is rather different from that of the traditional worker, but the overall *level* of electoral support may be as high as ever, providing that the Labour Party provides (or is expected to provide) the relevant pay-offs. In other words, the relationship between the worker and the Labour Party is a *contingent* one: while the affluent workers are disposed, for the reasons given above, to prefer collectivist policies of the kind that the Labour Party has typically espoused, the party needs to deliver the goods if support is to be maintained. Support is conditional, not unconditional.

AFFLUENCE AND CLASS IDENTITY IN THE 1980s

Embourgeoisement theory received a knock with the Labour victories of 1964 and 1966, but the decline of the Labour vote in the 1970s and 1980s has tended to revive the theory and perhaps cast doubt on the *Affluent Worker* team's demolition of it. Has affluence eroded workers' class and political awareness after all?

We can explore this question using data from the British General Election Study of 1987. This is a national random probability sample, conducted in the weeks after the 1987 election.[1] It contains data on the respondents' class identity and voting behaviour, their 'objective' social class and their household income. Table 10.1 shows the relationship between objective social class, household income and subjective class identity.

We have divided income into three bands, representing the low-paid (including those on state pensions, etc.), the average paid and the well-paid. We have used Goldthorpe's seven-class schema (respondents being classified according to the head of household procedure) to measure 'objective social class' (Goldthorpe, 1980a). This schema is based on Lockwood's concepts of 'work' and 'market' situations (Lockwood, 1958). Classes I and II contain professional, managerial and administrative employees; Goldthorpe sometimes groups these two together to form the salariat or 'service class'. Class III contains routine non-manual workers, Class IV small employers and own account workers, and Class V foremen and technicians. These can be grouped together to form the 'intermediate classes'. Finally, Class VI contains skilled manual workers and Class VII semi- and unskilled manual workers. They constitute the working class proper.[2]

'Subjective social class' is measured by standard survey questions. Respondents are asked: Do you ever think of yourself as belonging to any particular class? [If yes] Which class is that? [If no] Most people say they belong either to the middle class or the working class. If you *had* to make a choice, would you call yourself middle- or working-class? Around half the respondents gave a middle- or working-class

Table 10.1 *Percentage of Respondents with Middle-Class Self-Image, 1987*

| Head of household's class | Household Income | | | |
	Less than £8,000	£8,000– £11,999	£12,000 and over	All
I Service class, higher grade	56	61	69	66
II Service class, lower grade	38	38	58	50
III Routine non-manual	31	22	44	35
IV Petty bourgeoisie	29	30	35	32
V Foremen and technicians	18	13	28	20
VI Skilled manual	17	13	17	16
VII Semi- and unskilled manual	13	20	25	17

Source: British General Election Study, 1987.

self-description spontaneously. The great majority of the remainder assented to a middle- or working-class label if they had to make a choice. In Table 10.1 the answers to the 'spontaneous' and the 'forced' parts of the questions have been combined.

As we can see from the table there is a clear relationship between 'objective' social class (as measured by Goldthorpe's schema) and 'subjective social class'. The three manual classes (V, VI, and VII) differ little in their class self-image, but they are clearly different from the non-manual classes (I, II, III and IV), while members of the higher level of the service class (Class I) stand out as being particularly likely to have a middle-class self-image. Thus 20 per cent (or fewer) of the working classes have middle-class self-images, rising to 50 per cent and more in the service class. There is quite a strong association between objective class and income, but the relation between objective and subjective class persists even when we control for household income. Indeed, controlling for income has little effect on the differences between the classes in their self-images. Thus the overall gap between Classes I and VII in the proportion with a middle-class self-image is 49 points (column 4); this gap falls to 43 points among the low-paid (column 1), 41 points among the average paid (column 2), and 44 points among the well-paid (column 3).

This brings out a point that is very important both to the *Affluent Worker* team and in John Goldthorpe's later work, namely that class cannot be reduced to income differences. If class were merely a matter of income, then we would expect the class differences in self-image to disappear once we controlled for income. Quite clearly, they do not. Goldthorpe's measure of class, therefore, must be tapping something other than, and in some senses more fundamental than, income alone. As Goldthorpe himself explains, class is more a matter of the *conditions* under which income is earned than of the *level* of income. That is, the classes differ in their degree of economic security, their prospects for individual economic advancement, and their location within the system of authority (Goldthorpe, 1980a: 39). Within the social classes there are also some differences in self-image according to income level, although these do not always reach statistical significance. In general, the differences between income categories are much less than those between the objective social classes.

These results support rather strongly the suggestion of the *Affluent Worker* team that affluence on its own does not necessarily lead to a middle-class identity. Even the well-paid members of the 'aristocracy of labour' (Class V) fall well short of the poorest paid members of the service class in their proportion with a middle-class identity. The *Affluent Worker* team had suggested that an understanding of working-class politics is to be found, first and foremost, in the structure of the worker's group attachments (*op. cit.*: 82). Table 10.2 pursues this theme.

Instead of presenting a series of multi-way cross-tabulations, we have followed the simpler strategy of using multivariate logit models (for further details, see Fienberg, 1980). The first column of Table 10.2 shows the results of the logit model when class identity is predicted by household income and by head of household's class. In effect, it shows the results of fitting a logit model to the data of Table 10.1. More formally, we fit the following model (using Fienberg's notation):

$$\ln(m_{ij1}/m_{ij2}) = w + w_{(A)i} + w_{(B)j}$$

where the dependent variable is a binary variable coded 1 (middle-class identity) or 2 (working-class identity), the independent variable *A* represents household income

Table 10.2 *Logit Models: Class Identity of Respondents, 1987*

		1	2	3	4
Constant		0.38(0.03)	−0.31(0.03)	−0.28(0.03)	−0.23(0.03)
Income	1	−0.10(0.04)	−0.02(0.04)	−0.08(0.04)	−0.00(0.04)
	2	−0.09(0.04)	−0.09(0.04)	−0.12(0.04)	−0.12(0.05)
Head of house-	1	0.66(0.05)	0.61(0.06)	0.58(0.06)	0.56(0.06)
hold's class	2	0.33(0.05)	0.29(0.06)	0.27(0.05)	0.26(0.06)
	3	0.07(0.08)	−0.01(0.09)	0.02(0.08)	−0.06(0.10)
	4	0.00(0.06)	−0.01(0.06)	−0.00(0.06)	−0.02(0.07)
	5	−0.31(0.07)	−0.25(0.08)	−0.24(0.08)	−0.19(0.08)
	6	−0.41(0.06)	−0.38(0.07)	−0.35(0.06)	−0.35(0.07)
Wife's class	1		0.28(0.04)		0.25(0.05)
	2		−0.01(0.04)		0.01(0.04)
Father's class	1			0.35(0.04)	0.33(0.05)
	2			−0.06(0.04)	−0.08(0.04)
N		2581	2117	2337	1923
Chi Square		11.3	64.3	47.4	190.6
df		12	52	52	169
p		0.50	0.12	0.65	0.12

Note: Figures in brackets give the standard errors.
Source: *British General Election Study*, 1987.

(three categories as in Table 10.1) and variable B represents head of household's class (seven categories as in Table 10.1). Note that in the SPSSX parameterization which we have used, the parameters for a given variable sum to zero.

The results of this first logit model confirm our analysis of Table 10.1: household income does have a significant relation with class identity, but it is substantially weaker than that of head of household's class. The parameters for the latter variable are much the larger. (Alternative codings for income do not change the picture greatly.) We then add to the analysis, in column 2, wife's class and, in column 3, father's class. To avoid too many empty cells in the underlying table, wife's class and father's class have been collapsed into three categories with Classes I–II (the service class) constituting one category, Classes III–V constituting the second (the intermediate classes) and Classes VI–VII (the working class) the third. As we can see from column 2, wife's class does have a significant relationship with class identity, net of the other variables in the model, and its inclusion in the model tends to reduce the size of the other parameters. (Since we are predicting respondent's class image, the effect of wife's class is sometimes the effect of the wife's class on her own identity, net of her husband's class, and sometimes it is the effect of wife's class on the husband's identity, net of his own class.) Similarly, we see from column 3 that father's class also has a significant relationship with class identity, although its inclusion in the model does not affect the size of the income parameters. The final analysis, the results of which are given in column 4, adds both father's and wife's class to the model. They continue to have significant relationships with class identity. Household income also continues to have a significant relationship with class identity, but the relationship is considerably weaker than the relationships with the three class variables.

These results offer strong support for the ideas advanced by John Goldthorpe and his colleagues over twenty years ago. Despite the great differences in the nature of the samples and in the statistical methods used, and despite the social changes of the last quarter-century, we still find that affluence *per se* has only a small role to play in understanding class identity.

AFFLUENCE AND VOTING BEHAVIOUR IN THE 1980s

We now turn from class identity to voting behaviour. Table 10.3 shows the relationship between Labour voting, household income and head of household's class. The results are somewhat similar to those of Table 10.1, although in general the relationship between household income and vote is rather stronger than was the relationship with class identity. The main change concerns the low-paid. In the case of class identity the differences between respondents on low and average income tended to be small (or actually in the wrong direction), and it was only those on high income who were more likely to have a middle-class identity. In the case of voting, on the other hand, there is a significant difference between the low-paid and the average-paid (as well as between the average-paid and the well-paid). This can be seen more clearly from the logit analysis of Table 10.4.

Compare the income parameters in column 1 of Tables 10.2 and 10.4. In Table 10.2 the parameters for low and average income are not significantly different from each other (being -0.10 and -0.09 respectively), although they are lower than that for high income ($+0.19$). In Table 10.4, on the other hand, all three parameters are significantly different from each other (being 0.21, 0.04 and -0.25). (The change in the signs is due to the fact that we move from predicting middle-class identity in Table 10.2 to Labour vote in Table 10.4.)

Table 10.3 *Percentage Voting Labour by Class and Income, 1987*

| Head of household's class | Household Income | | | |
	Less than £8,000	£8,000– £11,999	£12,000 and over	All
I Service class, higher grade	18	7	12	12
II Service class, lower grade	22	20	14	17
III Routine non-manual	36	29	15	26
IV Petty bourgeoisie	28	30	10	20
V Foremen and technicians	52	40	16	37
VI Skilled manual	60	49	35	51
VII Semi- and unskilled manual	56	40	29	4

Source: *British General Election Study*, 1987.

Table 10.4 *Logit Models: Labour Voting, 1987*

		1	2	3	4
Constant		−0.58(0.03)	−0.64(0.04)	−0.66(0.03)	−0.69(0.04)
Income	1	0.21(0.03)	0.19(0.04)	0.19(0.03)	0.18(0.04)
	2	0.04(0.04)	0.04(0.04)	0.05(0.04)	0.04(0.04)
H Class	1	−0.35(0.07)	−0.25(0.08)	−0.30(0.08)	−0.23(0.08)
	2	−0.22(0.06)	−0.20(0.07)	−0.20(0.07)	−0.20(0.08)
	3	−0.06(0.09)	−0.09(0.11)	−0.01(0.09)	−0.03(0.11)
	4	−0.21(0.07)	−0.22(0.08)	−0.19(0.08)	−0.20(0.08)
	5	0.16(0.06)	0.16(0.07)	0.14(0.07)	0.17(0.08)
	6	0.41(0.05)	0.39(0.06)	0.35(0.05)	0.35(0.06)
W Class	1		−0.12(0.06)		−0.09(0.06)
	2		−0.08(0.04)		−0.09(0.05)
F Class	1			−0.20(0.05)	−0.17(0.06)
	2			−0.01(0.04)	−0.00(0.05)
N		2648	2159	2393	1958
Chi Square		17.7	61.1	103.9	228.3
df		12	52	52	169
p		0.12	0.18	0.00	0.002

Note: Figures in brackets give the standard errors.
Source: *British General Election Study*, 1987.

EXPLAINING WORKING-CLASS POLITICAL BEHAVIOUR TODAY

How are we to explain the difference between the two sets of tables? Why does income have a stronger relationship with voting, net of 'objective' class, than it does with class identity?

The answer almost certainly lies in the distinction which the *Affluent Worker* team made between solidaristic collectivism and instrumental collectivism. In the case of the 'traditional worker' it was suggested that Labour voting was merely one way in which communal solidarity was expressed: 'party allegiance is less a conscious and deliberate choice than a by-product of the more primitive forms of collectivism in which he is involved at the workplace ...' (*op. cit.*: 75). Under these conditions we would expect a close relationship between class identity and class voting. The two are simply different expressions of the same underlying communal sociability of everyday life. In contrast, in the case of the 'privatized' workers studied by the *Affluent Worker* team in Luton there is no expectation that class identity and Labour voting will necessarily be associated. Voting is less expressive, more instrumental, and is thus more contingent on the actual pay-offs received from the Labour Party and, it should be added, from the Conservative Party. Conservative voting, therefore, does not necessarily indicate that the working class has become 'bourgeois' and abandoned working-class values; rather, it may indicate that the Labour Party has failed to deliver the collective benefits expected of it.

It is not entirely clear how many traditional and privatized workers there were in the electorate in the 1960s or how much the mix has changed over the years. I suspect that the traditional worker with his solidaristic collectivism was always a **rather rare phenomenon** and that instrumental collectivism has been the predominant orientation of working-class Labour voters for most of the post-war period.[3] At any rate there can be little doubt that instrumental orientations to politics are widespread today and that we must look to the pay-offs which the parties provide, or are expected to provide, in understanding working-class political behaviour. As emphasized in *How Britain Votes* (Heath, Jowell and Curtice, 1985), in explaining the fall in working-class support for Labour we should not assume that the answer lies in the changed nature of the working class, but should consider the possibility that it lies in the actions of the political parties themselves.

On the Labour side it is not difficult to think of actions that might have upset their voters in the working class, particularly the better paid. Thus the Labour defeat in 1970 can plausibly be ascribed to the failure of the Labour Government to pursue working-class interests. Both its move away from indicative planning to Conservative methods of economic management and its policies on trade union reform (particularly the *In Place of Strife* White Paper) may well have cost it working-class support. Similarly, Labour's defeat in 1979 may have been due in part to its incomes policy, which particularly hurt better-paid workers, culminating in the notorious 'winter of discontent' (see Heath, Evans and Payne, 1989).

On the Conservative side, too, it is easy to suggest relevant political actions. Under Mrs Thatcher the Conservative Party has not followed the 'one-nation' policies that it did under Macmillan or Douglas-Home. Workers on low incomes and people on state benefits have suffered particularly. In this way the actions of the Conservative Party may have highlighted the fact that Labour is the party that will provide collective solutions to the problems of the low-paid, the unemployed and those on social security, and it may well be that these are the people who have been most ready to stay with Labour during its period of division and disarray.

In short, the pay-offs which different income categories can expect from the parties may have changed. In the early 1960s, the Labour Party may have offered collective benefits to the working class as a whole, hence receiving high levels of support from affluent manual workers. The record of the Conservative and Labour parties since that time, however, may have led many affluent workers to question their support for Labour. But this does not mean that there is a *necessary* relation between affluence and the decline of Labour voting, much less between affluence and *embourgeoisement*. As the data of Tables 10.1 and 10.2 emphasize, most affluent workers continue to think of themselves as members of the class of 'ordinary workers'. If Conservative management of the economy goes awry, of if Labour can demonstrate its determination to provide collective benefits to the working class as whole, the relation between class, income and vote may change.

NOTES

1 The British General Election Study, 1987, was a joint venture between SCPR and Nuffield College, Oxford, and was funded by the ESRC, the Sainsbury Trusts and Pergamon Press.

2 For further details of the class schema, see Goldthorpe (1987a: 40–3). For its use in political research, see Heath, Jowell and Curtice (1985) and for a comparison with other class schei as, see Marshall, Newby *et al.* (1988) [and Marshall's own contribution to this volume, Chapter 4, eds].

3 A number of political scientists have argued that there has been a decline in the importance of habitual party loyalty in voting behaviour and that the electorate has become more volatile and more inclined to vote on the basis of issues or party record (see, for example, Crewe, 1984; Franklin, 1985; Rose and McAllister, 1986). However, more systematic research fails to detect any major changes in volatility, issue voting or the explanatory force of party identification (see Heath and Macdonald, 1988; Heath, Jowell and Curtice, 1988; Heath, 1988).

11. Ideology, Sociology and the Strategy of the British Labour Party

DENNIS KAVANAGH

There is no doubt that the work of John Goldthorpe deservedly commands attention among economists and political scientists as well as among sociologists. His work is characterized by a concern to define key concepts rigorously, to address major substantive problems and to link empirical research with significant issues of theory. He has also shown a refreshing willingness to relate his work to issues which cross disciplinary boundaries. He and his various collaborators have made a major contribution to the study of social class, particularly in clarifying concepts and testing fashionable ideas by empirical research. Not much of Goldthorpe's work on social class addresses itself primarily to political behaviour. Where it does, it is mainly concerned with the nature of change in the working class and its political implications for the British Labour Party.

This chapter is not concerned with the question of whether social class has declined in importance as a shaper of electoral choice. The literature is already immense and I regard the evidence as conclusive and affirmative. Rather, I wish to examine critically Goldthorpe's contribution to the debate. This article will consider, first, the work of Goldthorpe on the affluent working class and his recommendations for the Labour Party, and then his recent work on social mobility and, again, his recommendations for Labour.

It is possible to discern a remarkable consistency in Goldthorpe's work on class and political behaviour from *The Affluent Worker* in 1968 (Goldthorpe *et al.*, 1968b) to the second edition of *Social Mobility and Class Structure in Modern Britain* in 1987 (Goldthorpe, 1987a). Three persistent themes are worth noting:

1 Suggestions of a change in the working class are much exaggerated, be it affluence leading to *embourgeoisement* (or workers becoming middle-class in lifestyle, values or voting Conservative); the reduced propensity of the working class to vote Labour; the increased rates of social mobility in

twentieth century Britain proving that Britain is now a more 'open' society; or the working-class acceptance of the 'fairness' of many of the social and economic outcomes in a capitalist society. Goldthorpe has pointed to the shortcomings in these claims and the lack of supporting evidence. He has been an effective demolisher of much conventional wisdom about social structure and political behaviour.

2   Despite the sharp reduction in the size of the manual working class and in Labour's electoral strength, Labour should not pursue 'the middle ground' or de-emphasize its class orientation. Goldthorpe has consistently argued that, by promoting radical egalitarian policies, Labour may mobilize a larger electoral coalition.

3   Much discussion of the relationship between social structure and political behaviour has been marred by a 'reverse sociologism', i.e. the tendency to move from the analysis of political events and trends to supposed changes in social structure and processes 'which, it is believed, the events and tendencies must betoken' (Goldthorpe, 1987a: 347). Goldthorpe claims that analyses, particularly by political scientists, of *embourgeoisement* in the early 1960s, of 'class dealignment' in the 1980s and the consequent decline of Labour as a working-class party, have taken this form. He finds the work of many political scientists on voting behaviour careless, value-laden and technically deficient. They do not meet the Goldthorpe standard.

AFFLUENCE AND LABOUR'S DECLINE

From 1962, in various journal articles and subsequently in book form, Goldthorpe and David Lockwood exposed a number of shortcomings in the thesis of *embourgeoisement*. In 1951, 1955 and 1959 the Labour Party had lost three successive general elections, the last two with a reduced share of the vote. The party had done particularly badly in the new towns and among prosperous workers. Commentators argued at the time that, because white-collar employment was increasing and the manual working class was declining in size, Labour, as the party of that class, would decline with it. It was also claimed that the spread of home ownership and other symbols of affluence to working-class families would weaken their class consciousness and their propensity to vote Labour. Broader social changes seemed to 'fit' Labour's electoral decline. Although Goldthorpe and Lockwood made pointed observations on the logical and empirical shortcomings of the original *embourgeoisement* thesis, the idea became increasingly important in Labour's internal debates about electoral strategy, policy and political leadership. Revisionism, until then a strategy for managing capitalism rather than replacing it with public ownership, became a strategy for satisfying working-class hopes of middle-class styles of consumption. By implication, the Labour Party had to become a 'catch-all' party rather than one oriented to the working class, industrial trade unions and council estates.

    The Goldthorpe and Lockwood survey of Luton car assembly workers in the early 1960s was a critical case to test the thesis. Such workers, at the time, were regarded as excellent examples of the newly affluent workers. The authors drew attention to three of their findings. The first was that workers on higher incomes did not adopt middle-class values and middle-class friends. In other words, one had to distinguish the economic from the relational and normative aspects of *embourgeoisement*. They discovered, second, a very high level of Labour voting among their sample. At 80 per cent it was appreciably higher than national levels of Labour voting among the skilled working class, at the time about 60–65 per cent. These affluent workers were not defecting from Labour. Third, they found no trend to increased Conservative voting in recent elections among their sample of workers. The thesis of *embourgeoisement* was more complex and even doubtful in the light of the Luton study. When Labour won the 1964 and 1966 general elections, that apparently disconfirmed the claims about *embourgeoisement* and Labour's decline.

But before awarding game, set and match to the *Affluent Worker* study, one should enter some reservations. The term '*embourgeoisement*' was indeed stretched by commentators in the 1960s to encompass a variety of allegedly interrelated features, including higher levels of prosperity for workers; weakening loyalty to Labour; growth of white-collar employment and decline of manual work; and the integration of the working class into society or the weakening intensity of its loyalty to Labour. One may regret that the term had different usages, but it is worth noting that Goldthorpe and Lockwood are tackling only one aspect of the *embourgeoisement* case, namely that prosperous workers are less likely to vote Labour. It can be seen from Table 11.1 that the electoral decline of Labour was only halted, not reversed. Except for the 1966 election Labour has never again come near to reaching the 44.1 per cent it gained then. Labour managed to win the 1964 and 1966 general elections in defiance of the advice of Goldthorpe and Lockwood, which was to appeal to the working class. The landmark survey study by Butler and Stokes (1969) showed that Labour gained by conveying the impression of being more 'new' and 'modern' than the Conservatives. The rhetoric of Labour leaders, particularly of Harold Wilson in 1964 and 1966, was addressed to all classes and the party's programme was based on its plan for economic growth and greater efficiency. Butler and Stokes also found that the major swings to Labour between the 1964 and 1966 general elections were among those who felt their economic positions had improved under the Labour Government (*ibid*.: 405).

Table 11.1 *Labour's Share of the Vote in General Elections, 1945–87* (percentages)

1945	48.3
1950	46.1
1951	48.8
1955	46.4
1959	43.8
1964	44.1
1966	47.9
1970	43.0
1974 (Feb.)	37.1
1974 (Oct.)	39.2
1979	37.0
1983	27.6
1987	30.8

Source: Butler and Kavanagh (1988: 283).

The Luton study may also have oversold its findings. The authors claim: 'The most important single fact to emerge relating to the politics of the affluent workers we studied was that the large majorities were, and generally had been, Labour supporters ... a notable feature was the *stability* of Labour support' (*op. cit.*: 172). The year in which the interviews were conducted (1963) was the worst in terms of public standing for the Conservative Party since regular opinion polls were conducted after 1945. The party was running between ten and fifteen points behind Labour throughout the year and was dogged by the Profumo scandal and divisions over the leadership. This makes it all the more surprising that, in spite of Labour's national popularity in 1963, the Luton study found that Labour voting among the sample actually fell from 83 per cent in 1955 to 79 per cent in 1963 (Crewe, 1973: 32). All the indications would lead one to expect it to have increased.

One of the most striking claims of the study was that a gradual change from 'proletarian traditionalism' to 'instrumentalism' among workers was taking place. The former, often found in such industries as mining, shipbuilding and docking, is described as voting Labour on the basis of class loyalty, while 'instrumentalism' is described as voting Labour on the basis of personal self-interest (Goldthorpe *et al.*, 1968b: 74–80). If *embourgeoisement* was not occurring, then, it was claimed, this subtle shift in orientation was. In fact, such a shift was included in some of the statements of *embourgeoisement* which Goldthorpe had attacked. However, neither the distinction nor the *evidence* for the shift is persuasive. As Heath, Jowell and Curtice observe, class loyalty itself may rest on self-interest (1985: 9). Many of the responses in the Luton sample show that workers offer a mix of both instrumental and traditional reasons for voting Labour. The evidence for such instrumentalism in the study is hardly conclusive. The authors point to the widespread disapproval among their sample of the party's link with the trade unions as well as the support for the unions' role in gaining workplace benefits (rather than in promoting wider social and political change) and the belief that a Labour Government is more likely than a Conservative one to provide benefits. The authors claim that such mixed views would 'tend to undermine a genuinely "labour" orientation—or, at least do not readily co-exist with a radical and highly partisan political outlook' (1969: 177). Such a statement is more a very loose interpretation of the data than an actual finding. It is also worth noting that such instrumentalism among the working class was widely found among contemporary studies of deferential working-class Conservatives by McKenzie and Silver (1968), by Nordlinger (1967), and in the *Must Labour Lose?* survey (see Abrams, Rose and Hinden, 1960).

POLITICAL AND ELECTORAL STRATEGY: WHAT SHOULD LABOUR DO?

When working-class parties have performed poorly at the polls, there have usually been two reactions. One (usually on the right of the party) has been to claim that the party should move to the 'middle ground' and dilute policies which are regarded as extremist or sectional. Usually this has meant qualifying or abandoning socialist policies and presenting itself as a national rather than a class party. The other reaction (usually on the left) has called for greater socialism or a programme which advances the interests of the working class. After the 1959 election defeat and again after the election losses since 1979, the working-class-based Labour Party has faced the problems of coping with socio-economic change which appears to weaken support for the party. Should it adapt to such change (and presumably seek the elusive middle ground) or should it try even harder to educate the electorate to its socialist values?

John Goldthorpe has argued from the second standpoint in the debates about Labour's electoral strategy both in the early 1960s and in the 1980s. On the first occasion the growth of affluence was a central plank of the school of commentators and politicians who envisaged the end of ideology and a decline of class politics, propositions which Goldthorpe has rejected. Many of the same themes have been voiced again in the 1980s in the wake of the steady decline in the size of the manual working class and of Labour's electoral following. On both occasions Goldthorpe (and co-authors) have rejected the middle ground strategy. Instead, they have emphasized the opportunities for creative political leadership which may offset any adverse social trends, 'that is, to purposive action on the part of elites and organisations, aimed at giving a specific and politically relevant meaning to grievances, demands and aspirations, which have hitherto been of a sub-political kind, and thus mobilising support for a programme or movement' (1969: 189). Goldthorpe has consistently emphasized active political choice over passive social determinism and argued that Labour leaders should follow a left-wing strategy rather than a centrist one. 'Far from reflecting, as is often claimed, a hard-headed recognition of "the end of ideology", the strategy of winning the middle ground must be seen as being in fact inspired as much by ideology as by sociology' (*ibid.*: 191). Ideas of *embourgeoisement* have been a convenient and plausible legitimation for the strategy. Goldthorpe and his colleagues also argued that Labour should reject 'the—essentially Conservative—doctrine that the efficient management of the economy is the key to electoral success' (*ibid.*: 193). That was the enemy's terrain. Instead, the party should fight on a radical, egalitarian and class-based programme. It should have a commitment '... to the interests of the mass of wage-earning, rank-and-file employees, and an endeavour to advance these interests not merely by promoting general economic expansion but also by thorough-going egalitarian measures over a wide-front' (*ibid.*).

Three points are worth making about the recommended strategy. First, there was hardly any evidence in the Luton survey, or other surveys for that matter, that a significant proportion of the working class strongly supported such policies. Indeed, the authors probably realize this when they go on to recommend that Labour should not merely respond to wants and expectations already manifest among its potential supporters, '... but expand and diversify such wants and expectations in ways that would carry radical implications' (*ibid.*: 194). Discussion of these alleged vote-winning policies is unfortunately brief. They include more public provision for recreation and leisure, an improved urban environment, better education, industrial democracy and more democratic decision-making all round. It is all rather thin. There is no acknowledgment that affluent workers, for example, might be alienated from Labour by its espousal of 'thoroughgoing egalitarian measures over a wide front' or that Labour for long has attracted support from highly *conservative* voters (Harrop, 1982). The recommendations also fly in the face of the authors' emphasis on the instrumentalism and the 'pay-off' outlook of many working-class Labour voters. Labour lost much working-class support in 1970 and 1979 because it failed to satisfy such instrumental demands. There was a backlash among skilled workers over tax rates in the 1979 election (and in other Western countries at the time). In spite of Goldthorpe's claims to the contrary, it has been poor management of the economy (and the resultant lack of 'pay-off' for working-class voters) that has so often damaged Labour governments at the polls.

CLASS DEALIGNMENT AND LABOUR'S DECLINE: NOTHING CHANGES

Nearly twenty years later much has changed both in social structure and in electoral behaviour. The scale of Labour's electoral decline (from 44.1 per cent in 1964 to 27.6 per cent in 1983 or 30.8 per cent in 1987) is greater than that suffered by any other major West European socialist party in the post-war period (and is surpassed only by the electoral decline of the French Communist Party). Second, there has been a remorseless decline in the size of the manual working class—from two-thirds to half the working population between 1964 and 1983, according to the British Market Research Society (BMRS) social grading, or from 47 to 34 per cent on the Goldthorpe criteria of social class (see below). Finally, in the 1980s there has been a return to mass unemployment, largely affecting the manual working class.

The social group which has defected most from Labour is the skilled working class, the C2 group. Table 11.2 shows that this group (30 per cent of the electorate) was regularly voting nearly 2-1 in favour of Labour between 1964 and 1974. By 1979 the Conservatives had drawn level with Labour and then took a clear lead in the general elections of 1983 and 1987. The C2 group has certainly become more bourgeois in material terms; between 1979 and 1987 possession of a telephone spread from 35 per cent to 85 per cent, car ownership from 30 to 60 per cent and home ownership from 45 to 70 per cent, according to Robert Worcester of MORI. A different way to make the same point is to refer to Labour's long-term decline in the affluent south, and the erosion of its working-class support in the region. In 1987 the Conservative share of the national vote was almost identical to that of 1964 (42.3 and 43.4 per cent respectively), but Labour had lost substantial ground in such new towns as Billericay, Epping and Hitchen. In spite of these significant social and electoral changes, Goldthorpe's views have hardly altered. In the 1960s *embour-*

Table 11.2 *Proportion of Skilled Working Class (C2) Voting Labour, 1964–87* (percentages)

	Voting Labour	Labour Lead over Conservative
1964	54.5	20.5
1966	58.5	26.0
1970	55.5	21
1974	49	23
1979	41	0
1983	32	− 8
1987	36	− 4

Source: Nuffield *British General Election* series, reporting Market and Opinion Research International for 1974–87; National Opinion Polls for 1964–70.

geoisement was the dragon to be slain by a sociology of the centre-left, in the 1980s it has been 'class dealignment'.

At this stage one must refer to Heath, Jowell and Curtice's major survey study of the 1983 general election, *How Britain Votes* (1985). The study largely accepts Goldthorpe's ideas about how social class should be conceptualized and measured. Indeed, one of the authors, Anthony Heath, had earlier collaborated with Goldthorpe on the Oxford Social Mobility Study, which allocates people to social classes on the basis of their authority and autonomy at work. *How Britain Votes* detaches the self-employed, technicians and foremen from the working class, so that the working class amounts to only 34 per cent of the working population. The groups they have excluded from the working class are those most likely to be home-owning and affluent. We are left with a smaller and more solidly proletarian working class, which we would expect to be more solidly Labour. Compared to other surveys, which show working-class support for Labour at 38 per cent in the 1983 election, *How Britain Votes* finds that 49 per cent of its working class supports Labour. The methodology and arguments of *How Britain Votes* have received a mixed reception; this has been discussed elsewhere (Crewe, 1986; Dunleavy, 1987; Kavanagh, 1986). Goldthorpe, in turn, in the second edition of his *Social Mobility and Class Structure in Modern Britain* (1987a), quotes approvingly many of the arguments of *How Britain Votes* in support of his views as against those of Crewe and others. It seems justifiable, therefore, to use this study as a surrogate for some of the views of Goldthorpe.

Goldthorpe (like Heath, Jowell and Curtice) accepts that there has been an *absolute* decline in class alignment in the sense that the proportions of working class voting Labour and middle class voting Conservative have fallen steadily in the last twenty years (see Table 11.3). For example, on the BMRS criteria working-class support for Labour fell from two-thirds in 1964–66 to 42 per cent in 1983, and on the Goldthorpe-Heath criteria from 70 to 49 per cent. This decrease in the proportion of manual workers voting Labour and non-manuals voting Conservative is what most scholars have meant in talking about the decline of class politics since 1964. A perceptive critique of *How Britain Votes* by Dunleavy suggests: 'The

Table 11.3 *Labour's Share of the Manual Working-Class Vote* (British Market Research Society categories; percentages)

1964	64
1966	69
1970	58
1974	57
1979	50
1983	42
1987	43

Source: For 1964–83 Heath, Jowell and Curtice, (1985: 30; see their note of explanation on page 40); for 1987 MORI.

"intuitive" meaning of class dealignment is simply that non-manual and manual class have become more similar or less contrasting in their voting patterns over time' (Dunleavy, 1987: 414). Goldthorpe and *How Britain Votes*, however, do not accept that there has been any *relative* decline. Relative class voting is *cross-class* voting, i.e. the combined shares of the working class voting Conservative and middle class voting Labour. It is measured by the Conservative-Labour odds in the non-manual group divided by the same odds among manual workers. On this criterion of odds ratios there has been no class dealignment. Class dealignment is spurious, 'an artefact of the inadequate manual non-manual dichotomy', according to Heath, Jowell and Curtice (1985: 34). They mean, of course, that *relative* class dealignment has not occurred. Goldthorpe dismisses the political scientists' claims that there has been a decline in class voting and complains that they do not use the superior analytical techniques and data which are now available (1987a: 347). *How Britain Votes* argues that Labour's problem is not that it is losing support among the working class (the argument advanced by most political scientists), but that the working class has shrunk. If class politics is still alive, Labour has no need to dilute its class policies.

One problem concerns the treatment of those voters who voted for the Liberal-Social Democratic 'Alliance'. The growth of substantial electoral support for the Alliance in the 1980s is bound to weaken the relationship between the two parties and the two classes. In four of the last five general elections support for the Conservative and Labour parties has been confined to three-quarters or less of the electorate, compared to the usual 90 per cent for elections between 1950 and 1970. To exclude (as Heath, Jowell and Curtice do) such a large third party fraction of the electorate in an analysis of social and political change is highly questionable; indeed, the rise of third-party voting is surely an important aspect of the decline of class voting and regarded as such by political scientists.

We are now faced with two different definitions of class dealignment and a clash of statistical techniques. The recent exchanges of views between rival schools reflect the *impasse*. Goldthorpe is roughly dismissive of those who disagree: 'But what is not credible is to seek to maintain the class dealignment thesis on the basis of arguments which either ignore, or show a fundamental lack of understanding of, results achieved via the new techniques' (1987a: 354). Proponents of other approaches and different statistical techniques continue to disagree. Leaving the scholarly debate aside, surely the electoral decline of Labour, the reduction in the size of the working class (however defined) and the fall in working-class support for Labour are among the most significant features of British society and politics in the past two decades. In all the rarified debate over whether we should measure absolute or relative class dealignment, or over the merits of odds-ratios, we are in danger of throwing the baby out with the bathwater, overlooking the dramatic decline in Labour support.

POLITICAL STRATEGY: NOTHING CHANGES

Scholarly disagreements about dealignment are one thing; consequences for the real world are another. As in the *Affluent Worker* studies, Labour is again warned against accepting claims about an end to class politics and pursuing the middle ground. In a remarkable echo of Goldthorpe nearly two decades earlier, Heath, Jowell and Curtice claim that 'Labour might be able to survive whilst remaining a class party' and, by pursuing an egalitarian strategy, might 'shape the social potentials' (1985: 174). It could do this by fighting on the 'working-class issues' of job security, pensions, unemployment and working conditions, and making an appeal on the basis of social justice. As evidence of the continuing high level of class consciousness among the working class, the authors report the impressive majorities in 1983 for egalitarian responses on three out of four survey questions, covering measures to promote redistribution, tackle poverty and foster industrial democracy. The average positive response for the three was 74 per cent (Heath, Jowell and Curtice, 1987a: 276). In optimistic language, again redolent of the *Affluent Worker* studies, the authors interpret the results as confirmation that 'unrealised potentials for class action may remain within the working class'.

I agree with Crewe (1986) when he argues that the three attitude questions are poor indicators of class consciousness or a left-wing outlook. The values are largely consensual. Who would declare against redistribution towards ordinary working people, or spending more money to get rid of poverty, or giving more say to people at work? Many 'One Nation' Conservatives would accept such policies, as would many Liberals and Social Democrats. Although Labour campaigned on policies which were targeted towards redistribution and attacking poverty in the 1983 and 1987 general elections, both elections produced the party's worst results in the post-war period. It is true that many reasons contributed to Labour's election defeats and perhaps its radical programme made little difference one way or the other. I would conclude that the electorate does not doubt that Labour favours such policies, but that they are not major influences on voting behaviour.

Goldthorpe's strategy also assumes that Labour can be a strong campaigning party, i.e. that it has the resources to 'educate' the electorate. This is doubtful. The Labour movement as an educational movement—based on the Workers' Educational Association, socialist Sunday schools, a Labour press, working men's clubs with libraries, socialist lecture series and 'chapel'—has more or less disappeared. The press is hostile and television neutral. Moreover, it is much easier for parties in government, with their access to information and a civil service machine, to shift public opinion than it is for an opposition party, which must rely on its own inadequate research staff. The only remaining major vehicle for grassroots campaigning available to the Labour Party is the trade unions, and the evidence so far is that they are singularly unsuccessful (Minkin, 1986).

The issue once again becomes that of the relative importance of the voters' perceptions of a party in terms of its competence in managing the economy or its egalitarianism. According to a survey conducted in 1971–72, 'the greater part of Labour supporters would appear to have been broadly satisfied with its existing degree of commitment to egalitarian objectives' (Gallie, 1983: 137–8). The same study found that the number who criticized Labour for being too moderate was balanced by those who thought it was too dependent on the trade unions and discouraged individual effort. Above all there was dissatisfaction based on the perception that the party was economically incompetent. Surveys after the 1983 and 1987 elections found a similar concern. More recently, Rose and McAllister have found that socialist principles actually divide the working class. Although approval for socialist principles increased somewhat among Labour voters (from 50 to 61 per cent) from 1979 to 1983, as the party's vote has fallen, it is likely to decrease if and when the party's vote expands. There is no evidence that socialism will be a vote-winner for the party. Indeed, Goldthorpe's latest words on the subject acknowledge that 'social inequality has ... been effectively removed from the political agenda' and 'its restoration in the foreseeable future is highly uncertain' (1987a: 346). Goldthorpe also allowed for such an eventuality in the final sentence of *The Affluent Worker in the Class Structure*. If the Labour leadership opted for consensus rather than radical policies, then this would help to de-radicalize the working class and 'it will to some degree be also attributable to the fact that the political leaders of the working class *chose* this future for it' (1969: 195).

Goldthorpe's work correctly reminds us of the openness of many social trends for voting behaviour and the opportunities for political choice. Indeed, during the 1960s and 1970s one may point to the increases in numbers renting council houses, in the proportion of male employees in trade unions (from 53 per cent in 1961 to 66 per cent in 1979) and in public employment as a proportion of the workforce (from 24 per cent in 1961 to 31 per cent in 1981). In other words, social changes have not been uniformly disadvantageous for Labour. There have been such remarkable shifts in political allegiances in recent years that social change alone is an inadequate explanation of Labour's decline. In the 1979 Parliament, for example, all three political parties saw their support in the polls vary between 50 per cent and percentages in the low 20s. Heath, Jowell and Curtice are surely correct in claiming that the abrupt decline of Labour owes more to political factors than to social changes.

Goldthorpe (and Heath, Jowell and Curtice) correctly observe that Labour is still overwhelmingly a working-class party; it draws four-fifths of its support from the working class. It does not make much sense to seek new voters at the expense of alienating existing supporters. It is inconceivable for the present-day Labour Party not to advocate better public services, to promote the interests of the disadvantaged, to seek a bigger role for the trade unions and so on. Moreover, a programmatic, let alone an ideological, party cannot adopt and then abandon policies willy-nilly. But there are two uncomfortable features in a Labour strategy continuing to rely on this class-based heartland. One is that, even among the 'pure' working class of Heath, Jowell and Curtice, only 49 per cent voted Labour in 1983 and the proportion would not be much higher in 1987. Labour's electoral performance as a class party is poor. Second, Heath, Jowell and Curtice also show that the working class shrank from 47 per cent in 1964 to little more than a third in 1983. Even if Labour does better among the working class, it still has to look elsewhere for electoral salvation.

Goldthorpe argues that the party should still follow a class strategy and seek support in classes proximate to the working class, i.e. those in 'jobs' rather than in 'careers' (1987a: 350). It should particularly seek support among Class III (routine clerical and other service workers) and the lower level of Class IV (lower level of technicians and supervisors), two groups which amount to a quarter of the electorate but of which only a quarter voted Labour in 1983. (The recommendation sits oddly with the insistence of Goldthorpe—and of Heath, Jowell and Curtice—on regarding these as quite separate classes, with different interests, for the purposes of class analysis.) Predictably, this will be done by radical policies which appeal to the shared interests of these classes. Equally predictably, these policies are not spelled out. If they cover more progressive taxation, no incomes policies, restoring pre-1979 trade union rights, reducing mortgage tax relief and opposing the sale of council houses, sceptics will note that such policies have been remarkable for dividing the working class and Labour supporters.

CONCLUSION

Four points are worth emphasizing in this discussion of Goldthorpe's work about social class and Labour partisanship:

1   Social change has reduced the size of the working class and with it Labour's core constituency. There has been at least one form of *embourgeoisement* since the 1960s, in that society is more white-collar and middle-class and that a substantial minority of white-collar and 'service-class' people come from working-class origins. This social change has occurred at the same time as a steep decline in support for the Labour Party.
2   Goldthorpe's early suggestion about the instrumental attachment of many workers to the trade unions and the Labour Party has been confirmed. Many subsequent surveys have shown that there has long been public support for the role of trade unions in workplace bargaining and generally defending the rights of workers against employers, but little for the unions playing a larger political role. Tables 11.3, 11.4 and 11.5 make interesting reading. Table 11.4 shows the steady increase in membership of trade unions between 1964 and 1979, Table 11.3 shows the sharp decline in Labour's post-war vote over the same period and Table 11.5 shows the

Table 11.4   *Changes in Trade Union Membership, 1964–83*

	Membership (millions)	Density (percentages)
1964	10.1	44.0
1966	10.2	44.0
1970	11.2	47.7
1974	11.8	49.6
1979	13.3	51.1
1983	11.3	41.6

Source: *Department of Employment Gazettes.*

Table 11.5   *Proportion of Trade Unionists Voting Labour, 1974–87* (percentages)

	Voting Labour	Labour Lead over Conservative
1974 (Oct.)	55	32
1979	50	15
1983	39	8
1987	42	12

Source: Butler and Kavanagh, *British General Election* series, reporting MORI data.

declining proportion of trade unionists voting Labour in these years. Since 1979 Labour support among manual workers in trade unions has fallen by almost twice the rate of Labour's national decline. Increasingly, union members are found in middle-class jobs and are home-owners (*Gallup,* September 1987). Moreover, trade union campaign activity, as distinct from union leaders' public statements of support on behalf of Labour, is feeble. The tables make explicit the implicit point of Goldthorpe and his colleagues on the *Affluent Worker* study about the dissociation between workplace behaviour and political attitudes.

In the light of these tables it is interesting that Heath and Macdonald (1987) have recently argued that the British Labour Party should draw on one feature of the Scandinavian model. They suggest that Labour should promote trade union membership as a means of gaining votes. In Scandinavian countries affluence co-exists with a much higher trade union density and Social Democratic dominance of the political system. In fact, Tables 11.4 and 11.5 show the opposite relationship. Labour's absolute vote and its proportion of the electorate were appreciably higher in the 1950s and 1960s, when trade union membership was lower. (There is a good debunking piece to be written on the alleged 'lessons' which Sweden has for the British Labour Party.) Trade unionists do not vote just as trade unionists; they are also consumers, parents and home-owners (Webb, 1987). Subsequent electoral research has confirmed the importance of the economy's performance—though the measures of performance (e.g. unemployment, inflation, or prosperity) vary over time—and instrumental voting (Alt, 1978). There is little evidence, however, that the policy and strategy recommendations of Goldthorpe or Heath and co-authors will improve Labour's chances of electoral success. The recommendations derive more from ideology than sociology.

3   It is perhaps unfortunate that Goldthorpe's studies of changes in social class have been so narrowly related to the electoral prospects of the Labour Party. Such a concern perpetuates a longstanding feature of much political sociology in Britain, i.e. the greater body of research and commentary on the Labour Party compared to that on the Conservative Party. Many of the early studies of the deferential working-class Conservatives took as their starting point that it was 'natural' for workers to vote Labour. One was, therefore, dealing with *deviant* political behaviour.

4   A problem for political and sociological analysis is why Labour has been doing so much worse electorally than most other centre-left parties in Western Europe. Compared to its Continental counterparts, Labour has had many advantages. Since 1919 it has competed in a predominantly two-party system; social class has overwhelmingly been the main cleavage (religion, language and nationalism were weak); and the electoral system has meant that even with 40 per cent of the vote it could form a government on its own. In addition, Labour (and the TUC) has not been shadowed by a substantial Communist Party, splitting the left politically and industrially. Yet most Continental Socialist parties have coped better than the British Labour Party with affluence and the decline of the manual working class. Most of these parties live with proportional electoral systems and multi-party politics and have to settle for a share of power in government. It may

be that these parties have had to be more innovative than Labour in making alliances with other parties, modifying their ideological commitments and appealing beyond the ranks of industrial workers. Peter Pulzer notes that all West European left parties have had to adapt to social change: 'All have found this difficult but few have failed as spectacularly as the British Labour Party' (1987: 383). In this respect the warnings of Goldthorpe and of Heath and colleagues against social determinism are apt. What is unconvincing are the policy prescriptions for reversing the decline.

Interchange

HEATH REPLIES TO KAVANAGH

Kavanagh's piece sprays assertions, arguments and evidence all over the place—some directed at Goldthorpe's work, some at my own. Inevitably, some are correct, others are inconsistent and some are simply wrong.

For example, Kavanagh is certainly correct to draw attention to the 'remorseless decline in the size of the manual working class', although I wish he used more authoritative sources such as the Census (as in Heath and Macdonald, 1987) rather than opinion polls.[1] On the other hand, he is inconsistent when he says that, 'In all the rarefied debate over whether we should measure absolute or relative class dealignment ... we are in danger of throwing the baby out with the bathwater', but then accepts our conclusion that Labour's decline must be explained by political factors and not by social change alone—a conclusion which arose directly from our distinction between absolute and relative class dealignment and one that was not widely accepted before. But he is simply wrong when he says that I excluded the centre parties in my analysis of social and political change in *How Britain Votes*. He has clearly not taken the trouble to read the relevant literature carefully.[2]

Rather than continue point by point, I intend to focus on the implications of our work for Labour Party strategy, something which I did not deal with in my earlier piece but to which Kavanagh rightly draws attention. Kavanagh's central attack is on Goldthorpe's (and my) suggestion that Labour's electoral strategy might be to promote working-class interests, particularly those of an egalitarian kind. He says that the recommendation arises more from ideology than sociology (although Kavanagh is probably quite ignorant of my own ideology.)

First, in support of this recommendation I have shown in another publication (Heath, Jowell and Curtice, 1987a) that there are large majorities in the working class for measures to promote redistribution, tackle poverty and foster industrial democracy. Kavanagh criticizes this on the grounds that these are consensual issues.[3] This seems to be an extraordinary *non sequitur*. If these are consensual, then by adopting these policies surely Labour would win votes from all classes alike and thus maximize its electoral chances. Perhaps Kavanagh means that, because these are consensual, they cannot be working-class interests. As it happens, he is also wrong. On all three issues there are class differences, and on redistribution they are among the largest that I have found.

Second, Kavanagh brings up Labour's defeats in 1983 and 1987 as relevant evidence. He writes: 'Although Labour campaigned on policies which were targeted towards redistribution and attacking poverty in the 1983 and 1987 general elections,

184

both elections produced the party's worst results in the post-war period'. Here and elsewhere Kavanagh confuses cross-sectional analysis with time-series analysis. To explain Labour's decline between 1979 and 1983, we must look at *changes* in Labour's policy, not at cross-sectional analysis. Kavanagh brings forward no evidence that Labour was fighting on more radical egalitarian policies in 1983 and 1987 than it was before, and so the fact that Labour fared worse in 1983 than in 1987 tells us absolutely nothing about the electoral consequences of egalitarian policies. Interestingly, there is some evidence from the British Election Surveys about public perceptions of Labour's position on nationalization in these three elections. This evidence shows that Labour was perceived to have moved towards the centre on this particular issue between 1979 and 1983, not away from it.

Third, we urged in *How Britain Votes* against a one-dimensional approach to political attitudes. Kavanagh does not seem to have learned this lesson. Nowhere does he distinguish between Labour's policies on economic issues and those on, for example, nuclear disarmament. As Neil Kinnock, if not Dennis Kavanagh, is very well aware, the major change between 1979 and 1983 in Labour's policy was the introduction of unilateralism. Whatever our personal ideologies may be, nowhere do Goldthorpe or myself suggest that unilateralism is a specifically working-class interest; nothing in our sociological analysis suggests that unilateralism will improve Labour's electoral prospects in the working class. (For evidence which suggests the contrary, see Heath and Evans, 1988.)

Finally, the main thrust of Kavanagh's analysis seems to be that Labour should concentrate on managing the economy efficiently rather than on pursuing egalitarian measures. For example, he writes: 'The issue once again becomes that of the relative importance of the voters' perceptions of a party in terms of its competence in managing the economy or its egalitarianism'. I must confess that I cannot understand why the issue should be posed in this way. Neither Goldthorpe's arguments in the *Affluent Worker* study nor my own analysis in *How Britain Votes* suggests that there is a trade-off between managerial efficiency and egalitarianism. The *Affluent Worker* study emphasized the importance of 'delivering the goods' to the instrumental manual voters, and in *How Britain Votes* we took managerial competence seriously as a source of short-run fluctuations. Thus we wrote:

> The dissensus issues such as nationalisation and defence, on which the parties take fundamentally different stands, may be the sources of the long-run continuities of support. But the consensus issues, such as the management of the economy, may be the sources of short-run change. Even the inhabitants of the heartland who agree with their party's ideology may be disillusioned by evidence of incompetence. (*ibid.*: 160)

Indeed, it might be argued that managerial competence is a help to egalitarians, not a hindrance. Managerial incompetence which leads to high levels of inflation or balance of payments crises is likely to subvert egalitarianism, not promote it. The tight fiscal and monetary policies which almost inevitably follow such crises tend to have inegalitarian consequences in themselves and, by inhibiting growth, produce a zero-sum situation in which the political opposition to redistribution will be all the greater.

NOTES

1 I do not, however, know of any sources from the 1960s that use the term *'embourgeoisement'* to refer
   to the growth of white-collar employment and the decline of manual work. Kavanagh asserts that the
   term was used in this way at that time, and I would be grateful for a reference.
2 The point is made very clearly in Heath, Jowell and Curtice (1987a: 267–9) that our log-linear models
   included the centre parties. Indeed, that is one of their strengths. Kavanagh may disagree with our use
   of log-linear models (although it is a pity that he does not give any arguments against their use), but he
   should at least represent them correctly.
3 Kavanagh says that he agrees with Crewe (1986) that these three questions are poor indicators of class
   consciousness or a left-wing outlook. I have not been able to find any reference in Crewe (1986) to this
   effect, which is perhaps not surprising since I did not introduce these three questions into the
   argument until my *reply* to Crewe's piece.

KAVANAGH REPLIES TO HEATH

My comments on Anthony Heath's chapter will be brief, for I agree with much of
what he says. We agree on the importance of the *Affluent Worker* studies for an
understanding of the persisting themes in the work of John Goldthorpe. I agree also
with Heath's assertion that level of income alone is inadequate for an understanding
of a person's class identity. He shows that objective class is in many respects more
significant. He does show, however, that income level is more important in
correlating with voting. Perhaps our understanding of class identity is poor or
poorly operationalized. Alternatively, perhaps the large minority voters no longer
connect class and party vote in ways that social scientists would expect.

There may be something in the distinction between privatized and solidaristic
types of workers. We do not have good evidence of how people think of politics and
how they connect them to their class positions. Nor do we have a good understanding of how this might have changed over the past 30 or 40 years. After all, high levels
of working-class Conservative voting have been a feature of much of the twentieth
century.

The lack of expected connection between class and vote may also have been
stimulated by the policies which the parties in government pursued in recent years,
as Heath suggests. This is a big subject, little researched and therefore perhaps often
brought in as a residual explanation. I think this may apply to Heath's last three
paragraphs. What does he mean when he refers to 'working-class interests'? Do
these apply equally to home-owners and council tenants, the affluent and poor, and
employees in the private and public sectors, among the working class? What is the
evidence that the abandonment of economic planning and the pursuit of trade union
reform—as opposed to the minuscule rise in living standards—lost the Labour Party
support among working-class voters in the 1970 election? As for developments since
1979, one wonders if the benefits stemming from wider home ownership, share
ownership and tax cuts among the affluent working class may have affected their
partisanship. There may not be an increase in Conservative voting among affluent
workers, but their sense of distance from the Labour Party—including both
instrumental and solidaristic motives—may well have increased.

VII. CLASS AND INDUSTRIAL RELATIONS

12. Social Class, Social Integration and Industrial Relations

WILLIAM ROCHE

In his writings on industrial relations John Goldthorpe has presented a sustained critique of major arguments and orthodoxies which fail to take sufficient account of the influence of social stratification on worker attitudes, systems of industrial control and the institutions which mediate relations between employees and managements. The common strand running through Goldthorpe's writings on industrial relations—defined thus broadly—is a concern with the effects of social inequality and class formation on social integration in industrial life.

This chapter will outline Goldthorpe's ideas on social class and industrial relations and examine the merits of the major criticisms these ideas have encountered. It will suggest that his work can be regarded as having considered the effects of class inequality on industrial relations in two related ways. In one group of writings he has examined the effects of long-run changes in social stratification on worker attitudes and priorities. Other writings, however, have been concerned with the effects of the British class structure on the character of industrial relations at various points during the 1960s, 1970s and 1980s. The essay will argue that many criticisms levelled against his work fail to stand up to critical scrutiny. A number of questions and problems will be highlighted. Several of these are conceptual problems that arise from the very abstract character of some of the central arguments in Goldthorpe's work. Others are more substantive and concern the implications for his ideas of economic and sociological changes in recent years. The essay will conclude that as a corpus John Goldthorpe's ideas on industrial relations stand up well to critical scrutiny.

THE CONSEQUENCES OF LONG-RUN CHANGES IN SOCIAL STRATIFICATION

The 1963 Paper with David Lockwood

It has always been a feature of John Goldthorpe's work that it has raised major objections to dominant or orthodox approaches to understanding industrial relations and developments in the working class. One of his earliest papers, written in collaboration with David Lockwood, cast doubt on the claim of the *embourgeoisement* thesis which held that 'affluent' manual workers in post-war Britain were becoming progressively more 'middle-class' in their material standards of living and their social values and priorities (Goldthorpe and Lockwood, 1963). This early paper and the subsequent *Affluent Worker* studies, in which Goldthorpe, Lockwood and a group of collaborators conducted an empirical study of working-class attitudes and behaviour, contain the core ideas of Goldthorpe's analysis of changes in worker attitudes and industrial relations.

In their 1963 paper Goldthorpe and Lockwood argued that the literature on working-class *embourgeoisement* was conceptually, theoretically and empirically loose and imprecise. Any meaningful hypothesis that affluent workers were becoming middle-class, they argued, presumed that three claims could be substantiated empirically. First, it was necessary to establish that the economic dimension of social stratification was changing, such that affluent manual workers and their families were acquiring a standard of living, in terms of income and material possessions, that put them on a par with the lower strata of the middle class. Second, it had to be shown that these same workers were developing recognizably middle-class norms and values. Finally, it had to be shown that class relations were also changing as members of the middle class accepted affluent workers as social equals in both formal and informal social interaction (*ibid.*: 136).

From a review of research purporting to demonstrate trends towards *embourgeoisement*, Goldthorpe and Lockwood concluded that these dimensions of the theoretical claim that affluent manual workers were becoming middle-class had not in fact been substantiated. In the same paper an alternative theory of the long-run contours of change in social stratification was elaborated on the basis of a different interpretation of the results of existing research. Goldthorpe and Lockwood's theory of 'normative convergence' suggested that normative changes were occurring among manual *and* white-collar workers as the normative frameworks that had traditionally characterized both the working class and the lower middle class were adjusting to changes in the market and the wider social situation of both groups. Specifically, Goldthorpe and Lockwood argued that urban redevelopment, structural shifts in the industrial composition of the workforce, the growing scale of industrial and commercial organizations and increased geographical mobility had weakened the 'solidaristic collectivism' that had characterized the 'traditional working class' and the 'radical individualism' of lower-level white-collar workers. With the breakdown of distinct working-class communities, it was suggested, progressively more manual workers could be expected to shift their aspirations and allegiances from the level of the communities in which they lived to that of their immediate nuclear families. In the same way they would increasingly look on collective action as little more than an 'instrumental means' to their 'privatized' aspirations. In the case of white-collar workers, industrial and administrative concentration and chronic inflation threatened employment conditions and standards of living, predisposing growing numbers towards collectivist strategies for advancing their privatized career aspirations (*ibid.*: 150–5).

The Luton Studies and the *Affluent Worker* Thesis

Some of these early ideas were refined in the *Affluent Worker* studies, based on fieldwork conducted between 1962 and 1964 and published in the late 1960s. As is well known, the research on which these studies were based was conducted in Luton, Bedfordshire. For Goldthorpe and his collaborators, Luton in the early 1960s represented an urban setting highly suited to a 'critical test' of the *embourgeoisement* thesis. The city's demographic, economic and social features approximated closely to the theoretical conditions supposedly conducive to working-class assimilation into middle-class society. If *embourgeoisement* was not evident in Luton—as proved to be the case—it was reasonable to conclude with some confidence that it was unlikely to have been a pervasive social trend (Goldthorpe *et al.*, 1969: Ch. 2).

In the 1960s industrial sociology was still practically synonymous with theoretical approaches which held that behaviour at work was determined above all else by industrial structure and technology. The 'human relations tradition', originating in the work of Elton Mayo, had long argued that workers had a deep-seated 'need' for 'social gratification' and esteem that might be satisfied or blocked depending on whether industrial structures and supervisory styles fostered social integration in organizations—and, in particular, permitted informal work groups to form and operate. In contrast, the approach of the 'technological implications' school put particular emphasis on the importance of technology in determining behaviour at work (for a review of these approaches, see Goldthorpe *et al.*, 1968a: 178–86). Goldthorpe *et al.* claimed to have been initially critical of these approaches on axiomatic grounds; their dissatisfaction arose from the manner in which both approaches neglected the way in which workers' own definitions of the work situation might significantly affect their behaviour, as well as the possibility that these definitions might be anchored in workers' wider social lives (*ibid.*: 45).

Though not designed to test the validity of alternative approaches to explaining industrial behaviour, the Luton survey of affluent workers' attitudes to employment appeared to Goldthorpe *et al.* to undermine empirically the view that attitudes to work were determined primarily within the sphere of work itself. The survey established that few workers in the sample participated in informal work groups or showed any interest in 'affective' involvement with workmates. It also suggested that lack of interest in work-group activity could not be accounted for by the limitations imposed on social interaction by the technologies of the plants in which those interviewed were employed (*ibid.*: Ch. 3). The results confirmed that technology was indeed the major factor determining the level of intrinsic satisfaction that the workers were able to derive from their jobs: car assembly workers, process workers and machinists, performing relatively unskilled and monotonous jobs, were least satisfied with the intrinsic features of their jobs, while maintenance craftsmen and semi-skilled setters were relatively highly satisfied (*ibid.*: Ch. 2). Nevertheless, attitudes to employment more generally were not found to vary with technology.

Irrespective of the levels of intrinsic satisfaction permitted by different technologies, attitudes to the firm and to conditions of employment among those interviewed revealed a high level of uniformity. The affluent workers appeared satisfied with the firms in which they worked and with their pay and conditions (*ibid.*: Ch. 4). Moreover, there was evidence that workers had in the main *chosen* their current jobs because they offered above all a high level of pay and good security (*ibid.*: 25–36). In interpreting these two results, Goldthorpe and his collaborators introduced a concept that was to become strongly associated with the Luton studies.

> The main conclusion we would wish to draw ... is, then, the following: that the question of *satisfaction from* work cannot in the end be usefully considered except in relation to the more basic question of what we would term *orientation towards* work. Until one knows something of the way in which workers order their wants and expectations relative to their employment—until one knows what *meaning* work has for them—one is not in a position to understand what overall assessment of their job satisfaction may most appropriately be made in their case. In seeking to become 'affluent workers', the machinists and assemblers in our sample have, no doubt with varying degrees of self-awareness, given primacy to extrinsic satisfaction from work, and have therefore chosen jobs of a kind which would enable them to come near to maximising the economic returns from their labour. (*ibid.*: 36)

Though variations in 'orientation to work' could be identified in the replies of the Luton sample, Goldthorpe *et al.* concluded that an 'instrumental orientation to work' was dominant among the great majority of the workers interviewed. This orientation accounted for the low level of involvement in work groups. It also accounted for the finding that the affluent workers were interested in trade union activity only insofar as it directly affected their pay and conditions of employment (*ibid.*: Ch. 5).

The survey results also indicated that the affluent workers desired, and were confident of enjoying, ever-increasing consumer power, though they had little faith in 'individualistic' advancement through promotion (*ibid.*: 136–43). Questions regarding their aspirations and pattern of sociability revealed that they led 'privatized' social lives and possessed outlooks that were distinct from those associated with either the 'traditional working class' or the 'traditional middle class' (Goldthorpe *et al.*, 1969: Chs 4–5). It appeared to Goldthorpe *et al.* that these attitudes and orientations to work were of wider significance than simply representing a refutation of existing approaches to industrial sociology and of the *embourgeoisement* thesis. In adopting an instrumental orientation to work and a privatized approach to home and community life, the Luton workers were, it was argued, 'prototypical' of the emerging British manual working class. The attitudes revealed in Luton reflected changes underway in the wider system of social stratification in Great Britain. This important argument, the so-called 'affluent worker thesis', was advanced by inference from several sources: from survey evidence on the social correlates of instrumental orientations, from existing studies of traditional working-class life and from observable demographic changes then underway.

One of the more obvious determinants of instrumentalism in the Luton sample was the life-cycle position of those interviewed. In line with the original objective of devising a critical test of the *embourgeoisement* thesis, the sample had been limited to married men between the ages of 21 and 46; over 80 per cent of those interviewed had one or more dependent children. In consequence, the workers interviewed occupied a position in the life-cycle where they had to cope with major financial demands and family responsibilities. Goldthorpe *et al.* argued, however, that this alone could not account for the prevalence of instrumentalism among the Luton sample. From what was known about traditional working-class communities, it appeared that the family roles of those in a similar life-cycle position had not been interpreted in such a manner as to give them general priority over commitments to workmates or work organizations (Goldthorpe *et al.*, 1968a: 149). Moreover, there existed the alternative possibility of accepting a fall off in living standards to preserve other social commitments. The life-cycle hypothesis alone could not account either for evidence in the surveys of a wider concern among the affluent workers to maintain a rising standard of living. The *inclination* towards a family-centred style of living, apparent among the Luton workers, also had to be presumed to vary sociologically and to require explanation.

The pattern of replies in the survey suggested that instrumentalism was correlated with the affluent workers' experience of geographical and social mobility. Some 70 per cent of the Luton sample had migrated to the town in search of employment, attracted by prospects of higher wages and better living conditions. The sample was therefore to a major degree 'self-selected' on the basis of a high level of motivation towards material advancement (*ibid.*: 150–4). However, Goldthorpe *et al.* argued that the circumstances of life in Luton probably reinforced significantly any such orientations formed before migration to the town. The costs associated with migration, principally separation from kin and friends, would have increased migrants' stake in reaping the benefits of their decision by maintaining a high standard of living. Then the very experience of living in a town characterized by a large number of geographically mobile persons would be expected to have reinforced instrumental attitudes by fostering a privatized pattern of social life, centred on the home and conjugal family (*ibid.*: 154–5). A high proportion of the sample also appeared to have experienced downward social mobility. It was hypothesized that this might have engendered feelings of relative deprivation, with the result that those concerned would have been further motivated to attain a higher standard of living. They might also have experienced 'status incongruency' in their work organizations, fostering a strict separation between work and home life and encouraging a privatized pattern of community life (*ibid.*: 155–68).

It could be concluded that the instrumentalism and privatism evident among the Luton workers would become more widely prevalent as urban redevelopment and greater geographical mobility affected the working class generally. The analysis of downward social mobility was not generalized in the same way by Goldthorpe *et al.*, most likely because the survey evidence on the mobility effect was little more than suggestive and there was no reason to expect structural change to increase the level of downward social mobility; the opposite must have seemed more likely. Other structural changes were also linked to growing instrumentalism and privatism. It was suggested that changes in the family were leading to more 'companionate' relations between spouses and between parents and children, further enhancing home life. The scale of work organizations seemed set to go on increasing, further reducing the probability that workers might seek to identify with enterprises in a 'moral' sense (*ibid.*: 174–6). In the light of these findings and projections Goldthorpe *et al.* argued that unions, no less than enterprises, would increasingly be viewed in an instrumental light by their members. At the same time the erosion of working-class traditionalism and the new concern to increase the material rewards of work would have the effect of intensifying members' interest in union activity at the workplace, or at whatever other level pay and conditions were determined. Anticipating a theme to which Goldthorpe would return at greater length, the study noted among its conclusions that 'greater aggressiveness' on the part of unions in the field of 'cash-based bargaining' was a very probable consequence of the changes in social stratification outlined in the study (*ibid.*: 176–7).

Confirmation and Criticism

It is remarkable that in the twenty years since the first of the *Affluent Worker* studies was published few of their conclusions on the direction and character of change in working-class attitudes and behaviour have been subjected to challenge, and no compelling alternative interpretation of working-class change has appeared. Reflecting the influence of the *Affluent Worker* thesis, a critique, published in 1981, claimed that *The Affluent Worker* remained one of the most important works, if not *the* most important work, in British sociology a decade after publication (Grieco, 1981: 62). The same paper noted that many studies during that decade had endorsed the conclusions of Goldthorpe *et al.*'s research (*ibid.*: 82, notes 1–5, lists the studies in question).

Nevertheless, a problem that arises when considering the validity of the *Affluent Worker* thesis is that until now no research has been undertaken for the specific purpose of replicating the Luton research or of testing the various strands of what remains a complex and subtle argument. Among the questions that might now be raised—and which research alone can effectively decide—the following appear to merit particular attention. First, is it the case that the structural developments identified by Goldthorpe *et al.* have the rather pronounced attitudinal and behavioural effects that were postulated in the Luton studies? Second, could other structural changes, evident since the studies were undertaken, have counterbalanced these hypothesized effects, leading to a more diverse or different pattern of attitudes among sections of the working class in the vanguard of socio-economic change? Among the factors that might have led, or that might yet lead, to a culturally more diverse working class are such developments as de-industrialization, new patterns of urban planning, the growing popularity of industrial location in 'green-field' sites, falling plant size and industrial relations decentralization. The emergence of so-called 'strong culture', or commitment-oriented management philosophies, especially in transnational corporations, and their growing popularity among indigenous employers, might also have the effect of tempering instrumentalism among significant sections of the working class employed in 'flagship' companies and industries. *The Affluent Worker* suggested that instrumental orientations to work and privatism were related in some degree to the effect of post-war affluence *per se* on expectations and thereby on worker motivations. That is, the studies distinguished implicitly between the effects of prolonged economic affluence on worker orientations and the effects of the structural changes with which post-war affluence had been associated (see Goldthorpe *et al.*, 1968a: esp. 142–3, 177–8). A question that then arises is whether the severe and prolonged dip in the business cycle which began in Britain in 1974 might have dampened working-class expectations of continuous material and employment security, thereby affecting the relative priority accorded to job rewards.

A final question that might be raised concerns the validity, when viewed from the vantage point of the late 1980s and early 1990s, of the claim that the affluent workers of early 1960s Luton were prototypical of the emerging working class. The structural developments identified by Goldthorpe *et al.* may indeed have resulted in progressively larger relative numbers of workers with orientations and attitudes similar to those revealed in *The Affluent Worker*. At the same time, to return to a point made earlier, other developments may have led to the ‘growth of other segments or strata within the working class with significantly different attitudes. The issue is not whether workers *within* what may be regarded as the ‘core’ sectors of the labour market have developed the attitudes revealed in Luton, but rather whether workers in the apparently growing ‘peripheral’ areas of the labour market would reveal the same attitudes and priorities. Even if we leave aside the case of migrant workers, an important section of secondary labour markets in a number of countries, the question arises as to whether the pattern of attitudes evident in Luton was in any way prototypical of other groups of indigenous secondary workers which have emerged in the British working class. Indications of answers to some of these questions can be obtained from existing research on social stratification and worker orientations. While again it has to be borne in mind that we must rely for confirmation of the *Affluent Worker* thesis on surveys undertaken at different times, for different purposes, in different sociological settings and using different research instruments, it can still be concluded that more recent studies and interpretations of change in the British working class are not in major respects inconsistent with the ideas developed during the 1960s by Goldthorpe and his colleagues.

The concept of ‘orientation to work’ has received more direct empirical attention in subsequent research in industrial sociology than any other aspect of the Luton studies. This can be attributed to the obvious relevance of workers’ definitions of work to the much researched question of job satisfaction. In a review of a sizeable number of studies conducted in Britain between 1963 and 1983 on job satisfaction, employment attitudes and orientations to work, Richard Brown *et al.* (1983: 47) concluded that there was some evidence that orientations to work had become ‘more narrowly preoccupied with pay and security and similar “economistic” considerations’. The evidence most directly relevant to the *Affluent Worker* thesis came, in fact, from the authors’ own studies of change in orientations to employment on Tyneside. From these they concluded that a long-term trend towards more economistic orientations to work was associated with the decline of distinctive ‘occupational identities’ that had characterized traditional working-class industrial areas (*ibid.*: Chs 5–6). On the balance of the evidence available Brown *et al.* (*ibid.*: 46) underscored the *Affluent Worker* thesis that the decline of industries and occupations in which workers could develop a strong sense of occupational identity could give rise to an increasingly calculative involvement in work. The studies reviewed were split into pre-1973 and post-1973 groups to examine whether there was any evidence that the advent of recession after the 1973 oil crisis had influenced orientations to work. The evidence (*ibid.*: 22–8, 40–2), though far from decisive, suggested that in conditions of relatively high inflation and rising unemployment after 1972 workers began to show an increasing concern with pay and job security. The studies reviewed by Brown *et al.* also reinforced the findings in the Luton survey that work orientations vary with occupation, age, family life-cycle position and other socio-demographic factors.

The most important subsequent study dealing with orientations to work and their social context is Blackburn and Mann's research on the labour market in Peterborough (Blackburn and Mann, 1979). On the basis of a survey of 951 non-skilled male workers, Blackburn and Mann distinguish between 'strong' and 'weak' orientations to work. They argue that the concept of orientation to work developed in *The Affluent Worker: Industrial Attitudes and Behaviour* (Goldthorpe *et al.*, 1968a) posited the existence of an outlook in which one type of work reward dominated to the exclusion of all others (*ibid.*: 144–5). This they term a 'strong' orientation to work. In the Peterborough survey they were unable to find compelling evidence that strong orientations existed. Evidence could, however, be found for the existence of 'weak' orientations, which they define as a set of relative priorities concerning work rewards (*ibid.*: Chs 6–8). Blackburn and Mann's findings represent empirical confirmation that employees approach work with a 'central organizing principle', or at least a set of central organizing priorities, influenced by their experience in all areas of social life. This accords with the essential feature of the definition of orientation to work developed in *The Affluent Worker*. Goldthorpe had admitted that the concept, as developed in the Luton studies, was no more than a hypothesis adequate for interpreting the data produced by the survey of attitudes to work and employment (Goldthorpe *et al.*, 1968a: Chs 3–6; and see Goldthorpe, 1970a, 1972a). The existence and explanatory significance of orientations to work had later been called into question on a variety of grounds (see esp. Daniel, 1969, 1971; Whelan, 1976; other critical works are reviewed in Brown *et al.*, 1983).

Blackburn and Mann (1979: Ch. 8) identified a variety of 'weak' orientations to work among the Peterborough sample and attempted to establish the 'background factors' with which they were associated. An 'economistic orientation', they suggested, had a high probability of being found among young married workers with dependents and also appeared to be associated with family-centredness (*ibid.*: 221). However, those with economistic orientations also appeared to have held 'radical' attitudes towards industrial relations and to have had a high level of union involvement (of an unspecified character). No evidence was found that 'alienated instrumentalism', as Blackburn and Mann describe this orientation, was associated with downward social mobility. Other weak orientations were identified among the Peterborough workers, though their relative incidence and implications for the *Affluent Worker* thesis were not highlighted.

More recent reviews of research on working-class change have also largely underscored the *Affluent Worker* thesis. Marshall, Rose *et al.*, for example, echo Brown and his colleagues in their interpretation of the impact of recession on worker attitudes and orientations:[1]

> It seems that a lengthy period of inflation *and* recession during the past twenty years has exacerbated rather than diminished the pecuniary attitude to work. ... Indeed, when it is recalled that the impact of recession has been thrown principally onto the unemployed and unwaged and that many of those continuously in work will have experienced an increase in real living standards, then arguments about affluence and recession converge. (1985: 271)

It would appear, therefore, that the recessionary conditions prevailing during much of the 1970s and 1980s have not reduced the priority workers accord to material rewards from work, through any impact they may have had on their expectations.

The *Affluent Worker* studies have nonetheless been criticized on theoretical and empirical grounds. Mackenzie (1974) criticized the studies above all for departing from the theory of social class advanced in earlier writings by Goldthorpe and

Lockwood. In these writings, Mackenzie points out (*ibid*.: 239–42), people's 'position in the division of labour', that is, their 'market' and 'work' situation, was taken to be *the* crucial determinant of their class position. Mackenzie argued that Goldthorpe and Lockwood departed from this position in *The Affluent Worker* by using orientation to work to explain industrial behaviour, thus making relatively little use of workers' market and work situations as independent variables with which to analyze the survey data. However, equating the idea that position in the division of labour should be regarded as *the* determinant of class situation with the view that variables measuring workers' current market and work situations should have explanatory primacy in accounting for industrial attitudes involves the 'fallacy of misplaced concreteness'. From their earliest writings, as Mackenzie recognizes (*ibid*.: 240), Goldthorpe and Lockwood had outlined how people's location in the division of labour made them subject to a variety of sociological constraints, some internal to the organizations in which they worked, others originating in the community settings in which they lived. Moreover, these earlier writings contained many suggestions as to how community settings were influenced by the jobs of the people who lived in them. Nothing presented in the three volumes of the *Affluent Worker* studies appears inconsistent with this understanding of class and class structure.

The most detailed and highly critical evaluation of *The Affluent Worker* is found in a paper by Margaret Grieco (Grieco, 1981). She argued that the attitudes of the affluent workers surveyed by the Luton research group were neither typical of the attitudes of affluent manual workers nor prototypical of the value changes then being wrought by social structural and economic developments. The attitudes that emerged in the Luton surveys, according to Grieco, reflected the decision of the companies whose employees were surveyed to attract labour from 'peripheral' areas of the British economy, characterized by high unemployment, low levels of union membership and malleable individualist workforces. Grieco's thesis was that the attitudes and priorities reflected in the Luton surveys were formed in the communities in which the majority of the workers interviewed had lived *prior to migrating to Luton*. As such, they bore no relationship to the social circumstances of life and employment in the city, nor to the kinds of macro-social and economic influences and trends outlined by Goldthorpe and his colleagues.

Grieco's argument in support of this contention is marred by empirical, logical and theoretical shortcomings. To begin with, she pointed out (*ibid*.: 62, 66) that the labour force of Luton had not been recruited purely from the traditional working class, with the result that the attitudes that came to light in the surveys could not have been indicative of ongoing changes in working-class values. This is a confused reading of the *Affluent Worker* thesis. Goldthorpe *et al*.'s concern was to identify the structural and other reasons why the attitudes and values apparent among the affluent workers differed from those which existing research had shown to be characteristic of the traditional working class. As such, the fact that those interviewed were not themselves from traditional working-class backgrounds is in itself quite irrelevant. More serious concern could be expressed regarding the representativeness of Grieco's own data. Evidence regarding the recruitment policies of Luton employers during the 1960s is based on an interview Grieco conducted ten years after the publication of *The Affluent Worker* with a personnel officer at Vauxhall, as well as on Grieco's doctoral fieldwork on migration patterns in Corby. But only 38 per cent of the Luton sample had been employed by Vauxhall and little attempt was made to establish whether Vauxhall's practices were typical of all the companies from which Goldthorpe *et al.* had drawn their sample.

As outlined, Grieco claimed that instrumentalism was in some degree present prior to migration in the case of many of those interviewed in the Luton studies (*ibid.*: 66). This, however, was accepted by Goldthorpe *et al.* (1968a: 154); indeed, it was part of their explanation for the attitudes revealed in the surveys. The important point is that the Luton researchers attempted to show how such a predisposition, whatever its origins, might be powerfully reinforced by the social circumstances of Luton. However convincing the analysis here might appear, it is central to the 'prototypicality' claim rejected by Grieco, and yet she ignores it.[2] Elsewhere Grieco appears to want to advance the opposite claim that the workers interviewed could not have chosen Luton in accordance with an instrumental orientation because they would not have had sufficient information on the pay and conditions offered by Luton employers (*ibid.*: 70–4). This is flatly contradicted by the survey data, which revealed that by far the most important reasons given for moving to Luton by those who had migrated to the city were higher wages and better housing (see Goldthorpe *et al.*, 1968a: 152–3). The argument that the Luton workers had been recruited from a malleable individualist workforce is not substantiated and is again difficult to square with the survey results. Grieco accused Goldthorpe *et al.* of what she termed the 'full employment error' in failing to recognize that even in the full-employment economy of the 1960s there existed pockets of regional unemployment and that it was from areas characterized by relatively high unemployment that Luton employers recruited their workforces (Grieco, 1981: 64–55). While full employment is a statistical artefact, it has to be concluded that it is Grieco and not Goldthorpe *et al.* who falls prey to the 'fallacy of combination'—the fallacy of presuming that aggregate statistics disaggregate into uniform cases—in concluding that people from regions of relatively high unemployment have *ipso facto* been 'exposed to an atmosphere of employment insecurity' (*ibid.*: 65). The claim that 'economic coercion' rather than choice in accordance with an instrumental orientation was a major reason why many of those interviewed had migrated to Luton is not borne out by the survey results: 88 per cent of the Luton workers had never experienced unemployment and from the pattern of replies there was no evidence that previous experience had conditioned them to feelings of job insecurity (see Goldthorpe *et al.*, 1968a: 116–19). The supposed individualism, which according to Grieco had been fostered by the areas from which the majority of those interviewed had migrated, is hard to reconcile with survey findings which established that some 90 per cent of those interviewed were trade union members; 58 per cent had been trade union members on joining their present firm; only 20 per cent claimed to have joined a union because of the existence of a closed shop or other coercive pressures; and the majority of trade union members were extensively involved in workplace union activity (*ibid.*: Ch. 5). The remainder of Grieco's critique relies on inferences from secondary sources on migration which have little bearing on the *Affluent Worker* thesis.

Changes in Social Stratification and Worker Militancy

Goldthorpe returned to the theme of long-run changes in social stratification and their implications for worker attitudes in his paper on the sociology of inflation

(Goldthorpe, 1978) and in later work on the political economy of capitalist nations (Goldthorpe, 1984b, 1987b). The most detailed treatment of his more recent ideas on this theme is found in the paper on inflation. Here he argued that the inflationary pressures experienced by Western capitalist nations during the 1960s and 1970s reflected a situation in which conflict between social groups and strata had become more intense and more equally matched as a result of three major lines of change in social stratification. According to Goldthorpe, the class inequalities of capitalist societies had in the past derived legitimation from 'interactional status orders' which had developed in 'pre-capitalist' social milieux. Interactional status orders had normatively constrained worker expectations by institutionalizing notions of social inferiority among the working class. Status orders of this kind had been subject to long-run decay as the local communities in which they had originated were eroded by urbanization and increased geographical mobility. The decay of status had also been accelerated by the 'commercialization' of social relations in general (Goldthorpe, 1978: 197–200). As status decayed, groups of workers began to press claims for better pay and conditions closer to the limits of the actual power at their disposal. This development had contributed to the increased trade union militancy associated with inflation:

> what the mass of wage- and salary-earners have learnt from capitalism is not acquisitiveness *per se*—which they probably never lacked—but, of far greater consequence, the practice of exploiting one's market position to the full. This includes, of course, maximizing the gains to be had from any 'strategic' advantage that may present itself; and, more importantly still, using the power of organization to improve a weak position or to reinforce and maintain a strong one. (*ibid*: 200–1)

A second important sociological change that had led to increased 'worker pushfulness' was the realization of working-class 'citizenship rights' in the political and industrial spheres of advanced societies. The development of citizenship enhanced worker power, threatened to weaken further the acceptability of market inequalities and made it more difficult for governments to pursue standard deflationary policies. Finally, Goldthorpe pointed to the emergence of 'mature' working classes as an 'objective' sociological change which bolstered the subjective redefinitions of social reality reflected in the decay of status orders and the realization of citizenship. A mature working class—whose closest empirical approximation was to be found in the British working class—was defined as a class that is demographically homogeneous, or composed of members from urban social backgrounds and patterns of life experience, and socio-politically reliant on trade unions and the labour movement to defend and improve working conditions and standards of living (*ibid*.: 204–8). In line with this analytical scheme Goldthorpe interpreted inflation as an expression of more intense and more equal 'distributional conflict' in modern societies.

These ideas have proved to be more controversial than the *Affluent Worker* thesis. Sociological critiques of Goldthorpe's theory have been advanced by Eric Batstone (1984) and by Marshall, Vogler *et al.* (1987) (see also the debate between Goldthorpe and Smith: Smith, 1982, 1985; Goldthorpe, 1983c). Batstone (1984: 317, 320–2) criticized Goldthorpe first of all for not advancing a complete theory of inflation which took account of the role of economic and institutional factors and was capable of explaining the precise timing of inflation and differences in the inflation rates of different nations (see also Smith, 1982). This is fair enough, except that Goldthorpe indicated that his paper was exploratory and concerned above all to treat the 'residual categories' of economists' theories of inflation in a sociologically informed manner (Goldthorpe, 1978: 197, 213n7). Sceptical of the priority accorded to citizenship by trade unions, Batstone noted that citizenship rights had been under attack since 1979 by British Conservative governments and, relatedly, that standard deflationary policies had been pursued without provoking a concerted response from the working class. In part, the working-class reaction had been muted because aspects of 'industrial citizenship'—such as redundancy legislation, along with welfare state provisions, more generally—had cushioned the impact of state action. At the same time, Batsone noted, the very sectionalism promoted by inflation had further reduced the capacity of the working class to adopt a concerted response to reversals in citizenship rights.

It is hard to dispute Batstone's criticisms of the sociological significance of citizenship for worker militancy in the light of the Conservatives' further victory in the 1987 general election, the reversals in citizenship and curbs on trade union power imposed in recent years and the growing division which has arisen in the TUC as unions have tried to respond to the effects of prolonged recession and political hostility. Batstone's criticisms of the other two strands of Goldthorpe's theory point to conceptual problems. Citing Lockwood's well known paper on working-class images of society, Batstone argued that far from being exclusively pre-capitalist in origin, interactional status systems could be created by industrialization and were found in traditional working-class communities. Morever, traditional working-class groups, he observed, had been at the forefront of wage demands that had resulted in inflationary pressure (*ibid.*: 317–18). It seems clear, however, that interactional status, in the sense understood by Goldthorpe, is inconsistent with the features of traditional working-class communities identified in the research literature. The research paper cited by Goldthorpe in defining interactional status had concluded that social status of this kind had not been evident in urban working-class areas of Britain (see Plowman *et al.*, 1962: esp. 177–86). Lockwood's paper, on the other hand, is not entirely consistent, but on balance appears to support Goldthorpe.[3]

When this confusion is removed, another more serious problem comes to light. If the demands of traditional working-class groups had not been constrained by interactional status structures, it becomes difficult to see how the decay of status could have had anything more than a quite peripheral impact on the build up of inflationary pressure during the post-war period. For it has to be recognized, as Batstone suggested, that the militancy of traditional working-class groups was central to the wages and prices 'explosion'. So too, it might be added, was increased assertiveness among many occupational groups, manual and non-manual. As such, the plausibility of Goldthorpe's hypothesis would seem to depend on whether developments in social status can be related to changes in the attitudes and expectations of a wide spectrum of occupational groups. It is clear that Goldthorpe believed that the idea of status decay had much wider relevance than might appear from the conceptual range suggested by the works cited in defining the concept. The decay of status might, he suggested, explain why the pay claims of different groups of workers had expanded and why groups of workers seemed to have begun 'punching their weight'; it might also explain increased unionization and militancy among white-collar workers (*ibid.*: 196, 200 and 213n10; see also Goldthorpe and Bevan, 1977: 319).

It can be argued that these and other developments become intelligible in terms of the status decay hypothesis when it is related conceptually to three issues which have received considerable attention in the literature on industrial relations and industrial sociology. The issues are, first, the role of 'fairness' in wage bargaining and union policy; second, the influence of managerial 'prerogative' on effort bargaining; and, third, the attitudes of various occupational groups, in particular white-collar groups, to the 'propriety' of exercising their collective power through the full range of industrial sanctions that might be available to them (for a detailed theoretical discussion of these issues and their bearing on the idea of social status, see Roche, 1987: Chs 1–4).

The issue of fairness in pay bargaining is related to social status—though not necessarily to 'interactional social status'—in a rather obvious sense. What comes to be regarded by workers as a fair rate of pay, a fair pay increase, or a fair relativity may depend on their attitudes and expectations regarding the levels of pay and pay differentials thought to be appropriate to different occupations and categories of employees. Similarly, groups of workers may defer to management authority and the exercise of managerial 'prerogative' out of respect for managers' general social status, or, relatedly, out of deference to their 'right' to manage.

Looked at in this way, the decay of status might be evident in such things as more 'fluid' or strategic uses of 'fair comparisons' by unions. It might also be reflected in the erosion of managerial prerogative and, relatedly, in the emergence of worker and union practices in which 'effort bargaining' becomes more instrumental, or more concerned with selling effort 'at the margin' in return for discrete cash awards. Little empirical work has been addressed to the question of whether such trends have been apparent in the long-run development of collective bargaining among different groups of workers in Britain. Indeed, remarkably few studies have been conducted in Britain on the evolution of wage policy in different unions. On the other hand, indications of strategic positioning in wage rounds can be found, the tactical or instrumental use of comparisons—as occurs, for example, in 'pattern bargaining'—is not unknown, and there is no shortage of commentary on endemic 'leapfrogging' (see Knowles and Robinson, 1964: Eliott, 1976; *The Times*, 25 February 1977; Thomson and Beaumont, 1978; Eliott and Fallick, 1981). That the Goldthorpe hypothesis has a good deal of plausibility is also clear from various reviews of the causes and consequences of inflation (see, for example, Phelps Brown, 1973, 1975, 1983: Ch. 9; but cf. also Jones, 1973; Brittan and Lilley, 1977; Meade, 1982; Noble, 1985). The idea of status decay is also consistent with Batstone's review of evidence on the operation of productivity bargaining and other strategies of industrial relations reform in Britain, as Batstone himself recognized (see Batstone, 1984: esp. Ch. 4). My own study of the changing policies of unions organizing electricity generating station workers in the Irish Republic (Roche, 1987) also provided empirical support for the status decay hypothesis.

If little is directly known about how change in social status may have affected the bargaining objectives and strategies of unions, more is known about the attitudes of white-collar unions to the use of sanctions in industrial relations. It is well established that at least some groups of white-collar workers traditionally looked on militant collectivism, and even unionization itself, as normatively inconsistent with middle-class social status. In this way views regarding 'occupational propriety', as it were, rooted in the system of social status, acted as a constraint on the methods they were prepared to countenance in pursuing their interests in the labour market (cf. Bain, 1970: 48–9).[4] The progressive breakdown of such normative constraints, the emergence of more 'unionate' forms of collective action, and the growing militancy and assertiveness of sections of the white-collar workforce are major themes in the sociological literature on white-collar trade unionism (see esp. Wright Mills, 1953; Lockwood, 1958; Prandy, 1965; Blackburn, 1967; Blain, 1972; Roberts *et al.*, 1972; Kelly, 1980).

In the paper on the sociology of inflation Goldthorpe suggested that the decay of status was only one aspect of a more general process of decay in the 'moral legacy' derived by capitalism from pre-capitalist social relations (1978: 199). This suggestion accords with a large literature on developments in post-war economies. It has long been recognized that the 'effective' exercise of management depends on employees being prepared to accept normative rules and conventions which, though not themselves part of the employment contract, nonetheless constitute important 'non-contractual elements' of contract (cf. Baldamus, 1961; Bendix, 1963; Storey, 1983: Ch. 6). It has also been recognized that these aspects of social integration in economic relations may themselves be subject to 'social erosion' (cf., for example, Kristol, 1971; Fox, 1974; Hirsch, 1977). Insofar as social values and attributes like trust, cooperativeness, flexibility, enthusiasm, loyalty and consistency remain non-contractual elements of individual contracts and collective agreements, buttressed by general social norms, employees may be satisfied to concede them to managements in an important sense as 'free goods'. As a result of what Goldthorpe (1978: 199) described as the spread into an ever-enlarged area of social life of 'market relations and the principle of "equal exchange"', such social values can acquire 'price tags' and become part of the 'cash nexus'. Such a trend was outlined in the case of British industrial relations by Batstone (1984: Ch. 4), who saw it, indeed, as an aspect of the decay of status which resulted from the institutionalization of union representation at workplace level and the professionalization of management. This more general 'social erosion' thesis, as we term it, has been applied by social scientists of widely varying traditions to interpret long-run change in economic and labour market behaviour in Western capitalist societies (cf., for example, Brittan, 1973, 1975; Bell, 1976; Habermas, 1971, 1976; Hayek, 1976).

The idea that increased distributional conflict in labour markets is symptomatic of the intensified individualism, sectionalism and privatism resulting from the erosion of capitalism's 'moral order' has been disputed in virtually all its strands by Marshall, Vogler *et al.* (1987).[5] However, as an attempt to refute the social erosion thesis, at least as it might be applied to developments in the United Kingdom, their argument is open to serious criticism. First, their treatment of what they referred to as the 'developing consensus' among social scientists that moral erosion had occurred badly distorts the works in question. The article claims that these works locate the major point of change in worker attitudes and values in the economic recession of the second half of the 1970s and the 1980s (*ibid.*: 55). This is not the case. Most of the works cited by Marshall *et al.* are similar to Goldthorpe's paper in pointing quite clearly to a process of long-run change, and many were written before the advent of the recession. In adducing data from post-war British research (*ibid.*: 57–8, 66–8) to argue that 'neither proletarian sectionalism nor pecuniary privatism' were 'recent inventions of economic recession', Marshall *et al.* were thus knocking down a straw man. Nor is it the case that the works in question treated sectionalism and privatism as the 'obverse of class consciousness' (*ibid.*: 62). Most of the works cited, for example, those of Hirsch, Bell, Habermas, Brittan and Hayek, were not in any sense concerned with the question of class consciousness. Goldthorpe, on the other hand, who might be said to have been concerned with this issue, clearly made no such simplistic assumption.

Marshall, Vogler *et al.*'s attempt to demonstrate empirically that sectionalism and privatism could be found in early British capitalism is also open to serious objection. The evidence presented consists of a case study of the 'aristocracy of labour' in mid-nineteenth century Britain. However, their reliance on this case study as empirical refutation of the social erosion thesis is open to a number of objections. First, and most obviously, the group in question was a small—if, in a number of respects, very significant—section of the working class, whereas the social erosion thesis is explicitly concerned with how acquisitiveness and its concomitants had become both more *intense* and more *widely prevalent* among the working class. Second, as will be clear from the quotation from Goldthorpe's paper presented earlier, a social erosion thesis need not presume that the working class lacked 'acquisitiveness' at some early stage. Of much greater importance is the question of whether groups of workers were prepared to pursue their labour market interests in a normatively unrestrained fashion, unencumbered by socially prevailing views of their 'due', or by any concern to avoid being seen to be violating norms of 'proper' conduct. Such a sociological distinction between 'acquisitiveness' and similar motives and the rational pursuit of economic objectives has been developed most famously by Max Weber (1923) and is fundamental to Goldthorpe's argument. Marshall, Vogler *et al.*'s historical material fails to address this issue and, what is more, the case of the labour aristocracy in the mid-nineteenth century could just as reasonably be interpreted as supporting Goldthorpe's version of the social erosion thesis. One of the features of the labour aristocracy which has received particular emphasis in historical research was their apparent concern to uphold some variant of prevailing standards of lower-middle-class Victorian morality. This may in part have been due to the involvement of labour aristocrats in social intercourse with lower-middle-class groups (cf. Hobsbawm, 1964). It appears that the material aspirations of groups of labour aristocrats were in important respects morally circumscribed by social norms arising from their sense of 'place' in the social hierarchy. In this sense historical research gives grounds at least for reasonable doubt that craft unions and their members felt at liberty to 'punch their weight' to the full as a matter of routine practice.[6]

In relation to the arguments in Goldthorpe's paper it can be suggested that the idea that gives rise to the greatest difficulty is one that has received least attention from his critics: that is, the idea of working-class maturity. In the first instance the problem is a conceptual one. In *The Affluent Worker* it was argued that the breakdown of 'traditional' working-class communities fostered growing instrumentalism and 'greater aggressiveness in the field of cash-based bargaining' by releasing worker expectations from local bounds and by dispelling fatalism (Goldthorpe, 1968a: 176–7). In the paper on inflation Goldthorpe suggested that the emergence of 'mature' working-class communities reinforced other sociological trends leading to greater worker militancy and union 'aggressiveness'. The distinction between the 'traditional' working class of *The Affluent Worker* and the 'mature' working class of Goldthorpe's later paper is unclear. Batstone's critique (1984: 319) treats them as one and the same thing, and there are grounds for this in Goldthorpe's discussion. In defining working-class maturity, Goldthorpe suggests that the British working class had attained 'demographic' maturity by the mid-twentieth century at least. The vast majority of the industrial workforce were by then second-generation urban dwellers who had lived their lives within 'working-class and neighbourhood cultures' (1978: 205–6). In terms of its undisturbed experience of 'citizenship rights' and reliance on trade unions, the British working class had also, for some time past, attained 'socio-political' maturity (*ibid.*: 206–7).

In both how it is defined and where it is located in time, the mature working class seems very similar to the 'traditional working class' portrayed in Goldthorpe's earlier works. Three problems then emerge. First, it had been suggested in earlier writings by Goldthorpe that such features of traditional working-class communities as localism, fatalism and traditionalism had served to contain worker expectations. Second, it had also been been pointed out that working-class communities with these characteristics were breaking down in the wake of social and demographic change. But if this was the case, growing working-class assertiveness and union militancy during the long boom of post-war British capitalism was associated—at least in point of time—with the disappearance rather than the maturation of communities of the kind sketched by Goldthorpe in the paper on inflation. Third, it seems more plausible theoretically to argue, as Goldthorpe had done in *The Affluent Worker*, that the emergence of new—one could even say 'second-generation'—forms of working-class communities, characterized by privatized social relations and more 'cosmopolitan' social outlooks and expectations, had fostered increased working-class assertiveness and wage militancy (see Lockwood, 1966: 366–72). Such communities could still be regarded as 'mature' insofar as they comprised second-generation urban dwellers and a 'self-recruited' working class. On the other hand, as Goldthorpe *et al.* had shown in *The Affluent Worker*, the neighbourhood and family cultures found in communities of the kind represented by Luton, along with the socio-political orientations of their members, are different from those which characterized the 'traditional' working-class.

While representing a major contribution, then, the ideas on the social roots of worker militancy advanced in Goldthorpe's paper on the sociology of inflation pose several serious conceptual problems. In its exploration of (decaying) non-rational constraints on working-class assertiveness, this paper adds to the theory advanced in *The Affluent Worker*. Depending on how the concept of working-class maturity is interpreted, however, the paper might be regarded as inconsistent in important respects with Goldthorpe's earlier ideas.

SOCIAL INEQUALITY AND SOCIAL INTEGRATION IN INDUSTRIAL RELATIONS

Thus far we have considered Goldthorpe's ideas on the effects of long-run changes in social stratification on worker attitudes and industrial relations. In two highly influential papers Goldthorpe turned his attention to the implications of social inequality for social integration in industrial relations and for attempts to reform British industrial relations through institutional reconstruction. Both papers challenged the dominant theoretical tradition in British industrial relations during the 1960s and 1970s: the so-called 'Oxford school'. In the first of these papers Goldthorpe (1974a) argued that prevailing patterns of social inequality in Britain were associated with the state of 'anomie' prevailing in industrial relations, particularly in the field of wage bargaining. Goldthorpe defined 'anomie' in the Durkheimian sense as a situation in which there was a lack of moral regulation over the wants and goals held by individuals (*ibid*.: 222). By definition, anomie is the antithesis of social integration, understood as consensus among individuals and groups on the normative standards which ought to guide behaviour. The idea of anomie had earlier been used by two influential Oxford school figures, Alan Fox and Allan Flanders, to interpret the breakdown of 'orderly' collective bargaining in Britain over the post-war period (cf. Fox and Flanders, 1970). Goldthorpe argued that Fox and Flanders's analysis failed to follow Durkheim in relating the problem of anomie to inequality. However anomie may have arisen, Goldthorpe argued that the facts of inequality render it very difficult to introduce 'order' into industrial relations. Anomie in British industrial relations, it was argued, would prove intractable because the structure of economic inequality was perceived by wage-earners as having 'no rationale whatsoever' (Goldthorpe, 1974a: 224). Observing that incomes policy was usually regarded by reformists as a means of introducing order into pay determination, Goldthorpe pointed to a serious problem it must inevitably confront:

> An industrial worker seeking a wage increase might be prepared to recognise that his claim was weak in comparison with that of, say, certain of his low-paid workmates; but he would have no difficulty in finding other groups, possibly outside the working class, in relation to whom his claim could be justified—even assuming that his range of reference groups was not extensive. (*ibid*.: 224)

Groups of workers would have no difficulty making a case for special treatment, or finding a reason to justify evading pay norms, precisely because the existing order of pay differentials was 'unprincipled' or riddled with anomalies. This was because the inequalities thrown up by the market had no rationale and were incapable of being morally justified in any coherent and consistent way (see also Goldthorpe, 1978: 198). But Goldthorpe went further and suggested that because the administration of incomes policies necessarily involved the investigation of existing pay inequalities and pronouncements on whether they were deemed to be 'fair', such policies could intensify anomie by making more transparent the anomalous nature of prevailing patterns of pay. Such an outcome was even more likely because there appeared to be no consensus on the principles which *ought* to govern pay inequality (*ibid*.: 226–9). This argument was supported by a review of research and commentaries on the British experience of implementing and administering incomes policies.

In the second paper (Goldthorpe, 1974b) a similar line of argument was advanced to question the viability of the industrial relations reform proposals put forward in the late 1960s by the Donovan Commission, in which members of the Oxford school had been extensively involved. Here Goldthorpe was also concerned with unearthing the *ex parte* features of the 'liberal pluralist' reform proposals championed by the Oxford school. The liberal pluralist position, which advocated rationalizing industrial relations institutions, sought to represent itself as an essentially technocratic problem-solving approach to a state of disorder experienced by unions, management and employees alike. In a critique of the liberal pluralist analysis of industrial relations disorder in Britain, Goldthorpe attempted to show that liberal pluralist reform proposals amounted to an essentially managerialist strategy, geared to increasing management control of industrial relations by fostering institutions and procedures which would give employees and their unions, at best, power to contest management decisions at the margin (*ibid.*: 427–38). The pluralist suggestion that disorder had arisen due to a loss of management authority in industrial relations was challenged by Goldthorpe on conceptual grounds. The legal authority of management, he argued, had not changed; what had changed was the *de facto* power available to management to control employees. This had declined as a result of the growth of bargaining awareness and confidence on the part of workers over the post-war period. Change in worker attitudes could in turn be linked to the emergence of tighter labour markets in a period of full employment and the erosion of the 'symbolic power' that had been derived by managers from their superior social prestige (*ibid.*: 427–30).

Using research data available to the Donovan Commission, Goldthorpe argued that two major 'problems' or symptoms of 'disorder' identified by the pluralists, namely, systematic overtime working and the decay of payment-by-results systems, were not regarded as problems by employees themselves. On the contrary, both features of British industrial relations resulted from an attempt by employees to improve the 'money for effort bargain' which they made with their employers (*ibid.*: 432–8). Donovan and post-Donovan reforms also appeared from research evidence reviewed by Goldthorpe to have been considerably less effective than anticipated. The major weakness in the liberal pluralist analysis, Goldthorpe again contended, was its failure to inquire into the 'social relationships and modes of action' which put strain on industrial relations institutions and which created and expressed social conflict (*ibid.*: 449). Any such line of inquiry would inevitably lead to a consideration of class inequality and its effect on shaping employees' interests and their attitudes to the labour market and to systems of industrial control. The 'problems' which had exercised the Donovan reformers would then be seen as an outcome of industrial relations with little normative basis which compelled employees to exploit their position as best they could.

The track record of incomes policy and reform measures in Britain in the period since these papers were published seems to confirm Goldthorpe's thesis regarding the 'pre-institutional' roots of industrial relations disorder. Batstone's (1984) study of two decades of workplace industrial relations in Britain concluded that post-Donovan reforms had, in effect, 'backfired' and compounded the problems faced by British managers in controlling industrial relations. The social contract of 1974–9 proved as unsuccessful as previous exercises in incomes policy and appeared, moreover, to have crumbled in much the same way as earlier initiatives and for the same reasons (cf. Boston, 1983). Surprisingly, Goldthorpe's critique has not been countered by academics in the liberal pluralist tradition. The main criticism of Goldthorpe's ideas on industrial relations disorder has come from a sociologist, Ian Maitland, in a comparative study of industrial relations in a British and a West German factory (Maitland, 1983). Maitland's observations in this study of the effects on workplace industrial relations of the contrasting union and employer organizations and institutional frameworks of Britain and Germany are unexceptionable. What has to be questioned is whether Maitland's research represents an adequate test of the Goldthorpe thesis.

Maitland rejects the argument that the roots of disorder in industrial relations are to be found in the structure of inequality. His critique is focused at several levels. The study begins by dismissing the argument on the basis of macro-level data on inequality in each country. 'On a variety of indices', he suggests, Britain appears to be among the most egalitarian of advanced industrial societies. Thus, following the logic of Goldthorpe's analysis, British industrial relations should be least prone to disorder (*ibid.*: 4). Comparing Britain and West Germany, he argues that in spite of the higher level of social inequality in Germany, that society's industrial relations are considerably more 'orderly' than Britain's. This claim is open to question. As is well known, international comparisons of levels of inequality are highly problematic. The study cited in support of his argument by Maitland points to a more complex pattern of inequality than suggested by his conclusions (cf. Roberti, 1978). A comparative study of pay differentials in Western Europe by Saunders and Marsden (1981), on the other hand, concluded that West Germany was the most egalitarian of the six nations studied, while Britain was among the most inegalitarian. Shifting to a conceptual line of attack, Maitland (1983: 4) cites a number of surveys to show that, contrary to what Goldthorpe had suggested, comparative reference groups had not widened in Britain during the period of deepening 'disorder'. This is an egregious misinterpretation of Goldthorpe's argument. Goldthorpe had clearly indicated (1974a: 224, 236n15; 1978: 200, 213n10) that no such trend was implied by his argument.[7]

The two case studies of workplace industrial relations that make up Maitland's micro-level critique of Goldthorpe serve his purpose little better. It is not clear how a hypothesis suggesting that the legitimacy of social inequality had weakened over a long period—in Britain at any rate—can be tested empirically on the basis of Maitland's four weeks of participant observation in a factory. Nevertheless, Maitland's research data on the proximate role of such 'external factors' as productivity bargaining, incomes policy and inflation in bringing about the 'demoralization' of the pay system in his British factory could reasonably be interpreted as providing support for the Goldthorpe thesis (*ibid.*: 83–6; and cf. Batstone, 1984, who presented such an interpretation of similar developments in workplace industrial relations). If, on the other hand, the main intention was to show that attitudes to inequality had no relationship to order or disorder in the factories during the period covered by the fieldwork, Maitland's research design was seriously and rather obviously flawed in failing to introduce any systematic data on worker attitudes to pay differentials inside the British and West German factories, or to the wider structure of inequality prevailing in each country. What Maitland succeeds in presenting is a plausible argument on how different institutional frameworks may countervail or intensify essentially pre-institutional social and economic pressures. As a test of the Goldthorpe thesis, the merits of the study are few.

CONCLUSION

John Goldthorpe's ideas on the influence of social class on worker attitudes and industrial relations are a major contribution to scholarship and debate in this field. Indeed, Goldthorpe can be said to have focused much of the scholarship and debate in British industrial relations and industrial sociology over more than two decades. The long-run trends in social stratification which he identified in *The Affluent Worker* are still regarded as the major influences on change in worker attitudes and behaviour. His arguments on the decay of status and on the more proximate sources of strain on British industrial relations institutions have yet to be refuted; and no convincing alternative line of argument has emerged. On the whole then, Goldthorpe's thought stands up very well to critical scrutiny in a discipline where theories —particularly when they address major questions of social and political concern—are not noted for their longevity.

NOTES

1   At least some of the arguments presented in this paper, however, contradict those outlined in a subsequent paper by the same authors (Marshall, Vogler *et al.*, 1987) which will be examined below.
2   A similar criticism was advanced by Mackenzie (1974: 246–7), who again ignored this important theoretical argument.
3   Drawing on Plowman *et al.*'s paper, Lockwood (1966: 369) introduced the idea of interactional status when discussing the outlook and social milieu of 'traditional deferential' workers (*ibid.*: 364), though in a schematic summary of his argument he appeared to suggest that 'traditional-proletarian' communities *were* also characterized by interactional status (*ibid.*: 369). Such a suggestion sits uneasily with Lockwood's comments on both interactional status and working-class communities. Interactional status, he pointed out, occurred when people from middle-class and working-class backgrounds engaged in day-to-day and face-to-face relations of deference and derogation. As such, interactional status orders tended to form in small towns and rural areas, characterized by social heterogeneity and a high level of regular social contact—in work and leisure—between people from different class backgrounds (*ibid.*: 364). Traditional working-class communities, in contrast, were portrayed by Lockwood as socially homogeneous and geographically isolated from middle-class society (*ibid.*: 361; see also Goldthorpe and Bevan, 1977: 301).
4   Bain quotes David Lockwood's caution against regarding variations in attitudes to social status as the sole determinant of white-collar unionization. However, the fact that, as Bain puts it, 'there is no general correlation between social status and the extent of trade unionism' (*ibid.*: 50) does nothing to invalidate the suggestion of many researchers on white-collar trade unionism, Lockwood included, that attitudes to social status have been among the factors influencing white-collar unionization and the policies of white-collar unions.
5   Surprisingly, there was little discussion of Goldthorpe's argument in Marshall, Vogler *et al.*'s paper. Aside from presenting one of the most sociologically sophisticated treatments of the question in which they are interested, Goldthorpe's paper is not open to a number of the criticisms they have levelled at other works. It was also addressed, like their argument, to the British experience and clearly influenced the terminology they used in their paper.
6   This should not be taken as proposing that craft unions were wedded to 'industrial pacifism'. Any such claim would be invalid. Of particular interest in this regard, however, and possibly of some significance, are indications that craft unions were ideologically or normatively ambivalent on the question of militancy (cf. the review of historical research presented in Grey, 1981: Chs 5–6).
7   Maitland (*ibid.*: 126n2) claims to be unable to follow Goldthorpe's reasoning here but, rather disingenuously, still interprets his comments in precisely the sense Goldthorpe had been careful to dismiss.

13. Class and Industrial Relations: Sociological Bricks without Institutional Straw

WILLIAM BROWN

The events of the 1980s cast a harsh critical light on earlier analyses of British labour relations. High unemployment and official hostility to collective bargaining have caused an upheaval which mocks much that was written in the 1970s. From the tumult of those years, when Edward Heath and James Callaghan both had their governments broken by industrial unrest, the achievement of an eerie calm in the late 1980s would have seemed inconceivable. In any comments on John Goldthorpe's analysis it is difficult to separate criticism that might be fair in the light of the facts then available from an arid carping informed only by the privilege of hindsight.

However they may appear in retrospect, there is no doubt that Goldthorpe's two major contributions to industrial relations were widely considered to be important at the time as seminal statements of opposition to dominant orthodoxies. Both are still to be found in academic reading lists from which many of the publications they criticize have long been dumped. The first contribution, 'Industrial Relations in Great Britain: A Critique of Reformism' (henceforth referred to here as the 'Critique'), was first published in *Politics and Society* in 1974 (Goldthorpe, 1974b), but later reprinted for a much larger audience (Clarke and Clements, 1977). The second, 'The Current Inflation: Towards a Sociological Account', was presented at a conference in 1977 and published in *The Political Economy of Inflation* (Hirsch and Goldthorpe, 1978: 186–214).

Although there are many British sociologists interested in economic issues, and probably even more engaged in industrial relations research, they generally fall into one of two traps. Some fail to approach their analysis primarily as sociologists, abandoning the full analytic strength of their discipline and opting merely to add sociological footnotes and insights to what are essentially asociological ways of thinking. Others apply their sociology to crude misunderstandings of the intentions of the other subject. Goldthorpe avoids these pitfalls with distinction, his work revealing a scholarly care in reading deeply and sympathetically into the literature he criticizes. Indeed, a central strength of both these papers is that he succeeds in identifying what it is that is distinctive, and hence what he wishes to take issue with, about the methodologies of mainstream economists and industrial relations analysts.

How successful are the results? That they are important analyses which enrich the subjects they tackle need hardly be said. If this reviewer is only willing to give them two cheers, it is primarily because neither attempt comes fully to terms with the political character of the employment relationship, of payment, and of the process of collective bargaining through which they are generally managed. Although more peripheral themes could be pursued, it is this neglect of what are often called institutional features with which the argument will be concerned, commencing with Goldthorpe's 'Critique'.

THE CRITIQUE OF LIBERAL-PLURALISM

The 'Critique' was written after it had become clear that Edward Heath's *Industrial Relations Act* of 1971 had not only failed, but had also become an embarrassing obstacle to trade union cooperation in incomes policy. It was written, presumably, before the shaking of the international post-war order by the first oil price rise in 1973 and also before the constitutional challenge posed by the destruction of Heath's Government by the miners' strike of 1973–74.

Credit should be given, therefore, for the perceptiveness of the 'Critique's' recognition of the realism of what he called the 'Tory' approach to reform, one that aimed directly at undermining trade union power. Academics and politicians of all complexions were to go on believing that to be a pipe-dream, until Margaret Thatcher embarked on her electorally triumphant 'step-by-step' progress of labour legislation. Even then it has been some years before the full debilitating significance of narrowed trade union 'immunities' has become clear. When Goldthorpe was writing this paper, there was a century of history that appeared to suggest that no British government would consider it practical, even if desirable, to encourage employers to spurn collective bargaining altogether, as opposed to making its conduct more orderly.

With the 'Tory' approach in apparently eternal eclipse, the 'Critique' concentrates its attention on what it calls the 'liberal-pluralists', the most influential of whom were, or had been, at Goldthorpe's own Nuffield College: Allan Flanders, Hugh Clegg and Bill McCarthy. Many of the inadequacies of their analysis are seen to stem from the tendency of their approach to be fundamentally too 'problem'-oriented. It is not a new criticism and it perhaps reveals undue expectations of the subject.

An essential feature of the academic study of industrial relations and one of its major strengths is precisely that it is concerned with problems. It is not a discipline, in the sense of a distinct set of methodologies linked to a coherent conceptual structure, but rather a field of study, centred upon the employment relationship, to which many disciplines contribute. There is no shortage of its exponents who call for their subject to have more theory (it is one of the most familiar cries throughout the social sciences), but their attempts in that direction rarely endure. Like Antaeus, what strength the subject has comes from its contact with the ground, the constantly changing world of employment. Its development has not been shaped by internal theoretical questions so much as by externally defined 'problems'.

It would be dreadful if all social sciences were like that. But, on the other hand, their grip on the employment relationship would be weaker if they did not have data and understandings that have been, as it were, pre-digested by industrial relations specialists. There are some aspects of society that are so complex that 'problem-solving' makes a fruitful heuristic. It should not be disparaged, so long as it is seen as the start, and not the end, of the effort of understanding.

The 'Critique's' argument, at risk of oversimplifying, is that this problem-solving approach, being detached from any broader conception of society, uncritically adopts as its starting point a view of the key problems of British industrial relations that is essentially managerial. The central problems of the 1960s were accepted by the liberal-pluralists as unofficial strikes, inefficient working practices and wage drift. These were seen by them, and by the 1968 Royal Commission on Trade Unions and Employers' Associations chaired by Lord Donovan, which they successfully hijacked, as symptoms of what Goldthorpe describes as 'institutional lag'.

Their diagnosis was that formal authority to bargain had been denied to the organizational levels at which bargaining was in fact taking place. If this were to be rectified, there would have to be procedural reform which fully accepted the impotence of many long-established industry-wide (multi-employer) agreements, and which transferred their legitimacy to factory or company (single-employer) negotiations. Strikes and labour inefficiency were no more than symptoms of the underlying institutional inadequacy.

This view, the 'Critique' argues, is naïve. Interests are not common to both sides. Management's problems are not the same as their employees' problems. Well-padded inefficiency, for example, may be a highly valued aspect of an employee's working life. The eradication of the supposedly deplorable symptoms does involve a potential clash of interests. Consequently, it cannot be achieved simply by shifting the locus of authority to become more congruent with the locus of power and allowing rational discussion to do the rest. The problem arises precisely because power and influence have shifted, with the consequence that a different, non-managerial set of priorities has been imposed.

The liberal-pluralists should come clean, the argument goes, and admit that they want to shift power back towards management. But if they did so, they would have to face up to the fact that they cannot presume that employers will be able to win the willing cooperation of employees in reform, nor to educate them successfully into greater 'responsibility' or 'enlightened' self-interest. Whether or not one agrees with the liberal-pluralists' covert managerial values, their reform proposals are starry-eyed, misguided and doomed to failure.

A DEFENCE OF LIBERAL-PLURALISM

There are several grounds for finding Goldthorpe's 'Critique' unpersuasive. As a preliminary it is worth noting the common misperception of the pluralist position in industrial relations writing. Although debated in many shapes and forms, the way those who are characterized as pluralists apply it in their policy prescriptions is essentially as a rather weak theory of the manner in which power is exercised in society. It is a relativistic, fluid view. It has none of the certainties offered by, on the one hand, the self-righteousness of managerial unitarism, or, on the other, a belief in the practicality of some sort of worker-controlled unitarism. Nor does it espouse any idea of a balance of industrial power. Instead it observes that, as market, technical and organizational circumstances change, so also does the nature of interdependence between employers and employees, and with it their capacity for inflicting mutual damage. To the extent to which one side can and does exploit its temporary advantage, the frontier of control and reward may shift.

Because instability may have generally damaging consequences, both sides usually see advantage in establishing negotiating procedures which, by bestowing at least temporary legitimacy on particular agreements or agents, provide a workable inertia to the relationship. The more effective the negotiators, and the stronger their bargaining relationship, the less likely it is that they will have to embark on costly sanctions to test or demonstrate a shift in relative power. It is usually better in the long run to beat a strategic retreat than to suffer a predictable defeat. The 'Critique's' implication of a sharp contrast between the roles of shop steward and full-time trade union official overlooks these dynamics.

Nor does this pluralist analysis imply that all interests get equal, or indeed any, hearing. Potential interest groups that cannot become sufficiently organized to be either needed or a nuisance are ignored. Consequently, the liberal-pluralist view is not, as the 'Critique' implies, that a willing consensus is a necessary prerequisite for industrial change, and that nothing can be achieved without employee cooperation. It is merely that, to the extent that it can be achieved, the change is less costly for both sides.

A recurring point of the 'Critique' is that the liberal-pluralists ignore, in both their frame of reference and their research, the wishes of the rank-and-file. Attention is drawn to the finding of the Donovan surveys that the existing system of industrial relations was felt by participants at the lower levels to be 'comfortable', and to the fact that institutionalized overtime is often popular. Drawing on the present writer's study of workplace industrial relations in the engineering industry, entitled *Piecework Bargaining* (Brown, 1973), Goldthorpe points out that disorderly piecework systems provide a high level of employee control. He considers it self-evident that their reform may be contrary to the pieceworkers' interests: 'why should it be thought that they too will regard the existing state of affairs as being in evident need of reform?' In his vivid metaphor such reform would make it easier for management to fill in the silences in the employment contract to its own advantage.

Assertions about the wants and aspirations of individuals always raise notorious methodological difficulties with which Goldthorpe will have been more than familiar. But they are difficulties which here fundamentally weaken his argument. For in the context of collective bargaining, the subjective statements of individual workers are so misleading as a guide to their future decisions and actions that it is generally impossible to give them the primacy he would wish. The charge that the liberal-pluralists neglect the interests of the rank-and-file is one which itself neglects the political processes through which the rank-and-file's interests are expressed.

This is a point that is well illustrated by the example of workplace bargaining in disorderly piecework systems. A notable characteristic of such bargaining is the very active role played by shop stewards, pieceworkers themselves, representing the small constituencies in which they work. Goldthorpe is critical of research on the bargaining process (especially that of the present writer) which concentrates on interviews with shop stewards rather than with the rank-and-file they represent. Certainly, shop stewards in these circumstances tend to reveal different concerns from their constituents. They have to if they are to be effective representatives. The individualism of a piecework system creates profound problems for the worker collectivity, being prone to constantly disturbed pay differentials which divide and weaken the workforce. Individual shop stewards are generally less concerned to exploit the anomalies than to uphold some degree of unity. This tendency is amplified through workplace shop steward organizations. Some of the most effective of these have used extreme measures such as strike-breaking and fining in their efforts to prevent individual worker opportunism weakening their strategic influence.

This argument is best supported by the outstanding study, *Shop Stewards in Action*, by Eric Batstone and his colleagues (Batstone, Boraston and Frenkel, 1977). Using data from hundreds of rank-and-file workers as well as stewards themselves, they demonstrated clearly that the 'populist' stewards who attempted passively to reflect the wishes of their members tended to achieve relatively little for them. It was the more strategic, calculative, 'leader' stewards who obtained more successful results and who were also more likely to be re-elected. They did so by working together, cultivating links with management and, paradoxically, by tending to distance themselves more from their constituents than the 'populists'. Batstone's work did not please those sociologists who had exalted the class purity of the shop steward in the 1970s, but his analysis has survived far better in the 1980s. Rather than gauge the wants of workers on the basis of optimistic expressions of opinion, is it not more useful to rely on the outcome of a political process, especially of one as responsive as that of a pre-1980s shop steward body? Is it not more informative to see how elected representatives seek to negotiate order and shape opinion?

There is a further point to be made in defence of the liberal-pluralist analysis. It is nothing short of patronizing to suggest that employees are uncritical of managerial incompetence, even if they may exploit it. Successive waves of plant closures have underlined the economic naïvety of the view that workers' interests are best served by short-term managerial indulgency. Thus, if the problems of British industrial relations that were identified by liberal-pluralists were also seen as problems by perceptive managers, it is in large part because they were concerned with economic survival. They were similarly identified at the time by all but the most purblind of trade union activists. People who take advantage of a state of disorder which they are in no position to rectify should not be assumed to be in favour of it, especially when it is widely perceived to be a fatal malaise. Long after the silencing of so many shipyards, engineering works, steel mills and printing houses where a shop-floor union organization was once strong, an enduring research memory of this writer is that at the time their shop stewards had not been complacent, but bitterly outspoken, about what they readily perceived as management weakness.

In retrospect it is evident that the liberal-pluralist analysis was rather better than its policy prescription, at least as it was expressed by the Donovan Commission. In many ways it was a surprising analysis. At the time it was bold and controversial for the Commissioners to argue that the problem of 'institutional lag' should be resolved by the abandoning of those national multi-employer bargaining arrangements which appeared to be becoming ineffective. It was equally contentious to argue that the then supposedly notorious role played by shop stewards could be tamed by enhancing their procedural status. But how right the Commissioners were. Two decades later it is only a minority of employers who even partially follow national agreements, and it is the shop stewards who now usually take the lead on the union side in negotiating the single-employer agreements that have displaced them.

The Donovan diagnosis probably had some catalytic effect in this institutional revolution. At the very least some credit should be given to reformers astute enough to point clearly in the direction in which people were already beginning to move. For the next decade the pace of change was to be slow. But far less reasonable forces were to accelerate it into the 1980s: harsher international product market pressures, new powers to inflict penalties on trade unions and, in the public services, a government largely contemptuous of collective bargaining.

To a historian of ideas, this may be where the liberal-pluralists will be seen to have the clearest advantage over the opposing 'radical' school of industrial relations analysis. The Donovan Commission had been unanimous in its robust argument for the defence and extension of collective bargaining, with all its libertarian and redistributive implications. Barely acknowledged at the time, this moral position shines out in retrospect. In the late 1980s defending the role of trade unions has become as suspect in Britain as has describing oneself as a liberal in America. The radical sociological writings of the 1970s have an almost pathetic irrelevance in retrospect. They certainly appealed to many of that decade's students, but they provided little to guide them in the harshness of the 1980s when faced with a divided union movement and with a Tory-voting rank-and-file that is far removed from any sentimental ideal.

THE SOCIOLOGY OF INFLATION

By 1977 the 'current inflation' of Goldthorpe's second work under review here (Goldthorpe, 1978) had been gathering pace for a decade. It was a worldwide inflation, primed by the cost of the Vietnam War in the 1960s, encouraged by the indiscipline of floating exchange rates after 1971 and accelerated by a concerted upswing in the world economy in 1973. Most dramatically, later that year the Yom Kippur War brought OPEC sufficient solidarity to force a massive rise in oil prices. For Britain, it had been a decade of almost incessant government incomes policies, imposed at great electoral cost and with limited success. It had also been a decade in which a growing public sector, which had given the Donovan Commission no cause for disquiet in 1968, had become increasingly strike-prone.

It is important to recall these circumstances before engaging with any general discussion of inflation. Price inflation has many, varied, interactive causes and this rules out simple explanations. The inflation of the 1970s was particularly complex, with some of the extraordinary contributory factors just mentioned. It is important also to recall that by the mid-1980s inflation was to fall substantially in both Britain and the world. When Goldthorpe presented his paper in 1977, the annual inflation rate for the OECD as a whole was 9 per cent and for Britain 16 per cent; ten years later the figures were to be respectively 3 per cent and 4 per cent.

Goldthorpe starts his argument fruitfully with a survey of the degrees of discomfort of different economists' theories of inflation. He identifies the 'residual' factors that they acknowledge to be important but cannot fit in and thus generally condemn as 'irrational'. This is, and should be, anathema to a sociologist. An explanation should not be grounded in 'error, ignorance and unreason on the part of the actors involved', but rather 'in on-going changes in social structures and processes', and it should then go on to show how actions are still intelligible, 'that is to say, express a logic which is adequate from the actor's point of view, in the situation in which he finds himself, and which at the same time is apprehensible by the "outside" observer'. This is a humane and fruitful approach, and it is a sad fact that it has been ignored in so much social science and especially in economics. It recalls the admirable statement of Samuel Taylor Coleridge that 'until you understand a writer's ignorance, presume yourself ignorant of his understanding'.

Goldthorpe's explanation is that the then current inflation was grounded in changes in the form of stratification, in the structures of social advantage and power. Rising inflation had intensified the conflict between social groups, made them more easily matched and more willing to use their full bargaining strength, thereby amplifying the inflationary process in a cumulative way.

He identifies three processes of change as being of particular importance to Britain. The first is that conceptions of social status have been decaying, giving rise to a less deferential, more hard-headed and more realistic appreciation of class inequalities. The second process is a growing awareness of a common body of rights, despite class inequalities, which militates against the notion of labour as a commodity. He argues that this rules out any solution to inflationary pressures that implies a substantial rise in unemployment; the consequence would be electoral damage, industrial unrest and the collapse of tripartism. Third and finally, Britain has achieved a 'mature' working class, in the sense that it is stable and reasonably homogeneous in social background and life experience. Its members remain, however, relatively uncommitted to a capitalist system based on 'free' market forces. Their major commitment is to the directly contrary features of greater citizenship rights and an effective labour movement.

The problem that confronts a British government as a result of these three processes is not just inflation, he concludes, but also the wider threat that the social antagonisms arising from 'an increasingly delegitimated structure of class inequality will prove no longer capable of institutional containment'. The economic phenomenon of inflation is to an important degree epiphenomenal, and a satisfactory explanation of it requires an understanding of the underlying relationships between social groupings.

THE PROBLEM OF INSTITUTIONAL NEGLECT

The passage of years has been unkind to this account. Unemployment trebled, there was an unprecedented increase in the dispersion of income and wealth and a substantial erosion of public services. Accompanying this massive increase in inequality, the annual number of strikes more than halved, inflation declined fourfold, trade union membership fell by a quarter and the Conservative Government enjoyed repeated electoral success. If one avoids the question of causation, it is a pattern of events remote from that discussed in Goldthorpe's account.

'I'm a good Popperian' he said disarmingly in the published discussion of the paper, 'I don't believe in historicist predictions about what's going to happen in the future, or in developmental laws of society—that's why I'm not a Marxist .... I don't know what will happen, and I can't see any point in pretending that I do' (Goldthorpe, 1978: 215). As was said at the outset, back in 1977 no other analyst would have predicted these developments or disputed the view that unemployment at 1930s levels was politically unthinkable. It could be claimed that within four years there was to be so substantial an alteration in the power relationship between classes that the processes he outlined have been suspended. The pertinent question for this discussion is how persuasive his account was at the time.

The memory retained by this writer of the Warwick conference at which the paper was presented, sustained by reading it when the proceedings were published, is one of disappointment. The generally narrow conceptions of most economists' theories were long overdue for sociological criticism, and the paper set them up for analysis so carefully, yet the explanation advanced seemed both weak and implausible. By tackling the underlying social circumstances at so high a level of generalization, it seemed to grip nothing tangible. Of course, how satisfying an explanation is felt to be depends very much upon the beholder, so such a criticism is inevitably personal. To this writer the account was constructed of sociological bricks without institutional straw and, as a consequence, seemed hard to validate and hard to act upon.

Before one tackles the major question of the relationship between class structure and economic performance, there are the three interrelated processes of change that Goldthorpe identified in 1970s Britain. The one that seemed least substantial at the time was that of the emergence of a 'mature' working class. Behind the image of 'Scargillism'[1] carefully nurtured by the trade union left, the reality seemed far less substantial. Some of the strongest traditional areas of trade unionism, in manufacturing and transport industries, were contracting, and the new trade unionism was increasingly management-sponsored and shallow. The idea of an effective trade union movement was being sapped by growing dependence upon shop steward committees with their factory-based chauvinism and overdependence upon management resources. It was trade unionism on the cheap, effective only so long as the chief shop steward could get into the manager's office and trade union leaders could get into Downing Street. In any case, the workforce was changing, with a clear threat in every respect to the dominance of the male, white, full-time, manual worker. There was diminishing, not increasing, homogeneity.

It was also difficult to accept the idea of the decay of the status order. Within the employment relationship, managers devote considerable resources to building status structures, and trade unions and professional associations fight hard to defend them. Some do decay, and some of the criteria whereby status is measured fall out of use, but what is remarkable to the observer is the constant process of regeneration, in which collective bargaining plays an important part. Goldthorpe accepts that considerations of status play a part 'in shaping patterns of intimate association', which presumably he intends to encompass employment relationships. He directs his argument primarily towards integrated status structures for society as a whole, arguing that a feature of their decay is a willingness of people to make pay comparisons with a socially broader range of comparative reference groups than hitherto. But it is hard to see what such a view might be based upon. The evidence of research on pay bargaining suggests that the most powerful points of comparison remain very local, both spatially and socially. The substantial spread of job evaluation systems in the 1970s, doing much to contain and channel pay comparisons within the bargaining unit, suggests that, whatever the rhetoric of union leaders, notions of pay fairness continued to be born at, or close to, the place of work.

Throughout the history of labour, inflationary periods have always brought, and been nourished by, industrial unrest. With it has come a greater rhetoric of rights and an increased extravagance of comparison. But they have been passing phases, and it has been remarkable how, even after the upheaval of war, the generally conservative and cautious scope of social comparison has subsequently returned. One question this raises is whether there is, or ever has been, an integrated and overarching popular conception of society's status structure—other, that is, than in a trivial, Ambridge sense.[2] Might it not be more realistic to describe a forest of locally grown status structures? Inflationary gales may shake and break their branches without altering the shape of the forest. With the benefit of hindsight, another doubt raised about the 'Sociological Account' is whether it is appropriate to use the long-term trend implied in Goldthorpe's three processes of change as an explanation for an inflationary episode which was soon to be ended.

The British inflation of the 1970s was part of a world inflation for which the country's domestic social structures could hardly be blamed. But recent economic research does suggest that they may have contributed to the British susceptibility to amplify the inflation it imports. The studies by A. Brown (1985) of world inflation since 1950 and by Bruno and Sachs (1985) of the response of OECD countries to the 1974 and 1979 oil price shocks both conclude that the source of different countries' inflationary potential lies in their labour markets and in the way in which they fix wages. To oversimplify complex arguments, it appears that among those with more than about a quarter of their workforce unionized, the countries less subject to extreme inflation are those for which bargaining is in some way centralized and coordinated—Sweden, West Germany, and Austria have at times exemplified this. Those with more fragmented bargaining, such as Italy, France and Britain, suffer from frantic second-guessing among individual bargainers, with the consequence that inflation is exacerbated by the pay settlements that are trying to match it.

What is notable about this inflationary process is that it is not, in the first instance, the result of class antagonisms, but of sectional division quite apart from class: division by company, industry, occupation, region, etc. Where class notions may come in is in helping to explain why in some countries the employers are able to form an effective united front against labour, and thereby either exclude bargaining (as in much of the United States) or centralize it (as in West Germany), and why elsewhere labour is able to forge an alliance with a social democratic government with much the same effect (as in Australia). In short, it is not class antagonisms *per se* but the institutional structures that contain and channel class antagonisms that appear to be a major source of differential inflationary experience.

CONCLUSION

It is a common failing among economists that they dismiss institutions as no more than the mechanisms whereby market forces are translated into social action: a source of lags, ignorance and inefficiency, but little else. They fail to appreciate that markets are themselves social constructs, that institutions interact with them and that most economics is enhanced by an appreciation of political processes. Goldthorpe, by trying to keep his analysis at a level of generality that deals only with class, and by failing to raise the question of the institutional forms whereby class interests are mobilized and obstructed, is vulnerable to a similar criticism. His 'Sociological Account' is accordingly weakened.

A decade of hindsight makes for a smug critic, and this writer concludes his appointed task uncomfortably. It is so easy to forget the context of a debate; it is so easy to forget that the best social science has always been shaped by contemporary social concerns and should not be judged in isolation from them. If only more serious sociological work were done on economic and industrial relations issues, both subjects would be greatly enriched. John Goldthorpe should return to these matters.

ACKNOWLEDGMENT

The author is grateful for the helpful comments of Hugh Clegg, Paul Edwards and Peter Nolan.

EDITOR'S NOTES

1   Scargillism denotes militant trade unionism of an uncompromising kind, named after Arthur Scargill, a leading figure in the British National Union of Mineworkers in the 1970s and 1980s.
2   Ambridge is a fictional agricultural village in the English Midlands, the setting for the longest running daily British radio 'soap'.

Interchange

ROCHE REPLIES TO BROWN

Willy Brown's stimulating chapter concentrates on the two works by Goldthorpe dealing with the reform of collective bargaining in Britain and the sociology of inflation. Some of the criticisms of Goldthorpe's work advanced by Brown are similar to those outlined in my own contribution, and his contention that sociological bricks should be reinforced where appropriate with institutional straw is one with which I would concur. I wish, however, to make three observations on the argument developed by Brown.

To begin with, the manner of Brown's critique of Goldthorpe brings out the major point of divergence between sociologists and industrial relations specialists in tackling the analysis of collective bargaining. Sociologists look for pre-institutional social roots of industrial relations and economic disorder and often treat institutions in residual categories. Industrial relations specialists tend to locate their explanations in the complexities and dynamics of institutional arrangements and treat social trends and structures in residual categories. This state of affairs has resulted in much mutual pegging of bricks at windows and seems to be due more to the disciplinary division of labour in Britain than to any genuinely sustainable analytical difference at a fundamental level in the approaches of scholars in each tradition. Differences of starting point cannot be supported axiomatically or resolved at a general level. Rather, it seems evident that social trends and divisions can undermine institutional arrangements, as argued in a major work in the institutionalist tradition (Fox and Flanders, 1970); may render institutions very difficult to reform and reconstruct, as Goldthorpe has contended; and that institutions may in certain circumstances auto-destruct, so to speak, as shown by Brown himself in his classic study of piecework bargaining (Brown, 1973). It also seems evident that institutional arrangements can greatly exacerbate social and economic disorder, as argued in different ways in the literature on political economy cited by Brown and in Batstone's work on post-Donovan reforms in Britain (Batstone, 1984, 1988a).

The upshot of this is that the bricks of sociological argument may or may not require institutional straw and likewise that institutionalists may sometimes validly ignore the wider social context of collective bargaining—sometimes, though not always, and perhaps even not often. It could then be argued that a failure to engage the complexities of collective bargaining institutions is more limiting in Goldthorpe's paper on the sociology of inflation than in his paper on reformism in British industrial relations, where surely sufficient attention is paid to the character—and, what is more, to the political character—of collective bargaining. To suggest that a failure to engage institutions somehow vitiates Goldthorpe's work on industrial relations *tout court* hardly seems valid.

Second, while Brown's defence of liberal pluralism makes important observations, it is not compelling as a response to Goldthorpe's criticisms. The nub of Goldthorpe's position was not so much that liberal reformism was 'problem-focused', and therefore not concerned to develop theory, as that the manner in which it identified industrial relations problems, as well as its suggestions as to how they should be resolved, were *ex parte* in terms of analysis and prescription. Brown appears to suggest that Goldthorpe attributed some kind of ultimate analytical—and even moral—priority to worker motivations and orientations to the neglect of the way in which institutional arrangements can shape or mediate orientations and to the neglect of the interests workers acquire as employees of companies facing more or less competitive conditions. Here he makes some telling points on the problem of adducing worker objectives and decisions from attitudinal data. But Goldthorpe was well aware of the complex interplay of subjective attitudes and objective conditions as they affect industrial relations disorder and reform (cf. Goldthorpe, 1974b: 427, 438, 447–8). Indeed, he repeatedly underscored the institutionalist observation that industrial relations disorder might have damaging consequences for the objective interests of workers and managers as stakeholders in industrial enterprises. His argument was that there was nonetheless a balance of advantage in 'disorderly' arrangements and likewise that reconstruction, even if deemed to be desirable on objective grounds, inevitably raised difficult questions of relative advantage as between management and unions and as between different levels within each side. Reform would raise the prospect of employees having to cede some of their autonomy, of unions gaining greater formal control over the activities of shop steward organizations and of management having to give up aspects of their 'prerogative'. Liberal pluralism, as Goldthorpe suggested, did propose one model of how this realignment of advantage might be achieved; this model was unavoidably *ex parte*, and was reasonably described, without political disparagement, as 'managerialism' (for a similar view, cf. Crouch, 1977: Ch. 8).

Against this background to imply that Goldthorpe's argument amounted to championing, analytically and prescriptively, some kind of shop-floor 'populism', as Brown appears to do, is wide of the mark. By the same token Goldthorpe's major theme that reform, no less than disorder, inevitably involved issues of power and advantage hardly reflects an approach that fails to come to terms 'with the political character of the employment relationship, of payment, and of the process of collective bargaining through which they are generally managed'. Rather, it could be suggested that the argument that Goldthorpe ignores the political character of industrial relations rebounds on Brown's defence of pluralism, which skirts these issues through a highly abstract, if suggestive, discussion of the place of power in liberal pluralism. Dismissing the 'radical sociological writings of the 1970s' on grounds of their 'almost pathetic irrelevance' to the agenda for industrial relations reform in the 1980s and their appeal to that 'decade's (naïve) students' amounts to rejection by association. That arguments may influence the politically naïve does not at the same time make them naïve arguments. Brown's argument here does little to advance the debate on the merits of Goldthorpe's essential thesis, but instead tilts at a straw man of Brown's own contrivance. It hardly needs stressing that Goldthorpe was not writing a viable political programme for reforming British industrial relations along social democratic lines. That he did not provide a programme of reform viable in the 1980s appears to trouble Brown. This is a rather exacting standard to apply when assessing the merits of a piece of social scientific writing; it also ignores the findings of research which has called into question the achievement of post-Donovan reforms, and the current political hostility towards liberal-pluralist models of industrial relations.

Finally, it can be argued that there *is* institutional straw in existing British industrial relations and sociological research to reinforce the fabric of Goldthorpe's argument. In commenting on the paper on inflation Brown is unhappy with the high level of generalization and abstraction that characterizes Goldthorpe's argument. It is true that the argument of this paper is developed at a highly abstract and general level; though it might be noted *en passant*—and it is clear from Brown's own paper—that sociologists hardly possess a monopoly of the abstract or the general in the debate on industrial relations disorder and reform. It is also the case that Goldthorpe's argument can be given institutional, or in any case operational, substance through research on several more concrete industrial relations trends and issues. The major contention of Goldthorpe's thesis is that an increase in 'worker pushfulness' or hard-headedness that arose as a consequence of secular sociological changes was one important feature of inflation and stagflation during the 1970s. I am at one with Brown in doubting some of the arguments Goldthorpe deployed in support of this view. We are also at one in doubting, most of all, some of the sociological as distinct from institutional pivots of the thesis. It will be clear, however, that I believe that changes in the class structure and the disappearance of pre-capitalist social constraints on worker militancy, including social status, may have been an important ingredient in the wages explosion and its concomitants. I have also tried to give operational focus to this hypothesis in my chapter, though not in a manner that Goldthorpe might necessarily endorse. Whatever its merits, this at least shows that from Goldthorpe's highly original, if exploratory, thesis there can be developed the fabric of an argument built on sociological bricks reinforced with institutional straw.

BROWN REPLIES TO ROCHE

The breadth of Bill Roche's advocacy reveals the narrow basis of my criticisms. I should neither wish nor venture to take issue with the bulk of the writing and arguments that he defends. I certainly would not wish to defend the arguments of most of the critics with whom he disagrees. It requires extreme caution for an outsider to make a constructive contribution to another discipline's controversies.

It is hardly surprising that his chapter makes no points that send me rushing to amend or defend my own. As he very fairly complains, 'Goldthorpe's critique has not been countered by academics in the liberal-pluralist tradition'. I hope my belated response provides sociologists with a clear enough target.

VIII. CAPITALISM AND CORPORATISM

14. Capitalism and Corporatism: The Political Economy of Advanced Capitalist Societies

NIAMH HARDIMAN

Goldthorpe's interest in the political economy of advanced capitalist societies can be traced through many of his writings, beginning with the *Affluent Worker* study (Goldthorpe *et al.*, 1968a, 1968b, 1969). However, his major contribution to political economy takes the form of two lengthy and stimulating essays published in the 1980s. Both take a broad comparative perspective, having been written for collaborative research projects on Western Europe. They survey the previous decades of the 'post-war era' which were characterized by the 'long boom' extending from 1945 to the mid-1970s, and they look ahead to the emergent trends in political economy in the 1980s. The first, 'Problems of Political Economy after the Post-War Period' (1987b), discusses the nature of the economic crisis of the 1970s, and investigates the logic and prospects of the dramatically divergent options apparent in economic management strategies in the 1980s. This paper was originally written in 1981 and revised in 1983. However, publishing delays meant that it did not appear until 1987. The second study, 'The End of Convergence: Corporatist and Dualist Tendencies in Modern Western Societies' (1984b), begins with a critique of liberal pluralist convergence theories, aspects of which Goldthorpe had discussed elsewhere (1964, 1971); it complements the earlier essay in its discussion of the very different trends in political economy emerging in the 1980s. These essays also take up themes developed in an earlier essay, 'The Current Inflation: Towards a Sociological Account' (1978). This analyzes the social and institutional context of heightened distributive conflict in the 1960s and 1970s and its significance for economic outcomes.

Goldthorpe argues that the political economy of the post-war period up to the mid-1970s was dominated by Keynesian economics. This involved a new form of accommodating the class-based social and economic conflicts which capitalism continually generates:

> The establishment of Keynesianism within the Western democracies ... represented
> more than simply the acceptance of a new body of economic theory and techniques.
> Also involved was a major political development: in effect, a historical compromise
> between contending ideologies and opposing class interests ... government ... took
> upon itself responsibility for ensuring the success of the economy, as defined by the twin
> criteria of full employment and growth. (1987b: 364)

For Goldthorpe, the main problems of political economy in the post-war
decades arose from the need to regulate inflation while maintaining steady growth
and supporting full employment. This was the economic context in which corporatist agreements came to be negotiated in a number of countries. However, the
decades of the 'long boom' came to an end with the economic crises of the 1970s,
and Keynesian approaches to fiscal and demand management policy lost a good deal
of their credibility. Goldthorpe's interpretation of the failings of the Keynesian era
sets the scene for his analysis of the emergent trends in the 1980s. The political
economy of the 'post-Keynesian era' is to a large extent the story of the variety of
responses to the conflicts of the preceding decades.

This chapter seeks to set Goldthorpe's views on capitalism and corporatism in
the context of his understanding of political economy more generally. The second
section sets out his approach to the problems of the decades of the 'long boom', and
the third section discusses more fully his projection of trends in the 1980s.

THE POST-WAR KEYNESIAN ERA

Goldthorpe's writings on the political economy of the post-war era up to the
economic crises of the 1970s take as their central issue the significance of organized
labour for economic performance. He is sympathetic to a 'cost-push' understanding
of inflation for the post-war decades; his analysis of inflation is therefore central to
his understanding of why and under what conditions corporatist arrangements came
into being. This section examines Goldthorpe's account of the origins of inflation,
and then moves on to his analysis of corporatism.

Inflation and Distributional Dissent

Goldthorpe argues that the inflationary surge of the 1970s, and the options facing
governments after the end of the 'Keynesian era', cannot adequately be accounted
for without recognizing the endogenous contributions to inflationary tendencies
within Western economies during the post-war decades: 'the problems of inflation
and of "stagflation" with which these economies are now beset are ones that have to
a significant extent been produced endogenously within the societies of the Western
world, and through processes *which were already in train during the post-war
period*' (1984b: 317; original emphasis). He argues convincingly that monetarist
economists fail to take the social structural sources of inflation seriously enough
(1978: 186–94), and defends 'an alternative analysis, in which inflation in modern
Western societies is represented as primarily the monetary expression of distributional dissent: or, to be more precise, of a heightening of such dissent' (1987b: 369).

Distributive outcomes are always subject to challenge, Goldthorpe holds, because inequalities lack normative legitimation. But over the post-war period there emerged 'a new "maximising" militancy in collective bargaining, encouraged ... by the weakening of traditional legitimations of class inequalities and traditional limitations on wants and life-styles, as well as by the rising confidence of trade-unionists in the bases of their organised power' (1984b: 322). The post-war period saw an 'organisational revolution' in which many interests, but especially labour, came to be more effectively organized (*ibid.*). Under full employment, wages became 'downwardly sticky'. Inflation in the sense of a general rise in the price level is 'a means of accommodating ... conflict which has indeed some attraction from a governmental standpoint: that is, in avoiding direct sociopolitical confrontations' (1987b: 373). Inflation may thus be seen as a manifestation of the changed balance of social and economic power in Western societies.

His interpretation of distributive conflict leads Goldthorpe to criticize the optimistic assumption which had prevailed in liberal-pluralist theory in the 1950s that a genuinely consensual basis for the integration of trade unions in capitalism had been found. The free association of workers had been taken to be the guarantee of the political integration of the working class; relatively low levels of industrial militancy had been assumed to prove the permanent severance of economic from political conflicts. However, Goldthorpe points out that these assumptions came increasingly to be seen as valid only for the earlier post-war decades (1984b: 318–21). In the course of the 1960s and 1970s widespread industrial conflict became common across Western Europe, and the significance of organized economic interests and distributive conflict for the functioning of the market economy once again became a political issue (Gourevitch *et al.*, 1984; Barkin, 1983; Crouch and Pizzorno, 1978: Vol. 1).

Goldthorpe's analysis of heightened distributional dissent and the growth of trade union 'pushfulness' applies primarily to Britain in the mid- to late 1970s. It was there, he contends, that these developments were most evident, and sociological analyses may reveal analogous processes at work elsewhere (1978: 197). His later essays make it clear that he believes that his observations about trade union militancy can indeed be generalized across Western Europe (1984b: 319–20; 1987b: 369).

He identifies three reasons for these developments. First, he argues that the older status order which had helped to legitimate social inequalities was in decline.[1] This laid the distribution of advantages and disadvantages through the market more open to question (1978: 200–1). Second, Goldthorpe argues, drawing on work by T. H. Marshall, that the post-war decades witnessed the extension of concepts of citizenship (*ibid.*: 201–4). Statutory extension of welfare entitlements had helped to offset some of the disadvantages associated with class position and exposure to market uncertainties. Labour now had a degree of protection against being treated as a factor of production like any other commodity (cf. Esping-Andersen and Korpi, 1984; Esping-Andersen, 1985). But where Marshall anticipated that this would help to promote the political integration of the working class in capitalist societies, Goldthorpe points out that it may well be a double-edged development (1978: 202). Welfare policies may contribute to evening out inequalities between the two sides in collective bargaining. Most significantly, Goldthorpe argues, the post-war decades saw the strengthening of the belief in Western European societies that unemployment would not be used as an instrument of economic policy by any government, a belief which gained not just an empirical but a normative status (1978: 203; 1987b: 322–3). The belief came to be widely shared—up to the mid-1980s at any rate, a point to which we shall return—that no government could survive the electoral consequences of permitting unemployment to increase unchecked. Third, social mobility studies reveal that the working class was now more homogeneous than ever before and therefore possessed what Goldthorpe terms 'socio-political maturity' (1978: 206).

All these factors, along with the new organizational capacity of the trade unions, increased unions' preparedness to 'punch their weight' (*ibid.*: 196) in pursuit of their own economic advantage. Goldthorpe points out that there is no particular reason why unions should be expected to restrain their market strength and refrain from striking for purely altruistic reasons (1987b: 387). If trade union cooperation is to be secured in a strategy to control inflation, this must be a bargained agreement, with all the contingencies associated with this. Thus the increased organizational and bargaining power of the trade unions provided the stimulus to government to try to secure wage restraint through corporatist agreements.

Corporatism and Capitalism

Having looked at Goldthorpe's analysis of the endogenous sources of inflation and 'stagflation' in Western economies, we can now turn to his conception of corporatism as a means of containing it.

Corporatist political arrangements, according to Goldthorpe, generally originate with governments, as a means of bringing 'some degree of order, and hence of predictability, not only into their own relations with particular organised interests, but further into the relations prevailing *among* these interests, where their aims and their strategies for pursuing these aims are, in some way or other, interdependent' (1984b: 324). Other authors had already noted that problems of effectiveness and consent, indeed of 'governability', led governments to draw organized interests more closely into processes of policy-making while obliging them to assume some responsibility for policy implementation. Corporatism was taken by many to represent a distinctive mode of 'interest intermediation' which could arise in any policy area (Schmitter, 1979, 1981; Schmitter and Streeck, 1985; Lehmbruch, 1979; see also Ross Martin, 1983, and response by Crouch, 1983; Panitch, 1981). However, Goldthorpe notes that corporatism is most typically found as an outgrowth from attempts to implement incomes policies:[2]

> In so far as Western governments have had to face recurrent crises of effectiveness and, perhaps, of consent in the recent past, these have in fact by far most frequently arisen in connection with the management of the economy, and in consequence of the actions of organizations representing major economic interests: that is, business and employer organizations and trade unions. (1984b: 324)

Corporatism is an attempt to find an institutional and political means of overcoming problems of economic performance, specifically problems arising from distributive conflict. Goldthorpe supports the conception of corporatism advanced by Lehmbruch, for whom 'corporatist concentration' is distinguished by two essential features (1984b: 324–50):

> i. it involves not just a single organised interest with privileged access to government but rather a plurality of organisations usually representing antagonistic interests; and

ii. these organisations manage their conflicts and co-ordinate their action with that of government expressly in regard to the systemic (*gesamtwirtschaftliche*) requirements of the national economy. (Lehmbruch, 1984: 62)

Wage restraint has been seen as necessary, according to Goldthorpe, to facilitate economic adjustment policies based on full employment: 'to allow government to introduce expansionist policies aimed at sustaining employment without producing disastrously high rates of inflation; or, conversely, to allow them to introduce restrictionist policies aimed at curbing inflation without producing disastrously high rates of unemployment' (1984b: 325). The incomes policy element of corporatist agreements requires trade unions to 'under-utilise their market power—that is, the power they can express in collective bargaining in labour markets—in exchange for the opportunity for their leaders to exercise political power or, at all events, political influence' (*ibid.*). Control of inflation has the character of a 'public good', requiring the cooperation of the great majority of bargaining groups to make it effective (1987b: 405n37). But this involves risk for trade unions: there is no certainty that economic performance will be better than would otherwise be the case. The government input to the agreements aims to offset this uncertainty.

Goldthorpe's discussion of trade union involvement in corporatist agreements involves two issues. First, the trade union movement must be able to act strategically and to mobilize its members behind a relevant conception of where their interests lie. Second, the trade union movement must possess the capacity, both organizational and ideological, to become involved in political bargaining.

If they are to be able to commit their memberships to corporatist agreements, trade unions and employers' associations must be able to exercise a representative function which can overcome sectionalism and internal divisions within their own organizations (1984b: 325). This is likely to present a significantly greater problem to the trade union leadership. It must be able to convince its members that their interests are not exclusively confined to higher wages and improved working conditions in the short term, but that there is a sense in which they share collective interests such as control of inflation, full employment and better welfare provisions.[3] The longer-term, more generalized benefits negotiated by the trade union leadership accrue to everyone in the society whether or not they have contributed to the strategy,[4] and, indeed, whether or not they are trade union members. Effective coordination requires that the trade union movement constitute what Olson calls an 'encompassing organisation' which can transcend sectionalism and represent the whole constituency of its interest (1984b: 325). Goldthorpe's view is consistent with empirical findings that countries with highly centralized, authoritatively coordinated trade union federations, with high membership density, are best suited to developing corporatist agreements (Headey, 1970; Schmitter, 1981; Schmidt, 1982b; Visser, 1984).

One of the factors which may destabilize corporatist agreements is the disaffection of trade union members. Authors such as Lange (1984) and Przeworski (1985b), drawing on rational choice analysis, argue that there need be no opposition of interest between trade union leaders and their members. A centralized trade union movement seems to have an important function in helping to bridge the time scale of members' rational expectations, from short-term to medium-term (Lange, 1984). On this view the centralization and authoritative coordination of the trade union movement needed to negotiate corporatist agreements may be an asset, rather than the instrument of an authoritarian and oligarchic leadership as some have argued (Sabel, 1981; Panitch, 1979).

However, Goldthorpe correctly stresses the uncertainties of a strategy of involvement in corporatist agreements, and the internal conflicts likely to be generated. Too much importance can be attached to the organizational preconditions for corporatist involvement: trade unions must also develop a suitable ideological orientation, which Goldthorpe sees in terms of a new 'collective identity' (cf. Pizzorno, 1978), with reference to which the benefits obtainable through a centralized strategy can be made meaningful for the membership. For Goldthorpe, this means that they must act on a class-wide definition of shared interests (1984b: 327; 1987b: 388–9).

Goldthorpe is fully aware of how difficult it is for trade unions to adopt such a strategy: we shall return to this point. It is sufficient here to note that he regards the concept of 'interests' as problematic. Like a number of other recent scholars, Goldthorpe is dissatisfied alike with liberal-pluralist and Marxist approaches to analyzing interests (see Berger, 1981):

> In corporatist practice, interests are clearly not treated simply as sociological 'givens', and the function of representative organisations is not merely to express, but actually to formulate interests, in response to pressure from both their memberships *and* from their bargaining partners, and also in the light of their leaders' own conceptions of appropriate strategies. (1984b: 326)

Corporatist agreements involve the trade union movement in direct negotiations with government about the terms on which wage restraint will be forthcoming. This 'political bargaining' or 'political exchange' is central to Goldthorpe's conception of corporatism.[5] Involvement in political bargaining gives the trade union movement the opportunity to convert economic strength into political influence (1984b: 325). In 'exchange' for wage restraint the government may commit itself to a variety of policies favourable to trade union interests (*ibid.*: 325–7, 383–4). These may involve short-term compensations for earnings foregone, in the form of tax concessions and price controls, but they may also involve longer-term and more generalized benefits such as improved welfare entitlements and measures to guarantee the maintenance of full or high employment levels (*ibid.*: 327). Understandably, the trade union movement is likely to have greater confidence that a government of the left will be sympathetic to its priorities (*ibid.*: 329). This point has been borne out empirically. The countries in which a corporatist approach to wage formation came to be most stably institutionalized, Sweden, Austria, Norway, all had strong participation in government of left-wing parties sympathetic to the strategy of 'political bargaining' (A. Martin, 1985; Schmidt, 1982a; Korpi and Shalev, 1979, 1980; Cameron, 1984).[6]

Goldthorpe's depiction of political bargaining is congruent with the 'power resources' model of labour strategies (Korpi, 1978, 1983; Korpi and Shalev, 1979, 1980), a model which draws to some degree on the Swedish experience. Goldthorpe has had a long-standing interest in Swedish political economy and in the theoretical as well as empirical implications of Scandinavian approaches to wage formation. This is apparent in his overall evaluation of the potential significance of corporatist wage bargaining for working-class interests:

> It would seem quite inadequate to regard corporatist tendencies in modern societies in the manner of more orthodox Marxist writers, as reflecting no more than the latest or

'highest' form of the social control of labour under capitalism and as quite lacking in radical potential (e.g. Panitch, 1979, 1981; Jessop, 1978a). What corporatist institutions can be said to provide is a distinctive context within which the class conflicts of a capitalist society may be carried on. The eventual outcome of such conflicts will depend on the relative success of contending organizational leaderships in mobilizing and sustaining support within their constituencies: but under corporatism as here understood, labour attains a position in which it can at least make the attempt to convert its market strength into political measures designed to advance working-class interests in a wider-ranging and more permanent manner than could be achieved through action in the industrial sphere alone. (1984b: 339)

THE POST-KEYNESIAN ERA

The Keynesianism of the post-war period, as we have already noted, was inadequate to the new economic situation of the mid-1970s and after. Spiralling prices fuelled wage claims, and for the first time government intervention seemed to be powerless to restore equilibrium (cf. Lindberg and Maier, 1985: Part 3). 'Stagflation' seemed an intractable problem and full employment seemed to be at an end in many countries. Unemployment was worsened by the structural decline in heavy industries and by rapid technological changes and new production methods. Economic management options no longer ranged around a basic consensus on policy methods. But more fundamentally, Goldthorpe points out, new disagreements opened up on the correct or desirable objectives of economic policy. He identifies three possible strategies which could be adopted in response to the Keynesian 'impasse'; he discusses the internal logic of each and the difficulties it is likely to encounter were it to be followed to its logical conclusion. These are as follows:

1 'new interventionism', or a further development of the corporatist approaches to economic management already familiar in Western societies;
2 'new laissez-faire', involving a radical reversal of the trend towards state regulation of the market;
3 'dualism', a decentralized strategy whereby employers seek means of escaping the consequences of effective trade union organization.

Each of these alternatives is discussed primarily in terms of the government's approach to organized labour, revealing the centrality Goldthorpe attributes to organized labour as a vital shaping force in the political economy of Western European countries. Neither employers' strategies nor the international and domestic economic context receive much attention; they are largely taken for granted. This allows him to present a coherent and forceful analysis of the prospects for each strategy. It may be, however, that the explanatory weight Goldthorpe attributes to organized labour may need some modification in the light of developments in the years since his two major studies were completed.

Corporatism in the Post-Keynesian Era

Goldthorpe attaches considerable significance to the fact that corporatist agreements had not collapsed during years of economic recession in the countries in which they were well established, mainly Sweden and Austria. These countries also, as a consequence, differed notably from most other Western European countries in successfully maintaining into the 1980s their commitment to full employment (Johannesson and Schmid, 1980; Scharpf, 1984; Cameron, 1984; Rowthorn, 1986). Goldthorpe's views on the prospects for corporatist strategies in the 1980s were evidently also influenced by the debate on the left of the British Labour Party in the early 1980s about the 'Alternative Economic Strategy', which proposed, among other measures, import controls, a move towards more central planning and a greater degree of nationalization, in a strategy aimed at an eventual transition to socialism (1987b: 404n323).

Goldthorpe argues that if full employment were to be retained as the first objective of public policy in the 1980s, an effective incomes policy would be essential. This would be the case whether corporatism is thought of as a means of stabilizing capitalism, or as a radical means of 'transcending' it (*ibid.*: 383–4). Therefore, the problems likely to arise in implementing a corporatist strategy, Goldthorpe projects, will be those involved in securing a stable incomes policy. Two issues will be particularly important: the continuation of distributional dissent, and the problems of securing trade union commitment to a strategy of political bargaining.

Distributional dissent will not cease causing problems in centralized wage agreements, Goldthorpe argues; income differentials will rather obviously be the result of planning decisions, and the criteria used will be open to question (1987b: 386). The need to overcome discontent from this quarter could drive upwards the price of unions' continued participation in an incomes policy. Goldthorpe notes that 'those national incomes policies which "succeeded" in the 1950s and 1960s, in the minimal sense of achieving relatively long-term political acceptability (whatever their economic results), were generally complemented by attempts at price control and dividend limitation and formed part of an overall economic strategy aimed at full employment and expansion' (*ibid.*: 386). The trade union movement would be likely to claim, in addition, that they had 'some legitimate interest in the way the profits that are retained are actually used—or in other words, in the amount and type of investment that is undertaken' (*ibid.*: 388).

This strategy, as Goldthorpe notes, was most highly developed in Sweden. In the latter half of the 1970s the main trade union federation proposed a form of collective wage-earner equity to be financed out of company profits. The plan (called the 'Meidner' plan after its main architect) was devised in response to the tensions generated by the unions' 'solidaristic' wages policy which had helped to generate extra profits in some industries (*ibid.*). The logic of Goldthorpe's projection is compelling in theory: there would appear to be a natural progression of this sort in the logic of 'political bargaining'. So far, however, Sweden remains the only country which has experimented with union influence over investment control, even to the rather limited degree provided by the wage-earner funds established in the early 1980s (Crouch, 1980; A. Martin, 1985; Pontusson, 1987).

Resistance to corporatist policies, or to trade union adoption of any fuller strategy of political bargaining, Goldthorpe notes, may come from the membership itself. As noted earlier, he argues that political bargaining requires the trade union leadership to adopt a class-wide frame of reference and an explicitly political orientation. However, trade unions may be unable or unwilling—or both—to adopt this new strategy (1987b: 392). Trade unionism developed in response to the conditions of capitalist economies, and is very much a product of liberal capitalism (*ibid.*: 391). In many countries, Goldthorpe acknowledges, a strategy of political bargaining or 'new interventionism' would require traditional trade unionism to be 'radicalized' (*ibid.*: 395–6). But this may not be perceived as either feasible or desirable, and the familiar problem of an 'interpretation gap' between leaders and members may undermine a commitment to political bargaining (*ibid.*: 393).

Goldthorpe's outline of the problems facing a corporatist strategy is incisive and convincing, and has been borne out in the experiences of a number of Western European countries. However, the unions' strategies in the 1980s have to be explained with reference to changes in their economic environment which were less evident when Goldthorpe was writing and which fall outside his main range of concerns. Employers' strategies on the one hand, and the general economic situation on the other, help to explain more fully the problems of organized labour's involvement in corporatist agreements.

Both factors help to explain the unsteady course of centralized bargaining in Sweden in the 1980s. The labour movement grew more differentiated with changes in the composition of the workforce, resulting in growing problems of trade union coordination during the 1970s, very much as might be expected from Goldthorpe's analysis (*Current Sweden*, 1985). During the recession of the early 1980s the main employers' federation determined to seek wage agreements more closely attuned to particular industries' conditions, and the wage agreements in 1983 and 1985 were more decentralized than normal (Swedish Institute, 1986). However, the networks of close relationships between the representative organizations of labour and employers, and between them and government, remained intact, and a new nationwide central agreement was concluded in 1986. Wage pressures and inflation were widely recognized as the most significant problem facing the Swedish economy in the years of economic upturn in the mid-1980s (*Current Sweden*, 1988). But this is broadly tolerated as a consequence of Sweden's successful commitment to full employment policies; unemployment peaked at 3.5 per cent in 1983, and was under 2 per cent in the late 1980s.

In Austria, too, economic and social changes brought new sources of tension into its corporatist arrangements. During the 1970s and 1980s the close interlocking ties between organized interests and political parties, so characteristic of Austrian 'consociational' corporatism in the post-war period, were gradually loosening, allowing new policy options to be discussed outside the constitutional tripartite economic institutions (Marin, 1983; Gerlich, Grande and Müller, 1988). The post-war methods of maintaining full employment, through expensive subsidies to the large state-owned industrial sector, became an increasingly heavy burden on Austria's public finances. By the mid-1980s the fiscal drain and uncompetitive performance represented by much of the state sector led to an unprecedented decision to introduce phased redundancies and a measure of privatization. The international economic climate and problems of structural adaptation of the domestic economy set the agenda to which the trade union movement was obliged to respond.

Nevertheless, centralized and political bargaining is not fundamentally threatened in either country. This may be due in part to policy inertia: once all the compromises and trade-offs have been worked out between the bargaining parties, and a functioning set of agreements has been stably institutionalized and proven its usefulness over time, employers as well as trade unions may seek to press their respective advantage within these institutions, but without fundamentally altering existing arrangements (cf. Scharpf, 1981, 1984).

Several other countries in which corporatism had not previously been stably institutionalized also implemented corporatist agreements during the 1980s. These can be explained in terms of Goldthorpe's conception of corporatism as a means of containing trade-offs between inflation and unemployment (1984b: 325). But in countries such as Australia and New Zealand on the one hand, and Spain, Portugal and Greece on the other, corporatist agreements have been negotiated in what might be thought of as rather unpropitious economic conditions, and have played an important role in facilitating structural economic adaptation (see the annual OECD *Economic Survey* on each country). In Australia and New Zealand Labour governments—supported increasingly by business as well as by their traditional bases among employees—have presided over a range of 'free market' policies, including deregulating the financial system, floating the currency, reforming the tax system and promoting export competitiveness. The 'national accord' in Australia, negotiated in 1983, held wages below inflation between 1985 and 1988, even after the reduction of indexation and cutbacks in public spending to curb a large budget deficit. The accord is credited with increasing net employment significantly. The support of the trade union movement remained firm into a third Labour period in government: its leadership believes that the best prospects for the unions and for workers in general lie in supporting Labour's adjustment strategy (see Glyn, 1988). In New Zealand, a country in the throes of economic contraction between 1985 and 1988, the trade union movement expressed rather more discontent with the policy of support for the Labour government: nevertheless, the Labour government was re-elected to a second term of office.

Both Spain and Portugal also faced considerable problems of structural adjustment in the 1980s, as they prepared to compete in the European Community; the same was true of Greece. Spain and Portugal needed to reduce the battery of protective measures inherited from the fascist era. In both countries the main section of the trade union movement supported economic reconstruction measures which included alteration of labour laws to permit greater market flexibility, and implementing incomes policies. Between 1982 and 1986 the Socialist government in Spain had firm support from close union allies, the UGT. Despite austerity measures and a very rapid increase in unemployment, wages were held below inflation (Perez-Diaz, 1986). Between 1986 and 1988, however, relations grew rapidly worse: as might be anticipated from Goldthorpe's analysis, the conflict centred on the costs to trade union members of continuing wage restraint. But the unions had little opportunity to press a more developed style of political bargaining, and the conflict was expressed in the form of massive and recurring industrial protest. Similar outbreaks of strikes, between unions and the centre-right government, were evident in Portugal in 1987–88, especially among public sector workers. The Greek Socialist government negotiated an incomes policy with the trade union leadership in 1985, which held firm until 1987. But here, too, the vulnerability of incomes policies to membership dissatisfaction is borne out, and mass protests and strikes were held at the end of 1987 to secure greater concessions in the 1988 budgetary proposals.

New Laissez-Faire

The new laissez-faire, or new monetarism, entered political debate in various Western European countries in the 1970s, but its most thorough realization, besides the United States, was undoubtedly in Britain. For the incoming Conservative Government in 1979, the widespread industrial action in 1978–79 not only indicated the failure of Labour's social contract to provide economic stability and growth or to control inflation; it also signalled the exhaustion of any strategy of political 'inclusion' of the trade union movement (P. Hall, 1986).

The new laissez-faire, in Goldthorpe's analysis, entails increasing the sphere in which market forces operate freely. Control of inflation would be the highest objective of policy, and control of the money supply the principal means of achieving it. This would involve a departure not only from the techniques but also from the objectives of Keynesianism, because:

> to overcome inflation via monetarist policies requires, as monetarists themselves acknowledge, a 'stabilization crisis', in which unemployment unavoidably rises—to an extent and for a period that cannot be accurately predicted. And, furthermore, it is seen as essential to long-term price stability, and, indeed, to the possibility of any return to full employment, that government should provide *no guarantees* of full employment. (1987b: 366)

Rather, market disciplines would reassert themselves: the market strength of trade unions would also have to be reduced, both through the effects of unemployment and through statutory controls. A basic minimum of public responsibility for health and welfare would continue to be taken for granted (*ibid.*: 367). But otherwise, the logic of the new laissez-faire set out by Goldthorpe implies that capitalism should come to be accepted as a quasi-natural system, in which market outcomes are not subjected to criticism in ethical terms, but accepted merely as signals of the state of supply and demand for goods, services and skills.

Goldthorpe once again considers the difficulties which would be encountered by a full-scale implementation of this strategy in terms of the resistance offered by organized labour: first, through its contribution to distributional dissent; second, from its direct opposition, both industrial and political, to any government adopting such a strategy. He argues plausibly that distributional dissent cannot be eliminated totally: even if it is contained for a time by unemployment severe enough and of long enough duration to alter trade union expectations, there is no guarantee that it will not re-emerge with improved economic performance.[7] 'Differences in incomes and other rewards are indeed very frequently and readily assessed in terms of their "fairness"—in relation to ability and effort, and also to other criteria such as individual or family need, or the inherent deprivations or the "social value" of different occupations' (*ibid.*: 371). Moreover, the argument that market outcomes are ethically neutral undercuts another claim made by some new laissez-faire theorists, which is that economic rewards are meritocratic, based on individual hard work and effort. In this view the market provides a just reward for past effort. However, Goldthorpe argues that the meritocratic legitimation of market outcomes is no more likely to gain widespread acceptance, as people perceive that unemployment can happen not because of individuals' attributes but in virtue of membership of a particular category or collectivity or residence in a particular region. The class basis of disadvantage or benefit may become all the more apparent to people the more insistently it is denied (*ibid.*: 371–2). The government may wish to cultivate a fatalistic acceptance of market-based distribution among the electorate.[8] But Goldthorpe holds that established concepts of 'citizenship' would prevent this happening: the normative endorsement of government intervention in the economy has strong roots. He cites evidence from the 1983 general election campaign in

Britain to argue that it offered 'little support for the idea that public concern over high rates of unemployment is tending to diminish: on the contrary, poll data consistently revealed unemployment to be the leading issue' (*ibid*.: 375).

Goldthorpe also projects that a government adopting thoroughgoing policies of 'new laissez-faire' will be likely to invite a 'trial of strength' with organized labour, resulting in 'a heightening of industrial conflict of a clear political significance: for as well as in some cases involving government directly as the employer in the public sector, such conflict will in any event be seen as stemming ultimately from the constraints that government's economic strategy imposes' (*ibid*.: 374). The possibility also exists that trade unions' recourse to market power may cause business itself to lose confidence in the government in the course of the 'stabilization crisis'. Goldthorpe concludes that 'if widespread, and thus a source of major disruption in the economy, such conflict could itself undermine the political viability of a laissez-faire program. However, a more serious threat is that likely to be posed by an adverse electoral reaction, in particular to the return of large-scale and long-term unemployment' (*ibid*.: 374).

Goldthorpe's analysis of the prospects of a strategy of new laissez-faire provides a stimulating framework for interpreting Britain's experience, though the resistance of organized labour has been less successful than he anticipated in the early 1980s, and the strategy of deregulation, privatization and otherwise expanding the role of the market has progressed much further than anyone might then have expected.

The problems likely to be encountered by a strategy of new laissez-faire were expected to emanate primarily from organized labour. Goldthorpe correctly anticipated 'trials of strength' between the government and the trade unions. The biggest confrontation, that of the miners' strike in 1984–85, was seen very much in these terms by the government. It was thus prepared to endure a bitter and very costly conflict because the view expressed by Nigel Lawson, Chancellor of the Exchequer, was shared by the government as a whole, that whatever the cost of the strike, resisting the miners was 'an excellent investment' (*Sunday Times*, 1985: 25). Unemployment brought rapid loss of membership to the British trade unions: from a peak of 13.3 million in 1979 they lost some two million members by the mid-1980s, or 17 per cent of the total (see e.g. Longstreth, 1988: 419). The new economic and political circumstances of the 1980s not only weakened the unions' political influence and market strength, but also contributed to sharp internal divisions on the best strategic response to the new situation.

However, the degree to which trade union power has been curtailed is the subject of some disagreement. Studies of workplace industrial relations indicate that trade union organizational capacity and bargaining strength remained considerable during the 1980s, though varying by sector (Batstone, 1988a; Millward and Stevens, 1986; MacInnes, 1987; Longstreth, 1988). Real earnings for those in work increased steadily in the years after 1981–82. It appears that Goldthorpe was correct to doubt that continuing high levels of unemployment would guarantee a permanent abatement of distributional conflict (1987b: 379). Furthermore, these findings suggest that his analysis of 'dualist' tendencies (see below) was well founded: many employers are clearly prepared to accept relatively rapid increases in earnings to secure a well trained and stable 'core' workforce.

Goldthorpe projected that large-scale unemployment would, over the longer term, prove intolerable to the electorate, because it violated established notions of 'citizenship'. He attributes the Conservatives' electoral victory in 1983 to political factors—chiefly the disunity and lack of credibility of the opposition—rather than to any fundamental change in shared political values (*ibid.*: 375). Recent studies such as that of Heath, Jowell and Curtice (1985) support his claim that full employment, improved health and welfare services and increased government intervention in the economy command widespread electoral sympathy. This would imply that the Conservatives' success is predominantly a consequence of the continuing divisions and weaknesses which characterize the political opposition. Britain's political institutions are such that opposition parties have relatively little role in shaping policy (Scharpf, 1981). Those sections of the population most seriously disadvantaged thus constitute no political or electoral threat to the Conservative Government. However, the possibility remains that the relative prosperity experienced by a considerable proportion of the electorate in the 1980s may effect a more permanent shift in voting behaviour, and that important elements of the Conservatives' radical neo-liberal strategy may themselves gain not merely empirical but also normative acceptance.[9] In any event, the Conservatives have been more successful in seizing the initiative and altering the 'balance of class power' to their advantage than was apparent to anyone in the early 1980s.

Dualism

Goldthorpe notes that few countries have adopted fully fledged versions of the stark options outlined above, either of which would entail according a decisive advantage to either one side or the other in socio-political confrontations (1987b: 399). Thus 'the Keynesian compromise may have broken down, but what might be described as the Keynesian impasse—with an attendant high level of economic discomfort—could well persist' (*ibid.*: 366). This might lead to a continuing 'after-life' of Keynesian policy intervention, where governments would be drawn into attempting to regulate economic performance in a piecemeal way, to 'give priority to the avoidance of serious conflict' (*ibid.*: 401). Yet this could result in an inability to deal effectively with either inflation or unemployment (see also Lange and Garrett, 1985): 'To future observers of the Western capitalist world, it may well appear that the failure of a nation to achieve decisive modifications of the pluralist model—in one direction or another—is the typical concomitant of persisting economic decline' (1984b: 341).

Goldthorpe discusses another trend observable in the political economy of Western European countries in the post-Keynesian era, which represents a rather different 'third way'. This is 'dualism', where employers seek to 'enlarge the areas of the economy within which market forces and associated relations of authority and control are able to operate more freely than in others' (1984b: 329).[10] Where labour is effectively organized, it can cause rigidities in the supply of labour and the terms on which it is employed, and can limit managerial discretion over deployment and dismissal decisions. Thus employers may try to find sources of labour that are more 'flexible' and kinds of work processes that are not subject to such restrictions. This is an important contribution to the analysis of the political economy of Western Europe in the 1980s, with far-reaching implications for the capacity for collective action of organized labour.

Migrant workers are among the most significant new sources of labour supply in a number of Western European countries, representing between 5 and 15 per cent of the workforce in most of the major countries, yet no more than a quarter are likely to be trade union members (1984b: 331; see also 1972b: 357–8). They frequently lack political rights, and trade unions may see little benefit to their own indigenous members from organizing them. Their status as a new 'industrial reserve army' appears to be borne out by the fact that they suffered most heavily during recessionary years: countries such as West Germany, Austria and Switzerland 'exported' a sizeable proportion of their unemployment in the late 1970s and 1980s (see e.g. Webber, 1986: 24).

Non-standard forms of work, Goldthorpe points out, far from declining as liberal-pluralist theory anticipated, are increasing, often quite rapidly. Part-time employment is the most rapidly growing sector of employment in Britain in the 1980s, and the vast majority of those working part-time in Britain are women (Department of Employment *Employment Gazette*, various dates; OECD, 1983: Table 18). Women workers, like workers from outside the national community, have been seen as adding significantly to 'flexible' sources of labour (1984b: 333). Subcontracting appears to vary in significance in different countries. As Goldthorpe notes, it is well established in France and Italy, but while the scale of subcontracting in Britain increased during the 1980s, it remained of limited significance (Batstone, 1988a: 186–7). Non-'standard' employment typically enjoys less favourable statutory protections, and until very recently, especially in the case of women workers, trade unions have not accorded a high priority to improving the pay or terms and conditions of employment of workers in these categories. What all these categories of employees and types of employment share in common is that they fall outside the 'web of rules' of employment relationships (Goldthorpe, 1984b: 334); labour can more easily be treated as a commodity, to be taken on and laid off as market conditions dictate. Goldthorpe correctly recognizes the dependence of effective 'citizenship rights' in the workplace on collective organization and statutory protection.

Dualism in Goldthorpe's sense can co-exist with a well organized workforce in 'core' employments, but he also points out that each model of employment relations carries ideological implications (*ibid.*: 335). The extension of a poorly organized or non-organized sector of the labour market could undermine any capacity for collective action on the part of the trade union movement, resulting in unions' defensive concentration on sectional interests above all others (on the challenges facing West Germany's unions, see Streeck, 1984; Jacobi *et al.*, 1986; Kastendiek *et al.*, 1986; for a discussion of changing prospects in Britain, see W. Brown, 1986; Longstreth, 1988). As Goldthorpe prophetically noted, unions' responses to these new challenges may be decisive for their viability as an economic and political force in the 1980s and beyond.

CONCLUSION

Goldthorpe's work on capitalism and corporatism, and more generally his work on political economy, represents a landmark in scholarly studies in this area. He provides an authoritative interpretation of post-war political economy in the developed Western countries, and at the very moment when the 'post-war settlement' was breaking down offered a framework for understanding the diversity of emergent trends. Not all the elements of his analysis have proved, with hindsight, to be of equal significance; in particular, the central importance attached to organized labour may need to be modified in the light of the experience of the 1980s. Nevertheless, Goldthorpe's essays on political economy command attention for the clarity and rigour of their argument and the wealth of insight they contain.

NOTES

1 As Goldthorpe notes, similar arguments about the depleting moral legacy of capitalism have been advanced by theorists working in very different theoretical traditions, including Habermas, Hirsch, and Brittan (1978: 213n8).

2 As the debate on corporatism developed during the 1970s, various Marxist scholars also took the view that it was a phenomenon peculiarly associated with incomes policies: see Panitch (1976, 1979, 1980, 1981); Jessop (1979). Goldthorpe concurs with this, but would disagree with their conception of the purposes it serves, as will be seen below.

3 The problematic character of the interests of the working class in capitalist societies has been discussed in comparable terms, contrasting short-term with long-term, and short-range or sectional interests with collective interests, by Offe and Wiesenthal (1980).

4 There will probably always be an incentive for the strongest bargaining groups to 'free-ride', pursuing sectional wage gains while hoping that the general benefits will also come about through others' cooperation. Even in Sweden it has long been held that a considerable amount of additional wage drift at workplace level is a tolerable price to pay for the other successes of the 'solidaristic' wages policy and the associated highly interventionist labour market policy (Hart and Otter, 1976; Gourevitch *et al.*, 1984; cf. on the Norwegian case, Schwerin, 1980, 1981).

5 The term 'political exchange' was coined by Pizzorno (1978) in connection with the political bargaining of the main Italian trade union federations in the 1970s. On this experience, see Regini (1984); on the situation in the 1980s, see Jacobi *et al.* (1986: Part 3); also Kreile (1988).

6 But, as Goldthorpe also points out, these preconditions are neither necessary nor sufficient: agreements which share many of the features of corporatism were implemented at times in countries, most notably the Netherlands, West Germany and Finland, which did not have strong left governments; and other factors prevented them from functioning stably under Labour governments in Britain (1984b: 329; see Flanagan, Soskice and Ulman, 1983).

7 Goldthorpe cites Hirsch's work on 'positional goods' and status competition to support the claim that economic growth will not reduce the concern with questions of distribution and redistribution (1987b: 371–2).

8 An example cited by Goldthorpe is the slogan of the British Conservative Government that 'There Is No Alternative'.

9 This may already be the case with the sale of council houses and privatization of major industries. Other issues targeted by the Conservatives in their third term of office include the poll tax, pension schemes, and local authority control of education (see Rogaly, 1988). Nevertheless, health and social welfare provisions were not to experience major change—an indication, perhaps, of the current limits to the possibility of rolling back established 'citizenship rights'.

10 Goldthorpe explicitly distinguishes his conception of 'dualism' from that of segmented labour market analysis. He is primarily interested in the degree to which labour is 'commodified' (1984b: 342n6).

15. Post-Fordist Capitalism?: Corporatism and Dualism in Britain and West Germany*

JOSEF ESSER

In his criticism of the theoretical model of 'pluralistic industrialism', John Goldthorpe has pointed out that, despite their pluralist structure of political interest representation, liberal-democratic industrial societies of the West continue to operate on the basis of an economic system organized in the interests of private capital (Goldthorpe, 1984a, 1984b). He argues further that:

> In their advanced form, such societies in various ways promote the extensive and effective organization of economic interests—with labour gaining in particular in its capacity to engage in distributional conflict. But all such organization is essentially organization against market forces, on the operation of which the efficiency of capitalist economies, even when 'mixed' and 'managed', must still ultimately depend. (1984a: 12)

However, he also suggests that the organizational capabilities of powerful economic interests, particularly those of capital and labour, may threaten the governability of the state and the controllability of the economy.

Goldthorpe distinguishes analytically between two solutions to these problems. The *corporatist* solution, which

> can be understood as a response in which governments attempt to cope with intensifying problems of inflation and stagflation by bringing the major economic actors, and most crucially organised labour, into processes of policy formation and implementation. In other words, institutional and ultimately political substitutes are sought for market mechanisms, in order to aggregate and concert different interests and to render their pursuit consistent with policy goals. (*ibid.*)

As far as labour is concerned, Goldthorpe talks here of an 'inclusionary' strategy. In

---

* Translated from the German by Jon Clark.

contrast to this the *dualist* solution entails the exclusion of labour:

> That is, the creation of a sizable work-force whose members are in one way or another marginal to the key institutions of the plural society and who therefore lack effective organisation and the resources to achieve it. To the extent, then, that areas of the economy are developed within which market forces can operate with considerable freedom, the rigidities that prevail elsewhere may be offset. (*ibid.*)

In this context Goldthorpe also criticizes most mainstream Marxist analyses of recent developments in the political economies of Western European nations as seriously inadequate, particularly in their treatment of corporatist institutions: 'The view that such institutions can be understood as the latest or "highest" form of the social control of labour under capitalism is repeatedly challenged' (*ibid.*: 13).

I regard Goldthorpe's criticism of 'pluralistic industrialism' and its convergence thesis as convincing. I also find his distinction between corporatist and dualist tendencies extremely fruitful for the comparative analysis of liberal-capitalist industrial societies. What I miss, though, is a conceptual framework, grounded in social theory, which could explain why in liberal-capitalist societies one or other tendency (or hybrid forms between them) predominates and which particular set of political and economic conditions generates which particular outcomes. I would like to present here, from a Marxist perspective, an outline of such an explanatory framework which alone, I believe, demonstrates the fruitfulness of the categories corporatist and dualist. I hope thereby to counter Goldthorpe's claim that Marxist analysis is inadequate. To the extent that Marxist analysts have described corporatism as the latest or highest form of the social control of labour under capitalism, I would agree with Goldthorpe's criticism. What I find problematical is his contention that this criticism applies to most mainstream Marxist analyses.

FORDIST CAPITALISM: THE DOMINANCE OF CORPORATISM

Building on the work of Gramsci (1971) and the French 'Regulation School' (Aglietta, 1976; Lipietz, 1987; Boyer, 1986), I would characterize the historical period from 1945 to the mid-1970s (in which corporatism was established and became dominant) as 'Fordist'. Under the economic, political, military and ideological hegemony of the USA there developed during this period in all Western industrial societies, albeit at differing speeds and with differing penetration, a new type of capitalist society. It was distinguished by a specific *regime of accumulation*, a specific *mode of regulation* and a specific *hegemonial structure* (for an elaboration of these concepts, see Lipietz, 1985: 120ff.; Gramsci, 1971).

The most significant characteristic of the Fordist *regime of accumulation* is the systematic linking and interdependence of mass production and mass consumption. It involves the widespread use of semi-automated systems of continuous assembly production and Taylorist forms of work organization, particularly in those highly concentrated industries—automotive, electronics and chemical—which are so central to economic growth. Despite differences between largely deskilled production workers on the one hand and highly qualified skilled workers in the areas of maintenance, planning and supervision on the other, the Fordist accumulation regime sees the development of relatively homogeneous forms of labour market segmentation. This creates favourable preconditions for a growth in trade union membership and density as well as the development of comprehensive systems of conflict regulation between capital and labour. Parallel to this there occurs a generalization of consumption norms based on mass production, both through the extension of the supply of consumer goods (particularly consumer durables) and through an increase in overall demand in the economy. This in turn presupposes an increase in both money and real wages as well as the establishment and extension of consumer credit.

The close and systematic relationship between mass production and mass consumption in the Fordist accumulation regime requires a particular *mode of regulation*, above all the successful long-term regulation of the relation between capital and labour and the creation of new links between the state, society and the economy in the form of interventionist economic and social policy. During the Fordist phase we find in all capitalist countries—admittedly to different degrees and modified by different historical traditions—an institutionalized system of industrial relations with strong trade unions and employers' associations and the creation of cooperative arrangements or forms of concertation between trade unions, employers' organizations and state bodies. Even where they differ in their length of duration, substantive form, degree of stability and economic success, they all represent an attempt to harmonize the interests of the social partners with state social and economic policy (and sometimes industrial and structural policy too).

In this situation the 'Keynesian state' (Buci-Glucksmann and Therborn, 1982) does not function—as left Keynesians had hoped—as a societal instrument to overcome structural contradictions within capitalism. Rather, it expresses, in its internal structure and method of functioning, the social balance of power at a particular time and its conflicts and contradictions. It makes continuous use of a range of financial and organizational measures and ideological discourses to stabilize the existing accumulation regime and its institutionalized methods of regulation. The state is thus both an integral component of social production and reproduction in the context of the world capitalist market and simultaneously the organizer of a particular socially constituted hegemonial '*project*'. It is at one and the same time social and welfare state, law-and-order and surveillance state, but also 'discourse state' (Poulantzas, 1978; J. Hirsch, 1980). Equally, this Fordist phase of capitalist development under US hegemony is protected internationally by a multi-layered system of institutional frameworks and controls of an economic, political and military kind (for a detailed account, see Arrighi, 1986).

The cooperative structure which is written into Fordist capitalism grants the trade unions a significant increase in their areas of economic and political jurisdiction. Only strong unions, acting concertedly and equipped with an efficient bureaucracy and firm leadership from above, are able to mediate smoothly and effectively as a reliable social partner between the interests of the capitalist system and individual union members, thereby eliminating the 'Achilles heel of corporatism' (Teubner, 1979; see also Weitbrecht, 1969). Accordingly, we find in different capitalist countries different strategies—irrespective of whether it is Social Democrats, Conservatives or Christian Democrats who are in government—which aim to give the trade unions organizational, legal or financial support for the execution of this role. The strategies include the juridification of industrial relations, strengthening of trade union bureaucracies via so-called industry laws, social contracts, political exchange packages and co-determination.

It must be noted, however, that this corporatist mode of regulation and the importance of trade unions within it varies from country to country and assumes considerably different forms over time. For this reason only empirically and historically comparative investigations can determine their exact method of functioning and effectiveness (Lehmbruch, 1983, 1985). Overall, though, until the mid-1970s such 'monopolistic' forms of regulation were on the political agenda in all Western capitalist societies and the trade unions were correspondingly 'cultivated'. It is also true that by and large the trade unions' own policies promoted such developments, even when in many countries these policies were challenged temporarily by periods of intense industrial conflict.

CRISIS OF FORDISM = CRISIS OF CORPORATISM

Since the 1970s Fordist capitalism has entered a worldwide 'secular crisis'. The present phase is characterized by intense debates about a fundamental restructuring of capitalist societies. What is at stake is the implementation of a 'post-Fordist' mode of accumulation and regulation, for traditional methods are no longer able to guarantee the reproduction of capitalism, i.e. the continuous increase in the rate of profit, at a macro-societal level:

- In the spheres of *production and work organization* Taylorism proves to be too rigid to allow the optimal use of the technical and social possibilities of new information and communication technologies.
- In the spheres of *plant and company organization* the predominance of economies of scale over economies of scope is preventing enterprises from adapting flexibly to changes in the structure of demand on the world market and from pushing ahead with the required technological restructuring of mass production. In addition, traditional forms of organization prove to be unsuitable for implementing a stronger industrialization of the service sector and its integration with production processes through the introduction of microelectronic and information technology.
- In the system of *industrial relations* the centralized corporatist mechanisms for bargaining over wages and working conditions have consistently increased real wages and unit labour costs at the cost of labour productivity. In addition, the collective bargaining power of worker representatives at plant and industry level has impeded the required manpower reductions, the flexibilization of working time and changes in pay and grading structures.
- The existing 'welfare state' (*Sozialstaat*) is exposed to an ever-increasing range of demands and proves to be too expensive and bureaucratically inefficient. Since its activities have to be financed from ever-increasing tariffs on the employment of labour (e.g. national insurance contributions), labour productivity and company profitability come under increasing pressure from this quarter too.

However the conventional capitalist wisdom may argue on specific points, the crisis is clearly a *political* one. The ossified and inflexible structures of the monopolist mode of regulation, with its powerful trade unions, civil service bureaucracies and institutionalized interest groups, all impede increases in profitability. For these reasons a fundamental change of institutional structures, and the power relations crystallized in them, is required. The core of the political attack is directed at the union goals of *equalization* and *collectivization*—of qualifications, working conditions, and pay and grading structures—and state-guaranteed support for the sick, the disabled and the retired. This is to be replaced by an increased 'flexibilization' and differentiation, including the exclusion of specific employee groups from 'corporatist' structures and the fragmentation of employee interests and interest representation.

Flexibilization in the use of machine plant and the organization of production, conditioned by the primacy of the market economy and enabled by new technology, is accompanied by the flexibilization of labour in conformity with the functional demands of capital utilization. Recent research in industrial sociology has already identified at both plant and supra-plant level the *re-professionalization* of a highly qualified technical intelligentsia with relatively secure jobs. This is in contrast to a growing number of deskilled, poorly paid workers, who are employed in monotonous, machine-determined tasks and permanently threatened by dismissal (Kern and Schumann, 1985). Such work is carried out by a new type of 'mass worker', no longer tied to a particular workplace or faced with uniform working conditions, but highly individualized, flexibilized and fragmented.

On top of this, as a result of the structurally determined oversupply of cheap labour, employers are able to extend the use of insecure part-time, home and subcontracting work which is seldom protected by collectively agreed terms and conditions of employment. Simultaneously, because of the high potential for rationalization, the number of permanently employed staff in the core sectors of industrial production, administration and services is in ever-increasing decline. This perceptible differentiation within the labour force is enhanced by the '*tertiarization*' of industrial production, in which an increasing number of jobs are transferred from the factory floor to the office, in other words from production to pre- and post-production functional areas. The growing 'scientization' (*Verwissenschaftlichung*) of the production process intensifies this trend. This is accompanied by an increase in the proportion of graduate employees both inside and outside research and development departments, which in turn exacerbates the gap between highly qualified and less well qualified employee groups (Hack and Hack, 1985). Both strong centralized unions and Keynesian social policy are obstacles to this increasing trend towards the dualization and segmentation of the occupational and social structure. Correspondingly, the attack in all capitalist societies is directed at trade unions and policies which continue to favour the equalization of working and living conditions.

My central argument against John Goldthorpe is therefore the following. In all liberal-capitalist industrial societies there is a trend towards a hybrid relationship between corporatism and dualism. However, the form, content and degree of hybridity, and the nature of particular strategies and their relative success, are all dependent on the specific economic, social and political conditions in particular countries and can only be identified through comparative empirical investigation. In attempting to summarize country-specific differences on a more systematic level, it is possible to identify two different basic patterns:

1 disenfranchisement and exclusion of the trade unions from processes of conflict regulation and consensus-building at plant and macro-policy levels (labour exclusion);

2 selective incorporation of privileged trade unions or senior workplace representatives, with the exclusion of underprivileged groups.

Britain is a prime example of the first pattern (Crouch, 1986; Goldthorpe, 1984a; Hyman, 1986), the Federal Republic of Germany of the second (Esser, 1986; Kastendiek and Kastendiek, 1985).

GREAT BRITAIN: LABOUR EXCLUSION AND COMPANY UNIONISM

The economic policy of the Conservative Government in Britain since 1979 can be characterized as the use of a strong, albeit de-Keynesianized administrative state to give full and free rein to world market forces within the British economy. The aim is to promote the further modernization and specialization of the finance and service sector, primarily located in the south of England, and to make it into the flagship of 'post-industrial' British capitalism. Second, it is intended that multinational commercial and industrial capital, particularly of US-American, Japanese and West German origin, should find attractive capital investment opportunities in Britain, not least in order to arrest the decades of decline in British industry and to help bring about a process of re-industrialization. British industry itself, which the Thatcher Government does not really believe to be capable of adapting to changed world market conditions, is therefore to be exposed to relentless international competition.

The post-war model of 'social democracy' (Jessop, 1978b), including a powerful role for trade unions, is held to bear the main responsibility for the decline in the British economy. The Conservative Party's systematically applied authoritarian populist discourse (Hall and Jacques, 1983), aimed particularly at undermining the legitimacy of strong independent trade unions, is also directed against the 'nationalization of society', the 'obstruction of market forces by state intervention and large collective organizations', the nannying of individuals by the welfare state and the 'undermining of entrepreneurial initiative and the ability to innovate'. This 'discursive strategy' has led to a major reduction in the political influence of the trade unions and a weakening of their ability to strike and represent the interests of their members.

The policy of the Thatcher Government towards the unions is particularly well illustrated by its employment and trade union legislation. Five particular objectives can be identified (see Crouch, 1986):

1 weakening of unions *vis-à-vis* the employer by making most forms of sympathy and solidarity strikes actionable in law and by reducing state social security benefits for strikers' families by an assumed amount of strike pay (most British unions do not pay strike pay because of their low level of subscriptions);

2 strengthening the position of union members and non-unionists *vis-à-vis* the union bureaucracy by requiring secret ballots on closed shops, in union elections and before strikes;

3 undermining of the traditionally close links between the trade unions and the Labour Party—the collective affiliation of unions to the Party, an essential component of its organizational and financial strength, must now be subject to review by secret ballot every ten years;

4 abolition of a number of statutory bodies and committees which had previously made it possible to achieve a largely peaceful resolution of basic wages and conditions for particular sectors and occupational groups;

5 substantial narrowing of the criminal and civil immunities of the trade unions—many of the new provisions increase their legal liabilities and are intended to force them to renounce forms of action which have been regarded for decades as lawful.

Many of these measures have long been a component of the industrial relations system in countries with traditionally more juridified systems. In the British context, however, they are intended to destroy the traditionally highly informal system, to the sole disadvantage of the unions, without replacing it by an alternative set of positive legal rights. For example, the duty to carry out a secret ballot before a strike prevents the unions from reacting instantaneously to actions by the employer in the absence of simultaneous provision for legally enforceable collective agreements with fixed terms. Even those legal measures which strengthen the membership *vis-à-vis* the union bureaucracy lose much of their rank-and-file democratic innocence when they simultaneously weaken the position of trade unions and workplace representatives *vis-à-vis* the employer (Kastendiek, 1988).

It must remain an open question whether this policy of 'labour exclusion' will be successful in the longer term. It should be noted, however, that trade union membership has declined by three million between 1979 and 1986, that the incidence of strikes (apart from the unsuccessful miners' strike of 1984/85) has declined significantly and that employers have been able to make major modifications to traditional working practices at plant level (W. Brown, 1986; Hyman, 1986). Neither the unions nor representative bodies in the workplace have been able to mount concerted opposition to these fundamental changes in the production and labour processes.

The introduction of new technologies has also been used by managements to make major changes in the organization of work and to undermine existing bargaining structures. Attempts by trade unions to negotiate 'new technology agreements' with employers have met with little or no success, with the result that neither unions nor shop stewards have exerted any real influence on the introduction and use of new technologies. One important by-product of this development, possibly intended by the government and promoted in particular by multinational companies setting up new factories on green-field sites, is the extension of 'company unionism' and moves towards a 'micro-corporatism' on the Japanese model (Hyman, 1986). The focus of employee representation is shifted increasingly from the sectoral and occupational to the company level, thereby intensifying pluralist fragmentation and the subordination of workplace employee representation to market forces.

FEDERAL REPUBLIC OF GERMANY: SELECTIVE CORPORATIST LABOUR INCLUSION

In a characterization of the post-Fordist accumulation strategy in the Federal Republic of Germany the distinction which is often made between 'de-industrialization' (transfer of specific company activities and functions to other parts of the world), 're-industrialization' (regaining of a country's own industrial base) and 'neo-industrialization' (establishment of high-technology industries) proves to be problematical. In fact, German employers are united in their commitment to defending the existing specialist industrial profile and the traditional sectoral coherence of the economy as a whole.

This strategy means, first, that the core industries, already highly competitive and internationalized in the 1960s and 1970s, particularly the technologically advanced sectors (machine, vehicle and plant construction, chemical, plastics and petroleum processing, electrical engineering, electronics and opto-electronics), should be further modernized, specialized and flexibilized. Second, the high level of coordination between all sectors of industry, characteristic of the German model from the outset, should be further strengthened. In particular, small and medium-sized companies should become more strongly aligned to the process and product innovations of the large companies operating in the world market, and the functional and structural interconnections between the manufacturing and tertiary sectors should be increased considerably. The whole of the industrial core sector should profit from the benefits of the micro-electronic and information technology revolutions, and the sectoral coherence of all industries and sectors, including the so-called traditional industries, should be retained and strengthened rather than sacrificed in favour of concentration on fewer products (on the Japanese model) or on 'service' industries (on the American model).

Since this strategy shows more similarities with the Social Democratic Party's *Modell Deutschland* than the fashionable talk of the neo-conservative sea-change (*Wende*) would have us believe, there is no real break between the trade union policy of the Conservative-Liberal coalition after 1982 and that of its Social Democratic predecessor. The SPD's 'modernisation of the economy through the formation of corporatist blocks' (Esser, 1982) had led before 1982 to a cleavage in West German society between an economically healthy core of internationally competitive industries together with their appropriate service functions on the one hand, and a marginal surplus population on the other, economically superfluous, politically controlled and ideologically isolated. This has been the structural basis for the gradual weakening of the unions' 'integration capacity', organizational stability and fighting strength. In addition, union readiness (through participation in the formation of corporatist blocks) to be party to the exclusion of particular social groups and individuals from economic activity has contributed to the splitting of the working class into two powerless groups, one not prepared to risk losing their jobs, the other with no social power at their disposal.

The CDU-FDP coalition has been able to build on this development in a kind of dual strategy. On the one hand, it gives political and ideological support to all employer measures intended to bring about an effective flexibilization of work organization, working time, wages, labour markets, industries, regions and companies, and opposes all demands for state employment programmes and an across-the-board reduction in working hours (weekly and lifetime) aimed at uniting the interests of the employed and the unemployed. On the other hand, the coalition government is well aware that the preparedness of workers, works councils and trade unions to hold back on wage demands and to work cooperatively with employers when there is a need to introduce new technologies quickly and effectively represents an important international competitive advantage for the West German economy. For this reason a kind of reduced participation is offered to those trade unions regarded as fundamental to the micro-electronic restructuring of the economy and its functionally necessary political legitimation. This reduced participation takes place, of course, not with the intention of improving the present position of unions, but of cementing their present organizational weakness.

The government believes it can cope politically with this dual strategy because it can rely on the weakness and fragmentation of employees (brought about by the economic crisis) and need not fear any concerted opposition from the unions. Despite a few spectacular conflicts the unions continue to direct their efforts towards cooperation with employers and government. They are still geared to securing the international competitive position of the West German economy and to maintaining their organizational strength by extending their potential membership to include the 'winners' from the current changes in industrial and employment structure.

One effect of this development could be that the trade unions will become corporatist representative bodies of privileged groups of workers. By relinquishing *de facto* the principle of industrial unionism (one union for employees of all companies in a particular industry), they could well intensify pluralist fragmentation in the Federal Republic of Germany. An additional effect might be, as in Great Britain, the development of 'micro-corporatism'. The processes of flexibilization, differentiation and division within and between sectors, industries, regions, companies, workplaces and workforces are already in train and, without any need for political intervention from above, could result in the 'spontaneous' metamorphosis of national occupational unionism into company unionism. A union wage policy determined solely by the autonomous decisions of privileged groups of employees at company level would represent a complete reversal in the traditional relationship between works council and union, with the former rather than the latter calling the tune.

CONCLUSION

My central argument in this chapter is that, in the wake of the world economic crisis of the early 1970s, all liberal-capitalist industrial societies are undergoing a period of fundamental transformation whose eventual outcome still remains open. What can be said with some certainty, however, is that the model of Fordist capitalism together with its mode of regulation and hegemonial structure has reached its end and that the future lies in some form of 'post-Fordist' model of capitalist development and growth. John Goldthorpe's analyses of corporatist and dualist tendencies/strategies represent an important contribution to our comparative understanding of the relationship between the state, capital and labour in 'post-Fordist' capitalism.

My argument against Goldthorpe is that his distinction between corporatism and dualism needs to be underpinned by a theory of contemporary capitalism which would allow us to explain why one or other tendency (or a hybrid form between the two) is successful in particular countries. My distinction between Fordist and 'post-Fordist' capitalism, and its empirical differentiation as applied to Great Britain and the Federal Republic of Germany, leads to the provisional conclusion that in both countries the traditional centralized corporatist processes of interest mediation and conflict regulation between the state, capital and the unions no longer exist. In both countries the political attack of the state and capital is directed at trade union goals such as the equalization and collectivization of qualifications, working conditions and wage and employment relationships, as well as at guaranteed levels of social security benefits in cases of illness, disability and retirement. In both countries the intention is to use flexibilization and differentiation to divide the working population socially and weaken it politically. The ultimate aim is to bring about a fundamental change in political-institutional structures and in the strong bargaining power of trade unions crystallized in them. In 'union-hostile' Great Britain this strategy conforms increasingly to the basic model of 'labour exclusion', albeit complemented by micro-corporatist company unionism. In the more 'union-friendly' Federal Republic of Germany macro-political corporatism is being replaced by a selective corporatist 'incorporation' of privileged trade unions accompanied by a simultaneous strengthening of micro-corporatist tendencies in important large companies.

Whichever basic model proves to be generally more successful for post-Fordist capitalism, the result will be division and the weakening of solidaristic collective interest representation of the working population as a whole in particular countries. For this reason trade unions (and political parties closely associated with them) which see themselves as collective representatives of the interests of all employees, including the unemployed and 'marginalized' workers, must oppose the post-Fordist model of capitalism and develop their own alternative social and political 'project'. This will almost certainly need to go beyond the traditional model of political Keynesianism. If they fail to develop such an alternative or even go along actively with the current strategy of capital, then they themselves will have played an important role in ensuring the worldwide victory of a post-Fordist capitalist structure and a post-Fordist political and ideological hegemony.

Interchange

HARDIMAN REPLIES TO ESSER

Josef Esser's stimulating chapter on capitalism and corporatism concentrates not on a critique of Goldthorpe's work, but on developing an alternative analysis which, he suggests, constitutes a necessary corrective to Goldthorpe's studies of corporatism and dualism. Indeed, he states that he agrees with the substance of much of Goldthorpe's work on corporatism and dualism. But something crucial is missing in this work: 'a conceptual framework, grounded in social theory, which could explain why in liberal-capitalist societies one or other tendency [viz. corporatism and dualism]... predominates and which particular set of political and economic conditions generates which particular outcomes'. Goldthorpe criticizes those Marxist theorists who would see corporatism as 'the latest or highest form of the social control of labour under capitalism'. Esser, though writing within a Marxist tradition himself, agrees with the substance of this criticism; yet in his view not all Marxist analysis can be so easily dealt with. The main part of his contribution is devoted to setting out an alternative framework which, he argues, can provide a fuller theoretical account of the phenomena analyzed by Goldthorpe.

However, it is clear that what Esser means by 'social theory' is very different from Goldthorpe's conception. Esser's approach is characterized by a functional approach to explaining variations across industrial societies. This is allied with a high degree of theoretical abstraction which, I shall argue, results in an under-specification of the variables which are relevant to any comparative discussion. For these reasons his approach, rather than expanding or improving upon Goldthorpe's, in my view serves only to obscure the issues which Esser wishes to explain. Three issues focus the differences between the two authors: first, approaches to social explanation, functionalist versus actor-centred; second, the scope for politics to shape economic outcomes; and third, the purpose of model-building as a guide to social theory. The first of these is the most important area of disagreement; the other two considerations follow from the position taken with regard to this issue.

EXPLANATION IN THE SOCIAL SCIENCES

Esser makes it quite clear that his account has a functionalist cast. He argues that the requirements of maintaining capitalist accumulation at a satisfactory level dictate the necessity of the social processes we can observe empirically. Esser sets out his threefold specification of Fordism as 'a specific regime of accumulation', 'a mode of regulation' and 'a hegemonial structure'. Taylorist modes of labour organization favour the development of trade unionism; further, the link between mass production and mass consumption is 'systematic' and 'interdependent' such that, Esser argues, there also develop 'comprehensive systems of conflict regulation between capital and labour'. These are required: 'successful long-term regulation of the relation between capital and labour and the creation of new links between the state, society and economy in the form of interventionist economic and social policy' are needed to ensure stable capitalist production. This need somehow calls forth its own satisfaction. A similar point recurs later, where Esser argues that the 'secular crisis' of Fordism arises because traditional methods are unable to guarantee the reproduction of capitalism.

These formulations seem to present a great difficulty, in two respects. First, Esser purports to be able to identify the functional requirements of capitalism as a global mode of production. Second, the specific features of social organization which he discusses are held to be the necessary response to these functional requirements. However, the first issue raises the question of the appropriateness of functional explanation in the social sciences. I wish to defend the view, implicit in Goldthorpe's work, that functional explanation has only a limited and highly circumscribed role in sociological explanation. On the whole, as Elster argues, 'functionalist explanation in sociology rests upon an ill-conceived analogy from biology, and... a closer analysis of purported functionalist explanations shows that in virtually all cases one or more of the defining features are lacking' (1984: 28). A key defining feature is the existence of a 'causal feedback loop', that is, some mechanism whereby the requirements of the whole are made manifest such that the adaptive behaviour can be demonstrated to be necessary. The mere existence of 'unintended, unrecognized and beneficial effects' (*ibid.*: 32) is not sufficient to explain why a certain pattern exists and persists (see also Elster, 1982, 1985: 27–36, 1986). Esser wishes to invoke a functionalist explanation of certain features of capitalist organization in what seems to be an illegitimate fashion. He offers no indication of how we are to conceive of the whole, that is, the capitalist mode of production in its national manifestations, nor does he show how social and political patterns may be regarded as functional for its viability: he cannot identify any plausible 'causal feedback loop'.

Second, Esser offers no argument for why the *particular* observed functional adaptations are necessary, rather than any others. Why, for example, was it 'necessary' to develop corporatist patterns of industrial relations rather than any other? And if 'comprehensive systems of conflict regulation' were 'required' in the post-war period, why were such wide variations evident in the manner in which these were implemented—or not implemented—in, say, Britain, Sweden, Germany, France or the United States? Esser notes that 'the Keynesian state' continues to reflect 'the social balance of power at a particular time and its conflicts and contradictions', but he offers no indication of how this may be investigated or what relationship it bears to the basic functionalist analysis of the adaptive processes of 'capitalism'. He writes of corporatism as something 'granted' to trade unions. What his functionalist approach prevents him from seeing is the frequent contingency of trade union involvement in such agreements, and the lack of controlling power by government or employers over trade unions' activities. In short, he neglects the conflictual and bargained nature of corporatism where it existed, and altogether ignores the cases where it was either weak or non-existent. Esser's approach, intended to provide a framework for comparative investigation, paradoxically hinders investigation of all the interesting cross-national variations.

In contrast, Goldthorpe's starting point in patterns of economic regulation enables us to identify reasons for the development of Keynesian approaches and corporatist patterns of industrial relations in various countries. Furthermore, his interest in the organized power of economic interests (akin to the 'power resources' approach of authors such as Korpi, 1978, 1983, 1986), provides clear indicators of how cross-national variations can be explained. The reasons for the breakdown of the 'Keynesian consensus', and the divergent paths of development evident in different countries, are similarly capable of being analyzed with reference to the general conditions Goldthorpe sets out.

Goldthorpe's analysis is rooted in an 'actor-centred' approach to social explanation. This in no way precludes exploration of social structural features or economic constraints on action. But it enables us to investigate outcomes in terms of reasons for actions under various conditions. This avoids the pitfalls of functionalist explanation, provides ample scope for exploring empirical variations, and takes the motivations and perceptions of social actors more seriously than Esser can.

THE POSSIBILITY OF POLITICS

This observation leads directly to the second point of conflict between the two perspectives, that is, the scope and discretion of political choice in shaping social and economic outcomes. Esser's approach leads directly to determinist conclusions; Goldthorpe's allows a necessary degree of indeterminacy and takes seriously the differences between conflicting political interests and ideological orientations.

Esser describes the 'crisis' of Fordism as 'a *political* one'. The response to this crisis seems to entail a (necessary?) political attack on trade union goals of 'equalization and collectivization', favouring reduction in support for the welfare state, and promoting the 'flexibilization and differentiation' of the workforce. These responses arise from technical exigencies, from the 'functional demands of capital utilization', which now requires the differentiation of a 'deskilled' workforce from a 're-professionalized' technical intelligentsia.

The theoretical terms in which he describes changes in the workforce and the empirical accuracy of the thesis of a deskilled working class may be disputed (see, for example, Batstone *et al.*, 1987; Daniel, 1987; Gallie, 1988c; Roderick Martin, 1988). But the trends towards a decline in the relative size of the manual working class and the expansion of various categories of white-collar employment are evident in all Western capitalist societies. However, Esser concentrates exclusively on the technical aspects of these changes, and is altogether uninterested in the consequences for patterns of worker organization and the variations these may exhibit cross-nationally. In contrast, Goldthorpe sees as the key issue the socio-political implications of these changes in social structure. He identifies the nature of the shared interests on which organization is based—whether sectional and divisive, or overarching and approximating to 'class-wide mobilization'—as vital for the capacity for collective action and the general political orientation of labour movements. Furthermore, Goldthorpe stresses the importance of the ideological orientation of government for the strategic choices it makes with regard to economic management decisions. A range of responses may be evident across different countries on questions such as support for welfare programmes, relations with organized labour and the political toleration of high levels of unemployment. Esser appears to regard these outcomes as economically determined; Goldthorpe, more realistically, allows that a discussion of the partisanship of government may be vital for any adequate explanation of observed variations.

THE USE OF MODELS AND IDEAL-TYPES

The third point of contrast between Esser's and Goldthorpe's approach concerns the way in which ideal-types are constructed to assist in explaining variations in social and political patterns.

Esser identifies 'two different basic patterns' of post-Fordist adaptation. These involve respectively 'disenfranchisement and exclusion of the trade unions from processes of conflict regulation and consensus-building at plant and macro-policy levels (labour exclusion)'; and 'selective incorporation of privileged trade unions or senior workplace representatives, with the exclusion of underprivileged groups'. Britain is said to be 'an example' of the first, the Federal Republic of Germany 'an example' of the second. But the way in which these models are constructed seems decidedly *ad hoc* and arbitrary: no reasons are given for the inclusion of these elements and not others. Quite apart from the adequacy of these categories to describe the two countries mentioned, their utility as general typologies must be called into question. Most other Western advanced capitalist countries will not fit either pattern. The weakness of these two models follows directly from Esser's earlier failure to provide adequate methods of comparing the empirical variations he purports to acknowledge, a failure which springs directly from his functionalist approach to the whole question of how to identify patterns of political and social change. In contrast, Goldthorpe's use of the models of corporatism, neo-laissez-faire and dualism is firmly rooted in his basic commitment to explanation in terms of an action frame of reference.

CONCLUSION

There are various points of detail in Esser's discussion of the experiences of Britain and Germany which could be debated further. But my main concern here has been to draw out the essential contrast between his approach and that of Goldthorpe, which hinges on very different conceptions of what is implied by sociological theory. A general theory of capitalism is what Esser claims to miss in Goldthorpe's approach. However, when examined in further detail, Esser's general theory appears to be based on questionable premises; as a consequence, therefore, doubt is cast upon its utility both as explanation and as a tool of sociological analysis.

ESSER REPLIES TO HARDIMAN*

It is not intended simply as an act of courtesy when I say that Niamh Hardiman's contribution is an outstandingly successful defence of Goldthorpe's conception of the relationship between capitalism and corporatism. Her systematic presentation and development of Goldthorpe's argument show clearly the strengths of his analytical approach. Her impressive evaluation of the empirical literature demonstrates convincingly the fruitfulness of the distinction between 'corporatist' and 'dualist' tendencies in Western capitalist industrial societies, although I do have some difficulties in talking of a 'neo-laissez-faire' strategy in Britain. As I attempted to show in my own contribution, developments in Britain are perhaps better interpreted as a particular kind of hybrid relationship between micro-corporatist and macro-dualist (i.e. labour exclusion at the macro level) tendencies.

As one might expect, my objections to her analysis are on the same lines as my criticism of John Goldthorpe, namely that, despite the profusion of facts and empirical analyses from many different countries, their classification and interpretation will remain imprecise as long as they are not rooted in a theoretically grounded periodization of the historical development of the world capitalist system. More exactly, since every capitalist country (societal formation) is an integral component of world capitalist society (Wallerstein, 1979), bound into its historical dynamic and thus dependent on its structural constraints, the analysis of every individual country and the conditions under which its strategic actors (governments, parties, employers, employers' associations, trade unions, etc.) behave must be in the context of this historical dynamic and its concomitant structural constraints.

On my analysis the concepts used by Goldthorpe and Hardiman, namely 'post-war Keynesianism' versus 'post-Keynesianism', do not enable us to grasp the economic, social, political and ideological complexity of this connection between individual capitalist countries and world capitalist developments. In fact, they are much more 'reductionist' and 'economistic' than the theory of capitalism based on the Marxian critique of political economy, which is continually, one might say almost ritualistically, accused of such sins. My intention in introducing the concepts of 'Fordism' and the emergent contours of 'post-Fordist' production on a world-capitalist scale is precisely to suggest a theoretically grounded periodization of the historical development of the world capitalist system which could (and should) avoid all forms of reductionism as well as enabling us to comprehend the 'dialectic' between structural constraints and possibilities for action. It should perhaps be emphasized here that the concepts of Fordism and post-Fordism should be understood heuristically and are still far from achieving a convincing theoretical grounding. In fact, at one point in her contribution Hardiman herself alludes to the need for a more all-embracing theoretical frame of reference, without however building this systematically into her own analysis:

> Each of these alternatives is discussed primarily in terms of the government's approach to organized labour, revealing the centrality Goldthorpe attributes to organized labour as a vital shaping force in the political economy of Western European countries. Neither employers' strategies, nor the international and domestic economic context receive much attention; they are largely taken for granted.

---

* Translated from the German by Jon Clark.

If I understand it rightly, both Goldthorpe and Hardiman favour, implicitly if not explicitly, the 'rational choice' approach (Elster, 1983b, 1984; Przeworski, 1985a, 1986)—at present extremely fashionable among critical social scientists in the Anglo-Saxon world—and its philosophical basis, methodological individualism. I do not wish to play down the undoubted merits of the rational choice discussion, above all its insistence that structural theories in social science will remain unsatisfactory as long as they prove unable to explain the logic of individual or collective action, as long, in other words, as structural theory and action theory are not adequately linked with one another.

Without being able to demonstrate this in detail here, I nevertheless have major doubts as to whether approaches based on methodological individualism, and utilizing its operationalizations derived from game theory, are able to deliver the action-theoretical foundations of an historically oriented theory of capitalism. On the contrary I would argue that such approaches almost always depart either implicitly or explicitly from structural theory and analyze the logic of individual and collective action without reference to their constitutive structural constraints. It is significant that both Goldthorpe and Hardiman talk much about concrete strategies and actors, but little about the specific historical structure of the world market and its hierarchies, little about strategies of capital and forms of wage labour, little about capital accumulation and tendencies to crisis and so on. It is significant, too, that neither is able to explain why macro-corporatism, which appeared to be so stable in the 1970s, is now beginning to come under threat in the so-called model countries of corporatism, Austria and Sweden, as well as in Britain, West Germany and France.

I have often asked myself why so-called 'grand theories' or structural theories are much less beloved of social scientists in Britain than on the European Continent, and why extensive detailed empirical research is always regarded as more important than attempts to link social theory and the empirical world systematically with one another and to see both as equally important. Britain has its internationally recognized theoretical research, for example, the work of Anthony Giddens, G. A. Cohen, Bob Jessop, to name but a few from the field under discussion here. But do they represent the mainstream? I think not.

If my suspicion is correct, namely that much of what remains in dispute between Goldthorpe/Hardiman and myself can be traced back to the difference in social scientific 'cultures', it would perhaps be extremely fruitful for both sides to confront these different cultures—their respective strengths and weaknesses—with each other more systematically. Perhaps the outcome of our debate in this volume will be that this discussion will be conducted more widely. Both sides would stand to gain from it.

IX. CORPORATISM AND NEO-LIBERALISM

16. Sociology, Political Philosophy and Distributive Justice

RAYMOND PLANT

Behind the smokescreen of the monetarist controversy, therefore, lies a much more serious argument between rival views of human society ... which was papered over by several decades of good fortune and money illusion. (Samuel Brittan, 1983: 256)

My own position ... is that there may indeed be technical problems that one can treat in technical terms, but that, ultimately, the problem of inflation is a political problem: one's approach to it depends on what kind of society one wants to have .... What I object to is economists thinking that inflation is just a technical matter and that they, in the light of economic science, can tell us what to do. (John Goldthorpe, 1978: 215)

John Goldthorpe's work has set an exacting standard of empirical rigour and analysis which makes him a formidable model for any social scientist. However, while his work is concerned with empirical explanation, this does not mean that it does not have considerable salience for social and political philosophy. It is on its importance in this field that I want to concentrate in this chapter. As a self-confessed good Popperian in his approach to science, he has been concerned to preserve three precepts as central to scientific method: the search for hypotheses which are capable of being falsified by empirical evidence; the rejection of historicism, i.e. that there can be no way of predicting the future state of society by discovering some large-scale trends at work in society; and the separation of facts and values. He says that, *qua* sociologist, he has no more and no less to say about the desirable state of human society than the man who cleans his street. A social and political vision cannot be derived from sociology, it is a matter for political action which, it would appear, depends upon the preferences of individuals. In this context the social scientist has no particular authority.

However, in his own work sociological explanation and analysis can and do make clearer the nature of the choices facing members of Western societies. This becomes particularly apparent in his account of the nature of inflation in his contribution to *The Political Economy of Inflation*, a book which he edited with Fred Hirsch just before the latter's untimely death (Hirsch and Goldthorpe, 1978). I want to raise some of the issues for social and political philosophy implicit in this essay, which itself draws implicitly but extensively from the central areas of his work which have been discussed at length elsewhere in this volume. I shall argue that

Goldthorpe provides us with a very acute account of the dilemmas facing modern Western societies, but that his own refusal *qua* sociologist to take on normative questions, because these are inherently subjective, fails to point towards a way out of the dilemmas he has identified. Indeed, I shall argue that his refusal goes some way to supporting implicitly a neo-liberal view of the economy, which is a long way from his own political orientation.

A central theme of the inflation essay is that inflation is not just a technical problem, which if we knew enough economics we could solve or, if governments were not so obtuse they could solve by following economists' advice. In his view accounts of the nature of inflation raise major questions about the role of government, citizenship and interest groups in civil society, which lie deep in the present stage of development of Western societies, but which also raise normative questions about the desirable shape of the societies.

Since 1978, when the book was published, we have experienced the coming to power of a government in Britain which has taken over a good deal of neo-liberal economic analysis and the policy prescriptions arising from this analysis. On the surface these policy prescriptions look as if they are attempts at technical solutions to problems raised in the diagnosis. In fact they are policies which embody a view about the desirable role of government, the nature of citizenship and the role of interest groups, a point to which Samuel Brittan alludes in the first epigraph to this chapter. I want first of all to identify what the diagnosis is, partly by drawing upon Goldthorpe's own work, and then to look at the policy prescriptions to draw out their normative implications. I will conclude by discussing some of the issues raised by the normative aspect of modern neo-liberal political economy.

THE NEO-LIBERAL DIAGNOSIS OF INFLATION

There are several aspects to the neo-liberal diagnosis of the problems which were thought to beset British society in the mid-1970s, of which inflation was both a symbol and a consequence. Goldthorpe treats these aspects separately, which is important for analytical purposes, although they run together in the politics of the issues. These aspects are: monetarism and the general question of the causation of inflation; the role of interest groups and their effect on government; and the decline in what might be called civic virtue or what, referring to an older German tradition, might be called *Sittlichkeit*—ethical life or a set of shared values. There are links between these phenomena, and politically they have added up to a powerful political position which has put parties of the non-Marxist left in Britain on the defensive. In fact, the neo-liberal diagnosis has put a major question mark against social democratic political assumptions, assumptions which received their most extensive and plausible political statement in Anthony Crosland's *The Future of Socialism* (1956).

On the narrow interpretation, monetarism is a theory about the nature of the causation of inflation which rests upon the quality of money theory. The monetarist holds that the main determinant of monetary demand, or the total level of spending and thus the main influence on gross domestic product (GDP), is the quantity of money circulating in the economy. This can be expressed in the following equation:

$$MV = PQ$$

M is the quantity of money in the economy, V is the average velocity with which this money circulates, Q is the output produced, P is the price of this output. PQ is the nominal domestic product measured in cash terms, and this must equal the amount of money in the economy multiplied by the velocity of its circulation. Since the velocity is assumed to be constant, it follows that the quantity of money equals GDP at current prices. It is also part of the monetarist thesis that there is a clear definition of money compared with other financial assets and that this can be controlled by central banks and monetary authorities. Hence the relation between money supply and GDP can be made predictable and stable.

Given the relationship between the quantity of money and GDP at current prices, the crucial question then is whether an increase in money supply causes a rise in the price or quantity of goods. Will the real resources in the economy increase or will there simply be a rise in the price level of these resources? It is the central thesis of monetarism that any increase in the supply of money divorced from increases in real output will push up prices and hence be inflationary. Any regime which seeks to reduce or eliminate inflation will seek to expand money supply only in line with real increases in output. Any increase beyond the real level of output will increase inflation. Given that money supply is in the control of monetary authorities, it follows that inflation is essentially a political phenomenon caused by a government increasing the supply of money beyond the level of real output, essentially by running deficits in its own expenditure rather than cutting back its own expenditure or eliminating such deficits by raising taxes. Inflation is crucially a political choice, a fact which brings us to the more sociological factors which push governments into running deficits rather than either cutting government expenditure or raising taxes to cover deficits.

The political choices which cause governments to expand money supply are not the result of stupidity or obtuseness on their part, the failure, for example, to follow the advice of monetary economists, which would be the technical view of the inflation problem (severely criticized by Goldthorpe.) Rather, government is subject to deep pressures within society with regard to its own spending, arising to a great degree from 'unprincipled' interest group pressures. On the neo-liberal view, once government is involved in the social democratic project of seeking to secure a just distribution of resources through public expenditure on health, education, welfare, housing and so forth, it is inevitable that interest groups will press for expenditure on those resources which each regards as essential to its own view of what justice, or social and economic rights, or a commitment to citizenship, requires. Goldthorpe is surely correct in arguing that pluralist theorists have been much too sanguine in their claims about how interest groups work for the public good and about the extent to which the interests which they represent can both be harmonized and made compatible with what is still basically a capitalist economic system. He argues, correctly in my view, that critics of pluralism have now come to recognize two crucial facts:

> ... first, that interest groups, as they operate in the economic sphere, aim primarily at strengthening their members' market position through action that is taken in some sense against market forces, for example, via organisation, regulation, legislation, etc.; and secondly, that such interest groups are concerned very largely with distributional issues of a zero sum kind, in which their members' interests can only be protected or advanced to the extent that those of other groups are threatened or damaged.

Thus, as the number of interest groups and the amount of interest group activity increase, it must be expected that the market mechanisms on which the efficient functioning of the capitalist economy depends will work less freely and that distributional conflict within society will be heightened. This in turn will add to the difficulties of carrying through remedial economic policies. (Goldthorpe, 1984b: 321)

THE NORMATIVE IMPLICATIONS OF THE NEO-LIBERAL VIEW

There is a deep issue here in the neo-liberal view about social values. The non-Marxist left has come to define the goals of socialism or social democracy in distributive terms, usually in terms of greater equality to try to secure, as Goldthorpe has pointed out, a greater equality in the social rights of citizenship to match the formal equality in political and civil rights. This idea of citizenship as a status independent of the market, which should secure to citizens social and economic rights in both welfare and industrial relations and which will match political with civil rights (which are also independent of the market), is an idea and a demand which is now part and parcel of British society. However, in the view of the neo-liberal it is a malign and politically disruptive idea which has clear inflationary effects, above all because the commitment to social and economic rights is open-ended and incapable of being constrained by consensual social values. In the neo-liberal view we live in a morally fragmented society, in which there is no agreement on the criteria of social justice—whether in terms of need, merit, desert or entitlement—which could constrain the demands on the resources of society that the idea of the social and economic rights of citizenship would imply. So, for example, John Gray argues as follows:

> Ideas of social justice and of basic needs, which form the threadbare clothing of contemporary social democratic movements, are of minimal help here. Criteria of desert and merit, such as enter into popular conceptions of social justice, are not objective or publicly corrigible, but rather express private judgments grounded in varying moral traditions. Conceptions of merit are not shared as a common moral inheritance, neutrally available to the inner city Moslem population of Birmingham and the secularized professional classes of Hampstead, but instead reflect radically different cultural traditions and styles of life .... The objectivity of basic needs is equally delusive. Needs can be given no plausible cross cultural content, but instead are seen to vary across different moral traditions. (Gray, 1983: 181–2)

In short, the distributional side of interest group competition is essentially unprincipled. It is a zero sum struggle unconstrained by any shared distributive values.

The neo-liberal view therefore challenges in a direct way Goldthorpe's argument in an earlier essay about the way in which the lack of principle in the reward structure of British society produces a disorderly effect on British industrial relations. In 1974 he wrote:

> Such a consensus cannot be achieved without the entire structure of power and advantage becoming principled—becoming, that is, capable of being given consistent moral justification ... in other words the advancement of social justice has to be seen not as some lofty and impractical ideal ... but as an important precondition of mitigating current economic difficulties. (Goldthorpe, 1974a: 228)

In the view of the neo-liberal this demand is false on a number of counts. First, in a morally diverse society we cannot expect to find agreement concerning social justice which would make the struggle for resources principled. There are many criteria of social justice: need, entitlement, desert, merit, contribution, and so forth. We cannot achieve agreement on what is basic, or, if we believe in some balance of these criteria, we cannot achieve agreement on what the relative weightings should be. This is simply a sociological fact of our moral diversity in a modern society.

Second, in the absence of a consensus within society on these matters, which neo-liberals take to be a fact, it is vain to think that there is some kind of rational solution to be attained through reasoning about the nature of social justice. This point represents a rejection of the demand which Goldthorpe makes in the passage just quoted, and indeed the neo-liberal will argue that the reason why there is no rational solution to the problem is to be found precisely in Goldthorpe's own approach to questions of political morality. In the discussion printed at the end of his inflation essay (Goldthorpe, 1978: 214–16), he seems to argue—and this would be consistent with his Popperian position—that questions of political morality, because they are to do with ends and not means, are not amenable to rational, expert, technical solution. They are matters of subjective preference rather than reason, so that *qua* sociologist Goldthorpe has no more authority than his street cleaner to propose solutions to such problems. It is my contention that, by adopting this position, Goldthorpe reinforces the neo-liberal claim that there can be no rational way of constraining the distributional struggle.

The neo-liberal will argue further that the experience in Britain in the 1970s bears out this claim. Corporatist arrangements which sought to manage the economy and secure compliance to incomes policies could not work in an ethical vacuum in which there is no agreement about distributive issues. Groups of workers who, from their own subjective point of view, regard themselves as special cases, will seek to break incomes policies in their own interests, whatever union elites may do through corporatist arrangements with government. As Goldthorpe himself argues, corporatist arrangements require that interest groups, particularly unions, have to take on a role which transcends their sectional interests. This in turn requires that individual members of unions have to be prepared to accept this role. However, in the view of the neo-liberal this was shown by the events of the late 1970s, culminating in the 'winter of discontent', to be impossible. There is factually no agreement about who should get what, and in the absence of a real social consensus one cannot be built on rational grounds for the very reason that morality is, as Goldthorpe himself argues, a matter of individual preference. In this view there is no possibility of attaining some consensus on distributional norms to make the structure of power and advantage more principled.

From this various things follow. Given the view that inflation is inherently a political phenomenon caused by pressure on governments to expand the money supply ahead of output, and given that this pressure is much worse in a social democratic state, which is committed through the idea of citizenship to extending open-ended social and economic rights, a fairer distribution of resources and a more principled structure of power and advantage, then given that this pressure cannot be constrained by distributive consensus, it follows that it will add inexorably to inflationary pressures within the economy. This can only be eased by reversing the social democratic project. This is to be done by government getting out of the distributive arena, and viewing welfare not as an instrument of social justice and the securing of status outside the market, but as the maintenance of some minimum standard. It is done by government retrenching the rights of citizenship so that they are restricted to civil and political rights. It is done by eschewing corporatist arrangements as a means of managing the economy according to illusory consensual norms. It is also done by extending the role of the market as the institutional counterpart to moral subjectivism. The market is the mechanism which allows an individual and his or her goods and services to be measured not by some political method of securing a status and a sense of worth, but by what others from their own subjective point of view regard as an appropriate price to be paid for what the individual has to sell. The view that individuals have no basic right to an economic status which cannot be secured through the market embodies precisely the subjective preferences which Goldthorpe endorses, albeit with very different intentions.

Of course, all this is ideal. However, it has been and is a real factor in modern politics since 1979 in Britain and is to be found in the writings not only of theorists such as Hayek and Friedman, but also in *Let Our Children Grow Tall* (1977) by Margaret Thatcher, in *Stranded on the Middle Ground* (1976), *Monetarism Is Not Enough* (n.d.) and *Equality* (1979) by Sir Keith Joseph, and in *The New Conservatism* (1980) and *The Tide of Ideas from Attlee to Thatcher* (1987) by Nigel Lawson. It is to be found in the publications of various right-wing 'think tanks', such as the Institute for Economic Affairs, the Centre for Policy Studies, the Adam Smith Institute, and is part of the neo-liberal economic commentaries to be found in *The Times, The Financial Times, The Economist* and so on. It forms part of what has come to be called the 'hegemonic project' of modern conservatism, and hopes to become the new political common sense of our society to replace the social democratic assumptions which dominated British politics since 1945.

ALTERNATIVES TO THE NEO-LIBERAL PROJECT

Those wishing to challenge this 'project' have to take these ideas seriously, and in my view there are really only two general strategies open, each of which brings with it parallel problems. One, which has come to be known as market socialism, accepts a good deal of what has been said by the neo-liberals. It is concerned to adopt the market strategy, but at the same time to bring about a degree of redistribution to ensure that people enter the market on fairer terms. This approach avoids the problem of defining and justifying a set of end-state values of the sort that Goldthorpe has in mind when he talks about the structure of power and advantage becoming more principled, since the market socialist is prepared to accept that markets will produce inequalities which may be acceptable if the initial conditions of market entry are made fairer among individuals. Nevertheless, there are problems here about justifying distributive norms, not in terms of the outcomes of markets but in terms of defining what are the fair initial conditions of market entry and redistribution of property and capital which this would require.

The second approach is to attempt to revitalize some kind of corporatist arrangement. However, it is clear from our previous discussion that there is a dire need for distributive justice to be a shared value if the concentration of interests is to be a positive sum consensus rather than an unprincipled zero sum competition. Certainly, Labour's deputy leader, Roy Hattersley, was right when he argued recently that 'the main task now facing politicians of the left is to provide and to popularize an acceptable theory of distribution which is both consistent with egalitarian principles of socialism and with the realities of the modern economy' (quoted in Hoover and Plant, 1988: 321). The dilemma addressed here is central. A serious attempt to produce such a set of principles seems to be the only real alternative to the neo-liberal project, because both 'market' and 'corporate' socialism depend upon it. The current failure to do this has given the neo-liberal a very strong hand to play.

However, even in these terms the neo-liberal position has substantial defects. I have discussed these at some length elsewhere, but for the purposes of this chapter, I shall confine myself to just one feature, because it has a bearing on an important aspect of what Goldthorpe argues in his inflation essay. As I have argued, it is central to the neo-liberal case to lessen interest group pressures on government, particularly from the trade unions, because without this inflation will rise. However, while it may now be part of the present British government's policy to eschew social justice and distributive politics, as long as the public service sector remains at its current size, the same pressures will be at work, even if the long-term aim of public spending is to secure minimum standards rather than social justice. Just as we have no consensual norms relating to social justice, if the neo-liberal is to be believed, equally we have no such norms defining a minimum standard, say, in health and education, which form a large part of welfare expenditure.

In the absence of such norms, so-called basic provision is always capable of being bid up by interest group pressures, just as resources can be bid up when they are concerned with social justice or citizenship. It would follow that inflation can only be controlled, according to the neo-liberal belief, if governments were able to go back to the basic ideas of classical liberalism in which the role of government was not seen in terms of resource provision at all, never mind distributive justice. On this view the role of government is concerned solely with the provision of public goods in the technical economist's sense. This idea is to be found in Adam Smith's *The Wealth of Nations* of 1776:

> According to the system of natural liberty the sovereign has only three duties to attend to ... first the duty of protecting the society from the violence and invasion of other independent societies; secondly the duty of protecting as far as possible every member of society from the injustice or oppression of any other member of it, or the duty of establishing an exact administration of justice; and thirdly the duty of erecting and maintaining certain public works and certain public institutions which it can never be for the interest of any individual or small group of individuals to erect or maintain; because the profit could never repay the expense to any individual, or small number of individuals, though it may frequently do much more than repay it to a great society. (Smith, 1980: 27)

This classical liberal assumption about the role of government would certainly make government immune from interest group pressures in terms of the provision and distribution of resources to individuals and groups, and while it has been endorsed by some, it is scarcely practical politics, even in late 1980s Britain. Thus we have to consider ways of making the provision of resources more principled, since there is no practical way of government withdrawing altogether from this aspect of its twentieth century function. Expectations have been raised over a very long period about the resourcing role of government. There appears to be no way of going back on this, and so modern societies have to meet the challenge of making this function of government more principled and confronting the neo-liberal claim that there is no way of doing this.

CONCLUSION

This brings us back to the normative issues with which I started this chapter. I agree with Goldthorpe's demand that the reward structure of modern society should become more principled, and the neo-liberal project cannot avoid this question either, given that there appears to be no possibility of going back to the state of classical liberalism. However, we are in a hopeless position in trying to meet this challenge (1) if we accept the neo-liberal claim that it is in the nature of modern society that there is no social consensus, and (2) if we accept Goldthorpe's own view that moral norms such as distributive justice are simply a matter of personal preference. The analysis of the problems of modern society cannot avoid tackling normative questions. I do not believe that social and political inquiry can avoid being concerned with ends rather than means, as Goldthorpe suggests.

X. SOCIAL MOBILITY IN BRITAIN

17. Social Mobility in Britain

JOHN WESTERGAARD

RESEARCH ON SOCIAL MOBILITY: CHARACTER AND PURPOSES

Social mobility has a curious place in modern sociological scholarship: it looms both large and small. On the one hand, research on the subject is one of sociology's success stories—one of many, I hasten to add, lest I be taken to damn our much maligned discipline by faint praise; but a distinct success story all the same, as it will be part of my purpose to show. On the other hand, I doubt whether many professional sociologists—other than specialists in this neck of the woods itself—would spontaneously put inquiry into social mobility high on their lists, if challenged to enumerate sociology's main achievements in recent decades. I doubt especially whether most students of sociology—British undergraduates at least—emerge from their programmes of study with more than a hazy and fragmented understanding of the central findings from the now substantial body of work on social mobility.

These are impressionistic comments; but they are not entirely idiosyncratic. Both the principal authors of the recent major British studies in the field—respectively the subject of this volume and my 'better half' in this section's contribution to it—begin their chief reports by noting something like the paradox with which I have started (Goldthorpe, 1980a:1; Payne, 1987a: ix). Despite differences between them otherwise, they make the point in common that, insofar as the study of social mobility has become marginalized from 'mainstream sociology', this reflects a failure on the part of many of its practitioners to identify and pursue the sociological purposes of mobility research with sufficient clarity. I agree; and I shall argue here that it is among Goldthorpe's signal achievements to have reiterated, demonstrated and pressed home the central relevance of mapping social mobility for understanding social structure, continuity and change.

Just what that relevance is can, of course, be disputed. Goldthorpe's focus is firmly set on the bearing which patterns and trends of mobility have for the relationships, tensions and political potentialities of class structure: class formation and mobilization are his themes. These preoccupations have been challenged as too single-minded, and also as rather skew in relation to the data assembled. Payne in particular (1987a, 1987b) derives an argument for a widening of perspective, and a shift of emphasis, in part from a familiar operational feature of research in this field. For pressing practical reasons—especially the difficulty of obtaining more comprehensive information about individuals' socio-economic circumstances well back in the past—what counts as 'social' mobility is usually at best movement between different occupational categories, employment statuses and sectors of the economy. But if this tends to turn down the intensity of light which the results can shed on movement between 'classes', it also has its own advantages for illuminating the processes of economic change—of growth and contraction of economic sectors, occupational groups and modes of recruitment to them—which have gone to shape contemporary social structure and the patterns of mobility to be found at successive points of time. Those processes of historical change, Payne argues, both can and should be targets of inquiry in their own right: they should not be left aside—as he claims that Goldthorpe and many others leave them aside—as mere shifts in the parameters for numerical computation of mobility.

There is some substance to the point and Payne puts it to good effect, not least in explanation of one striking finding from the Scottish mobility survey. This shows a levelling off, from the late 1950s, in the entry of young men from manual working-class families into first employment in white-collar work—in a period when the volume of such work overall was in marked growth and young men from *non*-manual families were able to find first jobs of this sort in concomitantly growing numbers. Persuasively, Payne finds the explanation for this sign of widening class disparity of opportunity—puzzling as it seems at first, for a time of aggregate expansion of opportunity—in 'sectoral shift': an accelerated growth of 'service' activities, where recruitment to non-manual employment more often requires formal educational qualifications than it does, or at least did, in manufacturing (Payne, 1987a: 132–45).

Yet I see no good case made here against a prime focus on class. Close attention to historical shifts of economic activity, and of modes of personnel recruitment, can throw new light on trends and patterns of mobility between classes. But if the work of Goldthorpe and not a few others does have gaps on this front—with differences of recruitment to public and private sector employment, for instance, yet another dimension so far little explored—the gaps do not represent total neglect. To take just one example, Goldthorpe has a good deal to say about the implications, in comparative perspective, of Britain's early and protracted experience of industrialization for present patterns of class recruitment, especially to the manual working class (1987a: e.g. 314–15, 322–3, 344, 350). More to the point, class stays centre-stage even when a spotlight from the angle of sectoral change over time is brought on to define it more sharply. Payne's work underlines the point, since for all his protestation he returns recurrently in both overlapping volumes (1987a, 1987b) to treatment of his data as data about mobility between classes: rightly so and inexorably so; for what else, in the end, can give wider sociological justification to specialist inquiry into individual mobility than the bearing of its findings on the perennial issues of societal division and cohesion?

No doubt, in one way or another, these issues have been in the minds of most practitioners of mobility research. But in analysis and presentation of the results they have often been pushed well into the background or even largely out of sight. The editor and authors of the report on the pioneer national study in Britain, for example, were abstemious in social commentary on their data—at least beyond the question of equality or inequality of opportunity prompted especially by the recent passage of the 1944 *Education Act*—and even their presentation of the data was some way from being user-friendly for readers who might wish to pursue the implications for class structure and change (Glass, 1954). If this latter problem was already at work at a time when the techniques of statistical analysis applied in social mobility research were still quite simple, subsequent sophistication on that front has added considerably to the barrier of communication which often seems to obstruct incorporation of work in the field into 'mainstream sociology'. The international literature on the subject has become cluttered with papers whose mathematical notation discourages the uninitiated; and where—to more serious effect, since the first may be a sign only of deplorable if now dwindling innumeracy on the part of non-specialist sociologists—summary statistical measures at several removes from the original data (indices of indices of indices) are left with little or no translation back into terms that bear tangibly on the social realities from which they derive. But this is only the other face of the same coin: a failure of explicit and sustained attention to sociological purpose. When, to boot, the discipline has gone through a phase of widespread aversion to 'positivism'—an aversion little less 'mindless' than its purported target, but now thankfully on the whole passed—it is not entirely surprising that research on social mobility tended to become an esoteric mystery on the fringe of analysis of social, and most paradoxically of class, structure.

If that insulation of the subject is now set to break down, Goldthorpe can take much of the credit for the change. Of course, this has been no single-person enterprise; and much of his work has been collaborative: with colleagues in this country for the major inquiry in 1972 (Goldthorpe, 1980a) and its sequel in 1983 (Goldthorpe, 1987a: Chs 9–10); and with colleagues abroad in comparative analysis of mobility data from a number of countries (valuably brought together, in summary digest, in *ibid.*: Ch. 11). Nor will all readers of either edition of this *magnum opus* have found the density of detail, whether statistical or textual, easy to absorb. But they will have been able to rely on Goldthorpe for firmness of guidance through the thickets: for clear direction—notably at the outset and at the end, but also often *en route* when attention might otherwise stray—to the issues which drive the analysis. Those issues all concern the question, put briefly, of how far the patterns of individual mobility between different socio-economic positions—both from one generation to the next and within the span of single working lives—may be such as to turn inequalities of condition into cleavages between classes, distinct from each other in their members' typical experiences of economic life, and so the more open to political mobilization around distinctive class interests; or, conversely, to make for affinity of experience across the ostensible divisions of class, and for heterogeneity of experience within them, in such a manner as to reduce the potential for collective conflict which might otherwise be read into the persistence of economic inequality.

THE 1972 SURVEY

The 1972 mobility survey took a first and important step towards clearer focus on such issues of class 'structuration' (to use Giddens's term: see Giddens, 1973) by devising a new classification of groups between which movement was to be measured. Occupation was still taken as the prime indicator of socio-economic position on the 'Hope-Goldthorpe' scale: there was, and is, no ready alternative, even though it leaves out ownership of property as a significant dimension of class. But the new scale broke definitively with the practice—controversially adopted in the 1949 national British study (Glass, 1954), for example—of attempted classification of occupations by the 'prestige' generally associated with them. The new scale was intended instead to group occupations by circumstances of economic life that go typically with them; and it added to differentiation by occupation, in the conventional sense, also some differentiation by employment status. On the latter score it met one objection to 'prestige' classification voiced already in the first post-Second World War wave of mobility research (cf., for example, Geiger, 1951): that such status grading is liable to combine indiscriminately, within a single band, groups as distinct from one another in economic place and possible attendant interests as small independent entrepreneurs on the one hand and either salaried managers or skilled craftsmen employed as wage labour on the other. On both scores the new scale—imperfect though it might still be—offered a classification a good deal better designed to address issues of class formation and mobilization.

The Nuffield College team's intention to address just those issues was made plain from the outset; and one of the first published papers setting out some of the results of the 1972 survey was a provocative exercise in demolition of myth (Goldthorpe and Llewellyn, 1977a; a later version constituted Chapter 2 of Goldthorpe, 1980a, 1987a). Appropriately set side by side with a sharp challenge to the validity of the database for the 1949 Glass survey from the Scottish Social Mobility Survey team (Payne, Ford and Robertson, 1977), Goldthorpe and Llewellyn sought to identify three theses expressed in the earlier British literature on mobility, and to use the new information collected to pick them apart. These theses, as presented there in 'ideal-typical' form, were: first, that the top groups in this country were largely closed to recruitment from below; second, that low-grade non-manual work constituted a 'buffer-zone', absorbing movement from above and below but allowing little passage right across it; and third, that a trend towards more upward mobility through expansion of educational opportunity had been counter-balanced by contraction of other channels of upward mobility (success in independent entrepreneurship and, more recently, career promotion on the basis of work experience alone as distinct from formal educational qualifications).

The new data certainly told against these propositions—in the form that Goldthorpe and Llewellyn gave the three theses. They did so in large part because of one fundamental finding from the 1972 survey: that upward mobility and occupational opportunity had been growing apace overall, through the expansion of non-manual work at all levels and in recent years especially at the upper levels to which the Nuffield College team attached the term 'service class'. The essential fault in the three theses was that they had drawn, in part or whole, on data from the 1949 survey which—collected over two decades earlier and in any case, as the parallel paper by Payne *et al.* now argued forcefully, flawed on just this score—had shown no such large shift of occupational structure.

The demolition exercise was impressive. Even so it needs more qualification than it has received, though some of the qualification needed appeared in the fine print of the original paper and its later versions. First, as Goldthorpe acknowledges, recruitment even to the upper grade of the 'service class' from markedly mixed origins does not preclude more restricted recruitment to small elite groups at its very top, of the sort shown in a number of specialized studies; and the 1949 survey's definition of its top group was narrower than the new classification's definition of 'service class' Level I.

Second, there is rather more than Goldthorpe has allowed to the 'buffer-zone' thesis, at least in a version of it that I myself put forward. This was that routine non-manual work constituted something of a mobility barrier or threshold, in the sense that men of skilled manual origin were less likely than men of routine white-collar origin to move *above* it, and more at risk of moving '*down*' to non-skilled manual work; and that, if still true, this would be one count against a hypothesis of 'clerical proletarianization' (Westergaard and Resler, 1975: 301–2). In fact, this *is* still true, from the most recent 1983 survey data at Goldthorpe's own hand—very distinctly so in the case of men, as before; but, as a matter of some importance, only to a more limited degree in the case of women, whether their current positions are defined by their husbands' or their own occupations (Goldthorpe, 1987a: 283, Table 10.2, 287, Table 10.4).

Third—and again I am an interested party—Goldthorpe concedes that the 'counter-balance' thesis holds if it is taken to postulate, not an *absolute* decline in upward mobility by means other than the possession of formal educational qualifications, but a *relative* decline in the importance of such mobility routes. True enough, relying on data which did not show the large shift of occupational structure which fed into the 1972 survey material, my co-author and I in the 1960s failed to make this distinction (Westergaard and Little, 1967: 227–8; see also Westergaard and Resler, 1975: 319–20, 324–7). But the trend, in relative terms, for education to displace formerly more important channels of mobility—confirmed as it is by the Nuffield College surveys—remains significant for the point to which the 'counter-balance' thesis was originally addressed: to help explain why expansion of educational opportunity had less impact on aggregate social mobility than often assumed. That point, moreover, is reinforced by Payne's recent explanation of an apparent widening of disparity of opportunity on first employment since the late 1950s, as between young Scottish men of manual and of non-manual origin (see earlier). He finds the explanation precisely in a sectoral shift of the economy which has entailed an enhanced premium in the mobility stakes for those who have formal educational qualifications, and a growing handicap for those who have not.

MOBILITY IN BRITAIN: A SKETCH OF CURRENT KNOWLEDGE

In these particular respects the work of the Nuffield College team in which Goldthorpe has taken the leading role has valuably refined rather than reversed conclusions to be drawn from earlier information on social mobility in Britain. In general it seems noteworthy how much of the picture to be drawn from the 1949 survey still holds together, for all the flaws of that first national study. But not only have the inquiries of 1972 and 1983 for England and Wales, complemented by their Scottish counterpart of 1975, significantly shifted the dimensions of that picture by bringing into it the rapid growth of non-manual work at all levels—and the contraction of blue-collar work—which have so accelerated since the mid-century.

They have substantially consolidated much previous knowledge and inference; and they have no less substantially added to it. The result is an impressively large and solid body of fact: not just of fact, however, but of information so assembled and dissected as to bring its implications for class formation and mobilization into clear relief. Controversial though some of his interpretations may be—and their basis is there for others to see and use in questioning them—Goldthorpe's contribution stands out for the lead he has taken in knitting facts and inference from them closely together.

Consider what, by way of crude sketch, it can be said we now know about social mobility in twentieth century Britain. Whatever the details of categorization and measurement employed, Britain is neither a 'closed' nor an 'open' society. There is a great deal of individual movement across those lines of inequality in socio-economic conditions which at least potentially divide the society: movement from one generation to the next; within working lives; and by marriage. The continuing occupational shift over several decades—even into the years of recession from the late 1970s—has, moreover, generated a large and enhanced upward flow of people to the comforts, security and influence of professional and managerial life. But while all this points to 'fluidity' and 'opportunity', it is held a long way back from 'openness' by the persistence of class inequalities of opportunity—and risk—which, in relative terms, remain little or no less marked now than they were as far back as this century's records can go. On that score, hopes that economic growth—helped along by educational policy—would painlessly loosen the links between individuals' origins and destinations in life have signally foundered. Those who start with privilege are still far more likely—and remarkably, with much the same proportionate premiums as before—to get a 'good deal' in life than those who start without it.

But since more people of all origins have now come to have a better chance of a 'good deal'—in terms of a fairly high and secure occupational position and all that goes with it—those who get it are a mixed lot. Managers, administrators and professionals today have come to where they are from diverse backgrounds and by various routes. This may give the 'service class' which they can be said to constitute less cohesiveness than either it was believed to possess before mobility research had taken account of the shift of structure which has made for its growth, or than is possessed by the much smaller and more closed elite groups at its very top. But diversity of origins and earlier experience does not seem to divide members of the 'service class'. They have much the same lifestyles and outlook in common, once they get to where they are; they are very unlikely to come unstuck from their positions, once they have reached them; and it makes sense to attribute to them a common interest in using their influence, as best they can, to pass on their own security and privilege to their children. Even so, many of them have relatives and at least former acquaintances in lower reaches of the class structure. The latter may be inspired by their example to hope for similar success, if not for themselves then for their children; or to take the others' success as evidence that the society does now offer fair chances for those who can make it.

There is much here to take away from the potential for conflict between classes. But, by contrast at the lower end of the class pile, manual workers are now very far from being a 'mixed lot'. Their numbers—falling as they are—have come to be drawn very much from families of their own kind. True, while young, they have quite a chance of making it to better things. But they have little chance of that after they have reached the age of 30 or so. Since there is also a fair amount of movement between skilled and non-skilled places in manual work; since—by contrast notably with West Germany—mobility profiles are much the same in Britain for men of skilled and of non-skilled manual beginnings; and since the skilled and non-skilled here seem to share similar lifestyles and outlook: on all these scores, the British blue-collar working class—excluding both independent craftsmen who are their own masters, and those in technical and supervisory posts—shows a lot of the internal homogeneity that can help to make for class solidarity.

The implications of this, however, might be muddied if people long or permanently out of work were to become separated by their poverty and insecurity from job-holding wage earners of the kind—blue-collar very predominantly—that they were themselves when they had work. The numbers of the unemployed, of course, had grown sizeably by the time of the 1983 survey to show an appreciable new 'downward' flow—downward, that is, if the able-bodied workless can be seen to have the makings of a distinct 'underclass'. On the other hand, wage-labour solidarity might come to extend to a number of people in 'intermediate' positions, between the manual working class and the 'service class'. But these prove to be people and positions of very mixed kinds. Some here—rather more in the 1980s than before—are small employers and own account workers, quite distinct from wage workers in economic place, mobility profiles, aspirations and outlook. Others are low-level technical workers and supervisors, classical examples of people 'betwixt and between'. Others again—very many women, far fewer men—are in routine-grade non-manual work. But the men among these, at least, are often there only by way of transient passage from or to other things: without the stability of place which, it can be argued, might more readily make for class mobilization around common interests.

ISSUES IN CONTEST

This quick sketch is the product of knowledge which has grown cumulatively. Apart from the multiple corollaries of the shift in occupational structure (admittedly a significant qualification), many features of the sketch were visible at least as hints, and had been noted, from work on social mobility in Britain before the Nuffield College surveys: not only from the 1949 survey, but also, for example, piecemeal from studies of recruitment to particular occupations and socio-economic groups and, more comprehensively but on the basis of limited numbers and crude occupational categorization, from secondary analysis of 1959 survey data collected for another purpose (Westergaard and Resler, 1975: 303–13). But the 1972 and 1983 surveys, and their analysis and digest at the hands of Goldthorpe and his colleagues, have updated, confirmed or modified, elaborated and extended what was previously known or reasonably to be inferred, in such a way as to give knowledge now in this field impressive weight and range. The second edition of the main report (Goldthorpe, 1987a), moreover, adds to the first not only by extending the coverage by another decade—a decade of halted economic growth, mounting unemployment and political shift—but also in two other and important respects.

For one thing, Goldthorpe here (Ch. 11) brings in a synthesis of his work with others on comparison of mobility patterns between a number of countries. The conclusions, in summary, are to confirm a suggestion that there is a broad 'family resemblance' between mobility regimes in present-day industrial societies, once allowance is made for national differences in the historical phasing of economic development; to indicate that, if anything, the mobility regime in modern Britain is prototypical rather than peculiar—it is thus not peculiarly 'closed', as one long-standing legend likes to have it; but also to point up some cross-national differences. If 'openness' is the focus of interest on the latter score, the USA is probably not the model, as another longstanding legend likes to have it; but rather Sweden, where class inequalities of opportunity and risk have quite recently narrowed—a demonstration, so Goldthorpe plausibly speculates, of the impact which political organization and action can have in modifying social recruitment patterns within a generally common cross-national framework.

For another thing, Goldthorpe together with his main British collaborator, Clive Payne, now uses the 1983 survey data—collected principally for the British Election Survey of that year—to add an analysis of mobility among women (Goldthorpe, 1987a: Ch. 10). This is not the first work in Britain on the subject (see Heath, 1981: Ch. 4; Payne, Payne and Chapman, 1983). But the Nuffield College survey of 1972 had, of course, come under fierce criticism for its exclusion of women: a decision taken then essentially for reasons of 'sample economy', but based in turn on an assumption that to add women into the account was unlikely to result in substantial amendment of the conclusions to be drawn from detailed study of mobility among men only. The weight of emphasis in the new analysis is on confirmation of that assumption. The argument to this effect relies especially on a broad similarity—though not identity—found between the *relative* class disparities of opportunity and risk which apply to men and those which apply to women, when intergenerational mobility among the latter is measured by various alternative means. One means is 'conventional', to trace married women from father's to husband's occupational position; another traces women 'in their own right', still from father's occupational position but now to their own work positions, present or most recent; a third involves use of a formula to classify a married woman by reference to her husband only if the latter's position can be judged economically more influential for the couple's circumstances than her own. The middle measure, of course, in *absolute* terms shows far more downward movement among women than men, since women in paid work are thinly represented in the upper reaches of the occupational structure and are massively concentrated in low-grade non-manual employment. In as much as this might represent a phenomenon of 'proletarianization' significantly overlooked in accounts of mobility confined to men, however, Goldthorpe and Payne (Goldthorpe, 1987a: 289) counter that inference by noting the very high proportion of such women whose own low economic place could be said to be diluted by their husband's higher place.

This and some associated points—from one early and 'benchmark' type of analysis on a subject where there is a great deal more to be explored in the future—need some concluding comment here. But before I come to that, I should also say a little in general about Goldthorpe's use of relative measures of mobility: the ratios of class disparity in opportunity and risk which the Nuffield College surveys, like earlier work in Britain, have shown to be so markedly constant over time. That finding has been noticeably played down in a good deal of commentary—for example, in Heath's otherwise excellent synthesis of, and supplement to, work in this field (Heath, 1981). Payne (1987a: e.g. 118–22) has chided Goldthorpe for an emphasis on such measures of relative disparity which, he argues, over-stresses inequality at the expense of fluidity. The basic case for giving little weight to relative disparities of opportunity and risk is that they are very likely to be socially invisible. What will matter to people of humble beginnings, so this point goes, is that their chances of making it to better things have transparently improved—opportunity has boomed in absolute terms. Never mind, then, that the chances of a good and secure life have boomed just as much for others—for those who start off with distinctly more privilege already in hand—and that in relative terms the gap in fortunes between the different groups remains as marked as it was before. However dramatically statistical measures can show this, it will not come much into people's personal experience and perceptions.

Criticism of Goldthorpe—and others—on this score is in my view quite misguided. Not only is his overall interpretation even-handed between emphasis on fluidity and emphasis on inequality. He also explicitly and repeatedly makes the point himself (e.g. 1987a: Ch. 12) that the persistence of relative class disparities is unlikely to figure in people's minds. Indeed, he rather bends over backwards here in neglecting the possibility that such disparities may sometimes and perhaps increas-ingly become visible where there are institutional mechanisms for mobility, particu-larly in selection for education and for career promotion. This apart, however, patterns and trends of relative class disparity in mobility are of high significance on two scores, regardless of their low everyday profile: sociologically because they help to identify the contours of social structure, tenacious over time as these prove to be in this respect; politically—as Goldthorpe underlines—because they bear on the enterprise of achieving 'openness', a distinctly failed undertaking so far in most countries.

There could be little substance to any charge against Goldthorpe of excessively highlighting findings which support his own political predilections. Though quite explicitly not a Marxist, he is a radical who hopes for class mobilization to the effect of a more equal social order. But his hopes are shot through with scepticism: realistically so, but perhaps a little more than is warranted. Part of his scepticism comes from the lack of evidence he finds for 'proletarianization' outside the blue-collar working class, itself a group of dwindling size; another part comes from the possibility that people durably out of paid work may come to form a separate 'underclass'. The latter prospect, however, is still far from a certain scenario. It may prove to be countered by ties of mobility and affinity between the familiar world of regular wage-labour and the re-emerging worlds of irregular employment and non-employment, much as there have been for much longer such ties between the worlds of skilled and non-skilled manual work in this country. There are too many imponderables here for comprehensive conclusions as yet (cf. Harris, 1987; Wester-gaard, Noble and Walker, 1989).

Scepticism about 'white-collar proletarianization' seems well justified in the case of men (Goldthorpe, 1987a: esp. 271–2). It is more open to question in the case of women. Goldthorpe, as noted earlier, sees whatever 'radical' potential there may be to women's employment situations, 'in their own right', as weakened by the fact that so many women in low-grade jobs are married to men in higher-grade work. Though his data show roughly as many 'cross-class' marriages overall as some earlier material (Britten and Heath, 1983), they yield a good many more marriages of just this sort, and conversely fewer between manual-worker husbands and wives in routine-grade 'white-blouse' work. (I derive this point from reconstruction of the base data in Goldthorpe, 1987a: 289, Table 10.6; with allowance for differences between this source and others in classifying 'housewives only'.) This seems the consequence partly of the Nuffield College survey's reassignment of some jobs—mainly women's jobs—from routine non-manual to non-skilled wage-labour; but chiefly of that survey's assignment of petty-entrepreneurial, low-level technical and manual supervisory work—mainly involving men—to 'intermediate' places in the class structure. Both classifactory decisions make sense (though for want of the means to a more comprehensive reclassification, the first still leaves the great majority of women office workers undifferentiated, as routine-grade non-manual workers, in an intermediate position on the occupational scale). But if one result is to yield more marriages in which wage-labouring women may, on Goldthorpe's assumption, be influenced in conservative direction by their husband's better positions, there are corollaries worth noting to possible opposite effect as well.

One is to indicate a greater degree of class homogeneity in marriages where the husband is a manual worker than had seemed the case from the earlier data. Given the tighter definition of 'manual', this is a smaller group; but its composition again displays the features tending to blue-collar social cohesion which Goldthorpe has noted on other scores. A second corollary is to put a question mark against the inference possible from the earlier data that wives in routine non-manual jobs have a politically conservative influence on their blue-collar husbands' voting habits (Britten and Heath, 1983: 58–60). For the tighter Nuffield College definition of 'manual' is a reminder that the Conservative-leaning husbands in question may have included a good many independent craftsmen, technicians and foremen. From parallel evidence (Heath, Jowell and Curtice, 1985: esp. 20–2, 26–7, 33) it is clear that, though to varying degrees, these incline distinctly to the political right anyway, by contrast with both skilled and non-skilled blue-collar workers in ordinary wage-labour jobs.

Once more there are many questions still open: not least about the character and internal make-up, differential promotion prospects and class affinities of that large block of routine-grade office jobs which are typically staffed by women. But to end by underlining a set of questions yet to be pursued in depth is also, by implication, to note how many other questions now have quite firm answers. A very good part of the credit for that, in this field, belongs to John Goldthorpe.

18. Social Mobility in Britain: A Contrary View

GEOFF PAYNE

In its earliest appearances as a topic for sociological investigation, social mobility took two main forms: the study of the changing composition of ruling groups—in particular, the 'circulation of elites'—and the study of groups and individuals in general during times of rapid social upheaval. This second view, exemplified by the work of Sorokin, did not exclude the analysis of power and inequality: instead it placed them in a wider context of many types of mobility (Sorokin, 1927). The vertical dimension of this social space was subdivided into such subclasses as wealth, occupation and political power, each of which implied the examination of particular social institutions as the 'channels' through which individuals moved up and down. Despite the evident attractions of this comprehensive model, British mobility research has drawn more on the other source for inspiration, focusing narrowly on class inequality and power.

This is largely attributable to the influence of Glass's *Social Mobility in Britain*, which ignored the plurality of Sorokin's mobility processes in favour of a concentration on 'the formation and structure of the "middle classes"' (Glass, 1954: 3), and the impact of the 1944 Education Act. The results of this study were widely used by subsequent mainstream writers on social class, such as Bottomore, Miliband, Westergaard, Parkin and Giddens, although little new empirical research on mobility was done for over twenty years. This left social mobility defined as movements between occupationally defined classes, in the course of a generation: a (male) person's mobility was defined by the comparison of his own class, as given by his occupation, with that of his father when the respondent was completing his compulsory education, i.e. 14 years old. Although there was some interest in other formulations such as movement within a career (intragenerational mobility), the essential perspective of class movements between generations, as influenced by education, was set.

In Britain, then, the debate about mobility was characterized, on the one hand, by an emphasis on class analysis and, on the other, by a relative dearth of new empirical research between 1949 and the early 1970s. The Nuffield study of England and Wales filled a gap in our knowledge, and its combination of new data and explicit treatment of social class has been centrally important to the debates both on mobility and on class. It is in this tradition of British mobility and class analysis, with its strengths and weaknesses, that Goldthorpe is located, and which largely explains both its influence on him and his influence on a new generation of sociologists.

CLASS AND CLASS MOBILITY

Consequently, it should be recognized that in Goldthorpe's work the link between class and mobility is even more dominant than usual, to the extent that we find 'social mobility' largely replaced by the concept of 'class mobility'. His major contribution, *Social Mobility and Class Structure in Modern Britain*, starts with a chapter chiefly addressed to Marx's view on class, and then uses the term 'class mobility' in five of its other eight chapter headings (Goldthorpe, 1980a). In the second edition of the book (1987a) the three completely new chapters all refer to class mobility, not social mobility. As he has recently written,

> it is ultimately an interest in the historical role of class, both in shaping life-chances and as a potential basis for collective action, that underlies the way in which we have opted to view mobility—that is, to define, observe and measure it.... The chances—or risks—of individuals being mobile between, or remaining immobile within, different class positions represent one important aspect of life-chances in general.... At the same time to establish the rates and patterns of the mobility of individuals that prevail within such a (class) structure is of major relevance to the question of whether class-based collective action is likely to emerge. (Erikson and Goldthorpe, 1988a: 6–7).

Casting mobility in a class mould does not *in principle* raise insurmountable difficulties. Many sociologists find no problem with a class formulation, and even those who might ultimately operate within the frameworks of liberalism, or a social hierarchy, can adapt much of what Goldthorpe reports. However, *in practice* there are three difficulties which Goldthorpe's position gives us.

First, as he says, the theoretical framework determines how we 'define, observe and measure' mobility. Mobility is not a given: operational decisions are needed about which kinds of social movement are selected for classification as mobility. As we shall see below, 'the rates and patterns of the mobility of individuals' depend on how we choose to measure them.

Second, as in all academic writing, our interest leads us to write about some parts of our results rather than others, or more precisely, to spend more time discussing some aspects rather than others. Goldthorpe's narrow focus on class leads to an emphasis on relative chances of mobility which, while very important, can inadvertently create an impression of contemporary Britain as an even more closed society than it actually is.

The third difficulty may at first sight seem surprising in the light of Goldthorpe's other areas of interest, as indicated by the contents of the present volume. The focus on class brings with it a negative view of 'occupational mobility', so that he pays relatively little attention to the occupational processes which shape the individual moves comprising mobility rates. He therefore takes insufficient account of the structural changes in employment that are part of the defining characteristics of modern society. 'Structural mobility', the mobility which is connected to the expansion of non-manual employment opportunities, receives too little attention in his work. This is not to say that Goldthorpe ignores occupational transition (for example, see Goldthorpe, 1987a: 59–63): however, his underconceptualized treatment of the structural results of economic development leaves Goldthorpe with too narrow an approach to mobility and a position on measurement and observation that is strictly limited.

STRUCTURES OF ECONOMIC DEVELOPMENT

Both Marxist and liberal writing about economic development contains the central theme of a changing industrial activity and its associated changing occupational needs. On the one hand, Marx writes about the emergent forms of capitalism creating both a new proletariat and the conditions for proletarian revolution. The minor strata of state functionaries, small traders and industrial managers are explained as structural products of monopoly capitalism; their creation and destruction are structural changes in occupations caused by economic development. We can think of the people who are caught up in these processes as being mobile; upward at first, but ultimately downward. When, in challenging the view that mobility research is a bourgeois diversion, Goldthorpe quotes Marx, it is to this process that his selected references connect. Ranging over the *Communist Manifesto*, the *Eighteenth Brumaire*, *Theories of Surplus Value* and *Capital* (Goldthorpe, 1987a: 4–9), they deal with class formation on a wholesale basis, rather than the retail level of individual movements across a relatively constant structure. It follows that the intellectual pedigree that Goldthorpe is seeking is indeed present in embryonic terms in Marx's own ideas, but not in the form of class mobility that Goldthorpe wishes to emphasize. The extensive literature on the 'new middle classes' which has developed to fill the vacuum created by Marx is testament to this (see Payne, 1987a: 30–46).

By contrast, the liberal tradition which produced the theories of modernization, convergence and post-industrial society has given greater significance to structural and occupational change. Although currently out of fashion, and probably fatally flawed by their associations with post-war American expansion, most of these contributions recognized in some form the overwhelming evidence for technological innovation, the growth of technical knowledge and the creation of new categories of white-collar employment (*ibid.*: 51–63). The expansion of service industries and the availability of new types and numbers of occupations generate the conditions for social mobility. The new posts cannot—at least at first—be inherited from father to son, and by their very nature demand levels of intellectual competence constituting such 'an intellectual assault course' that the dense children of the old middle class 'will continue to stumble' (Parkin, 1979: 61).

British sociology was concerned in the main with how this phenomenon increased technical *content* in the new jobs, and hence the importance attached to educational qualifications as the key to entry. The American literature paid more attention to the *scale* of the changes, i.e. the number of new positions created, a view which allows for greater social fluidity in the filling of these jobs, rather than an underlying assumption of increased competition for a limited supply of posts (Payne, 1987b: 124–7).

Because of this orientation, the scale of industrial and occupational transition in Britain this century has been one of the most underestimated features in contemporary sociology. For example, between 1921 and 1971 the industrial sectors of distribution, commerce, professional and miscellaneous services in England and Wales expanded from 24 per cent of male employment to 29 per cent, whereas primary and 'heavy' secondary sectors contracted from 24 to 9 per cent. In particular areas these changes were even more dramatic: in Scotland services expanded from 19 to 27 per cent, while the primary and the mining, steel and shipbuilding secondary sectors fell from 38 to 14 per cent. In other words, a major redistribution of types of employment has been under way.

In recent years these trends have intensified. By 1986, 40 per cent of UK jobs were in the service sector, while in the south-east of England the figure was 46 per cent (*Regional Trends*, 1987). The previous seven years had seen a national contraction of manufacturing by 7 per cent, to match a 7 per cent expansion in services. The type of employment and its location have continued to change in response to economic and technological development, thus creating and destroying the framework of occupations against which mobility is measured.

In direct occupational terms several groups have seen marked growth or contraction. Although few have changed in a simple monotonic way, we can observe that the socio-economic groups of managers, professionals and semi-professionals (which approximate quite well to Goldthorpe's service class) have grown from about 12 per cent at the end of the First World War to 26 per cent in the 1981 Census, while junior non-manual work has grown from 12 to 22 per cent (Payne, 1987b; Kendrick, 1986). In contrast, skilled manual employment has fallen from 30 to 17 per cent, and the manual sector as a whole has dropped from 67 to 41 per cent. The picture is also complicated, as we shall see below, by the growth of female labour force participation, part-time employment and unemployment.

The significance of this occupational transition for social mobility is twofold. First, the groupings which make up the structure of opportunity have changed in size. Therefore, the processes by which people are recruited to these groupings must also change, with more people being recruited to some, and fewer to others. It remains to be seen *how* these processes have actually operated, but we cannot hope to explain mobility outcomes unless we take account of such structural change. In short, occupational transition within economic development is to be seen as important as a *cause* of mobility. In the second place, the results of structurally induced mobility must produce different life experiences for the population, and the dynamics of relationships between occupationally defined groupings are likely to change. Thus the increased social fluidity itself becomes a characteristic feature of modern society which needs to be integrated into class theory.

THE OPERATIONALIZATION OF CLASS MOBILITY

At the heart of this problem is the way in which Goldthorpe has operationalized social class. Despite the precise details being different, his class schema follows the conventional British practice of *approximating* social classes by using occupational groups. To put it simply, a person's job determines the social class to which he (we are dealing with male mobility) is allocated by the sociologist. In Goldthorpe's analysis, as we saw above, we can take the Registrar-General's socio-economic groups 1 to 5 as being very close to the definition of the service class, although Goldthorpe is attributing to the category more than just socio-economic similarity. By the same token, we do not greatly distort either the class specification or its associated historical experience of occupational transition if we approximate Goldthorpe's Classes VI and VII to the Registrar-General's socio-economic groups 9, 10, 11 and 15.

It follows that we can now say that since about 1921, the service class has expanded from 12 to 26 per cent (or about 10 to about 30 per cent if we limit ourselves to working males only), that the manual working class has contracted from 67 to 41 per cent (73 to 45 per cent) and Goldthorpe's intermediate classes have gone from 21 to 33 per cent (17 to 25 per cent). It is more difficult to connect the socio-economic groups neatly with Goldthorpe's more elaborated seven-class schema, or the eight-class schema used in his more recent work, but at the simplified level, say, of his analysis of counter-mobility, we have evidence of what presumably is a sharp upheaval in the British class structure as he defines it.

The point that is being emphasized here is the nature of this upheaval. For the present purposes it does not matter which conceptual framework is used, so long as it ultimately uses occupation as the signifier. We could equally well take occupational groupings based on lifestyle similarity (the socio-economic groups themselves) or on occupational gradings (e.g. the method used by the Scottish Mobility Study to formulate its 'classes', Payne, 1987b: 195–6). The detailed outcomes would change by a few percentage points, but the changes would still clearly show through.

Once the scale of this change is recognized, the importance of studying *processes of mobility* becomes more apparent. If 'class membership' is defined in terms of possessing a job which falls within a theoretically conceptualized group of occupations, then access to class membership depends just as much on access to that job as on the conceptualization of the groupings. To take one example where Goldthorpe *has* confronted this issue, the class of agricultural labourers displays characteristic mobility patterns because of its social situation. The sons of agricultural labourers typically grow up in locations where the educational system is relatively impoverished, where employment in agriculture is the main occupation on offer, and where competition from the sons of the urban industrial proletariat is reduced by both physical distance and differences in cultural values (Erikson and Goldthorpe, 1987a, 1987b). The result is high levels of class immobility in terms of the membership of the contemporary class of agricultural labourers. However, there is also a high flow out of that class of origin, as other sons of agricultural labourers move off the land and take up manual work in the cities. The latter has more to do with processes of economic development (the decline of the primary sector) than the class situation of agricultural labourers. In other words, if we are to understand the mobility of agricultural labourers, we need to know something about *both* their class *and* occupational positions. A similar view can be taken of other occupationally derived classes, such as farmers, owners of small businesses, managers and manual workers in traditional industries. The sons of farmers and owners of small businesses need capital if they are to follow their fathers: they are more likely to have that requisite capital than sons with fathers in employed positions. Managers who have achieved their positions without educational qualifications have a high probability of having sons with fee-paying secondary schooling and experience of post-secondary education (Payne *et al.*, 1979). Manual workers in traditional heavy industry such as mining, the docks or the shipyards would 'speak for' their sons, using their personal contacts with a foreman or manager to ensure jobs for their boys.

The question is, to what extent are these recruitment processes to be defined as 'class mobility' as against 'occupational mobility'? Most members of most classes do not in a direct sense exercise influence over the size of their class. Junior white-collar workers are not responsible for the expansion of their class, nor skilled manual workers for the contraction of their share of the labour market. It *could* be argued that the latter have had some collective influence: on the one hand, craft union protectionism could be said to have inflated salaries to a position where employers were driven to substitute cheaper forms of labour, and on the other, the struggle over numbers and control of apprenticeships might be seen as a manipulation of entry processes. But neither seems adequate to account for the flight from manufacturing industry (and in particular from the 'old staples') which explains the real reduction in numbers of skilled workers.

It is true, however, that classes may be said to have an indirect effect on economic development. Support for political parties espousing policies of development has been widespread since the Second World War. A culture of rising expectations, respect for technical knowledge and acceptance of credentialism has become dominant. As Parkin has argued, the middle classes have embraced strategies of occupational closure based on formal qualifications, to the cost of some of their offspring. But again, this is less a matter of specific or conscious class strategy than an acceptance of a generalized ideology of credentialism.

At the heart of the matter is the control over capital and decisions about its use and location. The collapse of employment in the old staples and the growth of a south-east of England services industry are largely to be explained as the outcome of many separate decisions by those who can influence the allocation of capital. This is not to say that the outcome is one that is consciously sought, but rather to make the point that the many component decisions that lead to it are taken by groupings of people that are distinct from the vast majority of those contained in Goldthorpe's class schemas for mobility analysis. While it is not the case that the decision-makers choose to expand or contract a class, that is the result of their activity. We can thus attribute the pattern of economic development and occupational transition to class processes, but only in this indirect sense. To treat mobility only as 'class mobility' is to obscure the significance of this underlying industrial and occupational dimension: it may help to identify the importance of access to credentials and petty capital, but it misses the power of the occupational machine to drive mobility.

In other words, the problem is not that Goldthorpe is interested in class, in mobility's 'implication for class formation and action', or even in demonstrating the need for 'collective action on the part of those in inferior positions' (Goldthorpe, 1987a: 28, 29), but rather that he is *too narrowly* interested in it. When he begins to analyze the specific work and market situations of certain classes or strata, as in the case of agricultural labourers or the petty bourgeoisie, his explanations of mobility are persuasive as far as they go. However, mobility between classes is not a phenomenon that can be explained purely in class terms, unless the many indirect connections between classes and economic and political processes are spelled out to a greater degree than is presently possible. In particular, the occupational processes which shape careers, while strongly conditioned by class, are more complex and powerful than a simple class analysis allows, and their complexity and power need to be taken into account in their own right (as, for example, Mach and Wesolowski, 1986—writing in a class tradition—propose). This is most important in taking on board the idea of occupational transition, but also applies to the work experience and life-cycle of the individual. It is a consideration which has profound effects on the way in which we *explain* mobility, but it also determines the basic framework that is used to identify which social movements come to be described as mobility in the first place.

MEASURING AND REPORTING MOBILITY

The 'marxisant' orientation (*ibid.*: 28) of Goldthorpe's work naturally influences his definitions, measurements and emphasis in the reporting of mobility. Because his attention, and that of the audience he addresses in Chapter 1 of *Social Mobility and Class Structure in Modern Britain*, is drawn towards the differences and barriers between classes, he is less interested in the relatively high levels of occupational fluidity he discovers (43 per cent of the Nuffield sample had moved at least one class step in a generally 'upward' direction, while 28 per cent had moved at least one step in the other direction: calculated from *ibid.*: 45, Table 2.1). If a majority of people have made such a move—leaving aside for the movement the question of whether it is 'up' or 'down' in a simple hierarchy—and if in turn the sons of the Nuffield sample also experience high mobility rates, then a very substantial part of the population will have experienced occupational mobility either for themselves or for someone in their immediate family.

This raises three issues for class analysis. To what extent can we talk about class formation and consciousness, if the membership of each class (and Goldthorpe's occupational groupings are classes) is changing in this way? Unless there is some degree of 'demographic consistency' in membership, it is hard to see how class-based action is possible. Second, it points to a much more dynamic model of class structure and class relations, because although the structure can be abstractly conceptualized independent of its members, in practice members are actively changing their locations, quite apart from the structural changes discussed in the previous section. Third, we need to investigate what effect mobility experience has on class-based attitudes and behaviour, as the scale of the movements threatens to undermine more traditional models of the class system.

These problems do not disappear even if we stick more closely to mobility as occupational mobility. However, one advantage is that there is a less dense thicket of ideas to negotiate in the field of occupational fluidity, not least the absence of any ideological commitment to a Marxist approach to class inequality. This freedom to operate also relates to concepts of the hierarchy which is formed by the social classes. Goldthorpe prefers an agnostic view of hierarchy, sharing with Giddens the view that classes do not neatly differ from each other in an easily visualized set of stratified layers. Rather than 'a consistently hierarchical form', Goldthorpe's class schema does not assume uniformity or ordinality. This means that he speaks of 'upward mobility only in the case of movement into Class I and II, whether from the intermediate classes or from Classes VI and VII, and conversely of downward mobility only in the case of movement out of classes I and II' (*ibid.*: 43). This view contrasts with, for example, that of the Scottish Mobility Study, where the 'occupational classes' are explicitly derived from the occupational ranking exercises used in the Hope-Goldthorpe scale (Payne, 1987b: 196).

In practice, Goldthorpe's position reduces the level of mobility perceived. It was noted above that the Nuffield sample had 43 per cent upward mobility and 28 per cent downward mobility, i.e. provided that 'up' and 'down' one-stage steps are defined as mobility. In Goldthorpe's terms, however, the more restricted model requires in most cases larger steps (e.g. from Class IV to Class I or II, etc.), while eliminating some moves as neither up nor down but presumably sideways. Thus 43 per cent upward mobility becomes 17.4 per cent, and 28 per cent downward mobility becomes 5.5 per cent. The lower figures may both be theoretically sound or sensibly conservative as an estimate, but the picture of only 23 per cent of mobile people misses the very real encounter with mobility which another 48 per cent (71 minus 23 per cent) of the population experience.

The picture is also complicated by the emphasis this gives to the service class as against the intermediate classes. The latter are destinations for many sons of manual workers: in the Scottish Mobility Study carried out at roughly the same time, using almost identical research methods and only a slightly different classification of the intermediate classes, these classes accounted for at least one-third of all upward mobility (Payne, 1987b: 65). The importance of these types of movements is minimized in Goldthorpe's commentary, which understandably concentrates on the service class.

The upper middle classes have always been a major topic for research, from Glass onwards, because of their strategic position in society (see Payne, 1987b: 78–89). Goldthorpe's formulation of the class structure as dominated by the service class is distinctive and requires him to devote more attention to exposition and analysis of its character. For example, in his examination of mobility patterns in Chapter 2 of *Social Mobility and Class Structure in Modern Britain*, movements to and from Classes I and II (which make up the service class) are commented upon roughly five times as often as the other five classes. The data are, of course, *reported* in the tables: it is the proportion of the narrative that directs attention to one subset of the total mobility processes.

This picture is further complicated by the emphasis which Goldthorpe gives to relative rather than absolute mobility. Absolute mobility is a straightforward report of what percentage of the sample has moved in a particular way, whereas relative mobility relates movements to the size of origin or destination categories. The log-linear models based on odds-ratios, which Goldthorpe employs extensively, are a particular version of this.

Goldthorpe himself does not see his work as drawing disproportionately on relative mobility:

> the greater part of the analyses that we present are in fact ones of absolute rates—of their overall patterns, of trends through time, of the relation between inter- and intra-generational movement etc. We do, none the less, also give a good deal of attention to relative mobility rates—or, as we would alternatively say, relative mobility chances—expressed in various ways. (*ibid.*: 29)

In fairness, this must be recognized as an accurate statement as far as breadth of coverage is concerned. However, that is not to say that the emphasis and orientation are so equally balanced: to this reader at least the message that seems to predominate is that relative mobility rates show a lack of change, a continuation of class inequality in opportunity and a corrective to an overoptimistic reading of the absolute mobility findings of high fluidity. Indeed, there is a pleasing paradox which Goldthorpe elegantly exploits, trading off the evidence of new-found greater absolute fluidity against the hidden patterns of continued relative disadvantage.

He is, of course, right to make much of this, both because it is a less than obvious outcome and because of the light it throws on inequalities of opportunity. Nonetheless, it needs to be taken on board with the observation that the numbers of people affected are changing: those with relatively lower chances of mobility are declining in number, while those with relatively higher chances are increasing. In other words the manual working class's disadvantage compared with the sons of the service class may continue to be as extreme as before (worse than one-third of the likelihood of getting a service-class job), but the numbers of people disadvantaged by these chances are declining. For example, in the Nuffield sample the sons of the manual working class were a 5 per cent smaller proportion of the workforce in the youngest cohort compared with the oldest (*ibid.*: 71). At the same time the absolute mobility rates show a rise in the numbers 'escaping' from manual origin.

It is important that we do not lose sight of this fact that the numbers of mobile people are large. Furthermore, these mobile people—and indeed the immobile too—do not encounter mobility as a relative chance but rather as mobility or non-mobility. In terms of class formation and consciousness the latter is probably more important than the valuable analytical insight about relative mobility. The Goldthorpe approach remains trapped in the traditional view that wishes to discard the changes in occupational structure: while he rejects the old-style partitioning of mobility in structural and exchange mobility, and the dubious indices associated with that (*ibid.*: 74–5), he has not taken the final step towards embracing structural change as a central issue in mobility research. The introduction of log-linear modelling, which has been a valuable contribution to the slow growth of numeracy in British sociology, has slightly confused the relative/absolute problem. Its technical character as a method and the power of its analysis have opened up a gap of comprehension between the specialist and the 'general' sociologist, a vacuum that has inevitably been filled by an acceptance of the conclusions highlighted in Goldthorpe's discussion.

SOME CONCLUDING OBSERVATIONS

Although the second edition of *Social Mobility and Class Structure in Modern Britain*, the articles in *Sociology* based on the British Election Study (Goldthorpe and Payne, 1986a, 1986b) and the work emerging from the CASMIN Project (e.g. Erikson and Goldthorpe, 1987a, 1987b) demonstrate the technical sophistication of the late 1980s, Goldthorpe's basic orientation has remained that of the Glass tradition that he inherited in the early 1970s. The emphasis on 'relative class mobility' among males has shown little sign of opening up to other conceptions of what mobility might mean. In addition to the central issue of occupational transition, there are at least four other dimensions which Goldthorpe has not fully integrated into his analysis.

The most widely recognized of these is in his treatment of female mobility. As the debate in *Sociology* between 1983 and 1985 shows, Goldthorpe is unhappy with the idea of married women having a class identity of their own separate from their husband. Not surprisingly, he evinces little interest in the mobility experiences of women. Characteristically, he concludes that when women are allocated an individual class position, it is only in *absolute* terms that there are any distinctive female features of mobility (1987a: 294–5). Goldthorpe is right to defend studies of male mobility for what they can tell us about *male* mobility, but his narrow conception of mobility results in a lack of information about the patterns and the *experience* of women's mobility. As others have argued (Payne *et al.*, 1983; Dex, 1987), gender segregation of labour markets means an average probability of early career downward intergenerational mobility, followed by upward career and marriage mobility, concluding in late career downward mobility in part-time work during or following childrearing. Not only can such a perspective expand our concept of mobility by linking it to labour markets and life-cycle processes (Payne and Abbott, 1990), it also points to the neglected importance of *subjective* experience in the generation of class consciousness.

This last point also applies to early career experience and unemployment. Following Registrar-General's conventions, Goldthorpe classifies trainee and apprenticeship positions as if they were the positions obtained after qualification. This misses the real inferiority of apprentices and their genuine upward mobility on becoming skilled craftsmen. Similarly, unemployed respondents were coded to occupational groups according to previous jobs, thus defining work and unemployment as equal in class terms. With the stagflation of the late 1970s and 1980s, this previously minor imprecision has become a more serious conceptual difficulty.

Even if the burden of this critique, that Goldthorpe has been too narrowly preoccupied with class mobility *per se*, is not accepted, one key shortcoming remains. The mainstream tradition of British mobility research has linked mobility to education, with qualifications being seen as the explanation of why some *individuals* are mobile, and others are not, within an overall distribution of mobility opportunities. Sadly, the main output from the Nuffield Study has been Halsey *et al.*'s work on origins and educational access (1980), and quite separately, Goldthorpe's work on origins and destinations (1980a). We still await even a basic treatment of education and mobility. While the problems of gender, unemployment and subjective experience are ones which Goldthorpe shares with most other contemporary mobility analysts (in Britain at least), the absence of a rounded, more sociological analysis in his work is most obviously shown in this division of labour within the Nuffield team. It provides a graphic illustration of the fashion in which, ironically, Goldthorpe's detailed and powerful development of class mobility analysis has ultimately diverted attention away from the fascinating and ultimately more fruitful questions of the interplay between occupational transition, occupational and social mobility and the wider issues of modern capitalism.

Interchange

WESTERGAARD REPLIES TO PAYNE

The format of this book encourages knock-about *ad hominem* argument; and Geoff Payne has certainly responded vigorously to editorial requirements. My immediate inclination is to make little of the opportunity for rejoinder: this for two reasons. First, I think I have already anticipated the essence of Payne's case. Second, that case seems to me to rely too much on the setting up and knocking down of Aunt Sallies to advance work on social mobility as far as it might. But this point, at least, probably does need elaboration.

Payne's location of the Nuffield College team's work in 'the Glass tradition' is one Aunt Sally. Of course, there are continuities; how otherwise, given the pioneer character of the 1949 survey? But the discontinuities are surely no less significant, and go beyond matters of method. Above all, Goldthorpe and his colleagues have given a theoretical focus to research on the subject which was singularly lacking—or at least hard to detect—in the work from LSE some 40 years ago. That focus—on the features of individual mobility and immobility which bear on class formation and mobilization—may still be too limited, as Payne argues. But its clarity contrasts with the fact—commonly recognized, even by Payne himself elsewhere—that the authors of the earlier work played their 'class cards' so close to the chest that it was left, in good part, to others to put them on the table.

Payne's charge that Goldthorpe 'underplays social fluidity' and creates 'an impression of contemporary Britain as an even more closed society than it actually is' comes now with some ostensible caution; as a personal interpretation of 'the message that seems to predominate'. But he still makes much of it. I find it as hard as ever to square with Goldthorpe's evident even-handedness in formal presentation; or with his no less evident worry, when it comes to interpretation, that the balance between features of closure and of openness—including fluidity in respect of those intermediate socio-economic categories in which Payne claims he shows little interest—is all too likely to work against class mobilization for political change 'from below'. It is ironic, incidentally, that one of Payne's own findings from Scotland—concerning class inequalities of entry into white-collar work from the late 1950s on—suggests rather more weight to features of closure than the Nuffield College analysis had detected.

If another of Payne's charges is not an Aunt Sally, it must be an odd slip of the pen. One of Goldthorpe's blindspots, he says, concerns unemployment; and with 'the stagflation of the late 1970s and 1980s', coding of the unemployed by their previous jobs 'has become a more serious conceptual difficulty'. In fact, the second edition of *Social Mobility and Class Structure* extends into just this period, includes a distinct coding for the unemployed, traces their recruitment, and discusses the implications at some length—if, as I have suggested, to debatable conclusions. The point goes to confirm my sense of a degree of fixation on Payne's part.

This is not to dismiss all that he has to say. While I do not share the view that Goldthorpe's stance in the class-gender debate represents a continuing blindness to the distinct circumstances and experiences of women—since this view itself tends to lose sight of the serious complexities of evidence and argument involved—the recent addition of some analysis of women's mobility to the Nuffield College team's work leaves a good many issues still wide open: I point to a few in my main contribution; Payne to others, and more, in his. His prime charge, however, seems to concern the lack of attention he finds, in the work from Oxford, to the processes of economic transformation which have given changing shape to mobility profiles and experience. I confess I cannot readily follow Payne's arguments here about the causes of these processes and their mobility outcomes. If he is attributing to Goldthorpe (or the Glass tradition) assumptions that, for example 'mobility between classes ... can be explained purely in class terms' or that 'classes ... *directly* control or cause mobility', this seems to me another—though rather impenetrable—way of setting up Aunt Sallies: I, at least, am too dim to fathom his meaning. His points remain good, however, that recruitment patterns and experiences change as the structures of economies change; that educational provision, opportunity and experience have bearings in this connection on mobility, which the division of labour within the Oxford team indeed seems to have left too much out on a limb; and that all this has a sociological salience—for inferences about class formation and mobilization as well as other things—which warrants much further exploration.

Payne himself has contributed to such exploration. But advocacy for more of that does not justify his verdict that the effect of the ground-breaking work from Nuffield College has been 'to narrow contemporary ideas of mobility'. The advocacy is sidetracked rather than advanced when it proceeds by putting up and shaking down straw men: I can recognize little of John Goldthorpe in Geoff Payne's images of him.

PAYNE REPLIES TO WESTERGAARD

John Westergaard accurately identifies the central difference between John Goldthorpe's (and his own) position and mine as being the relationship between social class and social mobility. The difference *per se* is in some ways small, and therefore needs clarification, whereas its significance for how one conceptualizes mobility is more substantial. Several of my relatively minor criticisms of Goldthorpe's work also stem from this, and so it is with class that we must start.

First, there are several points of agreement between us. Westergaard sees the significance of mobility as its capacity 'to turn inequalities of condition into cleavages between classes ... or make for affinity of experience across the ostensible divisions of class', with consequences for increased or decreased class-based political action. I share his concern with the ways in which society handles 'the persistence of economic inequality', which paraphrases my quotation from Goldthorpe's concerns about the potential for collective action (Goldthorpe, 1987a: 6–7). I may be more sceptical about that potential, in the light of how I read patterns of mobility, but in as far as we are talking about the *consequences* of mobility, there is little disagreement between us.

Where we do differ is in the *causes* of mobility. Both Goldthorpe, and to a lesser extent Westergaard, treat mobility as a product of class relations, to the virtual exclusion of other causal forces. In contrast, I regard occupational transition as an independent cause of such importance that it must always be included with class in any analysis. This is not to deny that class provides part of the explanation we seek. For example, the inheritance of petty capital, the availability of cultural capital in the child's home environment, the exercise of credentialist strategies of closure by professional associations and trade unions, and the capacity of fathers to 'speak for' their sons to employers, are clear examples of how the class system operates directly on the chances of mobility. But what we require is more analysis of these processes, so that we can discover how class acts as an *agent* to determine mobility.

In this respect I have argued that occupational transition is certainly not a conscious and direct outcome of class action. I accept that a case could be made for some kind of indirect or unintended connection, but even this calls for an account of those sociological processes which result in occupational change, an account that is still inadequate. In a very real sense the growth of non-manual posts calls for changes in recruitment patterns: it is the single most important mechanism for changing mobility rates. Goldthorpe does not address the causes of occupational mobility, because he addresses patterns and consequences of mobility rather than its causes. This may be a result of the division of labour between Goldthorpe and other members of the Nuffield team. Unlike, say, Westergaard or Parkin, Goldthorpe does not examine how educational opportunity modifies individuals' chances of riding the escalator of occupational mobility. His interest is coherent, organized and specific: contemporary manifestations of mobility and their implications.

As a further illustration of this narrowness of focus, the reader may care to compare Goldthorpe's work with Westergaard and Resler's *Class in a Capitalist Society* (1975). Although I would not embrace everything in the latter, it is a valuable demonstration of how class as a system operates in a number of ways, including how it controls life chances. The difference between Goldthorpe and Westergaard is not that the former is more specialized, so much as the latter is more rounded in his sociology of class and mobility. While accepting Westergaard's evaluation that Goldthorpe has re-established 'the central relevance of mapping social mobility for understanding social structure', I also feel that Westergaard is unduly modest about his own contribution to this realignment of our sociological endeavours. In short, Westergaard is right to point out that the alternative to Goldthorpe's position offered in my own work 'returns recurrently ... to treatment of (my) data as data about mobility between classes'. The difference lies in my search for the causes, rather than a fixation with the consequences, of mobility.

This difference permeates one's whole approach to the subject, from operationalization, through interpretation, to eventual evaluation and integration into sociological wisdom. As discussed in my initial contribution, Goldthorpe's limited definition of upward mobility results from his uncertainty about class hierarchy. In part this flows from the way he abandoned the rank ordering of the Hope-Goldthorpe scale (to a greater extent than Westergaard implies in his chapter; see also Payne *et al.*, 1976). The occupational ordering of the Scottish Mobility Study is based much more directly on the Hope-Goldthorpe scale, and, therefore, having more confidence in what most people see as up and down, the Scottish Study tends to define a higher proportion of movements as mobility. In the interpretation of these movements an occupational perspective makes it easier to accept the key finding of high social fluidity and to focus on absolute rates of mobility. A straight class perspective, while preventing overoptimism about the openness of modern society, can dwell excessively on the more pessimistic relative measures of mobility. Indeed, it could be argued that the technical sophistication of statistical analyses based on relative measures diverts attention away from the kinds of broader sociological explanation for which the present author has argued above (e.g. Müller's recent work, compared with Goldthorpe and Erikson's earlier contributions to the CASMIN Project).

The overall outcome of Goldthorpe's approach is, sadly, precisely what Westergaard says: his work 'has valuably refined rather than reversed conclusions to be drawn from earlier information on social mobility'. While, strictly speaking, a reversal was not to be expected, a more substantial refining of our understanding was not only desirable but also possible. Despite his new class schema and the techniques of analysis (which must not be undervalued, for all my doubts about their application), Goldthorpe's main contribution in the form of the first edition of *Social Mobility and Class Structure in Modern Britain* seems trapped in a time warp with Glass's *Social Mobility in Britain*. Only in the second edition of 1987 do we begin to get the sense of contemporary society, and contemporary sociology, impinging on mobility analysis. The issues of women, of the unemployed, of subjective response to mobility begin to emerge. Goldthorpe still attempts to cope with these issues in a class framework, but they point towards the need for a broadening of class analysis and a more radical reappraisal of our concepts. Our models of class structure, such as the mobility threshold, require more test than against data for men only, as Westergaard shows in his contribution (see also Abbott and Sapsford, 1987). More saliently for Goldthorpe's own expressed interests, the emergence of a new centralist political party and the redesign of the Labour Party in the late 1980s must surely have something to do with life chances and experiences of social mobility as well as with other aspects of class change. Credit is due, as Westergaard concludes, for the firm answers to many questions which Goldthorpe has provided. A slightly different approach might have left fewer questions yet to be pursued.

XI. COMPARATIVE SOCIAL MOBILITY

19. Social Mobility in Industrial Nations

WALTER MÜLLER

Ever since the classical texts of Marx, Pareto and Weber, social mobility has been of central interest in the study of industrial societies. A mass of data has been collected for this purpose and the most advanced techniques of statistical analysis have been developed and applied in the field of social mobility research. Many claims have been made that the scholarly returns on these endeavours have been limited (Mayer and Müller, 1971; Coser, 1975; Sørensen, 1986). However, such general criticisms can no longer be sustained. In a state of the art review Kurz and Müller (1987) observe that comparative social mobility research has now achieved a state of maturity. It is no exaggeration, in the light of the specific aim of this chapter (to argue pro John Goldthorpe), if I claim that John Goldthorpe is the person to whom the breakthrough and the new synthesis are due. The attentive reader of our earlier article (Kurz and Müller, 1987) will already have recognized this assessment.

Here I will elaborate more explicitly on John Goldthorpe's merits in three respects: (1) he has revitalized and established systematically the class perspective of mobility research and thereby integrated the study of mobility into the wider sociological debate by making it a central element of the class analysis of industrial societies; (2) he has made a crucial contribution to the improvement of the methodological and empirical grounds for the comparative study of social mobility; and (3) he has provided firm answers to a long debate on the nature and the impact of social mobility in industrial nations.

THE CLASS FRAMEWORK FOR THE STUDY OF SOCIAL MOBILITY

When Goldthorpe first entered the field at the end of the 1960s, social mobility research was dominated by the status attainment approach (Blau and Duncan,

1967). Goldthorpe was soon to become one of its most fervent opponents. He criticized this approach not only because of the inherent problems of path analysis (Goldthorpe, 1971), but above all due to its links to the 'pluralist industrialism' model of modern societies—links which he also finds in other variants of what he calls the vertical or hierarchical context of mobility.

More clearly than any of the representatives of the vertical approach themselves, Goldthorpe (1964, 1971, 1985b, 1990) and Erikson and Goldthorpe (1988f) have outlined the close relationship between this approach and the wider set of assumptions about industrial societies held by the theory of pluralist industrialism. According to this approach, mobility is seen as occurring among a set of positions whose principal or even unique property is their respective location along a finely graduated vertical continuum of the dimension of prestige or some other measure of social or economic status. By the very nature of this gradual conception of inequality, industrial or post-industrial societies are assumed to be classless societies. Immobility, on the other hand, appears as a defect from the normative ideal of a completely open society, an ideal towards which industrial societies are assumed to move in the course of the full development of their basic properties. The generally large and increasing amount of mobility is understood in turn as one of the major factors responsible for the lack of class formation.

Against this perspective Goldthorpe has clarified theoretically, and demonstrated empirically, the potential of the class context in mobility analysis. He has systematically derived the research agenda from this larger theoretical framework and, most crucially, has replaced the often arbitrary definition of the positions between which mobility is observed by an explicit and theoretically well-grounded schema of the basic class positions existing in advanced industrial societies.

Mobility researchers adhering to the class framework and those following the vertical approach do have some common interests. Both attempt to monitor the degree of openness prevailing in given societies and to analyze the mechanisms through which mobility occurs and immobility is secured. A crucial objective of mobility research in a class perspective, however, is the systematic study of the implications of mobility for class formation. It is linked to a central objective of class analysis, namely, to investigate the conditions under which a 'class in itself' becomes a 'class for itself', that is, 'the conditions under which individuals who hold similar class positions do actually come to define their interests in class terms and to act collectively—for example, through class-based movements and organizations—in their pursuit' (Erikson and Goldthorpe, 1988a: 5). Here mobility plays a crucial role, since, as Goldthorpe has argued convincingly, classes 'must have some degree of demographic identity before they can acquire a socio-cultural identity or provide a basis for collective action' (Goldthorpe, 1984d: 20). For if classes rapidly exchange their members and if an individual's class membership is only of an ephemeral duration, it cannot be expected that class-specific association patterns and lifestyles develop, nor that individual interests can be organized on a class basis. Independent of other factors affecting the formation of classes, mobility research is thus concerned with the *conditio sine qua non* of class formation.

However, the study of mobility will only contribute to the understanding of processes of class formation if the positions between which mobility is observed are defined in the light of this goal. They must be defined in a way that their holders can be assumed to share common interests from which class formation at the social and political level can be expected to occur. In this respect the characterization of positions solely according to their location on a vertical scale of prestige or socio-economic status is certainly not helpful.

The class schema developed by Goldthorpe (1980a), and more extensively described by Erikson and Goldthorpe (1988a), classifies individuals according to the *employment relations* in which they are involved. In its concrete form it adopts the classical criterion of whether individuals sell (their) labour or buy labour (of others) or do neither. Accordingly, it distinguishes between employees, employers and the self-employed. However, only by making further subdivisions within these three basic class positions can account be taken of the full range of significant variations in labour market conditions and employment relations.

Goldthorpe's most important contribution in this respect consists in the elaboration of the concept of the 'service class' (see Renner, 1953), its particular position in the organization of labour in advanced industrial societies and the implications for mobility which result from this position. In its purest form the notion of the service class relates to employees who 'exercise *delegated authority or specialized knowledge and expertise* in the interests of their employing organisation' (Erikson and Goldthorpe 1988a: 20). These new forms of employer-employee relations that expand rapidly with the increasing growth of corporate ownership and large-scale organization have been described in Weber's treatment of bureaucracy. Goldthorpe (1982) has shown that the 'service relationship' is not only apt to secure cooperation and control in the new type of work organization, but that the market and work situation characteristic of employees in such relationships is so markedly different from the 'typical' wage labourer that it has to be considered as constituting a distinct class. The service relationship is not only distinguished by higher remuneration but—more crucial for mobility patterns—by qualitatively different elements: by long-term salaries (instead of wages for labour) and rewards of an essentially prospective kind (salary increments, employment security and career prospects). Linked to their class location, at least according to evidence available for Britain, members of the service class differ from other classes in political values and affiliations as well (Heath, Jowell and Curtice, 1985; Gallie and Vogler, 1988).

The resulting class schema, as it could be operationalized for the comparative study of mobility, is summarized in Table 19.1. In contrast to a hierarchical framework, the class framework turns out to possess a number of advantages for studying mobility processes.

- Even though the definition of classes is independent of the pattern of mobility processes occurring between them, the properties of specific classes have implications for the frequency with which specific moves can be expected to occur. For example, prospects of promotion and employment security, characteristic of the service-class employment relationship, can be considered as quasi-guarantees against degradation once such a position is attained, and the generally high levels of education and income of holders of such positions constitute important resources for transferring the advantageous class position to their offspring.

- Different classes can provide their offspring not only with different *amounts* but also with different *kinds* of resources needed for access to different class positions. While ownership of at least some amount of physical or financial capital or land is a precondition for access to the propertied classes of employers and farmers, access to the service classes normally presupposes

Table 19.1   Ten- and Seven-Category Versions of the Goldthorpe Class Schema

Ten-category version		Seven-category version
I	Higher-grade professionals, administrators and officials; managers in large industrial establishments; large proprietors	
II	Lower-grade professionals, administrators and officials; higher-grade technicians; managers in small industrial establishments; supervisors of non-manual employees	I + II 'service class'
III	Routine non-manual employees in administration and commerce; sales personnel; other rank-and-file service workers	III 'routine non-manual'
IVa	Small proprietors, artisans, etc. with employees	IVa + IVb 'petty bourgeoisie'
IVb	Small proprietors, artisans, etc. without employees	
IVc	Farmers and small holders; other self-employed workers in primary production	IVc 'farmers'
V	Lower-grade technicians; supervisors of manual workers	V + VI 'skilled workers'
VI	Skilled manual workers	
VIIa	Semi- and unskilled manual workers (not in agriculture, etc.)	VIIa 'non-skilled workers'
VIIb	Agricultural and other workers in primary production	VIIb 'farm workers'

Source: Erikson and Goldthorpe (1987a: 58).

possession of an extended amount of human capital in the form of education, occupational qualifications or organizational skills. The hierarchical framework tends to amalgamate in strictly hierarchical terms occupational positions that are heterogeneous with respect to the resources on which their holders can draw in supporting their offspring in the competition for desirable class locations.

● A longstanding concern of mobility research has been with the changes in the amount and pattern of social mobility occurring in the course of the economic development of societies, associated with economic growth, advancing production technologies and changing organization of production and labour. As a result of these developments shifts in employment between sectors, industries and occupations occur that are directly related to the contraction and expansion of the different classes. These changes in class structure in turn strongly affect mobility opportunities. Thus, from a class perspective, the structural constraints on mobility can be traced back quite directly to concomitant developments in the economic system or to political interventions in the economy and the labour market. Within a hierarchical framework, linking mobility processes to their causal conditions appears to be much more difficult. Economic transformations and political interventions affect classes such as farmers, the petty bourgeoisie, the working class and the service class rather than occupations of particular socio-economic status or prestige. Occupations classified on similar hierarchical levels may be affected in quite different ways through particular structural transformations with, for example, farmers on the one side and service workers on the other.

ESTABLISHING THE DATABASE FOR COMPARATIVE RESEARCH

Goldthorpe's conception of class will be of particular importance for future research, since it is one of the very few class models that has been worked out to allow concrete empirical operationalizations on a cross-national comparative basis (for a competing project, see the discussion of Wright's class analysis in Chapters 4 and 5 of this volume). Previous work on comparative social mobility has not only suffered from a lack of clear theoretical ideas, but also from the fact that the empirical basis for comparative research was less than satisfactory. Practically all of the major comparative studies have been based predominantly on the use of the published results of studies carried out independently in different countries. Most of these studies have used different procedures in defining the categories between which mobility was observed. Comparability was established by collapsing the nation-specific classifications into a smaller set of categories—mostly into the manual/non-manual/farm distinction. However, neither a satisfactory degree of differentiation nor adequate comparability was achieved in this way (for discussion of these problems, see Goldthorpe, 1985a; Erikson and Goldthorpe, 1985, 1988a).

Starting with comparative work on England, France and Sweden (Erikson, Goldthorpe and Portocarero, 1979, 1982, 1983) and followed by a considerably wider range of nations in the CASMIN Project (Goldthorpe and Müller, 1982), Goldthorpe has pursued the more appropriate—although much more tedious and demanding—strategy of achieving comparability through secondary analysis of the original individual-based records of each national data set included in the comparisons. Following this strategy, Goldthorpe and his colleagues in the CASMIN Project have achieved a degree of comparability and of differentiation in the empirical base for the comparative study of social mobility which goes far beyond pre-CASMIN standards. The enormous improvement results from two main conditions. First, in establishing comparative classifications they were able to start from theoretically well developed and explicitly formulated criteria. Second, in each single nation the operationalization of the class schema was based on very detailed occupational classifications as well as additional information on employment status, number of employees or size of farm. In the CASMIN Project this schema has been developed for Australia, England, France, the Federal Republic of Germany, Hungary, Ireland, Japan, Northern Ireland, Poland, Scotland, Sweden and, on a lower level of comparability, the United States.

The fact that the number of nations for which the schema is available has quickly expanded through the work of colleagues outside the CASMIN Project (Pöntinen *et al.*, 1983; Dessens *et al.*, 1985; Jones and Davis, 1986; Luijkx and Ganzeboom, 1989) indicates that, building on the solid Goldthorpian foundations, the study of class structure in advanced industrial societies can now enter the stage of promising empirically based comparative analysis.

THE SYNTHESIS ON SOCIAL MOBILITY IN INDUSTRIAL NATIONS

The house to be built on these solid foundations will undoubtedly have several wings and many floors. With his own comparative work on social mobility Goldthorpe has already contributed an impressive segment of that building himself. His work shows him as a master of clearly designed architecture and full of scepticism about the work of earlier bricklayers. In fact, his work over the years has been an unceasing cannonade against the two grand theories of industrial society. First, Goldthorpe has forcefully defended the relevance of the mobility of individuals for understanding why processes of class formation occur or do not occur against Marxist assumptions regarding collective proletarianization as the main trend in the development of class structure in capitalist societies. The other side of the battlefield—as already indicated—involves assumptions contained in the vision of 'pluralist industrialism'.

Though much of the previous research on social mobility is associated with the latter battalions, there is no uniform formulation of the industrialism-mobility relationship. However, Goldthorpe has given precise characterizations of the different variants proposed in the literature. Conceiving higher rates of mobility either as a precondition for the take-off of industrial development (Davis, 1962) or as its consequence (Lipset and Zetterberg, 1959), a first variant postulates a historic increase in mobility with the transition from pre-industrial to industrial society. Other variants assume a steady increase in mobility as industrialism advances. They assume a fundamental trend towards rationalism and universalism inherent in industrial technology, work organization and the selection of personnel for employment positions. Rates of social mobility are expected to *increase* the more the economy grows and the more the assumed achievement-based stratification processes in industrialized societies become dominant, thereby replacing the earlier ascriptive principle (Blau and Duncan, 1967; Treiman, 1970). A further variant—found particularly in the convergence thesis of Kerr *et al.* (1960) and Kerr (1983)—stresses the standardizing tendencies inherent in advanced technologies and other elements of industrialism, thus assuming an increasing *uniformity* of social structures and patterns of social mobility in industrial societies. One far-reaching conclusion of this approach has been that in such societies the very basis for class solidarity and class action disappears (Blau and Duncan, 1967). Apart from these different conceptions of the links between advancing industrialism and mobility, there has also been a repeated defence of the thesis which postulates *exceptionally* high rates of mobility for specific societies, particularly those not burdened by the legacy of the European feudal past or its class-based stratification system, such as the USA, Australia or Japan.

Starting with his early critique of the convergence thesis (Goldthorpe, 1964), Goldthorpe has seriously questioned the underlying assumptions of these general hypotheses and has restated them in a series of papers in more precise form, confronting them with empirical evidence from the nations included in the CASMIN Project. Admittedly, this selection of nations does not correspond to the ideal sample were there to be no research restrictions.[1] However, the sample is heterogeneous enough to cover the variations in economic, political, social and cultural conditions existing in industrial societies for the period under investigation.[2] Space limitations permit only a crude summary of the achievements I consider most important in the empirical analysis of this data. I will focus on findings relating to intergenerational mobility, concentrating on the following aspects: the debate on similarities and variations in social mobility in industrial societies, and the theoretical formulation of common patterns of social fluidity and the paradigm of comparative macro-sociology.

Similarities and Variations in Social Mobility in Industrial Societies

Much of the earlier work on comparative mobility has been flawed by inadequate conceptualization or measurement of different aspects of mobility as they relate to different theoretical problems. If problems of class formation are at issue, the proper reference is to the *absolute* amounts of mobility or immobility as measured, for instance, by the total proportion of mobile persons or by indicators of the composition of given classes in terms of the class of origin of their members. With regard to questions of the degree of openness of the class structure or, as Goldthorpe calls it, the degree of *social fluidity*, the proper measures are *relative* rates. Relative rates express the pattern of association between origin and destination, measured independently of the size of classes of origin and destination. Absolute rates, on the contrary, can be conceived as resulting from the pattern of social fluidity and the opportunities created for mobility by the distribution in the relative size of the various classes and changes in this distribution through the contraction or expansion of particular classes. The need for this fundamental distinction has been recognized at least since the early 1950s (Rogoff, 1953), but a proper methodological solution had not been found. The status attainment models have rightly been criticized precisely for not having adequately controlled structural constraints. Only the methodological advances of log-linear modelling techniques introduced into the field of mobility research mainly through the pioneering work of Goodman (1969, 1978) and Hauser (1978) have indicated proper ways for measuring relative rates and for modelling patterns of social fluidity.

In the productive cooperation between John Goldthorpe and Robert Erikson in the CASMIN Project these tools have been used innovatively and with great insight. But this is not the main merit of their work. The most important implication for the future of the field is that these authors have formulated precisely the proper questions to be addressed concerning the different ways in which social mobility can and cannot be linked to the development of industrial societies. They have produced solid empirical knowledge to answer these questions and, with a powerful intellectual vigour, they have evaluated the implications of the empirical evidence for the theory of industrial societies (see particularly Erikson and Goldthorpe, 1987a, 1987b, 1988f; Goldthorpe, 1988b; and Chapter 11 in Goldthorpe, 1987a).

From this evidence it is quite clear that, if measured in *absolute* rates, the amount and pattern of mobility in industrial societies display a considerable degree of variation. Absolute rates of mobility do differ between societies, between subgroups of a given society and in the course of economic development of a society. These differences in absolute rates of mobility occur because class structures differ between societies, between subgroups of societies and in the rate of their change in the course of societal development. This contradicts Lipset and Zetterberg's conclusion from their analysis of absolute mobility that 'the overall pattern of social mobility appears to be much the same in the industrial societies of various Western countries' (1959: 13). It also contradicts convergence theories which had assumed similar absolute rates of mobility as a consequence of the convergence of class structures. There is only one consistent relationship between the absolute amount of mobility and industrial development: since immobility in the agricultural sector is known to be especially high, societies tend to attain a higher absolute level of mobility in the period of their economic transformation in which the agricultural sector contracts quickly.

In contrast to absolute rates, which vary quite substantially, the data give 'a good deal of empirical support' (Goldthorpe, 1988b: 15) to the reformulation of the Lipset-Zetterberg hypothesis by Featherman, Jones and Hauser (1975), who assume a basic similarity in *relative* rates, that is, in the pattern of social fluidity. Goldthorpe summarizes the evidence here as follows:

> First, that if taken in its strictest form, as claiming a complete uniformity in cross-national patterns of social fluidity, the hypothesis is not sustainable, but secondly, that it can find far more support if understood in a sense which, though less strict, is still informative. That is, as claiming that fluidity patterns display a very large commonality, across a wide range of industrial and industrializing societies. (1987a: 303)

Moreover, subgroups of populations differ little in their *relative* rates. This is particularly true for differences in social fluidity between men and women. Furthermore, the pattern of marital mobility of women is similar to the pattern of occupational mobility of men. Thus hypotheses postulating that marriage markets are less class-bound than labour markets cannot be sustained (Erikson and Goldthorpe, 1988b).

The data also contradict the hypothesis of a trend towards a general increase in social fluidity. If changes over time in relative mobility rates occur, such changes correspond most closely to the assumption of 'trendless fluctuation' suggested by Sorokin (1927). Industrial development is not automatically paralleled by increasing social fluidity. If changes do occur in that direction, they occur in the course of political intervention explicitly pursuing this aim. Therefore, they tend to be episodic. Trend data for relative rates also contradict the convergence hypothesis: at least until the 1970s variation between different societies did not lessen in the course of societal development. Finally, hypotheses postulating exceptionalism in mobility rates for the new nations or Japan cannot be sustained in a systematic way (Erikson and Goldthorpe, 1985, 1988e; Ishida *et al.*, 1988).[3]

In sum, Erikson and Goldthorpe's results are negative with respect to most of the assertions advanced by earlier writers linking patterns of social mobility with other characteristics of industrial societies and their development. Even the 'FJH hypothesis' cannot be accepted in an unqualified way. Although the pattern of social fluidity in industrial nations is characterized by a large degree of cross-national and between-group similarity as well as of temporal stability, there is also variation. This variation cannot be neglected, but it cannot be explained by the theories advanced to date. Although the reader may at times feel uncertain as to whether the deviations from uniformity displayed in the data should be taken as still indicating similarity or as being large enough to be understood as substantial variation, the general conclusions drawn from the empirical evidence are convincing. There are two principal reasons why this is so. First, Erikson and Goldthorpe adopt a strategy of comparative research particularly well designed to test hypotheses of similarity or variation among a number of nations. Second, their account is based on an explicit theoretical model of the pattern of social fluidity in industrial nations whose formulation they have already advanced a long way. In the following section I will discuss these two points in more detail.

Common Patterns of Social Fluidity and the Paradigm of Macro-Sociology

Given that the evidence provided by Goldthorpe and Erikson is at odds with most of the hypotheses advanced by earlier writers, how do they themselves integrate their findings into a consistent model? They accept that industrial societies do share common properties, although not in the sense of a complete uniformity, more in terms of a 'family resemblance' allowing for variation within each individual society. Put in more musical terms, they argue that 'there is a strong and well defined theme, but one on which national variations may be played' (Erikson and Goldthorpe, 1987a: 61). Given this expectation, the task of the analyst is first to establish the common theme as the core of similarity and then to show how and why particular nations deviate from that core.

In their core model of social fluidity Erikson and Goldthorpe (1987a) consider four types of effects as constituting the common pattern of the observed relative rates of mobility: 'inheritance' effects, 'hierarchy' effects, 'sector' effects and 'affinity' effects. This well-grounded theoretical model cannot be elaborated in detail here. However, from the point of view of class analysis it is most important to stress that one thing the model explicitly does not do is to reduce the theoretical explanation of mobility to a simple consequence of vertical distances in the sense of 'the further away, the less mobility'. Rather, it shows that classes which overlap in terms of vertical location are nevertheless divided from each other by strong barriers of mobility. This is particularly true for the barrier between sectors of industry. Similarly, the special inheritance effects, as well as several of the affinity effects, found for the propertied and service classes point to the clear significance of the class factor in generating and inhibiting mobility.

The model fits the data well for those nations which Erikson and Goldthorpe find to be most typical for the core of social fluidity in industrial nations. These core nations are England and France. Having established the core pattern, Erikson and Goldthorpe can examine the specific ways other nations deviate from this core and the factors accounting for such deviations. The crucial point of this analysis is that it appears impossible to explain the deviations straightforwardly as a consequence of macro-sociological factors. There is no evidence, for instance, of social fluidity increasing or decreasing in any linear way with the level of economic development of a society or with the rate of economic growth. Nor is there evidence that the pattern of social fluidity is systematically linked to distinct types of societies, for example, to the Western capitalist societies as opposed to the Eastern European socialist societies. From Erikson and Goldthorpe's results it seems unrealistic to expect that deviations of single nations from the core could be explained if—following Przeworski and Teune's (1970) recommendation—names of countries were replaced by values on specific variables. Deviations arise from the more or less idiosyncratic peculiarities of single nations. However, such peculiarities can be linked in a theoretically consistent way with the presence of other identifiable nation-specific conditions. These conditions are found in the peculiarities of a nation's economic, social and political history or in the particular institutional arrangements which have developed, for instance in the educational system, the labour market or other institutions which shape particular elements of the pattern of social fluidity.[4]

The conclusion I consider most significant for the general theory of industrial societies concerns the political factor. Political interventions appear in fact to matter—be they specific measures taken in the periods of socialist transformation in Eastern European societies or the long-term equalizing policies pursued by social democratic governments in Sweden. To put it very generally, the transmission of advantages to one's offspring, which are rooted in the solidarity of the family and the economic laws of the market, can be understood as the driving forces behind the commonalities in inequality found. Such forces, however, are not immutable constraints but susceptible to being moulded by political will.

In Goldthorpe's strategy of comparative sociology the elaboration and theoretical foundation of a core pattern, which can be seen as an exercise in general theory, has to be supplemented by the case-study-like reconstitution of historically contingent associated conditions which account for the deviations from the common pattern. Both general sociological theory and history have to be given their proper due. With the 'commonality and variation' papers, Erikson and Goldthorpe (1987a, 1987b) have provided lucid examples of a paradigm of comparative research which appears to be promising well beyond the narrow confines of comparative mobility research (for similar approaches in recent research on the welfare state, see Korpi, 1988).

CONCLUSION

I had originally planned to conclude this chapter with a section emphasizing the relationship between mobility analysis and class analysis. For several reasons I have decided otherwise. First, these two aspects are so intimately linked that the topic is presented throughout my entire contribution. The core model of social fluidity, in particular, shows that the pattern of association between origin and destination is strongly influenced by class factors. Second, if one wanted to follow the line of argument the other way round, that is, to ask how mobility patterns affect class formation, one would need to write an additional paper. On that topic the empirical evidence is not yet solid enough to treat the question on a comparative level. In many of the mobility data sets the central dependent variables—such as patterns of social association, participation in collective organizations, political attitudes and political affiliation—are still missing. Goldthorpe's own British study is among the very few in which the respective data have been collected, and his *Social Mobility and Class Structure in Modern Britain* documents the rich gains to be achieved from following that line of investigation. So it can only be hoped that future researchers collecting data on social mobility will be aware of this. Only then will sociology be able to use the full potential of the class framework for mobility research.

Social mobility research has often been attacked for its lack of theory, its empiricist number-crunching and a mania for ever more refined statistical models, all of which make most of its work accessible only to a tiny community of specialists. This is no longer true. Goldthorpe has provided us with a masterpiece of comparative macro-sociology. It demonstrates what little other work in sociology does, namely, how real advances can be made in our understanding of industrial societies through mutual interpenetration and accumulation in the formulation of theoretically guided research questions; through the elaboration or more precise concepts; through the establishment with stubborn energy of a satisfactory database; through the development of formal models appropriate to test precise hypotheses; and through linking research results with an historically based knowledge both of specific institutions and of the political, social and economic history of particular societies.

NOTES

1 The most serious restrictions result from the lack of reliable and comparable data. For this reason, no nation from Southern Europe is included. Furthermore, in some instances a theoretically important factor is found in but one country. Sweden, for example, is the only nation in the sample with a long tradition of social democratic political hegemony.
2 The data were collected at the beginning of the 1970s and cover a period preceded by economic transformation and growth perhaps unique in the history of industrial nations. The data therefore refer to a period in history in which conditions were particularly well suited to confirm a hypothesis assuming increasing mobility with economic growth and developing industrialism.
3 Only Australia, but not the USA or Japan, deviates clearly from the core pattern in the direction of more openness. However, Australia is not completely outside the range of the European nations, ranking second only to Sweden in the degree of fluidity.
4 For findings stressing the relevance of nation-specific institutional regulations see, for example, Müller *et al*. (1988) on education.

20. The Failure of a Paradigm: Log-linear Models of Social Mobility

JONATHAN KELLEY

There has been a revolution in the study of social mobility: the once dominant Blau-Duncan paradigm has been overthrown by log-linear modelling. The techniques were first developed by Goodman (1978) in statistics and applied to mobility problems by Goodman, Hauser, Featherman, Duncan, Goldthorpe and many others. The log-linear revolution was a noble experiment, and at first seemed to offer a bright new future beyond Blau and Duncan. Goldthorpe and his colleagues elaborated a particular version of the paradigm, combining log-linear methods, cross-cultural data and a particular schema for measuring class position (Goldthorpe, 1971, 1980a, 1985a; Erikson, Goldthorpe and Portocarero, 1983; Erikson and Goldthorpe, 1985). They have done impressive work with it; that is freely conceded even in this critical appraisal. Their Herculean labours in data preparation are ambitious in scope and commendable in quality. Their analytic methods are modern, employed with agreeable technical virtuosity and presented with commendable clarity. There is much good here.

But there are also fatal flaws. Some are flaws of the log-linear paradigm in general, in particular, the method's limited statistical power in dealing with questions of hierarchy and strength of association; the necessity of using crude categories instead of continuous measurement; and the difficulty of incorporating education, income and the myriad other variables relevant to social mobility in the model. Other fatal flaws are specific to Goldthorpe's variant of the paradigm, particularly the narrow range of countries and his crude typological measurement. In the end one must judge the new paradigm by its substantive fruits: what has the log-linear paradigm discovered about the real world? What new insights do we have, and with what implications for sociology?

In the end I believe Goldthorpe's experiment has failed. A decade and more has passed. Endless models have been fitted; legions of design matrices passed in review; chi-squares marshalled. But we have learnt little new of substance. Frequencies in a crude cross-classification of father's occupation by son's occupation are described in loving detail, with some *ad hoc* interpretation but little theory. The models are, for the most part, mere data smoothing. This compares poorly with the statistically simpler but conceptually more sophisticated results of the Blau-Duncan paradigm. It is too high a price to pay for statistical elegance. Let us trace the story, from its promising beginning as an alternative to the Blau-Duncan paradigm to its sad conclusion.

THE SETTING: BIRTH OF THE BLAU-DUNCAN PARADIGM

When Goldthorpe began his work on stratification, the Blau-Duncan paradigm (Blau and Duncan, 1967; Duncan and Hodge, 1963; Duncan, 1966) was in its heyday, having advanced study of social stratification from its speculative and non-cumulative beginning to the status of a normal science (Colclough and Horan, 1983). Goldthorpe was, from the beginning, a stern critic, arguing against Blau and Duncan and in favour of a new approach. This is the background in which Goldthorpe's work should be set, the state of the art from which his new departure must be judged. The key aspects were as follows:

Good data. Analyses were based on large, representative, national sample surveys, not on small samples, nor on local ones, nor ones unrepresentative of the population as a whole.

New variables. Blau and Duncan developed more revealing ways of looking at old problems. Departing from the older focus on the simple cross-tabulation of father's occupation by son's occupation, they opened up the black box of 'mobility' and disentangled the processes that link the generations. First, they treated father's occupation as one distinct variable and son's occupation as another, rather than treating them as a composite 'mobility' variable (Duncan, 1966). This was a simple step, but one with real statistical advantages. Then they explicitly measured other important links between parent and child, particularly education. They measured father's education and showed that its effects were separate and distinct from father's occupation. They measured son's education and showed it to be the key link between family background and occupational success—typically, about half of the advantages of birth come about because children born to privileged families get a better education than children born into poor families. Then Blau and Duncan expanded the paradigm to new related issues, looking at the effect of education and family background on occupational success and also on income. They found many similarities, but also important differences: family background has a substantial impact on earnings, but the effects were weaker and entirely indirect through education and occupation.

Detailed continuous measurement. An unglamorous but absolutely essential innovation was the development of precise and detailed measurement, particularly of occupational status (Duncan, 1961). Earlier researchers had generally used three crude categories: white-collar/blue-collar/farm. Later analyses were only slightly better, often distinguishing upper white workers/routine white-collar/skilled blue-collar workers/unskilled workers/farmers/and farm labourers. These broad categories conceal vital differences. The white-collar category, for example, includes doctors as well as the lab technicians who work for them and the clerks who file the results; it includes state governors and cabinet ministers dispensing millions, but also minor bureaucrats dispatching garbage trucks; skilled and highly paid salesmen in heavy industry, but also impoverished sales clerks in corner shops; owners of large businesses and hot dog stand proprietors; university professors and religious quacks.

Duncan, Treiman and others discovered the details of the occupational hierarchy, ranking hundreds of occupations. They showed that the hierarchy was much the same in all sections of society—men and women, rich and poor, old and young—and the same throughout the world. Their scales provided much more accurate measurement of occupational rank than had been available before.

New (to sociology) methods. Blau and Duncan adopted the powerful methods of the general linear model, especially ordinary least squares regression. These powerful and robust methods were, at the time, rarely used in sociology. Much of the success of the paradigm came from them; they turned out to be extremely well suited to sociological problems in general, and to social mobility in particular. They were robust, so that minor differences in models and measurement made little difference to the results. But they were also sensitive to small but important substantive differences, for example, in distinguishing the effects of father's education from father's occupational status, which are distinct in their consequences although closely correlated. They were capable of dealing with the highly multivariate models appropriate to the sociological world of many small overlapping influences. Much of the early success of the model came from these new methods and much of its lasting influence from their spread into all corners of the sociological realm. There was not much else new in the Blau-Duncan model. There were no new theories—the old Sorokin, Lipset, Smelser and Kerr arguments about development and convergence among industrial societies were recycled. But its many strengths offset that one weakness.

The result. The result was a flowering of research unprecedented in sociology. Robust findings about stratification emerged first for the USA (Blau and Duncan, 1967; Duncan, Featherman and Duncan, 1972) and soon afterward for many other countries, including Britain and Australia in the Western industrial world (Treiman and Terrell, 1975b; Broom and Jones, 1969); Poland and Hungary in Eastern Europe (Zagorski, 1984); and developing and even tribal societies (Pastore, Haller and Gomez, 1975; Kelley, 1971, 1978). A Kuhnian (1962) 'normal science' of social stratification was born and the field had its golden age.

NEW DEVELOPMENTS: THE BLAU-DUNCAN PARADIGM EXPANDS

By the time Goldthorpe became involved the Blau-Duncan paradigm had finished its first flowering but flourished on as new extensions branched out in many directions.

Data. There was little change in the paradigm's preferred data. The importance of good, large, representative national samples remained clear.

New variables.

> *education*—there were further improvements and desegregation of variables related to education. New studies focused on early success in school, on the transition from grade to grade in school, and the transition from school to university. Much of sociology of education adopted elements of the Blau-Duncan paradigm. The range of variables expanded to include social-psychological elements, notably encouragement by parents, teachers and peers; intelligence; teachers' perceptions and school quality; and many other things (Haller and Portes, 1973; Duncan, Featherman and Duncan, 1972; Hauser, 1969).
>
> *income*—new variables were added in the analysis of income, notably labour force experience. Industry differences appeared under a variety of guises (core versus periphery, primary versus secondary labour market), mostly distinguishing between jobs in large, prosperous, generally unionized, capital intensive industries and jobs in smaller, more vulnerable and competitive industries where pay was lower and employment less secure. Much of this new work converged with labour economists' work on human capital.
>
> *new aspects of class*—the paradigm originally focused just on occupational status (or prestige), but other aspects soon came to the fore, notably ownership, authority and government (versus private) employment. This overlapped with the new school of 'multiple regression Marxists' (Wright and Perrone, 1977), who adapted the methods of Blau and Duncan to a very different theoretical stance. Suggestions for outright convergence between the schools soon appeared (Robinson and Kelley, 1979). There was even a revival of some venerable aspects of class, not so much as competitors for occupational status and ownership but as additional aspects of a complex whole. Among them were subjective class identification and the venerable blue-collar/white-collar/farm distinction; these ultimately proved more potent for voting and other political issues than for stratification proper (Jackman and Jackman, 1982; Kelley, McAllister and Mughan, 1985).

Better measurement. There were gradual but important improvements in measurement. Education, measured in crude categories in Blau and Duncan's original work, was instead measured in years of schooling. Progress was made in sorting out mere credentialism from genuine educational skills and human capital. New occupational measures were developed, including SES-type scales for other countries, analogous to Duncan's US original (e.g. Duncan-Jones, 1972); prestige scores for many countries throughout the world; and Treiman's (1977) worldwide Standard International Prestige Scale.

Methods: gradual improvements. The original methods were gradually improved. Sets of dummy (dichotomous) variables were used when linearity could **not** be assumed (for example, in the distinction between private, public and church schools). Curvilinear relations were catered for (e.g. with quadratic terms as well as linear). Converging with econometric methods, more complex models were estimated where OLS was no longer appropriate, notably instrumental variable and two-stage least squares models. Converging with psychometric methods, explicit measurement models were estimated including multiple indicators (e.g. Featherman, Jones and Hauser, 1975) and corrections for attenuation due to random measurement error (e.g. Kelley, 1973). Finally, and perhaps most promising, was the convergence of these two traditions in LISREL models combining both the economists' structural equation methods and psychometric measurement models (Jöreskog, 1978).

Comparison of different populations. A very fruitful line of development was the application of Blau-Duncan models to separate groups, notably men versus women (e.g. Treiman and Terrell, 1975a), ethnic minorities (Duncan, 1968) and immigrants (Broom *et al.*, 1980). Methods for systematically comparing groups were soon developed (Duncan, 1968; Jones and Kelley, 1984) and new variables especially appropriate to such comparisons, such as language skill (e.g. Evans, 1987), were introduced. The analysis of 'discrimination' became a major field in itself, and remains so to this day, with a vast and flourishing literature.

Another natural expansion, logically very similar, was application of the paradigm to separate countries or—what is much the same—to the same country at different time periods. This began with cohort comparisons in Blau and Duncan's original analysis and subsequent comparisons of their survey with later ones—particularly Featherman and Hauser's (1976) 'OCG-II' replication of the Blau-Duncan original. The requisite large, representative national sample was replicated in many countries—among them Goldthorpe's excellent Oxford Mobility Study. The extension to an explicit comparison between two or three countries was almost immediate, for example in the perennial favourite US-British comparison (Treiman and Terrell, 1975b; Robinson and Kelley, 1979).

This cross-cultural extension is a natural and very promising one: it attempts to discover what is common to all countries (and so presumably to be explained by factors common to all); what is common only to countries similar in level of economic development or political system (and so presumably to be explained by that); and what is unique to each (and so presumably to be explained by factors unique to each country). Moreover, it is a traditional question in social stratification (e.g. Sorokin, 1927), where there is a longstanding concern with the effects of economic development. The usual questions are whether economic development makes for greater openness, greater social mobility, and whether there are differences in openness between 'old' traditional Europe and 'new' modern America.

The usual empirical finding was that fundamental differences between advanced industrial societies are small. There are surface differences due to variation in occupational distributions, particularly the size of the farm sector, but the fundamental patterns (as revealed by metric regression coefficients and the like) are similar. This confirms, with far more persuasive measurement and analysis, the longstanding claims of Lipset and Zetterberg (1959) (see Treiman and Terrell, 1975b; Robinson and Kelley, 1979). One of the best comparisons in this tradition made the point strongly enough to give a new name to this longstanding conjecture and it now commonly appears in the literature as the 'FJH hypothesis' (Featherman, Jones and Hauser, 1975).

The stage is set: stagnation in the Blau-Duncan paradigm. Then progress stalled, with the usual Blau-Duncan model apparently applying to most industrial societies without any interesting or systematic variation among them. There were dissenting claims, particularly concerning developing societies (e.g. Kelley, 1978) and the role of education in socialist societies (e.g. Zagorski, 1984), but nothing to overturn the prevailing consensus. In this inauspicious situation log-linear models offered a new approach.

A NEW PARADIGM: GOLDTHORPE AND LOG-LINEAR ANALYSIS

Goodman (1969, 1978), Hauser (1978), Featherman *et al.* (1975), Duncan (1979), Goldthorpe (1971, 1980a) and others suggested a bold departure from the Blau-Duncan paradigm. Much of its success came from the power of its methods, but they suggested abandoning them in favour of the newly developed log-linear methods.

The new paradigm. Goldthorpe and Erikson then, quite logically, proceeded to use these new methods to analyze cross-national patterns of stratification using data from their CASMIN (Comparative Analysis of Social Mobility in Industrial Nations) Project. They began by recoding individual-level data from almost a dozen societies, using (so far as possible) exactly the same definitions and measurement, in particular converting the original occupation codes into the seven (or sometimes nine) categories of the Goldthorpe-Hope classification. This combination of log-linear models and good data from the CASMIN Project, comparably coded into the Goldthorpe-Hope classification, is Goldthorpe's fundamental paradigm. Adopting it was a good gamble but, I shall argue, a gamble that failed.

Data.

> *occupations: achieving comparability*—Goldthorpe's paradigm retains the Blau-Duncan emphasis on good data from large representative samples. The CASMIN Project's reworking of individual-level data for nearly a dozen countries is an excellent idea (and involved a great deal of work). Most other comparative studies rely on re-analysis of published tables, but that is far inferior: there are almost always substantial differences in the occupational classification, so important detail must be sacrificed for comparability's sake, usually all the way down to the primitive white-collar/blue-collar/farm tri-chotomy; the classification of particular occupations often differs (for example, whether supervisors of manual workers are white-collar or blue; whether a craftsman who works at his trade but also owns the business and has employees is manager or worker); only rarely are identical populations covered

(e.g. coverage begins at age 16 or 18 or 21); and the like. To get a sound cross-national comparison, it is necessary to decide such matters consistently and—sad but true—that means going back to the original survey data and doing it oneself. The CASMIN Project has done this, to its great credit.

narrow range of countries—the value of the laborious task of achieving comparability has been undermined by limiting the scope of the project to industrial countries, mainly northern Europe and its overseas offshoots. Only Japan among non-European industrial nations is included. There is also the quaint insistence that Scotland and Northern Ireland are separate countries: this raises the apparent—but not the real—number of countries being compared. The most important weakness is the lack of any of the 'newly industrializing' nations, such as Brazil, Korea or Taiwan, and the absence of any pre-industrial nations such as India, Malaysia or the Philippines. Good surveys are available for many of them. Without them, it is hard to test claims—such as in the key FJH hypothesis—that industrialization leads to convergence in mobility patterns. The absence of differences among industrial societies supports the theory only weakly, since 'no difference' hypotheses are particularly difficult to prove. The problem is that the lack of observed differences could be due to other causes, most conspicuously to weak measurement or to weak statistical methods—and we shall see that both are plausible candidates. If Goldthorpe could demonstrate that his measurement and methods reveal large differences among pre-industrial societies, smaller differences among newly industrializing ones and no differences among industrial ones, that would be much stronger evidence.

Measurement. One of the great strengths of the Blau-Duncan paradigm lay in its careful and detailed measurement, particularly of occupational status. Goldthorpe has abandoned this at a serious cost:

> *the lack of hierarchy*—we study social mobility in order to understand stratification, hierarchy and their links across generations. So a ranking of occupations from high status to low is essential: the fundamental social conflict is over who gets good jobs, with the high pay and good working conditions that go with them, and who gets poor ones, with the accompanying poverty, dirt and toil. The reason people study hard in school, invest in a university education and work hard at their first job is that they want to get a good job. The reason that governments agonize over how working-class children do in school, fund students from poor families at university, pass equal opportunity legislation and the like is that everyone wants good jobs, high incomes and high status, but only some can get it. Not to know who wins and who loses the competition is to miss the main point.

But, particularly in the earlier papers, Goldthorpe and his colleagues argue that their occupational classification is not hierarchical but a 'class' scheme and that this is somehow different. It is not clear how seriously they actually take this claim, nor is it clear what they mean by it. Certainly they cheerfully assume—quite correctly—that the hierarchical reasoning concerning occupational status underlying the key FJH hypothesis should apply directly to class. Much of their discussion implicitly assumes a hierarchy—for example, that people would take professional and higher white-collar jobs (their 'service' class) if they could and avoid unskilled work. Their later models explicitly include a (somewhat eccentric) hierarchical parameter. But, on the other hand, they offer little rationale for their implicit hierarchy and most of their analytic models make no assumption of hierarchy. Insofar as they ignore hierarchy, this is to miss the main point.

crude measurement—Goldthorpe distinguishes only seven classes. In hierarchical order these are the 'service' class (professionals, administrators, managers, large proprietors and such), lower white-collar (routine clerical and sales), petty bourgeoisie (small proprietors and middle-sized proprietors), farmers, skilled workers, unskilled workers and farm workers. As usual in mobility research, there is some difficulty about the position of farmers (they have high prestige and in the past were many and prosperous, but their children do poorly); in some later work Goldthorpe moves farm sons (but not fathers) down the hierarchy.

In broad outline Goldthorpe's occupational class scheme is standard old-fashioned stuff. It is more refined than the crude white-collar/blue-collar/farm distinction used by many researchers up to the 1950s, improving on that by splitting the white-collar group into two, splitting blue-collar workers into two, splitting the farm group into owners and labourers, and by separating (some) business owners into their own class. Save for that last, it is close to the venerable Edwards classification used by the US Census in bygone days.

Goldthorpe's is not a bad way of classifying occupations. But it is crude compared to the original Blau-Duncan classification and its variants in other countries (for example, Duncan-Jones, 1972, in Australia). It is also crude compared to prestige scores which distinguish literally hundreds of specific occupations and are, moreover, well documented and readily available throughout the world (Treiman, 1977). It may be that this crude measurement loses little of importance, but that is unlikely and certainly unproven.

This crude classification raises dangers of unmeasured heterogeneity. For example, there are large differences in Goldthorpe's 'petty bourgeoisie', which includes prosperous owners with capital, management skills and workers to supervise; small shopkeepers working long hours alone behind the counter of a mom-and-pop grocery; and blue-collar electricians with their own small business. There are also clear and systematic differences between the professionals and administrators lumped together in Goldthorpe's 'service' class. For instance, administrators include big business owners who can pass on a business to their children and prosperous managers who can buy one for them, but also professionals who do no such thing; a school teacher or engineer cannot pass on his job to anyone. So when Goldthorpe reports on inheritance in the 'service' class as a whole, his figures are wrong both for administrators (underestimating the role of money and inheritance) and for professionals (overstating it). For Eastern Europe, combining political administrators and intellectuals is dubious (Frentzel-Zagorska and Zagorski, 1989).

Too few variables. Goldthorpe's paradigm abandons one of the great strengths of Blau and Duncan's: the extension beyond the old cross-tabulation of father's occupation by son's occupation. Blau and Duncan included explicit unidimensional measures of father's education and son's education, separating two aspects of class conceptually and statistically. They extended the analysis to include pay as an additional—and very relevant—outcome. We have learned much from these and lose much by abandoning them.

Goldthorpe reverts to a simple cross-tabulation between father and son. The measure of family background is thus a very coarse grouping of only seven categories. Compared to the Blau-Duncan paradigm's categorization of family background jointly by dozens of status categories and half a dozen categories of father's education, this is crude. But it does have virtues in the (partial) inclusion of ownership and authority dimensions that were ignored in the original Blau-Duncan scheme (but not in its successors). Goldthorpe makes much of this, dignifying it as a class schema and denigrating Blau and Duncan's alternative. The matter is important and requires discussion; I will argue that, far from being a strength, Goldthorpe's class scheme is a grave weakness, inferior to the original Blau-Duncan scheme and far inferior to more recent alternatives.

the weakness of typologies—an essential difficulty is that Goldthorpe's occupational classification is a typology, not a set of variables each measuring a single dimension. An important conceptual advance in the Blau-Duncan paradigm was to treat each variable as (in principle) continuous and unidimensional. For example, occupations were scored by their status. Then other aspects of class were treated as separate unidimensional variables. Education, scored continuously from many years of schooling to few, was the first addition. But others are easily added—as were number of siblings in the earliest version of the paradigm and many other variables in later developments. The great strength of using unidimensional variables rather than typologies is that each conceptual variable can be treated separately and their separate effects assessed statistically. For example, Blau and Duncan give straightforward estimates of the separate effects of father's occupational status and father's education. This can be very informative.

But Goldthorpe's occupational classification goes back to the earlier tradition of typological measurement which does not allow such separate effects to be distinguished. For example, his highest class, the 'service' class, includes professionals and administrators (both high status), while routine white-collar workers (lower in status) are in the 'lower white-collar' class; so far this is a (crude) status scoring. But then the conceptually separate dimension of supervision enters: any routine white-collar worker who also supervises other white-collar workers is upgraded into the 'service' class. So supervision is part of the typology, but cannot be easily distinguished statistically (because supervisors are lumped together with many other 'service' workers, some of whom supervise and some of whom do not). Ownership is treated similarly.

There are times when a typological approach is justified, but this is not one of them. Sharp discontinuities may make categories clearer than continuous variables, but here there are few such. For example, if you classify occupations by status, you would find that the bottom of Goldthorpe's 'service' class merges smoothly into the top of his routine white-collar class, and so forth down the hierarchy. Also, massive statistical interactions may make typologies superior to unidimensional variables, but these do not exist here either, or at least none has been clearly demonstrated. For example, supervision and ownership have straightforward additive effects, not interactions (Robinson and Kelley, 1979).

ignoring the role of education—ignoring education is a savage loss. It is the primary mechanism by which advantages are handed down from one generation to another in most societies. It is particularly important to cross-national comparisons because educational attainments grow rapidly with time and economic development; furthermore, there are major differences between societies in its nature and importance. This neglect entails a serious theoretical cost. For example, in comparing white-collar workers with the petty bourgeoisie Goldthorpe is comparing apples and oranges: white-collar families provide their offspring with valuable skills in language and literature, in dealing with bureaucracies and a taste for learning; petty bourgeoisie provide theirs with ambition, a preference for self-employment and perhaps a going business. Those are very different ways of helping; they can be distinguished, measured and analyzed separately in Blau-Duncan style analyses, but in Goldthorpe's paradigm they are inextricably confounded.

only a crude treatment of ownership—Goldthorpe makes a distinction between owners and employees—a 'class' rather than 'status' distinction as some would label it. That is an advance on the original Blau-Duncan model, which ignored ownership—a point which Goldthorpe and the 'multiple regression Marxists' trumpeted, not without justice. But Goldthorpe's method of measuring ownership is crude and incomplete. Ownership and size of firm owned are used to distinguish large proprietors, who go into the 'service' class; small proprietors, who go into the 'petty bourgeoisie'; and non-owners, who go into various other classes depending on their job and whether they supervise. But large owners are lumped together with (much more numerous) non-owners in the 'service' class. Thus owners of businesses are distinguishable from ordinary workers only if they are small and unsuccessful (and so have few employees or none). Hence there is no clear statistical means of separating the effects of ownership from other things.

Furthermore, within Goldthorpe's petty bourgeoisie class small businessmen with employees—and so with managerial responsibilities and at least the possibility of, as Marx would have it, exploiting labour—are confounded with the (numerous) solo self-employed. This too is a real loss. Goldthorpe's classification also ignores occupational status distinctions within the petty bourgeoisie, including the basic gap between white-collar (e.g. wholesale proprietors) and blue-collar (e.g. a self-employed carpenter). It would thus be better to use a more detailed typology of classes that makes some of these distinctions (e.g. Wright and Perrone, 1977). But even better, I would argue, would be to measure ownership as an explicit separate variable—just as education is measured explicitly and separately from occupation in the Blau-Duncan paradigm—and use it in a multivariate analysis. One could, for example, distinguish large owners (say, with more than 25 employees), ordinary owners (say, 1 to 25 employees) and small owners (self-employed without employees). Then add 'father's ownership' to 'father's status' and 'father's education' as measures of family background in an analysis of son's education, ownership and status—effectively extending the Blau-Duncan paradigm to include ownership (Robinson and Kelley, 1979).

neglect of authority and power—another important aspect of class that is largely neglected by Goldthorpe is authority (Dahrendorf, 1959). He makes some use of it among white-collar jobs, putting supervisors in his top-ranking 'service' class (together with many non-supervisors) rather than among routine white-collar workers. In his older ten-class scheme he also used it to make a distinction among skilled workers (but not among the semi- or unskilled, where there are also many supervisors). But this is unsatisfactory. Because supervisors are lumped together with non-supervisors in the 'service' class, he cannot make a clear estimate of the effect of being a supervisor; nor can he make any estimate of supervision's effect among blue-collar workers. In fact, it seems that there is, among other things, a clear financial pay-off to being a supervisor in both classes. Again, I would argue that including supervision as an explicit and separate variable—like education—would be preferable, perhaps a variable distinguishing higher level supervisors (who supervise other supervisors), ordinary supervisors (who supervise only ordinary non-supervisory workers) and ordinary workers (Robinson and Kelley, 1979). Then the Blau-Duncan paradigm can be extended in the obvious way to include 'father supervisor' as well as other aspects of family background, and 'son supervisor' as well as son's education, status and ownership.

A similar and possibly useful distinction, not envisioned in Goldthorpe's classification, is between government employment and private enterprise: between, if you like, those who control the means of coercion and those who are subject to it (Djilas, 1957). This has class-like aspects, together with genuine effects on earnings and politics (Kelley and McAllister, 1985), and would be well worth investigating in the context of social mobility. That would be straightforward in the Blau-Duncan style, involving just the addition of another dichotomous variable for father and one for son, but cannot easily be done in Goldthorpe's style.

neglect of social-psychological variables—a weakness of the typological approach is that it is very difficult to add further factors that cross-cut existing distinctions; but some such factors look very promising in the study of social mobility. For example, the Wisconsin school has shown strong effects of aspiration and encouragement by parents and teachers (e.g. Sewell, Haller and Ohlendorf, 1970; Haller and Portes, 1973), and the importance of IQ is equally clear (e.g. Duncan, Featherman and Duncan, 1972). Such extensions are easily included in Blau-Duncan style models, but not in Goldthorpe's typological style, and that is a real cost.

an alternative to typologies—I would argue that Goldthorpe's models are arid in good part because of the conceptual and statistical difficulties of incorporating unidimensional concepts into typologies. To illustrate the strengths of the alternative approach using separate variables, consider the model shown in Figure 20.1. It is a straightforward extension of the original Blau-Duncan scheme to include concepts of ownership, authority and power—the traditional elements of 'class' models—as well as the traditional blue-collar/white-collar/farm distinction (Kelley and McAllister, 1985).

This simple approach gives clear estimates of the relative importance of

Figure 20.1 An Extended Blau-Duncan Model of Class

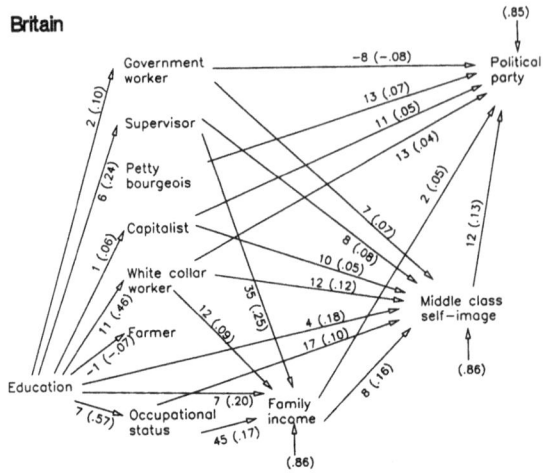

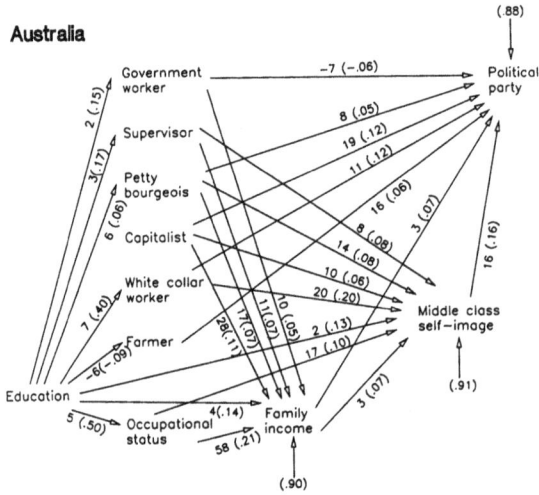

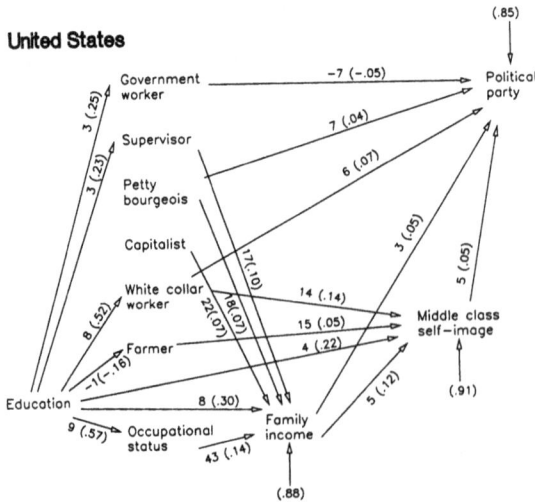

Britain

Government worker

Supervisor

Petty bourgeois

Capitalist

White collar worker

Farmer

Education

Occupational status

Family income

Middle class self-image

Political party

(.85)

(.86)

(.86)

−8 (−.08)
13 (.07)
11 (.05)
13 (.04)
2 (.05)
12 (.13)
2 (.10)
6 (.24)
1 (.06)
11 (.46)
−7 (−.07)
7 (.02)
8 (.08)
10 (.05)
12 (.12)
35 (.25)
12 (.09)
4 (.18)
17 (.10)
8 (.16)
7 (.20)
7 (.57)
45 (.17)

Australia

Government worker

Supervisor

Petty bourgeois

Capitalist

White collar worker

Farmer

Education

Occupational status

Family income

Middle class self-image

Political party

(.88)

(.91)

(.90)

−7 (−.06)
8 (.05)
19 (.12)
11 (.12)
16 (.06)
3 (.07)
8 (.08)
14 (.08)
10 (.06)
20 (.20)
2 (.13)
17 (.10)
16 (.16)
2 (.15)
3 (.17)
6 (.06)
7 (.40)
−6 (−.09)
10 (.05)
11 (.07)
17 (.07)
28 (.11)
3 (.07)
4 (.14)
5 (.50)
58 (.21)

United States

Government worker

Supervisor

Petty bourgeois

Capitalist

White collar worker

Farmer

Education

Occupational status

Family income

Middle class self-image

Political party

(.85)

(.91)

(.88)

−7 (−.05)
7 (.04)
6 (.07)
3 (.05)
5 (.05)
3 (.25)
3 (.23)
8 (.52)
−1 (−.16)
17 (.10)
22 (.07)
18 (.07)
14 (.14)
15 (.05)
4 (.22)
5 (.12)
8 (.30)
9 (.57)
43 (.14)

Notes: This contains metric regression coefficients (standardized in parentheses) for representative national samples of Britain, Australia and the United States. All variables scored 0 to 1 save for party (0 for left-wing through 100 for right-wing), education (in years) and income.

Source: Kelley and McAllister (1985).

different aspects of class, and of their differences and similarities in various contexts. Let us take some examples. Looking first at income: education and occupational status are its main determinants in all three countries, as Blau and Duncan would have it. Ownership and authority are of only secondary importance, Goldthorpe and his colleagues to the contrary notwithstanding, and the venerable white-collar/blue-collar dichotomy is irrelevant. But the picture is quite different for the subjective perception of class—something of which Goldthorpe makes a great deal—as measured by identification with the middle (versus working) class. Here all aspects of class matter: Blau and Duncan's familiar education-status-income trilogy; the venerable white-collar/blue-collar cleavage; but also ownership and authority. Thus people's subjective class identification is the sum of many small influences; no one school has any monopoly on the matter. Politically, the picture is quite different. Here the traditional Blau-Duncan variables matter little; people do not, by and large, vote as they do because of their status or education, nor even their incomes. Much more important is their subjective class position; whether they work at white-collar or blue-collar jobs; and whether they own the means of production.

In short, I would argue that extending Blau and Duncan's approach by explicitly including ownership, authority and the like is much more promising than the typological approach Goldthorpe has followed. Its main advantage is that it allows explicit consideration of many and diverse aspects of class and stratification, and statistically clear estimates of their separate effects. This is conceptually far superior to the muddle that comes from even the best typology. The main justification for using typologies with only a handful of categories rather than separate continuous variables is not conceptual but technical. Goldthorpe's preferred log-linear methods cannot easily cope with such variables, but are designed primarily for data in a small number of unordered categories. Are the statistical virtues of these methods sufficient to justify these heavy conceptual costs?

Methods: log-linear analysis. Log-linear methods are an intrinsic part of Goldthorpe's paradigm, a clear and important departure from the Blau-Duncan paradigm which leads in very different directions. The natural development of Blau and Duncan's techniques was to the structural equations methods of econometrics, the measurement methods of psychometrics and the combination of the two in LISREL and related techniques. But log-linear methods lead in other directions, some valuable and some exceedingly costly. I should say at the outset that log-linear methods have many virtues and have proved useful in many contexts (see the examples in Goodman, 1978, and elsewhere). They are also a great technical achievement. But they are not universal tools suited to all problems.

adjusting for differences in occupational structure—the greatest strength of log linear methods—or the one most stridently pushed by its advocates, possibly because there were so few other advantages—is its ability to adjust for differences in the marginals. Suppose, for example, we want to ask whether Britain is a more rigid and ascriptive society than the United States. The comparison is not straightforward because there are many differences in the occupational structure: more high status professionals and managers in the US, more unskilled workers in Britain, more farmers in the US and so forth. Log-linear models easily abstract away from these differences, showing the underlying pattern of association. This is a real advantage, albeit not so great an advantage as its proponents claim.

In the first place, regression and related methods do the same thing, although in a different way, by adjusting for differences in the means and standard deviations. So in the US-British comparison, for example, the abundance of high status professionals and comparative dearth of lower status workers make the US mean higher than the British and the standard deviation larger. But this is irrelevant to the key comparison: metric regression coefficients are unaffected by differences in the occupational structure, if the linear model is correct and still shows whether Britain is more (or less) ascriptive than the US. However, the standardized coefficients used earlier in the Blau-Duncan paradigm are affected and so are inappropriate for comparisons of this sort, as economists never tire of pointing out. Of course, the linear assumptions are never entirely correct, so differences in structure have some (usually modest) effect even on metric coefficients, but this is a difference of degree not kind. Furthermore, regression models which allow curvilinear relations (e.g. Kelley and McAllister, 1984) are even less sensitive to such differences.

Second, it is not clear that the occupational structure is really fixed, so that one ought to abstract away from it. The implicit 'bureaucratic' model is of fixed jobs into which workers are recruited. For example, if the US economy offers lots of high status professional jobs and the British economy few, that makes things better for US sons in a way that says nothing about them, or about social mobility, but is a mere consequence of the pre-existing economic differences. This is a perfectly sensible view for some jobs: each city has one mayor, one police chief and so forth; each position needs filling regardless of how many people are looking for work and what skills they have; the jobs exist regardless of the people who fill them. But many other jobs are created only because qualified people exist to fill them: in the 'economic' model jobs are created for workers. For example, the ample supply of college graduates in the US makes it profitable to establish high technology computer industries there rather than in Malaysia. On this model the number of jobs reflects the qualifications of workers and is not, therefore, something to be excluded from the analysis.

This 'economic' model reflects, I believe, the general pattern. Capital moves freely through the modern world, setting up jobs where the workers are. These adjustments are swift, not just long-run: the key characteristics of the labour force—which depend on family background and education—are clear long in advance, not something the economy must adjust to *ex post facto*. Indeed, economists have long argued that education is the primary driving force in economic development. On that argument the fundamental fact about social mobility is the regression line predicting occupational status from education and father's occupation: that is the true structural constraint, fixed by the underlying production function describing the technical means of production, not by the epiphenomenal distribution of jobs observed at any one time.

Even if one wants to adjust for differences in occupational structure, it is not clear that log-linear adjustments are the correct ones. They preserve odds-ratios, taking them to be the fundamental parameters; other things are adjusted in the way implied by the fixed odds-ratios. That may be sensible, but no one has yet made a very persuasive case for it in the mobility context. Other plausible models would not preserve odds-ratios. For example, if you take as fundamental the simple regression model (with error term), as the 'economic' model suggests, this too implies what would happen if the distribution of father's occupation changed but the fundamental regression equation did not. Equally, a 'queue' model in which potential workers are queued from most qualified to least and then fill the jobs in order of their qualifications (e.g. Thurow, 1975) would lead to yet a different prediction about what happens when the occupational structure differs. Thus there are many alternatives and the virtues of assuming fixed odds-ratios at least need to be argued, not blandly assumed.

Weaknesses of log-linear models. Log-linear models are principally designed to deal with categorical variables, especially dichotomies. This they do very well indeed, among other things overcoming serious statistical inefficiencies in the obvious alternative, ordinary least squares regression with dummy dependent variables. But log-linear methods are not well suited to continuous variables, nor to ones with a clear ordering from high to low, and so are, I will argue, inappropriate for the analysis of social mobility.

> *the necessity of crude measurement*—first, log-linear methods cannot success-fully cope with very many categories in any one variable—two or three categories are fine (for example, Protestant/Catholic/Jew), but a dozen or two are not (for example, years of education). The reason is that these methods require a reasonable number of cases in each cell of complete cross-tabulation of all variables included in the analysis (e.g. Bishop, Fienberg and Holland, 1977: Ch. 3). So, for example, if one is analyzing the effect of religion (three categories) on education (say, 12 categories), separately by age (say, five categories) and sex, then there are $3 \times 12 \times 5 \times 2 = 360$ categories. The usual rule of thumb is at least five cases per cell, and people are not uniformly distributed over all cells, so a huge sample would be required (to give, for example, five young Jewish men with no schooling). The upshot is that both the number of variables and the number of categories in each variable need to be severely restricted in most log-linear analyses. This is a serious weakness. For social mobility, it requires crude measurement of occupational status rather than more precise continuous measurement; crude treatment of owner-ship rather than a more refined measure like number of employees or capital value; a crude measure of authority rather than a refined one, like number of people supervised; and the like.
>
> *conceptual confounding*—this weakness means that conceptually separate variables cannot generally be treated separately. Suppose, for example, you wanted to measure only three aspects of class: status, ownership and authority (central, respectively, to the functionalist, Marxist and Dahrendorfian perspec-tives). Even if you are content to measure each crudely, the number of cells in a complete cross-classification quickly gets out of hand—say nine status groups

(professional, administrative, technical, clerical, sales, skilled worker, semi-skilled, unskilled worker, farm); three ownership groups (owners of large businesses, small businesses and non-owners); and three authority groups (those who have many subordinates, a few subordinates and no subordinates). That gives 81 categories ($9 \times 3 \times 3$). The usual mobility table cross-tabulating father's by son's class position would then have over 6500 categories (81×81). That is a wholly unmanageable number for log-linear methods. So to use these methods, the class description must be grossly simplified. We have seen that Goldthorpe, working with these same three variables, used not 81 but only seven categories, in the process necessarily glossing many and important differences.

no measure of openness or rigidity—a further difficulty with the log-linear methods that Goldthorpe uses is that they treat each category separately without any assumption of order or hierarchy (although newer log-linear 'association' models do assume order: Duncan, 1979). In some applications that is a strength (for example, in analyzing differences between Protestants, Catholics and Jews), but for social mobility it is a serious weakness. For that, hierarchy is the essence of the matter, as I argued before: we need to know who has the good jobs and who the poor; who has won and who has lost. Because they assume no hierarchy, the methods Goldthorpe uses have no simple association parameter—no analogue of regression's metric regression coefficient. So they provide no clear evidence on traditional questions of openness or rigidity: is there more social mobility in Britain or the United States, are industrial societies more open than developing ones, is there more social mobility now than there used to be?

Particular problems with Goldthorpe's models. Beyond the general weakness of log-linear models for studying problems like social mobility there are several particular problems with Goldthorpe's analyses.

    misleading treatment of inheritance—Goldthorpe, like most others using log-linear models of social mobility, treats the diagonal in a special way. He cross-tabulates father's occupation by son's occupation, measuring each in the same categories and (in a concession to hierarchy) the same ordering of the categories. The diagonal cells contain the sons who work in the same broad group of occupations their father did: the sons who 'inherited' their father's occupation. These Goldthorpe treats separately, fitting special inheritance parameters for them, on the undefended assumption that they got their jobs in a different way from other sons. For a few this is correct: there is a real difference between inheriting a widget factory in your father's will—Goldthorpe's image—and going to business school, saving money and buying one yourself. But this is a dangerously misleading image, because only a small minority of sons really inherit from their father. Most are in quite different jobs which happen to fall in the same broad classes in Goldthorpe's scheme—for example, a school teacher whose father was a business executive, laboratory technician or accountant. There is, for most, no inheritance: no business passed on when the father died, not even a business bought for money. Instead there are the usual processes of social mobility. In the example, the school teacher probably picked up a liking for reading from his family, did well in school, went to university and successfully applied for a post in a school far from home—little different from teachers who grew up in a clerk's family, or skilled machinist's or a grocer's. It would be more reasonable to treat separately people who went into *exactly* the same job as their father, for example teacher to teacher, or grocer to grocer, but even there genuine inheritance is probably still rare. Even better would be to ask explicitly about inheritance: did you take over your father's business, or did he buy you one? But to treat everyone in the same broad class as their father as inheriting their job is wrong.

Moreover, on many other models where inheritance plays no role at all there will be lots of people on the main diagonal. For example, suppose the world followed a simple regression model in the Blau-Duncan style, with son's status determined only by his father's status and with the usual assumptions about random error. With the cross-tabulation implied by this model (e.g. Pescosolido and Kelley, 1983), you have the heaviest concentration of cases along the main diagonal, just as Goldthorpe finds, even though there is nothing special about the diagonal at all. Similarly a 'queue' model along Thurow's (1975) lines would leave a heavy concentration along the main diagonal, even though inheritance plays no role in the model.

a grievous lack of statistical power—one difficulty with a relatively new statistical procedure like log-linear analysis is that some of its important properties are not yet known. Blau and Duncan had a great advantage in that their regression methods, although (fairly) new to sociology, had been used in other fields since the turn of the century and, in more recent decades, widely studied in econometrics. Goldthorpe was on more treacherous ground. He fell, I believe, into a serious pitfall: the models he uses have little statistical power to answer the questions he puts to them.

The key question is: do countries' social mobility patterns differ? To test this he estimated a straightforward 'common social fluidity' model in his earlier work and variants on that theme later. The procedure is to estimate a common model for the pooled data for several countries (for example, Britain and Sweden), which allows the occupational structure to differ in the two but estimates a single underlying pattern of association between father and son (defined by the odds-ratios) that is common to both. Then this common social fluidity model is compared to another model, otherwise similar, which adds a large set of 'interaction' terms permitting different patterns of association in (for example) Britain and Sweden. Insofar as the second model is (or is not) statistically preferable, Goldthorpe concludes that the pattern of mobility is (or is not) different in Britain and Sweden. Goldthorpe's basic answer is that these two countries, and indeed all the industrial countries he has studied, are not very different on this test.

But whether this conclusion is sound depends on the power of the statistical methods to detect differences of the relevant sort. To clarify the difficulty, consider a more familiar context: suppose we ask whether two animals are similar, say a St Bernard and a Yorkshire terrier. If we test them with scales used to weigh trucks, accurate to the nearest ton, we would find little difference: both weigh less than a ton. That is correct as far as it goes, but it does not go very far because our test is not very powerful. If instead we weigh them on scales accurate to the nearest 100 pounds, we would (just) find a difference. If we weighed them on scales accurate to the nearest pound, we would find a very clear difference. So our initial claim of 'no difference' should really read something like 'no difference to the nearest ton' and that is very different from a claim of 'no difference to the nearest pound'.

Is Goldthorpe's 'no difference' to the nearest ton or the nearest pound? While little is yet known about the power of log-linear methods for finding differences in social fluidity, the existing evidence suggests that Goldthorpe's 'no difference' is probably closer to the nearest ton than to the nearest pound (Pescosolido and Kelley, 1983). Suppose we create two hypothetical countries by Monte-Carlo simulation, one with a correlation between father and son of 0.1 (corresponding to a very open society indeed) and the other with a correlation of 0.6 (corresponding to an exceedingly rigid country, with six times as much ascription). There are 500 cases in each country, and the distribution of occupations in the two countries is quite different. Regression techniques have no difficulty detecting this difference in social fluidity ($p < .001$). We then compare the countries using Goldthorpe's common social fluidity methods. Do we find this huge difference? The answer is no: Goldthorpe's methods do not find even this extreme difference, saying that it is not significantly different from zero at $p < .05$ (see Table 20.1, Panel 1). That is, an astonishing difference to miss.

How well Goldthorpe's methods do depends on how different the occupational distributions are in the two countries. Despite the fact that he makes much of his method's virtues in adjusting for different distributions, they are statistically much less powerful when the distributions are very different. The previous example is admittedly extreme. But even in more prosaic cases Goldthorpe's methods are not powerful. In the simplest case

Table 20.1 *Differences in Social Fluidity: The Statistical Power of Log-Linear and Regression Methods* (Monte Carlo simulation of two societies)[1]

Difference in occupational structure[2]	Slope differences set in the simulation	Regression		Log-linear	
		t	sig. level	X2	sig. level
1 Large	.1 vs .6	7.0	p < .001	24	Not significant
	.1 vs .7	9.1	p < .001	35	p < .05
2 Medium	.1 vs .5	5.3	p < .001	19	Not significant
	.1 vs .6	6.8	p < .001	34	p < .05
3 Small	.1 vs .4	3.2	p < .01	24	Not significant
	.1 vs .5	5.3	p < .001	36	p < .05
4 None	.1 vs .3	2.1	p < .05	24	Not significant
	.1 vs .4	3.2	p < .01	33	p < .05

Notes:
1 Average of 12 repeated random trials with N = 1000 (500 per country). Likelihood ratio chi-square with 16 d.f. and t tests for regression, 1 d.f. 'Not statistically significant' is at the .05 level, i.e. p > .05.
2 Mean differences between countries, expressed in standard deviation units, for the 'occupational status' of 'father' and of 'son' are 2 and 2 respectively (Panel 1), 0 and 2, 0 and 1, and none (Panel 4).

Source: Pescosolido and Kelley (1983: Table 1).

where the occupational distributions are identical, he cannot detect a significant difference between a slope of 0.1 in one country and a slope of 0.3 in the
other (i.e. one country three times more ascriptive than the other; see Table
20.1, Panel 4). Other cases fall somewhere between the two extremes. But in
all, Goldthorpe's methods fail to detect large and substantively important
differences between countries.

Why Goldthorpe's methods have so little power to detect differences is not
entirely clear. Partly he puts too broad and unfocused a question, adding too
many parameters, rather than a more focused test adding a single parameter
(as in regression), but that is not all (Pescosolido and Kelley, 1983: 367–73).
However, this may be, the fact remains that they are exceedingly weak. Even
within the log-linear framework there are better alternatives in the newer
association models (Duncan, 1979). These bring log-linear models closer to
regression, albeit to the equivalent of bivariate regression, which still leaves a
long way to go.

THE FINDINGS: SIMILARITY AMONG INDUSTRIAL SOCIETIES?

The fundamental substantive question in this field is how social mobility varies
between one society and another, or how it varies in one society over time. In
particular, the central issue in most discussions has been whether society at some
times and places is more ascriptive (has less social mobility, is less open, less fluid,
less meritocratic) than in other times and places. The traditional debates are all
of this type. The traditional questions are, in logical sequence, three: (1) to begin,
are there any differences large enough to be worth worrying about? (2) if so, are they
systematic in any way that we can discover—that is, linked to some logical and
discernible general principles—or are they merely idiosyncratic? and (3) in particular, are differences linked to economic development, with rich industrial
societies less rigid and ascriptive than poor developing ones?

The null hypothesis. The obvious null hypotheses corresponding to these three
linked questions are (1) that there are no differences worth worrying about; (2) if
there are, they are not systematic but merely idiosyncratic; and (3) in particular,
economic development is irrelevant to whatever differences do exist.

With some notable exceptions (e.g. Sorokin, 1927), the null hypotheses have
held sway. In the early days of systematic analyses Lipset and Zetterberg (1959)
found surprising similarity among industrial societies. There are clearly differences
in occupational distribution—largely reflecting differences in level of economic
development—with the farm sector in particular much larger in some societies than
in others. But beyond that simple difference things look very much the same. Later
more sophisticated and more persuasive analyses in the Blau-Duncan tradition
mostly came to the same conclusion (e.g. Treiman and Terrell, 1975b), although
with some dissent concerning developing societies (Kelley, Robinson and Klein,
1981). One of the most persuasive analyses drew out these implications clearly and
gave the null hypothesis (in the 'no difference save due to occupational structure'
variant) its current name: the Featherman-Jones-Hauser hypothesis (1975).

Goldthorpe's work, using yet different methods, comes yet again to the null hypothesis. He finds some differences beyond those due to the occupational structure, but they are small, unsystematic and unrelated to economic development. However, this is unpersuasive. It is a sweeping generalization about all possible analyses and all possible comparisons, and there are good reasons to doubt it. First, weak measurement is a danger. If Goldthorpe's measurement is too crude to capture important differences, his results would wrongly support the null hypothesis. We have seen that this is a genuine possibility: he has measured class crudely with only seven categories: entirely ignored education; measured ownership and authority only partially; and ignored other aspects of class. Second, the narrow range of countries analyzed is a danger. Goldthorpe has less than a dozen, including none of the newly industrializing nations of the third world, and no developing nations. His sample of countries may be too narrow to show differences that would be clear in a broader sample. Third, weak statistics are a danger. If Goldthorpe's methods are not powerful enough to find differences, they would wrongly support the null hypothesis. We have just seen evidence that this, too, is a very real risk. Fourth, he may not have been looking for systematic differences in the right places. The old standby of industrialization is not the only possibility; I will suggest an alternative. Goldthorpe's basic findings in support of the FJH version of the null hypothesis are thus worth reconsidering. I will show that using better measurement, a wider sample of countries, more powerful statistics and an alternative to industrialization as the causal factor all provide substantial evidence against the null hypothesis.

AN ALTERNATIVE THESIS: INEQUALITY AND SOCIAL MOBILITY

Theory. In place of economic development, I would argue that inequality in the distribution of human and material capital is the key influence on social mobility (Kelley and Klein, 1982: Ch. 2 and Appendix 1). Let us begin by asking how it is that high status parents are able to provide advantages for their children? I argue that they do it mainly by giving their children scarce and valuable resources: concrete and tangible advantages that help in the competition for jobs. These are of two main kinds: human capital—education, knowledge, and skills in farming, crafts, language and the like—and material capital, including money and land. Sons compete for jobs on the basis of their human capital, material capital and various other things unrelated to family background (for example, interest and motivation). A few are able to buy jobs (for example, absentee landlords); more combine skills and money (for example, buying farms and businesses); and yet more get jobs on the basis of their skills. The job market is like a marriage market, simultaneously matching workers and jobs: every son wants the best jobs and every employer wants the most qualified worker, but in fact the best jobs go to sons with the most resources (they can buy the biggest farms, or offer the greatest skills to employers); middling jobs go to those with middling resources (for the better jobs are already taken by richer or more qualified sons, and the better employees already hired); and the worst jobs to sons with the fewest resources (for neither employers nor workers can do better).

Thus the advantage parents are able to pass on to their children, and so the amount of inherited privilege, depends on the amount of inequality among the parents in human and material capital. Consider two extreme cases. First, if there is great inequality, with parents at the top of the status hierarchy being (say) university graduates, while parents at the bottom are illiterate, being born into a high status family will be a huge advantage. University parents speak the dominant language well, understand schools and other bureaucracies, value education, and are able to help their children with school work, know how to look for jobs and so on; their children are well equipped in the competition for jobs. Illiterate parents can provide few such advantages, and their children therefore compete at a great disadvantage. Second, if inequality is small with only modest differences between high status and low status families—say a high school education at the top and eighth grade at the bottom—being born into a high status family is less of a disadvantage because differences in the help parents give their children are less. The same arguments apply to inequality in material capital: if high status families earn ten times as much as low (as in many developing societies), the advantages of birth will be greater than if high status families earn only twice as much as low (as in most industrial societies). For a detailed argument and the underlying mathematical model see Kelley and Klein (1982: 14–21 and Appendix 1). Thus:

> *Inequality hypothesis*: *The amount of inherited privilege in a society is proportional to inequality in human and material capital among parents.*

Data and method. This hypothesis can be tested using data from 15 societies which come from a larger project by Donald Treiman and myself. All of these societies have excellent data on father's and son's occupation, typically coded into three- or four- digit census codes. As Goldthorpe did with his CASMIN data, we obtained the individual-level, unit record data and recoded them in exactly comparable ways; a 40-page manual detailing our methods is available on request. For this analysis I coded occupations into the 14 categories of Treiman's occupational classification (Treiman, 1977: 203–8). I then assigned each of these categories a status score, based on my canonical analysis of data from 16 societies. I show that status is very similar throughout the world (correlations between status scores in different countries average over 0.8, slightly higher than correlations among prestige scores for different countries). That justifies constructing a Worldwide Status Score by averaging the separate scores for all 16 societies. These are status rather than prestige scores and are, for the US, virtually interchangeable with Duncan's SEI. For this analysis I measure social mobility simply by the correlation between father's and son's occupational status. But more elaborate measures produce essentially the same results, including one where all countries are adjusted to common occupational distributions using iterative proportional fitting and another using a log-linear association model. Educational inequality is measured, separately for each country, as the difference between the average education of professionals and the average education of farmers (in years of schooling). Income inequality is taken as a surrogate for all forms of inequality in material capital and measured conventionally by the Gini coefficient.

Results. These data show that there are clear differences in social mobility between countries (see Figure 20.2, Panel 1). The most rigid and ascriptive are Brazil and Bolivia among developing countries and the Netherlands in Europe. Then come

Figure 20.2   *Inequality and Inherited Privilege: Correlation between Father's and Son's Occupational Status*

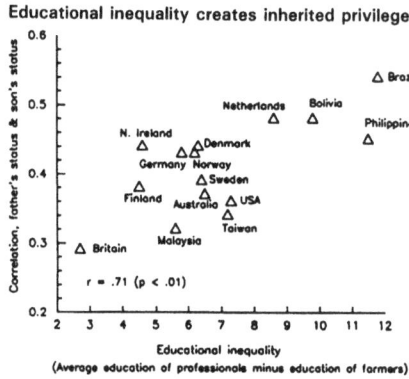

Educational inequality creates inherited privilege

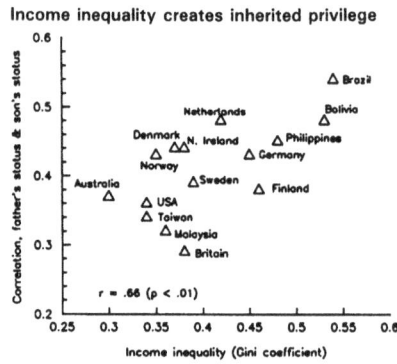

Income inequality creates inherited privilege

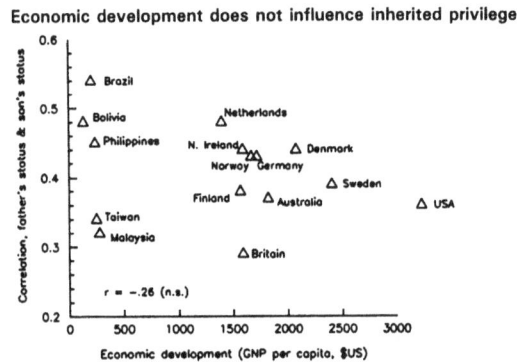

Economic development does not influence inherited privilege

Note: Individual-level data are taken from 15 representative national surveys; status in Kelley's Worldwide Scores. For further details on the data and methods underlying the cross-cultural analyses reported in this Figure, see the Appendix to this chapter.

the Philippines, Denmark, Northern Ireland and Norway. The US, Australia, Sweden and Finland come next, toward the more fluid and open end of the spectrum. Malaysia and Taiwan are even more open. The least rigid, most fluid society is, surprisingly Britain. In all, there is a wide range, the correlation between father's and son's status ranging from a high of over 0.5 to a low of half that, under 0.3.

Furthermore these differences are systematically related to inequality in the distribution of human and material capital. The correlation with educational inequality is strong: in societies where education is relatively equally distributed there is much less ascription, and in societies where education is unequally distributed—where there is a large educational gap between classes—there is much more. Computed over the 15 countries, the correlation between educational inequality and ascription is $r = 0.71$, which is statistically significant at $p < .01$. Similarly, income inequality is closely linked to ascription: in countries where there is more income inequality there is substantially more ascription ($r = 0.66$, $p < .01$). Thus these results offer strong support for my hypothesis that inequality creates inherited privilege. This is quite contrary to Goldthorpe's null hypothesis conclusion that industrial societies have very similar rates of social mobility. These results do, however, support Goldthorpe's claim that economic development is not systematically related to inequality (Figure 20.2, Panel 3); there is a slight downward trend, but it is not statistically significant. There is perhaps a suggestion of convergence in the course of industrialization.

This analysis clearly undermines most of Goldthorpe's fundamental conclusions. (1) His data, concepts and methods suggest no major differences exist between countries. I have shown that, to the contrary, there are large differences in the level of inherited privilege in different countries, with the most open having only half as much ascription as the most rigid. (2) Goldthorpe argues that such differences as do exist arc idiosyncratic, not systematic. I have shown that, on the contrary, the differences are systematically and strongly related to inequality in the distribution of human and material capital. (3) Goldthorpe claims that, contrary to much early theorizing, economic development does not create social mobility. My results are not unambiguous, but on this point alone tend to support Goldthorpe.

CONCLUSION

Log-linear modelling offered a new paradigm for the analysis of social mobility to replace the fading glories of the earlier Blau-Duncan paradigm and its many off-shoots. Goldthorpe's version of the paradigm extended it cross-culturally to analyze data from a dozen countries. That was all to the good. But Goldthorpe abandoned the detailed multi-variate measurement of the earlier paradigm in favour of a crude seven-category typology; he neglected hierarchy, ignored education and dealt with ownership and authority only crudely and partially. He abandoned the powerful and robust regression techniques of the original Blau-Duncan paradigm and its subsequent general linear model developments; ignored psychometric models of measurement error; ignored structural equation models borrowed from econometrics; and ignored LISREL models incorporating both. However valuable in other contexts, log-linear methods proved poorly suited to social mobility analyses, where variables are continuous, not discrete; where rank and hierarchy are of the essence, not to be neglected; where many variables are relevant, not few. In the end the log-linear paradigm was not fruitful, either in Goldthorpe's variant or in others. There was nothing like the heady excitement of the early days of the Blau-Duncan paradigm; nothing like the steady, satisfying normal science progress in its aftermath; no major insights. There was, to be sure, agreeable technical virtuosity and careful description.

After a decade the time of judgment is nigh: what have we learned about the world that we did not know before? The answer, I am afraid, is that we have learned very little. There is no stunning finding; no story to cry from the rooftops; precious little to show for a decade's work. Furthermore, the main tale we have been told from it is untrue. Goldthorpe and many others argued for the traditional null hypothesis of cross-cultural research: that the differences between societies in social fluidity are small, if they exist at all, and unsystematic. But I have shown that, measured more precisely and analyzed more appropriately, there are substantial and systematic differences between societies. In short, the log-linear paradigm for the analysis of social mobility is a failure. It was a brave departure from prevailing models, with new methods and good cross-cultural data. So it was a noble failure, but nonetheless a failure. It should be abandoned.

APPENDIX: DATA, METHODS AND A WORLDWIDE STATUS SCORE

This appendix gives details on the data and methods underlying the crucial cross-cultural analyses reported in Figure 20.2. Details on the analyses in Figure 20.1 and Table 20.1 are readily available elsewhere (Kelley and McAllister, 1985; Pescosolido and Kelley, 1983).

Data. The results are based on re-analyses of individual-level data from 16 representative national samples which include detailed information (generally three- or four-digit census codes) on respondent's occupation and his father's occupation. Analyses (and Ns given below) are for men, aged 20 to 64. In addition, I used several local samples in the analysis of occupational status reported below, but not for the mobility analysis of Figure 20.2. The data: Australia, 1967: N = 791; Bolivia, 1965: N = 1,125; Brazil, 1973: N = 62,127; Britain, 1964: N = 674; Denmark, 1972: N = 401; Finland, 1972: N = 345; Germany (West), 1976: N = 706; Hungary, 1973: N = 12,238; India, 1966–67: N = 1,916; Kenya (Nairobi), 1971: N = 1,410; Malaysia, 1966: N = 5,047; Netherlands, 1970: N = 829; Northern Ireland, 1968: N = 462; Norway, 1972: N = 395; Philippines, 1973: N = 4,703; Poland (Lodz), 1976: N = 960; Sweden, 1972: N = 390; Taiwan, 1970: N = 948; United States, 1973: N = 20,880.

Occupational classification. An occupational classification suitable for cross-cultural analysis is not easy to construct. A principal difficulty is balancing precision (which suggests many narrowly defined occupations) and practicality (which argues for a few broad groups to reconcile differences in the detailed classifications used in various countries). A good argument can be made for using essentially continuous measures using hundreds of specific titles—like Duncan's (1961) well known socio-economic scale for the US—but no suitable cross-cultural equivalent is available (or likely, given the different detailed occupational classifications used in various countries). Goldthorpe's seven-category classification errs, I have argued, too far in the opposite direction. A reasonable balance is, I believe, Treiman's (1977: 203–8) 14-category classification and I have used it in this analysis. It is based on the major groups of the International Labour Office's International Standard Classification of Occupations (ILO, 1968), with further distinctions within major groups based on Treiman's prestige scores.

Occupations were individually coded by prestige and ISCO major group. These were then recoded into Treiman's 14 (the status scores, described below, are not Treiman's, nor are the names; the specific occupations mentioned are illustrative, not exhaustive):

> Status Group (Definition: ISCO major group; Treiman prestige)
> 100   Higher professionals (ISCO 0 or 1; prestige 58 or more)
> —lawyers, doctors, dentists, pilots, engineers, accountants, academics, secondary school teachers, economists, etc.
> 75   Administrators and managers (ISCO 2; any prestige)
> —managing directors of companies, sales managers, bank managers, parliamentarians, high ranking bureaucrats, etc.

70 Technical employees (ISCO 0 or 1; prestige under 58)
—computer programmers, nurses, primary school teachers, librarians, artists, social workers, etc.

60 Higher clerical employees (ISCO 3; prestige 41 or more)
—clerks, secretaries, book-keepers, bank tellers, etc.

51 Higher sales employees (ISCO 4; prestige 40 or more)
—owners of retail stores, sales representatives, insurance agents, wholesale managers, etc.

38 Routine clerical workers (ISCO 3; prestige under 41)
—filing clerks, postal clerks, telephone operators, etc.

37 Skilled manual workers (ISCO 7, 8 or 9; prestige 38 or more)
—mechanics, machinists, master craftsmen, foremen, television repairmen, locomotive drivers, etc.

33 Skilled service workers (ISCO 5; prestige 27 or more)
—restaurant managers, policemen, cooks, hairdressers, etc.

32 Routine sales workers (ISCO 4; prestige under 40)
—shop assistants, sales clerks, etc.

24 Ordinary semi-skilled workers (ISCO 7, 8 or 9; prestige 26 to 37)
—carpenters, plumbers, sheetmetal workers, drivers, painters and decorators, bricklayers, etc.

18 Unskilled service workers (ISCO 5; prestige under 27)
—waiters, bartenders, cleaners, etc.

14 Unskilled manual workers (ISCO 7, 8 or 9; prestige under 26)
—labourers, porters, garbage collectors, etc.

10 Farmers (ISCO 6; prestige 34 or more)
—farm owners, farm foremen, etc.

0 Farm labourers (ISCO 6; prestige under 34)
—farm workers, tractor drivers, fishermen, etc.

Occupational status. Assigning sensible hierarchical scores to the occupational classification is theoretically crucial but in practice difficult and controversial. I have developed a worldwide score which is, I believe, the best yet available for cross-cultural analysis. Before describing it, let us briefly consider the main alternative.

The major alternative is Treiman's (1977) Standard International Occupational Prestige scores. But these are, I believe, unsuitable for cross-cultural analysis, greatly understating the amount of inherited privilege (in part because farmers have a prestige far exceeding their limited education, low income and their children's modest prospects in life). This shows up conspicuously in the low correlation between father's prestige and son's prestige compared to the correlation between father's status and son's status (as measured by my status scores):

	Prestige	Status
United States	.28	.36
Britain	.27	.30
The Philippines	.36	.45
Bolivia	.33	.49

Thus the weakness Featherman, Jones and Hauser (1975) found for prestige scores in the US does not appear to be unique to that country but, if anything, more pronounced in less developed nations.

In my 'World-wide Status Score' I assume that the true status of an occupation is intimately related to the education of incumbents (well educated people get the best jobs), to their income (high status jobs command larger rewards) and to the success of their children in the next generation (high status jobs provide resources that can be used to give children a head start in life). If so, and if Treiman's 14 categories give groups of occupations with similar status, then it follows that a scoring scheme (applied to the 14 categories) that maximizes the correlation between them and education, or income or occupation in another generation, would reflect the true status of occupations in each group. This scoring scheme can be found from a canonical (or, equivalently, discriminant) analysis—for example, Klatzky and Hodge's (1972) procedure using only occupation in two generations or Duncan-Jones's (1972) 'predictive' procedure using many variables. Rather than relying on a single pair of variables, I prefer a variant of Duncan-Jones's procedure predicting respondent's occupation (treated as a set of dummy variables without assumptions about rank) from education, income and father's occupation (also scored as a set of dummy variables without assumptions about rank). I applied this procedure to individual-level data from 16 countries, obtaining entirely independent scores for each. As the resulting scores are invariant under a linear transformation, there is no natural unit or zero point; I have therefore (arbitrarily but conveniently) normed them from a low of zero to a high of 100.

These results suggest that occupational status hierarchies are much the same throughout the world. Table 20.A1 shows the (product-moment) correlations

Table 20.A1 *Correlations among Socio-economic Status Scores for Sixteen Societies* (decimals omitted)[1]

	1	2	3	4	5	6	7	8	9	10	11	12	13	14	15
Industrial nations															
1. USA															
2. Australia	82														
3. Denmark	86	91													
4. Finland	63	28	73												
5. Germany	90	89	91	63											
6. Britain	92	91	93	43	99										
7. Netherlands	93	84	96	61	84	91									
8. N. Ireland	79	53	81	60	75	92	87								
9. Norway	88	82	90	67	87	89	92	78							
10. Poland	84	87	91	89	89	86	89	99	98						
11. Sweden	91	91	97	69	99	99	95	79	99	94					
Developing nations															
12. Bolivia	94	87	94	84	91	96	99	87	94	92	95				
13. Kenya	92	90	84	44	83	79	88	97	96	94	94	99			
14. Malaysia	79	63	72	70	62	77	80	93	84	93	78	84	96		
15. Philippines	89	70	81	57	73	84	92	94	93	93	93	98	97	89	
16. Taiwan	82	69	69	78	51	65	84	88	82	78	76	98	93	82	92

Note:
1 Computed over occupational groups, not individual respondents.

between hierarchies in 16 societies. The correlations are high, averaging 0.84. Indeed, this is slightly higher than the correlation Treiman found among prestige scores around the world. Furthermore, the similarity holds not just for Western industrial societies but is equally apparent for the developing societies of Latin America, Africa and Asia; correlations between industrial and developing societies average 0.82. Poland, though communist, is little different from the rest of the world. By far the lowest correlations involve Finland, but since the other three Scandinavian countries are in no way unusual and the Finnish sample is the smallest analyzed (N = 345), I attribute this to sampling error.

Since occupational status is essentially the same throughout the world, it is reasonable to construct a single scale for use throughout the world. I did this simply by averaging the scores for each country and norming the result to range again from zero to 100. These worldwide status scores are given in the text above and shown graphically in Figure 20.A1 below.

For the world as a whole, higher professionals—the traditional free professions—are clearly at the top of the hierarchy. Administrators are well behind, closely followed by technical employees, with higher clerical and higher sales employees coming next. Then there is a distinct gap; below that, the bottom of the white-collar hierarchy overlaps with skilled manual workers. Ordinary semi-skilled workers follow next, then unskilled, followed by farmers and farm labourers at the bottom. Note that the traditional white-collar/blue-collar correlation is poor because of the overlap between the bottom of white-collar and the top of blue, and that farmers are very low in status, although of middling prestige.

I believe this Worldwide Status Scale is the best presently available for cross-cultural comparisons and have used it in the analyses in this chapter.

Figure 20.A1 Worldwide Status Scale

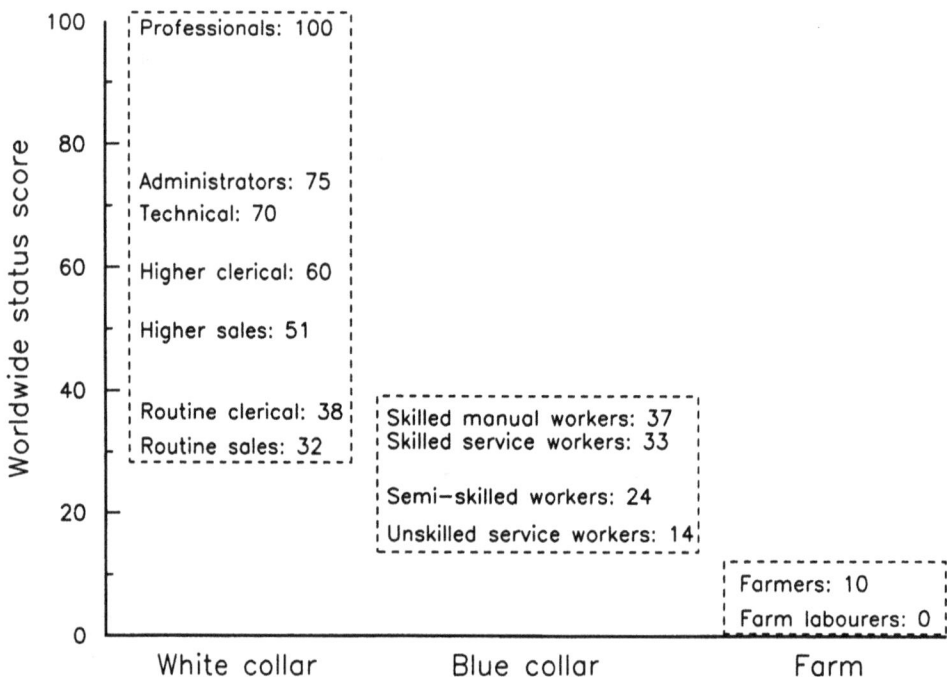

Interchange

MÜLLER REPLIES TO KELLEY

It is a rather disagreeable task to react to Jonathan Kelley's paper, not because his critical review of Goldthorpe's work on class mobility is convincing, but because he uses a large number of pages to distort Goldthorpe's work and then to shoot at a misrepresented enemy. In some instances Kelley's representation is exactly the contrary of what Goldthorpe really said, for instance, where Kelley states that Goldthorpe moves farm sons (but not fathers) down the hierarchy. Goldthorpe's main findings on cross-national variation in the pattern of social mobility are so heavily perverted in the direction of 'no difference' that one can no longer recognize them. Goldthorpe very carefully shows in which senses similarity prevails and in which ways dissimilarities and national peculiarities exist. I cannot list all the instances of misrepresentation, because that alone would need more space than is available here.

It is also disagreeable to comment on Kelley's paper because one does not learn anything new from it. Kelley merely heats up old meals. The dish with which he wants to seduce us is the Blau-Duncan paradigm, of which Kelley himself admits that it has gone stale since the mid-1970s. If I had to argue for an alternative approach to the one Goldthorpe has so forcefully put forward, I would turn to the dynamic models of life course analysis (see, for example, Carroll and Mayer, 1986; Sørensen, Allmendinger and Sørensen, 1986; Blossfeld, 1986). If the status attainment paradigm is to have a future, then solutions will need to be found to the various deficiencies that have been demonstrated.

In more detail, I will take up only a few points on which my views sharply oppose the ones presented by Kelley. First, Kelley's main theoretical and methodological criticism is based on the assertion: 'Insofar as they [Erikson and Goldthorpe] ignore hierarchy, this is to miss the main point'. There is both a factual and a theoretical answer to this argument. On the factual issue Kelley at no point refers to Erikson and Goldthorpe (1987a, 1987b), thereby neglecting altogether a serious evaluation of their most central contribution to the issue. In their 'Core Model' Erikson and Goldthorpe (1987b) do not ignore hierarchy; they give it its proper place, beside the other dimensions and barriers that structure the mobility process. From the class-theoretical perspective Goldthorpe adopts and in the questions he poses, hierarchy cannot be said to be the main point. Classes do not differ only—or even merely—in vertical location, but rather with respect to their position in the division of labour. The opposing interests created between classes such as farmers, the petty bourgeoisie and different fractions of wage workers and

347

salaried employees are certainly not captured by a simple measure of their location on a vertical scale.

Second, Kelley makes much of his assertion that the effects of third variables—particularly of education—on mobility patterns cannot be analyzed using the log-linear model approach. He concludes that the use of log-linear models for the study of intergenerational mobility has failed. This association can be easily refuted. Goldthorpe did not consider the effects of education simply because of a division of labour agreed upon in the CASMIN Project. Other related work (see Müller *et al.*, 1988) shows that within the log-linear approach it is perfectly possible to study the effects of education. The results fit very neatly with Goldthorpe's findings. One of the central points in this analysis, however, is that one does not get much insight by simply asking to what extent more education—expressed as years of schooling—is connected with higher socio-economic status or prestige. The effects of education on mobility patterns—and the cross-national variation thereof—appear only in detailed studies of the different educational systems that developed in different nations over many decades. As a result of this development there evolved different educational courses in different nations as well as different links between educational institutions and the class structure. As in the case of class positions we rather find different *types* of educational courses and credentials. Representing them by typologies appears to be more appropriate than reducing them all to quantitative dimensions.

Third, Kelley criticizes the narrow range of countries considered in Goldthorpe's work. He regrets the omission of 'newly industrializing' nations and of pre-industrial nations. Goldthorpe never pretended to study the whole world. His work is on industrial nations. Even though it would be better if good comparable data for more industrial nations could have been included in his work, a critical evaluation would have to show in what respect the inclusion of additional industrial nations would have altered the conclusions drawn from Goldthorpe's sample of nations. Kelley does not engage upon this demanding task. Furthermore, someone who reads Goldthorpe's papers carefully will soon appreciate the advantages of the strategy for which Goldthorpe has opted. Only by limiting the number of nations to a manageable extent does it appear possible to prepare the data carefully and enter into the details of the historical background and the institutional peculiarities that are indispensable for a valid interpretation of the findings of cross-national differences. The Thomas Cook approach of the 'Europe-in-one-day' tourist, which is inevitable for a whole-world analysis, is mercifully not to Goldthorpe's taste.

Fourth, to support his points Kelley includes selected 'sultanas' out of his own published work. I think he would have done better not to have referred to them, because they only demonstrate the weakness of his arguments:

● The comparison of regression methods and log-linear models in Table 20.1 is in no way adequate to prove his assertion that log-linear models favour 'no difference' hypotheses because of their lack of statistical power. The construction of the simulation exercise Kelley uses is heavily biased in favour of regression models. A fair comparison would require at the very least that a log-linear model is applied that considers the order and distance among the categories as the regression model does. Although such log-linear models are available, Pescosolido and Kelley use a log-linear model from which the result they wish to prove is already determined in advance. The careful reader will also observe that the *p*-values in Table 20.1 are reported in a form biased against the log-linear model. All significant *p*-values are stated as '$p < .05$'; in fact, using the same reporting rules as those adopted for the regression model, the correct statements would be either $p < .005$ or $p < .01$.

● I am not convinced at all by the results Kelley presents to illustrate the substantive yield of the regression methods which he prizes so much. With Figure 20.1 Kelley wants us to believe, for example, that only in Australia do capitalists behave as one would expect them to behave. In Britain, in contrast—when one controls for education and occupational status—there is no effect on family income from being a capitalist, whereas being a supervisor or a white-collar worker has positive effects. In the USA, on the other hand, there are no direct effects from being a capitalist on middle-class self-image and on voting behaviour. A number of other strange results in Figure 20.1 cast doubt on the validity of the findings, as do several findings in Figure 20.2. It is well known that—apart from the careful work in the LIS project (O'Higgins, Schmaus and Stephenson, 1985)—there are almost no solid comparative data on income inequality, even for the industrial world. According to the best data recently available from the LIS project, the US appears to be one of the most unequal industrial countries, whereas Sweden is among the most equal. But Kelley has no scruples about republishing results assuring us, for example, that income inequality in the USA and Malaysia is smaller than in Sweden. Without appearing to be troubled at all, he also observes in Figure 20.2 that educational inequality in Britain is smaller than in any other country investigated. This finding is partly an artefact of the way Kelley measures educational inequality, which he defines as the difference between the average education of sons of professionals and sons of farmers. Since the social position of the class of farmers varies substantially between countries, the inequality measure adopted is unfortunate for comparative purposes. For instance, the English class of farmers is clearly distinct from farmers in other countries because of its large proportion of relatively wealthy tenant farmers and land owners, and thus the low educational inequality there is at least partly a consequence of Kelley's particular measure of inequality.

I hope these short remarks make it clear that comparative research implies more than grabbing hold of what is quickly available from countries all over the world. It involves knowledge in depth about each country and a careful and critical use of data. John Goldthorpe's work has achieved exemplary standards in this respect, and I can only advise the reader to study Goldthorpe's original work and not to be misled by Kelley's comments.

KELLEY REPLIES TO MÜLLER

[*Editors' Note*: *This reply was submitted too late for consideration in John Goldthorpe's concluding response. It has been accepted for publication for reasons of symmetry within this section.*]

Walter Müller makes an ardent case for John Goldthorpe, arguing three main points. First, he argues that Goldthorpe's 'class' typology is far superior to Blau and Duncan's (1967) 'status' approach. Second, he points out great virtues in Goldthorpe's data, particularly those used in the CASMIN Project. Third, he extols Goldthorpe's findings about the (lack of) systematic cross-cultural variation in patterns of social mobility.

Müller's second point is true, and I would not contest it but acclaim it: Goldthorpe and his colleagues have certainly done commendable work in preparing data, a thankless but vital task. Müller's third point is false. As I argued in my initial contribution to this volume, Goldthorpe missed the key cross-cultural finding: that patterns of intergenerational social mobility are determined by inequality in the distribution of human and material capital (not by economic development). Having made those arguments in detail, I will not repeat them here.

But I would like to contest Müller's first point, on the virtues of Goldthorpe's class typology. Indeed, I must confess myself astonished that so much is made of it. There are very many virtues in Goldthorpe's work, but this is not one. Rather, I would expect it to have been passed over in embarrassed silence, save perhaps for a passing apology that so crude and simplified a scheme was necessitated by the restrictive demands of Goldthorpe's preferred log-linear methods. But it is not. Rather than silence, we hear the flourish of trumpets heralding a revolution against the old order: 'status' is dead, long live 'class'. I will argue for a restoration of the *ancien régime* and for a constitutional monarchy, with new class variables added as supplements to, not replacements for, the old regime.

GOLDTHORPE'S 'CLASS' TYPOLOGY VERSUS THE 'CLASS-STATUS-POWER' EXTENSION OF BLAU AND DUNCAN'S 'STATUS' MODEL

Class is certainly an important aspect of social stratification, not only in Marx's sense of the ownership of the means of production, but also in Dahrendorf's sense of exerting authority in the workplace, and also in Djilas's sense of controlling the powers of government. There have been many suggestions that class concepts should be included in research on stratification, either alone (most notably by Wright and Perrone, 1977, and their many followers) or as a supplement to Blau and Duncan's paradigm, rather than a replacement for it (Robinson and Kelley, 1979). Goldthorpe was quite right to consider both authority and ownership. As Müller notes, they have real implications for class formation. For example, in Britain, as we shall presently see, those who exercise authority or own the means of production differ in many ways from those who do not: most notably, they have higher incomes and more often identify with the middle class. It would be a pity to neglect these important differences, as the status tradition would.

Goldthorpe's class schema. The issue is how best to model the effects of ownership and authority. Wright and Perrone's scheme (and its later variants) are one way, but it has the great disadvantage of abandoning the even more important differences due to occupation and education that are central to Blau and Duncan's paradigm (Robinson and Kelley, 1979: 45–8). Goldthorpe does better, retaining many occupational differences as well as taking ownership and authority into account.

Stripped of its verbiage, his scheme comes surprisingly close to being an extension of a (much simplified) Blau-Duncan scheme, rather than a replacement for it. Where Blau and Duncan began with over a dozen occupational groups explicitly ranked from high to low, Goldthorpe begins with a simple six-group classification of ancient vintage—higher white-collar, lower white-collar, skilled manual, unskilled manual, farm owners, farm labourers—slightly relabelled (e.g. 'service' for 'higher white-collar'). There is an implicit hierarchy here, more evident in his later analyses than in his earlier rhetoric. Goldthorpe then adds two refinements. First, he uses the possession of authority to raise (some) people up a class from where they would be on the basis of occupation alone (*viz.* from unskilled to skilled manual, or from lower white-collar to higher). Second, he uses ownership as the basis for a separate class of small owners, his petty bourgeoisie, with large owners going into the service class.

The 'class-status-power' model. I will argue that this way of taking authority and ownership into account is not optimal. Instead, I suggest a simpler and more systematic way of combining them which easily incorporates them with Blau and Duncan's status model: rather than using authority and ownership to help define a typology, I treat them as conceptually distinct dimensions in a multi-variate model, adding separate ownership and authority variables to Blau and Duncan's status and education. Thus there are high status owners (e.g. professionals with their own practices, businessmen with their own firms); low status owners (e.g. carpet cleaners with their own small business, hairdressers with their own shops); and yet others in-between; equally there are high status employees (e.g. 'in-house' lawyers, government ministers) as well as low. Similarly, some owners are well educated (e.g. accountants with their own firm) and some poorly educated (e.g. owners of small construction companies). There are also high status workers who exercise authority (e.g. administrators) and those who do not (e.g. university lecturers); equally, there are low status workers who exercise authority (e.g. a bricklayer with an apprentice) as well as those who do not.

Treating ownership and authority as separate variables allows one to combine them with status and education in a model incorporating the insights of Marx and Dahrendorf with those of Blau and Duncan, rather than having to choose one approach at the cost of abandoning the other (Robinson and Kelley, 1979). Thus there is no need to abandon variables of known importance (as Goldthorpe abandons education) or to simplify variables drastically (as with Goldthorpe's six occupational groups). Equally important, the multi-variate approach allows one to compare the impact of the various aspects of stratification position in a given outcome (for example, finding whether authority matters more or less than ownership in determining income) *and* also to compare the effects of any one aspect across outcome variables (for example, finding whether ownership matters more in shaping class identification or in politics). One cannot do this with a typology.

There are several other variables that can be usefully added, giving the full 'class-status-power' model. In addition to distinguishing owners and employees, I suggest that it is useful to distinguish further among employees, between those who work for private enterprise and those who work for the government (Kelley and McAllister, 1985). This is because bureaucratic power, like ownership of private property, is a valuable resource and one that generates class interests just as ownership does (Djilas, 1957). Finally, the traditional white-collar versus manual boundary remains important. It is captured implicitly in Goldthorpe's typology, but needs explicit modelling in this multi-variate approach.

A multi-dimensional approach like this allows one to discover distinct social classes if they exist, but it also allows one to find looser groupings, partial groupings (when these people and those are in the same boat some of the time but not all of the time), fine graduations or many other possibilities. In other words, it treats social class boundaries (their existence, strength and location) as an empirical question meriting research. The typological approach, in contrast, typically treats them instead as a matter of faith and *a priori* definition—indeed, a serious weakness in Goldthorpe's work is his failure to justify empirically his *a priori* claims about class boundaries: that should be a matter of research, not pronouncements *ex cathedra*.

Empirical comparison of the models: the British case. Goldthorpe's class typology was originally developed for Britain and so I will use that as a test case. He has argued, at length and with vehemence, that his model is far superior to Blau and Duncan's, particularly in understanding class identification, class conflict and the politics of class. But I will argue that my straightforward extension of Blau and Duncan's model is noticeably superior, even on Goldthorpe's home ground. Table 20I.1 presents relevant data from the 1979 British Election Survey; technical details are given in the Appendix at the end of this contribution.

Income—the first column of the table shows the impact of class, as defined by Goldthorpe, on income. The service class, for example, typically has a family income 62 per cent higher than non-skilled workers, while skilled workers earn 20 per cent more and the petty bourgeoisie 25 per cent more. In all, class explains about 12 per cent of the variance in income.

The multi-dimensional class-status-power model does noticeably better (second column of the table). For example, professionals at the top of the status hierarchy earn 57 per cent more than workers at the bottom (farm labourers), with workers in-between earning in-between amounts. Education is the other important influence, each year increasing income by 4 per cent (net of status). Supervisors earn more too, some 33 per cent. In all, this model explains about 18 per cent of the variance. This is markedly better than Goldthorpe's model, fully 6 per cent higher (18 versus 12). So it seems that the Blau-Duncan model, as extended to include authority and ownership, gets closer to the essence of the matter than Goldthorpe's typology. This is shown dramatically in column 3, which predicts income simultaneously on the basis of Goldthorpe's typology, the class-status-power variables and a range of controls. The class-status-power variables remain important. But once they are taken into account, there are *no* statistically significant differences between Goldthorpe's classes at all. In short, income in Britain is determined by status, education, authority and ownership (and other things)—these fully capture the effects of class and the Goldthorpe typology adds no further information.

Subjective class identification—Goldthorpe (and Müller in his contribution) makes much of the conditions under which people come to identify with a class and make it a basis for collective political action. This is, indeed, a theoretically crucial matter. One rough but valuable indicator of class formation is

Table 20I.1 *Income and Subjective Class Identification in Britain*: The Explanatory Power of 'Class' and 'Class-Status-Power' Models (using metric partial regression coefficients)

Class scheme[1]	Log income[2]			Subjective class[3]		
	(1)	(2)	(3)	(4)	(5)	(6)
Goldthorpe's class typology (G)						
Service class	.62	—	ns	.50	—	ns
Routine non-manual	ns	—	ns	.22	—	ns
Petty bourgeoisie	.25	—	ns	.31	—	ns
Skilled workers	.20	—	ns	.08	—	ns
(Non-skilled workers)[4]	—	—	—	—	—	—
Farm owners	ns	—	ns	.40	—	ns
Farm workers	ns	—	ns	ns	—	ns
Class-status-power model (CSP)						
Status (0 to 1)[5]	—	.57	.39	—	.21	.21
Education (years)	—	.07	.04	—	.05	.05
Supervision	—	.33	.32	—	.13	.13
White-collar	—	.13	ns	—	.13	ns
Owner	—	ns	.31	—	.14	ns
Government employee	—	− .09	− .10	—	− .07	− .05
Controls[6]	—	—	*	—	—	*
Percentage variance explained, R2	11.9	17.7	25.0	17.0	20.8	23.4
Difference in R2		5.8, CSP higher			3.8, CSP higher	

Notes:
ns—not statistically significant at p < .05, two-tailed.
1   Refers to head of household.
2   Natural log of family income, so coefficients are proportional changes.
3   Scored 1 = middle class, 0 = working class.
4   Omitted (reference) category.
5   100s of status points.
6   Controlled but not shown are: sex, age, union membership, colour, Catholic, Welsh residence, parents' political party (columns 3 and 6 only).

Source: 1979 British Election Survey, N = 1893.

subjective identification with a class, as indexed by the familiar question on identifying with the 'working class' or the 'middle class'. In fact, Goldthorpe's concept of class is closely linked to this (Table 20I.1, column 4). For example, the service class is 50 per cent more likely to identify with the middle class than are non-skilled workers, and the petty bourgeoisie are 31 per cent more likely. In all, Goldthorpe's class explains 17 per cent of the variance.

But class in the multi-dimensional class-status-power (CSP) model explains even more, around 21 per cent of the variance, some 4 per cent more than Goldthorpe's typology (column 5). Status matters a great deal, with high professionals 21 per cent more likely to identify with the middle class than are farm workers at the bottom of the hierarchy. Each year of education increases middle-class identification by 5 per cent. Supervisors, owners and white-collar workers are (each) some 13 or 14 per cent more middle-class, and government workers 7 per cent more working-class.

More strikingly, when we consider Goldthorpe's class typology and the CSP variables jointly, it seems that the Goldthorpe typology adds no further explanation of subjective class (column 6). There is *no* statistically significant difference between Goldthorpe classes, while class differences in the CSP model remain large. In short, subjective identification with the middle or working class in Britain is determined by status, education, authority and ownership (and other things), while class in Goldthorpe's sense adds no further information.

Class and politics—a similar pattern holds for the links between class and politics (Table 201.2; for simplicity, I give only summary statistics, corresponding to the last two rows of Table 201.1). Goldthorpe's typology is less effective than the multi-dimensional CSP model in explaining party identification and economic ideology (rows 3 and 4). The differences are not as large as those we have seen for income and subjective class (rows 1 and 2), but are nonetheless appreciable.

Class and social mobility—the CSP model of class is just as effective as Goldthorpe's in explaining social mobility, or perhaps very slightly better. For example, a father's class in Goldthorpe's sense explains 19.2 per cent of the variance in his son's education (row 5). But father's class in the CSP sense explains just as much, or fractionally more, 19.5 per cent. Strikingly, the CSP model is no worse than Goldthorpe's, and perhaps better, in predicting whose sons get into *Goldthorpe's* service class (row 6). So even here, where Goldthorpe's class would be expected to be at its best, the CSP model is at least as good. Furthermore, these results on social mobility seriously understate the CSP model's power. This is because the data at hand have no measure of father's education, which is part of the CSP model but not Goldthorpe's, and is known to be very important here.

Table 201.2   *Class and Political Variables in Britain*: *The Explanatory Power of 'Class' and 'Class-Status-Power' Models* (percentage of variance explained in OLS regressions)[1]

Predictor and dependent variables	Goldthorpe typology (1)	Class-status-power model (2)	Difference, column 1 vs column 2 (3)
Respondent's class predicting:			
1 Family income	11.9	17.7	5.8, CSP higher
2 Subjective social class	17.0	20.8	3.8, CSP higher
3 Political party preference	10.1	10.8	0.7, CSP higher
4 Conservative ideology	6.9	7.9	1.3, CSP higher
Father's class predicting:			
5 Respondent's education[2]	19.2	19.5	0.2, CSP higher
6 Respondent in Goldthorpe's service class[2]	9.5	9.8	0.3, CSP higher

Notes:

1   See Table 201.1, columns 1 and 2, for variables included in each model. The results shown are from the last two lines of Table 201.1 and their analogues for other dependent variables.

2   Men only.

Source: *1979 British Election Survey*, N = 1893 (915 men).

The service class. One of the reasons Goldthorpe's class schema is rather less powerful than the Blau-Duncan status scheme, as extended in the class-status-power model, is that Goldthorpe uses only a small number of classes, some quite heterogeneous. The problems are two. First, the classes are large and so offer considerable scope for heterogeneity that could be directly measured in a scheme that has more classes, like Blau and Duncan's or the CSP scheme. For example, Goldthorpe's service class includes professionals, administrators, and technicians —all prosperous and high status, but nonetheless diverse. Because it is a typology, Goldthorpe's scheme makes no further distinctions within classes; for example, there are no distinctions between owners and employees in the service class, or between supervisors and non-supervisors there. In a multi-variate model such distinctions can be made; for example, distinguishing high status owners from high status employees (which allows us to isolate the effects of ownership from those of status).

The empirical question is whether there is anything to gain from such distinctions. Goldthorpe argues not, that his classes are homogeneous—and that this is a key difference between typological models and multi-variate ones. But, in fact, there are significant distinctions within Goldthorpe's service class (see Table 201.3). First, there are sharp differences in income (column 1). Administrators earn about 30 per cent more than technicians, and professionals some 20 per cent more. Furthermore, owners earn almost 50 per cent more than employees, and supervisors 30 per cent more than non-supervisors. These are substantial differences. Second, there are also real differences in subjective class identification, with administrators and professionals over 10 per cent more likely than technicians to identify with the middle class (column 2). Third, there are, however, no real political differences, at least none significant with a sample this small (under 500 cases: column 3). Fourth, there are, however, modest ideological differences with administrators and supervisors holding more conservative views about economic questions than others in the service class (column 4).

Thus there are real differences within Goldthorpe's service class, differences which the CSP model could, at least in part, capture. This is a notable weakness.

Table 201.3 *Class Differentiation within Goldthorpe's 'Service Class'* (metric partial regression coefficients predicting various dependent variables)

Class groups within the service class	Family income (1)	Subjective social class (2)	Political party (3)	Conservative ideology (4)
Administrators[1]	.30	.13	ns	.19
Professionals[2]	.20	.14	ns	ns
(Technicians)[3]	—	—	—	—
Owners	.47	ns	ns	ns
Supervisors	.32	ns	ns	.17

Notes:
1 International Standard Classification of Occupations (ISCO) major group.
2 ISCO professional with Treiman prestige $>= 58$.
3 ISCO professional with Treiman prestige < 58.

Source: 1979 British Election Survey, service class only (N = 432).

CONCLUSIONS

Goldthorpe has strenuously advocated his class typology as preferable to Blau and Duncan's status model, a view strongly endorsed by Müller. In taking ownership and authority into account, he is undoubtedly right: they were ignored in the original Blau-Duncan paradigm and are important in a variety of economic, social and political contexts. But Goldthorpe's way of incorporating ownership and authority was, I believe, disastrously wrong. He opted for a typology, losing the much greater refinement and precision possible in multi-variate models like Blau and Duncan's. Partly for this reason, he omitted education from his model, a truly grievous loss of a variable known to be central to social mobility, lifestyle and income inequality. He used only half a dozen occupational groups, in the process losing important distinctions at least among his large and heterogeneous service class. He used information on ownership and authority in only a limited way, again omitting important distinctions among the service class.

In fact, there are simpler and more powerful ways to incorporate ownership and authority (and other variables) into the Blau-Duncan model. I have described one, the class-status-power model, and shown that it is superior to Goldthorpe's model: it better explains income and subjective class identification, reducing the effects of Goldthorpe's classes to statistical insignificance. It explains politics and social mobility at least as well. Far from being a great advance on Blau and Duncan, Goldthorpe's class typology is inferior. It should be abandoned in favour of the conceptually simpler and statistically more powerful multi-variate approach of adding ownership, authority and other class variables to Blau and Duncan's education and status.

APPENDIX: TECHNICAL NOTES

These analyses are from the 1979 British Election Survey, a large representative national sample available from the data archive at the University of Essex. They are based on ordinary least squares regressions.

The definitions in the 'class-status-party' (CSP) model follow those given in my main contribution to this volume with further details in Kelley and McAllister (1985). The underlying occupational classification is from the International Labour Office (1968) and Treiman (1977: 203–8). For comparability and convenience, I have used these in defining boundaries for Goldthorpe classes as well (e.g. between non-manual and manual, or between skilled workers and semi-skilled). So there is some inexactness, but I strongly doubt that it makes any substantial difference. The most noticeable divergence appears to be on the boundary between skilled workers and other workers, where the ILO/Treiman boundary is more stringent than Goldthorpe's, counting fewer as skilled and correspondingly more as unskilled. Throughout, occupational variables refer to the head of household.

Income is the natural log of family income (individual earnings were not available). Subjective class is measured by a single question basically distinguishing working from middle class. Party preference is scored Conservative = 1; Liberal, etc. = 0.5; and Labour = 0. Conservative ideology is measured by a four-item additive scale derived from a factor analysis; it includes questions on inequality, nationalization, comprehensive education and the House of Lords. Education is in years.

XII. THEORY AND RESEARCH IN SOCIOLOGY

21. Theory, Rhetoric and Research: John Goldthorpe's Tennis Player View of Society and Sociology

KARL ULRICH MAYER

I met John Goldthorpe for the first time in 1969 when he was giving a lecture at the University of Constance. In this lecture he outlined his ideas for a programme of research on social mobility—a programme whose execution, ramifications and implications have occupied him ever since. Shortly before, I had written a similar assessment of the then current state of this field and was surprised about the convergence of our points of view. Since that time we have met once or more each year—often for purposes related to the activities of the Research Committee on Social Stratification and Mobility of the International Sociological Association. I was at Nuffield College, Oxford, as a visiting fellow in 1977–78, and in 1984 we jointly founded a new journal, the *European Sociological Review*. This project was based on our common conviction that European empirical social research needed its own forum. Through these experiences I can claim that in the role of a sympathetic observer from the Continent—unaffected by and mostly unaware of inner-British controversies—I have enjoyed for almost two decades the personal and intellectual pleasures, and suffered the intellectual irritations, of my acquaintance with John Goldthorpe.

The task of taking a positive stance on Goldthorpe's overall contribution to theory, methods and research in sociology provides me with the welcome cathartic opportunity of attempting to disentangle the problems posed by his sociology, and in so doing to disentangle what I find so intellectually fascinating and compelling about him—and what I do not. All this might seem to be very personal. I hope to make clear, however, that it is certainly not intended to be of idiosyncratic interest to myself only.

In the first and main part of what I write, I shall unabashedly celebrate John Goldthorpe's contribution as one of the best current examples of what sociology can and should be. I will take his intellectual career as the empirical basis for a study in epistemology: how must sociological analysis be conducted in order to be

361

scientifically valid, intellectually convincing, academically successful and politically meaningful? In the second part on the 'Tennis Player View of Sociology and Society' I will search for the key to Goldthorpe's sociology (and personality). This will provide an opportunity to discuss substantive aspects of his sociological theory in both a sympathetic and a critical manner. It will be a study from the perspective of semantics, metaphors and interaction ritual. In the third part, 'Rhetoric in Sociology: Goldthorpe as Writer', I will approach Goldthorpe's works from the point of view of communication theory and literary style. Here I am concerned with the non-textbook aspects of the bases of the acceptance of scientific arguments and empirical results. In the final section I will try to fit these three perspectives and their results into a coherent whole.

THEORY, METHODOLOGY AND EMPIRICAL RESEARCH IN SOCIOLOGY: AN EXEMPLARY TALE

John Goldthorpe's sociology is certainly one of the best current examples of what sociology can and should be. His work can be used as a 'critical case' to learn what it takes to perform a proper sociological analysis today, 100 years or so after this enterprise had its first beginnings. In the spirit of Paul Lazarsfeld, it is more useful to examine successful studies than to turn to the philosophy of science in the area of the epistemology of the social sciences. This is the task intended to be accomplished in this section. Although not neglecting his other contributions, our prime material will be his studies on social mobility in the class structure.

Over the last quarter of a century Goldthorpe has been extremely consistent and persistent in a single, but very complex, enterprise.

1 He has defined problems of a macro-sociological and historical nature, above all dealing with changes in contemporary class structure.
2 He has been very careful and explicit in situating these problems in the context of the history of ideas, i.e. of ideology and social theory, in current academic dispute and political debate (e.g. Goldthorpe, 1976; see also 1987a: Ch. 1).
3 As one of the last living and practising Popperians, he has always seen sociological analysis as a task of construction. Knowledge is only to be gained by the even-handed combination of theory-building, data collection and measurement as well as formal methods of data analysis. Theory-building, in the sense of developing strong, unambiguous and falsifiable hypotheses and the explication of basic assumptions and underlying intellectual traditions, is a *conditio sine qua non*. Although theory-building is the cornerstone of the whole undertaking, Goldthorpe has also followed the advice preached and practised by Reinhard Bendix: a little theory goes a long way. To be effective in terms of empirical test and communication in the scientific community, theory-building must be economical, almost ascetic in nature.
4 Goldthorpe has invested years of his life in establishing adequate databases for his studies as regards sampling quality, sample size and precision of measurement. Furthermore, he has made sure that the criteria of replicability and comparability are observed. The fruitfulness and gener-

ativity of the Nuffield Mobility Study lie not least in the fact that—in the best possible way—it can be related to the 1954 study by David Glass and his associates, that it served as a paradigm for the Scottish mobility study, that it was replicated in part about a decade later, and that—through deliberate intent and the personal investment of many years' work—it became the core study for cross-national comparisons.

5 One crucial element for measurement, replicability and comparability was the decision to construct a theory-driven classification of the class structure. Goldthorpe thus followed an essential and often neglected methodological rule in sociological analysis: the substantive fruitfulness of research depends not only on the proper specification and measurement of the dependent variable, but just as much on the meaningfulness of what are posited as independent variables. The Goldthorpe class scheme has become the standard tool in the field and has been a crucial precondition of doing cumulative science in it. For this important instrument, very precise measurement rules and extensive coding and recoding exercises have been as important as its explicit theoretical rationale.

6 This combination of history of social thought, theory-building, data collection and measurement is rare enough; but Goldthorpe has pushed this recipe yet one important step further. After some initial doubts and intercollegial dispute, the methodology of advanced multi-variate analysis in the form of log-linear modelling has become a major instrument in his empirical analysis. More than anyone else he has tried to ensure that formal methodology plays a more important role than the mere accounting of variance, that the formal aspects of models correspond as closely as possible to substantive criteria. The methodological tail has never wagged the substantive dog. In fact, the substantive dog has perhaps sometimes been too much in control of the wagging tail.

7 For macro-sociological purposes, survey methodology for nationally representative samples can be productive only if it is employed in rigorous cross-national comparisons. The CASMIN Project on comparative mobility, which Goldthorpe has masterminded and engineered as a small-group experiment, has been, in my opinion, the best and probably only good example where the high hopes of cross-national survey research have been realized, producing not only reliable but new knowledge (for a good review, see Kurz and Müller, 1987).

8 Goldthorpe has also fed his research results back into the area of general sociological discussion and the debate on the major characteristics and developments of contemporary society (for a recent example, see Goldthorpe, 1990). A second important strand in his intellectual career has been his fight against both the Marxist and the liberal '*terribles simplificateurs*', confronting them with socio-historical and nationally specific configurations emerging from his empirical studies. Here he has persistently played both the Weberian and the Popperian. Sociological theories provide only categories and guidelines for empirical analysis. Their deductive character can be applied only so far. Armchair sociology must always be barren. There is no 'logic' of industrialism, of capitalism or of pluralist differentiation which would allow us to know once and for all '*was die Welt im Innersten zusammenhält*'.[1]

Finally, both in the selection of research questions and in the interpretation of results, Goldthorpe has not forgotten his initial training as a historian.

Goldthorpe has thus demonstrated abundantly that there are no shortcuts to knowledge. There is no alternative but to take the long, painful and winding path through the whole cycle of intellectual history, theory, empirical measurement, macro-sociological and political interpretation. More importantly, one has to master each of these components at their most advanced level. One also has to push the enterprise through numerous single studies and papers which are necessary to arrive at a coherent whole. This takes tremendous commitment and decades of a scholar's life. Many individuals and groups have enjoyed speedier successes by concentrating on just one of these elements, being negligent or sloppy in the others. But this simply won't do. The hallmark of Goldthorpe's sociological career is steadfastness, almost stubbornness. He has been unperturbed by the fashions and fads of the discipline, apart from occasional scornful comments addressed to them. The drummer he has followed is himself, and he has invented his own melodies and rhythms (and even the drum, too!).

THE TENNIS PLAYER VIEW OF SOCIOLOGY AND SOCIETY[2]

My choice of a metaphor from the sphere of sport might give the impression that there is something improper and less than complimentary in this heading. The opposite is closer to my view. This heading originated in a casual remark by John Goldthorpe in the Nuffield quad about Max Weber having a tennis player view of society. Since I am no sportsman, it took me years to figure out what might be meant by that. On reflection, I realized that the image of the tennis match is an insightful metaphor for a basic premise in Max Weber's sociology, i.e. his view that social life is essentially struggle and strife, competition and selection, and these frequently shape the outcome of social processes. It is worth noting that the category of 'struggle' (*Kampf*) implies a strong theoretical orientation to 'social actors':

> A social relationship will be referred to as 'conflict' (*Kampf*) insofar as action is oriented intentionally to carrying out the actor's own will against the resistance of the other party or parties. A peaceful conflict is 'competition' insofar as it consists in a formally peaceful attempt to attain control over opportunities and advantages which are also desired by others. (Weber, 1978: 38)

In addition, Weber refers to social selection as the ever-present latent competition of human individuals for life chances or chances for survival (*Lebenschancen*), a struggle which is carried on without conscious pugnacious intent against others.

This tennis player view of society is characteristic not only for Max Weber[3] but also for the sociology of John Goldthorpe, and I assume—for him—quite consciously so. Social life is not primarily functional adaptation, harmonious cooperation, the explication and re-enactment of symbols and values or the rational implementation of means-goals relationships. On all levels—daily existence, party competition, labour markets and industrial conflict, intellectual and academic pursuits—it is a fight.

It is easy to see how this perspective leads to a preoccupation with class structure, class conflict (as the modern form of actor-related struggle) and social mobility as both an intentional and non-intentional process of social selection. It is worth noting that in his works Goldthorpe does not resolve the ambiguity of the intentional and non-intentional aspects of 'society as struggle' by falling into reductionism on one side or the other. He falls neither into the trap of structural-functionalism or systems analysis, nor of exclusive symbolic interactionism. Rather he attempts to combine a macro- and a micro-approach. In his studies of industrial sociology and in his contribution to the *Political Economy of Inflation* (Hirsch and Goldthorpe, 1978) he reconstructs the logic of individual and group action in terms of rational motives in given situations, whereas in the mobility studies he uncovers the institutional and often unintentional conditions and outcomes of competition and selection processes between social classes. It has been a basic premise in Goldthorpe's work that the social heterogeneity of classes, which is induced by mobility processes, determines their likelihood of operating as collective actors. This assumption must be seen as an attempt to bridge the actor-arena and the non-intentional process-world of society. It is also probably the weakest spot in his construction. In modern societies it is very hard to demonstrate that class composition (by class of origin) is important for class organization and class conflict. My own work (on class career mobility in Germany and Norway) seems to provide evidence for the independence of these two macro-variables (Mayer, Featherman, Selbee and Colbjørnsen, 1989). It is quite reasonable to argue—as Luhmann has done most extremely—that contemporary developed societies are distinctive precisely in regard to the dissolution of the links between institutional-organizational subsystems like the polity and the population. The welfare state creates its own clienteles and motives.

The fact that John Goldthorpe holds to a class-theoretical framework in his mobility studies is therefore not so much based on solid empirical arguments (of which there certainly are some), but is more an expression of his basic underlying premises about the nature of society. Here Goldthorpe reaches a limit which, to me, seems to be characteristic of even the best examples of current sociology. Empirically, it is nearly impossible to follow both an action framework and a macro-process framework at the same time. At best, we can follow one empirically and keep the other perspective theoretically in our and the readers' minds.[4]

The metaphor of the tennis match is precise and fruitful in other respects as well, which brings us back to Goldthorpe's tennis player view of sociology. For Goldthorpe, the view of (academic) life as a constant fight is, on the whole, not a deplorable fact; for him it is fun; and when there is no (intellectual) fight going on, he is sure to provoke one in his typically teasing and challenging manner. Here the metaphor of the tennis match illustrates vividly how Goldthorpe himself understands and plays the game. According to the rules of tennis, one has to make one 'serve' after another with the idea of placing the ball out of reach of the opponent. Goldthorpe has achieved a remarkable rate of aces in scholarly exchanges, and his opponents in argument have often been too stunned to come up instantly with (sometimes more correct) counter-arguments. The aim is to score unrelentingly and never to give up—one paper after the other, one well prepared presentation after the other. He has persistently pursued and attacked what he has called the logic of industrialism and versions of pluralism and deterministic Marxism. The others in the game—partners or adversaries—have either been beaten, did not have as much stamina, or were much faster at turning to the next interesting problem, while Goldthorpe was still on court making one serve after the other and staying there until he had won.

The tennis player view of doing sociology entails not only making one unreturnable serve after the other, hitting the balls as hard as possible and hitting them, i.e. the opponents' arguments, at the point where they are easiest to respond to, it also involves deuces. Goldthorpe has certainly been great in scholarly deuces. Repeatedly, he has turned around apparently decided academic controversies to come out as the winner. He has completely turned the sociology of social mobility from a US-dominated field, with an emphasis on individual achievement and a graduated stratification system, back to a macro-level analysis of transition regimes and to his own dominance, with its very British preconceptions about the pervasiveness of class structure. Status attainment and path analysis are now eliminated in this field, and even its former proponents apply Goldthorpe's class scheme (e.g. Featherman and Selbee, 1988). Goldthorpe has also succeeded in breaking up the solid belief in the similarity of patterns of intergenerational social mobility in advanced industrial societies (Erikson and Goldthorpe, 1987a, 1987b). Likewise Goldthorpe and his co-authors have reversed the argument of technologically based divisions in social consciousness and attitudes between groups of manual workers and invented the concept of instrumentalism in the *Affluent Worker* series (Goldthorpe *et al.*, 1969). More recently, Goldthorpe has achieved the advantage with regard to the conceptualization and measurement of women's class position (Goldthorpe, 1983a, 1984c; Goldthorpe and Payne, 1986b).

Another even more recent controversy is still undecided. With regard to the tradition of social mobility research, adherents of the life course approach have taken issue with the fundamentally flawed way in which conventional studies represent the mobility process, i.e. either as static comparisons in a single transition matrix or as a number of separate points in time as in status attainment studies. By contrast, it has now been asserted that mobility processes can, and must, be conceived and modelled as time-continuous event histories (see Mayer and Carroll, 1987; and Sørensen, 1986, for the life course side, and see Erikson and Goldthorpe, 1987c, for the mobility side of the controversy):

> The process ...is time-dependent; that is, the amount of movement that will take place will depend on the length of time the process has gone on ....The movement takes place in the labor force. Hence, the relevant period is the amount of time spent in the labor force... the destinations observed in a typical mobility table, then, are not destinations, but observations of a set of locations for people at different stages in their career. (Sørensen, 1986: 77)

Goldthorpe's strong counter-argument relies on the fact that, for a certain number of countries, variations in worklife mobility do not alter the overall mobility regime between class of origin and class of destination. (In this game I am on the other side, and of course I hope that he will lose it, but as things stand at the moment Erikson and Goldthorpe (1987c) have made the last return and the ball is in our court.) All these are remarkable examples of cases where Goldthorpe has joyfully challenged established points of view, managing at least to reopen the debate and often replacing them by his own.

RHETORIC IN SOCIOLOGY: GOLDTHORPE AS WRITER

It is all too rarely recognized that a particular style of arguing and writing is often not just a personal characteristic but may be a question of academic traditions and environment. Max Weber's *Economy and Society*, for instance, is easily misinterpreted if one is not aware of the fact that his way of phrasing paragraphs and collecting empirical examples of cases and subsuming them under a given theoretical concept is much the same as the way lawyers of his time presented their briefs and his contemporary fellow economists were expected to write their textbooks. For example, the significance of Weber's typology of social action has been greatly overestimated in its significance as a clue for the interpretation of his sociology, since it has not been generally recognized that every elementary textbook in economics of his time was expected to start with such basic definitions (Hennis, 1987).

Likewise Goldthorpe's style can hardly be appreciated if one does not recognize how it fits into, and was probably reinforced by, the Oxbridge tradition of arguing all day long—from the morning coffee break in the Junior Common Room through the college communal lunch, high table and evening wine-and-cheese-parties—in a game-like and adversarial manner. Goldthorpe's writing of even the dreariest reports of quantitative findings draws directly from this oral tradition. To paraphrase Clifford Geertz's (1988: 26) observations on Lévi-Strauss, what is most striking about Goldthorpe's voluminous articles and books is that, using the word in its non-censorious sense, they are an essentially rhetorical accomplishment.[5] It is not the mere facts or explanations invoked that make him an intellectual hero. It is the mode of discourse he has invented to display those facts and frame those explanations.

To understand the remarkable success of the sociology of Goldthorpe from the point of view of rhetoric, i.e. his efficacy as a speaker and as a writer, one finds additional material in a study by Ricca Edmondson (1984) on *Rhetoric in Sociology*, in which the *Affluent Worker* (Goldthorpe *et al.*, 1969) is used as an example. Edmondson argues and demonstrates convincingly that the task of sociological explanation must, among other things, be accomplished through persuasion and by drawing on the reader's prior knowledge and experience:

> The notion of rhetorical communication makes it possible to recognise that in presenting what he or she hopes approaches an adequate view of a situation, a sociological author is completing a whole of which the reader being addressed possesses a certain part; and complementing this part is very likely to dislodge some beliefs which the reader had previously associated with it... . However convinced sociologists may be of their analyses, they do not try to communicate them to everyone at once. The notion of correctness in their communication cannot be understood independently of that of appropriateness in interaction with this particular audience. Thus rhetorical communication is an integral part of what makes sociological texts explanatory. (Edmondson, 1984: 166)

Goldthorpe's persuasiveness, then, is a proper part of his sociological task.

Let me give two examples from Goldthorpe's and his co-authors' works to illustrate this perspective. Both the *Affluent Worker* series and the German study, *Industriearbeit und Arbeiterbewußtsein* by Horst Kern and Michael Schumann (1970), are concerned with the relationship between conditions of work and workers' attitudes. While Kern and Michael Schumann conclude that the assumption of a common workers' consciousness must be rejected, since different working conditions induce heterogeneous attitudes, Goldthorpe and his co-authors conclude that workers exhibit very similar orientations despite variations in the conditions of work. If one examines the empirical percentage differences between groups of workers (in answers to quite similar but unfortunately not identical survey questions), one finds that they are very similar in size. Clearly then, what are communicated and accepted as empirical statements of fact are not established by the empirical findings as such but through the manner in which they are translated into theoretical propositions. Another example is Goldthorpe and Erikson's conclusions about differences in patterns of social mobility within European nations. The empirical facts alone are open to emphasizing the similarities as much, if not more than, the differences (Erikson and Goldthorpe, 1987a, 1987b; Ganzeboom and Ultee, 1988).

If one considers the achievement of John Goldthorpe to be partly one of scientific communication, it is almost by direct implication that the question of audience arises. If what is offered and accepted as description and explanation depends, as Edmondson maintains, to a large extent on the prior knowledge of the audience, then the quality of the audience becomes a prerequisite for the quality of what is being written and communicated as scientific discourse: 'It seems to me probable that without the support of a community of reasonable people one is unlikely to reach reasonable conclusions; but this does not settle the question how one establishes the reasonableness of a group or its views' (Edmondson, 1984: 165–6). Goldthorpe has made special efforts and investments of time and energy in fostering and creating scientific audiences and improving their quality. For almost twenty years he has been committed to working with the Research Committee on Social Stratification and Mobility of the International Sociological Association, a body for which he served as president for many years and which has become the main forum for the discussion of Goldthorpe-style mobility research. This committee comprises most of the 'experts' who are able to follow and appreciate Goldthorpe's advances at the frontier of research, but it also has some of its most unrelenting critics. Goldthorpe has also been involved in two committees of the Social Science Research Council, those on Western Europe and comparative stratification. Additionally, his role as founder and editor of the *European Sociological Review* can be seen as one of 'audience'-building.

Even the most positive evaluation of the role of communication and rhetoric in scientific discourse must, however, reflect the possibility that communicative efficacy and the impressiveness of the speaker and writer may be greater than the truth value of the propositions advanced and empirically substantiated. But here I would like to claim that the kind of empirical research Goldthorpe practises is 'positivist' in the best meaning of this term (which as a scientific practice in sociology seems to be more and more lost in neo-Hegelian obscurantism). For him, the conceptual clarity of statements and hypotheses is taken to be a primary task, data collection procedures and operationalization are made fully explicit, data analyses are fully replicable and anybody can use the publicly accessible data to examine the assertions.

Much in line with Edmondson (1984), I see Goldthorpe as a good example of the methodological rule that efficient communication and the use of rhetoric are necessary complements to rigorous scientific procedures:

> I do not want to endorse the notion of a bare-bones sociology which argues without being rhetorical, but neither do I want to adopt a position which introduces notions such as those of 'degrees' of truth or of truth changing over time... . I have instead argued that there are different ways of perceiving what is true and different ways of truth-telling. This allows for more than one true account of a state of affairs but it by no means rules out that we should also claim to be able to identify some accounts which are definitely false. (Edmondson, 1984: 165)

In the process of dealing scientifically with sociological truth or error, rhetorical communication such as Goldthorpe's is an integral part of what is involved.

There is one final point which should be highlighted with regard to Goldthorpe as an author, and here again I will draw on Geertz (1988: 8–24). In arriving at his selection of anthropologists as exemplary authors, Geertz distinguishes between people who are writers of texts and authors who establish a tradition, who create a method of discourse in which other books and authors subsequently find their place. The significance of the latter in science goes beyond the adequacy of a particular statement or the appropriateness of a particular measure or model. Their impact is also likely to last even when more and better data, more advanced and sophisticated models, become available and even when some of their major conclusions or findings falter. Certainly Goldthorpe belongs to the category of 'authors' in social science.

THEORY AND RESEARCH IN SOCIOLOGY

It is now possible to summarize what it is that makes Goldthorpe's contribution to sociology so distinctive. First, despite the pressures of specialization and fragmentation, he has maintained the essential unity of the field in his writings. Macro-social problems, concepts of the social order, theory-building, empirical research and methodology have been kept together in all Goldthorpe has done. Second, with the stamina (and probably at times the loneliness) of the long distance runner he has pursued sociological problems just as long as it has taken to solve them, even if it took decades. He has—and this is extremely rare in science—both created a paradigm in the sense of Thomas Kuhn and carried it to its limits as a normal science. Third, he is a tower of strength (and stubbornness) in sticking to his view of society and sociological practice. He has always given an excellent performance and his performance has sometimes—though rarely—been better than his argument and evidence.

Thus it is easy to see why John H. Goldthorpe is so admirable and exemplary, but also occasionally infuriating as a scholar. He has not only done the right things, he has done them better and faster than others. As a result he not only wins the game, set and match, but also the tournament.

NOTES

1 *Editor's Note*: This is part of the famous monologue which opens the first scene of Goethe's *Faust Part I*. It could be translated roughly as 'what holds the world together in its innermost workings'. Robert David MacDonald's recent translation of *Faust* captures well the spirit and poetry of the original—herewith the relevant section including the three lines immediately preceding the words cited by Karl Ulrich Mayer:

And so the rules of Magic I rehearse,
To probe the secrets of the Universe,
To learn its mysteries and recognise,
The force that binds all Nature's energies.
(J. W. von Goethe, *Faust, Part I*, Trans. R. D. MacDonald. Birmingham, Oberon Books, 1988, p. 39)

2 By the use of this metaphor I engage in a form of presentation which Kenneth Burke calls 'perspectives by incongruity' (Burke, 1964).

3 Friedhelm Neidhardt has correctly reminded me that tennis is anything but a fight without rules, but rather a well ordered (he claims almost harmonious) game. I think that order and ritual are not alien to Weber's concept of society; harmony, of course, is.

4 This is the so-called micro-macro puzzle. For the attempts to apply the actor framework to macro-sociological analysis, see Roemer, 1982; Wiesenthal, 1987; Coleman, 1986; for the attempt to push the aspect of non-intentional population processes, see Carroll, 1988; Hannan and Freeman, 1989.

5 The reference here to Geertz's study of *Work and Lives: The Anthropologist as Author* and to his observations on Lévi-Strauss is to suggest neither an affinity of Goldthorpe's literary style and scientific epistemology to Lévi-Strauss in particular, nor an identity of the tasks of an ethnographer and a quantitative sociologist.

22. Ideology and Action in the Work of Goldthorpe

TERRY JOHNSON

John Goldthorpe has never been one to extend his undoubted belief in the potential scientific neutrality of sociology as a discipline to embrace the neutrality of his own position and work. In fact, he has always been at some pains to make clear his own value commitments. For example, in *Social Mobility and Class Structure in Modern Britain* he remarks:

> ...we would recognise, and insist upon the need to recognise, that mobility research is an ideologically loaded area—in the sense that underlying a research interest in it, one must expect there to be also an 'interest' of a different kind, which in some way derives from the researcher's own socio-political experience, values and commitments. (1980a: 2)

Goldthorpe's response to charges of ideological bias directed against mobility studies was to argue that a scientific 'interest' in such research was compatible with, and inspired by, a whole range of ideological 'interests', from liberalism to Marxism, and that in any case the real danger arose only when researchers concealed or failed to recognize the inevitable relationship which must exist between research 'interests' and 'interests' stemming 'from the researcher's own socio-political experiences, values and commitments' (*ibid.*).

Goldthorpe, therefore, regards this unavoidable interwining of political and research 'interests' as one of the strengths of sociological inquiry, parading subsequently for our inspection two such values which he recognizes as underlying and informing his own study of social mobility. The first of these he identifies as standing in the tradition of Fabianism and ethical socialism: '...we would ally ourselves with Tawney and the ethical socialists generally in seeing the degree of openness that actually prevails as an issue on which liberal ideology is highly vulnerable—in particular, of course, in respect of the claim that true equality of opportunity can co-exist with substantial inequalities of condition' (*ibid.*: 27). This 'interest' is, therefore, in 'greater openness' or 'greater equality of chances of access, for individuals of all social origins, to positions differently located within the social division of labour' (*ibid.*). It is an interest which presents itself as in direct ideological confrontation with a liberalism which equates individual freedom and opportunity with the 'good society', a view rejected by Goldthorpe on the grounds that the existence of structured inequalities hinders some individuals 'from realising their own full potential as citizens or indeed as human beings' (*ibid.*).

The second 'interest' revealed by Goldthorpe is of what he calls a 'marxisant' character: that is, it 'is from the standpoint of class formation and class action' (*ibid.*: 28). This recourse to Marxism does not, however, commit him to an historicist view, '... in which the working class and class conflict appear as the destined agency and means of revolutionary transition from capitalism to socialism' (*ibid.*). Nevertheless, while ethical socialism stressed the issues of equality and the significance of social mobility in its realization, it also underestimated the historical significance of class conflict, thereby failing to appreciate the extent to which the working class was '...the social vehicle through whose action, electoral *and otherwise*, their [ethical socialists] ideals have by far the best probability of being realised' (*ibid.*). Consequently, Goldthorpe admits to sharing, 'with students in the Marxian tradition, an interest in the dynamics of class relations' (*ibid.*). These Marxist credentials remain intact even while suggesting that what he means by 'class action' includes, crucially, social mobility. As we shall see later, it is this identification of mobility with class action that eventually undermines his 'marxisant' claims. For the moment the intention is merely to indicate the readiness with which Goldthorpe identifies his own ideological predilections and the way in which these are expressed in the mobility study.

It is also important to point out that Goldthorpe is equally insistent that such partisanship has no necessary consequence for the neutrality of sociology as a discipline which he sees, potentially at least, as conforming to the canons of scientificity developed by Popper. In respect of social mobility studies he is specific:

> ...we would maintain that whatever has actually been the case in mobility studies in the recent past, there is no *necessary* connection between a research interest in mobility and any specific ideological attachment, liberal or otherwise; and further, that the techniques that are commonly used in mobility research have, at all events, a much wider range of ideological neutrality than most critics have allowed... in fact, there is, in our view, no reason to regard it as in any way regrettable, or as detracting from the scientific standing of sociology, that interests in the sense in question should very generally lie behind the formulation of problems and the conduct of research. On the contrary, we would believe that if sociology is to fulfil its potential, and not only as a social science but as itself a mode of social consciousness, its practitioners must recognise that their problems—however much they may subsequently wish to redefine them—are to be taken far more 'exogenously', from the development of their society and their own response to this, than 'endogenously', from the development of their subject. (1980a: 2)

This recent expression of a personal value commitment to 'openness' allied with a strong belief in the potential of sociology as a science reiterates commitments which have been evident in Goldthorpe's work from the beginning. Such commitment to 'openness' in social mobility is, for example, a direct reflection of his more general and continuous commitment to 'freedom of choice', and its sociological reflection in the 'social action perspective', both of which he has frequently reasserted.

As a self-proclaimed 'socialist', then, Goldthorpe's work as a whole can be viewed as a continuous and insistent polemic confronting, on the one hand, the individualism of liberal dogma and, on the other, the inevitabilism of Marxist belief. At the same time he draws on what he conceives as the core virtues of each: individual freedom and collective action. These combined virtues he sees as both reflecting and overcoming the fundamental dilemma of sociology: action versus structure. Consequently, his sociological polemic, which matured under the dual hegemony of American functionalism and Continental Marxism, has stressed the 'social action perspective' as a counter to systems theory, while identifying in the open-ended operation of group conflict and action a rejection of the historicist fallacies of dogmatic Marxism.

In keeping with the Lawrentian principle 'never trust the author, trust the tale', I will in this chapter briefly, and selectively, trace some of the consequences of these expressed values as they affect Goldthorpe's theoretical and research writings. What I will suggest is that, while the central values of 'openness' and 'freedom' are expressed through a sociological commitment to an 'action perspective', this commitment is asserted and reasserted without becoming effectively represented in the sociological work. It appears neither as an elaborated theoretical position, nor as an analytical concept, nor as a set of research tools. It is, therefore, rendered assertive in theory, *ad hoc* in analysis, and *post hoc* in research. Consequently, 'social action' becomes incorporated into Goldthorpe's sociological work as a value assertion in analysis and as an interpretive gloss on data.

The corpus of Goldthorpe's writings is enlivened by the consistent polemic against determinism. From the early attack on historicism and functionalism in the paper on social policy delivered at the Fifth World Congress of Sociology (Goldthorpe, 1962a) to the broadside against sociological evolutionism and futurology (Goldthorpe, 1971) and the revised rejection of extreme liberalism and vulgar Marxism in his work on social class and mobility in 1980 (Goldthorpe, 1980a), Goldthorpe has expressed his anathema toward all social analysis that smacks of determinism as well as reiterating his commitment to the 'action frame of reference'.

THE NECESSITY OF THE PAST

By initial training an historian, Goldthorpe applied his new-found sociological expertise and enthusiasm to a field of historical study and explanation in his paper on the formation of social policy in the period 1800 to 1914 (1962a). The focus of this paper's critique was a revisionist historiography exemplified in the writings of Karl Polyani (1944), H. L. Beales (1946) and E. H. Carr (1951); all of these were characterized by Goldthorpe as sociologically biased accounts of the nineteenth century 'revolution in government' thesis, which in turn counteracted the previously dominating influence of Dicey's 'great men' thesis (1905) as well as constituting a 'collectivist' response to the extreme liberalism of such writers as von Mises (1936) and Hayek (1944). He identified in this historiographical departure theoretical errors common to functionalist explanations in sociology:

> Some form of relatively extensive public provision against the disruptive wasteful and debilitating tendencies within industrial and particularly capitalist society is taken as being in some sense a functional 'prerequisite' or 'imperative' for the continuing

existence and development of such society. In this view, then, the explanation of the growth of such provision is *ultimately* to be given not in terms of particular group interests and pressures; but rather, in terms of the objective 'demands' of certain social situations which are seen as virtually imposing particular courses of action. (1971: 50–1).

Polyani argued that had not the state intervened to protect society against the perils of the self-regulating market, a capitalist system 'would have physically destroyed man and transformed his surroundings into a wilderness' (quoted 1962a: 48). Goldthorpe identified in this an overreaction to the individualism of Dicey, as well as the liberalism of Hayek, rendering this new sociologically informed history equally untenable. While one might wish for a rather more moderate assessment of Polyani than is entailed in endowing this statement with the status of a general explanatory principle, it remains clear that Goldthorpe's critique was essentially directed against the commitment to *historical necessity* which defaced the new history and which, drawing on his sociological understanding, he rejected as an 'uncritical functionalism'.

Goldthorpe's response, which drew on the then current sociological critique of functionalism, was to reject such determinism by bringing back into account the 'ends of individuals or groups' (*ibid.*: 56). In short, functionalist explanations required to be refined and supplemented by way of an analysis informed by 'an action frame of reference', which would include the 'purposive actions of individuals and groups in pursuit of their ends' (*ibid.*: 55). Thus any adequate explanation of the development of social policy in the nineteenth century would have to make clear the conditions under which:

> ...decisive state intervention in economic and social affairs would tend to be regarded as imperative. In other words, they [the historians] must consider such questions as: what kind of case had reformers to be able to make out in order to prevail against vested interests opposed to reforms, or even simply inertia. What, in fact, were the ends to which social policy had convincingly to be related before its 'necessity' was accepted? (*ibid.*: 54)

Some might identify in this formulation a foreshadowing of the current claims of discourse theory or rhetoric analysis. If so, they would be disappointed by the subsequent direction of Goldthorpe's work. More important is his specification of the conditions in which such rhetoric would be likely to prove successful, which itself implies a 'less extreme' form of functionalism than that entailed in Polyani's statement:

> It is, one would suggest, that the development of social policy was necessary for the maintenance of a certain kind of society conducive to the achievement of certain ulterior ends held to a large extent in common by the members of that society... in other words, when it is said by historians that a particular social problem 'had to be dealt with' or that a particular piece of legislation was 'imperative' or 'inevitable' what, apparently, is meant is that the alternative to action of the kind taken was such as to be clearly incompatible with the ends of those, at least, who were in a position to make the effective decision. In this case, then, the argument is not that without the development of social policy in nineteenth century England the very existence of this society would have been threatened; but rather, that without this, certain goals to which a general public commitment had been made could not have been attained. (*ibid.*: 53–4)

This, suggested Goldthorpe, 'is the only useful way' (*ibid.*: 54) of conceiving of functional necessity; implying first, that explanation requires an analysis of the 'case' reformers had to make in order to convince the decision-makers of its necessity, but that, second, in the analysis of such 'ulterior ends' their potential diversity should be recognized, so taking into account those prevailing cleavages and tensions in society expressed in the actions of contending interest groups. For it is evident:

> ...that the pattern of institutional change was at all times and to an important degree determined by the shifting balance of power between rival factions, set in opposition to each other by differences of class, religion and culture as well as of politics... . Public health legislation, factory and labour legislation, the provisions made for social security were all to some degree or other created out of a process of struggle [*sic*] and compromise. (*ibid.*: 55)

Functionalist explanations of social history need to be modified, then, in several ways according to Goldthorpe: first, by an analysis which takes an 'action' frame of reference, that is, an analysis in terms of the ends of individuals and groups rather than in terms of the 'needs' of society considered as a whole; second, the 'necessity' of social policy must be related to 'certain ulterior objectives to which the members of society are committed' (*ibid.*: 56). Finally, the specific institutional forms through which social provision was made could only be specified in terms of the outcome of purposive action, but action 'directed towards a diversity of ends' (*ibid.*).

The significance of this argument was not that it provided, in any sense, an innovative response to functionalism. There is nothing here which could not have been derived from the influential Mertonian critique. Rather, its significance was in applying an existing sociological critique to historical explanation. Also important for us is that the paper laid the foundations of what one might call Goldthorpe's career values: the rejection of determinism and the embracing of the social action perspective.

I would also argue that this paper is characteristic of Goldthorpe's future writings in that it fails to explore in any depth the thorny issues of structure versus action which it raises. In short, Goldthorpe provides no clear indication of what his alternative mode of analysis would entail—theoretically or methodologically—consequently, the call to the flag of the 'action perspective' constitutes little more than an empty gestural response. As it is, Goldthorpe's suggested remedies for historical functionalism raise more problems than they resolve.

First, the explicit commitment to the 'action frame of reference' is never explicated except that it is identified as taking account of individual and group purposes. There is, second, an uninterrogated distinction made between the 'ulterior' goals to which all members of society would appear to be committed and the 'diversity of ends' and interests which feed the struggles out of which peculiar institutional forms emerge. Third, there is the attack on historical necessity combined with a failure to note the necessities to which his own analysis would be subject: that social action arises out of class interest, cultural values or religious belief. In short, the implied distinction between structure and action, between the conditions of action and available choices, is never recognized as requiring examination of a theoretical kind. There is only the most superficial recognition of what an action explanation would entail for historical analysis.

It may reasonably be contended that such expectations would be excessive in response to an article with only modest aims, written at the time it was. This would certainly be the case if it were not more generally indicative of Goldthorpe's subsequent failure to grapple with such problems. The argument is that, while remaining committed to the notions of openness, choice, action, etc., Goldthorpe never feels it incumbent upon himself to develop the theoretical or methodological means of realizing such values. Consequently, the attempts to distance himself from liberalism on the one hand, and Marxist determinism on the other, become merely polemics arising out of what he calls his 'general interest', rather than deriving from any systematic elaboration of his position. As a direct consequence, when it comes to his research, we find that, despite such values and interests, he is constantly to be found entangled in a determinism of his own making.

To justify this argument I will first consider Goldthorpe's position a decade later, in an article which was also directed polemically against the old enemy, 'determinism', or what he also called the 'recrudescence of historicism' (1971). In this case the enemy lurks in the 'evolutionist' writings of Talcott Parsons (1966), Clark Kerr (1962, 1968) and Daniel Bell (1967, 1968), as well as the 'future studies' of de Jouvenel (1967), Kahn and Wiener (1967) and Flechtheim (1966).

THE NECESSITY OF THE FUTURE

Again the critique was mounted to clear the ground for a reinstatement of the virtues of the 'social action perspective'. On this occasion Goldthorpe's critique derives more explicitly from Karl Popper's 'distinctive, liberal standpoint' (1971: 264). Popper's argument against any form of theoretical history allied to holism is marshalled to show that this work constitutes a form of evolutionary liberalism which is fundamentally tainted by determinism. Clark Kerr's attempt to identify a 'logic' of industrialism, arising out of the necessities of technological means and economic organization, and Parsons's effort to categorize those 'evolutionary universals' which he identifies as underlying the 'adaptive capacity' of all societies, are both castigated in these terms. Parsons's own effort to develop a distinctive 'voluntaristic theory of action' is ignored by Goldthorpe, and Kerr's efforts to disentangle himself from the charge of determinism are summarily dismissed: 'However...coyly...expressed, [the aim is] to make historical prediction, even if of a rather imprecise character' (1971: 267). Equally, despite the efforts to eschew historicism, the futurology of de Jouvenel and of Kahn and Wiener is condemned as committed in 'covert' and 'subtle' ways to the errors of historicism. This is despite the admitted claims of futurologists that the future is always the product of current choices and that future studies do not attempt to map the future but merely to 'provide a range of alternative potential maps, deriving from the logic of the choices made' (1971).

In particular, Goldthorpe argued, futurology is tainted by the pervading influence of 'technocratic historicism', which largely derives from its 'clear concentration on technological and economic forecasting' (*ibid.*: 280). The general lines of Goldthorpe's critique are clear, Popperian in inspiration and generally unexceptional.

All these theories—the logic of industrialism, Parsonian evolutionism and futurology—while inspired by nineteenth century attempts to comprehend the 'totality' of the historical or evolutionary process, are characterized by a modern emphasis on technocracy as the key to future post-industrial society. The agents of its realization are scientists, technologists, managers, etc. In Kerr's words the central problem of modern society is 'keeping...going without major disruption' (quoted in Goldthorpe, 1971: 269). Consequently, the 'management problem' becomes paramount, and 'keeping things on course' ensures a central role for the expert, as management problems are increasingly of an instrumental kind; political questions are subordinated to technical instrumental questions. Thus, Goldthorpe concludes, a seemingly neutral vision becomes politically committed to gradualism and there emerges a conservative attachment to piecemeal reform. Goldthorpe recognizes that there is a convergence here with Popper, ironically Goldthorpe's own inspiration for the critique. Two major elements of the Popperian critique of historicism are advanced by Goldthorpe as constituting a rejection of futurology and of evolutionary liberalism.

First, the shared commitment to the notion of invariant regularities or principles, comprehended as a scientific theory, simply misunderstands the nature of science as an activity. In Popper's argument there can be no science that is simultaneously both theoretical and historical. The totality of history is a unique process and cannot, therefore, be the subject of scientific theory, which is concerned with *recurrent* relationships between particular aspects of phenomena.

Second, the theories subjected to Goldthorpe's critique provide no justification for, or analysis of, the reasons why historical events or the anticipated future *should* follow the course observed in the past. Parsons's notion of adaptation cannot be taken for such a causal mechanism because (as with Kerr's logic of industrialism) it does not explain why social actors, through whose agency change occurs, *should* act in such ways and with such outcomes that the functional exigencies in question are, in fact, met (1971: 274).

Third, and less dependent on Popper, is Goldthorpe's claim that such theories involve a 'striking failure, or deliberate restriction, of the imagination' (*ibid.*: 278). Thus:

> ... the attempt is often made to rule out of court ideals and ideas which could point to genuine sociological and historical alternatives, and which, if more widely propagated and recognised, could significantly extend the *range of effective socio-political choice*. (*ibid.*, emphasis supplied)

Not that Goldthorpe is opposed to the possibilities of forecasting, that is, of identifying trends, sequences, cycles or other such social processes. Rather, his hostility is directed to the consequences of futurology as practised, of identifying empirical regularities arising out of the technological and economic constraints of industrialism or post-industrialism which take the form of historical prediction:

> As a corrective to this propensity, it would therefore seem essential that in the conduct of future studies there is automatically counterposed against the idea of process that of action; and against the activity of social forecasting, that of conjecturing and of what might be termed 'social designing'. (*ibid.*: 286)

Social forecasting would no longer be the object of such study; rather, the object would be to assess and identify the conceivable ways in which 'purposive, organized interventions, guided by different models of what the future *could* be like' (*ibid.*), might generate 'ranges of possibility'. Such a study would start not with observed empirical regularities leading to extrapolated historical prediction, but with 'conjectures' about possible futures, developed within the context of existing sociological, economic and psychological knowledge and data, rather than that derived from history.

This new discipline of 'social designing', Goldthorpe argues, could avoid historicist errors by starting with the assumption that 'the future is open, even though all things are not possible' (*ibid.*: 287). At the same time it is conceived as an activity providing alternative designs to serve as 'a basis for public debate and to show the diversity of goals that political action might rationally pursue' (*ibid.*: 288).

Once again, and here in rather more detail, Goldthorpe contrasts structural determinism with his own action perspective. A predicted and thereby closed future is contrasted with openness and political choice between alternatives. In the polemic against futurism he does attempt to develop a more elaborate alternative position, arising out of his social action perspective. This alternative approach, however, fails to overcome the problems identified in the social policy article of a decade earlier. What does Goldthorpe's 'action'-based alternative consist of? First, he agrees that some form of future studies is both possible and desirable, but that such studies should begin, not with historical extrapolations and the goal of social forecasting, but with 'action' and 'social designing'. By 'action' he means 'purposive, organized interventions, guided by different models of what the future *could* be like'. This fundamentally imaginative exercise he sees as being saved from Utopian fantasizing by subjecting it to 'the most critical appraisal possible in the light of relevant social scientific, and other knowledge' in order to determine their 'respective conditions and consequences and whether or not incompatibilities exist between them' (*ibid.*: 287): 'In this way, therefore, constraints—impossibilities—would certainly come to be recognized, and likewise the need to consider what these imply for the pursuit of any desired end: hence the notion of social designing' (*ibid.*: 287). Recognizing that the notion of ' constraints' and 'impossibilities' might be interpreted as involving the very same determinism which he sets out to criticize, Goldthorpe attempts to distance himself from any such charge by distinguishing between 'historical' constraints and those which are 'derived from sociological, psychological and economic analyses'. In short, he suggests an abstractive process which is entirely in keeping with the dismissed Parsonian theory, which also insists on a 'voluntaristic' action framework.

What is possibly the most surprising aspect of Goldthorpe's model for futurist studies is his insistence that it should move from mere forecasting to social action, from conjecture to social design, and from an attempt to understand, in some sense, the future to *making* the future:

> For the social designing approach is one clearly inimical to the technocratic acceptance of the *status quo* as given except where 'problems' are seen as calling for remedial action; and equally to the tendency to play down basic ideological or political issues or to present them as ones to be determined largely by expertise. To the extent that alternative futures really are spelled out (not just alternative forecasts or alternative 'solutions'), to that extent too there is revealed the true range of socio-political choice, the degree of existing social conflict, and the possibilities for future action. (*ibid.*)

While the project developed by Goldthorpe is again rather underdeveloped and ambiguous, the implications are literally mind-boggling. Goldthorpe is either conceiving of future studies as revolutionary practice or he is allying himself with the school of rational comprehensive planning. To deflate such pretensions, one merely has to ask *who* is to conceive of these conjectural alternative futures—sociologists, politicians? Whose futures are they to be? As Popper suggests, conjectures are unlimited except by the imagination. Also, once we convert such conjectures into scientifically informed social designs—which, Goldthorpe suggests, 'entail no presumption in favour of piecemeal social policies' (*ibid.*) as against designs of a more 'sweeping character'—we are unwittingly dumped into the world of Andreas

Faludi and rational comprehensive planning and all the consequent problems identified in such an approach by Camhis (1979).

Remarkably there is no discussion of the political conditions and consequences of such an activity, no suggestion of the problematic relation between intention and interest, no elaboration of the connection between action and power. There is a studied silence with regard to all those problems which have bedevilled the quest for a rational society. Goldthorpe's solution is an abstracted intellectual exercise which never begins to touch upon any realistic assessment of the relationships between action and structure. It has about it all the hallmarks of a naïve sociological idealism. Goldthorpe moves from an anti-determinist critique to an acceptance of comprehensive 'social designing' or planning by another name, which implies a level of determinism which is beyond anything to which a futurologist would knowingly admit.

> With, however, a greater emphasis on social designing, the specifically political relevance of future studies might be expected to become more widely appreciated— whether as a means of selecting new objectives or of *devising more effective strategies for the achievement of old ones.* (ibid.: 288; emphasis supplied)

This slide into such grandiose claims for social science is seemingly the product both of an unerring belief in its scientific mission and of Goldthorpe's failure to consider systematically what it is that he means by 'social action'. What are the requirements of a social action perspective as a form of explanation; what is the relationship between action and structure, knowledge and action, etc.? Most pertinent to this failure is that, while Goldthorpe briefly alludes to the relationship between power and action in the article on policy, he does not appear to conceive of its significance in the relationship between social designing and politics.

SOCIAL ACTION AT LUTON

In setting out with his research colleagues at Cambridge in the mid-1960s to test the thesis of working-class *embourgeoisement*, Goldthorpe was, for the first time, not only involved in relatively large-scale empirical research but coincidentally provided with the opportunity of putting into practice his social action approach. In deciding on a case study approach of one population of 'manual workers in one particular context at one particular time' (Goldthorpe *et al.*, 1969: 30), the research team were opting for an 'intensive' study which would allow them to collect detailed data relating to both work and non-work *milieux* as a basis for identifying those 'sequences of change' which appeared to be entailed in the claimed process of *embourgeoisement*. The ultimate aim was to identify the '*total* life-situations and life styles' (*ibid.*: 31) of the workers in this population. Ideally, this population would be found in a social setting conducive to a whole series of shifts in values, norms, reference groups and patterns of association which were implied in the notion of *embourgeoisement*'. Implied also was a new open community not bound by tradition, characterized by social heterogeneity and economic growth. The choice, as history reveals, was Luton.

The link between the *embourgeoisement* study and Goldthorpe's action perspective is difficult to discern in the outline of the research as presented in the major publications (Goldthorpe *et al.*, 1968a, 1968b, 1969). However, it is possible that 'interest' was operating in the decision to investigate a social setting 'conducive to .... shifts in values, norms, reference groups and patterns of association', reinforced by the claim that the *embourgeoisement* debate centred 'not on questions of income, standards of living, conditions of work or patterns of residence, but on questions of social values, social relationships and social consciousness' (Goldthorpe *et al.*, 1969: 21). While it is possible to draw such a conclusion from this emphasis on values and change in the research reports, there is no discussion of the centrality of social action nor any consideration of the research problems which might arise from adopting such a perspective; nor is there any identification of research procedures necessary to the adoption of an action approach.

Nevertheless, the Luton study does represent the closest Goldthorpe has come to identifying the way in which his avowed commitment might be expressed in research. This shaft of light broke upon the scene, not in the major co-authored research publications, but in an earlier article written by Goldthorpe alone (1966b), in which data from the Luton study were used to criticize previous studies of car assembly workers. This little illumination was subsequently fanned into a blaze of self-justification (Goldthorpe, 1970a) by the critical response of W. W. Daniel (1969), who argued in a rather oblique fashion that Goldthorpe's claim—to have developed an action approach as expressed in the Luton publications on industrial behaviour—was specious. In considering this exchange, we are not specifically concerned with Daniel's criticisms of the Luton study, nor with Goldthorpe's attempts to defend its conclusions. Rather, the focus is on Goldthorpe's attempt to explicate the 'action perspective'.

In the 1966 article Goldthorpe extracted from the Luton findings data on car assembly workers and used these to test the general conclusions of a mainly American literature on the subject. According to this literature, he argued, the attitudes and behaviour of car assembly workers towards their workmates, their supervisors and their firms were found to be 'remarkably' similar, from plant to plant and from country to country. Assembly workers were presented as a 'fairly well-defined type', distinctly conditioned by the technological environment of the place of work; 'almost as standardized as the vehicles (they) help to produce', the model of the self-estranged worker; the prototype of the 'mass man' and the 'militant worker' (1966b: 289).

The Luton findings, he argued, deviated from such conclusions, and the source of these deviations could be found in the unique attention which the Luton research gave to the 'prior orientations' toward employment exhibited by the assembly-line workers and the significance such orientations had for their choice of job, their definitions of the work situation and the meaning they gave to work. In short, Goldthorpe returns to his anti-determinist theme in rejecting the overemphasis in previous literature on the immediate technological environment as the determinant of workers' behaviour and attitudes. Such emphasis, he argued, effectively diverted attention from the orientations which workers brought with them into the work situation; orientations which mediated between the 'objective features' of that environment and workers' experiences of it. In short, he suggests, workers do not react passively to their (technological) environment; they react positively to it and they do so in terms of pre-existing attitudes, orientations generated outside the immediate work situation (*ibid.*: 240). That the Luton car workers were neither estranged nor militant, in accordance with the type defined in the previous literature, could then be explained by virture of the 'instrumental' orientations that they brought with them to the work situation as a result of previous non-work experience (*ibid.*), for example, their community relations, their place in the life (work-family) cycle and their experience of social mobility.

The approach developed by Goldthorpe to make intelligible the seemingly deviant attitudes and behaviour of the Luton workers (low strike rate, low level of disputes, low absence and turnover rates, low incidence of oppositional behaviour, etc.) was, he argues, a 'social action perspective' involving an investigation of the 'meanings given to work' and the significance which workers consequently attach to the objective technological environment. These orientations which workers bring to their employment and work experience must then, he argued, be regarded as 'a crucial independent variable to what occurs in the work situation' (*ibid.*: 241). Consequently, 'to account in turn for the particular nature of this orientation [instrumentalism], must mean investigating other non-work aspects of the social lives of the workers involved' (*ibid.*).

Goldthorpe effectively makes not one but three critical methodological points. First, and unexceptionably, is the view that workers' attitudes and behaviour cannot be fully understood as the outcome of the work situation—the plant environment—alone. Goldthorpe further suggests that situationally specific behaviour will be affected by orientations (we must take this to mean not merely discrete attitudes, but a structured coherent set of attitudes as suggested by the notion 'instrumentalism') generated prior to the situation under investigation. Again it is not earth-shattering to suggest that past experience will affect current behaviour, but neither would it be particularly innovative to suggest that current behaviour is affected by future expectations—a dimension which could be said to have altered radically in the industrial world of the 1980s as against the 1960s. However, the central issue which arises for Goldthorpe is that this argument is not an effective rejection of determinism. It merely recognizes the temporal and spatial diversity of the determinants. That is, workers' behaviour may not be determined in a situational, technologically induced, 'knee-jerk' way, but might, as Goldthorpe suggests, be determined by a broader cluster of social conditions which together result in instrumentalist attitudes. Finally, and most problematically, Goldthorpe argues that adequate analysis must allow for the 'positive' responses of the actors involved, by identifying how such prior orientations mediate between the 'objective features' of the environment and such responses. It is in this claim that the crucial *differentia specifica* of an action approach must be located. It is in the active mediation of the situation that the element of choice inheres, and it is in this sphere that Goldthorpe's argument and claims are at their weakest. The extent of Goldthorpe's inability to grasp the implications of what is required is brought out clearly in his exchange with Daniel.

DANIEL ENTERS THE LION'S DEN

Daniel's attack on Goldthorpe (1969) is disingenuously presented as an attack on the action frame of reference as generally applied to the analysis of industrial behaviour. It is disingenuous because, while the paper makes passing reference to other approaches, the only example considered is that of Goldthorpe and his co-workers and, in particular, the article and book on industrial behaviour. Daniel's strictures are as follows. The focus on the concept 'orientation to work' is a research commitment which raises the most 'elusive and intangible' (*ibid.*: 366) problems associated with the requirement to identify through adequate techniques of inquiry and measurement an actor's subjective definitions of work.

Goldthorpe's failure to match up to this task is, it is argued, rooted in his reliance on formal questionnaires, which are not capable of providing an adequate research basis either for the weight of analysis they are required to carry or for the conclusions arrived at. The procedure adopted by Goldthorpe *et al.* was to ask people 'why they chose a particular work situation, why they remained, and what features of the job they value' (*ibid.*: 367). From the responses elicited, categories of orientation to work were derived and these were then located on an instrumental-expressive scale. Workers are, therefore, seen as responding to work as providing either primarily intrinsic or extrinsic rewards. Daniel comments:

> This type of procedure would be perfectly unexceptionable (if somewhat obvious and circular) if such orientations were then used to explain or predict occupational choice or labour turnover. In practice they are extended and developed to explain all aspects of the work situation: for example, sources of gratification and deprivation in work, responses to different styles of supervision, relationships with other members of work groups, determinants of performance, and evaluations of the employer. (*ibid.*)

Daniel goes on to suggest that the factors attracting a person to a job are very different from those which determine their satisfactions, performance and behaviour. He proceeds to show how these general strictures apply to the specific conclusions reached in the Luton study. In particular it is argued:

> To justify the approach *via* orientation to work as relevant to the analysis of job behaviour, it must be convincingly shown that people with different orientations to work respond in different ways to the same work situation, and that people with similar orientations respond in similar ways to different work situations. (*ibid.*: 368)

This, it is implied, the Luton study signally fails to do.

Rather than follow the subsequent argument about the adequacy of the findings—Daniel's charges and Goldthorpe's responses—we will consider how Goldthorpe responds to the central charge of employing procedures and techniques (formal interviews) which cannot possibly lead to the desired end, namely, to identify how prior orientations positively mediate between the objective features of the environment and the actor's response.

Goldthorpe's first line of defence, and the core of his overall defensive strategy, is to suggest that Daniel does not understand the process of science, at least, not the Popperian version of science, which he presents as involving three neat stages (1970a: 199):

> *Phase 1* existing empirical data are found not to fit with the existing body of theoretical ideas, i.e. cannot be adequately explained or understood;
> *Phase 2* as the result of 'informed conjecture', existing theory is modified and renovated, the better to accommodate and account for the deviant empirical findings;
> *Phase 3* the new ideas, in turn, are subjected to critical scrutiny and explication and are empirically tested in the context of further research.

The Luton study was, according to Goldthorpe, 'to be taken as representative of phases 1 and 2' (*ibid*.: 200), so intimating that the process of 'conjecture' was the centrepiece of the project and implying, by default, that for some reason Daniel had no part to play in the third phase of 'critical scrutiny' and explication. Phase 3, it appears, must be seen as the responsibility of others, and Daniel is upbraided for failing to note subsequent studies such as those of Blackburn and Mann, which were taking the concept of 'orientation to work' to greater heights (*ibid*.: 201).

What concerns us here, however, is the extent to which Goldthorpe's response can be seen as absolving his own research from the charge of determinism which he so eagerly attacks. This focuses on a rather different, though related, problem to that of justifying the concept 'orientation to work' (which is at the centre of Daniel's concern). In self-justification, Goldthorpe claims that the research decision to draw respondents from occupational groups in three contrasting technological environments was based on the then current expectation (derived from Blauner, 1964; and Woodward, 1965) that some consistent variation in work attitudes and behaviour related to these socio-technical systems would be found. It was not. Rather, once skill level was held constant, there was a high degree of similarity in attitudes and behaviour. The resultant writings on industrial behaviour were the product of a joint decision by Goldthorpe and his colleagues to document and explore this 'failure to meet expectations', and the theory generated to account for such discrepancy was necessarily '*post factum*' (*ibid*.: 200–1). That is, an explanation of industrial behaviour was developed after the event; 'social action' was an afterthought: '... we arrived at the idea of the explanatory importance ... of orientations to employment ... as a factor influencing job choice, mediating the individual's experience of work-tasks and roles, and thus necessarily influencing his definition of the work situation and his conduct within it' (*ibid*.: 200). This tardy inspiration had problematic consequences: 'Obviously, in *this* case, no methods or techniques specifically adapted to the study of orientations were developed. Since the full possible significance of this factor was realized only after our data were collected and under examination ...' (*ibid*.: 201, original emphasis).

Goldthorpe's defensive strategy was to suggest:

- that Daniel had mistaken the nature of science;
- that the Luton study was an intervening aspect of the general scientific process, i.e. speculative and theoretical;
- that the recourse to an 'orientation to work' approach was dictated by the character and unexpected nature of the data emerging;
- that the 'interview schedule' used (not 'formal questionnaires', as Daniel had suggested) was adequate to such a task, particularly as 'complemented by ... other methods of inquiry, including observational work and interviews of a quite informal and unstructured character' (*ibid*.: 202).

Two points emerge from this exchange which render Goldthorpe's strategy problematic. First, it is surely remarkable that a researcher whose work had, from the very beginning, been pervaded by a value commitment to individual choice and a theoretical commitment to the social action perspective should suddenly discover, only after a major field inquiry had been completed, that that very same action approach was necessary for a full understanding of the emergent data. We are forced to conclude that either Goldthorpe had become overly defensive in the face of Daniel's attack, recognizing that the methodology was not consistent with the requirements of an action explanation, or that the design of the Luton study was an aberration in his otherwise consistent career position—the commitment to social action.

Now, as pointed out above, there is a difference between the notion of 'orientations to work' and the social action perspective which neither Goldthorpe nor Daniel disentangles. While Daniel focuses on subjective work orientations and the practical and methodological difficulties involved in analyzing them, Goldthorpe is able to counter effectively and simply by claiming that the interview and other techniques used were adequate to the task of identifying such orientations. For all the Luton study pretends to do is to recognize that the sources of such orientations are not located within the workplace but are external to the work situation. In short, Goldthorpe's response is to say that the *source of determination* was shifted by the Luton study. The source was no longer seen to reside in the technological or organizational conditions of the plant but, partially at least, in family and community contexts outside the plant. The point here is that identification of the variable structural conditions under which shared orientations to work arise has no necessary relationship to action theory at all. Goldthorpe's commitment to action, to choice, requires not a specification of the structural determinants of instrumental orientations, but an analysis of how these orientations mediate the 'objective features' of the work environment to generate responses. It is in the active mediation or negotiation of the situation that the specific character of action theory, if it is to be worthy of the name, inheres. It focuses on the way in which actors continuously negotiate changing situations in which they find themselves in accordance with such 'prior attitudes'. It is a positive, choosing, ongoing process. As I understand it, an action theorist places emphasis upon that process of choosing, and/or negotiation, not on established orientations, the implied logic of which provides only a speculative basis for an action explanation.

An action explanation involves a direct investigation of the process of action itself: the processes through which actors respond to, interpret and negotiate outcomes in the work situation. It is in this analysis of an open-ended process that action theory attempts to avoid the consequences of determinism. Goldthorpe's recourse to 'prior orientations' without such a complementary analysis merely shifts the location of the determination. That an action approach is necessarily the study of interpretive choosing processes is something which Goldthorpe does not appear to accept; consequently, he is never forced to identify the action perspective as anything other than what he happens to be doing at the time.

TALKING ABOUT A REVOLUTION

That Goldthorpe rejects the specific requirements of an action explanation becomes clearer in his review article—written in 1973—concerned with the then fashionable schools of phenomenology and ethnomethodology (Goldthorpe, 1973a). His attention was drawn to these schools, he suggested, because following a decade in which they had exhibited a studied 'indifference' to 'constructivist' sociology, ethnomethodology in particular was breaking out of the laager to compete with sociology, even seeking to replace it. Goldthorpe's response is presented as a somewhat benevolent attempt to overcome the potentially divisive consequences of this threatened 'revolution'. Division was implied, he argued, not merely in the phenomenological 'polemic' against sociology, but in the totalistic rejection of much of the counter-criticism directed by sociology at these schools. Consequently, Goldthorpe adopted a mediating reconciling role. While rejecting the radical claims of ethnomethodology to constitute a 'revolution' in sociology, he recognized that such a rejection was 'quite consistent with an appreciation of the force of certain methodological and theoretical arguments that are integral to this position' (*ibid*.: 450).

What is it about phenomenology that Goldthorpe 'appreciates'? First, while rejecting the phenomenological critique of conventional sociology, 'that it confounds topic and resource' to the extent of crucially damaging its claims as a discipline, Goldthorpe does accept the more limited critique that sociologists have 'been unduly complacent and unenquiring' about the extent to which they 'take for granted' the various practical activities in which they engage (*ibid*.: 452).

Significant in assessing Goldthorpe's general action perspective is the fact that he appears here to accept the phenomenological position that 'interpretative procedures are always involved in social interaction' (*ibid*.). Goldthorpe's account of the position must be quoted at some length.

> In conventional sociology, it is held, the basic assumption is that in most contexts of interaction there exists some shared, culturally-given set of values and definitions, equally available to participants and observers, and it is this assumption which is then exploited for descriptive purposes. For example, the investigator identifies particular structures of normative expectations and complexes of subjective orientations, and then seeks to use these as 'variables' by which observed patterns of social behaviour can be specified and, under given conditions, accounted for in terms of action. (*ibid*.: 452)

Such a description is coincident with Goldthorpe's own procedure in the analysis of work orientations. To develop such procedures, conventional sociologists, it is argued, must further assume that stable interaction is the result of different participants' discriminating situations and actions in much the same way—as a result of cognitive consensus—and that this shared cognition is the product of common socialization (i.e. the common community, family experience, etc. of Luton workers). The central issue, which Goldthorpe accepts, is that such an extension of the basic phenomenological assumption 'reduces actors to mere automata, programmed by their culture' (*ibid*.: 453). The ethnomethodologist resolves the issue of determinism by treating all interaction as, in principle, problematic: not the automatic product of pre-existing culturally established values but, rather, as a practical accomplishment within particular contexts. The ethnomethodological upshot of this principle is that the analysis of interpretive procedures must itself be conceived as an interpretive procedure; sociological work being interpetive descriptions and not literal ones. Thus *common reality* exists only as the continuous product of practical accomplishment and cannot be viewed as a pre-existing condition of action. Goldthorpe accepted the phenomenological position up to a point: ' ... The ethnomethodologists' refusal to accept sociological theory which is viable *only* if actors are taken to be complete "cultural dopes" is empirically well justified. So too is their insistence on the crucial but neglected role of cognitive processes in social interaction' (*ibid*.: 454).

Nevertheless, he contended that the phenomenological position was by no means revolutionary, being part and parcel of a major thematic of conventional sociology which has a perfectly acceptable solution to this central problem and is one which Goldthorpe is happy to go along with. He distances himself from the ethnomethodological conclusion that 'normative' (as against the interpretive) paradigm of sociology is, in principle, inoperable by claiming that how far or not actors *are* 'programmed' by their culture (with the programme being directly accessible to the investigator) is an 'empirical issue': 'Certainly it would seem open to suggest that in *some* situations the presuppositions of the normative paradigm, as a matter of fact, give a more or less adequate basis for the analyses of action in terms of variables and via deductive explanations' (*ibid.*).

In principle, then, according to Goldthorpe, action may be viewed as an interpretive process; in the long run there is freedom to choose. However, for practical purposes one can, as sociologist, proceed as though this were not the case, because empirically cultural dopes do exist. Moreover, we can determine who the 'cultural dopes' are:

> ... in any event, it may be held, where such presuppositions [of the 'normative' paradigm] are *not* valid, then, with a properly formulated explanation, this will be automatically shown up by its weakness or failure. Conversely, to the extent that explanations of the kind in question are successful, the appropriateness of the approach may be taken as confirmed. The ultimate proof of the pudding must be in the eating.
>
> Such a rejoinder to the ethnomethodological argument, it should be stressed, does not lead one to deny that interpretive procedures are always involved in social interaction: it rejects only the contention that the sociological analyst may never, to any extent, take these procedures for granted. (*ibid.*: 454)

The question which arises for us in this reaction to ethnomethodology is that in Goldthorpe's empirical work there exists no means, methodological or theoretical, which will admit of the significance of this interpretive process. Goldthorpe, in effect, reduces the phenomenological principle, which he agrees has force, to an empirical issue. His solution is an entirely empiricist one—'the proof of the pudding'—which exonerates him from the difficult theoretical and methodological tasks which face the action theorist or analyst. Also his response to phenomenology rejects the principled need to adopt an action perspective. Goldthorpe's position is that actors may be observed in a process of choosing, interpreting, negotiating, but that is an empirical question to be taken into account—presumably—after the event. It is certainly the case that Goldthorpe has never in his own work felt it necessary to focus on such interpretive procedures, so we can only conclude that he regards such action processes as relatively unimportant, despite his action rhetoric.

WHERE THE ACTION IS: CLASS AND MOBILITY

In identifying Goldthorpe's career commitment to the social action perspective we return to our starting point, the Oxford mobility study and its main findings published in 1980. As has already been shown, Goldthorpe presented his interpretation of these findings as essentially a product of his socialist 'interest' in social openness and equality. However, 'of prior importance has been an interest in mobility from the standpoint of its implications for class formation and class action' (1980a: 28). Once again the rhetoric of action is of central significance, and in this case the priority given to class action arises out of Goldthorpe's judgment that the socialist goal of the 'open' society can be realized only through the vehicle of working-class action. 'Change is therefore only likely to be brought about through collective action on the part of those in inferior positions, relying on their numbers and above all on solidarity and organization' (*ibid.*: 29). In making such a claim Goldthorpe recognizes an affinity with Marxists: 'To this extent we would agree with

Marx: that *if* class society is to be ended—or even radically modified—this can only be through conflict between classes in one form or another' (*ibid.*).

Crucial to Goldthorpe's argument is the distinction between absolute and relative mobility. He is able to show that the post-war period of economic growth saw a significant expansion in 'service-class' occupations at the expense of working-class occupations. An increase in the rate of upward social mobility was, therefore, necessary simply to fill the positions created by such changes in the occupational structure. Despite the consequential increase in the rate of mobility as a whole (absolute mobility), the *relative* chances of mobility between social classes remained stable—post-war British society was no more open than it had been previously. Despite the fact that post-war economic expansion had provided the ideal conditions for a reduction in inequality, there had been no such outcome, leading to grave doubts about the efficacy of socialist political strategy in '...seeking to attack social inequalities via legislative and administrative measures of a piecemeal kind that can be carried through without venturing too far beyond the limits of "consensus" politics' (*ibid.*: 252). The implications for Goldthorpe are clear; the goal of 'openness' can be achieved only through collective class action. Consequently, the bulk of the second half of the mobility text is geared:

> ...to examine the wider concomitants of such mobility as these may be found in aspects of men's lives outside the sphere of work—for example, in the accompanying degree of discontinuity in their social relations with kin, friends, leisure associates, etc.—and further, of course, to examine the extent to which the mobility which we would impute to individuals in fact corresponds with their own awareness of having been mobile. (*ibid.*: 143)

What emerges from the above quotation is that at this point the Marxist inspiration appears to evaporate. A conception of class action as sited in social organizations, political apparatuses and ideological practices fails to emerge. Hindess recognizes, for example, that from this point on the text

> ...pays not the slightest attention to the conditions and organisations of struggle in modern Britain: neither to the political parties, unions and professional associations, employers' organisations, state agencies and other bodies that define both the arenas and the principal agents of institutionalised political struggle, nor to the ideologies and forms of political calculation in terms of which those struggles are conducted and forces mobilized around them. (Hindess, 1981: 195–6)

Rather, Goldthorpe's focus of analysis is on factors that influence the emergence of 'shared beliefs, attitudes and sentiments that are required for concerted class action' (1980a: 265). The point of Hindess's critique is to reject the sociological reductionism of such an approach which assumes that to identify classes is also to identify the main political actors in society, so denying 'the specificity of parties, unions, state agencies and the multiplicity of other organisations and movements that constitute the field of political struggle' (Hindess, 1981: 196).

A related consequence of Goldthorpe's approach, however, and one which is central to our own concern with his proclaimed commitment to an action perspective, is that in identifying the issues of class formation and class action with 'shared beliefs, attitudes and sentiments' or social relations with 'kin, friends, [and] leisure associates', he is neglecting the crucial arenas of action, of struggle or resistance, which are admitted as being his prime interest. The issue here is very similar to that which arose in relation to the Luton study. To identify those attitudes and sentiments which arise out of the experience of mobility is in no sense to identify the mainsprings of class action or political struggle, the organizational and ideological contexts of which exert their own independent effects and are not reducible to prior attitudes. Such effects are situational in the sense which Goldthorpe rejected on a pragmatic basis in his attack on phenomenology.

One of the theoretical penalties of eliminating the sites of class or political action from his analysis is that Goldthorpe is forced to make a link between mobility, class formation and action which ends up looking increasingly like a reductionist single-factor theory. The logic of Goldthorpe's argument is as follows: class action arises out of the level of solidaristic class formation. However, solidarity in Goldthorpe's usage is reduced to 'homogeneity of origins', i.e. it is an outcome of the pattern of mobility. The pattern of mobility in (low) and out (high) of the working class in post-war Britain left a residual, stable, mature working class of 'hereditary proletarians', a solidary class, but one which evinced no 'overt and widespread resentment on account of their immobility' (1980a: 266), largely because the real level of inequality had a 'low social visibility'. The roots of class action are seen by Goldthorpe as anchored in 'homogeneity', which itself is a product of the pattern of mobility. Each element in the patterning of mobility is interrogated to determine its bearing on class formation and action.

The 'wide basis of recruitment to the service class', for example, is indicative of a very low degree of homogeneity (*ibid*.: 43). In particular, those individuals who have experienced long-range mobility from the working class are seen to be likely to maintain cross-class ties and to establish segmentary kinship relations, so posing problems of variant lifestyles and cultural heterogeneity within that class (*ibid*.: 147–74). At the same time the expansion of 'service-class' positions rendered 'strategies of exclusion... less necessary and less viable' (*ibid*.: 59), as well as creating 'favourable conditions for intergenerational stability', for having once obtained a 'service-class' niche, downward mobility is experienced by very few:

> ...there is no sign of any falling off in the capacity of its members to transmit social advantage to their offspring [given their established positions within bureaucratic structures]; and consequently, even while expanding, the service class has tended, so to speak, to 'solidify' in the sense that families have become less likely to be detached from it from one generation to the next. (*ibid*.: 256)

The implication is that, while collective action or class strategies such as professionalization are unnecessary and less viable (this without recourse to any analysis of the assumed decline of such processes), the action potential of the service class is to be explained either as a product of the unexamined authority structure of bureaucratic positions or the mobility experiences of individuals and families. The ideological tendencies of classes are read off from lifestyles (*ibid*.: 175–216), while the political capacities of classes are assessed in terms of the heterogeneity or homogeneity of social origins. The action potential of the working class is assessed entirely on the basis of the mobility experience.

> ...for those who fail to achieve mobility out of the working class, the goals that remain to be pursued—essentially the improvement of working and living standards within the context of wage-labour—are ones to which individual initiative can be only of secondary importance and which must by their nature be primarily achieved on a collective basis: that is, through participation in general economic advance *and* through organized action in pursuit of group and class interests. (*ibid*.: 267–8)

However, and again in line with the Luton conclusions, it is argued that this impetus to collective action deriving from the mobility experience (or lack of it) will be of a largely 'instrumental kind which centres on the wage-bargain' (*ibid.*: 267). Such conclusions are reached without consideration of any organizational, political or industrial contexts of action, but purely on the basis of attitudinal responses to non-mobility. Class action, thereby is conceived of as an individual response, a procedure which at the very least ignores the possibility of a disparity between the expression of individual goals and the resultant political consequences of such collective action, but also, significantly, confuses history with the intergenerational experience of mobility—the entire history of post-war Britain fails to raise even a ripple in the pool of class experience—and subordinates the complexities of structured class action to a single determinant: mobility. Goldthorpe's overall argument in the text slides inexorably from a claim that mobility must be seen to have some significance for class action to a position in which, by default, mobility takes on the role of prime cause. Once we link this with Goldthorpe's attendant claim that mobility-induced class conflict is central to social change, then we are close to straightforward prime-factor theory, in which action is assumed to be reducible to mobility experience.

Once again the claim by Goldthorpe to be primarily concerned with action is more observable in his rhetoric and his ideological interest than in his analysis. The site of action in the political sphere is squeezed out of the analysis by the assumption that the mobility experience as expressed in shared attitudes and sentiments will allow us to read off the implications for action. The existence of such capacities for action is not equivalent to the ways in which human agents act in a variety of organizational, political or historical contexts. Nor is it possible to argue that in the social formation of collectivities, whether of a class character or not, it can be assumed that these are constructed on the basis of a single factor, such as the experience of mobility.

CONCLUSION

This necessarily selective consideration of Goldthorpe's work suggests that it is possible to identify a continuity, a career commitment rooted in his ideological 'interest' in social openness and individual choice. The translation of this 'exogenous' interest into a sociological practice has involved Goldthorpe in generating a multi-directed critique of a variety of forms of determinism—functionalism, futurology and evolutionism, among others. Coincidentally, he has been a proselytizer for a social action approach as the only visible alternative to the inadequacies of individualism and holism.

Unfortunately, nowhere in the corpus of the work is it possible to find an adequate elaboration of what the social action perspective entails—its theoretical principles, its methodological implications or its research procedures. Consequently, Goldthorpe fails to articulate the relationship between what remains an ideological interest and its 'scientific' expression. It is a commitment which remains largely assertive, as in the case of the study of nineteenth century policy. As a form of social analysis it surfaces as a *post hoc* interpretive gloss on data, as in the Luton study. Finally, it exhibits the tendency to share elements equally with the objects of Goldthorpe's critique, such as evolutionary theory. In Goldthorpe's version the call to 'action' remains rhetorical. It begins and ends as an ideological interest.

Interchange

MAYER REPLIES TO JOHNSON

Although the title and introduction of Terry Johnson's critique of Goldthorpe raise the problems of both 'ideology' and 'action', he concentrates almost exclusively on a single issue: the way in which social action is treated by Goldthorpe both theoretically and empirically. By connecting the problem of action with the issue of ideological positions, Johnson seems to imply that certain methodological or theoretical practices have necessary connections with political or ideological orientations. If, as he tries to show, Goldthorpe does not succeed in transforming his action theory sufficiently into research practice, then Goldthorpe—Johnson seems to suggest—can also not be the proper socialist he claims to be.

The idea that methodology indicates ideology has for a long time been widespread in sociology. Mobility researchers are seen as market liberals, quantitative sociologists as conservatives, phenomenologists as progressives, etc. The so-called *Methodenstreit* in German sociology has greatly fostered such beliefs. However, the longer history of science and the shorter history of sociology should make us very cautious about drawing such inferences about the relation between political preferences and methodological positions. Self-styled progressives in sociology have shifted from system analysis within Marxist theory to hermeneutic approaches. And students of sociology should become very reflective if they realize that those who preached 'German' physics against 'Jewish' physics in the 1920s and 1930s used very similar arguments to those qualitative methodologists now use against quantitative researchers (Heilbron, 1986: 65, 114–15): that it is non-intuitive, too formal, too mathematical and removed from the real and directly observable processes in nature.

Since Johnson himself deals largely with the problem of 'action' in Goldthorpe's sociology, I also want mainly to comment on his arguments in this regard. Johnson's main thesis is that Goldthorpe professes to be an action theorist, but fails to employ a research methodology which would be adequate to such a theoretical position. Johnson states his main thesis as follows:

> What I will suggest is that, while the central values of 'openness' and 'freedom' are expressed through a sociological commitment to an 'action perspective', this commitment is asserted and reasserted without becoming effectively represented in the sociological work. It appears neither as an elaborated theoretical position, nor as an analytical concept, nor as a set of research tools. It is, therefore, rendered assertive in theory, *ad hoc* in analysis, and *post hoc* in research.

As my own comment shows, I would concede that Johnson has a point here.

Certainly, in Goldthorpe's mobility studies the relationships between degrees of class heterogeneity due to intergenerational mobility and class action are postulated theoretically rather than tested empirically. So far I would go along with Johnson. But Johnson beats his point to death in a very redundant and, in my view, erroneous manner. First, I fail utterly to see the legitimacy of the criticism directed against the *Affluent Worker* studies. To my mind Goldthorpe and his associates in these studies not only developed their theory as an action theory in a rarely found diligent manner, but also used their material in a very adequate manner to elucidate the 'vocabulary of motives' of the Luton workers. Johnson fails to demonstrate how the alternative research strategies he has in mind—obviously some kind of conversation analysis—would be superior both for the discovery and the test of the orientations of action.

More importantly, in regard to the mobility studies Johnson fails to make clear how he would go about bringing the micro level of individual action and orientations together empirically with macro-sociological patterns of relations and structures within the same study. I have dealt with this problem in my own comment. I know what I am talking about since I have carried out extensive (and separate) studies both on the qualitative aspects of images of society and mobility orientations (Mayer, 1975) and on the quantitative aspects of macro-structures of social mobility (Mayer, 1977). I think that Goldthorpe has done the proper things. In his micro-level studies he has kept a strong macro-sociological theoretical frame of reference and in his macro-sociological quantitative studies he has adhered theoretically to an action perspective. It is important to note here that proper adherence to a basic framework of social action does not mean imputing individual motives to objective measures of individual behaviour. The Oxford mobility project rightly started with a critique of the US tradition of status attainment studies with their model of the person with an ethos of upward mobility.

Why does Johnson become so confused about the connection between Goldthorpe's action perspective and what he thinks to be proper hermeneutic research procedures? It seems that Johnson has no notion of the distinction between a general and a differential sociology. We all agree—as he reiterates—that social actors are always communicating, negotiating and symbol-exchanging. This is a general condition of social life. From this universal fact, however, it does not follow that, in the analysis of market exchange, industrial action or patterns of intergenerational mobility, etc., we have to collect and analyze pieces of communication. Indeed, as Pareto, psychoanalysts and many others would agree, asking people about their motives can be highly misleading as to real causes. Or, proceeding, as Goldthorpe does, from the general assumption that the degree of inequality of opportunities may be subject to national differences in industrial development or social policies, it seems to me quite proper first to establish cross-national differences between, say, Britain and West Germany before one makes an investigation of party programmes and governmental action in the two countries. When we then find that differences in the institutions of academic training and in occupational training account for differences in mobility patterns, we can easily identify the actors and action arenas responsible. In this case, as so often, one has to go back a century or more to trace the origins of institutional differences. Among other things, one has to look at how the multitude of German dukes and princes tried to establish their sovereignty over their territories after the Thirty Years War by creating a civil service not drawn from the nobility but trained at universities. One has to look also at the unsuccessful struggles to liberate crafts during the nineteenth century. To suggest that in order to be faithful to an action perspective it is necessary to conduct open qualitative interviews with contemporary Germans and Britons is utter nonsense.

JOHNSON REPLIES TO MAYER

It has often been suggested that the pressures of professorial patronage in German academic life are conducive to the cult of personality; that scholarly relations conducted in the journals reek of both personal attachment and bitterness. Karl Ulrich Mayer's celebration of John Goldthorpe may not be explained as stemming from such a tradition, but it is noteworthy for the fact that the author finds it difficult to separate the work from the man. One comes away from reading the piece with the impression that Goldthorpe has imposed himself as a doyen of sociology by sheer force of personality and persistence: the common-room Margaret Thatcher; the Bjorn Borg of the academic baseline. For Mayer of the sporting metaphor, it is not the game that counts, but the way that Goldthorpe plays it.

This focus on the authorial subject does, however, provide Mayer with a neat rhetorical device distancing him from any necessary identification with the conclusions of Goldthorpe's work. In focusing on authorial qualities he avoids a commitment to the message. For example, in expounding on Goldthorpe's brilliance as a rhetorician—culturally rooted, it is claimed, in Oxford college coffee-breaks and communal meals—Mayer speaks of an 'intellectual hero' who has invented his own 'mode of discourse'. However, the absurdity of such an inflated claim is neatly deflated by the proffered example of such skill. The rhetorical skills of Goldthorpe lie in the fact that he has persuasively argued a contradictory case to that of Kern and Schumann regarding the existence of common worker consciousness, on the basis of near-identical data. While lauding the skill necessary to carry out such a feat, Mayer keeps his own counsel on the question of validity and further distances himself by adding the rider: '...communicative efficacy and the impressiveness of the speaker and writer may be greater than the truth value of the propositions advanced and empirically substantiated'. What Mayer actually thinks of the man is clear, what he thinks of the validity of the work is not. Even the naïve reader may be forced to seek a subtext where all is not sweetness and light.

It is fruitless to speculate why Mayer should have dredged from his memories of strolls in the quad with J.G. the metaphor of the tennis match as characterizing the celebrant's image of society. Is Mayer being ironical when he suggests that the image presented is of a society as riven with 'competition', 'struggle', 'conflict' and 'fight'? It may well be that for Mayer tennis does conjure up the bullish Boris Becker. However, in the all-England scene the cultural baggage of tennis metaphor is rather different. The irony of the metaphor arises out of the fact that tennis is a game for individual heroes rather than a collective team effort. In football the role of the social actor is more realistically difficult to disentangle from the web of interaction and rule structure. The simplistic effects of the tennis analogy, observed in Goldthorpe's work, are alluded to by Mayer himself when he identifies its implications for Goldthorpe's analysis of the class structure.

In particular, Mayer suggests that in the mobility studies Goldthorpe vainly attempts to bridge the divide between 'the actor-arena and the non-intentional process world' by claiming that the collective class actor can be induced from the effects of individual mobility on the composition of social classes. This, Mayer argues, is 'probably the weakest spot' in Goldthorpe's analysis: '...it is very hard to demonstrate that class composition (by class of origin) is important for class organization and class conflict'. Mayer, in effect, makes the very same point with recourse to Luhmann as I have in my own contribution with recourse to Hindess. That Mayer fails to pursue the point is a product of the personalized approach, concluding that if Goldthorpe has failed to achieve a satisfactory bridging of the 'macro-micro' divide, then it is probably not possible.

That Mayer's article is replete with such penetrating backhand(ed) compliment volleys suggests a personal ambivalence toward the hero. Maybe what we are glimpsing here is a subtext of family squabbles, surfacing above the layers of personalized praise. Like the modern marriage counsellor, I feel as though I should let them talk their problems through. We counsellors have heard versions of Mayer's underlying plaint so often: 'He's a wonderful man, but he's hell to live with'.

Part Three: Conclusion

23. A Response

JOHN H. GOLDTHORPE

INTRODUCTION

When the idea of this volume was first suggested to me by Jon Clark I was, of course, flattered but at the same time felt some misgivings. I was far from sure that it would be possible to recruit a sufficient number of suitable and genuinely willing contributors. The sociological community to which I belong—and which my inclusion in the series was intended to represent—is one of persons whose primary commitment is to sustained, systematic empirical research, usually organized on a team basis. Such sociologists live under severe time pressure. It is not only that their research is in its nature highly time-consuming; it has also to be conducted according to schedules that must meet the requirements and exigencies of various other parties—research institutions, funding bodies, fieldwork agencies, data processing services, etc. Furthermore, this is not a community whose members are likely to have much sympathy with a conception of sociology structured in terms of 'gurus' and 'schools'; their subculture is one favouring intellectual independence—indeed, irreverence—and puts the emphasis firmly on what is being said rather than on who is saying it. I feared, therefore, that the editors would be unable to induce enough of these sociologists to take time out from the research activities that would be their first and, as always, pressing priority in order to appear on the 'pro' or 'con' side of a collection of essays devoted to the work of a particular individual, and especially not if he were to be labelled as a 'master-mind'.

In the event such doubts turned out, for better or for worse, to be unfounded; and the editors in due course provided me with an impressive list of those who had agreed to participate. I was indeed gratified, but must confess that at this stage I was also aware of one set of misgivings being succeeded by another. On studying the list, it was borne in on me that while the 'cons' were a body who could certainly be relied upon to give a good account of themselves, the 'pros' represented, from my point of view, a rather less predictable force. They were, to be sure, largely collaborators, colleagues and former students, and indeed all dear friends. But within the subculture to which I have referred these are precisely the kinds of people with whom one gets into arguments, and I noted that with four out of my ten proposed defenders I had, in fact, engaged in public dispute. The famous remark of the Duke of Wellington on reviewing his troops came inevitably to mind: 'I do not know what they do to the enemy but, by God, they frighten me!'

In this last respect, I have to say, my apprehensions have proved to be not entirely groundless. Nonetheless, now that I have had the opportunity to read all the essays, 'pros' and 'cons' alike, my paramount feeling is one of deep appreciation. I must congratulate the editors on their success in getting the collection together in accordance, more or less, with their initial plans; and I most sincerely thank the contributors for the efforts they have devoted to the preparation of their essays which in some cases I know—indeed, have been forcefully informed—caused no little disruption to the real business of their lives. I have an obligation to respond to their commentaries with a similar seriousness of purpose, and this I seek to do in the pages that follow.

After some consideration, I have decided not to deal with each essay or exchange separately. I hope that I may do better justice to contributors, and at the same time produce a less repetitious and more coherent response, if I proceed, rather, by discussing together issues which arise in the foregoing chapters in several different contexts. To begin with, I will take up issues of a broad methodological character and then turn to more specific substantive ones. In regard to the former I find here the legitimation for setting out my position in a more explicit way than I have hitherto attempted, on account of a belief—which I now see may have been too naïve—that a methodological stance is best demonstrated in practice rather than through programmatic statements. In regard to the latter I will take the opportunity of re-examining, and of variously reaffirming and revising, my views in the light both of contributors' criticisms and of my own further research and reflection. Two further points should be noted. First, where I believe a critical point made by one contributor has been adequately answered by another, I have not returned to it. Second, in attempting to preserve the continuity of this response, I have had to relegate certain issues of importance to the notes, where, however, I have treated them at some length.

SOCIOLOGY AND POLITICS

The innocent reader of the preceding chapters could well be forgiven for feeling some uncertainty as to the true nature of my political beliefs and commitments. I am represented as one who has continued to advocate left-wing socialist policies in the face of clear evidence that they have little electoral appeal—but also as a radical whose scepticism may become excessive; as a persistent critic of Marxists—yet as a sociologist who cannot free himself from *marxisant* assumptions and expectations; as a visionary who must embrace either revolutionary practice or rational comprehensive planning—yet as an academic whose acceptance of the fact-value dichotomy lends support to the 'hegemonic project' of neo-liberalism. It might therefore prove helpful if I begin this section with an outline of my political views or, better, of their development over the last forty years or so. This should, however, be seen as subordinate to what is here my main concern: that is, the relationship between sociology and politics, not at the level of individual biography but, rather, as different kinds of intellectual and practical enterprise.

I grew up, in the late 1930s and 1940s, in a South Yorkshire mining village. My father was a colliery clerk, the son of a miner who became a colliery deputy; and my mother, a dressmaker before marriage, was the daughter of a local farmer who was also a quarryman and builder. Their politics, which were the politics of their parents and which I in turn inherited, could perhaps be described as those of Tory radicalism; but they were in effect the rather diffuse expression of an underlying set of more clearly defined moral beliefs and social attitudes that owed much to local traditions of Low Church Anglicanism. Of central importance was the conviction that individuals should assume responsibility for their own actions and thence for their own and their family's welfare—reinforced by a horror of what would now be called 'dependency'. However, such 'rugged individualism' did not preclude support for trade unions (my father joined the National Union of Mineworkers) or for cooperative societies—provided that these were understood as forms of self-help and not as vehicles of socialism; and it was also the source of frequent critical comment directed against all those who sought to make their way in the world through nepotism, 'connections' and sycophancy rather than through the exercise of their own abilities.

I was first led to question my parents' views during my sixth-form years. I came increasingly to reflect on the fact that at one educational branching-point after another—the 11-plus exam, the minimum school leaving age, sixth-form entry, university application—I had parted company with so many of my friends, including ones whose academic records were quite comparable to my own, as, out of often complex mixtures of choice and constraint, they had taken the educationally 'less eligible' paths. It was, I believe, chiefly as a result of the unease and puzzlement that I felt in this respect that when, as a history undergraduate, I was first exposed to the serious discussion of socialist ideas, I found more in them to attract me than I had expected. In particular, arguments in Tawney's *Equality* (1938) proved compelling. For a while I wished to retain (as I would still do) the value that my parents set on individual responsibility, my reading of history was leading me to an ever-greater awareness of the differences that could exist in the conditions—material, social and cultural—under which individuals lived, and which made the exercise of responsible choice a very different matter from one case to another.

After graduating from University College London in 1956, I went to the London School of Economics to study sociology, a move which had itself much more to do with my intellectual than my political development. However, during my year at the LSE my shift towards an acceptance of some kind of democratic socialism continued. The work of David Glass and his associates on social mobility and educational attainment (Glass, 1954), to which I was of course introduced, was one major influence. Apart from helping me make sense of my own experience, it provided, as I had occasion much later to point out (1987a: 21–3), direct and forceful empirical backing for Tawney's central contention that talk of equality of opportunity was hollow without a matching concern for equality of condition. But also important was my discovery of T. H. Marshall's *Citizenship and Social Class*

(1947), what I learnt in seminars about the work of Richard Titmuss and his group on social welfare (cf. Titmuss, 1958), and then my reading of C. A. R. Crosland's recently published *The Future of Socialism* (1956).

This last book came to represent the main focus of my political concerns for almost the next twenty years. I was entirely convinced (and so remain) by Crosland's 'revisionism' insofar as this related to the priorities of socialist politics: that is, by his argument that questions of the ownership and control of the means of production should be seen as subordinate to those of social equality, and that the key objective of a social democratic government should be to use fiscal, educational and a range of social policies in order to promote greater equality—in the interests of social justice and efficiency alike. However, I remained quite *un*convinced by the new electoral strategy that Crosland wished the British Labour Party to adopt, and that he urged more strongly following the Party's defeat in 1959; namely, that in order to gain the expanding 'middle ground' of British politics, Labour should cease to represent itself as a 'class' party, and should avoid formulating issues and policies in class terms or attempting to mobilize opinion on a class basis. Such a strategy was presented as simply that which sociological and political realism dictated. But this, I believed, concealed the fact that it was ideologically motivated, under the influence of what might be described as American 'cold war' liberalism (cf. Goldthorpe, 1979), and, moreover, was sociologically and politically mistaken.

My position was thus already in the 1960s somewhat unusual, and by the end of the decade it had become still more so with the post-1968 resurgence of new forms of Marxism, in left politics and sociology alike. I could now read both *Encounter* and the *New Left Review* with equal disagreement, and often distaste. While sharing in the disillusionment of the 'new' New Left with what had been achieved, or even attempted, by the Wilson administrations (1964–66, 1966–70), I found its own exhaustive analyses of 'the present crisis' no more convincing than the very sketchy accounts of the actual policies that it would favour or of the nature of the socialist society towards which these policies would supposedly lead. In particular, I objected to the apparent assumption that issues of social inequality were specifically ones of capitalism, and that 'come the revolution' they would, in some unexplained way, simply disappear.

By the 1970s, therefore, I was, and I have since remained, essentially 'homeless' so far as the British political scene is concerned. I retain the Croslandite view (even though the Labour Party itself would now seem uneasy with it) that the primary objective of socialist politics within a liberal capitalist society must be the creation of greater social equality—of both condition and opportunity together. But I would further hold, as against most non-Marxist opinion on the left, that socialist politics with this objective must, if they are to have any chance of success, remain in some sense class politics; that is, must rest on an awareness of class identities and interests and on the mobilization of class-based support. In my view it is naïve to suppose that democratic socialism is likely to prevail simply on the basis of some 'universal' moral appeal.

To be sure, I believe that arguments for egalitarian policies which have moral force can, and should, be deployed: to give but one example, the argument that especially 'inequalities before the market' (cf. Phelps Brown, 1977)—that is, those experienced by individuals within their families of origin and during their educational careers—not only operate as a systematic restriction on the supply side of the labour market, thus entailing massive distortions and loss of talent to society, but at the same time impose on many men and women gross limitations on their capacity to develop their human potential. Nonetheless, it needs to be recognized, first, that social inequality in its most pervasive and damaging forms is grounded in class; and, second, that those who hold superior class positions are unlikely to yield up the relative advantage and power that they thus enjoy in response to argument alone. Rather, a reduction in inequality will only be achieved through action on the part of those in less favoured positions that is politically directed towards this end—whether taken individually through the ballot box or collectively through representative organizations—and action that must therefore be expected to involve class politics and indeed class conflict in some form or other.[1]

The foregoing may perhaps help explain some of the wide variation that is apparent in perceptions of my political stance. Moreover, it will, I hope, serve as useful background in general and, more specifically, as I turn now to the issues concerning the relationship between sociology and politics that have been taken up when attention shifts, as Johnson would have it (p. 375), from the teller to the tale.

The basic question that arises here seems to me that of how far and in what ways sociology (or social science more generally) and politics are to be viewed as interdependent or independent pursuits. As regards their interdependence, it will already be evident that I would acknowledge—and without regret—the influence that sociology, as an academic discipline, may exert in forming political orientations. It must be no less clear that I would also recognize the part that political concerns may play—I believe quite legitimately—in determining the problems that sociologists choose to address, and even the hypotheses that they favour or contest. I would add that I see it as entirely proper and desirable that social science should be applied in attempts to promote particular political causes; and further that I find it no accident that in this respect the links between sociology and democratic socialism have been historically close.

However, I would on the other side wish to maintain, first, that political values cannot in any strict sense be *derived* from sociology, no more than from any other social science; and, second, that the choice of sociological problems or hypotheses on the basis of political interests need not compromise scientific procedure. This could be taken as an essentially Weberian position; but it also reflects my attachment to the philosophy of Popper, on which rather frequent comment has been made. Of direct relevance are, on the one hand, Popper's rejection of historicist theories of long-term social change as attempts to endow certain political ideas and beliefs with 'objective' validity—as those destined to be upheld by the course of history; and, on the other, his claim that the scientific status of an argument lies not in the nature of its motivation but rather in its form and, specifically, in its openness to falsification.

How, then, would my critics wish to question or oppose this position? An initial observation is that certain counters that might have been expected appear within the volume in only a limited or muted form. Thus, of those writing from a Marxist standpoint, only Crompton makes an attempt to defend theorizing of the kind I would regard as historicist, and even then, it would seem, rather on the retreat. Many Marxists, she tells us, now no longer adhere to the 'Stalinist' idea of 'iron laws of history', although they would still think it appropriate to judge certain groupings and movements within capitalist society as having greater 'transformative' potential than others (p. 105). What we are not told, however, is the nature of the criteria by which such judgments are made, nor whether they are regarded as being anything more than subjective assessments of probabilities. I would certainly agree that among Marxists today the shift that Crompton describes is quite common; indeed, I remarked upon it some time ago (1979: note 38) with special reference to Raymond Williams and E. P. Thompson. But, as I have also observed (1971) apropos of liberal theorists of industrialism, it is now difficult to present manifestly historicist arguments without losing intellectual credibility. The kinds of formulation that Crompton favours, which have evident similarities to those that led me to charge liberal authors such as Clark Kerr and Daniel Bell with 'crypto-historicism', must still leave doubts, in their incompleteness and ambiguity, as to whether they represent more than merely a tactical withdrawal, in the hope of more propitious times ahead in which the cry might once more be raised that 'history is on our side'.

Again, only one contributor, Kavanagh, gives any indication of wishing to join those who, from positions to the right of my own, have argued that, despite my view that a politically motivated choice of issues does not preclude serious social science, my own work does in fact carry a left-wing bias (e.g. Himsworth, 1984; Saunders, 1989). Kavanagh concludes that my prescriptions for the Labour Party's electoral strategy are so strongly contra-indicated by the evidence that they must 'derive more from ideology than sociology' (p. 182). However, the difference between us here would seem to be essentially one of the selection and interpretation of the results of attitude surveys; and for present purposes I need make only the minimal claim, on the basis of Heath's reply, that my position is certainly no more at variance with the evidence than is Kavanagh's own.[2] It is also pertinent to take up here Heath's objection to Kavanagh assuming that his (Heath's) ideological position—and, one could add, that of Jowell and Curtice also—is the same as mine (see pp. 177, 184–5). I would feel rather safe in asserting that the four of us together cover a non-negligible range of the political spectrum; but this does not prevent us from arriving at very similar conclusions about the relationship between class and political partisanship. What I suspect unites us—and at the same time separates us from Kavanagh—is not ideology but rather our approach to data analysis (see below).

If what could be regarded as standard reactions to my position are not, then, much rehearsed by my present critics, this is, I would say, more than compensated for by at least two lines of surprise attack. Thus, Johnson, an author known for his sympathies with structuralist Marxism (1977), finds an excessive determinism and too grandiose claims for the social sciences in my idea of 'social designing' as a complement to social forecasting (p. 380); while Plant, a fellow democratic socialist, points to the dangers that follow from my reluctance to accept that 'a social and political vision' can be derived from sociology and my refusal, qua sociologist, to 'take on' normative questions directly (p. 265).

To Johnson's critique, I find it hard to reply in any very constructive fashion, since it proceeds more by assertion than argument. I cannot see, and Johnson simply does not explain, *why* social designing as I would understand it (and he represents me quite accurately) *is* then simply 'planning by another name' and, hence, implies 'a level of determinism which is beyond anything to which a futurologist would knowingly admit' (p. 381). It should here be sufficient for me to remark that at the present time some of the most interesting and important attempts at social designing in my sense are those being made by Eastern European social scientists concerned with the question of how best—in terms of both efficiency and social conse-quences—to remodel centrally planned economies by the introduction of market mechanisms. Not only is the social science that they apply non-deterministic, but the questions of whether or not their projects will be allowed to influence policy and, if so, whether or not they will have their intended effects, are themselves only too clearly subject to resolution through political contingencies.

I have then some difficulty in taking seriously Johnson's suggestion that, inspired by my belief in the 'scientific mission' of sociology, I am just one more naïve idealist embarked on the hopeless quest for 'a rational society' (p. 381). However, what I would wish to maintain is that the application of social science can at all events contribute to a *greater* rationality in the fields of both public policy and politics alike: that is, in the formation and implementation of policy and also in devising the strategies that political actors pursue. I would add that over the last two decades or so British sociologists have often sold themselves badly short by promoting conceptions of their subject that would make such a role impossible—a consequence, I would suspect, of so many in the post-1968 generation preferring to flirt with whatever intellectual fashion might cross the English Channel rather than to acquire the basic technical skills of social inquiry (cf. Bulmer, 1989).

If Johnson believes that I claim too much for the social sciences and set too great a store on reason, Plant's objection is more or less the opposite: that I myself sell the social sciences short and unduly curtail the sphere of reason as against that of arbitrary preference. But I would not want to try to escape here by setting off one critic against another. Plant does put forward a very clear and cogent argument, to which an explicit response is due.

In one respect I have no alternative but to plead guilty as charged. I must confess that I *am* a 'subjectivist' so far as values, political or otherwise, are concerned; and that I would not believe, nor indeed wish, that in the last analysis I could account for my support for democratic socialism—rather than, say, neo-liberalism—as being anything other than a matter of commitment. However, there are at least two arguments that I would like to advance in mitigation: that is, by way of showing that my position is not so damaging to the democratic socialist case, nor as encouraging to the neo-liberal one, as Plant might fear.

First, while I do not believe that values 'exist' in any sense such that they might be 'revealed' or 'demonstrated' by social science, and thus endow, say, a theory of distributional justice with objective validity, I do believe that such normative theories can, and should, be *constructed*. They can be developed and expressed—or as his penchant for plosives would of course lead Labour's Deputy Leader Mr Hattersley to say, 'provided and popularized'—so that in certain societies over certain periods they hold sufficient sway to exert a political effect. Thus, I do not think that I am at all constrained to accept the neo-liberal contention that the moral diversity of modern societies makes any idea of consensus on distributional issues impossible, and that this is demonstrated by the failure of attempts at a 'social contract' in Britain in the 1970s. For I can point to a case such as that of Sweden where a larger measure of distributional consensus has for some time been established—as a political accomplishment and indeed as an element in an impressive piece of 'social designing'—and has helped provide the basis, most obviously via the solidaristic wages policy, for a form of political economy that stands as a challenging alternative to the neo-liberal model.

Second, the fact that I would be unwilling to give the social scientist any ultimate privilege in regard to the discussion of value questions does not mean that I regard such questions as entirely unarguable. Rather, I believe, as I have already sought to illustrate, that they can and should be argued, and that sociologists have here an important part to play. Thus, in the essay Plant cites (Goldthorpe, 1978), I make the case for trying to realize some conception of social justice by pointing to the consequences which, as a sociologist, I would see as following from the distribution of power and advantage remaining essentially *un*principled. Plant himself seems to be doing something very similar in indicating the practical difficulties that neo-liberals will themselves face in seeking to restrict state welfare to the provision of 'minimum standards' without some degree of consensus on norms defining the minimum. Note, however, that in these cases it would still be open for someone to accept the sociological arguments in full, and yet still to opt for the situation that would prevail where no normative theory could gain acceptance. All that one can seek to do *qua* sociologist is to make this option the more difficult to take, according to criteria of consistency, reasonableness and credibility at large.

In sum, I would say that, from our shared political standpoint, Plant and I are in entire agreement about 'what is to be done'—but that, from our opposing philosophical standpoints, we will probably have to describe it in different ways.

CONCEPTS AND HYPOTHESES

It seems often to be supposed that it is political differences that are at the bottom of most controversies among sociologists. However, while a good number of the controversies in which I have myself been involved have had a political aspect, I have found that disagreement—and often at the same time confusion—has more often arisen over concepts and conceptual approaches. Several controversies of this latter kind not surprisingly spill over into this volume, notably in regard to questions of class; and in taking them up in this section, I shall try to suggest how in conducting such controversies we might proceed to better advantage. I shall follow this with some remarks on the empirical testing of hypotheses that are likewise directed towards the goal not of eliminating, but rather of improving the quality of sociological disputes.

It may be useful to make at the outset the distinction between the advancing of a particular concept (or conceptual approach) as a *nominal* proposition and the advancing of a hypothesis as a *real* proposition. In the former case, it might be said, one is proposing that the world should be *viewed* in a certain way; in the latter, that it *is* a certain way. It is with hypotheses that we must be ultimately concerned; but hypotheses are dependent upon concepts in that some conceptual scheme is necessary before hypotheses can be formulated and, moreover, before relevant observations can be made (cf. Popper, 1976).

How then are we to evaluate concepts? Since concepts are tools, they must be judged essentially in terms of their utility. What we should ask are questions such as how well particular concepts help us to set out substantive problems that are of interest to us, and whether they lead us to pose rewarding questions and to collect illuminating information relevant to these problems. Thus the first point I wish to make is that some degree of 'conceptual pluralism' has surely to be accepted. Different conceptual approaches may be needed to address different kinds of problem, and while conceptual unification is in principle desirable, there is no point in seeking it by *fiat*.

In this connection Kelley's paper provides a good illustration of the kind of attitude and argument which is, in my view, futile and to be avoided. Kelley seeks to represent my approach to mobility research, which adopts the conceptual context of a class structure, as being not simply an alternative to the 'status attainment' tradition established by the work of Blau and Duncan but, rather, a 'new paradigm', specifically advanced with the intention of negating and superseding the old one. I was, Kelley writes, 'from the beginning, a stern critic, arguing against Blau and Duncan and in favour of a new approach. This is the background in which Goldthorpe's work should be set ...' (p. 320). Kelley goes on to claim that the new paradigm has failed, and that one important reason for this is its disregard for the idea of a status hierarchy of occupations, which must be central to any study of social mobility.

Now it is true that, along with not a few others, I had criticisms to make of Blau and Duncan, and of work in the 'status attainment' tradition generally, including Kelley's own. But I took up quite specific matters—such as the dubious definition and uncertain measurement of status, the inadequate treatment of structural constraints on 'attainment', and what seemed to me various slanted assumptions and interpretations deriving from the ideological commitments of American liberalism that I had criticized more generally elsewhere (cf. the papers by Gallie and Müller in this volume). Thus, while my arguments were, I hope, forceful, they did not aim at, nor did they entail, rejection of the status attainment approach as such. Indeed, in a paper that Kelley simply fails to mention (1984d), I sought to show how the alternatives of viewing mobility either within the conceptual context of a status hierarchy or within that of a class structure have actually been present in mobility research from its origins, and are taken up by investigators with interests in *different kinds of problem*. I explicitly concluded that the 'potential of [status attainment] research cannot be regarded as exhausted' (*ibid*.: 7).[3] However, what from this same pluralist standpoint I *would*, most certainly, reject is any attempt—such as that Kelley himself makes—at the 'pre-emptive definition' of what *the* problems, and hence *the* conceptual approach and methodology, of a field of research should be.

'We study social mobility', Kelley asserts, 'in order to understand stratification, hierarchy and their links across generations. So a ranking of occupations from high status to low is essential...' (p. 325); who gets the good jobs and who the bad within this hierarchy is the 'essence of the matter' (p. 334). To which one can only reply that this may be true for Kelley, but not necessarily for other people. If, as I pointed out in the paper that Kelley ignores, one's interests do lie in the questions of 'who gets ahead—and why', then a hierarchical perspective and a resort to the analytical methods pioneered by Blau and Duncan may well be found appropriate. But, as I also argued—and the papers by Müller and Westergaard remove any need for rehearsal here—various other questions which take their sense only from a class structural perspective have been, are and will continue to be no less central to mobility research, whether Kelley likes it or not.

However, while it would seem merely foolish to deny that different interests and substantive problems will lead to the adoption of different conceptual approaches, this does *not* mean that such approaches must, under all circumstances, be regarded as immune to assessment and comparative evaluation. Although concepts cannot, as purely nominal propositions, be set against data and then discussed as 'true' or 'false', they do remain in certain respects open to criticism of an empirically based kind. When applied to particular bodies of data, concepts have more or less determinate consequences so far as empirical 'results' are concerned. We can then, for purposes of evaluation, require two things: first, that, as tools, concepts should always be judged in terms of their empirical consequences—whatever other criteria it might also seem appropriate to invoke; and second, that they should be judged in the light of *all* the empirical results that are found to follow from their application, and not just those that may give their proponents greatest satisfaction. Several debates pursued in this volume concerning the conceptualization of class provide good opportunities for illustration of these points.

To begin with, I may take Ahrne's critique of the class schema which over the last decade or so I have developed with various collaborators, and his evident preference for the alternative conceptual approach, or in fact approaches—of an explicitly Marxist inspiration—that are to be found in the work of Erik Olin Wright (1978, 1985). Ahrne's main objection is that my schema is too 'common-sensical' and lacks a 'rigorous theoretical logic' (p. 69). I believe that, as the contributions by Marshall and by Müller indicate, this claim is exaggerated and neglects a good deal of what I have written, even though this may not have been explicitly labelled 'theory'.[4] However, this is not the issue on which I wish here to concentrate. Rather, I would want to agree with Ahrne that it is desirable that any such schema should possess as clear and coherent a theoretical rationale as possible—but then to add that, no matter what degree of theoretical refinement may be attained, the question of performance in application must still be seen as one of much greater importance than he would appear prepared to recognize.

Ahrne claims that my schema 'may work for certain mobility studies' but clearly thinks it of far less value so far as the main ambition of class analysis is concerned: namely, 'to connect scientifically the economic and social macro-structure with the everyday realities of human life' (p. 65). Leaving aside the point that I do not see how questions of class mobility could themselves be other than central to such a programme, I would argue that it is precisely in making the kinds of connection to which Ahrne refers that my class schema can claim the advantage over either of those proposed by Wright: that is, it will 'work' better in more clearly showing up variation in social attitudes and action that are of evident interest to class analysts—for example, in political partisanship, as Marshall, Newby *et al.* (1988: 236) have demonstrated. To say this is not to be excessively immodest; for the Wright schemata would seem to offer rather poor competition. Thus, so far as the analysis of British data on both political partisanship and class identification is concerned, they appear to compare unfavourably even with the much (and deservedly) maligned Registrar-General's 'Social Classes' (Marshall, 1988a).

It is open to Ahrne and others who favour the Wright approach to stick to their theoretical guns, and to argue that if patterns of social attitudes and action should turn out to be only rather weakly associated with class position, according to their conceptualization, then this must mean that in modern societies class has ceased to be a major influence on 'the everyday realities of human life'. Something like this conclusion would seem to be contemplated by the Norwegian team within the comparative class structure project that Wright has organized (Colbjørnson *et al.*, 1987). However, if other investigators using different conceptual approaches continue to find marked class effects, this position would appear an uncomfortable one—and not least for Marxists. It is obviously open to the comment that what has been discovered is not something new in social reality, but rather something wrong in the way in which this reality is being viewed. In other words, while concepts cannot be shown empirically to be 'false', the empirical results of their application can be a cause of some embarrassment.

As a second source of illustration, I turn to the debate on the class position of women, as resumed in this volume by Dex's contribution. Dex maintains that 'while Goldthorpe has argued for the debate to take place on empirical (or research) grounds, the main issues which separate Goldthorpe and his critics are conceptual' (p. 150). So they may be. But I would reply that empirical results are still highly relevant to their discussion, and are a good deal more consequential than Dex seems ready to allow in urging the potential value of different approaches within this area and in suggesting that I am too exclusive.

Thus, as regards conceptual schemes for the 'joint classification' of husbands and wives (see, for example, by Britten and Heath, 1983), which Dex thinks I should take more seriously because of their capacity to display socio-political and socio-cultural variation, I have set out (1983a, 1984c) two empirically based objections. The first is that there are good grounds for believing (Erikson, 1984) that this capacity is in part spurious, since it results from a confounding of class with life-cycle and family composition effects. Here it can be seen *why* it is important that a class schema should have not only an adequate theoretical basis but also one that is adequately operationalized. The second—and for present purposes more directly relevant—objection is that joint classification is bound to generate very high rates of class mobility (and this would still be so even allowing for the kinds of modification that Dex suggests). The point of the argument is not that joint classification should be placed under some kind of conceptual ban; but rather that those who favour this approach should be ready to take on board its empirical implications in full. What will not do is to opt for joint classification because, say, this seems to avoid being sexist and 'takes women's employment into account', and then to refuse to acknowledge that one is thereby committed to a view of present-day society as having far higher levels of class mobility than has hitherto been supposed, and so high in fact as to call the whole programme of class analysis into doubt.

I would make observations of a similar nature as regards the conceptual decision to reject the idea of the conjugal family as being the basic unit of class analysis and to determine the class position of married, as well as of single, women by reference to their own employment. Dex seems to misunderstand why I have analyzed women's intergenerational mobility using this approach. It was not because I wished to give even tacit approval to it, but simply to find out how the empirical results to which it led differed from those obtained via the 'conventional' approach—whether or not operationalized through the 'dominance' method.[5] The main difference is that if one accepts the 'individual' approach, then one has in turn to accept that downward class (as distinct from simply occupational) mobility is far more common than the conventional approach would imply.

For most of those who have advocated the individual approach, this outcome is itself unlikely to raise problems; it will rather be seen as testifying to the superiority of this approach in bringing out more clearly the extent of women's disadvantages (cf. Stanworth, 1984). However, the point I would then want to make is that there are other, probably less congenial, results that must also be accepted—and ones which do *not* follow from the conventional approach: most importantly, perhaps, that the propensity for class-based political partisanship is significantly lower among women than among men and that class identification is far more uncertain. This further difference results from the tendency for married women's partisanship and class identification alike to be more strongly associated with their *husband's* class position than with their own (that is, as determined through their own employment)—a tendency which emerges from empirical research far more consistently and robustly than Dex, or for that matter Payne, appears ready to concede (see, for example, Erikson and Goldthorpe, 1988b: Appendix). Some exponents of the individual approach (e.g. Marshall, Newby *et al.*, 1988: 135–6) have been prepared to face up to this implication, although with the accompaniment of signs of perplexity at the extent of women's 'false consciousness' rather than attempts at explanation. Here again it must be acknowledged that empirical results cannot be used to refute a conceptual choice; but here, too, the suggestion may be made that if only a change of glasses were to be accepted, the social world would be observed with a good deal less difficulty.[6]

So far, then, I have tried to show that a tolerance of conceptual pluralism can be allied with an awareness of possibilities for critical evaluation. If we do not restrict discussion simply to the theoretical—or ideological—antecedents of different conceptual approaches but attend rather to their empirical consequences, we can at least hope to bring out just what is at stake in opting for one rather than another. On this basis, I would suggest, we may expect, if not greater consensus, then at all events less confused and thus perhaps more fruitful disagreement than has so far prevailed in areas such as those to which I have referred.

To conclude this section, I move on from problems of evaluating concepts to those of evaluating hypotheses; that is, the real propositions that concepts are used to express. In this respect it might be supposed that the part to be played by empirical inquiry would need little arguing for: if hypotheses are not simply propositions about how we should look at the world that interests us but rather ones that claim to tell us how it actually is, then they should surely be tested by means of empirical inquiry into that world. However, in British sociology in particular, resistance to this position, stemming from the so-called 'reaction against positivism' of the late 1960s and 1970s, is still rather frequently found. What I refer to here is not a healthy awareness of the fact that hypothesis testing often turns out in practice to be a good deal less decisive and more messy than textbooks on 'scientific method' might suggest (cf. the discussion below of problems in evaluating the 'FJH hypothesis'). It is rather the concern to preserve, by one philosophical resort or another, the primacy of theory over inquiry, and in effect to blur the distinction between concepts and hypotheses, so that, apparently, rival 'interpretations' of the world may co-exist in number without any possibility of rational criticism or adjudication being allowed.

Against this propensity I would maintain that we would do better to see the problem we face as being not primarily philosophical but procedural: that is, the problem of how we can argue coherently and constructively with one another, so that there is at least the chance that our debates may in some sense *progress*. My own commitment to a Popperian 'falsificationist' approach stems from my belief that this offers the best solution available to this problem, despite all practical difficulties and even though I am well aware that, philosophically, falsificationism is far from being unassailable. For purposes of illustration here, I wish to take up Crompton's discussion of the present status of the thesis of continuing 'proletarianization' within modern capitalist societies. (Cf. the very apposite remarks in McRae's contribution on the explication and testing of arguments to the effect that sexual and class inequalities are cognate.)

Crompton, as a supporter of the proletarianization thesis, faces the difficulty that over recent years evidence telling against it has accumulated and, further, that one of its hitherto most resourceful defenders, Wright, has now unequivocally accepted that it is mistaken (Wright and Martin, 1987; cf. also Singelmann and Tienda, 1985).[7] Crompton's response is to embark on what I can only describe as an exercise in damage limitation. Her main resource here is the well-known 'anti-falsificationist' argument that since empirical observation must itself be in some degree theory-dependent, 'it does not always provide a secure base from which to reject theories' (p. 99). At least as presented, one need not be very impressed by this argument even at a philosophical level; but—as Crompton acknowledges in a footnote—my main reply would be that at the level of procedure the problem she raises can be overcome *by leaving it to the proponents of a hypothesis themselves* to decide what evidence, produced in what ways, *they* would accept as being adequate to invalidate it. To this Crompton replies that 'falsificationism is not thereby protected, as the theoretical proponents are at liberty to change their definitions' (p. 107). Indeed they are, and they might thus for ever preserve themselves in a condition of philosophical impregnability; but—and this is for me the important point—at the price of losing all credibility within their scientific community. For it would in this way become apparent enough that their primary concern was to 'save' their position at all costs rather than to cooperate in serious inquiry into its validity.

I would therefore continue to insist that if, as seems to be the case, Crompton still seeks to uphold the proletarianization thesis in some form or other, she should tell us what this is *and* indicate how, in *her* view, it could be appropriately tested through empirical investigation. Apart from anything else, I suspect that it may be only in this way that we shall ever come to a clear understanding of just what it is that she wishes to claim. The alternative is for her to follow Wright's example and to accept that the thesis is dead. Consistently, no doubt, with what Mayer refers to as my 'tennis player' view of the world, I am not in favour of the participants in academic controversy giving in easily. As Popper himself has remarked, it is important that proponents of hypotheses should defend them against attack, so as to ensure that they are not deemed to be false on inadequate grounds: *amour propre* and sheer bloody-mindedness may serve a useful scientific purpose. Nonetheless, it must be recognized that unless some 'rules of the game' are accepted, such as those of falsificationism on the lines I have suggested, then the question must arise of why we should bother to carry out empirical inquiry at all.

DATA AND ANALYSIS

The issues raised in the contributions to this volume which may be placed under the heading of 'Data and Analysis' are not numerous, but they are ones to which I would attach a large importance. As I have already suggested, many sociologists, especially in Britain, have contrived over the last two decades or so to get themselves into positions of considerable uncertainty, not to say difficulty, over the role and significance to be accorded to empirical inquiry; and although there are indications that some of the more bizarre epistemologies adopted during the heady days of the 'reaction against positivism' are now being abandoned, residues of that period persist. Two such residues are, I believe, reflected in criticisms to which I shall here respond: first, a feeling that if empirical work *is* to be undertaken, then this is somehow safer, more authentic, less open to distortions and in general 'less positivistic' if it takes the form of case studies rather than of survey research; and second, a suspicion of the quantitative analysis of data that aspires to any sophistication beyond, say, the calculation of a percentage. At the same time I wish to recognize, and with reference to Kelley's paper in particular, that exponents of quantitative analysis may in some cases take up positions which do unfortunately —because quite unnecessarily—reinforce anti-quantitative prejudices.

As regards data, I wish to return to Crompton's contribution: specifically, to her response to my critique of the use of case studies in evaluating macro-sociological arguments—such as the proletarianization thesis—and the closely related comments that she offers on the micro-sociological foundations of my class schema.

In both these respects Crompton's main contention is that 'random sample surveys of the population at large cannot provide conclusive evidence relating to organizational structures and processes...labour processes *have* substantive realities which cannot be described in their entirety via questions directed at decontextualized individuals' (p. 102). The drift of this argument is a familiar one to survey researchers; and to reply in similarly standard fashion, I would ask for further information about the techniques of data collection employed in case studies, which, while not directed at 'decontextualized individuals', are yet capable of producing 'conclusive evidence' and of describing social phenomena 'in their entirety'. Should one perhaps understand here a hidden reference to the magical method of 'ethnography'?[8]

However, Crompton's argument is largely irrelevant to the central point of my objection to case studies as a basis for addressing macro-sociological questions. This concerns difficulties which arise in drawing general conclusions from the results of such studies which cannot be resolved, as Crompton would have us believe, simply by appeal to 'common-sense notions of representativeness' (p. 101). Thus, as I have repeatedly pointed out—and as Gagliani also emphasizes—the proletarianization thesis has to be understood, and assessed, in terms of *net* effects at the level of the economy or society as a whole. No one, so far as I am aware, has ever sought to argue that *no* deskilling or degrading of work and occupations occurs; such processes would indeed be widely recognized as features of industrial capitalism, evident enough at least since the decline of the handloom weavers. The case of those who have opposed the proletarianization thesis has rather been that overall the deskilling and degrading that occur are offset—and more than offset—by upskilling and upgrading. The issue is therefore one which, in its nature, can be decided *only* at the aggregate, 'macro' level. Whether any particular case study shows degrading or upgrading can then be of little consequence for this issue, no matter how informative it may be in other respects and no matter how much talk may go on about the need to set 'holistic' approaches against the 'granular metaphysic'.

Crompton might still wish to maintain that it is only through certain methods of data collection which require a case study approach that the facts of degrading or upgrading can be established. But even if one were willing to concede this (I would not be), the crucial question would remain of how cases—firms, organizations or whatever—should be selected for study. Here I would argue that, rather than being chosen in ones and twos more or less *ad hoc* as seems usually to happen, it would be necessary for them to be in some way sampled from a theoretically defined universe.

For quite contrary to what Crompton suggests, the sample survey approach is in no way restricted to taking individuals, rather than other entities, as the units of analysis. However, her commitment to 'holism' is perhaps such that she would have as many problems with decontextualized organizations as with decontextualized individuals, and that nothing less than a 'world systems' approach to everything will suffice.

To reinforce her defence of case studies, Crompton further argues that any class schema such as that I have developed—although intended for use in macro-sociological analysis—must in its construction be dependent upon the results of 'micro'-level studies. She also suggests that my own schema has weaknesses which result in part from my reluctance to acknowledge this fact. Now, insofar as the contention is that, in aggregating combinations of occupational groupings and employment statuses to form the classes of the schema, my colleagues and I have ultimately to rely on empirical data about particular jobs, their associated conditions of employment, etc., I can only agree. I would also agree that the schema, as applied to Britain, or to any other nation, will be the more reliable, the more information of this kind that can be assembled. But I would disagree that it is specifically case study data that are crucial. The first requirement must once more be for data that have some claim to relate to the society at large; and Crompton is quite correct in supposing that we have drawn on other data, no matter how detailed they might be, only *faute de mieux*. However, in her comments Crompton again fails to recognize that the collection of data within particular firms or organizations can be combined with the survey approach through such 'cases' being taken as the units in a sampling exercise. In fact, the one study that was perhaps of greatest value in the initial construction of the class schema for Britain was of precisely this design: that by Craig and Wedderburn on the conditions of employment of men in manufacturing industry (Craig, 1969; Wedderburn and Craig, 1974).[9]

In sum, Crompton manages to increase rather than to assuage my concern that the attitudes of many British sociologists towards data collection show undue bias. A greater awareness would seem desirable, on the one hand, of the limitations of the case study approach, at least as usually practised and where macro-sociological issues are at stake; and, on the other, of the full range of possibilities that survey methods can offer.

Turning now to questions of data analysis, I would like to take up remarks made in the contributions of Payne and of Kavanagh. I will comment later on the merits of Payne's general critique of my work on social mobility in Britain and of his 'contrary view'. Here I wish to focus on one particular comment that he makes toward the end of his paper: namely, that the introduction of log-linear modelling into mobility analysis has 'slightly confused' the distinction between absolute and relative mobility rates, and has thus opened up a 'gap of comprehension' between specialists and others, which has in turn 'inevitably been filled' by an acceptance of the conclusions that I myself seek to stress (p. 297). This claim I would then bracket with that of Kavanagh, apropos of the application of log-linear modelling to data on class voting: 'In all the rarified debate over whether we should measure absolute or relative class dealignment, or over the merits of odds ratios, we are in danger of throwing the baby out with the bathwater, overlooking the dramatic decline in Labour support' (p. 178).

Both authors—though Kavanagh especially—present themselves in the guise of the 'plain man': advanced statistical analysis, they imply, may be all very well for those who fancy that kind of thing, but it is in the end peripheral to the really important issues, and may muddle our understanding of, or distract our attention from them. This position, I would hold, is both a mistaken and, so far as the future of the social sciences is concerned, a dangerous one. It is not, in truth, that of the 'plain man' but rather—and even if unintentionally—that of the academic Luddite. The fact is that in regard to the analysis of both mobility rates and class voting alike, log-linear modelling is not now something that one can simply take or leave, depending on whether one regards oneself as a specialist or not. It is quite integral to any worthwhile understanding of just what certain major *substantive* issues are. Rather than such modelling having 'confused' the distinction between absolute and relative mobility rates, it was this technique that first enabled the distinction to be satisfactorily made (and, as will be seen, Payne is not a little vulnerable in talking of confusion in this respect). Likewise, there can be no basis for the suggestion that log-linear modelling of the class-vote relationship in modern Britain encourages one to 'overlook' the decline in Labour support, since the technique not only highlights this decline but, moreover, has been applied primarily in order that the relative importance of different contributory factors to it may be reliably assessed—which could not be done before.

Payne does acknowledge the contribution that log-linear modelling has made to the understanding of social mobility. But Kavanagh is clearly unwilling to recognize any particular advance so far as the analysis of the class-vote relationship is concerned: the new techniques give different results from the old, but one can, apparently, after all the squabbling among the specialists is over, just carry on regardless, with one's previous firm grasp upon the obvious happily undisturbed (cf. Crewe, 1988: 31–2). This will not do. To put the matter shortly: I know of no multivariate analysis of British 'class × vote × election' tables that fails to confirm the conclusion of Heath, Jowell and Curtice (1985) that over time the *net* class-vote relationship changes little and shows no steadily weakening trend. This outcome creates evident problems for Kavanagh who, along with other regular commentators on British electoral politics, such as Butler, Crewe and Rose, has for long pushed the thesis of 'class dealignment' (see e.g. Butler and Kavanagh, 1984: 8). I find it hard to resist the conclusion that what chiefly underlies his lack of enthusiasm for log-linear modelling is not the nature of the technique *per se* but rather the result that it happens to have produced.[10]

If one were to inquire more generally into the reluctance of British sociologists to take quantitative analysis seriously, I suspect that a major factor would prove to be dislike, and indeed disdain, for what is thought of as 'American-style' sociology: that is, a sociology in which problems are effectively determined by methods, and in which the nature of social reality is so conceived as to provide maximum scope for techniques best capable of demonstrating the analyst's statistical virtuosity. This is not, I need scarcely add, an outlook that I share; British sociology would be much improved if more of its representatives did—indeed *could*—read the *American Sociological Review* and the *American Journal of Sociology*. However, I have to admit that when confronted with papers such as Kelley's, I can understand why such an outlook should exist.

Kelley seeks to argue that analyses of social mobility that envisage individuals moving along a series of continuous 'dimensions' of stratification and that apply regression techniques are inherently superior to those that envisage individuals moving between the categories of a classification (or, as he prefers to call it, a typology) and that resort to log-linear modelling. With the former approach mobility can be automatically understood in hierarchical or 'vertical' terms; each 'conceptual variable'—for example, each 'aspect of class'—can be treated separately; and, last but not least, questions of the degree of openness or rigidity of different societies can be determined by a single parameter! But, Kelley emphasizes, with the latter approach, at least as I implement it, none of these desiderata is achieved (pp. 327–31).

One reason why Kelley believes that his preferred methodology is superior is that it makes for better measurement—and this must be at once disputed. Thus Kelley maintains that the measurement of occupational status is one of the 'great strengths' of the Blau-Duncan paradigm: it might better be described as one of the great scandals, though Kelley and others have piously—and conveniently—averted their gaze from the various illogicalities and fudges that can readily be documented.[11] Again, Kelley tells us that the measurement of education has been improved by moving from 'crude categories' to the continuous variable of 'years of schooling' (p. 322). But for many nations which have highly diversified school systems, such a move is actually a backwards one: a categorical variable of 'type of schooling' or type of qualification, even if crude, makes far more sense.[12] In sum, while classification is often a problematic exercise, so too, and certainly to no lesser degree, is the projection of social attributes onto interval scales.

However, the real difficulty in Kelley's position stems from his one-eyed vision of the aims of mobility research on which I have already commented. He obviously finds it hard to appreciate that others may not share his preoccupation with the questions of 'who gets ahead and why?', and may have interests that are not well served by the idea of abstract stratification 'dimensions' over which individuals are distributed attributionally. Thus he cannot conceive that some investigators may find it far more appropriate to think of the distribution of individuals over sets of positions that are *relationally* defined within the social division of labour—or, in other words, to adopt a class structural perspective; and that this may be so because their primary interests lie *not* in individual 'attainment' but, for example, in the effects on mobility rates and patterns of economic development and also of political intervention and, in turn, in the consequences of mobility for class formation and action.

One must then point out to Kelley that neither economic development nor political decisions regarding, say, free trade or protection, collectivization or 'liberalization', or positive or negative educational discrimination, impact on occupations according to how they fare on the Duncan SEI, the Treiman international prestige scale or even Kelley's Worldwide Status Score. Such influences have to be seen, rather, as bearing on groupings such as farmers and peasants, industrial workers, artisans and the petty bourgeoisie, the salariat or intelligentsia (cf. Erikson and Goldthorpe, 1987a, 1987b). In turn it is these groupings, and not aggregates derived from slicing up interval scales, that must be regarded as the major collective actors, actual or potential, within modern societies.[13]

When mobility tables based on a class schema are analyzed through the application of log-linear models, two important possibilities are created. First, the effects of class structure, and of its historical development, on observed mobility rates (i.e. absolute rates) can be distinguished from the effects of the underlying 'mobility regime' (i.e. relative rates)—a task to which, despite Kelley's apologetics, regression techniques are far less suited. Second, one can examine, within the same conceptual framework, both absolute and relative mobility rates *in detail*. The 'one number' approach to describing the degree of openness of societies that Kelley favours is extraordinarily crude and conceals far more than it displays; the *pattern* of social fluidity within a society cannot be expressed in a single measure. Furthermore, to seek to overcome this difficulty by viewing mobility only in hierarchical terms is itself often restrictive and distorting. To take but one example: in the development of industrial societies the most important of all mobility flows, numerically at least, is that of peasants and small farmers and of their offspring into the industrial working class—which entails radical changes in their market and work relationships and usually in their entire way of life. Yet one of the *least* imaginative and revealing ways in which to treat such mobility is to ask simply whether it is 'upward' or 'downward' in direction (cf. Smelser and Lipset, 1966b; P. Johnson, 1981).

Kelley tries to make out that the main attraction of log-linear modelling in mobility research has been its technical novelty rather than its analytical value, but this argument will not stand up. Log-linear modelling and associated techniques represent one of a number of new possibilities in data analysis that have emerged in sociology over the last ten or fifteen years, and that have the advantage of being more suited to the kinds of data and of substantive problem with which sociologists are typically concerned than were techniques previously taken over from, say, experimental psychology or econometrics.[14] Kelley is clearly stuck in the techniques, and the problems, of the 1960s: he will do little harm there and perhaps some good. But attempts such as his to discredit new techniques by refusing to recognize that they are addressed to new problems, significantly different from the old ones, are likely to have an unwelcome, even if unintended, effect: that is, in reinforcing the—by now quite unjustified—notion that quantitative analysis in sociology is unduly limiting in the choice of problem, the conceptualization and the general 'image' of society that it imposes.

PROBLEMS AND THEORY

In this section I aim to respond to my critics on a number of theoretical issues that they have raised. I shall, however, approach these issues through a discussion of what, following Merton (1959), one might call the question of 'problem-finding' in sociology. A further practical consequence of Popper's philosophy of science which I have always thought valuable is the requirement that one should *begin* with problems, and then regard theory and empirical inquiry and analysis alike as means of arriving at their solution. However, despite Merton's attempt to give the matter greater priority, sociologists would seem to have devoted remarkably little consideration to just what *kinds* of problem their discipline should, and can, address; or, in other words, to what they should regard as appropriate *explananda*.

As I have already implied, this is an area in which any dogmatism is out of place. Sociologists can scarcely avoid the challenge of many problems that arise 'exogenously', from the development of the societies in which they live, as well as having to face those given 'endogenously', by the internal development of their discipline. Further, of course, the final judgment on whether or not a 'good' choice of problem has been made is possible only after the fact—that is, in the light of the results obtained from investigating it. Nonetheless, I would still maintain that sociologists do need to ask themselves more often and more seriously whether the problems they address—or encourage others to address—are in fact 'do-able'. Rather than attending to those who today urge us to have the ambition to tackle the 'big' problems of history, society and the human condition, we could, I believe, better learn a lesson from the natural scientists, who, as Medawar has pointed out, have recognized that 'if politics is the art of the possible, research is surely the art of the soluble' and that 'the spectacle of the scientist locked in combat with the forces of ignorance is not an inspiring one if, in the outcome, the scientist is routed' (1982: 2–3).

To illustrate here, I first return to Payne's paper. It is one of Payne's chief complaints that I have 'not taken the final step towards embracing structural change as a central issue in mobility research' and, more specifically, that I have not given sufficient attention to the process of occupational transition, within economic development, as a cause of mobility (pp. 297–8). Insofar as Payne's charge is that I do not recognize, or describe, the effects of structural change on mobility levels and patterns, then I find his account of my work—as indeed in other respects—difficult to accept. I would rather say that a concern with structural influences is pervasive. However, if what Payne really wishes to argue is that I do not attempt to provide a *theory* of 'occupational transition'—or, for that matter of class structural change —which would in turn be of major explanatory value in regard to (absolute) mobility rates, he is entirely correct. The reason I do not make this attempt is simply that I doubt if any very useful theory can in this respect be advanced. An obviously related scepticism, it may be added, underlies my differences with both Ahrne and Marshall, and also with Crompton and Dex, on the question of the tasks of class analysis. While they believe that sociologists should attempt to explain why class structures have the form they do, and why they vary over time and space, I would again take the view that these are not questions likely to provide much scope for the effective deployment of sociological theory.

My judgment would be that with both occupational and class structures alike, the diversity and moreover the specificity of the factors and of the conjunctions of factors that bear on them are such that we must look far more to *historical* accounts of their particular forms, patterns of change and diversity than to theoretical ones. Thus, so far as the analysis of mobility is concerned, structural effects, though requiring careful description and, so far as possible, quantitative assessment (cf. the results reported by McRae on the implications of women's labour force participation, pp. 122–4), will still have to be treated as essentially 'exogenous'; and class analysis must then take a given structural context as its starting point and concentrate on the elucidation of the processes occurring *within* that context, mobility included.[15]

I have no doubt that many sociologists will regard my position here as far too pessimistic, and will in particular be reluctant to accept the line that I evidently wish to draw between the uses in sociological analysis of history, on the one hand, and of theory on the other. However, it can scarcely be reasonable for those who do disagree to criticize me for failing to realize *their* programme until they have themselves produced rather better grounds for supposing that it is a viable one. To repeat the challenge that is quoted by McRae: let those who believe that general theories of class structural—or occupational—change can be developed set to work to produce them.

I have, then, referred to examples of what I would regard as 'bad' problem choices: but how would I seek to identify 'good' ones? I would offer two suggestions which I have, I think, tended to follow in my own work, even if in an essentially sleepwalking fashion. The first—which is, one would have thought, obvious enough—is that sociologists should concentrate their attention on regularities, not singularities; that is, on social actions and emergent processes which appear constant or recurrent under a range of conditions or which, if they do display change or variation, still do so in a trend-like or patterned way. The second suggestion is that sociologists should see an explanatory challenge—and opportunity—as arising to the extent that such regularities are 'opaque': that is, to the extent that they cannot be *directly* understood in terms of individuals either pursuing their own perceived interests or following well established, recognized and sanctioned norms. Thus not much would be gained from investigating such regularities as, say, the tendency for banks to attract more depositors if they increase interest rates, or for there to be fewer cars on the road between the hours of eight and nine on a Sunday than on a Monday morning. The challenge and opportunity come, rather, where the generation of the observed regularity at the level of individual action is not readily apparent—where the regularity has to be seen, in Boudon's apt phrase (1982: 198) as a 'synopsis of action', the detailed dynamics of which remain, however, obscure.

It is from *this* standpoint that I would acknowledge some justification for the suspicions that are voiced by both Payne and Dex that I have a greater interest in relative than in absolute mobility rates: *not* because I think them in any general sense 'more important' but because they do seem to me to constitute—in their degree of constancy over time and commonality over subpopulations (for example, men and women, different ethnic groups) and even national societies—precisely the kind of 'opaque' regularity for which sociologists should seek, and ought to be able to provide, some kind of explanation, if they are to continue to make theoretical claims at all. In contrast, I would regard absolute mobility rates as being far less promising *explananda*, since they do vary so greatly under the influence of structural effects of the kind which, on grounds already indicated, I would believe that one may be able to do little more than describe. Correspondingly, while I see no reason, *pace* Kavanagh, why a concern with the constancy over time of the class-vote relationship should lead one to overlook the 'more important' fact of declining support for Labour, I would regard this constancy—rather than historical fluctuations in the parties' share of the vote—as being the phenomenon on which, from a sociological standpoint, explanatory efforts could best be focused.

There is, I might add, a connection between the way I have sought here to characterize promising sociological *explananda* and the emphasis that I gave earlier to survey-based research and to quantitative analysis. Such methods would seem especially suited, and indeed in some cases essential, to demonstrating opaque regularities. Thus those that exist in relative mobility rates and in voting patterns alike could only be brought to light in the first place through the collection of data of an extensive kind, and through the analysis of these data in ways capable of showing up features of their structure that would just not be apparent from 'eyeballing' or the calculation of simple descriptive statistics. I believe that if more sociologists were ready to follow a similar approach, significant advances in problem-finding could be made in many other areas of research.

However, if those engaged in empirical inquiry could do more by way of clarifying just what it is that we might most fruitfully regard as 'problematic' and look to theory to help us explain, it is, I think, in regard to theory itself that improvement is most obviously needed. As Abell has recently observed (1990), sociology as a discipline is remarkably ill-served by its theorists. Most of what passes for theory is at best no more than 'meta-theory' and the elaboration of concepts, and at worst a mish-mash of second-rate philosophy, history of ideas and socio-cultural punditry: explanatory potential is what is conspicuously lacking. I make these remarks not gratuitously, but as a necessary preface to going on to respond in particular to Johnson's criticism of my failure to provide my own theoretical position—that is, my commitment to an 'action frame of reference' —with any systematic elaboration.

This is once again a charge to which, as stated, I must plead guilty; but it is also one which is presented in a rather disingenuous way. The first thing to say is that, so far at least, the systematic development of theory has not figured among the goals that I have pursued. Rather, I have concentrated my efforts on the empirical investigation of substantive issues, and have sought to *use* currently available theory to help make sense of my findings—which does, of course, at the same time imply testing it. In this respect I have experienced not a few disappointments.

For example, Johnson's account of my paper on the development of social policy does not sufficiently bring out the sense in which my critique of functionalist explanations was a regretful one. Such explanations did appear to me to mark a great improvement on those offered by more conventional historians, in particular in regard to the problem of why in nineteenth century industrial societies broadly similar kinds of social policy should have emerged out of very different political and ideological contexts. It was as a result of my concern with this problem that I first became interested in functionalist theories of industrial society in general, and hence in the issue of 'convergence'.

However, on grounds that Johnson indicates and that are more fully set out in Gallie's contribution, I came to the conclusion that, despite their initial intellectual appeal, such macro-functionalist theories had to be rejected. For in addition to empirically based objections that could be made to them, their inability in principle to explain why, as Gallie puts it, 'social actors ... *should* act in the particular ways that are deemed to be functional' (p. 30) was a fatal flaw. Consequently, I was pushed towards some kind of theory in which social action was more than simply epiphenomenal, and which would therefore, at the 'macro' level, permit one to treat both similarity *and* variation in social structure and process as to some extent the result of choice, and of the not entirely predetermined outcome of social conflicts—or as Hardiman puts it, in her parallel critique of Esser's *fonctionnalisme noir*, which would allow for 'the possibility of politics' (p. 257).

Likewise Johnson's discussion of the *Affluent Worker* studies (pp. 381–6) is in one crucial respect incomplete. He remarks that an 'action frame of reference' appears not to have guided the initial conception of the project; this theoretical approach he notes, did not emerge until my paper on the Vauxhall car workers (1966), in which it was argued that their attitudes and behaviour could not be understood as a direct response to assembly-line technology and related organizational features of the plant, but only from the standpoint of their 'orientations to work', which were generated largely outside the workplace and indeed prior to their employment at Vauxhall.

This is correct, so far as it goes. But what is *not* correct is to suggest, as Johnson then does, that the design of the Luton study was an 'aberration in [Goldthorpe's] otherwise consistent career position—the commitment to social action' (p. 386). For what Johnson fails to recognize—remarkably, in view of his determinedly historical approach—is that I came to the *Affluent Worker* project highly responsive to current theory (and research) which suggested that different forms of production technology *did* crucially condition workplace attitudes, behaviour and relationships (see, for example, Goldthorpe, 1959—my first published paper). It was *this* theory—in effect a form of micro-functionalism with psychological underpinnings (Woodward, 1958, 1965; Blauner, 1960, 1964; also Argyris, 1957)—which was reflected in various features of the design and conduct of the Luton research.[16] In the outcome, however, it proved to be of little value in explaining—and was indeed largely controverted by—the empirical findings. Most obviously, the degree of similarity in the attitudes, behaviour and relationships displayed by workers across the three technologically contrasting plants that were selected for study forced attention away from the effects of the differing workplace environments and towards what appeared to be their largely similar orientations to work, reflecting shared 'life projects' pursued within the shared constraints of their class situation.

Since the time of the *Affluent Worker* studies, I have then been convinced that useful sociological theory can only be some kind of action theory; that is, it must ultimately entail intentional, rather than either functional or causal explanation (cf. Elster, 1983a). I make no claim to distinction in having reached this conclusion —nor yet, to repeat, in having moved beyond it by way of any significant contribution to theory development. As, still, by preference a user—or would-be user—of theory, I looked in this respect to those who, with no little *fanfare*, did indeed take up the task of its 'reconstruction'. But, again, I have to record disappointment. Most of what has been put on offer by self-proclaimed theorists over the last decade or so seems to be of decidedly lower intellectual calibre than what went before. Thus, for example, if Johnson really believes that I have missed out on something of importance in 'discourse theory' or in the phenomenological or ethnomethodological movements, it is a pity that he did not say more clearly just what that might be or, better, give just one example of the theory in question doing explanatory work.[17]

The one development that I would at the present time regard as promising goes in a quite different direction: namely, the attempts being made by writers such as Boudon (1982, 1986, 1987), Elster (1983b, 1984, 1985) and Wippler and Lindenberg (1987) to adapt rational choice theory to sociological purposes. The possibility thus opened up is that 'opaque' regularities may be 'decomposed' by empirical analysis into their constituent sequences and patterns of individual action and interaction, which can then be rendered intelligible in terms of actors rationally pursuing their objectives under constraints of differing kinds, and including perhaps their own beliefs and value commitments.

This possibility emboldens me to conclude as follows. Johnson objects that I have pursued a 'career commitment' rooted in an ideological interest in social openness and individual choice and an opposition to all forms of determinism, yet have failed to translate this commitment into elaborated and coherent theory. I am sorry not to have lived up to his high expectations of me; but, since it is now evident enough that theory cannot be safely left to theorists, I will undertake to do better in future.[18]

SOCIAL MOBILITY

I now turn in this and the following two sections to more substantive matters. As regards social mobility, I shall first respond to criticisms made by Payne of my treatment of mobility, or fluidity, in present-day British society, and I shall then consider objections raised by Kelley to the results—or to what he supposes to be the results—of the comparative analyses of mobility that I have undertaken with Erikson.

As regards Payne's general interpretation of the objectives and emphases of *Social Mobility and Class Structure in Modern Britain*, I must concur with Westergaard in finding this not a little idiosyncratic; moreover, the exact point of Payne's criticisms is often difficult to discern. However, I take it that the main substantive charge that emerges is the following: that because of my class structural perspective, my concentration on relative rates, and my inadequate treatment of structural changes in employment, I 'create an impression'—albeit inadvertently—'of contemporary Britain as an even more closed society than it actually is' (p. 290). In no respect do I find this argument convincing.

First of all, Payne, like Kelley, seems reluctant to accept that mobility can actually occur other than within some kind of social hierarchy. Thus he argues that because I analyze mobility in the context of a class structure and do not wish to treat the classes I distinguish as being consistently ordered, this 'in practice ... reduces the level of mobility perceived' (p. 296; see also his reply to Westergaard, pp. 300–02). I can only describe this as bewildering, in particular, Payne's claim that *I* recognize only 23 per cent of the male population as having been mobile intergenerationally—since a further 48 per cent are discounted *by Payne* on the basis of *his* criterion that mobility must be 'vertical'. I have already pointed to the shift of labour from the farm sector into manual wage-earning jobs in industry as one major mobility flow within developing nations which will not be adequately understood if it is treated merely as movement along some 'vertical' dimension. Likewise in the British context movement between, say, skilled manual employment and routine white-collar positions, or between either of these categories and lower-level supervisory grades or self-employment and small entrepreneurship, will also imply changes in individuals' relations within labour markets and production units—that is, will imply *class* mobility—even while remaining only rather ambiguously interpretable in a 'vertical' sense.

Second, when Payne maintains that my emphasis on relative rates leads me to underplay the 'social fluidity' and 'openness' of British society (pp. 290ff.), it must be noted that he is using these terms in a way clearly different from that in which I use them. For Payne, so far as I can see, 'social fluidity' and 'social mobility' are synonymous and, further, a more mobile society is ipso facto a more 'open' society. However, I use both 'social fluidity' and 'openness'—in the way which has by now become more or less standard—to refer *only* to relative rates; and the criterion of fluidity or 'openness' is not then the simple amount of mobility occurring in a society as measured by some kind of absolute rate, but rather the *degree of equality* of relative rates. Or, to follow Gagliani, one might say openness increases to the extent to which there is 'an enhancement of the ability to compete of those for whom the dice were unfavourably loaded' (p. 90). Thus it is one of my central arguments—dependent, of course, on the distinction between absolute and relative rates—that although during the present century Britain may have become a somewhat more mobile society, as the result of structural change, it has *not* become a more fluid or a more open one: relative rates have not become more equal but have remained more or less constant. Payne presents no evidence to controvert this argument: what he does is to imply that it is overstated by making frequent references to examples of high 'social fluidity' which, however, in my terms are only ones of high (absolute) mobility, and on which there is no necessary disagreement. Payne is under no obligation to follow my usage, even if it is the standard one; but if he does not, then at least when discussing my work, he does have an obligation to recognize and point out the crucial differences that arise rather than trading on the confusion that is otherwise created.

Third, while I would reject Payne's claim that I give inadequate attention to structural effects on mobility, I would further observe that a concentration on such effects in the way that Payne advocates is itself likely to lead to a less than full appreciation of the extent of mobility in any modern society. As Duncan (1966) has pointed out, occupational or class structural change can be said to necessitate mobility only to the extent of the *net* redistribution of the population that it requires; however, once we move from an inter- to an intragenerational perspective, we see very clearly that the amount of mobility that occurs is much in excess of this necessary minimum. In *Social Mobility and Class Structure in Modern Britain* I discuss intragenerational, or worklife, mobility at some length (1987a, especially Chs 2 and 5), although a reader of Payne's paper would not realize this. Moreover, together with Erikson (1987c), I have presented analyses to show that, in comparative perspective, worklife mobility in Britain appears to be at a rather high level, even though both total intergenerational mobility and the pattern of intergenerational fluidity are in no way exceptional. Again, Payne makes no reference to this work.

In sum, I do not think that it is at all helpful to discuss my work on mobility in Britain in terms of the general 'impression' that it may, or may not, create.[19] Social mobility is a complex phenomenon, and I treated it as such; that is, I sought to make essential distinctions and to avoid 'one number', or 'one phrase', conclusions. Nonetheless, I believe that the conclusions that are reached will be clear enough to anyone who is ready to learn the techniques involved and to read the pages carefully.

I move on now to Kelley, and specifically to the question of the validity or otherwise of the 'FJH hypothesis': that is, the hypothesis advanced by Featherman, Jones and Hauser (1975; cf. also Grusky and Hauser, 1984) to the effect that while wide cross-national variation may be expected in absolute rates of intergenerational mobility, the underlying pattern of relative rates, or of social fluidity, will prove to be 'basically' the same in all societies, to the extent that a market economy and some kind of family system are in operation. Kelley's charge is that, in work arising out of the CASMIN Project, Erikson and I have given our support to the FJH hypothesis, but on the basis of quite insecure evidence. In particular, the log-linear analyses that we undertake have far too little statistical power: we accept the FJH hypothesis, taken as the null, but our methods could easily fail to detect cross-national differences in fluidity of a quite substantial kind (pp. 335–7).

Kelley's critique may at first sight appear formidable, and it would indeed merit being taken very seriously, were it not for one thing: namely, that the account Kelley gives of how Erikson and I seek to test the FJH hypothesis and of the conclusions that we arrive at is quite a number of years out of date. It would seem that this account is based on papers that we wrote with Portocarero (1982, 1983) on the basis of a three-nation study that ante-dated the CASMIN Project. Kelley makes no reference at all to the main publication thus far to emerge from this project, which is concerned precisely with the problems, statistical and otherwise, that are encountered in seeking to assess the FJH hypothesis on empirical grounds (Erikson and Goldthorpe, 1987a, 1987b).

In this paper—which I must assume Kelley simply does not know—Erikson and I present a log-linear model of 'core fluidity' in modern societies (see Müller's paper pp. 314–16, for a brief description) which, we believe, marks a major improvement on that we used in our earlier work. Among other things, this model allows for the FJH hypothesis to be tested with *differing degrees* of stringency. This would seem important in seeking to overcome the discrepancy that exists (but that Kelley overlooks) between the verbal expression of the hypothesis—the claim that relative rates will be 'basically' the same—and the formal model of the hypothesis that its authors themselves propose, that is, the 'constant social fluidity' model, which requires that relative rates be *identical*. Not surprisingly, then, the results we report from the application of our new model do not point to either a straightforward acceptance *or* rejection of the hypothesis, but rather to a more complex set of conclusions that might be summarized as follows:

1   *If* the FJH hypothesis is quite strictly interpreted as claiming that relative rates of intergenerational mobility show *no* cross-national variation, then it is surely mistaken: such variation is evident to an extent that is both statistically and sociologically significant. This conclusion, I might add, was also reached in our earlier work (Erikson, Goldthorpe and Portocarero, 1982), and Kelley thus exaggerates the extent of our commitment to the hypothesis even at that stage.

2   If, however, we use our model of 'core fluidity' to try to give meaning to the idea of a 'basic'—rather than a complete—similarity in relative rates, support for the hypothesis in this weaker form can be claimed in that cross-national differences do appear more as variations on the theme defined by the model rather than, say, as falling into a set of distinctive 'types' of mobility regime. Moreover, even though variation in relative rates cross-nationally is greater than that typically found over time or over subpopulations within the same national society, the extent of the commonality displayed is still impressive; and to ignore it, by considering the FJH hypothesis only *stricto sensu* and then dismissing it out of hand, would be to miss something—an 'opaque' regularity—of considerable sociological interest.

3   In some instances variation in 'core' fluidity, as represented by our model, would appear to result from highly specific, historically formed cultural or institutional features of a national society, and thus to lie largely beyond the reach of macro-sociological explanation. However, one more general source of such variation is indicated: that is, *political intervention*, based on the power of the modern state apparatus, which is aimed at modifyiำg the processes, or the outcomes of the processes, through which markets generate and families perpetuate social inequalities of condition and opportunity alike. Such intervention, it should be noted, does not necessarily lead to generally more egalitarian and 'open' societies, although it

may, as in the Swedish case. It is undertaken with widely differing objectives, degrees of success, and ultimate effects on fluidity patterns. Thus, for example, in Hungary and Poland the impact of political intervention on social fluidity during the post-war period of 'socialist reconstruction' would appear in the former case to have resulted chiefly from the collectivization of agriculture but in the latter from strategies of educational discrimination directed towards the creation of a 'people's intelligentsia'.

From the foregoing (and also from Müller's contribution), it should be apparent that what Kelley has to say about the treatment of the FJH hypothesis on the basis of results from the CASMIN Project bears little relationship to what Erikson and I have so far written on the matter (a book arising from the project is still in preparation). Although we would see the hypothesis in its weaker form as capturing a feature of modern societies that calls for serious sociological attention, we would at the same time most certainly regard cross-national differences in fluidity as being 'large enough to be worth worrying about' (p. 337). We have, after all, devoted a good deal of effort to modelling them (cf. also Goldthorpe, 1987a: Ch. 11). Furthermore, while we find no evidence for believing that such differences result in there being distinctive types of fluidity pattern, neither would we wish to dismiss them, or not all of them, as being 'merely idiosyncratic'.

However, if there remains a real difference with Kelley at the level of substance (as distinct from that of methodology, where, as we have seen, there are plenty), it appears to concern the extent to which cross-national variation in fluidity may be regarded as 'systematic'. Theoretically, and also 'ideologically', I am much attracted to Kelley's hypothesis that the degree of 'inherited privilege' in a society will be proportional to 'inequality in human and material capital' within the parental generation (pp. 338–41). Indeed, I have myself ventured what is essentially the same argument: that equality of opportunity and equality of condition will be found to be positively associated (Goldthorpe, 1987a: 320–1, 327–30). Nonetheless, I would still doubt whether a hypothesis of this kind will in the end be shown to account for all that much of cross-national variation in fluidity, if only because the degree of cross-national similarity in occupational or class inequalities in incomes, education, etc. would itself appear impressive (cf. Phelps Brown, 1977, 1988; Treiman, 1977). Moreover, the empirical results that Kelley presents do not fill me with great confidence.

Final judgment must be postponed until his work is published in a more complete form; that is, with full details of the analyses undertaken and the data sources used. However, apart from my strong reservations about the way Kelley measures status (see endnote 11), I find several peculiarities in what he reports in his present contribution. It is, for example, odd that it should make no difference to his results whether he measures mobility simply by the correlation between father's and son's status or uses techniques that control for marginal distributions. And yet more worrying is that his data should show both the USA and Great Britain as having *greater* income equality than Sweden; and again Britain as the most open country within the sample, while the Netherlands is one of the most rigid. Quite contrary indications are given by other data sets (see e.g. on income distribution, O'Higgins, Schmaus and Stephenson, 1985; Rainwater, Rein and Schwartz, 1986; and on the Netherlands, Luijkx and Ganzeboom, 1989) over which, I suspect, Kelley's cannot claim superiority. Note that for ten of his fifteen nations, the sample size is less than 1000, and for four less than 500.

Furthermore, in addition to such doubts about the empirical basis of Kelley's work, it is relevant to return to my earlier criticism of his attempt to represent the fluidity of a society by a single parameter. Much of the cross-national variation in fluidity that can be detected is not adequately described simply in terms of more or less 'inherited privilege' or 'equality of opportunity' overall: it occurs, rather, in relative rates of mobility between particular categories of origin and destination, as the model that Erikson and I have developed can show. In turn such variation often needs to be explained more specifically than by reference to the general structure of inequalities in social power and advantage. In other words, in exploiting his hierarchical perspective in order to produce 'one number' measures of fluidity, which can then be correlated with other 'global' measures of inequality, it is, ironically, Kelley himself who is the more likely to underestimate the extent to which from society to society the structure of mobility opportunities takes a different form.

CLASS FORMATION AND CLASS ACTION

In choosing to study social mobility within a class structural context, I aimed at reviving a tradition of research in which interest in mobility focused not solely on the fates of individuals, but further on the implications of mobility for the formation or decomposition of classes and thus for the potentialities for class-based collective action (cf. Goldthorpe, 1985b). This *démarche* meant not only breaking with the 'status attainment' approach, dominant within American liberal sociology, but also going beyond most Marxist sociologists, for whom—in the way that Ahrne's chapter well illustrates—mobility is a topic at best marginal to the concerns of class analysis.

What I sought to maintain was that any attempt to show how and to what extent a given class structure generates class action and conflict must call for a serious examination of mobility rates and patterns. For whether or not individuals take up specifically class identities and seek to realize specifically class interests will depend (among other things) on the degree of permanence with which they and their families have been, and expect in future to be, associated with certain sets of class positions. From such a standpoint, I hoped, the study of mobility and class analysis alike could be brought back into a closer relation with other major research areas within sociology. This appeared all the more important in view of the fact that within certain of these—electoral sociology and the sociology of industrial relations were of greatest interest to me—orthodoxies had emerged in which the treatment of class and its effects was in one way or another far from satisfactory. In this section I will be concerned with issues that arise out of my criticism of these orthodoxies and that refer chiefly to the British working class, although, in conclusion, questions of a more general kind are clearly involved.

At the source of most of this controversy is a line of argument that I developed, in effect linking the *Affluent Worker* studies with my later mobility research: that is, the argument that, far from the post-war period seeing the start of the decomposition of the British working class, it was only in this period that it reached a stage of 'maturity'. By a 'mature' working class, I meant one that is largely self-recruiting, and whose members are for the most part at least 'second-generation' urbanized industrial wage-workers and their families; and further one that has some lengthy collective experience of pursuing its industrial and political interests through its own organizations (see Goldthorpe, 1978: 204–7; cf. also 1987a: 335–45).[20]

One orthodoxy to which this argument was clearly inimical was that which claimed that in post-war Britain a general 'erosion of class' was progressively undermining the electoral prospects of the Labour Party, and would continue to do so as long as it sought to remain a distinctively 'class' party. This view, popular in the early 1960s, was challenged in the *Affluent Worker* studies (see Heath's paper, pp. 161–3), and with Labour's electoral successes of 1964, 1966 and 1974 became somewhat muted. However, following the Conservatives' return to power in 1979, and further victories in 1983 and 1987, it was strongly revived, largely on the basis of what I have called 'reverse sociologism': that is, the practice of arguing *from* shifts in parties' electoral fortunes *to* supposed underlying changes in social structure and process. Within a general hypothesis of 'class dealignment' in voting patterns, particular emphasis again came to be placed on the decline in support for Labour among the working class. This position is well illustrated in Kavanagh's contribution, in which his critique of my views on Labour Party strategy essentially depends on the contention that Labour's defeat in 1979 (and presumably their failure to recover at the two succeeding elections) reflects a process of working-class decomposition; that is, a relative decline in the propensity of workers, and especially of skilled workers, to vote for Labour as their 'natural' class party rather than for other parties.

Kavanagh appears somewhat put out that I should persist in my opposition to this kind of argument: 'Goldthorpe's views', he complains, 'have hardly altered. In the 1960s *embourgeoisement* was the dragon to be slain by a sociology of the centre-left, in the 1980s it has been 'class dealignment' (pp. 176–7). My reply can only be that my opposition has persisted because the attempt to show a secular decline in the political distinctiveness of the British working class has persisted—and is just as misguided now as it was in the 1960s.

As I have already observed, the demonstration by Heath, Jowell and Curtice (1985: Ch. 3) that patterns of net class-vote association display no more than small and trendless fluctuations over recent decades has not been seriously challenged. Rather, it is confirmed both by similar analyses of different data (Marshall, Newby *et al.*, 1988: Ch. 9) and by the application of different—though still technically appropriate—methods to both different and the same data (Hibbs, 1982; Weakliem, 1989). The direct implication is that manual wage-workers, whether skilled or unskilled, have *not* become relatively less likely to vote for Labour than for other parties.[21]

In explaining Labour's electoral failure since 1979, one sociological factor is relevant—and disputed only perhaps by die-hard supporters of the 'proletarianization' thesis: that is, the tendency for the working class to *contract in size* and for the 'service class' of salaried professional, administrative and managerial personnel correspondingly to expand and, one could add, to become itself more cohesive as a result of the increasing intergenerational stability of its membership (cf. Goldthorpe, 1982, 1987a: Ch. 12). In addition, a yet more important *political* factor has to be recognized: that is, the *general* unattractiveness of Labour as a party—on account of its internal divisions, poor leadership, unconvincing and unpopular policies, etc.—which has led to a reduction in the propensity to support Labour that is apparent *to a similar degree among voters of all classes alike.* The crucial point then is that, once these two factors are taken together, there is no need, and no basis, for any further claims concerning the 'class dealignment' of partisanship—whether overall or in regard to the working class specifically.

Moreover, Heath and his associates in their replies to critics and in other later work (including Heath's chapter in this volume) have presented further evidence to call into question the kinds of assumption that 'reverse sociologism' has typically encouraged: for example, that there has been 'a sea-change of attitudes within the proletariat' or 'a precipitous decline in the ideological consciousness and solidarity of the working class' (Crewe, 1986: 633). To the contrary, they show that in most respects working-class political attitudes display a high degree of stability; and that while levels of class awareness have indeed changed little among the population at large, within the working class there has been a 'quite remarkable' constancy (Heath, Jowell and Curtice, 1987a; cf. also Marshall, Newby *et al.*, 1988: Chs 5–8). Finally, they point out that, rather than any of these results being found surprising, they should be seen as essentially those that the main conclusions of mobility research in Britain would lead one to expect.

A second orthodoxy with which I was brought into conflict was that represented by the 'Oxford school' of industrial relations. The leading representatives of this school, while preoccupied—one might almost say obsessed—with the history and the organizations of the labour movement, showed remarkably little interest in the sociology of the working class, and clearly regarded this as having no great relevance for the understanding of industrial relations. Their analyses were conducted almost exclusively at an institutional level, and focused on the machinery and processes of collective bargaining between union representatives and employers or their managements. In the 1960s and 1970s this school achieved great prominence—and influence—in arguing that current problems of strikes, low productivity and inflation had a common origin in the 'disordered' nature of British industrial relations, and that a solution would have to be sought in extensive institutional reform. The arguments that I levelled against this position are summarized by Roche, and stressed what he aptly refers to as the 'pre-institutional' roots of the 'disorder' (p. 208), especially in changing class relations, and in turn the poor chances of success of institutional reforms that paid no attention to these changes. As Roche notes, no extended response to my critique was forthcoming (though see Clegg, 1975). However, Brown's contribution can now be regarded as serving this purpose, even though, as he very fairly acknowledges, with sufficient delay to give him some benefit of hindsight.

As a preliminary remark on Brown's paper, I would say that he appears to associate my position too closely with that of other—and yet more—'radical' critics of the Oxford or 'liberal-pluralist' tradition in industrial relations (e.g. Fox, 1973; Hyman and Brough, 1975). Thus I have never been an advocate of 'worker controlled unitarism' nor of any of the other *marxisant* nostrums of the 1970s that Brown now, understandably, finds of 'an almost pathetic irrelevance' (p. 218). Moreover, in advancing the idea of a mature working class, I was in no way seeking to underwrite what Brown refers to as 'Scargillism'. Rather, I wished to emphasize the importance of recognizing a working class not only more organized than before but one whose members were more homogeneous in their social backgrounds and worklife experience, more aware of their own bargaining strength, and more ready to exploit any bargaining advantage that they might possess—while still not, as I explicitly said, being in any sense 'revolutionary' (1978: 208).

Thus the differences between Brown and myself, so far at least as workplace industrial relations are concerned, are perhaps less than they might at first appear. I am very ready to accept that workers' 'interests' are not necessarily best defined by the wishes and demands that individuals express in specific 'here-and-now' situations, and in turn that shop stewards who do no more than simply respond to such wishes and demands may in the end achieve less for their members than those who take a longer view and a more calculated approach. But, as is now, I would have thought, well recognized (cf. Hardiman), to engage in such 'strategic' as opposed to more 'populist' forms of interest representation is at any level a high-risk undertaking. It is often subverted by 'free-riding' by individuals or groups within the rank-and-file, who try still to obtain immediate advantages for themselves even though this may threaten the achievement of 'collective goods'; and by 'crises of legitimacy' (cf. Regini, 1984) which arise if the rank-and-file come to doubt their representatives' ability to secure longer-term objectives and thus reject their leadership in favour of taking such gains as are readily available.

The key issue for me was not, therefore, whether industrial relations reformists were trying to make it easier for shop stewards to 'sell out' workers, as some critics on the left alleged. It was, rather, whether the proposed reforms could be effective—and even assuming 'strategic' rather than 'populist' shop stewards—when so many among the rank-and-file did not appear to see the need for reform and were evidently in a position to derive advantage, even if opportunistically, from those situations that reformers took as being most symptomatic of 'disorder'. Free-riding and other forms of opportunism are, after all, under many circumstances entirely rational courses of action.

Where I disagree with Brown is on his claim that 'the liberal-pluralist analysis was rather better than its policy prescription, at least as it was expressed by the Donovan Commission' (p. 217). In my view Donovan stands as an example of 'social designing' that was fatally flawed because of the inadequacies of the underlying analysis, and in particular because, as I previously argued (1974b), of the Commission's neglect of its own, as well as of other, research findings on the orientations and patterns of action of the individuals with whom it was chiefly concerned. Rather than making an effort to appreciate these as contextually rational, and thus as not perhaps readily modifiable, the Commission fashioned its proposals for a new institutional order according to its own lights, and then resorted to condemnations of 'ignorance' and appeals for 'more education'—sure signs, I would suggest, of would-be reformers in trouble.

I do not find it surprising that the most that Brown can say on the practical consequences of Donovan is that it 'probably had some catalytic effect' in regard to the shift away from national multi-employer to local single-employer agreements; nor, moreover, that he should also observe that the pace of change in this direction was quite slow until accelerated in the 1980s by the 'far less reasonable forces' of harsher market conditions and the anti-union policies of the Thatcher administrations (p. 218).

As regards inflation, I will have more to say on Brown's critique in the following section. Here it is relevant to note that in the paper to which he refers I was concerned with the problem of why, within a situation of world inflation, Britain should tend to have higher rates than most other advanced capitalist societies

(1978: 197). As an alternative to economists' views, I suggested (see the contributions by Hardiman and Roche) that, at least under certain conditions, inflation might better be understood as 'the monetary expression of distributional conflict'; and that Britain's comparatively high rates could in turn be taken as reflecting a situation in which such conflict 'has become *more intense* and also to some extent *more equally matched* with these two tendencies interacting in a mutually reinforcing way'. I then introduced the idea of the 'maturity' of the British working class, together with that of the decay of the status order and the realization of citizenship, to try to provide an—admittedly quite speculative—explanation of why distributional dissent should take on these distinctive features in the British case.

Brown finds this explanation to be 'constructed of sociological bricks without institutional straw' and, consistently, goes on to argue that it is in different labour market and wage-fixing institutions that the sources of cross-national variation in inflationary pressure are to be found. Among countries with more than about a quarter of their workforces unionized, those with centralized and coordinated wage bargaining are less likely to experience high inflation rates than those where bargaining is fragmented (see p. 221). I would broadly agree with this proposition; but it still seems to me that, as an explanation, it does not get one all that far. One needs to ask not only why (as Brown appears to accept) different institutional arrangements have developed; but why they persist and why those that appear more economically and socially efficient are not more widely copied. When these questions are raised, the importance of cross-national differences in, precisely, the degree and pattern of distributional dissent (cf. Plant) becomes once more apparent. Thus, for example, to take cases that Brown cites, the Austrian system of centralized bargaining, through which an effective incomes policy has been implemented and which has in turn permitted neo-Keynesian macro-economic policies, would seem ultimately dependent upon a remarkably low level of distributional dissent within the society at large (see Marin, 1985). Likewise, as I have earlier noted, the functioning of the Swedish system, in which a solidaristic wages policy has been crucial, has to rely on the continuing acceptance of what are, on a comparative view, very low pay differentials among the mass of wage and salary earners (see Scharpf, 1984).

I do not wish to assert that my account of how Britain's inflationary pressures are generated is the correct one; as I observed, to test it would require a comparative research programme—which remains to be undertaken. But I would claim that some account of this *type* is necessary: that is, one which goes beyond the institutional level to that of social action, at which institutions are treated as constraints but not as determinants, and at which intentional explanations can operate. I would still believe that in this context an understanding of how the dynamics of class, and of status, produce differing levels of 'effective' distributional dissent—that is, dissent that can find some forceful expression—will prove to be of central importance.[22]

In conclusion, I would stress that to argue thus is not to resort to the crude kind of 'sociological reductionism' that Johnson seeks to foist upon me. I do *not* regard mobility as the only factor in class formation, nor treat class action as purely a matter of 'individual response', nor try simply to 'read off' political action from social circumstances. Corrective statements of my position in these respects are, fortunately, well provided in the papers by Marshall, McRae and Hardiman especially (see also Goldthorpe, 1987a: 350–1). However, I would at the same time certainly wish to reject claims from such celebrated exponents of data-free social analysis as Hindess (quoted by Johnson) and Luhmann (cited by Mayer) to the effect that within the polities of modern societies we must recognize a complete 'dissolution of the linkage' between the institutional and organizational levels and mobility or other processes that determine the degree of class awareness among the population at large. The evidence of the—persisting—influence of class, including class mobility and the 'contextual' effects of class in neighbourhoods and communities, on the extent, direction and mode of individuals' involvements in the political and public realm generally is sufficiently massive to undermine the credibility of this stance. While it is surely true that the nature of the 'linkage' that exists will often be complex, and thus the task of bridging, in Mayer's phrase, 'the actor-arena and the non-intentional process world of society' extremely difficult, it is, as I have already argued, to exactly this task that sociologists must address themselves if they wish to create a discipline that is theoretical in any serious sense.

POLITICAL ECONOMY

In my essay on the sociology of inflation (1978) I argued that a mature working class generates inflationary pressure through its members being increasingly ready to 'punch their weight' in distributional conflicts; and, further, that it may constrain governments in pursuing anti-inflationary policies through its capacity to act, in a more solidaristic way, in defence of its economic and organizational power. In a later essay (1983b; also 1987b) I went on to suggest that the twin problems of distributional dissent and the power of organized labour created major difficulties for the implementation of *both* of the two main forms of political economy that appeared to be emerging out of the ending of the 'long boom' and the crisis of Keynesianism—'the new *laissez-faire*' and 'the new interventionism'.

However, already at the time when the first version of this essay was written the British case appeared not a little problematic. A Conservative Government committed to the new *laissez-faire*—and to the reduction of union power—had been elected in 1979 and was then re-elected four years later, despite what would have been previously regarded as 'politically unacceptable' levels of unemployment. A further election victory followed in 1987. In the first part of this section I thus take up the question of why in the face of the new *laissez-faire* in Britain 'the resistance of organized labour', as Hardiman puts it, 'has been less successful' (p. 240) than my analysis would suggest. I then consider related, though wider-ranging, issues concerning the new interventionism or, as it is now more commonly labelled, 'corporatism' or 'neo-corporatism', which are raised chiefly in Esser's paper, and with reference to a third essay (1984b) that I wrote in continuation of the two previous ones.

In pointing to the political difficulties faced by the new *laissez-faire*, I did make it clear that I regarded these as being formidable rather than insuperable. What this new political economy needed to bring about was a decisive shift in the balance of class power. If inflation resulted from distributional dissent becoming more effective as a result of a greater 'equality of conditions of conflict', then to control it meant cutting back the power of labour; and this could be achieved by government abandoning responsibility for maintaining a 'full employment' level of economic activity (and indeed pursuing monetarist 'stabilization' policies that would, at least for a time, push up unemployment) and further by legislation against the 'monopoly power' of unions and their freedom of action in organizing strikes. The crucial issue was that of the political, and specifically the electoral, viability of such a strategy. In the event Mrs Thatcher has in this respect been remarkably successful—but why?

In commenting on the situation after the 1983 election (1987a: 375–6), I suggested an explanation essentially in terms of political contingencies: the unremitting conflict within the Labour Party prevented much-needed new thinking on policy and electoral strategy alike, undermined the party's credibility, and led eventually, through the SDP breakaway, to a seriously divided opposition to Thatcherism—so that, given the peculiarities of the British electoral system, the Conservatives were able, with little more than 40 per cent of the popular vote, to wield more or less unchallenged political power. This position I would wish to maintain—as against the two alternative, more 'sociological', explanations that are to be found in contributions to this volume.

The first of these, on which I have already commented, is that of Kavanagh, to the effect that Labour suffered specifically from a loss of support within a decomposing working class. To repeat, the evidence goes contrary to this view—and in favour of that which sees Labour as a party that lacked electoral appeal 'across the board': that is, one that voters of all classes alike showed a similarly reduced propensity to support relative to other parties.

The second explanation comes from the Marxist left, represented here by Esser (but cf. Hall and Jacques, 1983; Hall, 1988). This claims that, by means of a 'discursive strategy' emphasizing 'authoritarian populist' beliefs and values, the Conservatives have established a new 'hegemony' over the British population, and have thus been able to undermine alike the industrial power of the unions and the electoral appeal of Labour. This I can only regard as another prime example of 'data-free' analysis. Not only is no evidence provided of the supposed 'hegemony' at work, but the argument for it involves ignoring the by now quite substantial findings to indicate that Thatcherism *cannot* be linked with any very significant belief and value changes within British society, and that many Conservative policies are well out of line with prevailing opinion (see e.g. Crewe, 1988).

In sum, while there is no doubt that a transformation in the political economy of Britain has taken place since 1979, one must be wary of what is for sociologists a major occupational hazard: that of supposing that great changes must always have great causes. Thatcherism is easily overinterpreted. To see its success as the result primarily of a failure of political opposition, rather than reflecting significant social structural or cultural shifts may, for some, be lacking in intellectual glamour or ideological resonance. But, as well as fitting best with the available evidence, this view is in accord with one conclusion that emerges from more general studies of 'the impact of parties' (see e.g. Castles, 1978, 1982): namely, that this impact will reflect not only the strength of ruling parties and their programmes but also the strength—or, rather, weakness—of the opposition that confronts them.

Furthermore, taking this view encourages one to ask just how far-reaching the 'Thatcherite revolution' has been, and how far it may be regarded as 'permanent'. Brown comments that 'the passage of years has been unkind' to my account of the sociology of British inflation, and generously offers me an escape route via the claim that 'so substantial an alteration in the power relationship between classes' has occurred that the processes I outlined 'have been suspended' (p. 220). But I am not at all sure that I would want to accept this way out. A shift in the balance of class power has certainly occurred; and obvious manifestations of this have been the inability of the unions to restrain or seriously impede Conservative policy, and indeed their virtual exclusion from the national political process. But clear indications of the distinctive pushfulness of British labour have continued to rise from the grassroots. Even under the conditions of the early 1980s wage rates showed a tendency to move well ahead of prices; and once strict monetarism was abandoned—in the run-up to the 1987 election—and economic activity increased and unemployment began to fall, Britain quickly resumed her accustomed place towards the top of the inflation league.

How far this reflects the durability of union organization and influence at workplace level is, as Hardiman notes, still a matter of debate, and the evidence remains insufficient for a conclusive answer (cf. Millward and Stevens, 1986). But the fact that high inflationary pressure persists—that monetarism did *not* solve the problem by a decisive squeezing out of 'inflationary expectations'—seems indisputable. In other words, despite the collapse of the power of organized labour considered either as a social movement or as a 'social partner', and despite high levels of unemployment, those workers who have remained in jobs have still been ready and able (cf. Roche) to engage effectively in distributional conflict. If the explanation of this source of inflationary pressure that I have suggested is not the correct one, then another remains to be found.[23]

I turn now to the main critical argument in Esser's contribution: namely, that my discussion of tendencies towards neo-corporatism and dualism in the political economies of modern capitalist societies lacks 'a conceptual framework, grounded in social theory' which could explain why in such societies one tendency or another—or particular 'hybrids'—should prevail (p. 246). From this formulation (and also from Esser's concluding comments in his reply to Hardiman, pp. 259–60) I suspect that Esser and I have differing ideas of the relationship between concepts and theory and also of what counts as explanation. But, leaving that aside, my initial response would be that Esser provides here a further example, to add to those I previously noted, of a social scientist choosing a dubious *explanandum*.

What *I* was trying to explain in my paper on corporatist and dualist tendencies in modern Western societies (1984b) was 'the end of convergence', in that capitalist societies appeared to be moving away, on two essentially divergent paths, from the 'pluralistic industrialism' that American liberal theory had seen as the ultimate goal of their long-term development. These tendencies towards neo-corporatism or dualism were, I argued, to be alike understood as reflecting attempts to overcome the serious incompatibilities that had emerged between the representation of organized interests—and not least, of course, of labour—within a fully developed pluralist polity and the efficient functioning of a market economy (cf. Scitovsky, 1980; Olson, 1982). I did not, and still would not, believe it a useful objective to try then to provide any *general* explanation of why developments within the political economies of particular nations have gone in one direction or another. One may note certain historically formed features of social structure or culture that are likely to facilitate or impede neo-corporatist or dualist tendencies; but still, and this was a point I was concerned to emphasize (1984b: 335), it is important that these contrasting responses be seen as embodying *real political and ideological alternat-*

ives—of the kind which, according to liberal theorists, the coming of advanced industrialism would progressively eliminate.

However, while Esser then promises to make good, from a Marxist standpoint, what he sees as the major deficiency of my analysis, he not only fails to fulfil this promise but further, as his paper progresses, moves to another position—one much the same as my own—which must surely deny the feasibility of any attempt to do so. After giving his interpretation of what he regards as a joint crisis of 'Fordism' *and* corporatism, Esser first advances a substantive argument—that in all capitalist societies there is 'a trend towards a hybrid relationship between corporatism and dualism'—and continues: 'However, the form, content and degree of hybridity, and the nature of particular strategies and their relative success, are all dependent on the specific economic, social and political conditions in particular countries and can only be identified through comparative empirical investigation' (p. 249). This I can only follow with a sincere 'Amen'—but linked, of course, with the obvious question: where, then, in this regard does theory enter in? What Esser goes on to provide is not theory in any sense, but simply a twofold typology in order, as he puts it, 'to summarize country-specific differences on a more systematic level': a strategy of labour exclusion plus some company-based 'micro-corporatism' is contrasted with one of 'selective' corporatism going together with the exclusion of a large 'secondary' workforce (pp. 249–54).

I would certainly accept that it might well be profitable to go beyond my analysis by examining further the suggestion I made that neo-corporatist and dualist tendencies 'can to some significant degree *co-exist* within the same society' but that, beyond a certain stage, this will 'give rise to increasing tension between them' because they imply different orientations in economic and social policy and reflect different balance-of-power situations. It is possible that I underestimated the extent to which co-existence might be taken.[24] Nonetheless, I still do not think that Esser's effort—considered as a typology and not a theory of national differences—is likely to add much to our understanding; and I would agree with Hardiman that its main weakness lies in Esser's essentially functionalist approach. Like many other Marxists before him, Esser tends to lurch between accounts of capitalist 'crisis' and of capitalist 'adaptation' that are equally exaggerated; and in turn neither his general analysis nor the typology he derives from it can allow sufficiently for the degree to which national capitalisms may *vary*, both in their institutional forms and in their degree of economic efficiency and 'success'.

Thus, to return to the British case, Esser's approach leads him to overestimate the extent to which a 'labour exclusion' strategy has been effectively implemented. As well as taking up the quite unsubstantiated idea of a Thatcherite ideological 'hegemony', Esser also relies on a very one-sided reading of the evidence on how far Conservative policies have succeeded in undermining union power at workplace level or the unions' political links with the Labour Party; and likewise on how far employers have generated dualism in labour markets.[25] Conversely, what he finds it difficult to consider is the possibility that British capitalism suffers more from chronic than from 'critical' problems, and that this condition results, in part at least, from the barriers which exist to neo-corporatist and dualist 'adaptations' alike, and through which, therefore, the 'perils of pluralism' are sustained.

Again, it is notable that Esser's typology makes no provision for cases where neo-corporatist strategies would appear to have survived the crisis of 'Fordism' (e.g. Austria or Sweden) or are presently being developed (e.g. Australia). Even cases where such strategies have had a chequered history but are still, so to speak, in the national political repertory (e.g. Italy, Finland, the Netherlands, Norway, Spain) are not easily accommodated. For, as Hardiman emphasizes, an interpretation here simply in terms of capitalist adaptation will not do; neo-corporatist arrangements of the kind in question must be seen as being actively 'bargained' between capital, labour and government, and not just as following from the functional prerequisites of a capitalist economy and society. Indeed, the maintenance of such arrangements must be taken as indicative of a high degree of working-class awareness and solidarity, since what is implied is the capacity of national labour movements to overcome 'free-riding' sectionalism; while, on the other hand, there is evidence that working classes can make real gains fromthe 'collective goods' that are the *quid pro quo* of their participation (Cameron, 1984; Goldthorpe, 1984b).

At the start of his chapter Esser disassociates himself from those Marxists who have characterized neo-corporatism as being no more than 'the latest or "highest" form of the social control of labour under capitalism' (p. 246). But the very logic of his Marxist functionalism would seem to force him back to a tacit version of this argument—in which the difficult cases simply disappear from sight. For such *fonctionnalisme noir* could scarcely allow that changes might be effected within capitalist society which would help overcome economic difficulties and at the same time reflect and express a *reduction* in inequalities in class power and advantage. Or, to put the matter more specifically, Esser simply does not have the theoretical resources to enable him to appreciate just *how* different are, say, present-day Britain and Sweden, *considered as* capitalist societies.

ENVOI

There can be little virtue in my attempting to end these remarks with any kind of summary or general conclusions. Despite the structure that I have sought to impose upon them, they have, in the nature of the case, had to be highly miscellaneous and—yet more to the point—they have already become too long. I can only hope that this will not be taken as indicative of an undue defensiveness or need for self-justification on my part, but rather as testimony to the range and importance of the issues that contributors have raised.

I will therefore make only one final observation, in the role attributed to me by Mayer—though I trust, mistakenly—as 'one of the last living and practising Popperians'. The theme of the series in which this book is included is 'Consensus and Controversy'. For Popper, these two modes of communicative action, implying 'friendly-hostile cooperation' among practitioners, are at the very heart of the scientific method, understood as a social and indeed a public process: scientists, including would-be social scientists, must 'try very seriously to speak one and the same language, even if they use different mother tongues', but at the same time they must seek to 'criticize everything' and be little deterred by 'authorities' (1945: ii, 217–18). Both endeavours have been admirably pursued in this volume, although, I naturally feel, the latter with yet greater enthusiasm than the former. I can therefore derive ultimate satisfaction from the fact that, even though they may not regard themselves as followers of Popper, my co-authors have nonetheless succeeded so well in underwriting and illuminating one of his most central arguments.

NOTES

1 It is largely on account of its reluctance to face up to this point that I have always felt uneasy with the English tradition of 'ethical socialism', as, for example, recently presented by Dennis and Halsey (1988). A marked and refreshing contrast is offered by the Scandinavian version of social democracy in its acceptance of class politics, although of a sophisticated kind that is not hampered by a narrow 'labourism', does not confuse industrial militancy with class consciousness and recognizes the need for 'class alliances'.

2 Kavanagh's representation of my position is misleading in that he equates my argument that Labour should retain its commitment to egalitarianism and should seek to politicize issues in class terms with an argument simply for 'more socialism'. There are many policies represented as 'socialist', at least by Labour's left wing, that have little to do with the reduction of class inequalities, that I would not support, and that, I would agree, have been electorally damaging. Unilateral nuclear disarmament is but the most conspicuous of these.

3 The CASMIN Working Paper referred to here was the first of a widely circulated series with which Kelley is obviously familiar; it was later published in German (Goldthorpe, 1985b).

4 Thus Ahrne fails to recognize that—as Marshall and Müller both make clear—the key idea underlying the class schema is that of differentiation in market and work situations or, as I now think it simpler to say, in employment relations (see esp. Goldthorpe, 1982). In this respect two further points may pertinently be made.

   First, while Ahrne, and likewise Crompton, describe the schema as being 'occupationally' based, it is important to note that occupation is always considered along with employment status and, moreover, that these are taken together as *indicators* of employment relations. Thus, when the schema is used in comparative work, similar combinations of occupation and employment status are not *automatically* allocated to the same class from one nation to another, but only if, in the light of available evidence, they would appear to be associated with similar employment relations. Although this turns out generally to be the case, in some instances—most notably perhaps with various public service occupations—similar combinations have been allocated to different classes because cross-national differences in employment relations are clearly present.

   Second, Ahrne raises—as does Kelley—the question of the inclusion of large proprietors and self-employed professionals in Classes I and II together with higher level salaried employees. However, as Marshall indicates, this is an issue that my colleagues and I have from the start recognized and discussed. We have pointed out that among professionals and managers especially, the line between self-employed and employee status is often difficult to draw and may, moreover, reflect legal and fiscal considerations as much as actual social relationships. Further, on the basis of data from the CASMIN Project one may say that large proprietors (or employers) account for only around 5 per cent of all men allocated to the service class (i.e. Classes I and II) in Western industrial societies, and cannot in any event be realistically seen as members of a capitalist elite or 'leaders of industry'. Rather, they turn out on examination to be most typically the owners of stores, hotels, restaurants, garages, small factories or transportation firms. It is, it should be noted, just such individuals who make up Wright's class of 'capitalists' or 'the bourgeoisie'—together with a rather arbitrary admixture of salaried managers who have some ownership interest in the firms they work for. See Marshall, Newby *et al.* (1988: 54–9), who conclude that 'Wright's operational definition of the bourgeoisie is derived from a nineteenth-century conception of family proprietorship which is wholly inadequate to the study of class processes in a late twentieth-century capitalist economy'.

5 As this formulation indicates, I see no theoretical discontinuity between the 'dominance' and the 'conventional' approaches. As I understand the latter, its essential postulate is that the family and not the individual constitutes the proper unit of class analysis. The dominance method is a relatively sophisticated way of implementing this position, which has obvious advantages where the labour force participation of married women becomes widespread *and*, one should add, to the extent that their disadvantages in the labour market are eliminated.

   I have myself made Dex's point that in using the dominance approach a sample of households is preferable to one of individuals (Goldthorpe, 1987a: 291); but I see no warrant for the critical intention of her claim that a lack of data from such samples, which would allow the production of 'complete' mobility tables, is attributable to 'the conventional view's traditional focus on men's social mobility' (p. 146). Dex much exaggerates the data problems with the complete tables that Erikson and I present, and is quite unspecific about *why* one 'cannot place any confidence' in our conclusion that they largely confirm the results of 'men only' tables (p. 146). I can see little reason for any serious sociologist to have doubted, at least until very recently, that 'men only' tables *would* be the most cost-effective way (and survey research inherently involves questions of cost-effectiveness) of determining rates and patterns of class mobility; and the evidence that Erikson and I adduce points clearly to the soundness of such a position.

6   A further consequence of following the 'individual' approach that has to be accepted is that women's and men's *relative* rates of class mobility prove to be essentially the *same*—with implications that, as McRae points out, will be unwelcome to those feminists who have sought to characterize women as being 'united in adversity' rather than divided by class to no lesser extent than men.

7   We are concerned here with the proletarianization thesis only in the version in which it refers to the degrading of jobs—and not to the *déclassement* of individuals. If considered in the latter, more extended version, then, as Gagliani makes clear, it becomes yet more problematic, not least because of the evidence of mobility studies (cf. Goldthorpe, 1987a: 335).

8   Crompton, it is true, argues that case studies 'need not be restricted to small-scale ethnographic work' and may indeed be 'quantitative' (p. 103). But she fails to say just what 'non-decontextualizing' alternatives to ethnography she has in mind.

9   It is difficult to think of any research project which would today throw greater light on the changing British class structure than a replication of the Craig-Wedderburn study—but extended to cover women as well as men, employing organizations in services as well as manufacturing and a wider range of features of employment relationships.

10 In general, the critical response to Heath, Jowell and Curtice's analysis of the class-vote relationship has been of an embarrassingly low technical standard (e.g. Crewe, 1986; Dunleavy, 1987). The results that they initially reported *could* have been reasonably queried on the grounds of the power of the test that they applied in investigating possible trends. (Kelley's illuminating 'dog-weighing' example is relevant here, pp. 335–6—although not, for reasons explained below, in the case in which he introduces it). However, in later work Heath and his associates have carried out further, more refined analyses which essentially confirm their original conclusions (see esp. Evans, Heath and Payne, 1989).

11 The Duncan Socio-Economic Index of occupations has a clear rationale *only* as a proxy measure for occupational *prestige*—which is what it was initially designed and presented as (Duncan, 1961). Taken as a measure of the 'socio-economic' status of occupations, it is quite arbitrary. Why should such a measure be based only on years of schooling and income (with almost, but not quite, equal weights)? Why should not other manifestly 'socio-economic' attributes also be reflected—such as vocational training, formal qualifications or wealth? Such questions have never received satisfactory answers. Moreover, when occupational categories have been hierarchically ordered, supposedly in accordance with the Index, modifications have been regularly made—though without any clear theoretical justification—so as, it would seem, to pick up opportunistically effects of class or of social status *stricto sensu* (see Blau and Duncan, 1967: 26; Featherman and Hauser, 1978: 27).

    I am no more impressed by Kelley's own 'Worldwide Status Score', which has the remarkable property of being explicitly based (see the Appendix to his chapter) on a set of assumptions which it is surely among the purposes of status attainment and mobility research to *test*. The hopeless circularity that this approach to status measurement entails led to earlier attempts in this direction being abandoned in the 1970s, and a return to it now can only be described as retrograde.

12 See, for example, the important results reported in Allmendinger (1989). Papers such as Müller *et al.* (1988) and Ishida and Ridge (1989) show that Kelley's charge that analyses of the effects of education cannot be readily accommodated within a class structural perspective on mobility is unfounded. Indeed, the fact that educational level does *not* enter into the construction of the class schema—which Kelley describes as 'a savage loss'—means that the role of education in mobility can then be investigated in a far more satisfactory way than via Kelley's status scale, which is itself influenced by educational level.

    As regards what might be seen as a similar complaint by Payne concerning the work of the Oxford Social Mobility Group on Britain—'We still await even a basic treatment of education and mobility' (p. 298)—I would note that this neglects inter alia Halsey (1977), Heath (1981: Chs 5 and 6) and Heath and Ridge (1983a, 1983b).

13 It was considerations of this kind which, as Marshall observes, were involved in my decision not to use the Hope-Goldthorpe scale of the prestige—or 'general desirability'—of occupations (Goldthorpe and Hope, 1974) as the basis of my work on mobility in modern Britain, and which led me to develop instead the initial version of the class schema (Goldthorpe and Llewellyn, 1977a). As a

matter simply of convenience, this made use of the categories, but *not* the values, of the H-G scale; and the later British version of the schema was developed without any reference whatever to the scale (Goldthorpe, 1987a: 255). I am therefore greatly disturbed by the confusion of these two instruments that appears to persist—[for example, the first draft of one of the contributions to this volume referred erroneously to 'the Hope-Goldthorpe class schema', eds]—and for which I feel I cannot accept responsibility.

I would further note, apropos of comments by Kelley, that supplementing analyses in terms of prestige or status by the introduction of further 'dimensions', such as 'authority' or 'ownership' (see pp. 329–31), only compounds the problem of moving from the 'macro' level and the discussion of the properties of societies to the level of social action. For in this way individuals are not merely 'decontextualized'; they are 'decomposed' into a series of attributes, treated as variables, and how we are to 'put Humpty Dumpty together again' is never explained (cf. Boudon, 1987: 61–2).

Finally, the suggestion made by Kelley (p. 331) and also by Ahrne (in his reply to Marshall, p. 76) that my shift to the class schema was 'technically' motivated—that is, by the appearance of log-linear models—is quite mistaken. This shift occurred more than a year before I first heard of log-linear models in a paper by Robert Hauser at the meeting of the ISA Research Committee on Social Stratification at Jablonna, Poland, in March 1974. I had been treating relative rates of class mobility by means of disparity ratios (cf. Miller, 1960), and the relevance of the much more powerful technique of log-linear modelling was then readily apparent in that disparity ratios were simply components of the odds ratios that provided the measure of association within log-linear models (see Goldthorpe, 1987a: 74–85).

14 Other examples would be provided by developments in multi-dimensional scaling, as, for example, in the study of status structures, the 'block modelling' of relationships in social network studies and techniques of event history analysis.

15 I find especially puzzling the position adopted by Marshall in his discussion of the effects of women's labour market participation, which can be instructively compared with McRae's. Marshall does not follow Crompton in her quite unjustified claim that I fail to recognize that the structure of men's employment—and thus of men's mobility chances—is affected by the structure of women's employment. Indeed, Marshall accepts that this is a point I do make (and, I might add, that I made with Llewellyn (1977a) before even Garnsey (1978) as cited by Dex). But Marshall then appears to believe that, under the rubric of class analysis, I should be ready to do something more than this, the nature of which escapes me. My puzzlement is all the greater since, in the end, Marshall simply comes back to the (uncontested) point that men and women compete with each other on the labour market—linked, however, to an analogy with blacks and whites in South Africa which further confuses me since it is a feature of that country that blacks and whites are distinctively *un*likely to marry each other. I can only conclude that Marshall is here assuming the validity of the 'individual' approach as a basis for arguing for it.

16 Woodward's work (1958), which directly influenced our choice of firms with assembly-line, batch and process production systems, did not explicitly use functionalist theory but offered nonetheless a classic functionalist explanation for variation in management structure and 'quality' of industrial relations with type of technology. Such micro-functionalism can more readily propose a 'feedback loop' of the kind which, as Hardiman notes, tends to be crucially lacking in macro-functionalist endeavours. Thus for Woodward, the empirical regularities that she claimed to observe came about because, to the extent that firms did *not* approximate to the modal organizational pattern and style functionally suited to their technology type, they would become inefficient and, in turn, would be less likely to survive—and hence to be observed—within a competitive business environment.

17 It is symptomatic of a crucial difference in orientation here that Johnson should advance it as a criticism of me that I seek to reduce 'the phenomenological principle' to an empirical issue, and that by adopting an 'entirely empiricist' (*sic*) solution to the problem of interpretive processes in social interaction, I avoid 'the difficult theoretical and methodological tasks which face the action theorist or analyst' (p. 388). I would have thought it a virtue to try to bring theoretical argument to some point of contact with the reality by reference to which its value must, I presume, be ultimately judged.

18 For what it is worth at this stage, I would see the most promising problem to tackle as being that of how one can gain the advantages and avoid the disadvantages of, on the one hand, the deductive approach of rational choice theory and, on the other, the ex post approach of the kind of 'rational reconstruction' of action proposed in differing versions by, for example, Popper (1972: Ch. 4) and von Wright (1971, 1972).

19 Payne also contends that 'Goldthorpe ... evinces little interest in the mobility experiences of women'

(p. 298). I think a sufficient answer is provided in the chapter by McRae or indeed in that by Dex. What perhaps Payne means is that the interest I show is not of the kind that can be decently acknowledged in wide areas of British sociology, where to display other than the most considered respect towards all self-styled feminist positions is to demonstrate a clearly 'unprogressive' attitude.

20   While I characterized the members of a mature working class as having 'a relatively high degree of homogeneity in their social backgrounds and patterns of life experience' (1978: 206), I would emphasize—to take up a point raised by Roche—that such homogeneity is not at all dependent on the existence of 'traditional' working-class communities. It is, rather, entirely compatible with considerable geographical and indeed occupational mobility which, as Westergaard and Resler (1975: 312) have emphasized, can contribute to the potential for class awareness and action by breaking down often competing solidarities of a communal, industrial or craft kind. This is, incidentally, a sociological point that has been well appreciated by the Swedish social democrats in favouring an 'active' labour market policy not only as a means of promoting full employment and economic efficiency generally, but also of encouraging the development of a specifically *class* identity among Swedish workers. Conversely, one may note the present tendency for employers in most Western capitalist societies to seek to create, at least among a 'core' workforce, an alternative competing solidarity—that based on the enterprise. Indeed, the encouragement of *Betriebsegoismus* may be given clear precedence over labour market flexibility.

21   It is important to recognize that, when the skilled and non-skilled sections of the working class are distinguished on the basis of my schema, their patterns of political partisanship are essentially the same—although, as would be expected, quite clear differences show up in other respects, such as income and qualifications. One source of this political homogeneity is, I would suggest, the large amount of worklife mobility that occurs in British society between skilled and non-skilled employment (cf. Goldthorpe, 1987a: Ch. 5).

     When Kavanagh echoes the wisdom of Sunday newspaper pundits in stressing the defection of skilled workers from Labour in recent elections, he is, like them, relying on the British Market Research Society's definition—which, however, includes both supervisory grades and self-employed manual workers. Apart from the theoretical incoherence of this category, the political heterogeneity of its constituent elements (supervisory grades and self-employed workers have distinctively high levels of Conservative voting) makes it a treacherous one to use in the study of change in voting patterns; for apparent temporal shifts may well be only compositional ones. Those associated with the 'class dealignment' thesis have again adopted the 'plain man' pose in seeking to suggest that the MRS definition is the obvious commonsensical one that everybody understands, as against the esoteric constructions of the sociologists. But this is scarcely convincing. Recall only the old Cockney version of the *The Red Flag* beginning:

> The working class can kiss my arse
> I've got the foreman's job at last.

22   If I were to extend my own commitments in large-scale comparative research, it would be to undertake a study of cross-national differences within Europe, specifically in the extent and nature of the decay of status structures—and the economic and political implications thereof—in the period since the Second World War.

23   In one respect of relevance here Brown seriously mistakes my argument. He supposes this to be that a consequence of the decay of status 'is a willingness of people to make pay comparisons with a socially broader range of ... reference groups than hitherto' (p. 220). However, I explicitly point out that my position 'does not require any claim of "expanding reference groups"'—which would seem empirically dubious' (1978: 213n10). The point is, rather, that as status structures decay, pay claims, and distributional conflict in general, tend to be pursued outside any normative context whatever, and on the basis simply of market, strategic and organizational power. I would, moreover, take the view that the reference groups that are invoked in pay claims are by now better regarded as being more of forensic than of motivational significance (for evidence on this point, see Roche, 1987).

24   I have been chiefly persuaded of this possibility as a result of discussions with Michael Shalev and his students on the case of Israel.

25   In this respect a consideration that Esser neglects is the influence of demographic change. Over the last decade or more the balance of power in labour markets has been tilted in favour of employers not only by depressed levels of economic activity and political intervention but further by the unusually large number of young people entering the workforce. But in the years ahead (as McRae points out) these numbers are set to fall very sharply, and in many sectors of the economy strong competition for new workers seems likely, with obvious implications for relative bargaining strengths.

Notes on Contributors

Göran Ahrne is currently Associate Professor of Sociology at the University of Stockholm. He is the director of a research project on the class structure in Sweden linked to an international comparative research project which began in 1979. He has published several books and articles, including a volume on changes in class society in Sweden. His most recent book in Swedish deals with politics and organization in the Swedish welfare bureaucracy. In 1988 he published in English (with R. Blom, H. Melin and J. Nicula) *Class and Social Organization in Finland, Sweden and Norway*.

William Brown has been Montague Burton Professor of Industrial Relations and Fellow of Wolfson College, University of Cambridge, since 1985. After completing a PPE degree at Wadham College, Oxford, he worked as an economist at the National Board for Prices and Incomes in London from 1966 to 1968 before moving to Warwick University. In 1970 he joined the Industrial Relations Research Unit at Warwick, becoming its Director from 1981 to 1985. His research has been concerned at different times with workplace bargaining, shop steward organization, payment systems, arbitration, incomes policies and pay determination. He has published books on *Piecework Bargaining* (1973) and *The Changing Contours of British Industrial Relations* (1981), as well as around 50 journal articles and chapters in books. He is currently writing a book on the pay policies of large firms. He was President of the British Universities Industrial Relations Association from 1986 to 1989 and acts as an arbitrator for the Advisory, Conciliation and Arbitration Service.

Jon Clark studied at the Universities of Birmingham (England), West Berlin and Bremen (West Germany), and was awarded a doctorate of the University of Bremen *summa cum laude* in 1979. He has held research posts at the London School of Economics and the Groupe de Sociologie du Travail, University of Paris, and was appointed in 1978 to the Department of Sociology and Social Policy at the University of Southampton, first as Lecturer, then in 1985 as Senior Lecturer. He has authored and co-authored a number of books, including *Trade Unions, National Politics and Economic Management* (1980); *Bruno Schönlank und die Arbeitersprechchorbewegung* (1984); and *The Process of Technological Change —New Technology and Social Choice in the Workplace* (1988). He has also co-edited *Culture and Crisis in Britain in the 30s* (1979); *Labour Law and Politics in the Weimar Republic* (1981); and *Labour Law and Industrial Relations* (1983). He is Principal Editor of the Falmer Sociology Series.

Rosemary Crompton has been Senior Lecturer in Sociology at the University of Kent since 1989. After completing a social science degree at the University of

London in 1964, she worked as a junior Research Officer in the Department of Applied Economics, University of Cambridge, from 1965 to 1967. From 1967 to 1989 she was successively Research Assistant, Lecturer and Senior Lecturer in Sociology at the University of East Anglia. Her publications include *Economy and Class Structure* (1978, with Jon Gubbay); *White Collar Proletariat* (1984, with Gareth Jones); and *Gendered Jobs and Social Change* (1990, with Kay Sanderson). She was also co-editor, with Michael Mann, of *Gender and Stratification* (1986). Her current research interests include occupational structuring, women's employment and stratification processes.

Shirley Dex is currently Senior Lecturer in Economics at the University of Keele. She was previously Lecturer in Economics at the University of Aston in Birmingham and a Tutor in Sociology at the University of Exeter. She is the author of *The Sexual Division of Work: Conceptual Revolutions in the Social Sciences* (1985); *British and American Women at Work: Do Equal Opportunities Matter?* (1986, with Lois B. Shaw); *Women's Occupational Mobility* (1987); and *Women's Attitudes towards Work* (1988).

Josef Esser has been Professor of Political Science at the University of Frankfurt am Main since 1981. He studied at the Free University of West Berlin and the University of Konstanz, where he completed his doctorate in 1974 and his 'habilitation' in 1981. He has held visiting professorships and fellowships at the Universities of Leiden, Leuven and Cambridge, and at Nuffield College, Oxford. His main publications include: *Einführung in die materialistiche Staatsanalyse* (1975); *Gewerkschaften in der Krise* (1982); *Krisenreguliering* (1983, with W. Fach and W. Väth); and *Die politische Ökonomie der Liebe* (1986, with A. Drescher and W. Fach). His current research interests are in the areas of state theory, industrial policy in international comparison, and the competitive position of Europe *vis-à-vis* Japan and the USA.

Giorgio Gagliani graduated from the University of Rome in 1965, was awarded an MA in Economics from the University of Chicago in 1969, and has been Professor of Labour Economics at the University of Calabria since 1981. He has held visiting fellowships at the Universities of California (Berkeley) and Oxford. He is the author of books and articles on the relations between personal and functional income distribution and economic development, trends in wage and salary differentials, and the structure of employment. Articles in English have appeared in the *European Economic Review* (1977), *American Journal of Sociology* (1981), *European Sociological Review* (1985) and *Annual Review of Sociology* (1987).

Duncan Gallie is currently an Official Fellow at Nuffield College, Oxford. Prior to this, he held appointments at the Universities of Warwick and Essex. In the 1970s he carried out comparative research in France and Britain on the implications of advanced technology for work experience and industrial relations (*In Search of the New Working Class*, 1978). This was followed by a study of the nature and determinants of attitudes to social inequality in the two countries (*Social Inequality and Class Radicalism in France and Britain*, 1983), which was awarded the American Sociological Association's Distinguished Contribution to Scholarship Award (Sorokin Prize). He has edited two books on labour market and employment experiences, *New Approaches to Economic Life* (1985, with Bryan Roberts and Ruth Finnegan) and *Employment in Britain* (1988). Since 1985 he has been national coordinator of the 'Social Change and Economic Life Initiative', a major inter-university and interdisciplinary research programme funded by the ESRC.

Niamh Hardiman is a Fellow of Somerville College, Oxford, where she teaches politics and sociology. She studied at University College, Dublin, and at Nuffield College, Oxford, and worked for a time at the Economic and Social Research Institute in Dublin. She is the author of *Pay, Politics and Economic Performance in Ireland*, 1970–1987 (1988), and of a number of articles on issues in contemporary political economy.

Anthony Heath is an Official Fellow at Nuffield College, Oxford. He read classics, then economics at Trinity College, Cambridge, achieving First Class Honours in both. He gained his PhD in sociology from Cambridge University, and was a Fellow of Jesus College, Oxford, from 1970 to 1986. He has published numerous articles and books, including *Rational Choice and Social Exchange* (1976); *Origins and Destinations* (1980, with A. H. Halsey and J. M. Ridge); *Social Mobility* (1981); and *How Britain Votes* (1985, with R. Jowell and J. Curtice). He was Co-director (with Roger Jowell of SCPR) of the 1987 British General Election Study, and is currently engaged (also with Roger Jowell) in an ESRC-funded project on understanding change in social and political attitudes in Britain.

Terry Johnson is at present Professor and Head of the Department of Sociology, University of Leicester. He has published widely on a range of topics in sociology, including *The Structure of Social Theory* (1984, with C. Dandeker and C. Ashworth) and *Professions and Power* (1972). His current research interest is in the effects of deregulation on the professions.

Dennis Kavanagh is Professor and Head of the Department of Politics at the University of Nottingham. He has also taught at the University of Hull, the University of Manchester and at a number of American universities. He is co-author of the last five Nuffield studies of British general elections. Among his recent publications are *Political Science and Political Behaviour* (1983); *British Politics: Continuities and Change* (1986); and *Thatcherism and British Politics: The End of Consensus?* (1987).

Jonathan Kelley was educated at Cambridge University, the Indian Institute of Technology, Kanpur, and the University of California (Berkeley), where he completed his doctorate in 1971. He has held posts at the University of California (Berkeley and Los Angeles), Yale University, Columbia University and the Aus-tralian National University (Canberra). Since 1982 he has been Director of the Australian National Social Science Survey based at ANU. He has published widely in the fields of social class, comparative social mobility, gender, electoral behaviour, and immigration and job discrimination, and his book *Revolution and the Rebirth of Inequality: A Theory Applied to the National Revolution in Bolivia* (with H. Klein) was awarded the American Association for the Advancement of Science Prize for Behavioral Science Research in 1977. His most recent book is *Australians' Attitudes to Overseas Aid* (1989).

Susan McRae is currently Senior Fellow and Women's Employment Programme Leader at the Policy Studies Institute, London. She has a BA from Simon Fraser University, an MA from the University of Toronto and a DPhil from the University of Oxford. Prior to her appointment at the Policy Studies Institute she was a Junior

Research Fellow at Nuffield College, Oxford. Her main publications include *Cross-Class Families—A Study of Wives' Occupational Superiority* (1986); *Young and Jobless—The Social and Personal Consequences of Long-term Youth Unemployment* (1987); and *Working Time and Family Life* (1989). She is currently working on a national survey of women which focuses on maternity rights and benefits and on employment changes over childbirth.

Gordon Marshall is currently Senior Lecturer in Sociology at the University of Essex. He was educated at the Universities of Stirling and Oxford before his appointment as Lecturer at Essex in 1978. His publications include *Presbyteries and Profits* (1980); *In Search of the Spirit of Capitalism* (1982); *Social Class in Modern Britain* (1988, with H. Newby, D. Rose and C. Vogler); and numerous articles on sociological theory and social stratification. His most recent book is *In Praise of Sociology* (1990).

Karl Ulrich Mayer has been, since 1983, Co-Director of the Max-Planck-Institute of Human Development and Education, West Berlin, and Head of its Centre on Education, Work and Societal Development. He has also been Professor of Sociology at the Free University, West Berlin, since 1984. He has studied sociology in the USA and West Germany, and has held posts and fellowships at the Universities of Frankfurt, Mannheim, Nuffield College (Oxford), Zürich and Harvard. He has also been Co-Director of the Mobility Project of the University of Mannheim since 1971. His main research interests are in social stratification and mobility, occupational careers and labour markets, and sociology of the life course. He is author and co-author of many books, including *Klassenlagen und Sozialstruktur* (1977, with J. Handl and W. Müller) and *Ereignisanalyse* (1986, with H.-P. Blossfeld and A. Hamerle). He is also co-editor of *Event History Analysis and Life Course Research* (1989, with N. Tuma), and has been editor of the *European Sociological Review* since its inception in 1984.

Walter Müller has been awarded degrees in philosophy, economics and sociology from the Universities of Leuven, Cologne, Konstanz and Mannheim, and has been Professor of Sociology at the University of Mannheim since 1980. He has also held posts or fellowships at the Universities of Konstanz, Frankfurt, Bielefeld, Geneva, Wisconsin (Madison), Nuffield College (Oxford) and the Center for Advanced Study in the Behavioral Sciences (Stanford). He was Director of the VASMA Research Unit for the Comparative Analysis of Social Structure at the University of Mannheim from 1978–85 and Co-ordinator (with John H. Goldthorpe) of the CASMIN-Project. His book publications include *Familie, Schule, Beruf* (1975); *Klassenlagen und Sozialstruktur* (1977, with J. Handl and K. U. Mayer); and *Strukturwandel der Frauenarbeit 1880–1980* (1983, with J. Handl and A. Wilms). His current research interests are in educational systems and class mobility in industrial nations and changing social structures in Western Europe.

Geoff Payne is Dean of the Faculty of Social Science and Professor of Social Research at the Polytechnic South-West in Plymouth. From 1973 to 1977 he was Director of the Scottish Mobility Study at Aberdeen University. His work on occupational and social mobility has appeared in numerous journals, and he is author of *Mobility and Change in Modern Society* (1987) and *Employment and Opportunity* (1987). His most recent book is an edited collection of papers (with P. Abbott) entitled *The Social Mobility of Women*, published by Falmer Press in 1990.

Raymond Plant has been Professor of Politics at the University of Southampton since 1979. He has a BA in Philosophy from King's College, London, a PhD from the University of Hull, and was Lecturer, then Senior Lecturer, in Philosophy at the University of Manchester from 1967 to 1979. He has been a member of a number of Social Science Research Council Committees (1979–84), chaired the British Council of Churches Working Party on Poverty in the UK (1981–82), and has been Chairman of the Political Studies Association (1985–89) and of the Standing Conference of Heads of Department of Politics (since 1988). He has published a number of books, including *Hegel* (1973); *Political Philosophy and Social Welfare* (1981, with H. Lesser and P. Taylor-Goodby); *Philosophy, Politics and Citizenship: The Life and Thought of the British Idealists* (1983, with A. Vincent); and *Conservative Capitalism in Britain and the United States: A Critical Appraisal* (1988, with K. Hoover).

William Roche is a graduate of University College, Dublin (MSocSc) and Oxford University (DPhil). A former Research Fellow of Nuffield College, Oxford, he is currently Senior Lecturer in Industrial Relations at University College, Dublin. He has published widely on industrial and economic sociology and industrial relations. He is currently Co-director of a comparative study, based at the University of Mannheim, of the Development of Trade Unions in the post-war West European democracies (the DUES Project).

John Westergaard, who is of Danish origin, graduated from the London School of Economics in 1951. After research at University College London (UCL) and Nottingham University, he returned to teach at the LSE from 1956 to 1975, when he became Professor of Sociological Studies at Sheffield University. He is still active in research there, though he retired from the chair in 1986. His earlier work focused on urban sociology (in association with the Centre for Urban Studies, UCL, and its Director, Ruth Glass), but his main concern for long has been class structure and change. His publications include *Class in a Capitalist Society* (1975, with Henrietta Resler) and *After Redundancy* (1989, with Iain Noble and Alan Walker).

John H. Goldthorpe: Outline Intellectual Biography

1935	Born 27 May
1946–53	Attends Wath-upon-Dearne Grammar School, Rotherham, Yorkshire
1953–56	Undergraduate student, University College, University of London
1956	Awarded BA Honours (First Class) in Modern History; Pollard prize for work in the sources of English history; Coal Industry Social Welfare Organization postgraduate scholarship for research in industrial sociology
1956–57	Research student in Department of Sociology, London School of Economics and Political Science
1957	Research Assistant in Department of Social Administration, LSE, in connection with a study of personnel policies in nationalized industries directed by John H. Smith
1957–60	Assistant Lecturer, Department of Sociology, University of Leicester
1959	Publishes first journal article on 'Technical Organization as a Factor in Supervision-Worker Conflict'
1960–69	Fellow, King's College, Cambridge
1961–69	Assistant Lecturer, then (from 1963) Lecturer, Faculty of Economics and Politics, University of Cambridge
1962	With David Lockwood initiates research project into the sociology of the affluent worker
1962–64	Undertakes fieldwork for *Affluent Worker* study with David Lockwood, Frank Bechhofer, Jennifer Platt (and the participation of many other research assistants, including Michael Rose and Rosemary Crompton)
1963	Publishes article (with David Lockwood) on 'Affluence and the British Class Structure'

1965–68   On establishment of Social Science Research Council becomes member of Sociology Committee

1966   Engages in debate in *Sociological Review* on 'Industrialisation and the Problem of "Convergence"'

1966–69   Member of first Editorial Board of *Sociology*, journal of the British Sociological Association

1967   Publishes article (with Lockwood, Bechhofer and Platt) on 'The Affluent Worker and the Thesis of Embourgeoisement'

1968   Publishes two books (with Lockwood, Bechhofer and Platt): *The Affluent Worker: Industrial Attitudes and Behaviour* and *The Affluent Worker: Political Attitudes and Behaviour*

1969   Publishes third book (with Lockwood, Bechhofer and Platt): *The Affluent Worker in the Class Structure*

1969-date   Appointed Official Fellow, Nuffield College, Oxford; joins 'Social Mobility Group', Nuffield College

1969   President, Section N (Sociology), British Association for the Advancement of Science

1969–72   Editor of *Sociology*

1970–72   Engages in debate with W. W. Daniel in *Journal of Management Studies* on the social action approach to industrial sociology

1971   Publishes article 'Theories of Industrial Society: Reflections on the Recrudescence of Historicism and the Future of Futurology'

1971-   Member, Research Committee on Social Stratification and Mobility, International Sociological Association; Vice-President (from 1974 to 1982), President (1982–85)

1972   With A. H. Halsey and Jean Floud directs 'Oxford Mobility Survey', which provides the main basis for his research project on occupational and social mobility in Britain

1972–74   With Keith Hope works on the development of a new approach to occupational grading

1974   Publishes book (with Keith Hope): *The Social Grading of Occupations: A New Approach and Scale*; also article 'Industrial Relations in Great Britain: A Critique of Reformism'

1977–78   Produces first publications (with Research Officer Catriona Llewellyn and Director of Nuffield Research Services Unit, Clive Payne) from research project on social mobility and the class structure

1977–78   Organizes multi-disciplinary international conference with economist Fred Hirsch on problems of inflation; joint editor (with Hirsch) of book arising from the conference, *The Political Economy of Inflation* (1978)

1979   Co-authors (with Robert Erikson and Lucienne Portocarero) first of three papers on class mobility in three countries: England, France and Sweden

1980   Publishes (with the assistance of Catriona Llewellyn and Clive Payne) first edition of *Social Mobility and Class Structure in Modern Britain*

1982   With Walter Müller inaugurates international CASMIN (Comparative Analysis of Social Mobility in Industrial Nations) research project; also publishes article 'On the Service Class, Its Formation and Future'

1982–83   Member of joint European and US-American study group on the political economy of Western European nations

1983–88   Publishes series of articles in *Sociology* on 'Women and Class Analysis'

1984   Edits book *Order and Conflict in Contemporary Capitalism* arising from joint European/US-American study group (see entry for 1982–83); author of concluding chapter, 'The End of Convergence: Corporatist and Dualist Tendencies in Modern Western Societies'

1984   Made Fellow of British Academy; awarded Helsinki University Medal

1984   With Karl Ulrich Mayer and Stein Ringen, founds *European Sociological Review* and becomes its Associate Editor (1984–89)

1986–89   Member of Social Affairs Committee and of Society and Politics Research Development Group, Economic and Social Research Council

1987   Publishes second, substantially extended and updated edition of *Social Mobility and Class Structure in Britain*; also first major journal publications (with Robert Erikson) from the CASMIN Project

1988   Made member of the Academia Europaea

1988-date   British Academy Assessor, Economic and Social Research Council

Bibliography

Abbott, P. and Sapsford, R. (1986) 'Class Identification of Married Working Women', *British Journal of Sociology*, Vol. 37, pp. 535–49.

Abbott, P. and Sapsford, R. (1987) *Women and Social Class*, London, Tavistock.

Abell, P. (1990) 'Methodological Achievements in Sociology over the Past Few Decades', in C. Bryant and H. Becker (eds), *What Has Sociology Achieved?*, London, Macmillan, forthcoming.

Abercrombie, N. and Urry, J. (1983) *Capital, Labour and the Middle Classes*, London, Allen and Unwin.

Abrams, M., Rose, R. and Hinden, R. (1960) *Must Labour Lose?*, Harmondsworth, Penguin Books.

Abrams, P., Deem, R., Finch, J. and Rock, P. (eds) (1980) *Practice and Progress: British Sociology 1950–1980*, London, George Allen and Unwin.

Acker, J. (1973) 'Women and Social Stratification: A Case of Intellectual Sexism', *American Journal of Sociology*, Vol. 78, No. 4, pp. 936–45.

Aglietta, M. (1976) *Régulation et crises du capitalisme*, Paris, Calmann-Levy.

Ahrne, G. and Leiulfsrud, H. (1984) *The State and the Class Structure in Sweden in 1980*, Comparative Project on Class Structure and Class Consciousness, Working Paper Series No. 20, Madison, University of Wisconsin, Department of Sociology.

Ahrne, G., Blom, R., Melin, H. and Nicula, J. (eds) (1988) *Class and Social Organisation in Finland, Sweden and Norway*, Uppsala, Almqvist and Wiksell.

Alexander, J., Giesen, B., Münch, R. and Smelser, N. (eds) (1987) *The Micro-Macro Link*, Berkeley, Calif., University of California Press.

Allen, S. (1982) 'Gender Inequality and Class Formation', in Giddens and Mackenzie (1982), pp. 137–47.

Allmendinger, J. (1989) 'Educational Systems and Labor Market Outcomes', *European Sociological Review*, Vol. 5, No. 3, pp. 231–50.

Alt, J. (1978) *The Politics of Economic Decline*, Cambridge, Cambridge University Press.

Argyris, C. (1957) *Personality and Organization*, New York, Harper.

Arrighi, G. (1986) 'Eine Krise der Hegemonie', in S. Amin *et al.*, *Dynamik der globalen Krise*, Opladen, Westdeutscher Verlag, pp. 36–75.

Ashburner, L. (1987) *The Effects of New Technology on Employment Structures in the Service Sector*, PhD, University of Aston.

Attewell, P. (1987) 'The Deskilling Controversy', *Work and Occupations*, Vol. 14, pp. 323–46.

Bain, G. (1970) *The Growth of White-Collar Unionism*, Oxford, Oxford University Press.

Baldamus, W. (1961) *Efficiency and Effort*, London, Tavistock.

Baldamus, W. (1976) *The Structure of Sociological Inference*, London, Martin Robertson.

Banks, J. (1969) 'Review' of Goldthorpe *et al.*, *The Affluent Worker: Political Attitudes and Behaviour*, *British Journal of Sociology*, Vol. 20, No. 1, pp. 90–2.

Barkin, S. (ed) (1983) *Worker Miltancy and Its Consequences*, 2nd ed., New York, Praeger.

Batstone, E. (1984) *Working Order*, Oxford, Blackwell.

Batstone, E. (1988a) *The Reform of Workplace Industrial Relations*, Oxford, Clarendon Press.

Batstone, E. (1988b) 'The Frontier of Control', in Gallie (1988a), pp. 218–47.

Batstone, E., Boraston, I. and Frenkel, S. (1977) *Shop Stewards in Action*, Oxford, Blackwell.

Batstone, E., Gourlay, I., Moore, R. and Levie, H. (1987) *New Technology and the Process of Labour Regulation*, Oxford, Clarendon Press.

Baumol, W. (1967) 'Macro-economics of Unbalanced Growth: The Anatomy of Urban Crisis', *American Economic Review*, Vol. 57, pp. 415–26.

451

Beales, L. (1946) 'The Making of Social Policy', Hobhouse Memorial Lecture No. 15, delivered on 23 May 1945, published by Geoffrey Cumberlege, Oxford University Press, London.

Bechhofer, F. (1986) 'Gender and Stratification: Some General Remarks', in Crompton and Mann (1986), pp. 224–30.

Beechey, V. and Perkins, T. (1987) *A Matter of Hours: Women, Part-time Work and the Labour Market*, Oxford, Blackwell.

Bell, D. (1967) 'Notes on the Post-Industrial Society', *The Public Interest*, No. 6, pp. 24–55, No. 7, pp. 102–08.

Bell, D. (1968) 'The Measurement of Knowledge and Technology', in E. Sheldon and W. Moore (eds), *Indicators of Social Change*, New York, Russell Sage Foundation, pp. 145–246.

Bell, D. (1973) *The Coming of Post-Industrial Society*, Harmondsworth, Penguin.

Bell, D. (1976) *The Cultural Contradictions of Capitalism*, London, Heinemann.

Bendix, R. (1963) *Work and Authority in Industry*, New York, Harper and Row.

Berger, S. (ed) (1981) *Organizing Interests in Western Europe*, Cambridge, Cambridge University Press, including editorial 'Introduction', pp. 1–23.

Berrington, H. (ed) (1984) *Change in British Politics*, London, Frank Cass.

Beynon, H. (1973) *Working for Ford*, London, Allen Lane.

Binswanger, H. and Ruttan, V. (1978) *Induced Innovation*, Baltimore, Md., Johns Hopkins University Press.

Bishop, Y., Fienberg, S. and Holland, P. (1977) *Discrete Multivariate Analysis: Theory and Practice*, Cambridge, Mass., MIT Press.

Blackburn, R. (1967) *Union Character and Social Class*, London, Batsford.

Blackburn, R. and Mann, M. (1979) *The Working Class in the Labour Market*, London, Macmillan.

Blain, A. (1972) *Pilots and Management: Industrial Relations in the UK Airlines*, London, George Allen and Unwin.

Blau, P. and Duncan, O. (1967) *The American Occupational Structure*, New York, Wiley.

Blauner, R. (1960) 'Work Satisfaction and Industrial Trends in Modern Society', in W. Galenson and S. M. Lipset (eds), *Labor and Trade Unionism*, New York, Wiley, pp. 339–60.

Blauner, R. (1964) *Alienation and Freedom*, Chicago, Ill., University of Chicago Press.

Blossfeld, H. (1986) 'Career Opportunities in the Federal Republic of Germany: A Dynamic Approach to the Study of Life Course, Cohort and Period Effects', *European Sociological Review*, Vol. 2, pp. 208–25.

Boston, J. (1983) *The Theory and Practice of Voluntary Incomes Policies with Particular Reference to the British Labour Government's Social Contract 1974–79*, DPhil Thesis, University of Oxford.

Boudon, R. (1982) *The Unintended Consequences of Social Action*, London, Macmillan.

Boudon, R. (1986) *Theories of Social Change*, Cambridge, Polity Press.

Boudon, R. (1987) 'The Individualistic Tradition in Sociology', in Alexander *et al.* (1987), pp. 45–70.

Bourdieu, P. (1984) *Distinction: A Social Critique of the Judgement of Taste*, Cambridge, Mass., Harvard University Press.

Boyer, R. (ed) (1986) *La théorie de la régulation*, Paris, Edition la Découverte.

Braverman, H. (1974) *Labor and Monopoly Capital*, New York/London, Monthly Review Press.

Brittan, S. (1973) *Capitalism and the Permissive Society*, London, Macmillan.

Brittan, S. (1975) 'The Economic Contradictions of Democracy', *British Journal of Political Science*, Vol. 5, pp. 129–59.

Brittan, S. (1983) *The Role and Limits of Government*, London, Temple Smith.

Brittan, S. and Lilley, P. (1977) *The Delusion of Incomes Policy*, London, Temple Smith.

Britten, N. and Heath, A. (1983) 'Women, Men and Social Class', in Gamarnikow *et al.* (1983), pp. 46–60.

Broom, L. and Jones, F. (1969) 'Father-to-Son Mobility: Australia in Comparative Perspective', *American Journal of Sociology*, Vol. 74, pp. 333–42.

Broom, L., Jones, F., McDonnell, P. and Williams, T. (1980) *The Inheritance of Inequality*, London, Routledge and Kegan Paul.

Brown, A. (1985) *World Inflation Since 1950*, Cambridge, Cambridge University Press.

Brown, R., Curran, M. and Cousins, J. (1983) *Changing Attitudes to Employment*, Research Paper No. 40, London, Department of Employment.

Brown, W. (1973) *Piecework Bargaining*, Oxford, Blackwell.

Brown, W. (1986) 'The Changing Role of Trade Unions in the Management of Labour', *British Journal of Industrial Relations*, Vol. 24, pp. 161–8.

Bruno, M. and Sachs, D. (1985) *The Economics of International Stagflation*, Oxford, Blackwell.

Brzezinski, Z. and Huntingdon, S. (1968) *Political Power: USA/USSR*, New York, Viking Press.

Buci-Glucksmann, C. and Therborn, G. (1982) *Der sozialdemokratische Staat*, Hamburg, VSA.

Bulmer, M. (1989) 'Successful Applications of Sociology: Can Britain Learn from Abroad?', Paper presented to the Annual Conference of the British Sociological Association, Plymouth.

Burawoy, M. (1987) 'The Limits of Wright's Analytical Marxism and an Alternative', *Berkeley Journal of Sociology*, Vol. 32, pp. 51–72.

Burke, K. (1964) *Perspectives by Incongruity*, Bloomington, Ind., University of Indiana Press.

Butler, D. and Kavanagh, D. (1984) *The British General Election of 1983*, London, Macmillan.

Butler, D. and Kavanagh, D. (1988) *The British General Election of 1987*, London, Macmillan.

Butler, D. and Stokes, D. (1969) *Political Change in Britain*, London, Macmillan; 2nd edition, 1974.

Cameron, D. (1984) 'Social Democracy, Corporatism, Labour Quiescence and the Representation of Economic Interests in Advanced Capitalist Society', in Goldthorpe (1984a), pp. 143–78.

Camhis, M. (1979) *Planning Theory and Philosophy*, London, Tavistock.

Carchedi, G. (1977) *On the Economic Identification of Social Classes*, London, Routledge and Kegan Paul.

Carr, E. (1951) *The New Society*, London, Macmillan.

Carr, E. (1964) *What Is History?*, Harmondsworth, Penguin.

Carroll, G. (ed) (1988) *Ecological Models of Organizations*, Cambridge, Mass., Ballinger.

Carroll, G. and Mayer, K. U. (1986) 'Job-shift Patterns in the Federal Republic of Germany: The Effects of Social Class, Industrial Sector and Organizational Size', *American Sociological Review*, Vol. 51, No. 3, pp. 323–41.

Castles, F. (1978) *The Social Democratic Image of Society*, London, Routledge and Kegan Paul.

Castles, F. (ed) (1982) *The Impact of Parties*, London, Sage.

Castles, S. and Kosack, G. (1973) *Immigrant Workers and Class Structure in Western Europe*, London, Oxford University Press.

Centre d'étude des revenus et des coûts (1985) *Les revenus des Français: la croissance et la crise (1960–1983)*, Paris, La Documentation Française.

Chalmers, A. (1982) *What Is This Thing Called Science?*, 2nd ed., Milton Keynes, Open University Press.

Chase, I. (1975) 'A Comparison of Men's and Women's Intergenerational Mobility in the United States', *American Sociological Review*, Vol. 40, pp. 483–505.

Child, J. and Partridge, B. (1982) *Lost Managers: Supervisors in Industry and Society*, Cambridge, Cambridge University Press.

Clarke, T. and Clements, L. (eds) (1977) *Trade Unions under Capitalism*, London, Fontana.

Clegg, H. (1975) 'Pluralism in Industrial Relations', *British Journal of Industrial Relations*, Vol. 13, No. 3, pp. 309–16.

Cockburn, C. (1986) 'The Relations of Technology: What Implications for Theories of Sex and Class?', in Crompton and Mann (1986), pp. 74–85.

Colbjørnsen, T., Birkelund, G., Hernes, G. and Knudsen, K. (1987) *Klassesamfunnet pa Hell*, Oslo, Universiteitsforlaget.

Colclough, G. and Horan, P. (1983) 'The Status Attainment Paradigm: An Application of a Kuhnian Perspective', *Sociological Quarterly*, Vol. 24, pp. 25–42.

Coleman, J. (1986) *Individual Interests and Collective Action: Selected Essays*, Cambridge, Mass., Cambridge University Press.

Coser, L. (1975) 'Two Methods in Search of Substance', *American Sociological Review*, Vol. 40, pp. 691–700.

Craig, C. (1969) *Men in Manufacturing Industry*, Cambridge, University of Cambridge, Department of Applied Economics.

Crewe, I. (1973) 'The Politics of "Affluent" and "Traditional" Workers in Britain: An Aggregate Data Analysis', *British Journal of Political Science*, Vol. 3, No. 1, pp. 29–52.

Crewe, I. (1984) 'Partisan Dealignment Ten Years On', in Berrington (1984), pp. 183–215.

Crewe, I. (1986) 'On the Death and Resurrection of Class Voting: Some Comments on *How Britain Votes*', *Political Studies*, Vol. 34, pp. 620–38.

Crewe, I. (1988) 'Has the Electorate Become Thatcherite?', in R. Skidelsky (ed), *Thatcherism*, London, Chatto and Windus, pp. 25–49.

Crompton, R. (1979) 'Trade Unionism and the Insurance Clerk', *Sociology*, Vol. 13, September, pp. 403–26.

Crompton, R. (1980) 'Class Mobility in Modern Britain', *Sociology*, Vol. 14, No. 1, pp. 117–19.

Crompton, R. (1986) 'Women and the "Service Class"', in Crompton and Mann (1986), pp. 119–36.

Crompton, R. (1988) 'Occupational Segregation', Working Paper No. 2, Social Change and Economic Life Initiative, London, ESRC.

Crompton, R. and Gubbay, J. (1977) *Economy and Class Structure*, London, Macmillan.

Crompton, R. and Jones, G. (1984) *White-collar Proletariat: Deskilling and Gender in Clerical Work*, London, Macmillan.

Crompton, R. and Jones, G. (1988) 'Doing Research in White-Collar Organisations', in A. Bryman (ed), *Doing Research in Organizations*, London, Routledge and Kegan Paul, pp. 68–81.

Crompton, R. and Mann, M. (eds) (1986) *Gender and Stratification*, Cambridge, Polity Press, including editorial 'Introduction'.

Crompton, R. and Sanderson, K. (1986) 'Credentials and Careers: Some Implications of the Increase of Professional Qualifications amongst Women', *Sociology*, Vol. 20, pp. 25–42.

Crosland, C. A. R. (1956) *The Future of Socialism*, London, Cape.

Crouch, C. (1977) *Class Conflict and the Industrial Relations Crisis*, London, Heinemann.

Crouch, C. (1980) 'Varieties of Trade Union Weakness: Organized Labour and Capital Formation in Britain, Federal Germany and Sweden', *West European Politics*, Vol. 3, No. 1, pp. 87–106.

Crouch, C. (1983) 'Pluralism and the New Corporatism: A Rejoinder', *Political Studies*, Vol. 31, pp. 452–60.

Crouch, C. (1986) 'Conservative Industrial Relations Policy: Towards Labour Exclusion?', in Jacobi *et al.* (1986), pp. 131–53.

Crouch, C. and Pizzorno, A. (eds) (1978) *The Resurgence of Class Conflict in Western Europe since 1968*, 2 vols, London, Macmillan.

CSO (1987) *Economic Trends*, London, HMSO.

CSO (1988) *Social Trends*, Vol. 18, London, HMSO.

Current Sweden (1985) 'The Swedish Collective Bargaining Model in Transition', No. 337, August.

Current Sweden (1988) 'Election Year 88: Economic Policy and the Election', No. 363, June.

Dahrendorf, R. (1959) *Class and Class Conflict in Industrial Society*, London, Routledge and Kegan Paul.

Daniel, W. (1969) 'Industrial Behaviour and Orientations to Work: A Critique', *Journal of Management Studies*, Vol. 6, pp. 366–75.

Daniel, W. (1971) 'Productivity Bargaining and Orientation to Work: A Rejoinder to Goldthorpe', *Journal of Management Studies*, Vol. 8, pp. 329–35.

Daniel, W. (1987) *Workplace Industrial Relations and Technical Change*, London, Frances Pinter.

Davis, K. (1962) 'The Role of Class Mobility in Economic Development', *Population Review*, Vol. 6, No. 2, pp. 67–73.

Delphy, C. (1981) 'Women in Stratification Studies', in H. Roberts (ed), *Doing Feminist Research*, London, Routledge and Kegan Paul, pp. 114–28.

Delphy, C. and Leonard, D. (1986) 'Class Analysis, Gender Analysis and the Family', in Crompton and Mann (1986), pp. 57–73.

Dennis, N. and Halsey, A. H. (1988) *English Ethical Socialism*, Oxford, Clarendon Press.

Department of Employment (DOE) (1988) *Employment Gazette*, London, HMSO, February.

Dessens, J. *et al.* (1985) 'Intergenerational Class Mobility in the Netherlands in Historical and Comparative Perspective', Paper presented at the Annual Meeting of the Stratification and Mobility Research Committee of the ISA, Harvard University.

Dex, S. (1984) *Women's Work Histories: An Analysis of the Women and Employment Survey*, Department of Employment Research Paper No. 46, London, HMSO.

Dex, S. (1985) *The Sexual Division of Work: Conceptual Revolutions in the Social Sciences*, Brighton, Wheatsheaf.

Dex, S. (1987) *Women's Occupational Mobility*, London, Macmillan.

Dicey, A. (1905) *Law and Public Opinion in England during the Nineteenth Century*, London, Macmillan.

Diprete, T. (1988) 'The Upgrading and Downgrading of Occupations: Status Redefinition vs. Deskilling as Alternative Theories of Change', *Social Forces*, Vol. 66, pp. 725–46.

Djilas, M. (1957/66) *The New Class: An Analysis of the Communist System*, New York, Praeger; London, George Allen and Unwin.

Dore, R. (1973) *British Factory—Japanese Factory*, London, George Allen and Unwin.

Duke, V. and Edgell, S. (1987) 'The Operationalisation of Class in British Sociology: Theoretical and Empirical Considerations', *British Journal of Sociology*, Vol. 38, No. 4, pp. 445–63.

Duncan, O. (1961) 'A Socioeconomic Index for All Occupations', in A. Reiss (ed), *Occupations and Social Status*, New York, Free Press, pp. 109–38.

Duncan, O. (1966) 'Methodological Issues in the Study of Social Mobility', in Smelser and Lipset (1966), pp. 51–97.

Duncan, O. (1968) 'Inheritance of Poverty or Inheritance of Race?', in D. Moynihan (ed), *On Understanding Poverty: Perspectives from the Social Sciences*, New York, Basic Books, pp. 85–110.

Duncan, O. (1979) 'How Destination Depends on Origin in the Occupational Mobility Table', *American Journal of Sociology*, Vol. 84, pp. 793–801.

Duncan, O., Featherman, D. and Duncan, B. (1972) *Socioeconomic Background and Achievement*, New York, Seminar.

Duncan, O. and Hodge, R. (1963) 'Education and Occupational Mobility', *American Journal of Sociology*, Vol. 67, pp. 629–44.

Duncan-Jones, P. (1972) 'Social Mobility, Canonical Scoring and Occupational Classification', in Hope (1972), pp. 191–210.

Dunleavy, P. (1987) 'Class Dealignment in Britain Revisited: Why Odds Ratios Give Odd Results', *West European Politics*, Vol. 10, pp. 400–19.

Edmondson, R. (1984) *Rhetoric in Sociology*, London, Macmillan.

Eichler, M. (1980) *The Double Standard: A Feminist Critique of Feminist Social Science*, London, Croom Helm.

Eisenstein, Z. (1979) *Capitalist Patriarchy and the Case for Socialist Feminism*, New York, Monthly Review Press.

Eldridge, J. (1980) *Recent British Sociology*, London, Macmillan.

Eliott, R. (1976) 'The National Wage Round in the United Kingdom: A Sceptical View', *Oxford Bulletin of Economics and Statistics*, Vol. 38, pp. 179–201.

Eliott, R. and Fallick, J. (1981) *Pay in the Public Sector*, London, Macmillan.

Elster, J. (1982) 'Marxism, Functionalism and Game Theory', *Theory and Society*, Vol. 11, pp. 453–82.

Elster, J. (1983a) *Explaining Technical Change*, Cambridge, Cambridge University Press.

Elster, J. (1983b) *Sour Grapes: Studies in the Subversion of Rationality*, Cambridge, Cambridge University Press.

Elster, J. (1984) *Ulysses and the Sirens: Studies in Rationality and Irrationality*, rev. ed., Cambridge, Cambridge University Press.

Elster, J. (1985) *Making Sense of Marx*, Cambridge, Cambridge University Press.

Elster, J. (1986) 'Further Thoughts on Marxism, Functionalism and Game Theory', in J. Roemer (ed), *Analytical Marxism*, Cambridge, Cambridge University Press, pp. 202–20.

Equal Opportunities Commission (EOC) (1986) *Men and Women in Britain: A Statistical Profile*, Manchester, Equal Opportunities Commission.

Erikson, R. (1984) 'Social Class of Men, Women and Families', *Sociology*, Vol. 18, pp. 500–14.

Erikson, R. and Goldthorpe, J. H. (1985) 'Are American Rates of Social Mobility Exceptionally High? New Evidence on an Old Issue', *European Sociological Review*, Vol. 1, pp. 1–22.

Erikson, R. and Goldthorpe, J. H. (1987a) 'Commonality and Variation in Social Fluidity in Industrial Nations. Part I: A Model for Evaluating the "FJH Hypothesis"', *European Sociological Review*, Vol. 3, No. 1, pp. 54–77.

Erikson, R. and Goldthorpe, J. H. (1987b) 'Commonality and Variation in Social Fluidity in Industrial Nations. Part II: The Model of Core Social Fluidity Applied', *European Sociological Review*, Vol. 3, No. 2, pp. 145–66.

Erikson, R. and Goldthorpe, J. H. (1987c) 'Worklife and Intergenerational Class Mobility: A Comparative Analysis', CASMIN Working Paper, No. 10, University of Mannheim.

Erikson, R. and Goldthorpe, J. H. (1988a) 'The Class Schema of the CASMIN Project', Paper prepared for the CASMIN Conference, Schloss Reisensburg, West Germany.

Erikson, R. and Goldthorpe, J. H. (1988b) 'Does the Class Mobility of Women Differ from that of Men? Cross-Sex Comparisons in Cross-National Perspective', CASMIN Working Paper No. 14, University of Mannheim.

Erikson, R. and Goldthorpe, J. H. (1988c) 'Women at Class Crossroads: A Critical Note', *Sociology*, Vol. 22, pp. 545–53.

Erikson, R. and Goldthorpe, J. H. (1988d) 'Trends in Class Mobility: A Test of Hypotheses against the European Experience', CASMIN Working Paper No. 13, University of Mannheim.

Erikson, R. and Goldthorpe, J. H. (1988e) 'A Note on a National Variant of the Core Model for the Australian Mobility Table', Paper prepared for the CASMIN Conference, Schloss Reisensburg, West Germany.

Erikson, R. and Goldthorpe, J. H. (1988f) 'Introduction: Industrial Society and Social Mobility', Manuscript, Stockholm, Swedish Institute for Social Research, and Oxford, Nuffield College. Draft introductory chapter for the book of the CASMIN Project.

Erikson, R., Goldthorpe, J. H. and Portocarero, L. (1979) 'Intergenerational Class Mobility in Three Western European Societies: England, France and Sweden', *British Journal of Sociology*, Vol. 30, pp. 415–41.

Erikson, R., Goldthorpe, J. H. and Portocarero, L. (1982) 'Social Fluidity in Industrial Nations', *British Journal of Sociology*, Vol. 33, No. 4, pp. 1–34.

Erikson, R., Goldthorpe, J. H. and Portocarero, L. (1983) 'Intergenerational Class Mobility and the Convergence Thesis: England, France and Sweden'. *British Journal of Sociology*, Vol. 34, No. 3, pp. 303–43.

Erikson, R. and Widerberg, K. (1988) 'Vardagslivets strukturering—klass och kön', in U. Himmelstrand and G. Svensson (eds), *Sverige—vardag och struktur*, Stockholm, Norstedts, pp. 315–48.

Esping-Andersen, G. (1985) *Politics against Markets*, Princeton, N.J., Princeton University Press.

Esping-Andersen, G. and Korpi, W. (1984) 'Social Policy as Class Politics in Post-War Capitalism: Scandinavia, Austria and Germany', in Goldthorpe (1984a), pp. 179–208.

Esser, J. (1982) *Gewerkschaften in der Krise*, Frankfurt, Suhrkamp.

Esser, J. (1986) 'State, Business and Trade Unions in West Germany after the Political *Wende*', *West European Politics*, Vol. 9, pp. 198–214.

Evans, G., Heath, A. and Payne, C. (1989) 'Modelling Trends in the Class-Party Relationship 1964–1987 Using Loglinear Analysis', Paper presented to the ECPR Workshop on Social Structure and Electoral Change in Liberal Democracies, Paris.

Evans, M. (1987) 'Language Skill, Language Usage, and Opportunity: Immigrants in the Australian Labour Market', *Sociology*, Vol. 21, pp. 253–74.

Family Expenditure Survey (1988) London, HMSO.

Featherman, D. and Hauser, R. (1976) 'Changes in the Socioeconomic Stratification of the Races 1962–1973', *American Journal of Sociology*, Vol. 82, pp. 621–51.

Featherman, D. and Hauser, R. (1978) *Opportunity and Change*, New York, Academic Press.

Featherman, D., Jones, F. and Hauser, R. (1975) 'Assumptions of Social Mobility Research in the US: The Case of Occupational Status', *Social Science Research*, Vol. 4, pp. 329–60.

Featherman, D. and Selbee, K. (1988) 'Class Formation and Class Mobility: A New Approach with Counts from Life History Data', in M. Riley and B. Huber (eds) (1988) *Social Structure and Human Lives*, Newbury Park, Sage, pp. 247–64.

Fienberg, S. (1980) *The Analysis of Cross-Classified Categorical Data*, Cambridge, Mass., MIT Press.

Flanagan, R., Soskice, D. and Ulman, L. (1983) *Unionism, Economic Stabilization and Incomes Policies: European Experience*, Washington, D.C., Brookings Institution.

Flechtheim, O. (1966) 'Futurology, the New Science of Probability', Ch. 5 of *idem*, *History and Futurology*, Meisenheim-am-Glan, Anton Hain, pp. 69–80.

Flora, P. (ed) (1986/88) *Growth to Limits: The Western European Welfare States Since World War II*, 5 vols, Berlin, de Gruyter.

Form, W. (1987) 'On the Degradation of Skills', *Annual Review of Sociology*, Vol. 13, pp. 29–47.

Fox, A. (1973) 'Industrial Relations: A Social Critique of Pluralist Ideology', in J. Child (ed), *Man and Organization*, London, Allen and Unwin, pp. 185–233.

Fox, A. (1974) *Beyond Contract: Work, Power and Trust Relations*, London, Faber.

Fox, A. and Flanders, A. (1969) 'The Reform of Collective Bargaining: From Donovan to Durkheim', *British Journal of Industrial Relations*, Vol. 7, pp. 151–80. See also *idem*, 1970.

Fox, A. and Flanders, A. (1970) 'The Reform of Collective Bargaining: From Donovan to Durkheim', in A. Flanders, *Management and Unions*, London, Faber, pp. 241–76.

Franklin, M. (1985) *The Decline of Class Voting in Britain*, Oxford, Clarendon Press.

Freeman, G. (1979) *Immigrant Labor and Racial Conflict in Industrial Societies: The French and British Experience 1945–1975*, Princeton, N.J., Princeton University Press.

Frentzel-Zagorska, J. and Zagorski, K. (1989) 'East European Intellectuals on the Road of Dissent: The Old Prophecy of a New Class Re-examined', *Politics and Society*, Vol. 17, pp. 89–113.

Gagliani, G. (1981) 'How Many Working Classes?', *American Journal of Sociology*, Vol. 87, pp. 259–85.

Gagliani, G. (1985) 'Long-term Changes in the Occupational Structure', *European Journal of Sociology*, Vol. 1, No. 3, pp. 183–210.

Gagliani, G. (1987) 'Income Inequality and Economic Development', *Annual Review of Sociology*, Vol. 13, pp. 313–34.

Gallie, D. (1978) *In Search of the New Working Class*, Cambridge, Cambridge University Press.

Gallie, D. (1983) *Social Inequality and Class Radicalism in France and Britain*, Cambridge, Cambridge University Press.

Gallie, D. (1985) '*Les lois Auroux*: The Reform of French Industrial Relations?', in H. Machin and V. Wright (eds), *Economic Policy and Policy-Making under the Mitterand Presidency 1981–84*, London, Frances Pinter. pp. 205–21.

Gallie, D. (ed) (1988a) *Employment in Britain*, Oxford, Blackwell.

Gallie, D. (1988b) 'Employment, Unemployment and Social Stratification', in Gallie (1988a), pp. 465–92.

Gallie, D. (1988c) 'Technological Change, Gender and Skill', Paper presented at Nuffield/PSI Conference, 'Developing the Labour Market', Nuffield College, Oxford, October.

Gallie, D. and Vogler, C. (1988) 'Labour Market Deprivation, Welfare and Collectivism', Manuscript, Oxford, Nuffield College.

Gamarnikow, E., Morgan, D., Purvis, J. and Taylorson, D. (eds) (1983), *Gender, Class and Work*, London, Heinemann.

Ganzeboom, H. and Ultee, W. (1988) 'Comparative Social Mobility in Industrial Nations: An Appraisal with Special Reference to Social Mobility in the Netherlands', Paper presented at the Conference on 'Class Formation and Comparative Social Mobility', Schloss Reisensburg, 16–19 March 1988.

Garnsey, E. (1978) 'Women's Work and Theories of Class Stratification', *Sociology*, Vol. 12, No. 2, pp. 220–43.

Geertz, C. (1988) *Works and Lives: The Anthropologist as Author*, Stanford, Calif., Stanford University Press.

Geiger, T. (1951) *Soziale Umschichtungen in einer dänischen Mittelstadt*, Aarhus, Aarhus University Press.

Gellner, E. (1985) 'Positivism against Hegelianism', in *idem*, *Relativism and the Social Sciences*, Cambridge, Cambridge University Press, pp. 4–67.

General Household Survey (1985) London, HMSO.

Geras, N. (1987) 'Post-Marxism?', *New Left Review*, No. 163, pp. 40–82.

Gerlich, P., Grande, E. and Müller, W. (1988) 'Corporatism in Crisis: Stability and Change of Social Partnership in Austria', *Political Studies*, Vol. 36, pp. 209–23.

Giddens, A. (1973) *The Class Structure of the Advanced Societies*, London, Hutchinson.

Giddens, A. and Mackenzie, G. (eds) (1982) *Classes and the Division of Labour*, Cambridge, Cambridge University Press.

Gill, C. (1986) *Work, Unemployment and New Technology*, Cambridge, Polity Press.

Glass, D. (ed) (1954) *Social Mobility in Britain*, London, Routledge and Kegan Paul.

Glenn, N., Ross A. and Tully, J. (1974) 'Patterns of Intergenerational Mobility of Females through Marriage', *American Sociological Review*, Vol. 39, No. 5, pp. 683–99.

Glyn, A. (1988) 'International Financial Markets and Economic Expansion: Australia 1983–87', Working Papers, Murdoch University.

Goldthorpe, J. H. (1959) 'Technical Organization as a Factor in Supervision-Worker Conflict: Some Preliminary Observations on a Study Made in the Mining Industry', *British Journal of Sociology*, Vol. 10, No. 3, pp. 213–30.

Goldthorpe, J. H. (1961) 'La conception de conflits du travail dans l'enseignement des relations humaines', *Sociologie du Travail*, Vol. 3, pp. 1–17.

Goldthorpe, J. H. (1962a) 'The Development of Social Policy in England, 1800–1914: Notes on a Sociological Approach to a Problem in Historical Explanation', Paper presented in 1962, published in 1964, in *Transactions of the Fifth World Congress of Sociology*, Washington, pp. 41–56. Fuller version (in French) in *Sociologie du Travail*, Vol. 5, 1963, pp. 105–20.

Goldthorpe, J. H. (1962b) 'The Relevance of History to Sociology', *Cambridge Opinion*, Vol. 28. Revised version, with 'Postscript', in M. Bulmer (ed), *Sociological Research Methods*, London, Macmillan, 1977, pp. 162–74.

Goldthorpe, J. H. (1964) 'Social Stratification in Industrial Society', in P. Halmos (ed), *The Development of Industrial Societies*, Sociological Review Monograph 8, University of Keele, pp. 97–122. See also Goldthorpe (1966c).

Goldthorpe, J. H. (1966a) 'Industrialisation and the Problem of "Convergence": A Reply to Dunning and Hopper', *Sociological Review*, Vol. 14, pp. 187–95.

Goldthorpe, J. H. (1966b) 'Attitudes and Behaviour of Car Assembly Workers: A Deviant Case and a Theoretical Critique', *British Journal of Sociology*, Vol. 17, No. 3, pp. 227–44.

Goldthorpe, J. H. (1966c) 'Social Stratification in Industrial Society', in R. Bendix and S. Lipset (eds), *Class, Status and Power*, London, Routledge and Kegan Paul, pp. 648–59.

Goldthorpe, J. H. (1968) Essays on 'Spencer' and 'Pareto' (and also 'Introductory Chapter') in T. Raison (ed), *The Founding Fathers of the Social Sciences*, Harmondsworth, Penguin. New enlarged edition, London, Scolar Press, 1979, pp. 76–83, 110–18 (and 9–16).

Goldthorpe, J. H. (1969) 'Social Inequality and Social Integration in Modern Britain', *The Advancement of Science*, Vol. 26, December, pp. 190–202. See also Goldthorpe (1974a).

Goldthorpe, J. H. (1970a) 'The Social Action Approach to Industrial Sociology: A Reply to Daniel', *Journal of Management Studies*, Vol. 7, pp. 199–208.

Goldthorpe, J. H. (1970b) 'L'image des classes chez les travailleurs manuels aisés', *Revue française de sociologie*, Vol. 11, pp. 311–38.

Goldthorpe, J. H. (1971) 'Theories of Industrial Society: Reflections on the Recrudescence of Historicism and the Future of Futurology', *Archives européenes de sociologie*, Vol. 12, pp. 263–88.

Goldthorpe, J. H. (1972a) 'Daniel on Orientations to Work: A Final Comment', *Journal of Management Studies*, Vol. 9, October, pp. 266–73.

Goldthorpe, J. H. (1972b) 'Class, Status and Party in Modern Britain: Some Recent Interpretations, Marxist and Marxisant', *Archives européenes de sociologie*, Vol. 13, pp. 342–72.

Goldthorpe, J. H. (1973a) 'A Revolution in Sociology', *Sociology*, Vol. 7, pp. 449–62.

Goldthorpe, J. H. (1973b) 'Contributions' to 'Discussion', in W. Müller and K. U. Mayer (eds) *Social Stratification and Career Mobility*, Paris, Mouton, pp. 359–90.

Goldthorpe, J. H. (1974a) 'Social Inequality and Social Integration in Modern Britain', in D. Wedderburn (ed), *Poverty, Inequality and the Class Structure*, Cambridge, Cambridge University Press, pp. 216–34. See also Goldthorpe (1969).

Goldthorpe, J. H. (1974b) 'Industrial Relations in Great Britain: A Critique of Reformism', *Politics and Society*, Vol. 4, pp. 419–52. Reprinted in Clarke and Clements (1977), pp. 184–224.

Goldthorpe, J. H. (1976) 'Mobilité sociale et intérêts sociaux', *Sociologie et Sociétés*, Vol. 8, pp. 7–36.

Goldthorpe, J. H. (1978) 'The Current Inflation: Towards a Sociological Account', in Hirsch and Goldthorpe (1978), pp. 186–214; plus an 'Addendum: On the Role of the Social Scientist' in the form of an exchange between John H. Goldthorpe, Alan Peacock and Samuel Brittan, pp. 214–16.

Goldthorpe, J. H. (1979) 'Intellectuals and the Working Class in Modern Britain', The Fuller Bequest Lecture, University of Essex. For reprint see Goldthorpe (1988a).

Goldthorpe, J. H. (1980a) *Social Mobility and Class Structure in Modern Britain*, Oxford, Clarendon Press (with the assistance of C. Llewellyn and C. Payne): 2nd rev. ed., see Goldthorpe (1987a).

Goldthorpe, J. H. (1980b) 'Reply to Crompton', *Sociology*, Vol. 14, No. 1, pp. 121–3.

Goldthorpe, J. H. (1981) 'The Class Schema of *Social Mobility and Class Structure in Modern Britain*: A Reply to Penn', *Sociology*, Vol. 15, pp. 272–80.

Goldthorpe, J. H. (1982) 'On the Service Class, Its Formation and Future', in Giddens and Mackenzie (1982), pp. 162–85.

Goldthorpe, J. H. (1983a) 'Women and Class Analysis: In Defence of the Conventional View', *Sociology*, Vol. 17, pp. 465–88.

Goldthorpe, J. H. (1983b) 'I problemi dell'economia politica alla fine del periode post-bellico', *Stato e Mercato*, 7 April, pp. 48–87; English version, see Goldthorpe (1987b).

Goldthorpe, J. H. (1983c) 'Sociology of Inflation: A Comment', *British Journal of Sociology*, Vol. 34, No. 4, p. 498.

Goldthorpe, J. H. (ed) (1984a) *Order and Conflict in Contemporary Capitalism: Studies in the Political Economy of Western European Nations*, Oxford, Clarendon Press, including an editorial 'Introduction', pp. 1–14.

Goldthorpe, J. H. (1984b) 'The End of Convergence: Corporatist and Dualist Tendencies in Modern Western Societies', in *idem* (1984a), pp. 315–43.

Goldthorpe, J. H. (1984c) 'Women and Class Analysis: A Reply to the Replies', *Sociology*, Vol. 18, pp. 491–9.

Goldthorpe, J. H. (1984d) 'Social Mobility and Class Formation: On the Renewal of a Tradition in Sociological Inquiry', CASMIN Working Paper No. 1, University of Mannheim. See Goldthorpe (1985b) for published version in German.

Goldthorpe, J. H. (1985a) 'On Economic Development and Social Mobility'. *British Journal of Sociology*, Vol. 36, pp. 549–73.

Goldthorpe, J. H. (1985b) 'Soziale Mobilität und Klassenbildung: Zur Erneuerung einer Tradition soziologischer Forschung', in J. H. Goldthorpe and H. Strasser (eds), *Die Analyse sozialer Ungleichheit*, Opladen, Westdeutscher Verlag, pp. 174–204. See also Goldthorpe (1984d).

Goldthorpe, J. H. (1987a) *Social Mobility and Class Structure in Modern Britain*, 2nd rev. and enlarged ed., Oxford, Clarendon Press (with the assistance of C. Llewellyn and C. Payne); 1st ed., see Goldthorpe (1980a).

Goldthorpe, J. H. (1987b) 'Problems of Political Economy after the Post-War Period', in C. Maier (ed), *The Changing Boundaries of the Political*, Cambridge, Cambridge University Press, pp. 363–407. First published in Italian, see Goldthorpe (1983b).

Goldthorpe, J. H. (1988a) 'Intellectuals and the Working Class in Modern Britain', in D. Rose (ed), *Social Stratification and Economic Change*, London, Hutchinson, pp. 39–56. See also Goldthorpe (1979).

Goldthorpe, J. H. (1988b) 'Current Issues in Social Mobility Research and the CASMIN Project', Lecture given to the Annual Conference of the Slovenian Sociological Association, Nova Gorica, 2 June 1988.

Goldthorpe, J. H. (1990) 'Employment, Class and Mobility: A Critique of Liberal and Marxist Theories of Long Term Change', in H. Haferkamp and N. Smelser (eds), *Modernization and Social Change*, Berkeley, Calif., University of California Press., forthcoming. Page references in the text are to the manuscript version.

Goldthorpe, J. H. and Bevan, P. (1977) 'The Study of Social Stratification in Great Britain: 1946–76', *Social Science Information*, Vol. 16, pp. 279–334. Published in an extended Italian version as *Lo Studio della stratificazione sociale in Gran Bretagna (1946–76)*, Torino, Fondazione Giovanni Agnelli.

Goldthorpe, J. H. and Hope, K. (1972) 'Occupational Grading and Occupational Prestige', in Hope (1972), pp. 19–79.

Goldthorpe, J. H. and Hope, K. (1974) *The Social Grading of Occupations: A New Approach and Scale*, Oxford, Clarendon Press.

Goldthorpe, J. H. and Llewellyn, C. (1977a) 'Class Mobility in Modern Britain: Three Theses Examined', *Sociology*, Vol. 11, pp. 257–87.

Goldthorpe, J. H. and Llewellyn, C. (1977b) 'Class Mobility: Intergenerational and Worklife Patterns', *British Journal of Sociology*, Vol. 28, pp. 269–302.

Goldthorpe, J. H., Llewellyn, C., and Payne, C. (1978) 'Trends in Class Mobility', *Sociology*, Vol. 12, pp. 441–68.

Goldthorpe, J. H. and Lockwood, D. (1963) 'Affluence and the British Class Structure', *Sociological Review*, Vol. 2, No. 2, pp. 133–63.

Goldthorpe, J. H., Lockwood, D., Bechhofer, F. and Platt, J. (1967) 'The Affluent Worker and the Thesis of Embourgeoisement: Some Preliminary Research Findings', *Sociology*, Vol. 1, pp. 11–31.

Goldthorpe, J. H., Lockwood, D., Bechhofer, F. and Platt, J. (1968a) *The Affluent Worker: Industrial Attitudes and Behaviour*, Cambridge, Cambridge University Press.

Goldthorpe, J. H., Lockwood, D., Bechhofer, F. and Platt, J. (1968b) *The Affluent Worker: Political Attitudes and Behaviour*, Cambridge, Cambridge University Press.

Goldthorpe, J. H., Lockwood, D., Bechhofer, F. and Platt, J. (1969) *The Affluent Worker in the Class Structure*, Cambridge, Cambridge University Press.

Goldthorpe, J. H. and Müller, W. (1982) 'Social Mobility and Class Formation in Industrial Nations: A Proposal for a Comparative Research Project', Nuffield College, Oxford and University of Mannheim.

Goldthorpe, J. H. and Payne, C. (1986a) 'Trends in Intergenerational Class Mobility in England and Wales, 1972–83', *Sociology*, Vol. 20, pp. 1–24.

Goldthorpe, J. H. and Payne, C. (1986b) 'On the Class Mobility of Women: Results from Different Approaches to the Analysis of Recent British Data', *Sociology*, Vol. 20, pp. 531–55.

Goldthorpe, J. H. and Portocarero, L. (1981) 'La mobilité sociale en France, 1953–70: nouvel examen', *Revue française de sociologie*, April-June, pp. 151–66.

Goodman, L. (1969) 'How to Ransack Social Mobility Tables and Other Kinds of Cross-classification Tables', *American Journal of Sociology*, Vol. 75, pp. 1–39.

Goodman, L. (1978) *Analyzing Qualitative/Categorical Data: Log-linear Models and Latent Structure Analysis*, Cambridge, Abt.

Gorz, A. (1982) *Farewell to the Working Class*, London, Pluto Press.

Gourevitch, P., Martin, A., Ross, G., Bernstein, S., Markovits, A. and Allen, C. (1984) *Unions and Economic Crisis: Britain, West Germany and Sweden*, London, George Allen and Unwin.

Gramsci, A. (1971) 'Americanism and Fordism', in Q. Hoare and G. Smith (eds), *Selections from the Prison Notebooks of Antonio Gramsci*, London, Lawrence and Wishart, pp. 277–318.

Gray, J. (1983) 'Classical Liberalism, Positional Goods and the Politicisation of Poverty', in A. Ellis and K. Kumar (eds), *Dilemmas of Liberal Democracies: Studies in Fred Hirsch's Social Limits to Growth*, London, Tavistock, pp. 174–84.

Grey, R. (1981) *The Aristocracy of Labour in Nineteenth Century Britain c. 1850–1914*, London, Macmillan.

Grieco, M. (1981) 'The Shaping of a Work Force: A Critique of the *Affluent Worker* Study', *International Journal of Sociology and Social Policy*, Vol. 1, No. 1, pp. 62–88.

Grusky, D. and Hauser, R. (1984) 'Comparative Social Mobility Revisited: Models of Convergence and Divergence in 16 Countries', *American Sociological Review*, Vol. 49, pp. 19–38.

Habermas, J. (1971) *Towards a Rational Society*, London, Heinemann.

Habermas, J. (1976) *Legitimation Crisis*, London, Heinemann.

Hack, L. and Hack, I. (1985) *Die Wirklichkeit, die Wissenschafft*, Frankfurt, Campus.

Hakim, C. (1980) 'Census Reports as Documentary Evidence: The Census Commentaries 1801–1951', *Sociological Review*, Vol. 28, No. 3, pp. 551–80.

Halfpenny, P. (1982) *Positivism and Sociology*, London, Allen and Unwin.

Hall, P. (1986) *Governing the Economy*, Cambridge, Polity Press.

Hall, S. (1988) *The Hard Road to Renewal*, London, Verso.

Hall, S. and Jacques, M. (eds) (1983) *The Politics of Thatcherism*, London, Verso.

Haller, A. and Portes, A. (1973) 'Status Attainment Approach', *Sociology of Education*, Vol. 46, pp. 51–91.

Halsey, A. (1977) 'Towards Meritocracy? The Case of Britain', in J. Karabel and A. Halsey (eds), *Power and Ideology in Education*, New York, Oxford University Press, pp. 173–86.

Halsey, A., Heath, A. and Ridge, J. (1980) *Origins and Destinations*, Oxford, Clarendon Press.

Hamilton, R. (1978) *The Liberation of Women: A Study of Patriarchy and Capitalism*, London, George Allen and Unwin.

Hannan, M. and Freeman, J. (1989) *Organizational Ecology*, Cambridge, Mass., Harvard University Press.

Harris, C. (1987) *Redundancy and Recession in South Wales*, Oxford, Blackwell.

Harrop, M. (1982) 'Labour-Voting Conservatives: Policy Differences between the Labour Party and Labour Voters', in R. Worcester and M. Harrop (eds) *Political Communications: The General Election Campaign of 1979*, London, Allen and Unwin, pp. 152–63.

Hart, H. and Otter, C. von (1976) 'The Determination of Wage Structures in Manufacturing Industry', in R. Scase (ed), *Readings in the Swedish Class Structure*, Oxford, Pergamon, pp. 99–118.

Hartmann, H. (1979) 'The Unhappy Marriage of Marxism and Feminism: Towards a More Progressive Union', *Capital and Class*, Vol. 8, pp. 1–33.

Hauser, R. (1969) 'Schools and the Stratification Process', *American Journal of Sociology*, Vol. 74, pp. 587–611.

Hauser, R. (1978) 'A Structural Model of the Mobility Table', *Social Forces*, Vol. 56, pp. 919–53.

Hayek, F. von (1944) *The Road to Serfdom*, London, Routledge.

Hayek, F. von (1976) *Law, Legislation and Liberty: The Mirage of Social Justice*, London, Routledge and Kegan Paul.

Headey, B. (1970) 'Trade Unions and National Wage Policies', *Journal of Politics*, Vol. 32, pp. 407–39.

Heath, A. (1981) *Social Mobility*, London, Fontana.

Heath, A. (1988) 'The Rise of the New Political Agenda?', Paper presented at the Annual Conference of the British Association for the Advancement of Science.

Heath, A. and Britten, N. (1984) 'Women's Jobs Do Make a Difference: A Reply to Goldthorpe', *Sociology*, Vol. 18, pp. 475–90.

Heath, A. and Edmondson, R. (1980) 'Oxbridge Sociology: The Development of Centres of Excellence?', in Abrams *et al.* (1980), pp. 39–52.

Heath, A. and Evans, G. (1988) 'Working-Class Conservatives and Middle-Class Socialists', in R. Jowell *et al.* (eds), *British Social Attitudes: The 5th Report*, Aldershot, Gower, pp. 53–69.

Heath, A., Evans, G. and Payne, C. (1989) 'Modelling the Relation between Class and Vote', Paper presented at the ECPR Conference, Paris.

Heath, A., Jowell, R. and Curtice, J. (1985) *How Britain Votes*, Oxford, Pergamon.

Heath, A., Jowell, R. and Curtice, J. (1987a) 'Trendless Fluctuation: A Reply to Crewe', *Political Studies*, Vol. 35, pp. 256–77.

Heath, A., Jowell, R. and Curtice, J. (1987b) 'Class Dealignment and the Explanation of Political Change: A Reply to Dunleavy', *West European Politics*, Vol. 11, pp. 146–8.

Heath, A., Jowell, R. and Curtice, J. (1988) 'Partisan Dealignment Revisited', Paper presented at the Annual Conference of the Political Studies Association.

Heath, A. and Macdonald, S.-K. (1987) 'Social Change and the Future of the Left', *Political Quarterly*, Vol. 58, pp. 364–77.

Heath, A. and Macdonald, S.-K. (1988) 'The Demise of Party Identification Theory?', *Electoral Studies*, Vol. 7, pp. 95–107.

Heath, A. and Ridge, J. (1983a) 'School Examinations and Occupational Attainment', in J. Purvis and M. Hales (eds), *Achievement and Inequality in Education*, London, Routledge, pp. 239–57.

Heath, A. and Ridge, J. (1983b) 'Social Mobility of Ethnic Minorities', *Journal of Biosocial Science*, Supplement 8, pp. 169–84.

Heilbron, J. (1986) *The Dilemmas of an Upright Man: Max Planck as Spokesman for German Science*, Berkeley, Calif., University of California Press.

Hennis, W. (1987) *Max Webers Fragestellung*, Tübingen, Mohr/Siebeck.

Hibbs, D. (1978) 'On the Political Economy of Long-Run Trends in Strike Activity', *British Journal of Political Science*, Vol. 8, pp. 153–75.

Hibbs, D. (1982) 'Economic Outcomes and Political Support for British Governments among the Occupational Classes', *American Political Science Review*, Vol. 76, No. 2, pp. 259–79.

Himsworth, H. (1984) 'Epidemiology, Genetics and Sociology', *Journal of Biosocial Science*, Vol. 16, No. 3, pp. 159–75.

Hindess, B. (1973) *The Use of Official Statistics in Sociology*, London, Macmillan.

Hindess, B. (1981) 'The Politics of Social Mobility', *Economy and Society*, Vol. 10, pp. 184–202.

Hindess, B. (1987) *Politics and Class Analysis*, Oxford, Blackwell.

Hirsch, F. (1977) *Social Limits to Growth*, London, Routledge and Kegan Paul.

Hirsch, F. and Goldthorpe, J. H. (eds) (1978) *The Political Economy of Inflation*, Oxford, Martin Robertson, including 'Prologue', pp. 1–11.

Hirsch, J. (1980) *Der Sicherheitsstaat*, Frankfurt, EVA.

Hirschman, A. (1973) 'The Changing Tolerance for Income Inequality in the Course of Economic Development', *World Development*, No. 1, pp. 29–36.

Hobsbawm, E. (1964) 'The Labour Aristocracy in Nineteenth-Century Britain', in *idem*, *Labouring Men: Studies in the History of Labour*, London, Weidenfeld and Nicolson, pp. 272–315.

Hoover, K. and Plant, R. (1988) *Conservative Capitalism in Britain and the US: A Critical Appraisal*, London, Routledge.

Hope, K. (ed) (1972) *The Analysis of Social Mobility: Methods and Approaches*, Oxford, Clarendon Press.

Hunt, A. (ed) (1977) *Class and Class Structure*, London, Lawrence and Wishart.

Husbands, C. (1980) 'The Anti-Quantitative Bias in Postwar British Sociology', in Abrams *et al.* (1980), pp. 88–104.

Hyman, R. (1986) 'British Industrial Relations: The Limits of Corporatism', in Jacobi *et al.* (1986), pp. 79–104.

Hyman, R. and Brough, I. (1975) *Social Values and Industrial Relations*, Oxford, Blackwell.

Incomes Data Services (IDS) (1988) *Report No. 519*, London, Incomes Data Services, April.

Inkeles, A. (1960) 'Social Stratification in the Modernization of Russia', in C. Black (ed), *The Transformation of Russian Society*, Cambridge, Mass., Harvard University Press, pp. 338–50.

Institute for Employment Research (IER) (1988) *Update on the Economy*, Coventry, University of Warwick, Institute for Employment Research.

International Labour Office (ILO) (1968) *International Standard Classification of Occupations*, Geneva, International Labour Office.

Ishida, H., Goldthorpe, J. H. and Erikson, R. (1988) 'Intergenerational Class Mobility in Post-War Japan: Conformity or Peculiarity in Cross-National Perspective?', CASMIN Working Paper No. 11, University of Mannheim.

Ishida, H. and Ridge, J. (1988) 'Class Origin, Class Destination and Education: A Cross-National Study of Industrial Nations', Paper presented to the CASMIN Conference, Schloss Reisensburg, West Germany.

Jackman, M. and Jackman, R. (1982) *Class Awareness in the United States*, Berkeley, Calif., University of California Press.

Jackson, P. and Sisson, K. (1976) 'Employers Confederations in Sweden and the UK', *British Journal of Industrial Relations*, Vol. 14, pp. 306–23.

Jacobi, O., Jessop, B., Kastendiek, H. and Regini, M. (eds) (1986) *Economic Crisis, Trade Unions and the State*, London, Croom Helm.

Jessop, B. (1978a) 'Capitalism and Democracy: The Best Possible Shell?', in G. Littlejohn *et al.* (eds), *Power and the State*, London, Croom Helm, pp. 10–51.

Jessop, B. (1978b) 'The Transformation of the State in Post-war Britain', in Scase (1978), pp. 23–93.

Jessop, B. (1979) 'Corporatism, Parliamentarism and Social Democracy', in Schmitter and Lehmbruch (1979), pp. 185–212.

Johannesson, J. and Schmid, G. (1980) 'The Development of Labour Market Flexibility in Sweden and

Germany: Competing or Converging Models to Combat Unemployment?', *European Journal of Political Research*, Vol. 8, No. 4, pp. 387–406.

Johnson, P. (1981) 'Changing Social Structure and the Political Role of Manual Workers', in J. Triska and C. Gati (eds), *Blue-Collar Workers in Eastern Europe*, London, Allen and Unwin, pp. 29–42.

Johnson, T. (1977) 'What Is to Be Known: The Structural Determination of Social Class', *Economy and Society*, Vol. 6, No. 2, pp. 194–233.

Johnson, T. and Rattansi, A. (1981) 'Social Mobility without Class', *Economy and Society*, Vol. 10, pp. 203–34.

Jones, A. (1973) *The New Inflation*, Harmondsworth, Penguin.

Jones, F. and Davis, P. (1986) *Models of Society: Class Stratification and Gender in Australia and New Zealand*, Sydney, Croom Helm.

Jones, F. and Kelley, J. (1984) 'Decomposing Differences between Groups: A Cautionary Note on Measuring Discrimination', *Sociological Methods and Research*, Vol. 12, pp. 323–43.

Jöreskog, K. (1978) 'Structural Analysis of Covariance and Correlation Matrices', *Psychometrika*, Vol. 43, pp. 443–77.

Joseph, G. (1983) *Women at Work*, Oxford, Philip Allan Publishers.

Joseph, Sir K. (1976) *Stranded on the Middle Ground*, London, Centre for Policy Studies.

Joseph, Sir K. (n.d.) *Monetarism Is Not Enough*, London, Centre for Policy Studies.

Joseph, Sir K. and Sumption, J. (1979) *Equality*, London, J. Murray.

Joshi, H., Layard, R. and Owen, S. (1983) *Why Are More Women Working in Britain?*, Centre for Labour Economics Discussion Paper No. 162, London School of Economics.

Joshi, H. and Newell, M.-L. (1987) *Family Responsibilities and Pay Differentials: Evidence from Men and Women Born in 1946*, CEPR Discussion Paper No. 157, London.

Jouvenel, B. de (ed) (1967) *The Art of Conjecture*, London, Weidenfeld and Nicolson.

Kahn, H. and Wiener, A. (1967) *The Year 2000: A Framework for Speculation on the Next Thirty-three Years*, New York, Macmillan.

Kastendiek, Hans (1988) 'Zwischen Ausgrenzung und krisenpolitischer Konditionierung: Zur Situation der britischen Gewerkschaften', in W. Müller-Jentsch (ed), *Gewerkschaften im Umbruch*, Frankfurt, Campus, pp. 160–90.

Kastendiek, Hans and Kastendiek, Hella (1985) 'Konservative Wende und industrielle Beziehungen in Grossbritannien und in der Bundesrepublik', *Politische Vierteljahresschrift*, Vol. 26, pp. 381–99.

Kastendiek, Hans, Kastendiek, Hella and Reister, H. (1986) 'Institutional Strategies for Trade Union Participation: An Assessment of the Incorporation Thesis', Jacobi *et al.* (1986), pp. 258–87.

Kavanagh, D. (1986) 'How We Vote Now', *Electoral Studies*, Vol. 5, pp. 19–28.

Kelley, J. (1971) 'Social Mobility in Toro: Some Preliminary Results from Western Uganda', *Economic Development and Cultural Change*, Vol. 19, pp. 204–21.

Kelley, J. (1973) 'Causal Chain Models for the Socioeconomic Career', *American Sociological Review*, Vol. 38, pp. 481–93.

Kelley, J. (1978) 'Wealth and Family Background in the Occupational Career: Theory and Cross-Cultural Data', *British Journal of Sociology*, Vol. 29, pp. 94–109.

Kelley, J. and Klein, H. (1982) *Revolution and the Rebirth of Inequality: A Theory Applied to the National Revolution in Bolivia*, Berkeley, Calif., University of California Press.

Kelley, J. and McAllister, I. (1984) 'The Genesis of Conflict: Religion and Status Attainment in Ulster, 1968', *Sociology*, Vol. 18, pp. 171–90.

Kelley, J. and McAllister, I. (1985) 'Class and Party in Australia: Comparison with Britain and the USA', *British Journal of Sociology*, Vol. 36, pp. 383–420.

Kelley, J., McAllister, I. and Mughan, A. (1985) 'The Decline of Class Revisited: Class and Party in England, 1964–1979', *American Political Science Review*, Vol. 79, pp. 719–37.

Kelley, J., Robinson, R. and Klein, H. (1981) 'A Theory of Social Mobility, with Data on Status Attainment in a Peasant Society', Treiman (1981), Vol. 1, pp. 27–66.

Kelly, M. (1980) *White-Collar Proletariat*, London, Routledge and Kegan Paul.

Kendrick, S. (1986) 'Occupational Change in Modern Scotland', in D. McCrone (ed), *The Scottish Government Year Book 1986*, Edinburgh, USGS.

Kern, H. and Schumann, M. (1970) *Industriearbeit und Arbeiterbewußtsein*, Frankfurt, EVA.

Kern, H. and Schumann, M. (1985) *Das Ende der Arbeitsteilung?*, 2nd ed., Munich, Beck.

Kerr, C. (1968) *Marshall, Marx and Modern Times*, Cambridge, Cambridge University Press.

Kerr, C. (1983) *The Future of Industrial Societies*, Cambridge, Mass., Harvard University Press.

Kerr, C., Dunlop, J., Harbison, F. and Myers, C. (1960/62) *Industrialism and Industrial Man*, Cambridge, Mass., Harvard University Press; London, Heinemann. See also Kerr *et al.* (1973).

Kerr, C., Dunlop, J., Harbison, F. and Myers, C. (1973) *Industrialism and Industrial Man*, 2nd ed., Harmondsworth, Penguin.

Klatzky, S. and Hodge, R. (1972) 'A Canonical Correlation Analysis of Occupational Mobility', *Journal of the American Statistical Association*, Vol. 66, pp. 16–22.

Knowles, K. and Robinson, D. (1964) 'Wage-Rounds 1949–1959', *Bulletin of the Oxford University Institute of Statistics*, Vol. 24, pp. 269–329.

Kornblum, W. (1974) *Blue Collar Community*, Chicago, Ill., University of Chicago Press.

Korpi, W. (1978) *The Working Class in Welfare Capitalism*, London, Routledge and Kegan Paul.

Korpi, W. (1983) *The Democratic Class Struggle*, London, Routledge and Kegan Paul.

Korpi, W. (1986) 'Power Resources Approach versus Action and Conflict', Reprint Series No. 155, Stockholm, Swedish Institute of Social Research.

Korpi, W. (1988) 'The Politics of Employment Policy: A Comparative Study of Unemployment Insurance, Unemployment, and Active Labour Policy in 18 OECD Countries', Manuscript, University of Stockholm, Swedish Institute for Social Research.

Korpi, W. and Shalev, M. (1979) 'Strikes, Industrial Relations and Class Conflict in Capitalist Societies', *British Journal of Sociology*, Vol. 30, pp. 164–87.

Korpi, W. and Shalev, M. (1980) 'Strikes, Power and Politics in the Western Nations, 1900–1976', *Political Power and Social Theory*, Vol. 1, pp. 299–332.

Kreile, M. (1988) 'The Crisis of Italian Trade Unionism in the 1980s', *West European Politics*, Vol. 11, pp. 54–67.

Kristol, I. (1971) 'When Virtue Loses All Her Loveliness: Some Reflections on Capitalism and "The Free Society"', in I. Kristol and D. Bell (eds), *Capitalism Today*, New York, Mentor Paperback, pp. 13–26.

Kuhn, A. and Wolpe, A. (1978) *Feminism and Materialism*, London, Routledge and Kegan Paul.

Kuhn, T. (1962) *The Structure of Scientific Revolutions*, Chicago, Ill., University of Chicago Press.

Kurz, K. and Müller, W. (1987) 'Class Mobility in the Industrial World', *Annual Review of Sociology*, Vol. 13, pp. 417–42.

Land, H. (1983) 'Poverty and Gender: The Distribution of Resources within the Family', in M. Brown (ed), *The Structure of Disadvantage*, London, Heinemann, pp. 49–71.

Lane, D. (1976) *The Socialist Industrial State*, London, George Allen and Unwin.

Lane, D. (1978) *Politics and Society in the USSR*, 2nd ed., London, Martin Robertson.

Lange, P. (1984) 'Unions, Workers and Wage Regulations: The Rational Bases of Consent', in Goldthorpe (1984a), pp. 98–123.

Lange, P. and Garrett, G. (1985) 'The Politics of Growth: Strategic Interaction and Economic Performance in the Advanced Industrial Democracies 1974–80', *Journal of Politics*, Vol. 47, pp. 792–827.

Lawson, N. (1980) *The New Conservatism*, London, Centre for Policy Studies.

Lawson, N. (1987) *The Tide of Ideas from Attlee to Thatcher*, London, Centre for Policy Studies.

Layard, R. *et al.* (1978) *The Causes of Poverty*, Background Paper No. 5, Royal Commission on the Distribution of Income and Wealth, London, HMSO.

Layton-Henry, Z. (1984) *The Politics of Race in Britain*, London, George Allen and Unwin.

Lee, D. (1981) 'Skill, Craft and Class: A Theoretical Critique and a Critical Case', *Sociology*, Vol. 15, pp. 56–78.

Lehmbruch, G. (1977) 'Liberal Corporatism and Party Government', *Comparative Political Studies*, Vol. 10, pp. 91–126.

Lehmbruch, G. (1979) 'Consociational Democracy, Class Conflict and the New Corporatism', in Schmitter and Lehmbruch (1979), pp. 53–62.

Lehmbruch, G. (1983) 'Neokorporatismus in Westeuropa: Hauptprobleme im internationalen Vergleich', *Journal für Sozialforschung*, Vol. 23, pp. 407–20.

Lehmbruch, G. (1984) 'Concertation and the Structure of Corporatist Networks', in Goldthorpe (1984a), pp. 60–80.

Lehmbruch, G. (1985) 'Sozialpartnerschaft in der vergleichenden Politikforschung', in P. Gerlich *et al.* (eds), *Sozialpartnerschaft in der Krise*, Vienna, Bohlau, pp. 85–107.

Lehmbruch, G. and Schmitter, P. (eds) (1982) *Patterns of Corporatist Policy-Making*, London, Sage.

Leiulfsrud, H. and Woodward, A. (1987) 'Women at Class Crossroads: Repudiating Conventional Theories of Family Class', *Sociology*, Vol. 21, pp. 393–412.

Levine, M. (1974) *The Socialist Economies*, London, Martin Robertson.

Lindberg, L. and Maier, C. (eds) (1985) *The Politics of Inflation and Economic Stagnation*, Washington, D.C., Brookings Institution.

Linhart, R. (1981) *The Assembly Line*, London, John Calder.

Lipietz, A. (1985) 'Akkumulation, Krisen und Auswege aus der Krise: Einige methodische Bemerkungen zum Begriff der "Regulation"', *Prokla*, No. 58, pp. 109–37.

Lipietz, A. (1987) *Mirages and Miracles: The Crisis of Global Fordism*, London, Verso.

Lipman-Blumen, J. (1973) 'Role De-differentiations as a System Response to Crisis: Occupational and Political Roles of Women', *Sociological Inquiry*, Vol. 42, No. 2, pp. 105–29.

Lipset, S. and Bendix, R. (eds) (1959) *Social Mobility in Industrial Societies*, Berkeley, Calif., University of California.

Lipset, S. and Zetterberg, H. (1959) 'Social Mobility in Industrial Societies', in Lipset and Bendix (1959), pp. 11–75.

Lockwood, D. (1958) *The Blackcoated Worker*, London, George Allen and Unwin.

Lockwood, D. (1966) 'Sources of Variation in Working Class Images of Society', *Sociological Review*, Vol. 14, pp. 249–67. See also Lockwood (1982).

Lockwood, D. (1981) 'The Weakest Link in the Chain?', in S. Simpson and I. Simpson (eds), *Research in the Sociology of Work*, Greenwich, Conn., JAI Press, pp. 435–81. Reprinted in D. Rose (ed), *Social Stratification and Economic Change*, London, Hutchinson, 1988, pp. 57–97.

Lockwood, D. (1982) 'Sources of Variation in Working Class Images of Society', in A. Giddens and D. Held (eds), *Class, Power and Conflict*, London, Macmillan, pp. 359–72. Reprint of Lockwood (1966).

Longstreth, F. (1988) 'From Corporatism to Dualism? Thatcherism and the Climacteric of British Trade Unions in the 1980s', *Political Studies*, Vol. 36, pp. 413–32.

Luijkx, R. and Ganzeboom, H. (1989) 'Intergenerational Class Mobility in the Netherlands between 1970 and 1985', in W. Jansen, J. Dronkers and K. Verrips (eds), *Similar or Different?*, Amsterdam, SISWO Publications, pp. 5–30.

Mach, B. and Wesolowski, W. (1986) *Social Mobility and Social Structure*, London, Routledge and Kegan Paul.

MacInnes, J. (1987) *Thatcherism at Work*, Milton Keynes, Open University Press.

Mackenzie, G. (1974) 'The "Affluent Worker" Study: An Evaluation and Critique', in F. Parkin (ed), *The Social Analysis of Class Structure*, London, Tavistock, pp. 237–56.

McKenzie, R. and Silver, A. (1968) *Angels in Marble*, London, Heinemann.

McRae, S. (1986) *Cross-Class Families*, Oxford, Clarendon Press.

Maitland, I. (1983) *The Causes of Industrial Disorder: A Comparison of a British and a German Factory*, London, Routledge and Kegan Paul.

Mann, M. (1986a) *The Sources of Social Power*, Vol. 1, Cambridge, Cambridge University Press.

Mann, M. (1986b) 'A Crisis in Stratification Theory?', in Crompton and Mann (1986), pp. 40–56.

Marshall, T. (1947) *Citizenship and Social Class*, Cambridge, Cambridge University Prss.

Marin, B. (1983) 'Organising Interests by Interest Organisation: Associational Prerequisites of Corporatism in Austria', *International Political Science Review*, Vol. 4, pp. 197–216.

Marin, B. (1985) 'Austria: The Paradigm Case of Liberal Corporatism', in W. Grant (ed), *The Political Economy of Corporatism*, London, Macmillan, pp. 89–125.

Marshall, G. (1988a) 'Classes in Britain: Marxist and Official', *European Sociological Review*, Vol. 4, pp. 141–54.

Marshall, G. (1988b) 'The Politics of the New Middle Class: History and Predictions', Paper presented at the Annual Conference of the British Sociological Association, March.

Marshall, G., Newby, H., Rose, D. and Vogler, C. (1988) *Social Class in Modern Britain*, London, Hutchinson.

Marshall, G., Rose, D., Vogler, C. and Newby, H. (1985) 'Class, Citizenship and Distributional Conflict in Modern Britain', *British Journal of Sociology*, Vol. 36, pp. 259–84.

Marshall, G., Vogler, C., Rose, D. and Newby, H. (1987) 'Distributional Struggle and Moral Order in a Market Society', *Sociology*, Vol. 21, pp. 55–73.

Marshall, T. (1947) *Citizenship and Social Class*, Cambridge, Cambridge University Press.

Martin, A. (1984) 'Trade Unions in Sweden: Strategic Responses to Change and Crisis', in Gourevitch *et al.* (1984), pp. 190–359.

Martin, A. (1985) 'Wages, Profits and Investment in Sweden', in Lindberg and Maier (1985), pp. 403–66.

Martin, J. (1986) 'Returning to Work after Childbearing: Evidence from the Women and Employment Survey', *Population Trends*, No. 43, pp. 23–30.

Martin, J. and Roberts, C. (1984) *Women and Employment: A Lifetime Perspective*, London, HMSO. This source is often referred to as the *Women and Employment Survey* or *WES*.

Martin, Roderick (1988) 'Technological Change and Manual Work', in Gallie (1988a), pp. 102–27.

Martin, Ross (1983) 'Pluralism and the New Corporatism', *Political Studies*, Vol. 31, pp. 86–102.

Marx, K. and Engels, F. (1962) 'Manifesto of the Communist Party', in *idem*, *Selected Works*, Moscow, Foreign Languages Publishing House, pp. 34–65.

Matthews, M. (1972) *Class and Society in Soviet Russia*, London, Allen Lane.

Mayer, K. U. (1975) *Soziale Ungleichheit und Mobilität im sozialen Bewußtsein*, Opladen, Westdeutscher Verlag.

Mayer, K. U. (1977) 'Ungleiche Chancen und Klassenbildung', *Soziale Welt*, Vol. 28, pp. 466–93.

Mayer, K. U. and Carroll, G. (1987) 'Jobs and Classes: Structural Constraints on Career Mobility', *European Sociological Review*, Vol. 3, No. 1, pp. 14–38.

Mayer, K. U., Featherman, D., Selbee, L. and Colbjørnsen, T. (1989) 'Class Mobility during the Working Life: A Cross-National Comparison of Germany and Norway', in M. Kohn (ed), *Cross-National Research in Sociology*, Newbury Park, Sage, pp. 218–39.

Mayer, K. U. and Müller, W. (1971) 'Progress in Social Mobility Research?', *Quality and Quantity*, Vol. 5, pp. 141–78.

Meade, J. (1982) *Wage Fixing*, London, Allen and Unwin.

Medawar, P. (1982) *Pluto's Republic*, Oxford, Oxford University Press.

Merton, R. K. (1959) 'Notes on Problem-Finding in Sociology', in R. K. Merton, L. Broom and L. Cottrell (eds), *Sociology Today: Problems and Prospects*, New York, Harper, pp. ix–xxxiv.

Millar, J. (1987) *Politics, Work and Daily Life in the USSR*, Cambridge, Cambridge University Press.

Miller, S. (1960) 'Comparative Social Mobility', *Current Sociology*, Vol. 9, pp. 1–89.

Millward, N. and Stevens, M. (1986) *British Workplace Industrial Relations 1980–84*, Aldershot, Gower.

Millward, N. and Stevens, M. (eds) (1987) 'Symposium: British Workplace Industrial Relations 1980–1984', *British Journal of Industrial Relations*, Vol. 25, pp. 275–94.

Minkin, L. (1986) 'Against the Tide: Trade Unions, Political Communications and the 1983 General Election', in I. Crewe and M. Harrop (eds), *Political Communications: The 1983 General Election Campaign*, Cambridge, Cambridge University Press, pp. 190–206.

Mises, L. von (1936) *Socialism—An Economic and Social Analysis*, London, Jonathan Cape.

Mitchell, C. (1983) 'Case and Situation Analysis', *Sociological Review*, Vol. 31, pp. 185–211.

Moore, Barrington (1966) *Social Origins of Dictatorship and Democracy*, Boston, Mass., Beacon Press.

Moore, W. (1963) 'Industrialization and Social Change', in B. Hoselitz and W. Moore (eds), *Industrialization and Society*, New York, Humanities Press, pp. 299–370.

Mosteller, F. and Tukey, J. (1977) *Data Analysis and Regression*, Reading, Mass., Addison-Wesley.

Mouzelis, N. (1988) 'Marxism or Post-Marxism?', *New Left Review*, No. 167, pp. 107–23.

Müller, W., Karle, W., König, W. and Lüttinger, P. (1988) 'Education and Class Mobility', CASMIN Working Paper No. 14, University of Mannheim.

National Economic Development Office (NEDO) (1988) *Young People and the Labour Market: A Challenge for the 1990s*, London, National Economic Development Office Books.

Nichols, T. (1979) 'Social Class: Official, Sociological and Marxist', in J. Irvine, I. Miles and J. Evans (eds), *Demystifying Social Statistics*, London, Pluto Press, pp. 152–71.

Noble, T. (1985) 'Inflation and Earnings Relativities in Britain after 1970', *British Journal of Sociology*, Vol. 36, pp. 238–58.

Nordlinger, E. (1967) *The Working Class Tories*, London, McGibbon and Key.

Nove, A. (1977) *The Soviet Economic System*, London, George Allen and Unwin.

Offe, C. and Wiesenthal, H. (1980) 'The Logic of Collective Action: Theoretical Notes on Social Class and Organizational Form', *Political Power and Social Theory*, Vol. 1, pp. 67–115.

Office of Population Censuses and Surveys (OPCS) (1982) *Labour Force Survey 1981*, produced by the OPCS, London, HMSO.

O'Higgins, M., Schmaus, G. and Stephenson, G. (1985) 'Income Distribution and Redistribution: A Microdata Analysis for Seven Countries', LIS-CEPS Working Paper Series, Walferdange, Luxembourg.

Olson, M. (1982) *The Rise and Decline of Nations*, New Haven, Conn., Yale University Press.

Oppenheimer, M. (1985) *White Collar Politics*, New York, Monthly Review Press.

Organisation for Economic Cooperation and Development (OECD) (1983) *Employment Outlook*, Paris, OECD.

Organisation for Economic Cooperation and Development (OECD) (1986) *Employment Outlook*, Paris, OECD.

Pahl, J. (1980) 'Patterns of Money Management within Marriage', *Journal of Social Policy*, Vol. 9, pp. 315–35.

Panitch, L. (1976) *Social Democracy and Industrial Militancy*, Cambridge, Cambridge University Press.

Panitch, L. (1977/79) 'The Development of Corporatism in Liberal Democracies', *Comparative Political Studies*, Vol. 10, 1977, pp. 61–90; also in Schmitter and Lehmbruch (1979), pp. 119–46.

Panitch, L. (1980) 'Recent Theorisations of Corporatism: Reflections on a Growth Industry', *British Journal of Sociology*, Vol. 31, pp. 159–87.

Panitch, L. (1981) 'Trade Unions and the Capitalist State', *New Left Review*, No. 125, pp. 21–43.

Parkin, F. (1967) 'Working Class Conservatives: A Theory of Political Deviance', *British Journal of Sociology*, Vol. 18, pp. 280–90.

Parkin, F. (1971) *Class Inequality and Political Order*, London, McGibbon and Key.

Parkin, F. (1979) *Marxism and Class Theory*, London, Tavistock.

Parsons, T. (1966) *Societies: Evolutionary and Comparative Perspectives*, Englewood Cliffs, N.J., Prentice-Hall.

Pasinetti, L. (1981) *Structural Change and Economic Growth*, Cambridge, Cambridge University Press.

Pastore, J., Haller, A. and Gomez, H. (1975) 'Wage Differentials in Sao Paulo's Labour Force', *Industrial Relations*, Vol. 14, pp. 345–57.

Payne, G. (1987a) *Mobility and Change in Modern Society*, London, Macmillan.

Payne, G. (1987b) *Employment and Opportunity*, London, Macmillan.

Payne, G. and Abbott, P. (eds) (1990) *The Social Mobility of Women*, London, Falmer Press.

Payne, G., Ford, G. and Robertson, C. (1976) *Occupational Groupings and Social Stratification*, SMS Working Paper No. 3, University of Aberdeen, Department of Sociology.

Payne, G., Ford, G. and Robertson, C. (1977) 'A Reappraisal of Social Mobility in Britain', *Sociology*, Vol. 11, pp. 289–310.

Payne, G., Ford, G. and Ulas, M. (1979) 'Education and Social Mobility', SIP Occasional Paper No. 8, Edinburgh.

Payne, G., Payne, J. and Chapman, T. (1983) 'Trends in Female Social Mobility', in Gamarnikow *et al.* (1983), pp. 61–76.

Penn, R. (1981) 'The Nuffield Class Categorization', *Sociology*, Vol. 15, pp. 265–71.

Perez-Diaz, V. (1986) 'Economic Policies and Social Pacts in Spain during the Transition: The Two Faces of Neo-Corporatism', *European Sociological Review*, Vol. 2, pp. 1–19.

Pescosolido, B. and Kelley, J. (1983) 'Confronting Sociological Theory with Data: Regression Analysis, Goodman's Log-linear Models and Comparative Research', *Sociology*, Vol. 17, pp. 359–79.

Phelps Brown, H. (1973) 'New Wine in Old Bottles: Reflections on the Changed Working of Collective Bargaining in Great Britain', *British Journal of Industrial Relations*, Vol. 11, pp. 329–37.

Phelps Brown, H. (1975) 'A Non-Monetarist View of the Pay Explosion', *Three Banks Review*, No. 105, pp. 3–25.

Phelps Brown, H. (1977) *The Inequality of Pay*, Oxford, Oxford University Press.

Phelps Brown, H. (1983) *The Origins of Trade Union Power*, Oxford, Clarendon Press.

Phelps Brown, H. (1988) *Egalitarianism and the Generation of Inequality*, Oxford, Clarendon Press.

Piore, M. and Sabel, C. (1984) *The Second Industrial Divide*, New York, Basic Books.

Pizzorno, A. (1978) 'Political Exchange and Collective Identity in Industrial Conflict', in Crouch and Pizzorno (1978), Vol. 2, pp. 277–98.

Platt, J. (1984) 'The Affluent Worker Re-Visited', in C. Bell and H. Roberts (eds), *Social Researching*, London, Routledge and Kegan Paul, pp. 179–98.

Plowman, D., Minchinton, W. and Stacey, M. (1962) 'Local Social Status in England and Wales', *Sociological Review*, Vol. 10, No. 2, pp. 161–202.

Polyani, K. (1944) *The Great Transformation*, Boston, Mass., Beacon Press.

Pöntinen, S., Alestalo, M. and Uusitalo, H. (1983) 'The Finnish Mobility Survey 1980: Data and First Results', Report No. 9, Helsinki, Suomen Gallup Oy.

Pontusson, J. (1987) 'The Story of Swedish Wage-Earner Funds', *New Left Review*, No. 165, pp. 5–33.

Popper, K. (1945) *The Open Society and Its Enemies*, London, Routledge and Kegan Paul.

Popper, K. (1957) *The Poverty of Historicism*, London, Routledge and Kegan Paul.

Popper, K. (1972) *Objective Knowledge*, Oxford, Clarendon Press.

Popper, K. (1976) 'The Logic of the Social Sciences', in T. Adorno *et al.*, *The Positivism Dispute in German Sociology*, London, Heinemann, pp. 87–104.

Poulantzas, N. (1974) *Les classes sociales dans le capitalisme d'aujourd'hui*, Paris, Seuil. See also Poulantzas (1975).

Poulantzas, N. (1975) *Classes in Contemporary Capitalism*, London, New Left Books. English version of Poulantzas (1974).

Poulantzas, N. (1978) *Staatstheorie*, Hamburg, VSA.

Prandy, K. (1965) *Professional Employees: A Study of Scientists and Engineers*, London, Faber.

Pryor, F. (1973) *Property and Industrial Organisation in Communist and Capitalist Nations*, Bloomington, Ind., Indiana University Press.

Przeworski, A. (1985a) *Capitalism and Social Democracy*, Cambridge, Cambridge University Press.

Przeworski, A. (1985b) 'Material Interests, Class Compromise and the State', in *idem* (1985a), pp. 171–203.

Przeworski, A. (1986) 'Methodologischer Individualismus als Herausforderung der marxistischen Theorie', *Prokla*, Vol. 16, pp. 120–43.

Przeworski, A. and Teune, H. (1970) *The Logic of Comparative Social Inquiry*, New York, Wiley.

Pulzer, P. (1987) 'The Paralysis of the Centre-Left', *Political Quarterly*, Vol. 58, No. 4, pp. 378–88.

Rainwater, L. (1984) 'Mothers' Contribution to the Family Money Economy in Europe and the USA', in P. Voydanoff (ed) *Work and Family*, Palo Alto, Mayfield, pp. 73–88.

Rainwater, L., Rein, M. and Schwartz, J. (1986) *Income Packaging in the Welfare State*, Oxford, Clarendon Press.

Rajan, A. (1987) *Services: The Second Industrial Revolution*, London, Butterworth.

Rajan, A. and Pearson, R. (eds) (1986) *UK Occupation and Employment Trends to 1990*, Brighton, Institute of Manpower Studies.

Regini, M. (1984) 'The Conditions for Political Exchange: How Concertation Emerged and Collapsed in Italy and Great Britain', in Goldthorpe (1984a), pp. 124–42.

Regional Trends (1987) London, HMSO.

Renner, K. (1953) *Wandlungen der modernen Gesellschaft*, Vienna, Verlag der Wiener Volksbuchhandlung.

Roberti, P. (1978) 'Income Inequality in Some Western Countries: Patterns and Trends', *International Journal of Social Economics*, Vol. 5, pp. 22–41.

Roberts, B., Loveridge, R., Gennard, J. and Eason, J. (1972) *Reluctant Militants: A Study of Industrial Technicians*, London, Heinemann.

Roberts, H. and Barker, R. (1986) 'The Social Classification of Women', Working Paper No. 46, London, City University, Social Statistics Unit.

Roberts, H. and Woodward, D. (1981) 'Changing Patterns of Women's Employment in Sociology, 1950–80', *British Journal of Sociology*, Vol. 32, No. 4, pp. 531–46.

Robinson, R. and Kelley, J. (1979) 'Class as Conceived by Marx and Dahrendorf: Effects on Income Inequality and Politics in the United States and Great Britain', *American Sociological Review*, Vol. 44, pp. 38–58.

Roche, W. (1987) *Social Integration and Strategic Power: The Development of Militancy among Electricity Generating Station Workers in the Republic of Ireland 1950–1982*, DPhil Thesis, University of Oxford.

Roemer, J. (1982) *A General Theory of Exploitation and Class*, Cambridge, Mass., Harvard University Press.

Rogaly, J. (1988) 'Mrs. Thatcher Knows How Far Is Too Far', *Financial Times*, 22 April.

Rogoff, N. (1953) *Recent Trends in Occupational Mobility*, Glencoe, Ill., Free Press.

Rose, D. and Marshall, G. (1986) 'Constructing the (W)right Classes', *Sociology*, Vol. 20, No. 3, pp. 440–55.

Rose, D., Marshall, G., Newby, H. and Vogler, C. (1987) 'Goodbye to Supervisors', *Work, Employment and Society*, Vol. 1, No. 1, pp. 7–24.

Rose, M. (1985) *Re-Working the Work Ethic*, London, Batsford.

Rose, R. (1980) 'Class Does Not Equal Party: The Decline of a Model', University of Strathclyde, Centre for the Study of Public Policy.

Rose, R. and McAllister, I. (1986) *Voters Begin to Choose*, London, Sage.

Ross, A. and Hartman, P. (1960) *The Changing Patterns of Industrial Conflict*, New York, Wiley.

Ross, G. (1978) 'Marxism and the New Middle Class', *Theory and Society*, Vol. 5, No. 2, pp. 163–90.

Rowthorn, B. (1986) 'Unemployment: A Resistable Force', *Marxism Today*, September.

Runciman, W. (1964) 'Embourgeoisement, Self-Rated Class and Party Preference', *Sociological Review*, Vol. 12, No, 2, pp. 137–54.

Sabel, C. (1981) 'The Internal Politics of Trade Unions', in Berger (1981), pp. 209–44.

Saunders, C. and Marsden, D. (1981) *Pay Inequalities in the European Communities*, London, Butterworth.

Saunders, P. (1989) 'Left Write in Sociology', *Network*, Bulletin of the British Sociological Association, No. 44.

Scase, R. (ed) (1978) *The State in Western Europe*, London, Croom Helm.

Scharpf, F. (1981) *The Political Economy of Inflation and Unemployment in Western Europe: An Outline*, Berlin, International Institute of Management.

Scharpf, F. (1984) 'Economic and Institutional Constraints on Full Employment Strategies: Sweden, Austria and West Germany 1973–1982', in Goldthorpe (1984a), pp. 257–90.

Schmidt, M. (1982a) 'The Role of Parties in Shaping Macroeconomic Policy', in F. Castles (1982), pp. 97–176.

Schmidt, M. (1982b) 'Does Corporatism Matter? Economic Crises, Politics and Rates of Unemployment in Capitalist Democracies in the 1970s', in Lehmbruch and Schmitter (1982), pp. 237–58.

Schmitter, P. (1979) 'Modes of Interest Intermediation and Models of Societal Change in Western Europe', in Schmitter and Lehmbruch (1979), pp. 63–94.

Schmitter, P. (1981) 'Interest Intermediation and Regime Governability', in Berger (1981), pp. 287–330.

Schmitter, P. and Lehmbruch, G. (eds) (1979) *Trends towards Corporatist Intermediation*, London, Sage.

Schmitter, P. and Streeck, W. (1985) 'Community, Market, State—and Associations? The Prospective Contribution of Interest Governance to Social Order', *European Sociological Review*, Vol. 1, pp. 119–38.

Schwerin, D. (1980) 'The Limits of Organisation as a Response to Wage-price Problems', in R. Rose (ed), *Challenge to Governance*, London, Sage, pp. 71–104.

Schwerin, D. (1981) *Corporatism and Protest: Organisational Politics in the Norwegian Trade Unions*, Kent, Ohio, Kent Popular Press.

Scitovsky, T. (1980) 'Can Capitalism Survive?—An Old Question in a New Setting', *American Economic Review*, Vol. 70, Part 2, Papers and Proceedings.

Sewell, W., Haller, A. and Ohlendorf, G. (1970) 'The Educational and Early Occupational Status Attainment Process: Replication and Revision', *American Sociological Review*, Vol. 35, pp. 1014–27.

Shorter, E. and Tilly, C. (1974) *Strikes in France 1830–1968*, New York, Cambridge University Press.

Siltanen, J. (1986) 'Domestic Responsibilities and the Structuring of Employment', in Crompton and Mann (1986), pp. 97–118.

Singelmann, J. (1978) *From Agriculture to Services: The Transformation of Industrial Employment*, Beverly Hills, Calif., Sage.

Singelmann, J. and Browning, H. (1980) 'Industrial Transformation and Occupational Change in the U.S., 1960–70', *Social Forces*, Vol. 59, pp. 246–64.

Singelmann, J. and Tienda, M. (1979) 'Changes in Industry Structure and Female Employment in Latin America: 1950–70', *Sociology and Social Research*, Vol. 63, pp. 745–70.

Singelmann, J. and Tienda, M. (1985) 'The Process of Occupational Change in a Service Society: The Case of the United States, 1960–1980', in B. Roberts, R. Finnegan and D. Gallie (eds), *New Approaches to Economic Life*, Manchester, Manchester University Press, pp. 48–67.

Smelser, N. and Lipset, S. (eds) (1966a) *Social Structure and Mobility in Economic Development*, London, Routledge and Kegan Paul.

Smelser, N. and Lipset, S. (1966b) 'Social Structure, Mobility and Development', in Smelser and Lipset (1966a), pp. 1–50.

Smith, A. (1980) *The Wealth of Nations* (first published 1776), Harmondsworth, Penguin.

Smith, M. R. (1982) 'Accounting for Inflation in Britain', *British Journal of Sociology*, Vol. 33, pp. 301–29.

Smith, M. R. (1985) 'Accounting for Inflation (Again)', *British Journal of Sociology*, Vol. 36, pp. 77–80.

Sørensen, A. B. (1986) 'Theory and Methodology in Stratification Research', in U. Himmelstrand (ed), *The Sociology of Structure and Action*, Vol. 1: *Sociology: From Crisis to Science?*, London, Sage, pp. 69–95.

Sørensen, A. B., Allmendinger, J. and Sørensen, A. (1986) 'Intergenerational Mobility as a Life Course Process', Paper presented at the meeting of American Sociological Association, New York.

Sorokin, P. (1927/59) *Social and Cultural Mobility*, New York, Harper; Glencoe, Ill., Free Press.

Stacey, M. (1980) 'The Division of Labour Revisited or Overcoming the Two Adams', in Abrams *et al.* (1980), pp. 172–90.

Stacey, M. (1986) 'Gender and Stratification: One Central Issue or Two?', in Crompton and Mann (1986), pp. 214–23.

Stanworth, M. (1984) 'Women and Class Analysis: A Reply to Goldthorpe', *Sociology*, Vol. 18, pp. 159–70.

Stanworth, P. and Giddens, A. (eds) (1974) *Elites and Power in British Society*, Cambridge, Cambridge University Press.

Stephens, J. (1979) *The Transition from Capitalism to Socialism*, London, Macmillan.

Stewart, A., Prandy, K. and Blackburn, R. M. (1980) *Social Stratification and Occupations*, London, Macmillan.

Storey, J. (1983) *Managerial Prerogative and the Question of Control*, London, Routledge and Kegan Paul.

Streeck, W. (1982) 'Organisational Consequences of Neo-Corporatism in West German Trade Unions', in Lehmbruch and Schmitter (1982), pp. 29–82.

Streeck, W. (1984) 'Neo-Corporatist Industrial Relations and the Economic Crisis in West Germany', in Goldthorpe (1984a), pp. 291–314.

Summers, R. and Heston, R. (1984) 'Improved International Comparisons of Real Product and Its Composition: 1950–80', *Review of Income and Wealth*, Vol. 30, pp. 207–62.

Sunday Times (1985) *Strike*, London, Coronet.

Swedish Institute (1986) 'Labour Relations in Sweden', October.

Swedish Institute (1988) 'Swedish Labour Market Policy', April.

Tawney, R. (1938) *Equality*, 3rd ed., London, Allen and Unwin.

Teubner, G. (1979) 'Neo-korporatistische Strategien rechtlicher Organisationssteuerung', *Zeitschrift für Parlamentsfragen*, Vol. 10, No. 4, pp. 487–506.

Thatcher, M. (1977) *Let Our Children Grow Tall*, London, Centre for Policy Studies.

Thomas, G., Meyer, J., Ramirez, F. and Boli, J. (1987) *Institutional Structure: Constituting State, Society and the Individual*, Newbury Park, Calif., Sage.

Thompson, P. (1983) *The Nature of Work*, London, Macmillan.

Thomson, A. and Beaumont, P. (1978) *Public Sector Bargaining: A Study of Relative Gain*, London, Saxon House.

Thurow, L. (1975) *Generating Inequality: Mechanisms of Distribution in the U.S. Economy*, New York, Basic Books.

Times Higher Education Supplement (*THES*) (1988) 'Firms Face Contest for Teenagers', *THES*, 5 June, p. 10.

Titmuss, R. (1958) *Essays on the Welfare State*, London, Allen and Unwin.

Treiman, D. (1970) 'Industrialization and Social Stratification', in E. Laumann (ed), *Stratification: Research and Theory for the 1970s*, New York, Bobbs-Merrill, pp. 207–34.

Treiman, D. (1977) *Occupational Prestige in Comparative Perspective*, New York, Academic Press.

Treiman, D. (ed) (1981) *Research in Social Stratification and Mobility*, Greenwich, Conn., JAI Press.

Treiman, D. and Terrell, K. (1975a) 'Sex and the Process of Status Attainment: A Comparison of Working Women and Men', *American Sociological Review*, Vol. 40, pp. 174–200.

Treiman, D. and Terrell, K. (1975b) 'The Process of Status Attainment in the United States and Great Britain', *American Journal of Sociology*, Vol. 81, pp. 563–83.

Visser, J. (1984) 'The Position of Central Confederations in the National Union Movements', Working Paper No. 102, Florence, European University Institute.

Walby, S. (1984) 'Gender, Class and Stratification: Towards a New Approach', Paper given at ESRC Symposium on Gender and Stratification, University of East Anglia, July.

Walby, S. (1986) 'Gender, Class and Stratification: Towards a New Approach', in Crompton and Mann (1986), pp. 23–39.

Wallerstein, I. (1979) *The Capitalist World Economy*, Cambridge, Cambridge University Press.

Watson, W. and Barth, E. (1964) 'Questionable Assumptions in the Theory of Social Stratification', *Pacific Sociological Review*, Vol. 7, pp. 10–16.

Weakliem, D. (1989) 'Class and Party in Britain, 1964–83', *Sociology*, Vol. 23, pp. 285–97.

Webb, R. (1987) 'Union, Party and Class in Britain: The Changing Electoral Relationship 1964–1983', *Politics*, Vol. 7, No. 2, pp. 15–21.

Webber, D. (1986) 'Social Democracy and the Re-emergence of Mass Unemployment in Western Europe', in W. Paterson and A. Thomas (eds), *The Future of Social Democracy*, Oxford, Clarendon Press, pp. 19–58.

Weber, M. (1923) *General Economic History*, London, George Allen and Unwin.

Weber, M. (1978) *Economy and Society*, edited by G. Roth and C. Wittich, 2 vols, Berkeley, Calif., University of California Press.

Wedderburn, D. and Craig, C. (1974) 'Relative Deprivation in Work', in Wedderburn (ed), *Poverty, Inequality and Class Structure*, Cambridge, Cambridge University Press, pp. 141–64.

Weitbrecht, H. (1969) *Effektivität und Legitimität der Tarifautonomie*, Berlin, Duncker and Humblot.

WES (1984) see Martin and Roberts (1984) for full reference.

Westergaard, J. (1970) 'The Rediscovery of the Cash Nexus', in R. Miliband and J. Saville (eds), *The Socialist Register*, London, Merlin, pp. 11–38.

Westergaard, J. and Little, A. (1967) 'Educational Opportunity and Social Selection in England and Wales', in H. Friis *et al.* (eds), *Social Objectives in Educational Planning*, Paris, OECD, pp. 215–32. (An earlier version appeared in 1964 in the *British Journal of Sociology*, Vol. 15, No. 4, pp. 301–16.)

Westergaard, J., Noble, I. and Walker, A. (1989) *After Redundancy*, Cambridge, Polity Press.

Westergaard, J. and Resler, H. (1975) *Class in a Capitalist Society*, London, Heinemann.

Whelan, C. (1976) 'Orientations to Work: Some Theoretical and Methodological Problems', *British Journal of Industrial Relations*, Vol. 14, pp. 142–58.

Wiesenthal, H. (1987) 'Rational Choice: Ein Überblick über Grundlinien, Theoriefelder und neuere Themenakquisition eines sozialwissenschaftlichen Paradigmas', *Zeitschrift für Soziologie*, Vol. 16, pp. 434–49.

Wilensky, H. (1975) *The Welfare State and Equality: Structural and Ideological Roots of Public Expenditures*, Berkeley, Calif., University of California Press.

Wilson, G. (1987) *Money in the Family*, Aldershot, Avebury.

Wippler, R. and Lindenberg, S. (1987) 'Collective Phenomena and Rational Choice', in Alexander *et al.* (1987), pp. 135–52.

Woodward, J. (1958) *Management and Technology*, London, HMSO.

Woodward, J. (1965) *Industrial Organisation: Theory and Practice*, Oxford, Oxford University Press.

Wright, E. (1978) *Class, Crisis and the State*, London, Verso.

Wright, E. (1980a) 'Class and Occupation', *Theory and Society*, Vol. 9, pp. 177–214.

Wright, E. (1980b) 'Varieties of Marxist Conceptions of Class Structure', *Politics and Society*, Vol. 9, pp. 323–76.

Wright, E. (1985) *Classes*, London, Verso.

Wright, E. and Martin, B. (1987) 'The Transformation of the American Class Structure, 1960–1980', *American Journal of Sociology*, Vol. 93, pp. 1–29.

Wright, E. and Perrone, L. (1977) 'Marxist Class Categories and Income Inequality', *American Sociological Review*, Vol. 42, pp. 32–5.

Wright, E. and Singelmann, J. (1982) 'Proletarianisation in the American Class Structure', in T. Skocpol and M. Burawoy (eds), *Marxist Inquiries*, Supplement to Vol. 88 of the *American Journal of Sociology*, pp. 176–209.

Wright, G. von (1971) *Explanation and Understanding*, London, Routledge and Kegan Paul.

Wright, G. von (1972) 'On So-Called Practical Inference', *Acta Sociologica*, Vol. 15, pp. 39–53.

Wright Mills, C. (1953) *White-Collar*, London, Oxford University Press.

Yanowitch, M. (1977) *Social and Economic Inequality in the Soviet Union*, New York, M. E. Sharpe Inc.

Zagorski, K. (1984) 'Comparisons of Social Mobility in Different Socio-economic Systems', in M. Niessen, J. Peschar and C. Kourilsky (eds), *International Comparative Research: Social Structures and Political Institutions in Eastern and Western Europe*, Oxford, Pergamon, pp. 13–42.

Zagorski, K. (1985) 'Class, Prestige and Status Attainment in Comparative Perspective', *International Journal of Comparative Sociology*, Vol. 26, pp. 167–80.

Author Index

Abbott, P.
  see Payne and Abbott
Abbott, P. and Sapsford, R., 126, 132n9, 136,
  152n12, 302
Abell, P., 419
Abercrombie, N. and Urry, J., 91n1
Åberg, 102
Abrams, M., Rose, R. and Hinden, R., 161–2,
  174
Acker, J., 121
Aglietta, M., 246
Ahrne, G., 7, 65–73, 74–6, 408, 417, 425,
  435n4, 437n13
Ahrne, G. and Leiulfsrud, H., 72
Ahrne, G., *et al.*, 71, 72
Allen, S., 136
Allmendinger, J., 436n12
  see also Sorensen *et al.*
Alt, J., 182
Anderson, P., 62n2
Argyris, C., 420
Arrighi, G., 247
Ashburner, L., 108n15
Attewell, P., 84

Bain, G., 203, 210n4
Baldamus, W., 204
Banks, J., 161
Barkin, S., 231
Barth, E.
  see Watson and Barth
Batstone, E., 40, 201, 202, 203, 204, 205, 208,
  209, 223, 240, 242, 257
Batstone, E., Boraston, I. and Frenkel, S., 217
Baumol, W., 92n15
Beales, H. L., 375
Beaumont, P.
  see Thomson and Beaumont
Bechhofer, F., 17, 118–19, 133n15, 161, 447
  see also Goldthorpe, Lockwood, Bechhofer
  and Platt
Beechey, V. and Perkins, T., 31
Bell, D., 5, 62n1, 204, 378, 404
Bendix, R., 204, 362

Bendix, R. and Lipset, S., 20
Berger, S., 234
Bevan, P.
  see Goldthorpe and Bevan
Beynon, H., 33
Binswanger, H. and Ruttan, V., 89
Bishop, Y., Fienberg, S. and Holland, P., 333
Blackburn, R., 204
Blackburn, R. and Mann, M., 198, 385
Blain, A., 204
Blau, P. and Duncan, O.D., 18–19, 53, 54, 308,
  312, 319, 320–35, 341–2, 347, 349–55, 356,
  407, 415, 436n11
Blauner, R., 29, 385, 420
Blossfeld, H., 347
Boraston, I.
  see Batstone *et al.*
Boston, J., 208
Bottomore, T., 289
Boudon, R., 418, 420, 437n13
Bourdieu, P., 66
Boyer, R., 246
Braverman, H., 62n2, 82, 97, 98, 104, 106
Brittan, S., 20, 204, 243n1, 265, 266
Brittan, S., and Lilley, P., 203
Britten, N. and Heath, A., 96, 132n8, 136, 140,
  142, 147, 152n9, 285, 286, 409
  see also Heath and Britten
Broom, L. and Jones, F., 321
Broom, L., *et al.*, 322
Brough, I.
  see Hyman and Brough
Brown, A., 221
Brown, R., *et al.*, 197, 198
Brown, W., 8, 213–22, 223–5, 242, 251, 427–9,
  431–2, 438n23
Browning, H.
  see Singelmann and Browning
Bruno, M, and Sachs, D., 221
Brzezinski, Z. and Huntingdon, S., 43
Buci-Glucksmann, C. and Therborn, G., 247
Bulmer, M., 405
Burawoy, M., 91n1
Burke, K., 370n2

471

Subject Index

Adam Smith Institute, 270
Affluent Worker: Industrial Attitudes and Behaviour, The, 17, 198
   see also *Affluent Worker* studies
Affluent Worker Political Attitudes and Behaviour, The, 17, 161, 171
   see also *Affluent Worker* studies
Affluent Worker in the Class Structure, The, 17–18, 97, 180
   see also *Affluent Worker* studies
Affluent Worker studies, 7–8, 15, 17–22, 24, 37, 52, 53, 97, 161–3, 168–9, 172–83, 192–210, 229, 366, 367, 381–6, 389–90, 393, 419–20, 425–6
   and action perspective, 18, 381–6, 419–20
   aims of, 17, 21, 22, 161, 381
   and choice of research site, 22, 162, 381; *see also* Luton
   and class and social conflict, 37
   as 'critical case' study, 21–2, 24, 52, 162, 172–3, 193, 381
   criticism of, 196–200
   and determinism, 385
   and *embourgeoisement thesis,* 17–18, 21–2, 52, 161–3, 164, 171–6, 181, 186n1, 192, 193–200, 381–3
   as example of Goldthorpe's sociology, 21–2
   findings of, 17–18, 162–3, 168–9, 172–4, 175–6, 193–210, 382–6, 419–20
   funding for, 17
   and influence of prior place of residence, 199–200
   and instrumental collectivism of workers, 163, 168–9, 174, 175–6, 193–210, 383–6
   and life-cycle hypothesis, 194–5
   methodology in, 17, 22, 162, 383–6
   occupational classification in, 19
   and orientation to work, 197–9, 419–20
   publications arising from, 17–18; *see also* individual titles under *Affluent Worker...*
   sample interviewed in, 17, 22, 27n5
   and social action, 18, 381–6
   staff employed on, 17, 161
   and theory of social class, 198–9
   theory underlying, 420
   and workers' geographical mobility, 195–6
   and workers and Labour Party, 162–3, 168–9, 172–83
   and workers' social mobility, 195–6
agricultural labourers
   and social mobility, 293
American Journal of Sociology, 414
American Occupational Structure, The, 53
American Sociological Review, 414
Australia
   corporatist agreements in, 238
   neo-corporatism in, 433
   social mobility in, 311, 317n3, 321, 349
   trade union movement and corporatism in, 238
Austria
   centralized bargaining in, 429
   corporatism in, 237
   neo-corporatism in, 433
   trade union movement and corporatism in, 237

Beveridge reforms [Britain], 54
Blackcoated Worker, The, 55
Blau-Duncan paradigm, 18–19, 49, 50, 308, 312, 319, 320–35, 341–2, 347, 349–57, 407, 415, 436n11
   characteristics of original, 320–1
   and comparative work, 323–4
   data in, 320, 322, 324
   and education as variable, 320, 322
   expansion of, 321–4, 329–31, 351–7
   and income as variable, 322
   and measurement, 320–1, 322, 325–6
   methods in, 321, 322–3, 331–2
   stagnation in, 324
   variables in, 320, 322, 326–9
BMRS
   see British Market Research Society
Britain
   see also British General Election Study; British General Election Surveys

479

For Product Safety Concerns and Information please contact our EU
representative GPSR@taylorandfrancis.com
Taylor & Francis Verlag GmbH, Kaufingerstraße 24, 80331 München, Germany